THE FIRST PRESIDENT JOHNSON

The Three Lives of the Seventeenth
President of the United States
of America

Also by Lately Thomas

THE VANISHING EVANGELIST
A DEBONAIR SCOUNDREL
SAM WARD: KING OF THE LOBBY
DELMONICO'S: A CENTURY OF SPLENDOR

Concerning the frontispiece. Painted before the Civil War, when Johnson was a senator, this portrait now hangs in the Johnson Homestead, Greeneville, Tennessee. When Johnson fled Tennessee at the start of the war and Confederates over-ran Greeneville, a neighbor cut the portrait out of its frame and took it to her house nearby, where she pasted newspaper over it and used it as a firescreen, thus saving it from mutilation or destruction by Confederate soldiers. After the war, she sent the picture to Johnson in Washington, and he had the paper removed and the painting touched up where it had become dented. Always afterward it was a favorite with him because of its history. The family always considered it a good likeness except for a slight narrowness in the forehead, Johnson's forehead being exceptionally wide.

THE FIRST PRESIDENT JOHNSON

JOHNSON

*The Three Lives
of the Seventeenth President
of the United States
of America*

BY LATELY THOMAS

William Morrow & Company, Inc.
NEW YORK 1968

Grateful acknowledgment is made to the following for permission to quote from the specified works: to the Illinois State Historical Library for *The Diary of Orville Hickman Browning*, edited by James G. Randall and Theodore C. Pease (Illinois State Historical Library Collections, Volumes 20 and 22); to W. W. Norton & Company, Inc. for *The Diary of Gideon Welles*, edited by Howard K. Beale, Norton, New York, 1960, Copyright © 1960 by W. W. Norton & Company, Inc.; to The Macmillan Company for *The Diary of George Templeton Strong*, edited by Allan Nevins and Milton H. Thomas, Macmillan, New York, 1962, Copyright © The Macmillan Company 1952, 1962; to Oxford University Press for *When the World Ended: The Diary of Emma LeConte*, edited by Earl Schenck Miers, Oxford, New York, 1957, Copyright © 1957 by Oxford University Press, Inc.; and to Houghton Mifflin Company for *The Education of Henry Adams*, by Henry Adams, Houghton Mifflin, Boston and New York, 1918, Copyright, 1918, by the Massachusetts Historical Society.

Published simultaneously in Canada by
George J. McLeod Limited, Toronto.

Printed in the United States of America.

Library of Congress Catalog Card Number 68-25487

TO

THE JOHNSONS
A Numerous and Remarkable Tribe

Contents

INTERLUDE

THE THIRD LIFE

In addition to the frontispiece, *photographs appear between pages 100-101, pages 196-197, and pages 292-293.*

"Therefore I purpose to tell a tale, no less true than lamentable; which albeit it sorted to a successful ending, yet notwithstanding, such and so many were the bitter thwartings, as hardly can I believe."

—Boccaccio, *The Decameron*

A BLOW OF FATE

It began on the day the President was shot.

For more than a week the city had been in a tumult of joy—parades, speeches, serenades—citizens and strangers celebrating the sudden, dramatic release from years of tension. The war was over, and the end of killing was in sight!

In a second-rate hotel at the corner of Pennsylvania Avenue and Twelfth Street one man was taking no part in the rowdy rejoicings of that evening. During the day perhaps not a dozen persons in town had given him a thought. His presence was not required at any official function, and the merrymakers—the theater parties, the groups weaving boisterously through the streets, singing, shouting, carousing in the bars along the Avenue—these had no reason to consider that superfluity, the Vice-President of the United States.

Weeks of sensational and exhausting events had drained the Vice-President's vitality, and he looked forward with relief to an early bedtime. Quietly and alone, he ate supper in the hotel dining room, then went to his rooms, suite 68, on the second floor. Nobody missed him. He read awhile, and about nine-thirty undressed, turned off the gas light, and settled himself in bed. Outside, the gaiety and hubbub kept up as he sank into sleep.

About an hour later he was aroused by a pounding on the door. Somebody in the hall was calling:

"Governor Johnson! If you are in this room I must see you!"

The voice seemed familiar. Throwing back the covers, the Vice-President struggled out of bed and, drugged with sleep, stepped into the parlor of the suite, not pausing to strike a light.

"Farwell," he called, "is that you?"

3

"Yes," came the desperate reply. "Let me in!"

The latch was turned, and the importunate visitor burst in, slammed the door shut behind him, and locked it.

Then he gasped appalling news. The President had been shot! In the theater, only two and a half blocks away! He had run all the way from there to warn the Vice-President to look to his safety! Murder was abroad—some dreadful conspiracy—perhaps aimed at assassinating the chief public officers and seizing the city!

The words tumbled out; the Vice-President heard them in stunned silence. Overwhelmed by the immensity of the catastrophe, he swayed, and the two men, falling against each other, clung together for mutual support.

In that blinding instant Andrew Johnson was whirled from the obscurity of an understudy's place into the principal role of a tumultuous drama—invested with responsibilities and powers exceeding those of any potentate on earth, in a moment of fearful crisis. A new world, a new life was created instantaneously for him in that darkened room.

Some hours later, at seven-thirty o'clock in the morning, the tolling of bells came mournfully through a drizzle of rain to confirm to Andrew Johnson that—by an assassin's bullet—he had become the seventeenth President of the United States.

All over the land, men and women, shuddering in their revulsion of grief, fear, pity, and horror at the deed of a hate-crazed killer, paused to consider anxiously the man who had been wrenched from the outer edge of the circle surrounding the lost leader and set down in the center, to occupy the chair so tragically emptied.

What sort of man was this new President—this man Johnson?

THE FIRST LIFE

"O world, how apt the poor are to be proud!"
—*Twelfth Night*

ONE

TO THE TUNE OF FIDDLES

ANDREW JOHNSON of Tennessee became the seventeenth President of the United States on April 15, 1865, without warning, but not without preparation. Of regular schooling he had none; but in experience of public affairs and the responsibilities of office he had been educated as have been few of the men who have attained the Presidency.

About the origins of men who become famous fables are sure to be spun, and this was the case with Andrew Johnson; especially so because the facts about his ancestry which can be authenticated are few, though they are significant.

The parallels between Andrew Johnson's and Abraham Lincoln's beginnings have not gone unnoticed. Both men were Southerners, born in border states. Johnson might have said, as Lincoln did say to certain well-wishers who proposed to endow him with a notable family tree: "I do not know who my grandfather was; I am more concerned with what his grandson shall be." And the remark a boyhood friend made about Johnson would have applied equally well to Lincoln: "Some people can boast of a grand start; I reckon he started underground." Both men overcame the most formidable handicaps and became President, significantly during the same crisis. In one respect Johnson outdid his predecessor: Lincoln did receive a trifle of formal schooling as a boy, but Andrew Johnson did not attend school a single day of his life.

He hardly knew who or what his grandfathers had been, and like Lincoln's, his start was so low in the scale of social recognition that it was almost out of sight. It was only late in life that Johnson established that his father, Jacob Johnson, a good-natured handyman in a country town, had been born in England, and had sailed from Newcastle for America about 1795. After

7

numerous adventures and aimless wandering, Jacob reached Raleigh, North Carolina. There he became an odd-jobs man, known as an easygoing, unambitious fellow, harmless but trustworthy.

Jacob Johnson was a "poor white," and seems not to have repined at his humble lot; even legend ascribes to him no attempt to improve it. He was employed at the principal tavern in Raleigh, operated by Peter Casso, the finest in that part of the country, situated on the main north-south highway. Raleigh was the state capital and boasted about a thousand inhabitants, a sizable place for the region and period. During court terms the inn was filled with lawyers and litigants; John Marshall, Chief Justice of the United States, presided at the circuit court there. The legislative sessions brought spectators and hangers-on, and experienced travelers who knew the accommodations along the road always made a point of stopping at Casso's, if possible. For an odd-jobs man there was plenty of work—errands to run, bags to tote, wood to bring in for fires, horses to be bedded down—and Jacob Johnson was a cheerful, willing servitor.

The region around Raleigh held a rustic aristocracy modeled upon those of Virginia and South Carolina, but neither so pretentious nor so prideful. In comfortable "big houses" the planters dispensed a rough-and-ready, open-handed hospitality, diverted themselves with hunting, shooting, and dancing, and discussed politics endlessly. Class lines were sharp, and Jacob Johnson belonged to a class that the aristocracy looked down upon.

Despite this he had the goodwill of influential citizens. Colonel William Knox Polk chose him to be the porter at Polk's new state bank, a position that implied reliability and honesty. (The Polks were prominent local gentry, though some of them already were moving with their slaves and households to the new lands in Tennessee.) Jacob Johnson also was appointed to ring the town bell for weddings, funerals, elections, and public announcements. He was elected captain of a company of workingmen like himself in the state militia, a position that carried honor but no more tangible benefits.

With all this, Jacob Johnson could neither read nor write. On September 9, 1801, he signed with his "mark" the bond that was required in order to obtain a license to marry Mary McDonough, whom everybody knew as "Polly." Illiterate like her husband, "Polly" nevertheless was a faithful and industrious wife, and eked out Jacob's slender support by taking in washing and mending the shirts of the "giants of the bar" (so designated by local pride) who argued their cases in the courthouse nearby.

Jacob and "Polly" lived in a little frame house on the grounds of Casso's; it was two stories high and contained one room on each floor. There, in 1803, the couple's first child, a son, was born. He was fair-haired and healthy, and they named him William.

Christmas was a season of jollity at Casso's tavern, the festivities keeping up for a week. Fiddlers could always be found to get up a dance, and according to tradition, a ball was in progress on the night of Thursday, December 29, 1808, when, in the cabin a few yards away, Mary McDonough Johnson gave birth to a second son. This boy was as dark as his brother was light, and he, too, gave promise of being strong and hardy.

It is said that Mary Johnson named this child, who had come into the world to the tune of fiddles and the stamping of a country dance, Andrew Jackson Johnson, in honor of the great hero of the region. If this was so (and in 1808, of course, the Battle of New Orleans had not been fought and Andrew Jackson was not yet a national figure), Andrew Johnson never used the name; plain Andrew, or even plainer "Andy," would be the name that he in turn would make known in every household.

The personal chronicle of Jacob Johnson between the appearance of his second son and 1811 is blank, so far as the record goes. In the spring of 1811, however, he made enough of an impression upon his fellow townsmen to become the subject of favorable talk, and even to be mentioned in the newspaper. Several well-to-do men organized a party to go fishing on Walnut Creek, and Jacob Johnson went along, probably to manage the food and drinkables and clean the fish. There was horseplay, in the midst of which Colonel Thomas Henderson (every man among the "quality" was either a "colonel," a "squire," or a "judge"), editor of the *Raleigh Star*, pushed off in a boat with two companions. One of these could not swim, and for a prank Henderson rocked the boat. It upset, and the non-swimmer sank, dragging Henderson with him.

Jacob Johnson was watching the tomfoolery from the bank. Without hesitation he dove into the icy water and after a hard struggle succeeded in getting both men safely to shore. But the exertion overtaxed his strength, his health was permanently impaired, and a few months later, early in January, 1812, he collapsed while ringing the town bell for a funeral. Shortly afterward he died.

One of the men whose lives he had saved, Colonel Henderson, published an obituary tribute in the *Star* of January 12, in which he attested that though Jacob Johnson had occupied "a humble but useful station in society," he had won the esteem of the community by his "honesty, integrity, and humane and friendly disposition." During his final illness, the report said, many of the town's "best people" had visited him, and "none lamented him more than the publisher of this paper, for he owes his life to Johnson's boldness and humanity."

Few "poor whites" received even as much notice as this when, after having lived in obscurity, they obscurely died.

Jacob Johnson was buried in the "citizens' cemetery," which was "potter's field" under another name. For half a century his grave would remain unmarked, "Polly" Johnson being too poor to afford even the simplest stone.

TWO

THE WILL TO SAY "NO"

WHEN in later life Andrew Johnson would say, "I have grappled with the gaunt and haggard monster called hunger," he was speaking the stark truth about his childhood. At his father's death Andrew had just turned three. His mother ("Aunt Polly," as Raleigh took to calling her) tried to feed and clothe her two lively boys, but her earnings as a washerwoman were not enough, and Andrew's earliest remembered sensations were of grinding poverty. Some of Jacob Johnson's friends helped now and then, and Colonel Henderson took Bill, nearly nine, as a printer's apprentice. But Henderson himself died shortly, and Bill was back on his mother's hands.

In her desperation, about 1814, "Polly" married again, a man named Turner Doughtry (or Daugherty), a "poor white" like herself. In his case the epithet usually associated with "poor white" ("shiftless") was deserved, and with a worthless husband also on her hands "Polly" found her lot worse than before. Education for either of her boys was out of the question; Raleigh had no free school, and she could not pay a teacher. So Andy ran wild. He was a vigorous, restless child, always on the go, ripping his clothes on fences and defying the power of soap and water to keep him scrubbed clean. But though he got into childish scrapes, a friend of that time described him as having "no *un*honorable traits."

In 1822 Andrew's mother found a means to provide for at least his upkeep until he should be grown, and also to acquire a trade, by apprenticing him to a tailor, James J. Selby, of Raleigh.

According to a journeyman in Selby's shop, a man named Tom Lumsden, Andrew was brought to Selby's notice by his eagerness to learn to read. Andy, said Lumsden, "was always pestering me out of work hours to read to him. He was a pert sort of boy, and

11

one fall business was brisk, and the boss wanted a 'prentice. He took in Andy, and the boy was right glad to get something to do to help his old mother."

The formalities entailed in articling an apprentice, to be taught a trade and work for his master until he was twenty-one, were soon dispatched. "Polly" and Turner Doughtry signed a statement of consent (each making the "mark" of an illiterate), and there was spread upon the minutes of the "Court of Pleas and Half Sessions begun & held for the County of Wake, at the Court House in Raleigh, on the third Monday of February A.D. 1822, being the 46th year of American Independence, & the 18th day of February," this indenture:

"Ordered

"That Andrew Johnson an orphan boy, the son of Jacob Johnson, deceased, 14 years of age, be bound to James J. Selby until he arrive at lawful age, to learn the trade of a Tailor."

Thus Andrew became bound to serve a man whom he was said to have described in afteryears as "a harsh and cruel master." His age was given incorrectly in the indenture, for he had barely turned thirteen. An arrangement was worked out whereby Andrew continued to live with his mother, and Selby paid her the equivalent of the boy's upkeep.

The apprentice laws in North Carolina were similar to those in other states, Massachusetts included, and they were strict. A "bound boy" was required to remain with his master until his term of apprenticeship expired; if he should run away, for whatever cause, he could be arrested and brought back like a runaway slave. The master, in turn, was required to maintain the apprentice and teach him his trade; refractory or unruly apprentices he was permitted to discipline by punishments including flogging.

Andrew's childhood of careless roaming came to an end. In Selby's shop he toiled from early morning to evening—sitting cross-legged on the tailor's bench, bending over a hot "goose," pressing, stitching, patching, cutting, binding, raveling—with no letup except for meals. After work he could still join in the skylarking of urchins as wild as himself, though at the risk of detection and punishment.

Unlike the other boys, however, he wanted to learn. He felt that he must master the ability to read, and there was nobody to instruct him. His brother Bill, who meanwhile had also been articled to Selby as an apprentice, was as letterless as himself. It was a custom to hire someone to read to the men while they worked, and there was one person of education, Dr. William G. Hill, or "Bill Hill," as he was generally called, who devoted his leisure to reading aloud in Selby's shop. His favorite book was a collection of the orations of Fox, Pitt, Burke, and other British statesmen, entitled variously, in different editions, *Enfield's Speaker, The United States Speaker, The American Speaker*, and otherwise.

Somehow Andrew managed to teach himself to read simple words. How he did this was never clearly explained; apparently he memorized words by sight, without reference to spelling or sentence structure. For a lad of fourteen or fifteen, with no one to help him, this was a feat requiring superior determination.

One day, after Hill had read a stirring passage from his *Speaker*, Andy begged to borrow the book. The doctor replied that if Andy could show that he could read, the book would be his to keep. Andrew thereupon did demonstrate that he could puzzle out words, and received the gift. It was his first book.

The subject matter of the speeches it contained dealt with lofty constitutional questions and government policy; abstract principles were set forth, defined, and pursued, in their practical application, to logical conclusions. Thus, while the style instilled a sense of grandeur in expression, the contents stimulated Andrew's reasoning faculties, and inclined his mind toward analysis and deduction. This was strong meat for an untutored youth, certainly not what an educator would prescribe as a balanced mental diet; but Andrew doggedly set himself to digest it.

Also in the book were instructive essays on the art of public speaking, with handy hints for the aspiring orator. One of these was an injunction to speak slowly and distinctly, and to cultivate that habit by reading aloud:

> Learn to speak slow, all other graces
> Will follow in their proper places.

This advice Andy sedulously adhered to, and in time he would develop a speaking voice of remarkable clarity, range, flexibility, and carrying force.

Apprentice though he was, Andrew was still full of the prankishness normal to a teen-ager, and in his second year with tailor Selby he found himself in a serious predicament, or so it appeared to him.

A widow who lived on the edge of town had two "right smart" daughters, and one night Andy and another apprentice "chunked" (threw stones at) the girls' window. The indignant mother found out who the culprits were and threatened to "persecute." This was a serious threat, for erring apprentices could be handled sharply by the law. Rather than run the risk, on the night of June 15, 1824, Andy and brother Bill quietly decamped, taking two other discontented apprentices with them. Heading south, they did not stop until they came to Carthage, a town fifty miles southwest of Raleigh. There they succeeded in obtaining the use of a shack and opened a tailoring business of their own.

Months went by and they were not molested, although their immunity was not due to neglect by Selby. He had promptly inserted an advertisement in the *Raleigh Star*, posting a reward for the recovery of the runaways, but perhaps by the typesetter's error the brothers' descriptions were reversed:

TEN DOLLARS REWARD

Ran away from the Subscriber, on the night of the 15th instant, two apprentice boys, legally bound, named WILLIAM and ANDREW JOHNSON. The former is of a dark complexion, black hair, eyes, and habits. They are much of a height, about 5 feet 4 or 5 inches. The latter is very fleshy, freckled face, light hair, and fair complexion. They went off with two other apprentices, advertised by Messrs. Wm. & Chas. Fowler. When they went away they were well clad—blue cloth coats, light homespun coats, and new hats . . . I will pay the above Reward to any person who will deliver said apprentices to me in Raleigh, or I will give the above Reward for Andrew Johnson alone.

Evidently Selby thought that in losing the services of Bill he was not losing much; but Andrew, despite his alleged "black habits," was another matter. It is possible that Selby bore Andrew a grudge because of the lad's refusal to kowtow; the forms of servility he simply would not observe.

Probably the truants learned of the reward outstanding for their arrest, and after six or seven months in Carthage they decided to flee farther. So, crossing the state line into South Carolina, they came to the town of Laurens, in the county of that name, where again they set up shop in an empty cabin. Knowing their trade, by diligence they managed to earn a living.

Andrew at fifteen was strong and well built, and he was exceptionally earnest for his age. Tradition has it that while in Laurens he fell in love with a girl named Sarah Work, and sentimentally helped her stitch a quilt. But Sarah's family frowned on the penniless tailor, and she turned down his offer of marriage. In despondency, it is said, he closed the shop in the autumn of 1825 and returned to Raleigh, intending to make his peace with Selby and work out the remainder of his apprenticeship honorably. He was then sixteen.

Selby had moved away from Raleigh, and Andrew trudged twenty miles to the tailor's new location to apply for reinstatement. But Selby was anything but reasonable. He would not take Andy back, nor would he release him from his indenture. The practical effect of this was to cut Andrew off from all employment, since any person harboring or hiring a runaway apprentice was liable to severe penalties under the law. The sentence Selby in effect passed upon the runaway was "starve and be damned." None of Andy's friends dared to give him work; and though penniless he was proud, and he would not beg. Throughout his whole life, when faced by any unjust assumption of superiority or power, both his instinct and his will forbade him to knuckle under.

His plight was serious. If he remained in Raleigh, he could degenerate into a handyman or vagabond; Turner Doughtry was a reminder in his own family of the fate that awaited a man who submitted to adverse conditions without fighting back. He was still able to say "No!"—and deprive the poor of the ability and readiness to say "No!" and they are degraded and defenseless indeed.

The only course open was to set out again, leave home and head for a region where he might be permitted to work out his destiny like a free man.

Often he had discussed with his brother and others the continuing movement of Carolinians into Tennessee, attracted by the fine farmlands there and the opportunities for employment in the settlements growing up beyond the mountains. Tennessee sounded like the country for an enterprising person, and it would be out of the reach of Selby. Tennessee was new; perhaps class distinctions were not drawn so rigidly there. In the older states there were the few at the top of the social heap, and the "others"; slaves didn't count. Sarah Work's family, no great shucks themselves, had contempt for a tailor, and likely it was the same in all the long-settled states. In Tennessee maybe a man could make his way on his own merits.

Not all these thoughts may have passed through Andrew Johnson's mind in such crystallized form as he worried over his predicament. But the ideas were in the air, he had heard others say things that he felt, and in part his decision was made for him. A "shiftless poor white" he was determined he would never be; he would push on, surmount the obstacles, and make a decent place for himself and be respected in the world.

About this time William Johnson took off by himself for Tennessee. He was headed for the Sequatchie Valley, in the southeastern part of that state, and soon was settled on a farm there. Andrew made up his mind to follow his brother.

Tom Lumsden, the journeyman tailor who had befriended Andy on numerous occasions, saw the lad off. It was a dismal leave-taking. As Lumsden described it:

"He was a gawky sort of boy and his clothes never did fit him. He had on a little cap, and a bundle of shirts and socks thrown over his shoulder. It was a bright moonlight night, and I walked out of town with him a matter of two miles. He was talking all the time about the great things he intended to do out West. When he shook hands, and he bade me good-bye, the tears just rolled down his cheeks."

For all his determination, Andrew felt utterly alone. He was penniless, he had no friends where he was going, and he was leaving his own people, to whom he was pathetically attached. Lumsden tried to strike a cheerful note.

"Cheer up, Andy," he urged. "Raleigh is no place for you. You'll succeed out there, and some day I hope to see you President, for you are bound to be a great man."

Such words were at least comforting, although that bit about becoming President was what was said to every American boy. Still, it was of some help that somebody believed in him.

Shouldering his bundle, Andrew set out along the moonlit highway. And such is the resiliency of youth, as he went he began to whistle.

Ahead of him lay—the future!

THREE

A HOME AND A HOPE

HIKING across the Appalachian Mountains would test a man's stamina, and Andrew Johnson sensibly accepted every ride he could hitch. At one point he was taken up by a Carolina gentleman who was traveling to Tennessee in state, with a train of wagons carrying his household and slaves. The man had been struck by Andy's forlorn appearance as he rested by the roadside in travel-stained clothes, his bundle between his feet; besides, there had been a mute, almost shy appeal in those piercing eyes that asked for sympathy and tenderness. Those eyes, small and intensely black, were the feature one noticed most, especially when Johnson fixed them unwaveringly (as his habit was becoming) upon the person he was addressing or listening to; they penetrated indifference and commanded attention.

Andrew traveled by road as far as Knoxville. There he boarded a flatboat and floated down the Tennessee and Little Tennessee Rivers to Decatur, Alabama, looking for work. Finding no opening, he struck out on foot across country and walked seventy miles to Columbia, Tennessee, where he was hired by Columbia's leading tailor, James Shelton.

Columbia was the county seat of a fat country, a region of wide-spreading tobacco and cotton plantations and manor houses, where the great landowners, possessors of hundreds of slaves, reproduced the spacious living of the older South from which they had come. Most of the planters around Columbia were from Virginia and North Carolina, and one of the district's most prominent men was James K. Polk, who came from Johnson's own district around Raleigh. Between Polk and the tailor's helper there was, of course, no communication; but Andrew did meet others of Tennessee's men of wealth and influence. Not far off was Andrew Jackson's home, The Hermitage; Jackson was the hero of New

Orleans, and the idol of young Andy Johnson's imaginings. Only a year before, Jackson had been defeated for the Presidency, when John Quincy Adams had taken the prize; but three years hence he would be installed triumphantly in the White House, and already in the Southwest he was a demigod.

Johnson's stay in Columbia was both pleasant and profitable. He was industrious and skillful, and had a knack for giving customers exactly that "snug fit" in which he took pride. Mrs. Shelton was drawn to the lonely youth and by little acts of kindliness earned his lasting gratitude. Many years later, when Johnson was President of the United States, Mrs. Shelton took to stating that she had taught Andrew Johnson to write. When a White House visitor asked the President about this, with an affectionate smile Johnson replied:

"She did not. But she seemed to get so much pleasure out of saying she did that I have not denied it. I am glad to give her all the pleasure that I can, for she was a mother to me when I lived with them and worked at my trade with her husband."

Andrew had been in Columbia six months when he learned that his mother was living in destitution in Raleigh, bad luck and Turner Doughtry having proved too much for her slender strength and means. Accepting without question this call to assume a manifest responsibility, he bade the Sheltons good-bye and headed back over the long, hard trail. Arriving in Raleigh, he took stock of the situation, and decided that his mother and stepfather should come to Tennessee with him. He was the head of the family now, and in some community in the West he was confident he could provide for all.

The few sticks of furniture and boiling kettles that "Polly" possessed were loaded into a two-wheeled cart, to which a gaunt, blind pony was harnessed, and the group set out. A tailor with the intriguing name of A. D. February accompanied them; their intended destination was the Sequatchie region where brother Bill was understood to be living.

Andy and friend February alternated with "Polly" and Turner in riding and walking—an hour on foot and an hour in the cart—because the starveling horse could not haul four at once; "ride and tie" was what poor folks called that method of travel.

Progress was slow—thirty miles the first day, sometimes only ten or fifteen after that, while crossing the mountains. Long afterward February wrote to Johnson recalling their adventures—"the panther that came and knocked the skillet off the fire where we camped one night"—the time "on top of the Blue Ridge, where you snapped your shotgun so often at a bear." The journey was replete with hazards, but through the dust and heat of August they followed the Daniel Boone trail. And one Saturday afternoon in September they arrived at the crest of a hill overlooking the little town of Greeneville, in East Tennessee.

The view from that eminence, had they been minded to take in scenic beauties, was thrilling. To the west, directly in their path, rose the Cumberland Mountains; in the distant northeast the Blue Ridge dreamed hazily on the horizon; while sixty miles to the southeast loomed the Great Smokies. In between were wooded hills and valleys, interlaced with a fretwork of clear-running streams with names as musical as their rushing waters—the Yadkin, the Eno, the Catawba, the Haw, the French Broad, the Pigeon, the Swannanoa, the Nolichucky. Below lay the placid village, with its millrace and mill, and its four squares joined by streets laid out primly at right angles.

The travel-worn party needed to rest before undertaking the final leg of their journey.

Descending the hill, Andrew asked a girl standing in front of an attractive dwelling whether there might be a vacant house or cabin where they could shelter. The girl, Eliza McArdle, answered that storekeeper Armitage had an empty cabin, and obligingly walked up the road a way to point out the store.

There Andy made inquiry and was given permission to use the cabin. More than that, Armitage, upon hearing Johnson's story, volunteered that he had a quantity of homespun on hand which he wanted to have made up into garments, and would Johnson like the job? Johnson would, and for several weeks he stitched for the storekeeper, while his family recuperated their strength, encamped near the "Gum Spring," a source of cool drinking water, through that sunny autumn of 1826.

There is a story which is unfailingly related in every account of Andrew Johnson's life. It goes that Eliza McArdle, when she came back from pointing out the way to the disreputable-looking tramp leading a scarecrow pony, was teased about acquiring a "new sweetheart." Tossing her head saucily, she is represented as retorting: "He's all right. I might marry him some day."

The story also is told that on that same day Andrew Johnson confided to his mother that the pretty girl who had spoken so kindly to them was the girl he was going to marry.

Whether these stories be true or not in fact, in sentiment they certainly are, as events proved.

Once the itinerant tailor had finished making up Armitage's cloth, there was no further occupation for Johnson in Greeneville. The town had a tailor, but he needed no helper. There was nothing to do but push on again; so the family's goods were loaded into the cart and the party resumed the journey westward. They kept on as far as Rutledge, a town forty miles beyond Greeneville, where Andrew found an opening. A lawyer who had been elected to Congress was leaving for Washington, and the little brick building he had used as an office was vacant. Johnson rented it for a tailor shop, and for six months he plied his needle in Rutledge.

Then came news that the tailor in Greeneville had closed his shop and moved on. Greeneville offered more advantages than Rutledge, and upon receipt of this word Johnson hitched up the decrepit pony, piled the furniture in the cart, and with his mother and stepfather hastened back. He arrived there in March, 1827, and immediately opened business in his own name. Then, in one of the few actions of his career which on the surface might appear precipitate, he married Eliza McArdle.

The license, issued at the courthouse on May 17, 1827, empowered "any authorized Minister of the Gospel or Justice of the Peace . . . to solemnize the Rights [sic] of Matrimony between Andrew Johnson and Eliza McArdle"; and that same day the knot was tied by the local "squire," Mordecai Lincoln, a tanner by trade and a distant cousin of Abraham. Johnson was eighteen and his bride was seventeen years old on their wedding day.

With this happy culmination of a brief and earnest courtship, the goddess of good fortune for once beamed her broadest smile upon the recent runaway apprentice; finding and marrying Eliza McArdle was to be the greatest stroke of good luck Andrew Johnson would ever have.

Eliza's father was dead. He had been a shoemaker. She had

been living with her widowed mother and contributing to their support by piecing together "crazy quilts" and making a rough sort of sandal with cloth uppers. Now Andrew took on the burden of helping Mrs. McArdle. The McArdles were Scotch-Irish, with more of the Scotch than the Irish in them—descendants, as were most of the people of East Tennessee, of the stern and unsubmissive Covenanters of Scotland. A mountain race, they were fearless, hardy, and self-reliant, proudly clannish, suspicious of outsiders, and given to fierce loyalties. Their confidence was not easily won, but once they gave their trust they were steadfast.

Eliza was an attractive girl, well formed and graceful. Her features expressed her character, a combination of strength, tact, gentleness, and patience. She had large hazel eyes, light brown hair, a generous mouth, and a brow indicative of intelligence and poise. She had received a good elementary education, and the dowry she brought her husband was the most precious gift, next to her love, that she could have bestowed—for she taught Andrew to write and cipher.

Who can describe the thrill experienced by a man avid of knowledge, who after years of fumbling efforts finds himself able to set down his thoughts in words, phrases, sentences? Andrew Johnson was far from childhood, and was the support of several dependents, with no resources except his skill as a tradesman to rely upon; and at the age of eighteen, at last, he was learning to communicate with others by a means other than speech. No wonder the covers of his carefully kept but simple account book became scrawled with practice signatures, in ink and pencil, written across and up and down the page—"And"—"Andrew"—"Andrew Johnson"—with a fanciful flourish underneath. Sometimes the writing of the entries in the book would waver and trail off like the unformed letters of a schoolboy. But as months went by it gained regularity. Spelling presented difficulties, and always would; but many an educated man of that day was indifferent to orthography. Did not Andrew Jackson growl at the secretary who called his attention to a misspelling of his own name that "it is a man of small imagination who cannot spell his name more than one way"?

Andrew and Eliza moved into a two-room frame and puncheonboard house on Greeneville's Main Street. The front room, twelve feet by twelve, was the shop, where Andy received customers and worked. The back room, about the same size, was the couple's home—their kitchen, bedroom, and parlor all in one.

In that back room, during the next two years, their first two children would be born—a son, Charles, and a daughter, Martha, who from infancy bore a striking resemblance to her father.

As a tailor Andrew was expert and even stylish, industrious and prompt. His custom widened until he was being patronized by some of the "best people" in town. Both he and Eliza had been brought up to live frugally; their tastes were simple, and from necessity they economized; and bit by bit they set aside a nest egg for their children's education. Before long, Andy was taking on assistants to help him in the increasing load of work.

Two years after settling in Greeneville he might have looked around with a certain satisfaction, for he had come far in that time. East Tennessee he liked; he liked the people and their democratic ways; in the main, they liked him. He was prospering in business, blessed in his wife, had started a family, and was rich in domestic affection. What more could he, the penniless outcast of Raleigh, the butt of a Selby's vindictive spite, what more could he desire? Yet there was something more, he felt, than a profitable business and a well-ordered life. Upon attaining that further goal he was about to embark, and not entirely by his own design. His introduction to public service was about to take place.

FOUR

FIRST STEPS

EAST Tennessee was a land of good omen for Andrew Johnson. The state was in effect three separate states, each having its own heritage, culture, and interests; and since these were often mutually antagonistic, the result was less a homogenous political entity than an uneasy coalition of basically hostile forces.

East Tennessee was a region of small homesteads and independent artisans. Its farmers plowed their fields and reaped their harvests by their own labor. They raised a diversity of crops, bred cattle and mules, and planted tobacco for the cash market. Their needs were nearly all supplied by themselves; even the cloth from which their garments were made was the product of their spinning wheels and looms. There were slaves in the region, but not many; families usually owned one or two for household help, for in fact domestic servants were obtainable in no other way. There was no widespread opposition to slavery, although there was some abolitionist sentiment in the area; but that issue was not crucial, and in East Tennessee manual labor was not held in disrepute.

The people of the district, many of them living on remote farms, cut off from human contacts for weeks and months at a time, were capable of turbulent emotional displays whenever they came together. Camp meeting revivals, with their hysterical frenzies, were popular in East Tennessee; the farmers and mountain folk, starved for any kind of human companionship, would gather from miles around to experience the supercharged excitements of shouting, stamping, roaring sanctification, whiplashed by the lurid verbosity of backwoods preachers.

The principal town of East Tennessee was Knoxville, and even that center retained an almost rustic simplicity. Social levels were observed in the towns somewhat more than in the countryside, and Greeneville had an aristocracy that was as self-consciously condescending toward social inferiors as were their counterparts elsewhere. The most important man in Greeneville was Dr. Alexander Williams, the Whig boss for the entire region; he lived in a style that enabled him to hunt with a pack of sixty foxhounds. The district's representative in Congress for years had been Colonel Thomas D. Arnold, the handsomest man in town and every inch a patrician. There were families like the Dicksons who could number their slaves by the dozens, and these were properly disdainful of plebeian neighbors.

The working class in East Tennessee—the smiths, the masons, and the builders—was numerous but politically ineffective. Both the laws and customs worked in their disfavor, the state constitution imposing disabilities that few manual laborers, however capable, were able to overcome.

In Middle Tennessee the prevailing conditions were quite different. That was a country of rolling uplands and bluegrass meadows, given over to plantations worked by gangs of slaves. The proprietors raised cotton and tobacco on a large scale, and shipped their produce to New Orleans for marketing. After the regulation of their domestic concerns, the attention and energies of these lordly planters were devoted to the conduct of public affairs. Having come mainly from the lowlands of the South Atlantic states, in their superb mansions they reproduced the spacious hospitality of the leisured South. Their social center was Nashville, which was also the capital of the state, and the government they dominated they looked upon as their responsibility, not to be shared with the "lower orders." But they accepted the obligations of office with the honors, and in most cases worked intelligently for the commonweal, as they viewed it.

To those who were excluded from their circle, of course, their pretentions seemed arrogant, and their monopoly of the public service was an obstacle to the attainment of a real democracy.

The state's third division was West Tennessee, whose hub was Memphis, on the Mississippi River. This district had been taken over by emigrants from the Gulf states of the deep South, a people cavalier in behavior and conservative in ideas. Side by side with the cotton magnates were the adventurers who swarm to any new frontier, drawn by the opportunities and excitement abounding there. Around Memphis the type of man known as the "Southron"—swaggering, high-tempered, scornful of inferiors, chivalrous toward women, generous to friends, implacable to enemies, disdainful of all who "played it safe"—this type was numerous. Since cotton raising was the principal activity, West Tennessee was heavily slave populated.

East Tennessee's individualists, with their rugged simplicity, suited Andrew Johnson. He became a tireless and tenacious reader, and customers would often find him seated cross-legged in his shop, an open book propped in front of him, to which his glance would travel thoughtfully while he worked. The supercilious were inclined to doubt that a tailor could comprehend Thomas Jefferson's messages to Congress, or Chatham's speeches, or the Constitution of the United States (which were the works he chiefly read), but Andrew was not deterred. The slow process by which his mind absorbed the printed page induced reflection, and a facial expression of furrowed concentration became habitual with him.

Greeneville was a center of such culture and learning as existed west of the mountains. The town had been the capital of the short-lived state of Franklin, which had preceded the formation of Tennessee, and Greeneville College had been founded as far back as 1794. It was the first institution of higher learning south of the Ohio River and west of the Appalachians, and in a period when books were scarce and costly its library contained three thousand volumes. Nearby were two other colleges, Washington and Tusculum.

To enroll in any of these schools was out of the question for young Johnson; he had neither the requisite elementary education nor the time or means to take up regular studies. But Greeneville and Tusculum had debating societies, which met once a week and argued philosophical and political questions. Johnson obtained permission to join the debates at Greeneville College.

Thereafter, every Friday, after his long day's work, he walked four miles to the college to take part in the debate, and four miles home again. This was a further step in his program of self-education, and enabled him to pit his wits against the minds of inquisitive students. Most of these were younger than Johnson, and they soon tended to cluster around him and listen attentively when he became earnest in expounding a point, speaking in the low, persuasive voice he had cultivated. He was always dead serious, and while he would not argue for argument's sake, he would grapple with a contradiction if by exposing its unsoundness he could penetrate to the central, basic principle involved. His thinking was abstract; good practical results, he would insist, must always be based on correct principles; whereas false principles, like will-o'-the-wisps, would lead one to destruction.

Johnson formed one of the few close friendships of his life at Greeneville College. This was with a tall, spare, thoughtful teacher named Sam Milligan.

Milligan had graduated from the College of William and Mary in Virginia, and was teaching by the time he was sixteen. Later he would study law and would practice. He had a judicial mind, was reserved in manner, and was accustomed to examining questions deliberately and dispassionately. His conclusions generally were sound and humane. The vitality of the ambitious Johnson attracted him, and he encouraged the latter to persevere in his mental training. In time Sam Milligan would come to occupy a unique place in Johnson's confidence, as his staunch friend and most valuable and trusted political and legal adviser.

After some time Greeneville College discontinued its debating society; then Johnson walked four miles out of the other side of town to attend the weekly sessions at Tusculum. And this weekly rubbing against student minds was not all. Johnson's shop had become a gathering place for some of the younger, more alert workingmen in town, men like Mordecai Lincoln, the tanner, and a plasterer named Blackston McDannel. These men, relegated to a submerged position in the prevalent society, often discussed the reasons for their enforced inferiority. The assumptions of the town's self-constituted ruling class they resented, and in their "bull sessions" they expressed this resentment bluntly. Johnson joined in rejecting caste prejudice, and he would enter into the men's talk while he worked. The doctrine that said the rich should rule was as pernicious as it was false, he contended; and he cited the snubs and slights to which his well-to-do patrons subjected him, often unconsciously and with no intention to offend. They were "stuck up" because custom made them so, he maintained. He himself was a plebeian and would always be one; there was no ignominy but honor in that title, so far as he was concerned; and he saw no reason why an honest workingman should bow down before any man whose claim to superiority was spurious. Worldly advantages did not create ability, and the denial of advantages could not keep it hidden. Blackston Mc-Dannel was every bit the equal in ability and intelligence of any of Greeneville's high and mighty, Johnson would declare, and the group would agree.

McDannel's good sense appealed to Johnson, and Blackston, on his side, understood Andrew's determination to make an honorable place for himself and his family in the world. McDannel was perceptive enough, too, to glimpse the sensitivity that underlay Johnson's brusque, severe exterior. His bitter boyhood had made Johnson suspicious of nearly everyone; he mistrusted men's motives, and would accept no proffer of friendship or loyalty on faith. For this reason he would open his thoughts and his inmost sentiments only rarely, and only to a chosen few. Tactiturn to the point of secretiveness, he confided in no one all the time—no one, that is, except Blackston McDannel and one or two others who had the key to his shy, recognition-hungry nature.

There was another town character against whom Johnson could sharpen his perceptions. This was a farmer of sorts named John Jones, who cared little for agriculture, and really was interested in two things—*reading* and *thinking*. Neighbors scoffed that Jones could "just sit and think" for hours on end; but his thinking was not daydreaming. His mind was analytical; he had studied law but did not practice; and he was constantly worrying ideas, dissecting them, reducing them to their elements, and rearranging them to arrive at ineluctable conclusions. He derived sensual pleasure from ferreting out fallacies, especially political fallacies. Any subject he considered worthy of attention he gave his undivided attention to. He was neither a scholar nor a public speaker, but a relentless reasoner in conversation. Johnson shared the propensity to analyze, and John Jones became another of his little circle of real friends.

Gradually, without his specifically designing it, a path was being opened to launch Johnson upon a course that would win him the recognition he craved. Greeneville's annual election of town officials was approaching. A clique of wealthy Greenevillians had monopolized the offices, electing each other with regularity year after year, but several of the young men who hung out at Johnson's tailor shop decided to try to win a voice for their kind in the town council. Without divulging their plan, they drew up a list of candidates of their choice, Johnson's name being put down with those of McDannel and Mordecai Lincoln. Ballots were prepared, and on election day the insurgents buttonholed voters on the way to the polls.

The result was a landslide victory for the entire slate; out of twenty-seven persons who received one or more votes for alderman, the top seven, who were elected, accounted for more than two-thirds of the votes cast. "B. McDannel," "M. Lincoln," and "A. Johnson" all were elected, McDannel and Lincoln standing next to the top of the tally, with twenty-six votes apiece, while Johnson just squeezed in, with eighteen votes. Winning by a hair would become a feature of Andrew Johnson's political career.

The election in 1829 having demonstrated the effectiveness of political organization, the next year the same group reelected their slate, Johnson included, and in 1831 they gave Andy a third term in the council. Then his friends pushed their audacity further and elected him mayor of Greeneville.

This was a real triumph for the tailor turned politician, and a severe jolt to the town's "well-bred." A farmer or a blacksmith as mayor they might countenance, but a tailor! . . . To have a fellow who would run up a pair of pantaloons on order representing the gentility of Greeneville was preposterous, was outrageous. The blot on the town's good name must be expunged, and twice in succession Andrew Johnson was marked for extinction. But each time instead he rode to another term.

His reputation rose with his political fortunes, and in 1832 the county court named Andrew Johnson, a man twenty-three years old who had never attended school, a trustee of Rhea Academy. Johnson would serve on the board with pride for years to come.

The year before he was first elected mayor, the budding tailor-politician acquired a real home for his family, a house that they owned. At an auction sale Johnson bid in a small brick dwelling on Water Street, with a "smith's shop" in the yard, paying somewhat less than one thousand dollars for the property. Soon after moving Eliza and the children into these larger quarters, Johnson bought a whitewashed clapboard building, containing a single room lighted by a door and two shuttered windows, and rolled it two and a half blocks to his own lot, where he fitted it up as a shop. Over the entrance he nailed a board lettered: "A. Johnson, Tailor." As long as he lived, that sign would not come down.

Ambition invited the young man to bid for a higher honor in 1835. He entered the race for a seat in the lower house of the Tennessee legislature, to represent the district embracing Greene and Washington counties.

At that time there were no nominating conventions, and the process of entering a political contest was Acadianly simple. One day "the boys" were lounging in the tailor shop, talking about the men likeliest to run for the Assembly seat. In the midst of the discussion, Johnson looked up from his work, and striking his hands together exclaimed, "Boys, count me in!"

His principal opponent was Major Matthew Stephenson, a well-known Whig leader. The campaign opened with a joint appearance of the candidates in Washington county, which was Stephenson's home ground; Johnson was scarcely known there. The Major made a straight Whig pitch, declaring himself in favor of internal improvements (public works, a later generation would call them), a high tariff to protect American industry, a national banking system, and other measures horrendous in the eyes of Jacksonian Democrats.

Johnson had allied himself with neither party formally, but he started his reply with a tribute to "old Hickory" for having scotched the serpent of Nullification and saved the Union—"the grandest government God ever made."

Then he laid down a fire of facts and statistics and questions that riddled his opponent's lofty claims. Where, he inquired sarcastically, were the industries in East Tennessee that needed the protection of a high tariff and high taxes? Had not Andrew Jackson, the hero of New Orleans, fought the monster—*The Bank*—

for years? Was it wise to resuscitate the octopus in a new form? Certainly not, was his view. He came before the people as no colonel, no major, and no criminal, either—but was that an offense? He earned his bread by the toil of his hands; and in the legislature he would be watchful to safeguard the interests of the common people, to whom he belonged and whom he would never desert. The Whigs, he cried scornfully, called for more laws, when the bane of the country was too many laws already. The only new laws that should be passed, in his opinion, would be laws to repeal some of the existing ones!

The speech was crude and it appealed to prejudice, but it had power. Johnson, Sam Milligan, and John Jones had moiled over it for weeks, and its array of facts was unanswerable. The campaign developed into a bruising ordeal for Stephenson, and on election day, by a narrow margin, Johnson carried off the victory. It was one rung higher on the political ladder.

When the legislative session convened at Nashville, Johnson took his seat as self-conscious spokesman for a faction which Middle Tennessee's patricians and the policy-makers of the west regarded as little more than a nuisance, a noisy minority tucked into the eastern corner of the state, to be endured only because of their votes.

Callow, unformed, jejune, with preternatural gravity Johnson entered upon this grander stage of public endeavor, and quickly came a cropper.

FIVE

AN AFFAIR TO FRIGHTEN HORSES

ANDREW JOHNSON'S first inconspicuous emergence at the state level of Tennessee politics coincided with the achievement of state constitutional reforms that in themselves were a reflection of the liberalizing tendency of the times. The constitution adopted in 1796 had impressed Thomas Jefferson as "the least imperfect and most republican" of any of the states. It granted the vote to every adult free man, including free Negroes, guaranteed freedom of press and speech, and forbade enactment of laws that would tend to encroach upon the "rights and privileges" of the people.

But there were restrictive clauses which were a legacy of the old aristocratic Federalist influence, and these discriminated against the "mechanic" class in particular. In 1833 Johnson had added his name to a call for a convention to revise the constitution, and the convention had met in 1834 and among other improvements had eliminated the property qualification for holding public office and abolished imprisonment for debt. Johnson welcomed both reforms, though his voice carried no weight in the final action. Nevertheless, it was a happy augury for his legislative baptism; and he made as clear as so unimportant an Assemblyman could that he felt himself a part of a great democratizing trend at work in the state. He announced that he stood for strict economy, adherence to constitutional principles, unfettered democracy, and justice for the laboring man.

His record of activity in the legislature during the next two years was feeble in concept and virtually nil in worthwhile results. Bumptious and bumpkin in appearance, he thought and acted like a rustic. His views were as ill-gaited as a sore-hocked horse, and he stressed their narrowness by airing them with solemn pertinacity. Fortunately the legislature did not take him seriously; it hardly regarded him at all.

32

He began by opposing the incorporation of the Hiwassee Rail-road—first, because it was a monopoly, and monopolies are bad, and then because it was an affair to affright horses, would put wayside taverns out of business, bankrupt stagecoach owners, ruin blacksmiths and wheelwrights, and end in causing grass to grow on the highways. He also opposed a bond issue to finance the construction of a network of macadamized turnpikes through-out the state, arguing that access to such large funds would tempt officials to steal, open the door of the treasury to corruption and graft, and anyway the proposition was plainly unconstitutional because it would tax the people without having obtained their consent in advance.

Relentless in following a principle to a *reductio ad absurdum*, he opposed the opening of the legislative sessions with prayer as a violation of the constitutional separation of church and state; there were churches nearby, he said, where legislators who felt the need of divine assistance could be accommodated at any time.

The worst of Johnson's blundering as a fledgling legislator was not that he exposed the confusion and immaturity of his own mind—that he was not yet at home in the realm of ideas, and put the cart of theory before the horse of practice with ludicrous results—but that he failed even to represent the interests of his constituents. More than any other section of Tennessee, the coun-ties in the east were dependent upon good roads; in their section there were few navigable rivers such as served Middle and West Tennessee for transport and travel, and highways were a neces-sity.

One might have expected that after so much earnest study, after coaching by Sam Milligan, and after exercising his mental powers in the rough forum of his "tailor shop crowd," Johnson would have comported himself less ineptly upon this first assump-tion of major public responsibilities. At home, in the township, where he was dealing with small-scale concerns that he under-stood, he had been an acceptable alderman and probably a better than average mayor. Confronted with problems of greater magni-tude and conditions of which he knew nothing except by report, he was out of his depth.

When Johnson returned home in 1837 and bid for a second

term in the Assembly, the voters retired him without hesitation to the platform of his tailor shop.

Obviously he had erred. The people had judged him and found him unsatisfactory, and then, as ever, he was convinced that in the long run the people are right. With characteristic persistence and thoroughness he set himself to find out why he had failed and to correct his mistakes.

In this task of reevaluation he called upon his farmer-philosopher friend. He asked John Jones to come into town, and taking him into his home, day after day he went over the problem with that clear thinker. Jones could show him where he had fallen down; Johnson had to absorb it and change accordingly, and that took time. But a practice was established by this intimate consultation which Johnson would follow for years: when confronted with a new question or issue, he would not take a stand until he had canvassed the whole matter with his friend Jones. Then, when he would finally announce his position, he would have so thorough a grasp of the subject that he could meet any attack with irresistible logic.

Meanwhile, he found some adherents among the practical politicians of Greene county. So far he had aligned himself with neither the Whigs nor the Democrats. The Whigs suspected that he was really with them, although cautious about going all the way and joining the party. On the other hand, the Democrats were beginning to claim him, and he was outspoken in his admiration of Jackson, that party's idol.

Tennessee was full of Jacksonian henchmen, fanatically loyal to the hero. There were some of these in Greeneville, among them the sheriff of Greene county, Richard M. Woods, and the clerk of the county court, George Foute. These men were veterans of many a hard-fought campaign, and they began to advise and guide young Johnson politically. This help was given partly on a personal basis, for Johnson seemed intent on making his own place, independent of party organization; yet he would not scruple to capitalize on Jackson's popularity by such devices as printing the hero's picture at the top of his ballots. For the time being, however, neither the party nor he made any overt commitment.

Consciously or not, Johnson was identifying himself with the people of East Tennessee—embodying in himself their interests, their mentality, their prejudices, and their aspirations. This really required no effort on his part, for their interests and their aspirations were his own; he spoke their language, and they spoke his homely idiom.

Although he seldom appeared on the streets (for he had to work, and a tailor's trade is confining), wherever there was a gathering, he would be on hand, moving among the crowd, conversing in his low, earnest voice, drawing around him recurrent clumps of attentive listeners. He rarely joked, and he had no small talk; but he could exchange gossip, and discuss the commonplace concerns of ordinary people.

On market days, when the country folk came into town, he was sure to appear, greeting friends, shaking hands, praising a farm wife's handiwork or the size of her eggs, talking politics with the men. Whatever subject he touched upon, he took up directly. He would dwell upon a point until his listener grasped it, then pass to the next point, and so on, driving the argument home. It was a way of educating his neighbors and educating himself, and it paid the expected dividend: after the two-year relegation to private life, in 1839 Johnson once more ran for election to the legislature, and beat the very man who at their last meeting had defeated him. With the tables turned, Johnson served another term in the Assembly.

This time, having learned his lesson, he remained gun shy in the face of controversial and complex issues. Upon his fellow lawmakers he made little impression. Nevertheless, he did introduce or support measures that earned him some minor admiration and also some potent disapproval. On the subject of internal improvements he had seen the light, and he voted for a program of public works that would be administered by a non-political board of trustees or commissioners. But generally he remained a quiet back-bencher, and succeeded in doing nothing that the "bunch back at the tailor shop" could not endorse.

The legislative sessions being brief, Johnson spent most of the two years in Greeneville. Materially he continued to prosper, for whatever the townspeople thought of him as a politician, as a tailor he was in demand. Several assistants now were needed to handle the volume of trade, and these journeymen became staunch admirers of their boss. He paid them fairly, worked side by side with them, and eventually set up some of them in shops of their own. More than one was taken into his home as a boarder. As early as 1831 his account book showed the entry, in writing like that of a child who was "trying hard": "Bob Powell commenced boarding February the 12th, 1831." Just below this was a record of monies due: "For making one Coat–$4 66"–"For making one vest–$1 00"–"For making one half coat–$2 33"–"Two pants–$1 00."

In that account book much of Johnson's personal life was revealed. Living expenses were carefully noted, and numerous entries showed that payment for tailoring had been taken in kind—a barter business. Mingled with the record of sums due and sums paid, exact to the halfpenny, were personal scribblings. On the reverse of one leaf was an entry written with obvious pride: "Martha Johnson commenced going to school to Chas. P. Byers July 17th, 1838." This was repeated, in part, directly underneath; that evidently was a memorable date for Andrew Johnson. There were no free schools in Greeneville and education had to be paid for. Johnson now was well able and overjoyed to pay for the tuition of his children, and Martha and Charles were being given the best teaching Greeneville could provide. More than that, when Martha started to bring home her lessons and textbooks, Andrew studied alongside her, not a bit abashed to "go to school" with his own daughter.

Martha and Charles, who was proving to be a sunny, likable boy, had been joined since the family moved into their own house by a second daughter, Mary, and another son, Robert. Mary was fair and cheerful, unlike Martha, whose dark gravity reflected that of her father. Robert would grow into a high-spirited, charming young man.

In the home, Johnson enforced a strict but not harsh discipline. There was abundance and kindliness, but no pampering and no waste. Plain speech was encouraged: "Tell it as it is or not at all," was the rule drilled into the children. Johnson kept his home apart from his public activities, and never allowed it to be used for political meetings; his shop was the place for that. His children were rather awed by their intense, stern father, but they did not fear him; he listened to their complaints and requests, was patient with their misdemeanors, and would always decide reasonably. During his absences on public service, Eliza managed the family's affairs efficiently, and in every respect she encouraged her restless husband to excel. Johnson had been able to purchase a small farm outside Greeneville, and on this he established his mother and stepfather; his relations with them appear to have been harmonious.

Domestic satisfaction, however, was offset by the continuing snobbery displayed by many of the "better element" of Greeneville. Their petty malice found expression in snubs which rankled with Johnson, much as he professed to despise their source. There was, for example, the grand banquet which Dr. Alexander Williams gave to a local Whig politician in 1836. Everybody of consequence in Greeneville was invited—except the town's three-times mayor. The affront was public and intentional, and Johnson was furious. Chancing to meet a neighbor on the street, he blurted out his sore resentment of "Alexander the Great," saying:

"Some day I'll show the stuck-up aristocrats who is running the country! A cheap, purse-proud set they are—not half as good as the man who earns his bread by the sweat of his brow!"

Johnson's pride would never down, and he would never cease to suffer from the snubs of snobs, reason them away as he might.

In 1840, while still only a middling large frog in a small pond, he at last took the step that landed him firmly in the ranks of the Democratic party. It was so extraordinary, and also so epitomized his personal power, that it is worth a chapter by itself.

SIX

SPELLBINDER

POLITICAL organizations in the 1830s were in flux. The Federalists, who had looked backward toward the "good old days" of royal prerogative and the subordination of the classes, had been swept aside; yet the Whigs who succeeded them were a conglomerate group providing only a partial replacement. The one unifying bond tying together the otherwise ill-assorted components of the Whig party was their almost pathological detestation of Andrew Jackson and everything the rugged, intemperate, belligerent warrior President represented or advocated. Jackson had pugnaciously championed the "common man"; therefore to the Whigs he was the epitome of wickedness, the "leveler," the inciter to anarchy, and the enemy of the rich, the privileged, and the socially powerful. By the natural law of opposites, the Jacksonian Democrats rallied the more solidly around "Old Hickory," the more vigorously the Whigs assailed him. Jackson's personality overshadowed every controversy.

The contest for the White House in 1840 was a purely personal fight between the Whigs' man and the Democrats' man, with party principles turned topsy-turvy on both sides. For President the Democrats nominated Jackson's personally designated heir, Martin Van Buren, who had already served one term as chief executive to the entire satisfaction of practically nobody, including himself. The Whigs bypassed the two stalwarts of their cause, Henry Clay and Daniel Webster, and nominated the lesser known William Henry Harrison, a gentleman of Indiana, tortuously linked with an ancient military exploit of doubtful authenticity. John Tyler of Virginia was chosen to be his running mate, and thus the slogan "Tippecanoe and Tyler too" was born.

Van Buren was attacked on the score of dandified ways and alleged luxurious living (he was suspected of scenting his whiskers with eau de Cologne), while the dignified, retiring Harrison was transformed into a gallused frontiersman, perched at the door of his log cabin drinking hard cider—the omnipresent friend of the "common man." The campaign involving these two rivals was one of the most bizarre and uproarious in Presidential history.

Tennessee was predominantly Whig; even in the eastern end of the state the Whigs were influential, although Jacksonism had its stronghold there. Andrew Johnson, perhaps prompted by Sheriff Woods and Court Clerk Foute, astute Jackson lieutenants, decided that the time had come to take sides. Characteristically, he had been exasperatingly slow in reaching that point, and he did not announce his decision in so many words. Instead, in the late winter or early spring of 1840 he issued a call for all Democrats of Greene county to rally at Greeneville on a given day.

That turnout would prove so sensationally successful, it would be repeated annually for years to come; and to comprehend Andrew Johnson's character and career, it is necessary to appreciate how he revealed himself there.

Witnesses of the event never recovered from their amazement. What had been expected to be just another political assembly unaccountably grew into an "irresistible outpouring" of mountain folk for twenty miles around. On foot and on horseback, in lumbering carts and creaking wagons, they jolted into town. There were no bands and no banners, but everywhere one felt a tingling of expectancy.

The proceedings had been carefully planned. Planks laid across empty boxes in the courthouse square provided a platform for the speaker, and between ten and eleven o'clock on the morning of the day designated, Johnson took his place there. Before him spread out the densely packed throng.

The meeting was opened by Foute, who read a set of resolutions that Johnson had drawn up. In some less primitive setting these would have sounded quaintly archaic, but for the backwoods audience they expressed eternal, never-to-be-denied truths. First they flayed the Federalists, and the arch Federalist of all, Alexander Hamilton. John Adams and his iniquitous Alien and Sedition Acts came under a scorching fire. Then Thomas Jefferson, inspired founder of the glorious Democracy, was eulogized, and by contrast, Henry Clay, base leader of the Whigs and exponent of abominable heresies, was excoriated for his asserted part in the "corrupt bargain" of 1824 that had elected John Quincy Adams President, and kept Andrew Jackson out of the White House for four years—a most damnable crime. Next "Old Hickory" was praised fulsomely as the second father of his country and the St. George who had killed the bloodsucking dragon, *The Bank*, and defended the rights of the people against the cunning machinations of aristocrats and reactionaries.

The resolutions drew roars of approval, and after they had been laid aside Johnson started his speech.

Let a man who observed the extraordinary occasion describe it. This man, Oliver P. Temple, was a Whig, and he never liked Johnson; in fact, he was so unfriendly that although he lived next door, he all but boasted that he had never stepped inside Johnson's house. As for Temple's feeling for the Democratic party, he expressed it in these words: "I am not certain whether I hate, or despise, or fear it most. I am sometimes tempted to think it is Antichrist." Yet Temple never withheld from Johnson a grudging admiration, and he never underrated Johnson's abilities. Temple was to meet most of the leading men of his day, but none of them, he recorded, "so impressed themselves on my young mind" as did Andrew Johnson.

In person, at this period, said Temple, Johnson was no ordinary man. He stood about five feet ten inches, and weighed about one hundred seventy-five pounds. "His limbs were strong and muscular, his movements active, indicating superior physical strength . . . His shoulders were large, his head massive, round and broad, his neck short and stout." Evidently a sedentary occupation had not made Johnson flabby, and his power of endurance was phenomenal. His step Temple called "quick and elastic, giving evidence of the energetic and restless spirit within." His complexion was "dark, his eyes black and piercing; his countenance, when in repose, gloomy; when lighted up by a smile, it became attractive . . . His voice was good and pleasant," and in ordinary conversation "soft and low." As time went by it would develop astonishing carrying power; helped by clear diction, it could be heard intelligibly from a great distance, possessing both range and flexibility. It seemed peculiarly adapted to speaking in the open air.

Temple described the speech as sheer prestidigitation, though all Johnson's speeches were "strong and sensational," this witness stressed. "His facts were presented in a bold and vigorous manner," and there was in them "that salt of bitterness, that impressive personality, that characterized him so markedly . . . His delivery, if not elegant, was at least easy, natural, and pleasing. His flow of language was wonderful, considering he was uneducated and [at the start] inexperienced in public speaking. There was nothing violent or spasmodic in his manner"; but the effect of his speeches upon East Tennessee audiences was like that of a hurricane.

The mountain people, isolated in their clearings, rarely seeing a stranger, rarely hearing news of the active world, built up frustrations that periodically demanded an outlet. To obtain this release some took to drink; others took to the more acrobatic forms of religion; but all took to politics. Their political pap they liked to have ladled up scalding hot, in copious doses, and the brand Andrew Johnson served stimulated them to frenzies that assuaged their repressions. It also riveted their loyalty upon him like an impervious armor. In Temple's phrase, "He knew their names and they knew his voice. He could lead them whithersoever he would."

Often he would tell them, with truth, that they formed the cornerstone of his career, that he owed everything he was to their faith and support. And, Temple added, "no granite foundation was surer or firmer . . . He took them as babes, and first by milk, and afterwards by strong meats, nurtured them into the stalwarts they became. He made of them a muscular race of men. He knew how to build men as well as how to clothe them . . . There was an exact fitness between him and these people. They were solid, compact, petrified. In vain opposition orators launched facts and arguments against these Greene county Democrats. The impact rang like an anvil struck with a hammer, but it left no impression.

"With almost a religious faith," these East Tennesseans had believed in Andrew Jackson, and when Jackson stepped aside they had feared that "all would be over with this government, and that there would be no one fit to rule . . . When Johnson appeared they were consoled with the hope that he might save the country."

At this initial rally (as afterward at each repetition), when Foute had concluded reading the resolutions, Johnson started his speech in his usual conversational tone. He interjected a few humorous touches (these he would discard gradually, for humor was not his forte) but his manner generally was serious and earnest. Carefully he developed his first point, and drove it home and clinched it before passing to the next. Sensitive to the temper of the crowd, he varied the tempo accordingly, and kept on for an hour, two hours, without pause. As he entered the third hour of the exhortation, his intensity rose in a long, sustained crescendo of denunciation of Whigs and Whiggery—that sum of all iniquities. He would call to mind those fearsome Federalists of old who had tried to steal the people's liberties, and with swelling voice would recite the words of the resolution that scourged those evil beings—traitors who in the War of 1812 had "hung out blue lights to the enemy," and had hoped to stifle the war by their infamous Hartford secession convention. The excitement infected even Temple himself. And when the speaker entreated his hearers to "stand firm on the Constitution" and with unwearied vigilance guard their rights, the crowd would "huddle closer together as if for mutual protection, and plant their feet firmly upon the ground, and would furtively glance around to see if anyone was trying to steal from them."

The philippic always included an appeal to stand fast, "hand in hand, shoulder to shoulder, foot to foot, and to make a long pull, a strong pull, and a pull together." The expression was drawn from the country custom of wagoners lending each other a hand to pull a wagon out of the mud; and when Andy uttered the familiar call, the delighted whoops of the wagoners and drovers could be heard far off; while the whole throng, catching the contagion, would clamor and shout and hurrah in an indescribable uproar.

No matter that by 1840 flesh-and-blood Federalists had become a historic memory; in East Tennessee they survived as ghosts, to be evoked by Andy Johnson's tirades against their diabolical schemes to oppress the "common man." Johnson's rallies became the high point of the year for thousands of Tennesseans, who awaited only his whistle to spring to his defense, and at any cost save him and themselves from political damnation. Laggard, awkward, and fumbling as he would for some time yet remain elsewhere, in his own bailiwick, at home, addressing his own people, Johnson early hit his stride and would maintain it.

SEVEN

GENTLEMEN AND DEMOCRATS

THE Greeneville rally of 1840 was fortunate for Johnson. It brought to the attention of Democratic chiefs throughout the state his hold upon the plain people of his section, and it underscored his effectiveness as a stump speaker. In consequence, that summer he was chosen to run as elector-at-large on the Van Buren ticket, drafted by the party to canvass the state. This was flattering recognition, for there were other able party orators, and Johnson threw himself into the epithet-studded fight with vim. His reputation was widened, and he began to be spoken of as a strong-minded partisan who could not be browbeaten, and who cut "not with a razor but with a case knife."

Whig speakers slashed back, and there was no dearth of dealers in the vocabulary of mayhem. Henry Clay invaded Nashville and addressed the Whig faithful not in hundreds or in thousands but in acres, and a fever of partisanship gripped every department of life—society, the church, the professions. Families were divided and partners became enemies; whole communities were set by the ears as the battle progressed. Politics in Tennessee was politics with the bark on, and a weakling was soon eliminated.

Realizing that he would be carrying the fight beyond the boundaries of Greene county, Johnson armed himself by subscribing to newspapers of every shade of opinion, and with the help of friends and his family, compiling scrapbooks of clippings which might prove useful in debate. The terrible *Jonesboro Whig*, mouthpiece of the opposition in East Tennessee, edited by "Parson" Brownlow, a preacher turned journalist who had few peers in using every term of denunciation, must be answered; so Sam Milligan undertook to edit a counter sheet, the *Greeneville Spy*, that carried the war into the *Whig*'s territory.

Apparently with some prescience of things to come, Johnson

also at this time began to insist that a complete, unbiased record be kept of his activities, whether political or domestic. No scrap of paper must be discarded, no matter how trivial, if it concerned him; everything must be preserved, intact and uncensored. It was not long before boxes stuffed with the motley collection were piled up in the little outbuilding that stood in the yard of his house.

The Presidential wrangle ended in defeat for Johnson's man. The mild-mannered Harrison entered the White House, and after one month of merciless badgering by place-hunters, he died, and John Tyler became the first Vice-President in the nation's history to succeed to the Presidency by reason of an incumbent's death. Johnson received the reward for his services in the campaign, however, by being elected to the State Senate in 1841. And there he offered what seemed positive proof of his having entered fully into the party's councils, amenable to party direction and submissive to the party's discipline. This was a novel departure.

Few persons in this world have managed to map out a course of action early in life, setting a goal and listing the successive steps by which to attain it, and then have successfully adhered to that program. The usual process—about all that can be expected in most cases—is to set one's face in the desired direction, forge ahead, and hope for the best.

This was the course of Andrew Johnson in his unoriented, often convulsive striving to break out of the bounds imposed by his mentally starved, inhibited youth. Fully escape he never would, and in reaction he soon learned to clothe his handicaps with the mantle of voluntary choice; to make of necessity not simply a virtue, but a distinction and a boast.

This seeming perversity in proclaiming and insisting upon his disadvantages puzzled and irritated many who could not grasp its motivation. Like every man endowed with superior abilities, Johnson was aware that he possessed unusual gifts; but how to use these fruitfully he still only imperfectly sensed. Circumstances had started him along the highway of politics, though he would more than once lament that such had not been his natural bent. Nevertheless, once launched upon that road, he plowed forward, regardless of obstacles and suiting his gait to the unevenness of whatever stretch he was at the moment traversing. This led to some strange shifts in his apparent direction, to temporary backtracking now and then; but these detours did not halt his steady forward progress.

In 1841 this pragmatic attitude toward present necessities cast him in the role of a party regular, loyally and ruthlessly carrying out a party decree, come rule, come ruin. It was a test of fortitude.

James Knox Polk, severe, dry aristocrat of Middle Tennessee, had been drafted by the Democrats in 1840 to run for governor; only he, it was felt, could redeem the state from the bondage to the Whigs under which (the Democrats contended) it had groaned too long. Polk had served in Congress and as Speaker of the House of Representatives, and an attempt was made to inflate his popular appeal by enthroning him as the inheritor of Jackson. He actually was dubbed "Young Hickory," incongruously, for no two men could have resembled each other less than Andrew Jackson and James Knox Polk. The former was all passion, impulse, and unpredictability; the latter was cold, pedantic, and reticent exactly where and when Jackson would have been rash, fiery, and outspoken.

Polk accepted the party's call and carried the election. Then he found himself caught in a dilemma not unusual among popular governments: he controlled the patronage, but the Whigs controlled the legislature. By the narrowest possible margin, it is true, and not in both branches; but the almost exactly equal division of strength strengthened the resolve of both parties not to acquiesce in a minority role.

In the Assembly the Whigs had a majority of two; but the Senate was held by the Democrats, by the slender margin of one vote—thirteen Democrats against twelve Whigs. Andrew Johnson was one of the thirteen Democrats.

When the regular legislative session opened early in 1841, the first order of business was to elect two United States senators. One incumbent's term was expiring, and a vacancy had been created by the death of the other. United States senators were chosen by a joint vote of the two houses of the legislature, and unless both houses consented to vote no election could be held.

The Democrats were bent upon capturing at least one of the seats at stake, and the Whigs were just as determined to prevent this from happening.

Before the session opened, deep were the conferences on both sides to devise a winning strategy. Johnson had taken a hand in this, writing to the governor (in a letter the orthography and handwriting of which must have made the scholarly Polk wince) that "unless I am rong [sic]," a special session would be the best way to "handle the matter." This unsolicited counsel from a hill-billy freshman senator Polk treated with silence.

The plan finally agreed upon by the Democrats was to prevent the taking of a vote; in a joint vote by the two branches, the Whigs would have a one-vote edge, and both prizes would be theirs.

Day after day, the clerk of the Assembly transmitted to the Senate a request to fix a date for a joint session, and day after day the thirteen Democrats voted in a block to refuse the request. The deadlock lasted through the whole session, and as a result, for the next two years Tennessee had no voice in the United States Senate.

The man most active in erecting and defending this roadblock was Andrew Johnson. He kept his colleagues in line, dragooned the waverers, resisted every pressure, and seemed impervious to temptation. It was a straight party fight, and so far as he was concerned no other question entered into it. The Democratic leaders were pleased by his generalship, and Polk so far revised his opinion of the Greeneville tailor as to suggest him for one of the contested Senate seats. Best of all, from The Hermitage came warmest commendation.

In East Tennessee, this victory of sorts and the praises of Jackson gave impetus to the talk already circulating there that Andy Johnson was the true successor to "Old Hickory" and was bound to wind up in the White House. This conviction became so deeply rooted in the minds of the people of that region that it was accepted as inevitable, something not to be questioned any more than one would question the rise and setting of the sun.

The satisfaction of the Democratic chiefs—members of the planter class and their spokesmen, all of them—over Johnson's apparent readiness to subserve the ends of the party was incomplete, however, because the young senator from East Tennessee entertained some unsettling ideas and persisted in recommending changes that would, in effect, overthrow the existing social and economic structure.

For example, Johnson submitted a resolution favoring the creation of a new state—the state of Frankland—out of contiguous portions of the mountain areas of Tennessee, Georgia, the Carolinas, and Virginia. The people in these regions were of common stock; they had mutual interests, not identical with those of the other portions of their states, and free white labor was the dominant pattern among them. Johnson's resolution was tabled by the preponderant representatives of Middle and West Tennessee, who had no intention of diminishing the area under their control.

Johnson's next proposal was even more revolutionary, for it struck at the source of the power wielded by the slaveholder oligarchy. The constitution of Tennessee, like that of the United States, apportioned population for purposes of taxation and representation by the so-called three-fifths rule. That is, slave population was counted as equal to three-fifths of the same number of free white population. This gave an immense leverage to the slave counties, and worked proportionately to the disadvantage of regions where slaves were few, as in East Tennessee. To illustrate: a county in West Tennessee containing 15,000 slaves and 1,000 free men was given a population figure of 10,000; while a county in East Tennessee that had 5,000 free men and only 1,000 slaves was given a population figure of 5,600. This manifest injustice aroused Johnson, and he proposed a constitutional amendment wiping out the three-fifths clause.

The majority of the legislature was dead against this; they saw the threat to their continued dominance of state affairs that the plan contained, and they looked askance at Johnson as a visionary, subversive of public order. Their estimate, of course, was erroneous: Johnson was profoundly conservative in his instincts and his actions. However, as he himself put it, while he advocated none of the revolutionary " 'isms' and 'schisms' " put forward by extremists, he was able to "understand when an injustice was done to the people," and attempt to right it.

The dignity of labor was a constant theme with him. In a memorial he drew up for a group of Greeneville mechanics he enumerated famous figures of legend and history who had toiled with their hands. Adam headed the list as the first tailor, for had he not, according to the Bible, sewed fig leaves together for an apron? "Tubal Cain was an artificer in brass and iron; Joseph, the husband of Mary, was a carpenter, and our Savior probably followed the same trade; the Apostle Paul was a tentmaker; Socrates was a sculptor; Archimedes was a mechanic; King Crispin was a shoemaker, and so was Roger Sherman, who helped to frame the Constitution." And was not General Greene of Revolutionary fame a tinker, and General Morgan, the frontier rifleman, a blacksmith?

These simple conceits delighted Johnson's naïve mind, and he would revert to them throughout his life; that his own craft traced back to Adam gave him particular satisfaction. By elaborating this laboring man's Pantheon, he constructed a mythology that substituted for the one to which he had never been introduced, in the form of fairy tales, as a child. But often as he reverted to them, these fantasies never obstructed or clouded his practical vision.

In the department of religion (a very, very important department in America at that period) Johnson came under suspicion of being a nonconformist, and possibly a dangerous one. Eliza and Martha were ardent Methodists, but they could not bring Andrew to regular churchgoing. Although reared loosely in Baptist doctrine, he belonged to no church, and his attitude toward all organized faiths was one of broad tolerance but little or no personal attachment. As a politician he was challenged on this subject many times, and he confined himself to replying that his creed was "the doctrines of the Bible, as taught and practiced by Jesus Christ." Nothing could move him beyond that honest though imprecise declaration. He read the Bible diligently, and he was much attached to a fine English edition, with clear, large type, which he carried in his journeys.

On this score he resembled Abraham Lincoln, whose simple Christianity failed to recommend him to the churchgoers and clergymen of rural Illinois. Both these men were passing through a preparatory stage, finding their bearings in a world not yet aware of their special qualities. In one respect, however, Lincoln was enjoying a decided advantage over Johnson, and this was the former's daily association with men of education and superior mental capacity. Lincoln had read for the bar and in 1840 was practicing law at Springfield, the state capital, where his associates were the most able lawyers in the region.

In the new states beyond the mountains the best-educated class of men, by and large, during the first decades of settlement, was the legal class. Pioneers cannot carry the impedimenta of culture with them when they strike into a virgin wilderness; the mere struggle to survive and take root absorbs all energies, and art, science, abstract thought, and social niceties have to wait. Books, however, are relatively easy to transport, and many pioneer families managed to bring along a volume or two—the Bible, a Shakespeare, *Pilgrim's Progress*, perhaps a digest of laws, or a collection of patriotic speeches. And the Constitution and the Declaration of Independence were read everywhere.

The nature of their profession required the lawyers to familiarize themselves with literature in general, the classics and the moderns; they were obliged to read, and their very work was an intellectual exercise. Lawyers, therefore, in the early settlements, comprised the intellectual class, and association with them on terms of intimacy was a humanizing influence and stimulus to mental development.

Such an association Andrew Johnson never enjoyed. His early intimacies were with workingmen, many of them uneducated like himself. Though sometimes endowed with natural shrewdness and penetrating minds, these men were untrained, unlearned, and not bred to systematic intellectual effort. Among Johnson's first instructors, Sam Milligan and John Jones were almost the sole exceptions to this class; the debates held in Johnson's tailor shop, while rich in common sense, were conducted, in the main, in the pungent, limited vocabulary of unlettered men.

To appreciate the effect of this lack of a daily intellectual stimulus, consider the background and condition, in 1840, of several men whose destinies were to converge with Andrew Johnson's in a few years, with consequences fateful to them all.

Across the Ohio River, in Illinois, Abraham Lincoln (three months younger than Johnson) was riding circuit in Sangamon County, living among lawyers and judges, some of whom had well-furnished, polished minds. Lincoln so far had had only the responsibilities of a single man to cope with, for he would not marry Mary Todd until two years later; in 1840, Andrew Johnson had been supporting a family for years, and had one son almost grown to manhood.

In northern Ohio, in the Western Reserve, settled by New Englanders, was a lawyer, eight years older than Johnson, who already had been elected to the lower house of the legislature, had been defeated once, and, like Johnson, would soon be returned to the State Senate. This bluff, rough-speaking Whig had made a name for himself by a powerful speech against strict enforcement of the hated Fugitive Slave Act. He, too, had run the gauntlet of poverty and hard usage, had worked at menial jobs while struggling to acquire an education, and would always carry scars from that period of hard knocks; but by 1840 he was educated and moving in the company of educated men. This man, who fascinated spectators by his odd stance when speaking—rising on his tiptoes and falling back sharply on his heels to emphasize a point in his hard-hitting arguments—was Benjamin Franklin Wade.

Further south in Ohio was a lawyer, a man of twenty-six, who, despite a penurious youth, had gone to college and was now practicing in Steubenville. Already he showed flashes of mental brilliance marred by signs of an emotional intensity that suggested some pathological instability; but he had tremendous drive, a fierce power of concentration, and was determined to rise in his profession. His name? Edwin McMasters Stanton.

Almost next door, in neighboring Indiana, in 1840 a bright twenty-three-year-old student was admitted to the bar. His Quaker forebears had left North Carolina because of antipathy to slavery, and in his surroundings intellectual attainments were held in esteem. This keen-witted, generous youth with a reforming urge was George Washington Julian.

Farther east, in Pennsylvania, in 1840 was a lawyer as craggy as his native Vermont, who was serving his last term in the state legislature, about to withdraw from politics in disgust at the timidity of politicians. Born desperately poor, he had known grinding toil, but he had gained an education. Always angered by the inequities that are placed upon the poor, he had risen to impassioned eloquence in a denunciation of the proposal to scrap Pennsylvania's system of free schools—"an act for branding and marking the poor," he called it. At forty-eight, Thaddeus Stevens was a frustrated idealist, wasting his powers in petty squabbles, and ready to quit.

These men, all lawyers, like Andrew Johnson had been born poor and in lowly condition, but unlike him, they had been able to get an education. For they lived in the North, where ignorance and poverty were not equated and the term "poor white" was not applicable; educational facilities of some sort had been within their reach. And there were others, like the Bostonian Charles Sumner, whose lives would coincide with that of the tailor of Tennessee. Sumner, a graduate of Harvard College and Harvard Law School, in 1840 was intellectual, erudite, Olympianly handsome, and still under thirty. To a political career he had given no thought, nor would he for some time to come.

A different type of Massachusetts man was a brash, pushing schoolteacher in Lowell. In 1840, at twenty-two, he was admitted to the bar, and by dint of cleverness, sharp practice, hard work, and boundless self-confidence he would rapidly pile up a fortune from a practice devoted mainly to defending criminals and unpopular causes, some of them undeniably worthy. This irrepressible controversialist responded to the name Benjamin Franklin Butler.

One whose career would impinge vitally upon that of Andrew Johnson was in 1840 no lawyer, no anything of much consequence yet; he was an eighteen-year-old cadet at West Point, remarkable for little except a power of taciturnity and a passion for horses. On the army rolls his name was entered, incorrectly, "Ulysses Simpson Grant."

And isolated on a plantation in Mississippi was a man exactly Johnson's age, a graduate of West Point, who in 1840 was immersed in a long course of cotton raising and intellectual study —a fastidious, high-principled, reserved, austere, Kentucky-born man named Jefferson Davis.

Not one of all these men, whose influence upon each other would have a fateful bearing upon the course of the nation as well as upon their own fulfillment—not one, with the exception of Andrew Johnson, had been confined, during their formative years, to the almost exclusive society of men whose native intelligence had never been sharpened and focused by systematic schooling. The effects were visible in all the cases; in Johnson's case, to his disadvantage. For the leaders of the Tennessee Democracy—the Polks, the Pillows, and their kind—while they praised Senator Johnson's adamancy in the crisis of the "Immortal Thirteen," could neither unreservedly accept nor personally like the out-of-character tailor. In brief, they found themselves unable, despite the best intentions, to welcome him as an equal. And the fault was as much his as theirs. There was something about him that held would-be friends at bay when they tried to bridge the chasm that separated them.

Johnson had no social life and appeared to desire none. He had no relaxations; when he was not working he was studying, or charily cultivating useful friendships among his own people. The hours that other men gave to diversions—social gatherings, the theater, hunting and fishing—Johnson gave to self-improvement. From the tentative advances of his "betters" he shrank, taking refuge in a fierce pride. He was not one of those who, when they rise in the social scale, kick out the ladder by which they have climbed; Johnson clung to it. A plebeian, he exulted in the designation. As was said in East Tennessee, "Andy Johnson never went back on his raisin'."

Within his party, the well-inclined ruminated on how far Andrew Johnson was to be trusted. Would he ever become a gentleman, or comport himself like one? The Whigs had their opinion about this, and it tied in with a standing Whig riddle: Can a Democrat be a gentleman? The reply given by a stately Virginian to this question seemed not too severe for many Whigs in Tennessee:

"Well, he is apt not to be; but if he is, he is in damned bad company."

Johnson recognized his exclusion from the innermost circles of his party and accepted it. Plainly he would have to make his own way, and he felt he could do this with the help of the sort of people who did not feel above him—*his* people of East Tennessee.

Without reference to the party hierarchy, therefore, he announced that he was a candidate for Congress from his district; and great was the disgruntlement of the "better element," Whig and Democrat alike, when, despite their heartiest efforts to head him off, he was elected.

EIGHT

NEITHER BOOR NOR PALADIN

IF the arrayed forces of conservatism in East Tennessee, Whig and Democrat, failed to stop Andrew Johnson on the threshold of Congress, it was not for want of trying. At first his own party leaders demurred at endorsing his candidacy. Then he threatened to run as an independent, and rather than risk losing all hold on him, the leaders yielded reluctantly. But in a covert alliance with the Whigs they trotted out a popular lawyer of Jonesboro, Colonel John Aiken, himself a Democrat, to finish off the tailor. It was Aiken who was beaten.

Johnson lost no time in traveling to Washington, and arrived there in late November, 1843. Martha was on hand to welcome him, for he had enrolled her a year before in the Female Seminary conducted by Roman Catholic nuns at Georgetown. There she would be a student for three terms.

Her father had chosen the school for reasons not known now, but possibly because of its academic reputation and its location in an atmosphere free from the prejudices of Greeneville. At home the child would be regarded as the daughter of "Andy the tailor"; at Georgetown she was the daughter of "the Hon. Andrew Johnson," a legislator of Tennessee. He wished Martha, whose intelligence and quiet dignity already were noticeable characteristics, to receive the best education procurable (which he was now well able to pay for), but one without frills—none of the "polite accomplishments" that were supposed to be indispensable to a young lady of rank and fashion. A bill submitted by the school made this clear.

At the bottom of the printed invoice four branches of instruction appeared (Music, French, Drawing, and Latin), but in the space left for filling in the charges for these subjects was carefully written "0.00." Martha's education should be useful, thorough, and practical. The bill, submitted on February 12, 1843, characteristically was endorsed "Paid" the same day. The main items included:

Board and Tuition, Dec. 2, 1842, to Feb. 12, 1843	-	$33.81
Extra for Lodging	-	1.59
Ditto for fuel, quills, ink, etc.	-	.39
Extra for Washing	-	3.95
Extra for 2 copy books, 12½ c. each	-	.25
		Total $39.99

Washington was the largest city Johnson had yet seen, except for a brief glimpse of Baltimore, when he had attended the Democratic convention there in 1840. The capital's population was about forty thousand, and it was strongly Southern in tone. During most of the year it dozed, though when Congress was in session it grew animated enough. The great party leaders maintained fine homes, but ordinary members of Congress "batched it" in boarding houses scattered below Capitol Hill. Theirs was an uncomfortable life, separated from their families and congregated in more or less congenial groups called "messes." Apart from the public buildings, a few of which were fine, the place was a hodgepodge of low brick and timber houses and ramshackle hotels. The streets were dusty and stank in summer, and turned to quagmires in winter. One feature the slatternly town did not lack was barrooms. Doubtless exposure to its squalor contributed to Andrew Johnson's conviction that "large cities are eyesores on the body politic." Like other inconspicuous congressmen, he found an inexpensive boardinghouse close to the Capitol, and set about familiarizing himself with his new environment.

His maiden speech had an immense success back in Tennessee. In his old age, Andrew Jackson was burdened by debts, and to provide some relief and rectify a long-standing injustice, Johnson introduced a resolution to repay to the battered hero a thousand-dollar fine for contempt of court which had been imposed on him at New Orleans, in the War of 1812. Jackson had seized a judge who dared to interfere with martial law, had conveyed him a dozen miles into the country, and dumped him down on the highway. Two days later the war ended, and the judge, resuming his bench, slapped on the fine.

Johnson's proposal was carried, and the money, with accumu-lated interest, was transmitted to The Hermitage. Tennessee Democrats praised the action, though the Whigs were far from jubilant.

The President when Johnson entered Congress was John Tyler, who had succeeded to the office on the death of President Harri-son. That crisis had necessitated the setting of a precedent, and there had been some attempt to withhold the title from Tyler; but he stuck to his claim and established the rule that would prevail thenceforth.

Tyler and Harrison had been elected by the Whigs, although Tyler had followed an independent course throughout his politi-cal career. He had backed Andrew Jackson in some of the latter's policies, particularly in the war on the United States Bank; but Tyler also had supported some of Clay's projects. The indignation of the Whigs overflowed when, upon becoming President, Tyler showed continued indifference to party direction; his firm opposi-tion to restoration of *The Bank* in any form—the issue on which Jackson had stirred up the most violent enmity—infuriated the party that elected him to the point of frenzy. Tyler vetoed in succession two bills for setting up a national banking system, and the Whigs howled "Treason!" Their anger in Tennessee was ex-pressed by the fulminating "Parson" Brownlow, who published in the *Whig* an open letter to the President, seething with invective.

"This abominable treachery," he told Tyler, "is only equalled by your hypocrisy in proclaiming a national fast, for the purpose of working the public mind up into a religious mood that they might bear that astounding and atrocious act of perfidy which you intended to commit . . . Oh! has Heaven no secret hidden thunderbolt, red with uncommon wrath, for such a vile traitor? Little did I think, when introduced to you last March, and while boarding with you for weeks together in Brown's Hotel, that I was in the society of such a cutthroat! . . . Resign! For the sake of the credit of your posterity, resign your seat, and let the party you have so shamefully betrayed fill it with a man on whom they can rely!"

Now posterity was a matter of concern to John Tyler, for by his first wife he had had seven children, and by his second, whom he had just married, he would have seven more; but he did not resign. Midway in his term, however, he had become a President without a party and a politician with a past but no future.

As a Democrat, Congressman Johnson was not unduly perturbed by Tyler's deviationism; on the crucial issues of hostility to a nationalized banking system, and of the annexation of Texas, he sided with the President. But Johnson's activities during this term in the House were confined mainly to voting for measures that jibed with his principles, and opposing those that did not.

He spent much time in study, haunting the Library of Congress, and the books he borrowed covered a wide range of topics. Often he received overdue notices from the librarian, for no subject in which he took an interest did he fail to plumb thoroughly and to brood upon before coming to a conclusion. He made few speeches and attracted few friends. His speeches, while hardhitting in content, in expression tended to be either clumsy or banal, for words did not come readily to him, and he was more inclined to lecture than to persuade. When writing to some crony at home, such as Blackston McDannel, he could lapse into the homely, rude, pungent speech of East Tennessee with evident relish. At the close of the term he presented himself for reelection, standing on his record.

"Parson" Brownlow took on the task of cutting the tailor down to size, egged on by the "better element" of the district, who were humiliated that a "boor" should represent them in Congress.

The "Parson" was a product of the frontier as unusual in many ways as Johnson. Born in the hills of western Virginia, Brownlow had come to East Tennessee as a youth and picked up an education by reading. At a camp meeting he became converted and joined the Methodist ministry, "riding circuit" through the Appalachian back country for ten years. Drawn irresistibly to politics, he launched his newspaper, the *Whig*, to serve the interests of Henry Clay in East Tennessee and confound all Democrats. His mastery of the lexicon of abuse was his greatest gift, and in his campaign against Johnson he exceeded himself. Aware that as a stump speaker he was overmatched, he fired his invective through the columns of the *Whig* while Johnson, on his side, hurled taunts as tellingly, in one speech calling his vituperative opponent a "hyena," "devil," and "coward."

This last was unforgivable, because "Parson" Brownlow feared nothing in human form. In a furious rejoinder, flaunted in capital letters, he termed Johnson a "VILE CALUMNIATOR, AN IN-FAMOUS DEMAGOGUE, A COMMON AND PUBLIC LIAR, AN IMPIOUS INFIDEL, AND AN UNMITIGATED VIL-LAIN," adding, to show that he was not hiding under his desk: "Mr. Johnson knows where to find me, at all times."

Next Brownlow accused Johnson of inciting a plot to assassinate him—and then questioned Johnson's parentage. Andy could not possibly be the son of that illiterate loafer, Jacob Johnson, Brownlow insinuated; wasn't he "the very spit" of Judge John Haywood's nephew at Raleigh? Andy must be a by-blow of the judge.

This accusation brought Johnson's anger to the boiling point; his mother, "Polly" Doughtry, was living near Greeneville and the charge reflected upon her. Taking time out, he went to Raleigh and collected affidavits which he published in an open letter concluding:

"These vandals and hyenas would dig up the grave of Jacob Johnson, my father, and charge my mother with bastardy."

Johnson won the election, in spite of Brownlow's last-minute springing of "Ten Reasons For Believing Andrew Johnson To Be An Atheist." This Johnson brushed aside, merely repeating his simple creed—the doctrines preached by Jesus.

The year 1844 had been momentous in Tennessee because it resulted in the election of James Knox Polk to the Presidency. Twice Polk had been defeated for a second term as governor, his opponent being "Lank Jimmy" Jones, a political buffoon of the sort that turns up periodically in American politics. By reducing the campaign to the level of farce, "Lank Jimmy," in the popular phrase, "made a monkey" of the dignified, serious-minded Polk. Then, in the face of two defeats at home, Polk won nationally in 1844 as the original "dark horse" Presidential candidate, defeating Henry Clay.

On March 4, 1845, a day of rain and mud, the new Democratic President took office, and three months later, on June 8, an era came to an end when the legendary Jackson died. For Democrats everywhere, but especially in Tennessee, a great light went out with the hero's passing; the Whigs shrugged that retribution had caught up with a hoary sinner. Brownlow paid an awesome tribute to "Old Hickory" in the *Whig:*

"After a life of eighty long years spent in the indulgence of the most bitter and vindictive passions, which disgrace human nature and distract the human mind, the existence of ANDREW JACKSON terminated . . . We would not if we could, turn aside the veil of the future to show his deluded followers and blind admirers what awaits him."

In Washington Johnson answered in his own way the "atheist" tag Brownlow had tried to tie on him. He introduced a resolution providing that "Congress shall be opened with sincere prayer to the Giver of all Good for His blessing, and that the same should be done upon the terms as laid down in the Gospel of Jesus Christ, without money and without price, except as shall be voluntarily contributed by the members of the House individually."

The resolution fell flat.

During this second term, Johnson increasingly tended to elude party control. His courage was not questioned, but his discretion was. He did not hesitate to twit even the venerable John Quincy Adams with hairsplitting and inconsistency. Adams, having become the first ex-President to be elected to Congress, was one of the most formidable debaters in the House, and he conceded in his diary that the brash young man from Tennessee possessed "great native ability."

It seemed to be impossible, however, to predict just what Johnson would say or do, except that he would probably do the unexpected, and that it quite likely would be something disagreeable. He declined to accept any man's opinion on faith; everything must be weighed, tested, and sifted in his analytical mind. He must ferret out the reason behind things, and since his mental processes were as slow as they were thorough, his conclusions were not reached hastily. Once arrived at, they could not be shaken. A contemporary set down that Johnson possessed "the virtue of candor in a much higher degree than most public men. There was no deceit in him. If he was an enemy, he was too independent and too bitter to conceal the fact. It was always well known what he thought of those around him." Complimentary or the reverse, the truth came out.

He had no compunction about defying the dictates of the party leaders when a principle was at stake. He would cross swords as readily with a Democrat as with a Whig. Although he claimed adherence to the Democratic party, he really was a guerrilla fighter within its ranks. When the question of excluding petitions advocating the abolition of slavery came to a head in the House, Johnson voted with the Southern bloc to exclude them; but when Joshua Giddings, fiery Ohio abolitionist, was shouted down in his attempt to justify the presentation of such petitions and the session was thrown into uproar, Johnson was the only Tennessee member who voted to let Giddings speak. There was no inconsistency in these actions. As the representative of a slaveholding state, Johnson took the side of the South on the general position. But his sense of justice forbade him to deny Giddings or any man the right to be heard.

Johnson had voted for the annexation of Texas, and when, in January, 1846, the question of admitting Oregon, a free state, came up, he voted in favor of admission, although roundly denounced for this by his Southern colleagues. It had been understood from the beginning, he said, that Texas and Oregon should come into the Union together, and he was for honoring the agreement.

When Thomas H. Bayly of Virginia, every inch a gentleman, an aristocrat and a large slaveholder, accused Johnson of being an "ally" of the abolitionists, he spurned the accusation so hotly that Bayly protested he was being misrepresented—"unintentionally, I presume," he interjected politely.

Johnson bristled:

"Will the gentleman specify in what way I have misrepresented him?"

Bayly sat silent, scowling, and Johnson went on scornfully:

"The gentleman's scowls and threats have no terrors for me. He may show his slaves how choleric he is, and make his bondsmen tremble!"

Such outbursts placed the tailor beyond the pale of gentlemanly consideration, a fact of which Johnson was reminded in floor clashes.

Thomas L. Clingman of North Carolina, a Whig who had once

shown a tendency toward party independence similar to Johnson's, but had been dragooned into line, was crushed by Clay's defeat, and in a bitter exchange shouted that the Democrats owed their victory to the Irish Catholics of New York City—"a lot of gamblers, pickpockets, thimble-riggers, droppers, barn-burners, quibblers, and repeaters." And there, he sneered, you have your Democrats, as opposed to the Whigs, who comprised "the intelligence and virtue of the country."

Religious bigotry always aroused Johnson's fighting blood. There were few Catholics in Tennessee, but he reminded Clingman that "the Catholics of this country had the right secured to them by the Constitution of worshipping the God of their fathers in the manner dictated by their own consciences. This country is not prepared to establish an inquisition and try to punish men for their religious beliefs."

Then turning to a second point, he asked, "How, then, stands this matter of intelligence?" Well, in the Democratic state of Pennsylvania, one person in every one hundred and twenty-two was unable to read or write; but in the Whig state of North Carolina—the state Clingman so *intelligently* represented—one person in every four was illiterate. The figures were not his, he explained; they were taken from the United States Census.

The use of the cudgel of fact to beat down an opponent earned Johnson a reputation for ungallantry and often of "perfidy" to his—the Southern—side of the House.

Legislation to aid the social class from which he sprang—the landless, rejected "poor white" and mechanic—was never far from Johnson's thoughts. Early in 1846 he introduced the bill upon which his reputation in Congress would ultimately rest—the so-called Homestead Bill. On March 27 of that year, in the first session of the Twenty-ninth Congress, he submitted a measure "to authorize every poor man in the United States, who is the head of a family, to enter one hundred and sixty acres of the public domain, 'without money and without price.' "

Johnson was not the first to propose a distribution of the public lands among settlers who would live on their holdings and cultivate them. The alternative was to sell the land to speculators, which meant the big money interests. The Louisiana Purchase had added millions of acres of uninhabited terrain to the public ownership, and the debate over the best way to dispose of this enormous expanse of property was to continue for years, and eventually the whole complex issue of slavery and disunion would be brought into the controversy.

Johnson's proposal, although in some ways anticipated by others, was the first to offer a homestead policy in a workable form, and as long as he remained in Congress he battled for its adoption.

His stand was clear: "Like the air or like the heat, the public domain is the property of all, intended to be used and enjoyed by all. Every man is entitled to a home, [and when] the government fails to supply a home it makes war on the interests of those it is bound to protect."*

Even when weighed in the economic scales, he maintained, settlement of the land by homesteaders would redound to the greater advantage of the government; for while selling the land would bring billions in revenue, placing it in permanent productivity would enrich the nation far more.

No measure he would sponsor would provoke more savage and sustained opposition than this Homestead Bill. The South denounced the plan as disastrous to its economy, for if free land for free men were to become the national policy, where could the slaveholder go with his property, to expand his system of labor? What man would buy a farm in North Carolina or Virginia if he could get a better one for nothing in the West? Johnson was lashed as an apostate, a renegade, a traitor, a demagogue of the deepest dye, and called "the greatest of national humbugs" for proposing this "infamous and nefarious scheme."

In 1846 his proposal sounded a preliminary alarm only, and it got no further than a committee pigeonhole; but it would be revived again and again.

Six weeks after he introduced the measure, a more urgent crisis intervened: on May 13 the President declared that a state of war existed between the United States and Mexico.

* This same doctrine would sound persuasively on the lips of another President Johnson, more than a century after Andrew Johnson's advocacy of it.

NINE

A CRY OF DESPAIR

"JACKSONIAN DEMOCRACY" had come to mean, among other fundamentals, adherence to the rule of political warfare that "to the victors belong the spoils." The term by which Andrew Johnson one day would designate Stephen A. Douglas ("the candidate of the cormorants") might have applied prospectively to any aspirant to the White House, regardless of party and regardless of intentions. Let him but be elected, and the cormorants would swoop down to snatch jobs, favors, and perquisites from his grasp.

This torment befell James Knox Polk in his turn, and so revolted him that he noted in his diary: "If I live, I shall tell the country about the hungry Congressmen who infest the city of Washington."

One hungry congressman was Johnson of East Tennessee, and his luck in fishing for appointments for his supporters at home was wretchedly poor. Middle and West Tennessee, the districts lorded over by the party's hierarchy, received the bulk of the federal patronage, and in consequence, Johnson's relations with the President became strained. As early as July 22, 1846, he wrote to Blackston McDannel:

"Take Polk's appointments all in all and they are the most *damnable* set that was ever made by any president since the government was organized, out of Tennessee as well as in it . . . He has a set of interested *parasites* about him, who flatter him until he does not know himself. He seems to be acting upon the principle of hanging an old friend for the purpose of making two new ones." Being deficient in moral courage, the President was not "competent to lead a great party," he went on, and his "duplicity" had cost him all respect.

"There is one thing I will say," Andy assured "Old Mac," "*I never betrayed a friend or [was] guilty of the black sin of ingratitude.* I fear Mr. Polk cannot say as much."

In this condemnation Johnson fell into an error common among his contemporaries. Polk was prickly of approach and firm-set in his policies, and he took few pains to ingratiate himself with party members. Having announced at the start that he would not accept a second term, he acted with the latitude of decision which that attitude seemed to confer. After an hour's frank discussion of the patronage situation with the truculent Johnson, Polk made another jotting in his diary to the effect that the discontented East Tennessean apparently "wished to play the demagogue . . . I would almost prefer to have two Whigs here." Thereafter Johnson's calls at the White House became fewer and fewer until they ceased altogether. After two years of struggle he was forced to confess to McDannel that he had "signally failed [in] getting every appointment" he had gone after.

"Things seemed to have taken a strange turn with the powers that be," he lamented. "The democracy in my district . . . seem to have fallen under the political displeasure of the administration . . . When such men as Bob Powell can get appointments over the heads of the best democrats in the country, it is time to call a hault."

Bob Powell, ne'er-do-well tailor, had boarded with the Johnsons back in 1831.

Martha Johnson, however, was a frequent White House guest of Mrs. Polk. Having no children of her own, the First Lady took an interest in the children of Tennesseans in the government, and she liked Martha.

Sarah Childress Polk was formidable in her own right. Endowed with regal stateliness and conscious of possessing the most high-toned manners, she personified what one admirer called "the aristocracy of virtue; an idea that, whatever the mass of society might consider themselves at liberty to do, it was indispensably due to her station to preserve inviolate the strict laws of decorum and of the purest principles." It was said in her praise that she had never been known to "discuss a subject in relation to which her sex was expected to be ignorant." In obedience to her stern Presbyterian faith, she banished dancing and other "light amusements" from the Executive Mansion, deeming them unbefitting its official character.

One point on which she and Martha Johnson met was the First

Lady's spotless housekeeping. Under some of its previous occupants the White House had become downright slatternly—cheese smeared on the upholstery in the East Room, and tobacco spittle bespeckling the Turkey carpets. Mrs. Polk made the mansion gleam, and this Martha could appreciate; since she herself had been old enough to attend school, she had been her mother's helper in taking care of their Greeneville home.

Johnson was grateful for the Polks' attentions to his daughter, but his estrangement from the President persisted, though Polk made clear that their differences were purely political, not personal, and that he was not aware of having intentionally offended his fellow Tennessean.

In regard to the war in Mexico, Johnson heartily supported the government. He voted to provide funds, but did express a wish that taxes might be so apportioned that the expenses of the war "should be borne by the rich whose property the government protected, and not by the poor and the laborer who received little at its hands." War or no war, Johnson continued to fight for economy in the government.

Sometimes this carried him to bizarre lengths, but the principle was what he pursued. When the purchase of the draft of Washington's *Farewell Address* was proposed, he moved that the price be pegged no higher than one thousand dollars; otherwise, he warned, "by-bidders and sweeteners" would run it up and up. He voted against an appropriation to add wings to the Patent Office, alleging that "great frauds" had been perpetrated in that department. He opposed the Smithsonian Institution and tried to have it changed into an industrial school "for training American mechanics throughout the United States for the duties of their trades." In this he again simply expressed his preference for the useful and practical, over the ornamental and theoretical.

In all his official actions his point of departure was the same— equal justice for all, high and low, mechanic or manufacturer— and equal distribution of public favors. He fought against the creation of a permanent military caste, and preached adherence to the Constitution, the lodestar by which the nation must steer. He urged a downward revision of the tariff (a revision carried out by Polk's Secretary of the Treasury, Robert J. Walker of Mississippi) as a step toward reducing the cost of necessities. To bills increasing the pay of government white-collar workers he tacked riders stipulating that the pay of manual laborers should be equal. He tried to scale down Congressional salaries and reduce the office staffs of members—"mere fugelmen," he called them, "going around the country blowing the horns of their bosses." Congressional perquisites, like free postage and free stationery, came under his censure as inducements to petty graft. On the floor of the House he said that he knew one congressman who had sold, for two hundred and fifty dollars, books and stationery taken from these help-yourself supplies, which had cost the government twice that sum. This particular attack his colleagues felt was letting down the system, and he was reproved.

His bent for economizing brought him into collision with a junior representative from Mississippi, Jefferson Davis. When the latter urged a larger appropriation for the Military Academy at West Point, his alma mater, Johnson disputed the necessity. Although concerned with furthering education, Johnson constitutionally mistrusted "experts," especially those who were self-qualified. Davis asked with disdain—alluding to a recent victory won by his father-in-law, General Zachary Taylor, in Mexico: "Can a blacksmith or a tailor construct the bastioned field-works opposite Matamoros? Can any but a trained man do this?"

Johnson's tinder-dry touchiness flared up at this implied slur, and he struck back savagely:

"I am a mechanic, and when a blow is struck at that class I resent it. I know we have an illegitimate, swaggering, bastard, scrub aristocracy who assume to know a good deal, but who, when the flowing veil of pretension is torn off from it, is seen to possess neither talents nor information on which one can rear a useful superstructure . . . Sir, I vindicate the mechanical profession!"

The "mechanical profession," interrupted Davis; what did he mean by the "workingman"?

"I mean," Johnson answered bluntly, "the man who earns his living by the work of his hands, and not by fatiguing his brain."

The next day, after cooling off, he explained to the House that he had not intended to be rude; but if the gentleman from Mississippi had not meant his remark to be personal, "why had he selected a tailor?"

Davis rejoined coldly, "I retract nothing that I said in that debate."

Shortly after this Jefferson Davis resigned his seat and, accepting a brigadier general's commission, went to Mexico, there to keep an eye surreptitiously (as a Democratic politician) upon Taylor, who was developing alarming availability as the next Whig candidate for President. An unforeseen result of this tour of duty would be Davis' contracting a lifelong delusion of military genius, a delusion that would prove costly to himself and to the Confederate States of America.

A fighting man who was acquiring no public reputation in the war was Captain Ulysses (or "Sam," as his messmates called him) Grant. He hated the war and considered it an outrage against Mexico, but as a soldier he was demonstrating the dogged tenacity that one day would lift him to the pinnacle of fame.

As in all wars, profiteers swarmed in Washington, and their voracity sickened Andrew Johnson. Oppressed by ill health and frustration, parted from his family, on whose moral support and encouragement he always depended, he grew morose. In letters to Greeneville he begged constantly for news, and more news, of what was happening there. His rupture with Polk had produced a bad effect at home, and rumors reached him that even Sam Milligan had turned critical as a result. His despondency, during the winter of 1846–47, at times grew unbearable. Reviewing his life, he saw one long, unremittent struggle; every step he had advanced had been against bitter odds. And now to be deserted by the people of Greene county!

One desolate day—January 10, 1847—he poured out his heart-sickness to Blackston McDannel—that "dear friend, *if there is one lefte* [*sic*] *that I dare call my friend.*" It was a cry of anguish, uttered without regard to form or phrasing, in the angular, earthy vernacular of East Tennessee.

"This is Sunday morning, and I must say it is one of the gloomiest that has passed over my head this many a day. This is a cold rough morning, the clouds look white and angry, indicating a snow storm. The government seems pushing on to destruction in spite of all that can be said and done. In connection with this my bones in general and my limbs in particular ache in the most excruciating manner—legs, arms, head, and heart all seem to have entered into a conspiracy against my peace and happiness, everything here seems to augur some ill. Even the letters received from home this morning bring with them indications of jealousy and ill will in the private circles there."

Then the gall of bitterness gushed out:

"When I reflect upon my past life and that of my family, and know that it has been my constant aim and desire to steer them and myself through society in as unoffending a manner as possible—when I sum up the many taunts, the jeers . . . and intended slights to me and mine, all without cause so far as I know, I wish from the bottom of my heart, that we were all blotted out of existence, and even the remembrance of things that were.

"I have tried to serve my friends, my principles, my party, and my country faithfully and conscientiously, but have failed in giving that satisfaction that has always been my highest ambition to give. . . .

"If only I had some friend here to talk with about these things —some one that I could unbosom myself to as I have to you on some occasions, it would at this time [be] like an *oasis* in a desert. I with to *God* you were here today that we could talk over everything . . . I used to think that Milligan was my friend, but how the matter really stands I have some doubts . . ."

Even his business affairs were going awry:

"The property that I bought at the sale some time since on the main street has been redeemed by McHenry as I understand. They make take and go to hell with it . . . I never want to own another foot of dirt in the DAMNED town while I live—The *God* damned 'Murrel' gang may take, and may a perfect 'pandemonium' of it, and headquarters for all the infernal spirits that are now out of hell, for I know of no place more suitable. If I should happen to die among the damned spirits that infest Greeneville, my last request before death would be for some friend (if I had no friend which is highly probable) I would bequeath the last dollar to some negro as pay to take my dirty, stinking carcas after death, out on some mountain peak and there leave it to be devoured by the vultures and wolves or make a fire sufficiently large to consume the smallest particle that it may pass off in smoke and ride upon the wind over the *God* forsaken and hell deserving, mony loving, hypocritical, back bighting, Sundy praying scoundrels of the town of Greeneville."

His pen dug into the paper, disregarding spelling and grammar, under the force of his remonstrance. Yet even so he could not free himself, or find release from the objects of his curses.

"Write to me all the news," he pleaded. "Your business, I am doing the best I can with it . . . Give me some new fangled oathes that I can more effectually damn some of that brood in and the town [sic]. I have no news of interest to give you, the democratic party is gone to hell no mistake . . . Write me . . ."

The fires that burned in Andrew Johnson were seldom so revealed. He would be called cold, secretive, distant, sullen, but his passions were fierce, and only by force of will did he tame and repress them. Even so, occasionally they would flare up and startle the beholder by their intensity.

Outwardly the congressman conformed to conventional tastes. No longer a raw-boned rustic, he was dignified and impressive in bearing and dressed immaculately. Being a tailor, he appreciated and demanded fine workmanship in his clothing. Until he went to Washington he had made his own suits, and they were well cut, well fitting, and always of the best fabrics. His linen was spotless; he was conspicuous for it. At his boardinghouse he was considered a nuisance because of his habit of taking a bath every day; once a week was the rule, and if a week should be skipped, why, nobody objected.

In public the former hobbledehoy now carried himself with dignity and spoke in a voice singularly pleasing. His vocabulary seldom gave way to the earthiness that marked his outpourings to McDannel. His manners were stiff but correct, and he observed the proprieties attaching to every occasion, social or official. But he was not society-oriented; he would never shake off entirely the awareness that in the race for education he had been left behind at the start, and must constantly strive to make up the lost ground. This was his "poor white" heritage, and at times it became a shirt of Nessus, scalding but impossible to shed.

With it all, in his conduct he could not, would not, change. Pride and innate stubbornness forbade him to abandon the quarrel with Polk, in which he felt justified, and one month after his despairing letter to Blackston McDannel he aggravated his offense by arraigning the administration from top to bottom as a monster of corruption. In a speech in the House, February 10, 1847, he exclaimed:

"I wish to Almighty God that the whole American people could be assembled in this city; that there was some kind of amphitheater constructed, capacious enough to contain the whole voting population of the United States; and that they were convened for a short period of time, and the veil that now conceals from view the many abuses could be drawn aside, and they be permitted to take one calm survey, one full and dispassionate view, of all the secret springs of the entire proceedings of things under this government, of all the intriguing officers in authority, from the highest to the lowest. I will not say that they would lay violent hands upon an edifice designed by its founders to be so sacred and perfect in all its parts, and tear it into a thousand pieces . . . I have too much confidence in their forbearance to believe it for a moment. But I feel well assured of one thing, and that is that they would rip and tear off some of those funguses that have been fixing, and have fixed themselves upon the vitals of this government for years gone by; and they would turn a mighty stream through the Augean stable until it was thoroughly cleansed of the abominable filth that had been preying upon the life-blood of the republic for too long."

This overstepped all bounds; spattering the President with "abominable filth" was too gross an affront to be condoned. It was reported that Johnson had read himself out of the party.

Another election was at hand, and in no buoyant mood, when Congress adjourned on March 4, 1847, Johnson headed back to Greene county in quest of a third term.

TEN

HISTORY MUFFED
AND HISTORY MENDED

THE trip home was by way of Nashville, where Charles Johnson was in training to become a pharmacist. Martha went with her father. Sister and brother had not seen each other for two years and there was much to talk about.

Johnson found Greeneville absorbed in the war. At the commencement of hostilities the President had called for forty-three thousand volunteers, and Tennessee, true to its sobriquet, "The Volunteer State," had responded enthusiastically. Johnson had tried to get fighting commissions for Milligan and McDannel, but had succeeded only in landing them in the commissary department of a company, Milligan as a captain and Blackston as a sergeant. Both now were in Mexico, though not at the front, and Johnson constituted himself a news bureau to give them the gossip of home. So many schools were opening in the town, "what a place this is coming to be for literature and profound learning!" he commented ironically. People's health seemed to be mostly good, "scandal of all sorts" was "abundant," and he assumed that "a fair proportion of whoring is carried on, by way of variety." Blackston was enjoined to reassure Milligan that his fiancée was waiting for him, and both were urged to write frequently.

In Tennessee everybody seemed to be raising companies, even Whigs, who scorched the Democrats for starting the fight, but couldn't resist getting into it. Over in Jonesboro, "Parson" Brownlow was raising a hullabaloo in the *Whig* about President Polk's appointment of two Roman Catholic priests as chaplains to Taylor's troops in Monterrey (at the general's request), and in fuliginous prose he rained down maledictions upon the President, the chaplains, the Catholic Church, the Army, and the entire war—

which, however, he could not actually oppose, because that would be unpatriotic. He joined a company of volunteers—"The Protestant Invincibles"—and was elected its lieutenant. The "Invincibles" sweated through drills but saw no active service, though they did hear many speeches by the "Parson." He had one set harangue, four hours long, which he delivered at camp meetings, recruiting rallies, and political picnics; let every man enlist, he would urge—but Democrats first, because it was their war.

"It is our country right or wrong," he would shout. "So go, go blindly!" But be sure to stipulate that no Catholics be appointed as *their* chaplains.

In his way the "Parson" was doing what a gangling congressman from Illinois, Abe Lincoln, was doing in his—playing "smart politics" with a question that meant life or death to thousands of nonpoliticians in uniform. Lincoln was counseling his fellow Whigs to cry up the iniquity of the conflict and pin the responsibility squarely on the Democrats—but be sure to vote all the men and money requested, because to do the contrary would arouse the wrath of the voters.

In the midst of the alarms, Johnson entered into his private fight to retain his Congressional seat. Twice he had triumphed against powerful odds; this time he felt confident of trouncing the youthful Whig who, it developed, was to oppose him, a fellow townsman named Oliver P. Temple.

Temple was twenty-seven, a lawyer for one year, with no business. It had been expected that a hard-hitting lawyer from Jonesboro—Landon C. Haynes—would face Johnson. Haynes was a rough-and-tumble fighter who had grappled with "Parson" Brownlow in a street scuffle and inflicted a leg wound on the tough and wiry editor; but he chose not to run, and Temple was drafted.

At first Temple was awed by the prospect of facing the redoubtable Greeneville tailor; but the excitement appealed to him, and he reflected that even if he did not win, the campaign would give him a reputation. Besides, he thought he had discovered a way to hit Johnson where it would hurt—through his pride.

The custom was for the candidates to make a joint canvass, speaking from the same platform in town after town. The campaign started at Taylorville on July 11. Johnson spoke first, and mentioned that Temple was present and would speak later, that was all. Johnson's cold allusion to "my juvenile competitor" annoyed Temple, and he was primed to strike back. Instead, therefore, of trying to beat down Johnson's sledgehammer arguments, Temple attacked his entire political career, accusing him of dishonesty to his party, of time-serving, and of hypocrisy in pretending to champion the welfare of the common man. How, demanded Temple, did Johnson square his vote against raising the pay of a private soldier from seven dollars to eight dollars *a month*, with his own "ease and luxury" in Washington, on his Congressional allowance of eight dollars *a day?* As a crusher, Temple read Johnson's February arraignment of the Polk administration, and put it to the Democrats in the crowd whether Andy Johnson was one of their own.

As Temple recounted it, the effect upon the crowd was sensational, and there were cries of "Give it to him!" "Lay on, Nancy!" Johnson, said Temple, could not deny the speech and "he was too proud to retract it." He could only plead that he was no grammarian, that when he said *"from* the highest" he thought that exempted Polk. But the explanation was lame, and "Parson" Brownlow crowed:

"Temple did lift the ticks off Johnson at a rate that was really distressing. Andy got black in the face."

Temple was young and pitiless, and he reserved what he thought would be a finishing stroke until the last appearance of the campaign. This was at Braylesville, near Washington College, where Temple had graduated. The faculty and student body of the college were to be on hand to hear him, and he was ready. As he explained:

"Johnson was very fond of showing off his little learning, and always had some scraps of it, in history, or more frequently mythology, which he repeated, in solemn pomp, at the close of his speeches. One of these was a beautiful and pathetic story of the unfortunate Regulus, a Roman general who was captured at Carthage . . . He had been repeating it for several days, but he had the story all wrong, and when told truly it did not fit his point at all."

Temple knew that Johnson was muddled, but he waited until

they were at Braylesville, in the presence of the professors and students of his school, to expose him.

"Sure enough," he recounted, "in his stately peroration [Johnson] told the Regulus story, in his softest, most impressive manner.

"In my reply, I corrected his history, and showed its total inapplicability to the point he was making. Then turning to him, and pointing my finger at him, I said in the most scornful manner: 'Now, sir, go and *learn* history before you presume to *teach* it to an intelligent people.' "

Johnson, said Temple, "seemed stunned as if by a blow."

The trick was cruel: to be humiliated—before a packed audience—as a man who had yielded to a human weakness, the desire to shine, and subjected to the sneers and ridicule of youths who had no comprehension of the handicaps he had been compelled to surmount—to have his educational shortcoming flung in his face—this was galling. Temple himself appears to have been uneasy in his conscience, for he justified his action by averring that Johnson had adopted an air of "haughty superiority . . . He never spoke a kind word to me or did a gracious act . . . I knew there was but one way to fight him—with his own weapons."

When the first election returns came in, it appeared that Temple had won, and the Whigs began celebrating. Both candidates were called out to thank their supporters, and Johnson, said Temple, "shed tears, almost broke down, he was so mortified, chagrined, and almost overwhelmed with shame." But the next day the complete returns gave Johnson the victory; not by his normal majority of fifteen hundred, however, but by only three hundred and thirteen votes.

Back he went to Washington, and Temple, by his own admission, prudently left town—"moved to Knoxville to get out of politics and to avoid another race which would result in defeat."

During this new term, Johnson made no anti-Polk speeches. He even came to the rescue of the President in regard to the latter's use of the veto power. This dissertation, tracing the inception of the veto back to early Roman times, must have tried the patience of the House, for it resembled a schoolmaster's lecture more than a political address. The people (Johnson instructed his fellow congressmen, who couldn't have cared less), becoming alarmed by patrician encroachments upon their privileges, had appointed tribunes, empowered to scrutinize the laws passed by the Senate and veto those that infringed upon popular rights. The veto thus was plainly of plebeian origin, Johnson deduced, and its inclusion in the Constitution was proper.

"At one time in my life I entertained some doubts as to the exercise of the veto power myself," he admitted; but prolonged study and investigation had led him to change his mind.

In that speech (which was distributed as a campaign document in the Presidential contest of 1848, when Zachary Taylor was elected) Johnson introduced a phrase that would haunt him. Alluding to President Tyler, he spoke of "John Tyler, called by some, but not by me, in derision, 'The Accidency President.'"

As time went on and the war ended, and California and the Pacific Northwest were cemented into the nation, the still unresolved problem of the disposition of the public lands became acute. The United States government was the largest landed proprietor in the world. Responding to the need, Johnson hammered away at his homestead plan, introducing bill after bill, only to see them defeated. But the sentiment in favor of free land for settlers was gathering strength, and Johnson attracted allies. Southerners generally were tooth and nail against the idea, but the new Free Soil party, with its slogan, "Free soil, free speech, free labor, and free men," rallied to its support. Free Soilers were against slavery, and the homestead plan provided a way to prevent its extension into the territories.

Not all Northerners favored homestead legislation. High tariff advocates denounced it because they were afraid the class of small freeholders it would build up would demand cuts in the tariff, to bring down prices. Although Thaddeus Stevens hated slavery, he was a high-tariff man and he opposed Johnson's Homestead Bill. Stevens now was in Congress, elected by the Whigs, and enlivening the debates with his grim gaiety and savage sarcasm. His stand against homesteadism placed him in caustic companionship with ultra intransigents like Jefferson Davis, who upon his return from the war had been elected to the Senate in 1847. It was a strange fellowship.

The rising American, or Know-Nothing, party fought against a free-land policy because it dreaded an influx of Irish Catholic immigrants. The Know-Nothings (so called because the party was a secret order, and to all inquiries about it the members were instructed to answer, "I know nothing about that") were anti-foreigner and anti-Catholic, and the party was strong in the border states.

Railroad promoters also fought the homestead scheme, because they hoped to get large grants of land as subsidies.

But Johnson found supporters for his plan, too. Ben Wade took his place in the Senate in 1851, and he was a mettlesome, combative antagonist on behalf of homesteadism. Wade fought with a broadsword. Entering the Senate that year was Charles Sumner of Massachusetts, who would become a sacrifice to Southern wrath, and both he and Congressman George Washington Julian of Indiana, an abolitionist of the most uncompromising stripe, spoke ardently for Johnson's plan. Johnson accepted help from any quarter, and bit by bit the country and Congress were educated to the merits of the policy.

Meanwhile, Johnson faced the periodic struggle to retain his seat. In 1849, when seeking a fourth term, he defeated his Whig rival by his normal majority; and in 1851 he carried on an exhausting struggle against Landon C. Haynes, his most formidable opponent to date. Observing that his opponents had almost all been lawyers, Johnson attacked the domination of the government by members of that profession.

"There are two hundred and twenty-three congressmen," he pointed out, "and of this number all are lawyers except twenty-three. The laboring man of America is ignored, he has no proportionate representation, though he constitutes a large majority of the voting population . . . For my part, I say let the mechanic and the laborer make our laws, rather than the idle and vicious aristocrat."

The clash with Haynes developed into a verbal brawl, in which no demagogic appeal was overlooked. At one point Johnson suggested to McDannel that "the expulsion of Haynes from the church might be sent to some of the counties." Their joint debates in the summer heat often lasted six hours, and the stamina of both men was taxed to the limit. In the end Johnson prevailed, and returned to Washington for a fifth term.

His mood was somewhat less belligerent. Now and then he

would let his guard down. In one letter to McDannel he grew almost wistful:

"Yesterday I was at the Navy de't and I find that Tennessee is entitled to the appointment of some midshipmen. How would you like for John to enter the Navy? . . . If I was in a situation I would like to have one of [my sons] in the Navy . . ."

His sons were not bringing satisfaction. Charles, who, with his sunny nature, was Eliza's favorite, gave signs of becoming an alcoholic. Andrew and Eliza accepted this misfortune philosophically, and did their best to help but never complained. Robert, the younger boy, was having lung hemorrhages that alarmed the doctors. Johnson needed the sustaining affection of his family, and when he was in Washington and did not hear from them he grew despondent.

"I think my family must all be dead for have not heard from any of them for 20 days," he wrote a friend. "Write to me and give me all the news . . . My health is far from being good and has not been this winter."

Unique in his correspondence was an account of a "night off" from public duties which he took in November of 1848, just before the Presidential election. McDannel got the story in a long letter, telling how, after a hard day, Johnson "got with G. W. McLane and two or three others of 'our old companions in arms,' and we got on a *Kinder* of a 'bust,'—not a big 'drunk,' and mounted in the 5 o'clock train of cars and were in Baltimore for supper at 7 o'clock."

This was the height of dissipation for these country-bred gallants, and they went the limit—after supper "to the 'Front Street theater,' and witnessed the 'Danseuses Viennoises.' This splendid performance . . . consists of 48 little girls—all dressed in the richest and most gaudy manner—performing every imaginable evolution, and arranging themselves in every circle and figure to be found in the fashionable world, and singing with a voice so sweet and dancing with a foot so light, that *Job* in the midst of his afflictions would have rejoiced at the scene. . . .

"The theater over and a fine oyster supper devoured, we returned to our 'virtuous couches,' and then a perfect quiet rested till 6 o'clock this morning, then rose, and *after* we had taken 'a drink' felt like 'giants refreshed with new wine.' At 7 o'clock a.m. we again took the cars and were in Washington by 9 o'clock a.m. And here I am now at 11 o'clock neither sick, drunk, nor groggy, finishing my paper to my old well tried and faithful friend."

That this excursion had not interfered with his discharge of routine duties was indicated in the postscript:

"I spend every day of my life during office hours at the War Dept., preparing my accounts . . . and yesterday—thanks be the Lord!—I got them through the 3d auditor's office."

Johnson's "Kinder of a 'bust' " was mild compared with the rum-soaked air of Washington common during the sessions, at least as told by Representative Julian. The intemperance prevalent in the Capitol itself shocked the conscientious Hoosier.

"The free use of intoxicating drinks by senators was too common to provoke remark," he elaborated in his memoirs. "It was still more common in the House."

He never forgot the debauch he witnessed in the House on the last day of the Thirty-first Congress, March 4, 1851:

"Some of the most important legislation, involving the expenditure of many millions, remained to be disposed of at that sitting; and as a preparation for the work, a large supply of whisky had been deposited in a room connecting with the Hall of Representatives, which was thronged by members at all hours of the night. The chairman of the Ways and Means Committee became so exhilarated that he had to be retired from his post; and some of his brethren, who had been calling him to order in a most disorderly manner, were quite as incapable of business as himself."

In the light of this sanctioned orgy, Andy Johnson's "night on the town," culminating in an evening at the theater and a blissful night's sleep, seems innocuously innocent.

And yet, with all its roughness, that period was susceptible to refining influences and refined surroundings. A great event at the White House was the introduction of gas for illumination. The first lights were turned on December 29, 1848 (a little more than one month after Johnson's Baltimore whirl), and the critical Mrs. Polk approved.

Amid distractions coarse or elegant, Johnson's attention to his homestead plan did not slacken, and during the first session of the Thirty-first Congress an amended measure introduced by him was engrossed under the heading, "AN ACT," and was endorsed, "Passed the House of Representatives, May 12, 1852," over the flowing signature, "Jno. Forney, Clerk." A ten-year fight had been won.

Then the bill was killed by the Senate.

This was a bitter setback, but more bitter still to Johnson was the device his enemies in Tennessee resorted to in their determination to eliminate him from Congress once and for all. Five times they had tried to defeat him in elections and had failed. All they had been able to do had been to shout "Tailor!" "Plebeian!" "Ignorant!" "Low-born!"

In 1853, however, with the Whigs in control of the legislature, Johnson was gerrymandered out of his district. Greene county, the seat of his greatest strength, was wrenched away and attached to a county overwhelmingly Whig.

Against the new odds, it seemed useless to contend, and Johnson, accepting the inevitability of his retirement from the national scene, set about winding up his accounts. In the process he did an unheard-of thing.

He had been appointed to a committee charged with investigating a case of asserted corruption in office. Such assignments were coveted because of the liberal mileage allowance they carried; quite a bit of money could be picked up in this way. Contrary to precedent, contrary (it seemed to his startled colleagues) even to common prudence, Johnson declined to accept pay for more than the number of days he had actually worked at the investigation. His claim and receipt read:

"For 96 days service during the late recess of Congress as a member of [the committee] . . . I claim and receive pay for 27 days—$216.

"Balance to which I am legally entitled—$552 . . .

"I have no doubt of the legality of the [total]charge of $768, but I doubt my *moral* right to more than pay for the days actually engaged in the service, and therefore decline to receive the balance."

When he took farewell of the House, where he had served for a decade, he was one of only six remaining from the first Congress he had sat in. His enemies at home he depicted as already squabbling over who should inherit his seat. "They have parted my garments, and for my vesture are casting lots," he remarked, not without scorn; then with ominous ambiguity added:

"But there is much in the future."

A tailor may know ways of cutting one's coat to fit one's cloth which others may not. Euchred out of Congress, after a period of strategic hesitation, Andrew Johnson boldly set his sights on the governorship of Tennessee.

ELEVEN

"HELL ALL DAY"

EVEN while the hitherto ineradicable tailor of Greeneville was in process of being scrubbed from the rolls of Congress, he had kept a sharp and brooding eye on national political developments, and his conclusions were foreboding. 1852 was a Presidential election year; Millard Fillmore, another "Accidency President," had filled out the term of the deceased Zachary Taylor without igniting much enthusiasm for electing him in his own right; although historically he had acquired merit by furnishing the upstairs room of the White House known as the "library" with what it had conspicuously lacked—some books.

Johnson kept friends at home apprised of his opinion of possible and actual candidates. Stephen A. Douglas he dismissed as already "a dead cock in the pit." Douglas, he said, was "a mere hotbed production . . . warmed into . . . existence by a set of interested plunderers that would, in the event of success, disembowel the treasury, disgrace the country, and damn the party to all eternity."

On the Whig side, he reported that "Dan the God-like" (Webster) was "considered out of the fight," and Winfield Scott would be the nominee of that party—"but without hope of success."

When the Democrats' choice fell on Franklin Pierce of New Hampshire, Johnson accepted the selection passively; but after Pierce was elected he saw breakers ahead. With the voice of a minor prophet crying "Woe!" he declared the President-elect lacked "that political preparation so necessary to prepare *ordinary* men" for the high office; his "transit has been too sudden." One good trait he did detect in Pierce on the eve of inauguration, of which he advised Blackston McDannel (in a communication endorsed both "Private" and "Burn These Letters"):

". . . There are one hundred and one speculations as to who will compose the Cabinet . . . No one knows here if the President-elect has determined himself as to who they shall be, and if he has, it is said . . . that he knows how to keep his own counsel, which is a very good trait in an executive officer."

At the same time, in another "Private" letter to David T. Patterson, a circuit judge at Greeneville, Andy exhaled gloom over East Tennessee's prospects of sharing in the distribution of federal patronage, "on account of behaving so badly in the late election for President and Vice-President." (Tennessee had gone for Scott and the Whigs.)

"In this connection," he wrote, "if there is anything within the gift of this administration (I mean the Pierce) that you desire, you should not let modesty keep you back. The time has been when modesty was considered commendable and respected as such, but that time has passed and gone, and pretensions to anything of the kind is looked upon as being very antiquated and in exceedingly bad taste."

In regard to the current Congress, his pessimism was abysmal —"the poorest," he told Sam Milligan, "I ever saw, it deserves the curse of every honest man."

In this frame of mind Johnson had turned his back on Washington and set himself to ponder the urgings of friends that he enter the race for governor of Tennessee. Characteristically, he made up his mind slowly, after viewing the problem from all angles. In December of 1852 he wrote Judge Patterson that he had been thinking "to wind up my political career on the 3rd of March next . . . I will not deny . . . I have my ambition; but while I freely make the admission, I have always been determined not to let it run me into excessive error or cause me to ask too much at the hands of the . . . friends who have long been my . . . supporters."

Nevertheless, he admitted that to be elected governor, after the Whigs had carried the state in two successive elections, and "after being legislated out of Congress by a proscriptive legislature," would be a source of satisfaction. So, under "certain contingencies," and with "the full approbation of the democratic party," and after "a full consultation with my immediate friends," he believed he might become a candidate.

"In fine," he concluded the long, involute letter which mirrored the deliberate movements of his mind, "on the subject for the present, I will say, under *proper* circumstances I would consent

to run . . . and make the sacrifice both as to *health* and money . . .
I wish you would consult Milligan on matters and things in general and tell him to write to me. . . ."

It was this habit of cautious deliberation, before adopting a
course, and avoiding at all costs rash and precipitate commit-
ments, that led Oliver Temple to observe that "successes were no
surprise to Andrew Johnson." They were, Temple believed, "just
what he had planned, worked for, dreamed of, [and] what he
thought he deserved"; once embarked upon a line of action, "he
never feared defeat."

The *"proper* circumstances" to which he alluded, of course,
included endorsement by the Democratic leaders of the state.
This was a stumbling block.

With the party's chiefs Johnson had no credit, and he knew it.
He had ridden over and humiliated them again and again. But
with the people, the common voters, he was strong, and he knew
that. His following, furthermore, while it was in the party, was
purely personal, and rested upon the same sort of blind loyalty
that Andrew Jackson had inspired.

Johnson based his strategy on this fact. The Democratic state
convention was to meet in April to select the nominees for office.
Johnson did not bother to attend. Instead, he sent word of his
availability into the counties, of which there were eighty-seven in
Tennessee. The county conventions, held to instruct the delegates
to the state gathering, were close to the people, and in county
after county Andy Johnson was named as the overwhelming popular choice.

The state leaders were in a quandary. They did not want Johnson; their choice was Andrew Ewing of Nashville, member of a
powerful political clan.

The day before the state convention opened, a secret caucus of
the delegates was held to determine their temper, and on three
successive ballots Johnson received more votes than all his competitors combined. Despite this plain showing, the leaders, who
controlled the convention machinery, the next day presented
Ewing as the choice of the caucus.

Turmoil erupted, and amid the uproar Ewing withdrew his
name. Thereupon Johnson was nominated unanimously, one of
the defeated leaders glumly remarking:

"It seems that Johnson is strong enough to run all the Democrats out of the convention, and can run Henry [the Whig candidate for governor] out of the state."

The campaign got under way on May 1 and extended into August. Gustavus A. Henry, the Whig nominee, was described by one well-wisher as "decidedly the most delightful orator, as well as one of the most elegant men in the state." But when it came to "logic, facts, and hard licks," he proved no match for Johnson, presenting himself as "a man of the people and the people's man."

In his electioneering, Johnson tried to take the measure of an opponent before opening fire, and then to go as far in personal attack as seemed safe. It was said that at the commencement of this campaign he inquired of a friend of the "Eagle Orator," as Henry was known, what sort of man he was facing—whether touchy on the point of honor or patient and little inclined to anger. The friend replied that Henry was remarkably peaceful, and would shrug off all but the grossest insults.

"In that case," retorted Johnson, "I'll give him hell all day."

And he did, from the mountains to the Mississippi, week after week, in their joint appearances. Playing on his opponent's name, he contended that he had not been "Gerry-mandered" out of Congress, but "Henry-mandered" out, because Gustavus Henry had introduced the redistricting resolution in the legislature. Johnson had a rough tongue and no humor, and though he could get a laugh by such labored sallies, the lack of a consistent, alleviating sense of comedy was a handicap. He could amuse the uncouth Tennessee audiences by singing a song which he said had been made up about him, and the boys in Greeneville used to chant:

> If you want a brand new coat,
> I'll tell you what to do;
> Go down to Andrew Johnson's shop
> And get a long-tail blue.

> If you want the girls to love you,
> To love you good and true,
> Go down to Andy's tailor shop
> And get a long-tail blue.

But the rendition of this crude ballad (in a clear baritone) was only an overflow of occasional high spirits, and it had a defiance in it, too.

Henry, on the other hand, had all the graces of the finished speaker. But no rhetoric could stand up against the force and steady courage shown by his antagonist, and the trenchant blows he dealt. A writer for a New York newspaper was awed by the way Johnson "cut and slashed right and left" on the stump, and "tore big wounds and left something behind to fester and be remembered . . . His phraseology may be uncouth, and there may be many false Anglicisms, but his views are easily understood and he talks strong thoughts and carefully culled facts . . . running his opponents through and through with a rusty jagged weapon; chopping to mincemeat or grinding to powder his luckless adversary."

As a stump speaker, Andrew Johnson was rated by his contemporaries without a peer.

The "Eagle Orator" was luckless, and in August Johnson was elected governor by 63, 413 votes to 61,163.

On October 17, 1853, he took the oath of office in Nashville, arriving for the ceremony on foot, having walked from his hotel to the Capitol, disdaining to use a carriage. Andrew Jackson had ridden to his inauguration on a Tennessee walking horse, and Andy Johnson, the "mechanic governor," wanted no pomp either.

Not that he entered upon his new duties either poor in spirit or depleted in purse. At the time Johnson became governor of Tennessee he was a man of substance, worth about fifty thousand dollars, acquired by toil and thrift. His tailoring business had never ceased to prosper, and for years it had been ably managed by "Squire" Lewis Self, a devoted follower. Eliza Johnson managed the family income shrewdly. In later years, describing the part she had played in her husband's rise, she would say that she had "remained at home, caring for the children and practicing the economy" necessitated by their straitened means. By the fifties Johnson was investing in property in Greeneville, and already owned several town lots and a small hotel. He also owned property in the form of slaves. As far back as 1837 he had purchased a

boy named Sam, and would acquire eight all told, male and female—"the product," he would say, "of my hard work and sav-
ings." They were housed in a building on one of his lots in town,
and were treated more like grown-up children than like responsible servants.

Johnson's liberality was instanced in a letter written to him in
Washington by his son Charles, reporting that Sam was demanding to keep *all* of his wages, instead of just half of them, whenever
he was hired out to work for neighbors. That Sam had been allowed to keep any portion was a testimonial to Johnson's generosity, for it violated custom. Sam was to become a familiar sight
in Washington as Johnson's valet and body servant. On state occasions he served as footman, standing behind his master's chair
in great dignity. He wore Johnson's cast-off coats, imitated his
speech and mannerisms, and would pompously announce himself
as "Mr. Johnson's first servant." In later years Johnson let Sam
have the Greeneville tailor shop on a nominal lease.

While Johnson was in Congress, he had bought a new home,
which would belong to the family permanently. It was in 1851
that an unfinished brick dwelling house on Main Street, in a good
residential part of town, came on the market when the owner was
unable to complete it. Johnson bought the house and lot for nine
hundred and fifty dollars, plus the deed to his old house on Water
Street.

The new house was simplicity itself. It stood flush with the
sidewalk, and had a lawn at the side and a large lot at the back,
containing fruit trees and a kitchen garden. There were two
rooms downstairs and two upstairs, divided by a hall running
from front to back. A lean-to pantry was attached to the rear, and
the kitchen, after the Southern fashion, was detached and at some
distance, to avoid heat and odors. The rooms were furnished with
the standard dark walnut and horsehair prescribed by sedate
tastes. There were framed photographs on the walls, a center
table in the parlor holding a Bible and an album, and flowered
carpets on the floors. Not by coincidence, behind the house was
the "Gum Spring" where Andy and his weary, begrimed family
had camped on their first night in Greeneville.

The Johnsons moved into this modestly spacious home in January, 1852, and shortly thereafter Mary Johnson was married to an East Tennessean named Daniel Stover, whose "spread of land" was in the Watauga Valley in Carter county, close to Greene.

Among his fellow townsmen, Johnson continued to be only moderately sociable. He was reputed to be "close" about money (a trait his detractors magnified into parsimony), but frugality had been drilled into him so early in life it had become an ingrained habit. He was not ungenerous; on the contrary, he was constantly performing acts of liberality, but so silently that knowledge of them seldom transpired. And he did not have the knack of doing gracious deeds gracefully. Sometimes his political enemies themselves inadvertently brought to light his generous actions. One instance of this occurred during the contest with Henry.

The latter, hoping to turn the Irish voters against Johnson, had reproached him with having voted in Congress against appropriating money for the relief of famine-stricken Ireland, and cried his wonder that anyone could be "so inhuman, so heartless."

Johnson was not fazed. Yes, he said, he had voted against using *the people's* money for that worthy purpose:

"But that is not all of the story. When I voted against that resolution I turned to my fellow congressmen and proposed to give fifty dollars of my own funds if they would give a like amount, and when they declined the proposition, I ran my hand in my pocket, Major Henry, and pulled out fifty dollars of good money which I donated to the cause. How much did you give, sir?"*

Another incident, well known in Greeneville, had to do with a friend who had gone to California to dig gold; he returned, broke, and appealed to Johnson for help. Johnson at once held out his purse, saying, "Here, Jim, take what you need"; whereupon the friend broke into laughter and disclosed that he really had brought back several thousand dollars, but wanted to find out whether the mean things being said about Andy were true.

---

* The executors of Johnson's estate turned up numerous promissory notes among his papers, signed by poor men whom Johnson had helped. Although they had possessed no assets, by letting them accept the money as a loan, he had saved their pride.

In the opinion of Oliver Temple, who knew Johnson during his entire political career, more bitter, malicious things were said about him than about any other public man in the United States.

Temple also went out of his way to attest to Johnson's perfect honesty and fidelity to his friends. "I am not aware of a single instance in which he promised a favor which he did not bestow," he wrote after Johnson's death.

A favor that Johnson did bestow, unwittingly, upon countless editorial writers and quipsters of the year 1853 came in the form of his inaugural address. This was a fledgling flight into the empyrean of hyperbolic imagery, by which Johnson invited, and suffered, the fate of Icarus. But it did bring him to the attention, in one way or another, of some who had not looked closely before at the tailor of Tennessee.

TWELVE

A MAN COULD STAND UP

JOHNSON'S victory was a severe blow to both the influence and the pride of the state's "leading Democrats," for it proved that his popularity with the mass of voters extended beyond his home grounds in East Tennessee. Once more, but on a larger scale, the leaders who mistrusted and disliked him had been routed. And his inaugural speech set the seal on their humiliation by exposing, as they thought, to nationwide derision the sort of visionary their party had boosted into the governor's chair.

Deeming himself the spokesman of his class, in his view the foundation of the nation, Governor Johnson on the day of his induction delivered himself of a paean to democracy, and a blast at those who held themselves above the level of the "honest working man." The speech scandalized the unco guid, but it hypnotized his true believers.

"I claim to belong to that division of the Democratic party," he began, with a side glance at the leaders who had opposed him, "which stands firmly by the combined and recorded judgment of the people, until changed or modified by them . . . [and] which is progressive, not in violation of, but in conformity with, the law and the Constitution." To the old, iniquitous Federalists, and to their inheritors, the Whigs, by contrast, the Constitution, he said, "was but a paper wall through which they could thrust their fingers at pleasure, or a piece of gum elastic, that could be expanded or contracted at [their] will or whim.

"There are some who lack confidence in the integrity and capacity of the people to govern themselves," he went on. "To all who entertain such fears I will most respectfully say that I entertain none."

Then he put a Socratic question which might be heard from campaign platforms a hundred years afterwards:

"If man is not . . . to be trusted with the government of himself, is he to be trusted with the government of others?"

This was a defensible political position; but from this the governor veered off to pay his disrespects to intellectual snobs, especially such as, he maintained, were being turned out by institutions of higher learning—those schools of wisdom that he had never attended.

Many of the "young men of our country," he averred, "while at our academies and colleges . . . imperceptibly imbibe notions prejudicial to Democracy. Their wealth, and too frequently their preceptors—many of whom are bigots and supercilious on account of their literary attainments and assumed superior information on most subjects—inspire their students with false ideas of their own superiority, mixed with a superabundance of self-esteem which causes them to feel that the great mass of mankind were intended by their Creator to be 'hewers of wood and drawers of water' . . . To this class of our young men I have a few remarks to make."

Make them he did, after disavowing the intention of launching into any "analytical or metaphysical disquisition upon the great principles of Democracy."

"In this principle of Democracy," he said, "consists [man's] capacity of self-government . . . to lift himself above all animal creation." This capacity he termed "the Divinity of Man."

"I hold that the Democratic party proper, of the world, and especially of the United States, has undertaken the political redemption of man, and sooner or later the great work will be accomplished. In the political world it corresponds to that of Christianity in the moral. They are going along, not in divergents, not in parallels, but in converging lines; the one purifying and elevating man religiously, the other politically. At what period of time they will have finished the work . . . is not for me to determine; but, when finished, these two lines will have approximated each other . . . [and] the Divinity of Man having now fully developed, it may be confidently and exultingly asserted that *the voice of the people is the voice of God*."

For the benefit of "all discerning young men" (others apparently were so far sunk in Whiggery as to be lost to reason), the governor offered pointers on how they might place themselves upon this ascending path leading to millennial beatitude. They would "readily perceive" that "Democracy is a ladder, corresponding in politics to the one spiritual which Jacob saw in his vision; one up which all, in proportion to their merit, may ascend. While it extends to the humblest of all created here below, it reaches to God on high; and it would seem that the class of young men to which I have alluded might find a position somewhere between the lower and upper extremes of this ladder . . . which they would occupy with honor to themselves and advantage to their country."

Upon reading this farrago, flaunted through the press as Governor Johnson's "Jacob's ladder speech," Whigs and conservative Democrats hung their heads in shame for Tennessee. The educated and fastidious spoke of "vulgarity" and "blasphemy," while the more outspoken denounced the new incumbent as "a natural leveler, leading a rabble against the better elements of society."

"Governor Johnson we think falls into a mistake (a pardonable one under the circumstances)," observed the *National Intelligencer* at Washington, in a two-column-long review, "in supposing that 'literary attainments' render their possessors 'bigoted and supercilious' . . . We have known politicians who . . . are quite as 'bigoted' *without* 'literary attainments,' as is the most 'supercilious' professor in Tennessee *with* them."

The speech, as something to be talked about, in praise or derogation, did spread an awareness of the "mechanic governor" into sections of the country where he had been unknown before. However fanciful the phrasing or inept the imagery of the manifesto-address, the sentiments it contained undoubtedly were his, deeply felt, and he never departed from them. He did not retract a word; he stood upon what he had said; and in some quarters outside his immediate following there was applause. Here and there labor journals and conventions of workingmen expressed their thankfulness that they could count on at least one friend in a place of authority. Johnson's own reaction to the howls of derision sent up by the high-toned and highborn may have been best "shadowed forth," as he would say, in the course he adhered to for the next two years—making no speeches at all.

It is possible that the harsh strictures against seats of higher learning and their "preceptors" had been to some extent provoked by the activities of a budding politician of Knoxville named Horace Maynard. A native of Massachusetts, Maynard had come to Knoxville to teach mathematics at East Tennessee College, after being graduated from Amherst College with high honors. Tall, straight, and swarthy, with long black hair that hung down to his shoulders, he was nicknamed "The Narragansett," and was supposed to have Indian blood. After giving up teaching and establishing himself in a law practice, he was taking a hand in Whig politics. He had campaigned against Johnson's election, and a year hence would himself seek election to Congress from East Tennessee, but would be defeated by the disclosure of a letter he had written, in which he spoke contemptuously of the "common herd," with whom, he said, he desired to have "no fellowship." Any man holding views like that—and a college professor, no less—would inevitably have stirred Andrew Johnson's bile.

All Johnson's entrances into successive new roles were unpropitious. In his first term in the state legislature he had appeared ignorant and cross-grained. His early performances in the House of Representatives (with the exception of the Homestead Bill) were ill-digested and sophomoric. The doctrinaire truculence with which he assumed the governorship repeated this pattern. But in each transition, after an unbecoming entrance, he quickly regained poise and acquitted himself well.

This time, he devoted two months to hard study of the problems of the state, then redeemed himself by submitting an able message to the legislature. This was remarkable on several points. And in place of the high-flown verbiage of his inaugural address, its language was plain, vigorous, and down-to-earth.

His first concern was with the state's wretchedly inadequate common schools. Among all the states, in respect to providing elementary education, "Tennessee ranks last, except for one," he said. "The time has surely arrived when the legislature and the people should lay hold of this important question with a strong and unfaltering hand." To supply the funds needed for a thorough overhaul of the system, he urged that a general tax be levied upon the whole people. No such tax existed in Tennessee at the time. Pointing to the millions being spent on completion of the new Capitol building (William Strickland's masterwork), with its "niches and rotundas for fine statues and generous paintings, and the exterior, grand with carved and massive columns," he asked, "can nothing be done to advance the great cause of education?"

He probed the state's indebtedness and made recommendations for reducing it. He urged the gradual liquidation of the Bank of Tennessee, and wanted the state to get out of the banking business altogether. He called for the creation of a Board of Agriculture and the underwriting of fairs to display the state's products and stimulate commerce. He struck at the competition of prison labor with free workers, and proposed greater state aid for railroad construction.

More controversially, he urged the adoption of resolutions calling for amendments to the United States Constitution that would provide for the direct election of the President and Vice-President, eliminating the Electoral College; for direct election of United States senators; and popular election of federal judges for terms of twelve years, instead of their appointment for life. All these reforms, which he would call for again and again, were expressions of his religiously held belief that the people really should rule; that there was no problem of government that the common man, through popularly elected representatives, could not grasp and solve.

But schemes so radical were condemned by conservatives, either profanely or in President Polk's curt rejection of Johnson's homestead plan as "not worthy of an answer." Nevertheless, although the legislature was divided, the Senate being Democratic and the Assembly controlled by Whigs, legislation—including the school tax—was enacted substantially along the lines laid down in the message. For here Johnson was on the safe ground of the practical and useful; no rapt mysticism was involved. And at the close of the session the *Nashville Daily Union and American* merely expressed the consensus when it commented that "rarely if ever has there been a more harmonious [one], and certainly never one which has transacted more important business." This was high praise for the leadership of the "mechanic governor."

There were, of course, malicious stories spread about Johnson's peculiar behavior. On New Year's Day, for instance, he declined an invitation to dine with Aaron V. Brown, a Democratic magnifico, in order to keep a previous engagement with a workingman. This was twisted into the governor's devouring "bacon and cabbage with his washerwoman." He was reported to be boarding in a livery stable, when actually he lived in a hotel, the Nashville Inn. But the wounds he had inflicted on his adversaries festered and inspired spiteful gossip. Landon C. Haynes, smarting from his defeat, when asked how the new governor was getting along, sneered that he was "living with a butcher and skinning cattle for his keep."

Johnson did find friends among the wealthy and cultivated, and some of Nashville's most elegant homes were thrown open to him. His rank-and-file followers idolized him, and in his party no one could withstand him; nor could any one hoping to advance dispense with his blessing. As an old campaigner he was full of sage advice. Judge Patterson, who was seeking election to another term on the circuit bench, was counseled:

"Be prudent, and go into the canvass in good earnest, and there will be no danger. It is not worthwhile to be scared at any rustling you hear in the leaves, for you must expect to hear of many things while you are a candidate that you never heard of before, and probably after it is over [will] never hear of them again."

In April, 1854, Eliza Johnson's mother died, and about this time another son was born to the Johnsons in their Greeneville home. The boy, so much younger than his brothers and sisters, was named Andrew, and he would become the pet of the family.

As governor, Johnson withdrew temporarily from national politics. He paid little attention to national issues and concentrated on the business of the state. This was one of the reasons for the success of his administration, this and the fact that he was the first governor of Tennessee to give practically all his time to the job.

In 1855 he let it be known that he would seek a second term, and at the state convention opening on March 27 he was renominated by acclamation. The leaders of the conservative wing did get in an oblique insult by pushing through a resolution praising the "enlightened and patriotic" administration of President

Pierce, and making no mention of Johnson's accomplishments. As Oliver Temple remembered the occasion, these leaders would have been delighted to shelve Johnson, but such was his support among the people they "did not dare to move a little finger against him."

That 1855 campaign was the hardest Johnson had yet undertaken. The reason was the phenomenal gains made by that mongrel political growth, the Know-Nothing, officially designated the American party. The basis of this party was hostility to foreign immigration and to Roman Catholics. As it spread, and as the Whig party disintegrated, it attracted men of all degrees of uprightness, for reasons which afterwards they themselves were sometimes unable to define; it was a hysteria, a blind reaction to a feared threat to established customs and entrenched interests. In Tennessee, by 1855, it had a hundred thousand members. This was the opposition Johnson faced in his second bid for the governorship.

The Know-Nothings held no conventions. Their leaders met in secret conclaves and chose the party's candidates. The candidates did not even acknowledge that they had been selected by the party; they simply issued a statement to the effect that in response to popular urging they were in the race. In 1855 the Know-Nothings of Tennessee selected Meredith P. Gentry as their choice for governor, and the Whigs, disorganized and dispirited, without bothering to hold a convention, endorsed Gentry also.

This notable Tennessean was a man of charm and culture. During his service in Congress he had been called by such judges of oratory as John Quincy Adams and Alexander H. Stephens of Georgia the finest speaker the Capitol had ever heard.

Now Gentry was coming out of retirement to contest the election, yielding, he said, to "the generous sentiments expressed for me"—by whom, he did not specify. In 1852, when Daniel Webster had been passed over by the Whigs in favor of Winfield Scott as their Presidential candidate, Gentry had quit public life in disgust, considering himself "excommunicated" by his party. Thenceforth, he said, he would live obscurely, on a farm "in a sequestered valley in the state of Tennessee . . . There I will go and pray for Rome."

The campaign schedule agreed upon mutually by the candidates opened at Murfreesboro on May 1, and was to close at Chattanooga on August 1. It called for sixty meetings, and demanded iron endurance, what with the heat, continual excitement, and lack of physical comforts while traveling.

The opening blows traded at Murfreesboro indicated the temper in which the battle would be fought. Johnson twitted Gentry upon the brevity of his retirement to "pray for Rome," and Gentry retorted that he would illustrate why he had left his "Sabine farm" with a true story.

There was a fearful drought in Spain, he recounted; cattle were dying and people were perishing. A pious priest, accompanied by a band of devout intercessors, traveled over the country, praying for rain. Presently they came to a field that was particularly dry and parched. The priest raised his hands and closed his eyes, and said nothing. Opening his eyes, he looked over the desolate field, closed his eyes again, raised his hands in supplication, but said nothing. A third time he repeated the action; then turning to his followers said: "My brethren, prayer is no good for soil so cursed and blighted as this is; this field must have *manure*."

"Alas! my fellow countrymen," Gentry thrust home. "The state of Tennessee does not need prayers; there is a curse resting on her, parching and drying up her prosperity, and that curse must first be removed. I have come forth from my retirement . . . to remove that curse—and that curse is *Andrew Johnson!*"

In view of the temper of the crowds that were worked upon by such appeals, courage was required to hit back. The Know-Nothings were the real opponents, Johnson realized; the Whigs no longer counted. Therefore he launched into savage denunciation of the whole secret order and its schemes—its passwords, its secret grips, its oaths and midnight gatherings, its narrowness and bigotry. He ridiculed the proposed residence requirement of twenty-one years for naturalization. He poured scorn on the asserted threat of a takeover by foreigners. In Tennessee, he pointed out, there were only 5,838 aliens, in a population of 756,536—a ratio of 134 to 1.

"It is not my nature," he exclaimed, "when the poor Irishman leaves his own country and seeks America, as the home of the oppressed and the asylum of the exile, to meet him on the shore and forbid him entrance."

The Know-Nothings' claim to fear the Roman Catholic Church he derided as sheer hypocrisy. Only one elective office in Tennessee was held by a Catholic, and it was absurd for "624,295 Protestants, with their 2,011 churches, to make war on 1,400 Catholics with their three churches." As for the argument that Roman Catholicism should be prohibited because of its "foreign origin," why, if that rule were to apply, only Mormonism would be allowed.

In this opening blast, Johnson cried in passionate remonstrance against intolerance:

"Show me a Know-Nothing and I will show you a loathsome reptile, on whose neck every honest man should set his foot!"

The crowd was largely composed of Know-Nothings. Witnesses reported that the audience "grew pale with rage and still as death." Shouts were heard, "It's a lie! It's a lie!", and there was an audible sound of pistols being cocked. "Men ceased to breathe, their hearts stopped beating, the suspense was terrible." Johnson was unmoved. He paused a moment, gazing steadily at the enraged crowd, then calmly resumed his speech with a cutting reproof to Protestant preachers who, he said, were going around praying for his opponent—"instead of preaching Christ crucified, they preach crucify the Catholics!"

The day after this close call, Johnson's campaign managers ordered him to tone down his attacks and stop defending Catholics, or they would lose the election; worse, he would be killed, for serious threats were being made. Johnson heard the deputation out; paced the floor a few moments, in deep thought, then gave his decision:

"Gentlemen, I will make that same speech tomorrow if it blows the Democratic party to hell!"

The next day he was due to speak in a town that was a hotbed of Know-Nothingism, and he went armed. The crowd was in an ugly mood. Johnson stepped to the speaker's desk, took out his pistol, laid it on the table in front of him, and began calmly:

"Fellow citizens, it is proper when free men assemble for the discussion of important public matters that everything should be done decently and in order. I have been informed that part of the business to be transacted on the present occasion is the assassination of the individual who now has the honor of addressing you . . . If any man has come here today for the purpose indicated, I do not say to him, let him speak, but let him *shoot*."

Resting his right hand on his pistol, with his left he flung open his coat, and stood waiting. After a moment he said quietly:

"Gentlemen, it appears that I have been misinformed. I will now procede to address you on the subject that has called us together."

In this spirit, with both sides daily expecting a "difficulty" that would erupt in bloodshed, the campaign—the bitterest yet waged in Tennessee—went on.

The temperance issue was injected. During the fifties a nation-wide crusade against alcoholic abuses made rapid headway, and the Sons of Temperance exerted great influence on politics. Gentry and Johnson were questioned on the issue, and Gentry replied evasively. Johnson, who in his own family was plagued by the all too common curse, his two sons Charles and Robert having fallen into habits of intemperance, replied point-blank to the double question: "Are you in favor of a law prohibiting the sale of intoxicating liquors as a beverage? Will you, if elected, recommend to the legislature the passage of such a law?"

No, he would not recommend the passage of such a law, Johnson answered. "Some of the leading provisions . . . are incompatible with the rights and privileges of free men," was his opinion, and they conflicted with the spirit, "if not with the very letter" of the state's constitution. Having given his answer, he drove it home with the assertion, "I hope that I have succeeded in making myself understood."

The temperance people endorsed Gentry, announcing that "temperance and Know-Nothingism are kindred enterprises."

For taking this position, and for defending Catholics, Johnson was belabored by the Whig press as a demagogue. "Parson" Brownlow was in the fray, trying to prove that Washington, Jefferson, Webster, Jackson, and Henry Clay all had been Know-Nothings, though knowing nothing about it. As an editor the "Parson" displayed a striking ambivalence on numerous subjects. For example, although he was a staunch Son of Temperance, and the worst insult he could hurl at a man was "whisky drinker" (an insult he never hurled at Andrew Johnson), he once printed in the *Whig* a recipe for making wine that was so good, he assured his readers, it would make any man smack his lips, though it would be even better with the addition of a little "pure French brandy."

Johnson reduced Brownlow's attacks against Catholics to absurdity, saying that inasmuch as the "Parson" hated Baptists, Presbyterians, and every other sect as heartily as he hated Catholics, he would never rest until all were wiped out and Methodism was made the state religion. Said Brownlow:

"He misrepresented us and used our books in a way we never intended—but he is the strongest man the Democrats have."

The campaign proved too much for Gentry; he gave out at Knoxville on July 26. Johnson was in fine fettle, but in fairness he consented to cancel the rest of the schedule.

On August 1 the election was held, and the strongly Protestant counties of East Tennessee gave Johnson such a majority that he carried the state. The appeal of Know-Nothingism, it turned out, was not strongest among the primitive Protestants after all, but among the cultured classes in Middle and West Tennessee.*

Johnson's backers celebrated with fanatical joy, by torchlight parades, mass meetings, and jubilees. And in Greeneville, Colonel Thomas A. Arnold—the aristocrat who once had looked down on the tailor who presumed to be mayor—presided over the jubilation enthusiastically.

---

* Years afterward, a close friend of George Washington Julian who in this campaign had joined the Know-Nothings, rising to membership in their highest councils, revealed that the leaders had used the cry of anti-Catholicism and anti-foreigner to mask their real aim, which was the consolidation of their power as slaveholders by halting the spread of free white labor. The friend confessed his shame at ever having consented "to act with that clap-trap organization that for a time overshadowed the whole horizon . . . the Know-Nothing tom-foolery. I got into it—I hardly know how—and was carried along with the irresistible tide, and found myself a member of its august Councils. I was sent to . . . New York, then to the National Council at Cincinnati. There the bubble burst and I shook the dust from my feet, for I there learned from the haughty chivalry who sat around me that the organization was looked upon as a mighty instrumentality to forward the interests of slavery. This was to be effected by a universal disfranchisement of our foreign population, who were declared to be anti-slavery in all their sympathies . . ."

Andrew Johnson's birthplace, Raleigh, North Carolina. *Credit: Mrs. Margaret Johnson Patterson Bartlett.*

The first home Andrew Johnson ever owned, in Greeneville, Tennessee.

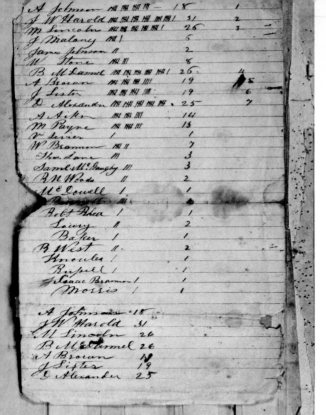

Andrew Johnson's first election tally sheet, when he was elected alderman of Greeneville. *Credit: Mrs. Margaret Johnson Patterson Bartlett.*

The Andrew Johnson tailor shop in Greeneville. When Johnson was village mayor, the town council met here to transact town business. The shop is now enclosed by a brick structure for preservation. *Credit: Mrs. Margaret Johnson Patterson Bartlett.*

Twin pictures, left and right in the two halves of a gold locket, Andrew and Eliza Johnson at the time Johnson first went to Congress, in the 1840's. This is the only picture of either of the couple known dating from that period, and never before published. The locket is in the possession of Mrs. Margaret Johnson Patterson Bartlett, President Johnson's great-granddaughter and last survivor of the family. *Copyright: Mrs. Margaret Johnson Patterson Bartlett.*

Andrew Johnson's "office" at Greeneville, situated in a yard some distance from the Homestead and quite separated from it. One room of the building was used as an office by Johnson when he was in Greeneville; the other was a depository for his boxes of papers and documents. *Credit: Mrs. Margaret Johnson Patterson Bartlett.*

Snow scene of Andrew Johnson's home from roughly 1850 on, in Greeneville, Tennessee. The house was acquired by Johnson about the time he became a United States senator. During the Civil War it was confiscated by the Confederates and used as a military hospital and barracks. The house has been carefully restored by the United States government to the condition of 1869 onward, when Johnson lived here. *Credit: Mrs. Margaret Johnson Patterson Bartlett.*

Entrance hall of Johnson Homestead, Greeneville. *Credit: Mrs. Margaret Johnson Patterson Bartlett.*

The parlor with portraits and furnishings of Johnson's time. *Credit: Mrs. Margaret Johnson Patterson Bartlett.*

Dining room of Johnson Homestead, Greeneville. New furniture for the entire house, left wrecked by the war, was purchased by Johnson in Washington just before he left the White House in 1869, and shipped to Greeneville. This furniture is part of the purchase. *Credit: Mrs. Margaret Johnson Patterson Bartlett.*

Johnson's bedroom in the Homestead, with relics of him, including his easy chair. *Credit: Mrs. Margaret Johnson Patterson Bartlett.*

Popular engraving of Senator
Johnson at outbreak of Civil War.
Credit: Library of Congress.

Rev. William Gannaway Brownlow ("Parson" Brownlow), Johnson's great Tennessee rival and opponent. About 1862, just after his
escape from the Confederacy.
Credit: Library of Congress.

Andrew Johnson as President of the United States. *Credit: Mrs. Margaret Johnson Patterson Bartlett.*

Eliza Johnson—the invalid of the White House. *Credit: Mrs. Margaret Johnson Patterson Bartlett.*

THIRTEEN

GREAT MAN OF TENNESSEE

THE fires of hatred lighted by the 1855 campaign did not die down at once. Hardly was Johnson installed in his second term when his friends received authentic warning that he was to be shot; the day and the place were named—in the street, on his way from the hotel to the Capitol. Urged to venture out only with a bodyguard, the governor declined to accept any escort, saying:

"If I am to be shot at, I want no man to be in the way of the bullet."

At the usual hour, alone and unhurried, he walked to the Capitol. He was not shot.

Amid the fervid public rejoicings over the great triumph, a family celebration occurred. On December 13, 1855, Martha, the Johnsons' eldest child, was married to Judge David T. Patterson. The judge was a steady-going, upright, conscientious man, slow and heavy in manner and thought, but devoted to Johnson; he had one weakness, an overaddiction to the bottle. Johnson bore with this failing, and the marriage proved congenial.

In February of the new year, 1856, Johnson's last link with his birthplace was snapped when "Polly" McDonough Doughtry, his mother, died. She had lived to see her orphan son honored as congressman and governor. Her elder son, Bill, had turned up in Greeneville from Texas once in a while, but he did not stay; truth to tell, he did not amount to much. Some of his children were reared in Greeneville under Andrew's care. Turner Doughtry, Johnson's stepfather, died soon after his wife and Johnson laid both to rest in the Baptist churchyard.

Shortly after his mother's death, Johnson figured in an episode which would have poignantly recalled to her his father's unassuming bravery. The hotel where Johnson was living caught fire, and a woman was trapped on the upper floor. At the risk of his life Johnson plunged through the smoke and succeeded in bringing her out safely. All his personal effects, however, with some $1,200 in cash, were lost. No medal was struck to commemorate this action, nor did the murderous threats taper off immediately.

Johnson's family was both a comfort and a trial to him during these exciting times. Mary Stover and her husband were living on their farm in Carter county and founding a family of their own—eventually including one boy and two girls. Martha and Judge Patterson lived on the edge of Greeneville, and Johnson was trying to bring her into town because of Eliza's health. Ever since the birth of little Andrew, she had been a semi-invalid; the doctor diagnosed phthisis, or "slow consumption," and recommended rest and abstention from physical strain. As much as possible, Martha relieved her mother of household responsibilities. Martha was her father's closest companion. Her mind reflected his, and the ties of affection between them ran strong and deep. Some of Johnson's friends averred that in shaping his public policy, he consulted his wife and his daughter more than he did anyone else. Certainly they, and almost they alone, had his entire and unreserved confidence.

Johnson's letters to Martha displayed this ease, this candor. In June 1856 he wrote her a long letter from Nashville, discussing his anxieties, about Charles, for instance, who had been drinking heavily, but seemed at last to have straightened out.

"You seem to think that [he] is trying to do something for himself," the governor wrote. "You could write no more pleasing intelligence than that. For you know it is a subject about which I have felt for many years a deep solicitude. I hope that he has reached the turning point in his history and that he will do well yet. I subjected myself [to] some inconvenience while at home to make the necessary arrangements for him and trust it will all work out right in the end.

"Your sister Mary," he went on, "I think is tolerably well satisfied, but she would prefer living a little nearer home than she does and where there is a little more society, etc., [that] she would be pleased with. I hope she will do well, at least until she can do better than she is now doing."

It was over young Andrew that his heart yearned most, however. Johnson was determined not to spoil the boy if it could be helped, but he could not resist humoring him.

"I cannot forget that young man you call Frank," he told Martha. "Tell him for his father, that if he cannot be '*where* his *father* is,' his father will soon be where he is, or in other words we shall soon be together. Tell him his father will not buy any more toys for him, but he will bring him a fine pair of boots and then he can keep from burning his feet on the stones when his curiosity takes him too far into things where he has no business."

A whimsical thought occurred: he would like to tailor a suit of clothes for the boy; but on second thought, a poor fit would be no credit to his skill as a craftsman, so he would forgo. With a smile, in all likelihood, he set down:

"If I could fit him I would bring him home a suit of clothes too. It would be rather hard to guess at, and would be as apt to miss as to hit it. Kiss him for his father and tell him he must be a good boy and to love his mother and obey her in all things. He must be broke of his conduct at table and now is the time to do it and bashfulness with strangers also should be corrected as soon as it can be done by proper means. If he should live and have no misfortune I think he has the elements of a very considerable man, and [you] should, as no doubt you do, feel it to be a part of your duty to contribute all that you can to the attainment of the end."

That "if he should live" carried poignancy, for the health of Robert, the Johnsons' second son, was causing alarm. Robert was reading law with Sam Milligan, but he continued to have hemorrhages, and the doctors were not hopeful. He also drank too much, and his father worried, confiding to Martha:

"I am afraid that Robert is to lose his health and disqualify him for the pursuit of his profession. I dislike these frequent returns of hemorrhage at the lungs and fear that it is permanent . . . You should urge upon him the propriety of exercising and carrying his chest erect, which will do more good than anything else."

The long chat concluded with advice on family investments.

"I had not heard of the purchase of the yard property till I received your letter . . . If the trade is closed I am glad of it, for the two pieces put together will make a first rate lot. If old Mrs. Good's could be bought at a fair price I would buy it also . . . Mrs. Good's property would do you to live in for a few years at least, and by that time we could know something more about our future. And you would be conve[n]ient to your mother also. Perhaps you could get on the right side of the old lady, and [if] she would sell to any one she would to you. I lived in worse property than that when I started in the world. And after a while when we saw our [way] clear we could build a good house on the lot. This is merely thrown out as a suggestion."*

His thoughts turning back to little Andy, he added: "Tell mother she must not neglect that pet of ours, for we must raise him if we can." Then saying that he had no news to transmit except that "Nashville is becoming somewhat sickly and is exceedingly hot," he signed the letter, *Your father devoted*, ANDREW JOHNSON," with a flourish underneath.

The day after this comfortable chat with Martha, Johnson wrote more succinctly to Robert, repeating his hope that "Charles will do well and commence now a new career in life." Regarding the new property acquisition: "Why would it not do for Patterson to move his office there and save paying the $30 or $40 rent which he is paying now?" If trees were planted around the door, the place would make a fine office, he thought.

"I intend to get off from here in about two weeks for Washington," the letter went on. "The weather is intensely hot and there is a good deal of sickness about Nashville. This morning I am very unwell and feel like I shall be laid up with a spell of sickness. I will take some of Arnold's Union Pills which you [know] is a sovereign remedy with me for all complaints."

Then the two subjects continually on his mind, Robert's health and little Andrew, were returned to:

"You must pay some attention to your little brother and im-

---

* Johnson may have suspected that the widow Good would not sell to him, for while in Congress he had once given Blackston McDannel his candid opinion of her late husband as "not worth the powder to blow him to hell."

prove him all that you can. He is your brother, and we must do the best we can with him. You will attend to the business of the family and give them whatever aid you can. I hope you will fix yourself comfortably at the office and go along as your health will permit and no faster—all valueless without health."

The mention of a trip to Washington was in connection with the forthcoming Presidential campaign. The Democrats, meeting in Cincinnati, had just nominated James Buchanan of Pennsylvania, and while Johnson had little liking for the nominee, he was prepared to pitch in and try to carry Tennessee for the party. Since Andrew Jackson's day the state had never gone for a Democratic Presidential candidate, and the occasion was a challenge to Johnson's natural pugnacity: although the party's high-toned leaders had been unable to carry the state, maybe the "mechanic governor" could.

Writing to Colonel William M. Lowery, a political associate, just after the nomination, Johnson refrained from commenting except to "express the hope that we can carry this state." But he did pay his disrespects to the self-important elite of the party:

"[Aaron V.] Brown, Pillow, and Humphreys seem to think they are the state and that nothing can be done unless they are in it somewhere. As to their democracy, there is no reliance to be placed in it."

With Robert Johnson, his father was more outspoken. Writing from Nashville, he said flatly:

"There is not much feeling with the democrats here for Buchanan. There is an acquiescence in his nomination but no decided zeal felt or manifested for him."

Nevertheless, as a Democrat, Johnson campaigned energetically, speaking outside the state also. In September, at the peak of the canvass, he told Robert that he had received "fifteen invitations to visit [Kentucky] and address the people, and among them one signed by 100 of the most responsible citizens to meet J. J. Crittenden at Bowling Green and have a regular setto or pitch battle which I am a great mind to accept and take the consequences." He had accepted engagements to speak at Huntsville, Tuscumbia, and elsewhere in Alabama, he said.

In November the Democrats swept Tennessee. Not only did

Buchanan win by a majority of seventy-five hundred, but both branches of the legislature were captured by the Democrats. It was a tremendous personal triumph for Andy Johnson, and established him beyond dispute as Tennessee's "great man."

The subsequent spectacle of the men who had *not* been able to carry the state preening themselves in expectation of patronage favors aroused his scorn.

"A. V. Brown," he wrote to Sam Milligan sourly, "is figuring a good deal and wants a Cabinet appointment or some other appointment (that is my opinion). He steps dignified, gestures gracefully, and looks wise far beyond the present into the distant future and will no doubt in a short time turn prognosticator. He is every day becoming more disgusting and contemptible and evincing the real elements of the man."

A. V. Brown would become Postmaster General in Buchanan's cabinet.

In January, 1857, Johnson went to Washington on an official errand which he undertook with pride. The Tennessee legislature had voted to buy Andrew Jackson's home, The Hermitage, including the tomb of "Old Hickory" and his wife Rachel, with five hundred acres of land, for forty-eight thousand dollars, and to offer the historic property to the United States, on the condition that it be used for a western military academy similar to West Point. The deed and resolution of the legislature Johnson personally carried to Washington. There he consulted President Pierce, who had little more than a month still to serve, and drafted a bill to be submitted to Congress accepting the gift. But the bill did not pass, and Tennessee retained the property.

The trip home proved nearly fatal to Johnson, when the train on which he was traveling left the tracks and he was badly injured. At first it was reported that he had been killed, and his family remained in suspense for days. Judge Patterson wrote anxiously to Robert Johnson, who was in Nashville with his father, "We hear so many conflicting statements . . . We all hope [his injury] is not a permanent one."

Robert replied that the injury was serious: "His right arm was broken just about an inch above the elbow. The joint of the elbow was very badly bruised and mashed—the whole arm badly bruised & when he reached this place it was [so] badly swoln [sic] that it was impossible to do anything to it for several days." However, there had been some improvement, and "in the course of two or three weeks he will be able to use it. I don't think there will be any permanent injury—perhaps a little stiffness."

Although the accident occurred in February, it was not until mid-July that Johnson was able to resume writing, and then his penmanship was a feeble, uneven tracing, little like the well-formed hand he had acquired after years of practice. The effects of the injury never would be entirely shaken off.

To crown his labors on behalf of the Democracy of Tennessee, in 1857 Johnson campaigned for the election of the party's nominee for governor, Isham G. Harris. Andy did not seek a third term; his ambition was set on the United States Senate, and with the Democrats in control of the legislature the time was opportune. Harris was elected, and on October 3, 1857, the legislature promoted the tailor-politician, the "mechanic governor," to the post he desired.

When the Thirty-fifth Congress met on December 7, 1857, Andrew Johnson took his place in the United States Senate, leaving behind him in Tennessee his pledge of gratitude:

"The people have never deserted me; and, God willing, I will never desert them."

THE SECOND LIFE

"Let us not be pygmies in a case that calls for men."
—DANIEL WEBSTER, *Seventh of March Speech*

ONE

NEW FACES, AND THE ISSUE

IN 1857 Andrew Johnson, aged forty-nine, was an anomaly in politics. He fitted no pattern; he traveled alone. Loyal as he was to the principles of the Democratic party, at heart he was not, he would never be, a party man. Whiggery, Know-Nothingism, and Federalism he loathed with a wholesome relish. "Parson" Brownlow once accused him of calling these elements "horse thieves and counterfeiters," although he had not; he simply, in a speech, had lumped the lot together in a common category of undesirables.

By assisting the election of Isham G. Harris, Johnson handed over the management of his party in Tennessee to the very group who had fought him unsuccessfully. And he did this without demur, almost, in fact, with relief. Harris was a West Tennessee slaveholder, who rode into the governorship not on his own strength, but on Andrew Johnson's popularity. Even after being installed, he would find it necessary, time and again, to call on Johnson to pull the party out of a hole, and Johnson would oblige.

Johnson's leadership was intensely personal. His followers, firm in their devotion, were loyal to him as an individual, and only in the second place loyal to the Democratic party which he represented. Unlike Abraham Lincoln, who could not function outside of a party organization, Johnson felt no need to maintain his grasp on the Democratic organization in Tennessee once he transferred his activities to Washington. His view was concentrated, never diffuse, and he had so often found ways to sidestep, outwit, or browbeat the state leaders into submission that he acquiesced in their restoration to control without an apparent qualm. The people, not the party, had elevated him to his honors, and he would continue to rely on the people. Apparently he did not feel any necessity to raise up a successor who would perpetuate his influence and his ideals; to such a need he seemed oblivious.

This blind spot in Andrew Johnson's political character would have a bearing on the crisis ahead. At the end of 1857, however, when he took his seat in the Senate, that time was still far off.

Both Johnson himself and the makeup of Congress had changed since his days in the House. His appearance had altered. He had taken on weight and sedateness, his compact figure now betokening strength and solidity. His movements were dignified, but not endowed with grace. His dress was the regulation uniform of a statesman of the period—black broadcloth coat, velvet waistcoat, doeskin trousers, all correct in cut and tailoring. An ample stock was wound around an old-fashioned collar, and he remained clean-shaven at a time when beards were beginning to sprout fashionably. His expression, especially in repose, was stern and melancholy, verging on grimness, but it would change startlingly when he smiled. A patient listener, he was extremely reticent, and in conversation with strangers, slow and cautious. When animated he would tend to declaim rather than converse, and sometimes in the heat of his enthusiasm would rise from his chair and make the equivalent of a speech.

His voice was well modulated, his enunciation clear, his tone in debate unusually low yet penetrating; he gestured seldom, and never violently; his poise while speaking was unruffled, no matter how vehement the language might become. As he fought, so he spoke—to win. He was always in dead earnest. Rugged honesty seemed to exude from him, and he had no charm except in the circle of his few trusted friends. With them, and with his family, he could be genial. His readiness for combat served as a deterrent to intimacy. His thoughts were square-cut and sturdy like the line of his lips, and in his courtesy was a tincture of reserve that chilled the newcomer and held the inquisitive at bay. Obviously a man of force, Johnson did not have the gift of making himself liked by most people; and his habit of proclaiming his lowly origin and identifying himself with the laboring masses irritated the cultured and genteel; they considered it an affectation. Lincoln and other men who had started under similar circumstances never made a point of their background, deeming it unimportant. Johnson, however, had suffered, and would continue to suffer, too keenly under the slights of his social betters to gloss over the disparity in their separate fates.

An able body of men was assembled around Andrew Johnson in the Senate in 1857, many of them relatively new to the national stage. Among the minority Republicans, comprising less than one-fifth of the membership, were such scholars as Lyman Trumbull of Illinois, and William Pitt Fessenden of Maine. Both had fine legal minds, and Fessenden was one of the most powerful debaters the Senate would ever know. These two were in their freshman terms, but already they were influential.

Thin and ascetic, Trumbull looked like a dyspeptic schoolmaster, with wispy beard, meditative eyes, and patient mouth; his tight lips bespoke intense convictions.

Fessenden, with his Maine angularity, his irascibility and positive opinions, suggested an angry parrot. Proud of his early associations with Daniel Webster (his godfather), in his grasp of the law he was masterly, and his devotion to duty was unbounded. Hot-tempered, he would treat an opponent with cutting sarcasm, but he never let prejudice overrule his zeal for justice in a crisis.

Another outstanding senator on the Republican side was Ben Wade, starting his second term. His first had made him one of the most detested and most feared men in public life. The bluntness of his speech had become proverbial, while his power of profanity compelled the admiration of even so straitlaced a Puritan as G. W. Julian; Wade's swearing, said the awed Julian, had "a spontaneity and fascination which made it almost seem the echo of a virtue."

With a tongue as rough as Andrew Johnson's, Wade had taken the measure of the blustering Southern chivalry, and he delighted in puncturing their flights of sentiment with knockdown rejoinders. Everybody knew how "Bluff Ben" had cut down the tremulous Senator George E. Badger of North Carolina, during debate on excluding slavery from the territories.

Why, Badger had asked in a tone of pathos, "if some Southern gentleman wishes to take the nurse who takes charge of his little baby, or the old woman who nursed him in childhood, and whom he called 'Mammy' until he returned from college, and perhaps afterwards, too, and whom he wishes to take with him in his old age when he is moving into one of these new territories for the betterment of the whole family—why, in the name of God, should anybody prevent it?"

"We have not the least objection . . . to the senator's migrating to Kansas and taking his old 'Mammy' along with him," Wade shot back. "We only insist that he shall not be empowered to *sell* her after taking her there."

"Bluff Ben" was never ill, never shirked a duty, was never tardy, and never failed to meet any foe, one or many. He was violent in his expressions and views, and at times moody and unpredictable. He, Trumbull, and Fessenden spoke for the new anti-slavery party that had contested the election of Buchanan the previous year, showing strength all through the North while pushing John Charles Frémont for the Presidency.

The acknowledged leader of the Republicans in Congress was suave, circuitous William Henry Seward of New York, another lawyer. After serving as governor of his state, Seward had entered the Senate in 1850, and at once raised the hackles of slaveholders by appealing to "a higher law" which forbade the protection of slavery. For this Seward had been subjected to the grossest abuse by Southern spokesmen. These attacks he met with an imperturbability which baffled his colleagues. Once when Robert Toombs, the fire-eater from Georgia, opened a tirade against Seward, the latter strolled to a cloakroom, lit a cigar, and standing in the doorway smoked it tranquilly, enjoying the performance.

Such passivity goaded Wade to the point of fury.

One face missing from the Senate in 1857 was that of Charles Sumner. In May of the previous year he had been assaulted in the Senate by Preston S. Brooks, a South Carolina congressman, in retaliation for a scathing arraignment of slavery and slaveholders. Sumner had been clubbed with a cane as he sat trapped by his desk, unable to rise and defend himself—clubbed so viciously that the cane was splintered, and his injuries were severe. Several senators had witnessed the atrocious assault without moving to interfere, and some even approved of it. Three of these—Toombs, Slidell of Louisiana, and Douglas of Illinois—defended their aloofness in speeches.

This was more than Ben Wade could stand. He declared war on such *"assassin-like, cowardly"* tactics. Alternately rising on the tips of his boots and sinking back with all his weight on his heels (his manner of driving home each blunt phrase), pounding his fist on the desk in front of him, he blazed that, outnumbered though the Republicans were, "I will vindicate the right and liberty of debate and the freedom of discussion upon this floor, so long as I live! If the principle now here announced prevail, let us come armed for the contest, and although you are four to one, *I am here to meet you!*"

Entering the Senate in 1857 as a future ally of Wade and Sumner was a former mayor of Detroit, Zachariah Chandler. "Old Zach" was a merchant, one of the richest men in Michigan. By despotic, bullying methods, and a coarse indifference to imputations of corruption, he had made himself boss of his state. He had subdued the Michigan legislature, his enemies said, first by whisky and then by bribery. One of the early organizers of the Republican party, Chandler opposed slavery with all his might, and although he won no distinction as a speaker, he would prove dangerous in lobbies and committee rooms, as a ruthless exponent of "practical politics." With him, party exigencies would always take precedence over abstract principles.

Ranged against this slender guard of Republicans and Free Soilers, on Johnson's side of the chamber, the Democratic, were the Southerners, the luminaries of the Senate. These formed a battalion of brilliance—violent, aggressive, extreme.

Though the scarred Toombs was a blowhard, he was that rare manifestation, a blowhard with ability. Bellicose and passionate, when defending what he thought was right he would work himself into a frenzy and become uncontrollable, though in cooler moments he tried to avoid hazardous positions and irrevocable decisions.

Patricianly James A. Hammond of South Carolina was a bold thinker and a graceful speaker, proud, amiable among his equals, and scornful of pretense. His courtesy could be devastating. Robert M. T. Hunter of Virginia, who held moderate views, was in favor with Northern Democrats; but he was sluggish in temperament and lacked personal attractiveness. His Virginia colleague, the pompously oracular James M. Mason, orgulous descendent of the author of the Bill of Rights, was almost burlesque in his assumption of superiority as he expectorated tobacco juice with lordly indifference to accuracy of aim.

Alfred Iverson of Georgia was so inflammable he was called

"Iverson the Terrible," but he was short-winded, fickle, and un-even. Alabama's Clement C. Clay, Jr., a cousin of the great Henry Clay, had inherited his seat from his father, and some of his colleagues put him down as narrow, opinionated, and apt to be vengeful; chronic ill health limited his activities. Alabama's sec-ond senator, Benjamin Fitzpatrick, owed his success as much to good looks and affability as to mental prowess; an easygoing middle-of-the-roader, he exerted little influence.

Louisiana's senators, John Slidell and Judah P. Benjamin, were studies in picturesque deviousness. Slidell, well characterized by the first syllable of his name, was astutely sly, an intriguer, self-centered, harsh, intolerant, and a source of bad counsels. Ben-jamin, West Indies-born and Yale-educated, was the perfect Devil's advocate: silken-tongued, with a wicked gift of plausi-bility, a brilliant mind, opportunistic, hardworking, and under surface charm remorseless in the prosecution of his aims.

Senator Albert G. Brown of Mississippi was a rarity, a Southern leader who spoke on behalf of the "poor whites." His views were completely Southern, and he was quick to defend them; oppo-nents found him dangerous to meddle with.

Extreme even among the fire-eaters (the name applied to Southern extremists) was swaggering Louis T. Wigfall of Texas—rash, violent, a dealer in taunts, copious in threats, ferocious and frequently vulgar. He had a special contempt for "doughfaces"—"faceless" men, that is, particularly Northern Democrats who meekly did the Southerners' bidding.

The Democratic group was leavened somewhat by men from the North and West, such as Stephen A. Douglas of Illinois, a shrewd, ambitious strategist, able in debate. California's David C. Broderick, the son of an Irish immigrant, reared in a New York slum, like Andrew Johnson had slugged his way to the top, but along a different route. Broderick's strength was not in appeal to the mass of voters, for he had never courted them; it was through his control of the Tammany-type political machine that he had built up in San Francisco. California's other senator, William Mc-Kendree Gwin, oddly was a Tennessean, born into the patrician class in Middle Tennessee. As a young man he had migrated to Mississippi, where he had been the protégé of Andrew Jackson.

While his sympathies were warmly Southern, they were tempered by his responsibilities as the representative of a free state.

The focus of the slavery clique was the Mississippian with whom Andrew Johnson had clashed in the House of Representatives, Jefferson Davis; he returned to the Senate in 1857 after four years as President Pierce's Secretary of War. Davis was not the most gifted member of his circle, nor the boldest or clearest thinker, but he was the steadiest. His rectitude was beyond question, while his devotion to principles was selfless and fixed. Except in relation to a few quixotic prejudices, he was incapable of acting from mean motives.

As Secretary of War, Davis had rendered valuable service, and during that time he probably had appeared at his best. Carl Schurz, a refugee German liberal, had met him at that period and had been struck by his fine presence—"tall, slender, erect," with "spare face, keen eyes, fine forehead . . . in his bearing a dignity which seemed entirely natural and unaffected—the kind of dignity which does not invite familiar approach." Other observers put their impressions less favorably, finding him cold, proud, and unforgiving. To G. W. Julian, he had "a military and magisterial look" and a self-estimate "so exalted that his ordinary demeanor towards others seemed like a personal condescension, if not an insinuation of contempt."

By the time Davis reappeared in the Senate his health had been lost, and he would be recurrently martyrized by a complexity of ailments, including neuralgia, nervous indigestion, and a painful disease of the eyes that eventually cost him the sight of one eye and threatened total blindness. As a speaker, there was no gainsaying his grace of diction and charm of voice.

He and Andrew Johnson lost no time in registering their total antipathy for each other. This was inevitable, for their fundamental views were diametrically opposite, and in personality each summed up a type that could have no relationship with the other except one of suspicion and hostility. Their class prejudices were reciprocal, directed as strongly against one as against the other. On issues of immediate action, however, sometimes the two men did stand together. Both were Southerners, tenacious of Southern rights. Both were slaveholders, and both supported the institution of slavery, although the quality and intensity of their support were widely different.

The issue of slavery Johnson found crowding out all others. No matter what proposition might be before Congress, slavery would find its way into the discussion. While governor of Tennessee, Johnson had watched this drift of events, and deplored it. After the election of Buchanan he had written to Sam Milligan:

"I have within the last few months thought much upon this subject and confess my apprehensions have become more alarming than at any former time . . . I feel this question is not ended and what it is to end in GOD only knows; its contemplation is dreadful and sickening to the heart of every one who loves his kind."

During the 1856 campaign, he had made his stand on the issue plain, in a speech to a large crowd at Nashville. Slavery, he said, existed not only in the South, where it was black, but in a more subtle form in the North, where it was white. The mill hand and wage earner of the North in some ways were worse off than the bond slave in the South, he contended. "Slavery exists . . . and it will continue to exist." He accepted the institution, and opposed making any further compromises that would whittle away the South's rights under the Constitution.

"We have been engaged in first one compromise and then another, until our rights have been all compromised away," he told the crowd. "For me, I have nothing to conceal in reference to my political sentiments; and when I say that I am no compromiser, I think there are many who agree with me."

This did not mean, he hastened to add, that he was one of those who were talking secession. Preston Brooks, Sumner's assailant, was such a man. At a public dinner given to him by the citizens of South Carolina, in honor of his assault upon Sumner, Brooks had declared, amid applause from the ten thousand present: "The Constitution of the United States should be torn to fragments, and a Southern Constitution formed in which every state should be a slave state!"

In Boston, William Lloyd Garrison, the fiery abolitionist, had burned the Constitution in public, reviling it as unclean, "a covenant with hell," and demanding that the righteous North sever all ties with the sinful South.

Johnson repudiated both these extremes. "I am no alarmist," he said, "but I speak what I think. This Union shall be preserved. Our Southern institutions depend upon the continuance of the Union, and upon noninterference."

In looking back upon the conflict over slavery, it is necessary for the present-day observer to rid his mind of present-day concepts. In the twentieth century, the thought of traffic in human beings is abhorrent; every instinct of humanity and justice condemns it. But in the 1850's men—good men—thought with different minds. Slavery existed, as Johnson said, not as a tolerated evil, but as a respectable condition of society. The Southern men who fought to preserve the institution fought in a bad cause, but they were not all bad men. Few persons manage to shake off the conceptions that have been bred into them as children, and that are confirmed, sustained, and fortified by every custom and every precept of the world they live in. Slavery was one of the conventions of the antebellum South, and it required an original and fearless mind on the part of a Southerner to question its validity.

Johnson felt and acted like the people of his time and place, the people among whom he had grown up and whose ideas he shared. Politically he stood with the South on the issue of slavery, without making a great point of it. In 1850 he had voted reluctantly for the compromises put forward by Henry Clay as a means of averting the imminent breakup of the Union, coupling his vote with an appeal to cease sectional strife—"to the North and to the South, to the East and to the West—to Whigs and to Democrats —to all—to come forward and join in one fraternal band and make one solemn resolve that we will stand by the Constitution." Unity and peace were his objectives then, and to obtain them he had compromised. But by 1857 he saw that compromises had failed.

"In 1820 we had a compromise [the Missouri Compromise]," he told the Senate. "The republic was agitated, a dissolution was threatened before it was made; and when it was effected it became a permanent subject of contention until it was repealed . . . In 1850 several measures were passed as compromise measures; they produced a great agitation, and dissolution of the Union was threatened; in 1854 some great pacificators came forward on another compromise [the Kansas-Nebraska scheme], and that compromise has been a continual and increasing source of agitation.

"Compromise! I almost wish the term were stricken out of the English language! . . . Let us . . . have no more compromises! . . . We have been compromised and conservatized until there is hardly any Constitution left . . ."

But now the issue was reaching a stage of crisis that compelled Johnson to take a deeper, harder look at the whole problem. How would he square his advocacy of free land for free men with the defense of slavery? Homesteadism meant death to the "peculiar institution," as everyone saw. Johnson's mind did not move quickly, and like other men, he was not all of a piece; he developed in stages, altering under pressure of changing conditions and ripening with experience. Hitherto (and still for a while to come), as between the slave and free sections of the nation, he had sided with his own; as between free labor and slave labor, he sided with free labor.

The position was self-defeating and untenable, but that decade was one of turbid thinking. Andrew Johnson had not yet found his cause—the cause that would lift him out of the ruck of politicians more or less earnestly pursuing personal fulfillment and common ends, and through him would provide the nation with a rallying point in a dark hour.

He thought, of course, he had found the cause in homesteadism, and on that he made his first stand in the Senate.

TWO

IMPENDING CRISIS

JOHNSON reintroduced his homestead plan, which had been rejected while he was in the House of Representatives, almost immediately upon entering the Senate, and then fought to get it considered. Other measures stood in the way, however, and his first speeches as a senator were upon unrelated topics. These brought him into renewed collision with his old antithesis, Jefferson Davis.

The administration was having trouble with the Mormons in Utah, and a military force was about to be dispatched to compel that stubborn sect to bow to the authority and customs of the United States. To carry out this mission, Davis proposed an increase in the number of regiments of the regular army. His bill encountered intense opposition from Northern senators, who feared that the additional force, under the control of the Democratic administration, would be used to impose slavery on the free territories. Senator Hale of New Hampshire had another objection: he scouted the notion that once the military establishment were increased, it would ever voluntarily go back to its original size, "as long as there was money or credit to maintain it." The idea was "too absurd to speak of," Hale scoffed, because "there are no backward tracks when our government begins to spend money."

Although the cleavage was between Northern and Southern interests, Johnson in this instance sided with the North in resisting the bill. He believed it not only involved needless expense, but was "against the spirit of the people."

"A standing army is an incubus, a canker, a fungus on the body politic. I want no rabble here on one hand, and I want no aristocracy on the other. Lop off the aristocracy at one end, and the rabble at the other, and all will be well with the republic."

Thanks in part to the defection of Johnson, Toombs, and a few other Southern senators, Davis' bill was defeated and the administration was obliged to accept a substitute authorizing an increase in the size of the existing companies, but not the creation of new regiments with their attendant swarm of commissioned officers.

Another measure which blocked speedy consideration of the Homestead Bill was the proposal to underwrite a railroad to the Pacific coast. This improvement had been sought ardently by Westerners ever since the acquisition of California. Both of that state's senators, Gwin and Broderick, had worked tirelessly to obtain the subsidies requisite for so gigantic a task. Johnson lined up on this issue with the Southerners, who were opposing the scheme for constitutional reasons and because of self-interest.

Broderick was arrogant in his demands. California, he said, was not standing "as a mendicant at the door of the Senate chamber, asking for an opportunity to build a railroad. The state of California has sent between six hundred and seven hundred million dollars to the Atlantic states, and what have you sent us in return for our gold? Nothing. If the state of California for fifty days should withhold her money from you, the banking interests, the commercial interests, and the manufacturing interests of thirty-one states on this side of the Rocky Mountains would be paralyzed."

Such boasting was too much for Tennessee pride, and Johnson replied. It seemed to him, he said, that the United States had been quite successful before California was ever acquired, and had "a good deal of manufacturing, a good deal of very successful banking and commerce" before that time.

"Where does the gold from California go to?" was his question. "All that gold, when it goes to New York or any other port, goes abroad . . . Cotton is just as necessary in commerce as gold . . . What would your country have done but for our rice, cotton, and tobacco . . . but for our manufactured articles? . . . While you are digging for gold, you must have something to eat and to wear . . . What would California have done for flour? . . . What would she have done for iron? . . . With the exception of gold, she would not have been much."

Johnson had never shown much patience with the gold fever

that had boomed California into existence as a state. Back in 1850, as congressman, he had written to Judge Patterson:

"I receive cords of letters in my mail upon the subject of California—information wanted, pamphlets, etc. Some of them will before all is over wish they had never seen California or heard tell of it."

Senator Gwin admonished Johnson that since the platform on which Buchanan had been elected had declared in favor of a Pacific railroad, that was the party's mandate, and it should be obeyed. Snapped Johnson, the Democratic convention by that action had "hung a millstone around the neck of the party . . . I am no party man, bound by no party platform, and will vote as I please." The political itch to sit in the White House, he hinted, was the real motive behind the advocacy of these grandiose schemes of expenditure. This was interpreted as a dig at Jefferson Davis, whose ambition to become President was well known. Let the people elect their Presidents and Vice-Presidents directly, Johnson recommended, and do away with the intriguing of national conventions.

"I think the people of the different states are as competent to judge of their own citizens, and their qualifications, as a national convention," he said. "And the chances are that they would be equally pure and as good men as would be brought forward by a national convention or a Congressional caucus . . . We have got into making Presidents, in modern times, so that nobody knows who is safe."

Jefferson Davis remarked that when Andrew Johnson got into the race, it would sink to "a pony race," and the latter flashed back:

"I do assure the senator that I prefer to discharge my duty faithfully as an honest representative of the state and the people. Occupying that position—the Senate will pardon me for the expression, but I do not use it in a profane sense—when contrasted with being President of the United States, I say, damn the Presidency!"

Detecting behind Davis' jab a covert sneer at his origins, Johnson declared without equivocation:

"It may be said that I am a plebeian and have made my way here from the ranks. Some gentlemen may say I contracted my prejudices there. I am a plebeian and I am proud of it. I know there are others who can boast of more favored circumstances; I have no objection. On the other hand, not to be egotistical, I thank Almighty God that He has endowed me with physical power, and with a tolerably healthy brain."

This speech produced some rancor in the Senate, but it was applauded in the nation's press.

Meanwhile, Johnson plied every parliamentary device to bring his Homestead Bill to the floor, but was blocked repeatedly by the omnipresent issue—slavery.

On March 4, 1858, South Carolina's Senator James A. Hammond spoke at length on this topic. Hammond had never bothered to veil his contempt for some of his colleagues—"a vulgar set of sharpshooters, county court lawyers, and newspaper politicians," he called them—and in replying to the condemnation of slavery by Northern speakers he applied the word "mudsill" to the poorly paid wage earners in the manufacturing North—"your whole hireling class of manual laborers and 'operatives,' as you call them—the very mudsills of society." These voiceless drudges, who performed the necessary but degraded tasks required by every community, he contended, were "essentially slaves."

Johnson was quick to resent the aspersion upon his class.

"Will it do to assume that any man who labors with his hands," he demanded, "is a slave? No, sir, that will not do. Will it do to assume that any man who does not own slaves, and has to live by his own labor, is a slave? That will not do. If this were true, it would be very unfortunate for many of us, and especially so for me. I am a laborer with my own hands, and I never considered myself a slave."

Hammond glanced aside in disdain, and other members of the "chivalry" shrugged that the "tailor plebeian" protested too much.

Finally in May, 1858, Johnson did get the Homestead Bill reported. Then the debate, with interruptions, dragged along for months. He stated all the old arguments, picturing the benefit the nation would derive from the transplanting of a million families from city slums, where they could barely sustain life, to their own freeholds, where they could become productive citizens.

Again his allies were incongruous, though he welcomed them all. Senator Wade fought for the measure, while the Southern contingent employed every means—attack, belittlement, obstruction—to defeat it.

Pending before the Senate was a proposal to purchase Cuba from Spain for thirty million dollars, and although the bill had no chance of passing, it served to stall off a vote on the homestead measure. Five times Wade moved to drop the Cuba matter and vote on homestead, and five times the motion was defeated. Once, when the result was a tie, Vice-President Breckinridge of Kentucky cast the deciding vote—for Cuba.

Seward lined up with Johnson in support of homesteadism, defining the issue cogently as "a question of homes for the homeless, land for the landless," while Cuba was "a question of slaves for the slaveholders."

Demagoguery! answered Toombs of Georgia. Why not be truthful? "If you don't want to give thirty millions for Cuba, say so, but don't sidetrack Cuba with your plea of 'land for the landless.' Don't divert us from a great public policy by pretext or by shivering in the wind of men in certain localities."

"We are shivering in the wind, are we, sir, over your Cuban question?" retorted Wade. "You may have occasion to shiver on that question before you are through with it. The question will be, 'Shall we give niggers to the niggerless, or land to the landless?'"

Wade yielded not an inch to bellicose opponents. Indeed, he and two other Republican senators—Zach Chandler of Michigan and Simon Cameron of Pennsylvania—had entered into a secret compact to treat insults offered by any Southern senator as personal affronts, and to incur the displeasure of their constituents rather than continue to avoid the "field of honor." The sentiment against dueling in the North was so strong, they realized that they risked political ruin if they engaged in such encounters; nevertheless, driven to desperation by the steady rain of "Southern insolence and browbeating," they drew up their agreement, signed it, and each retained a copy for his private files. Its text was not revealed until years later.

"Our constituents were well-nigh deprived of their rights in

Congress by the insolence of our political opponents," the secret memorandum stated. "Our very manhood was daily called into question . . . We consulted long and anxiously, and the result was a league by which we bound ourselves to resist any repetition of this [abusive] conduct by challenge to fight, and then, *to carry the quarrel into a coffin.*"

Although they did not publish the text of their resolve, the three parties to the agreement allowed knowledge of their determination to leak out; and in their words, "when it became known that some Northern senators were ready to fight for sufficient cause, the tone of their assailants was at once modified."

But not before Wade had accepted one challenge. The choice of weapons being his, he named "rifles at thirty paces, with a piece of white paper the size of a dollar pinned over each duelist's heart." Since Wade was a famous shot with a squirrel gun, the challenger declined. The "deep, smothered" fire that burned in Wade's black, unblinking eyes discouraged personal encounter.

Constant harping on the issue of slavery upset Johnson. Why could not his homestead plan be considered on its merits?

"Why lug slavery into the matter?" he appealed. And all this talk about "saving the Union!"

"I have never considered the Union in danger. I am for the Union, but in every little speech I have to make I do not deem it necessary to sing paeans and hosannahs to the Union. I think the Union will stand uninterrupted; it will go on as it has gone on, without my singing paeans to it . . . This thing of saving the Union . . . has been done so often that it has gotten to be entirely a business transaction."

So why the obsession with slavery?

"Round and round the giddy circle of slavery agitation have we gone, until our heads are reeling and our stomachs almost heaving," he went on. "It really seems to me that if some member of this body was to introduce the Ten Commandments for consideration . . . somebody would find a Negro in them somewhere; the slavery agitation would come up."

Obstructionism and the overriding issue were strong enough, however, to talk the Homestead Bill to death in the Thirty-fifth Congress. Johnson did not give up; promptly upon the convening of the Thirty-sixth Congress, in December, 1859, he introduced the bill once more, prepared to renew the struggle.

In the interim, he had lost confidence in President Buchanan; from "the old man" he now expected nothing but "grannyism."

"He is too timid to venture upon anything new or risk much upon anything old," Johnson had written his son Robert as early as January, 1858. "To hear him talk, one would think that he was quite bold and decided, but in practice he is timid and vacillating . . . I fear his administration will be a failure."

Nor did Johnson think much of his Whig colleague from Tennessee, John Bell. When Bell alluded slurringly to some of Johnson's political friends at home, the latter sprang to their defense, and in the course of his rebuttal spoke of Bell as "my competitor." This in turn drew an abrupt disclaimer from the irritated Whig: Andrew Johnson, he implied, was not big enough to be in that class.

At this Johnson's temper flared, and he informed Bell that he had met competitors "worthy of my steel, men who recognized me as such . . . A well-bred man will respect me; others I will make do it!" Jibing at Bell's weaseling on sectional issues, he quoted from *Hudibras:*

> "He wires in and wires out,
>   Leaving the people all in doubt
>   Whether the snake that made the track
>   Is going north or coming back."

The next day, having cooled off, both men apologized to the Senate for causing a scene, and became outwardly reconciled; but there was no friendship between them.

With the crisis deepening, minor issues were being shelved.

In June, 1858, Abraham Lincoln accepted the Republican nomination to the United States Senate, to run against Stephen A. Douglas, with a speech in which he quoted the Biblical admonition that "a house divided against itself cannot stand." Enlarging upon his thought, he said: "I believe this government cannot endure permanently half slave and half free."

In October, that same year, Senator Seward, who already was the leading contender for the Republican Presidential nomination in 1860, spoke in Rochester, and used the phrase that Southern hotheads construed as a virtual call to arms. Describing the sectional antagonism as "an irrepressible conflict between opposing and enduring forces," Seward interpreted it as meaning that "the United States must and will, sooner or later,· become either entirely a slaveholding nation or entirely a free-labor nation."

These sentiments Andrew Johnson did not share. He could foresee no dissolution of the Union. Although he had spent his life in promoting the interests of the masses against entrenched privilege, he admitted no right of Congress to interfere with slavery where it already existed under the highest legal sanction—the Constitution of the United States. Abolitionism he did fear and reject, on the grounds of both justice and expediency. Slavery was embedded in the fabric of the nation, and for the sake of social stability alone it should not be molested as long as it remained subordinate to the government. Should the institution, or any other sectarian, sectional, or class interest array itself against the government, that would be a different situation, and the government, in his view, must and should prevail. On the practical side, the slavery question was equally unsolvable by a mere fiat of emancipation, he held.

"If you liberate the Negro, what will be the next step?" he asked. "What will you do with two million Negroes in our midst? . . . Blood, rape and rapine will be our portion. You cannot get rid of the Negro except by holding him in slavery."

The "poor white's" mistrust of free Negroes and hostility to the Negro as a labor competitor, Johnson shared. And this feeling was common even among some proponents of abolition. Salmon P. Chase, governor of Ohio and a foremost defender of Negro rights, acted in near panic to head off a proposed plan to settle free Negroes in Ohio, declaring that he heartily wished not another Negro would enter the state, and if he had his way those already there would be got rid of somehow; they were a disturbing element. Other Northern governors took similar stands; free Negroes were resented almost everywhere.

When a bill was brought into the Tennessee legislature to expel all free Negroes from that state, Johnson wrote to his son Robert from Washington that "a cursory reading" led him to believe the measure was "in pretty good form," having been pruned of "everything like oppression or inhumanity to the free colored men . . . If they could be gotten clear of without violating the great principles of humanity it would be better for the country and especially for the slave states. I think the bill in its present shape will drive them from the state in a few years. I would give them a reasonable time to get away before the law commences operating."

It must be borne in mind that this attitude—the fantasy of some painless escape from a cruel dilemma—had been given substance and encouragement by that supreme legal fantasy, the Dred Scott decision, in which the United States Supreme Court held that a Negro, free or slave, could never be a citizen of the United States.

Where did Andrew Johnson and other conscientious men and women expect the Negroes to go? One solution was colonization —in Africa, Brazil, or elsewhere. This was a chimera, impossible of realization, though it would never be discarded entirely by many thoughtful leaders of the time, including Lincoln.

Another way out was based on a theory—a wistful hope rather than a settled conviction—that the Negroes might find a "gateway" through Texas to a warmer climate and unprejudiced surroundings in Latin America. Johnson long harbored this delusion, and in the 1840's had expressed the exact thought that "Texas in the end may prove to be the gateway out of which the sable sons of Africa are to pass from bondage to freedom, where they can be merged in a population congenial to themselves, who know and feel no discrimination in consequence of the various hues of skin or crosses of blood."

The skies were darkening over the whole nation; yet its responsible spokesmen—those in authority—strove to preserve an unruffled poise; on the verge of catastrophe they went through their usual offices and steadily discounted the danger.

On January 4, 1859, the Senate moved from the historic chamber where Calhoun, Webster, Clay, Benton, Hayne, Jackson, and other legendary giants of an earlier time had put together a nation, into more commodious quarters in the Capitol. The occasion was marked by solemn ceremonies. Vice-President Breckinridge delivered a eulogy to the past, and then looked forward to the future with unconcealed emotion:

"And now, senators, we leave this memorable chamber, bearing with us, unimpaired, the Constitution we received from our fore-fathers . . . The structures reared by man may yield to the cor-roding tooth of time. These marble halls must moulder into ruin; but the principles of constitutional liberty, guarded by wisdom and virtue . . . do not decay. Let us devoutly trust that another Senate, in another age, shall bear to a new and larger chamber this Constitution, vigorous and inviolate, and that the last genera-tion of posterity shall witness the deliberations of the American States still united, prosperous, and free."

It was a moving appeal, to which Andrew Johnson could return a fervid "Amen!" The time would soon come when that "Amen!" must be turned into action, and then Breckinridge's words would become his ultimate hope.

THREE

NOW HEAR THIS . . .

EVERYBODY was taking part in the great debate. In a wordy disputation on the righteousness or unrighteousness of slavery, "Parson" Brownlow in 1858 belabored a Calvinist antagonist, the Reverend Abram Pryne, with arguments defending the institution Biblically, historically, theologically, ethically, moralistically, economically, and politically. Although not a slaveholder himself, Brownlow was a Southerner. The debate, held in Philadelphia, extended over several days, and Pryne ran out of breath first. Brownlow breezed back to Tennessee and embedded his five-part argument in a book, in which he lambasted the inoffensive Pryne with every opprobrious name he could lay pen to. Pryne, he said, suffered from the spiritual heaves.

After a short spell of purely parochial fulminating, the "Parson" was catching his second wind as a large-scale scourger of error in the spheres of faith, morals, and politics, pleasantly confusing Democrats and the devil, to his own satisfaction and the edification of some ten to twelve thousand weekly readers of the *Whig*. A tri-weekly edition accounted for a circulation about as large, so the "Parson" had a considerable audience. He had moved his paper to Knoxville and rejoiced in the subsequent enlargement of his influence in East Tennessee.

Soon after the encounter with Pryne, Brownlow suffered the misfortune, in consequence of a severe attack of bronchitis, to lose his voice; but this merely added sparkle to his already Roman-candle prose.

In 1855 he had impulsively sold an interest in the *Whig* to a bookkeeper and a printer, just to get rid of the bother of publishing, retaining control (insofar as any control was discernible) of its contents. But in January, 1859, he bought back the full proprietorship, so as to be more at liberty to indulge a congenial latitude of expression. This event he imparted to his subscribers in the issue of January 9, 1859, in a bravura manifesto that concluded:

"In politics we will continue what we always have been, ONLY MORE SO. Being in *our own office building*, with a *Press, Type*, and other *Fixtures*, under our sole control, and being a *free white man of lawful age*, we shall come as nigh saying, writing, and publishing just what suits us as men usually do in this life! And neither . . . *Mining Companies and Political Organizations*, or any other *device of the Devil*, this side of *stopping our windpipe*, shall deter us from exposing corruption, unmasking villainy, and lashing rascals. Public interests call for this work; public justice requires its performance; and it shall be done, or we will perish in the attempt to execute it."

Authors were no more backward than editors in adding their voices to the clamor. By 1859 Harriet Beecher Stowe's *Uncle Tom's Cabin* was a perennial best seller. Published in '52, in the first few months it had sold more than a million copies, and its conquest of the reading public around the globe gave no sign of abating.

In 1857 a self-educated North Carolina "poor white," Hinton Rowan Helper, had published a patchwork compilation of statistics from the United States Census, by means of which he demonstrated that the curse of the South was slavery—not for humanitarian or moral reasons, because he hated the Negro, but on economic grounds. Titled *The Impending Crisis of the South: How to Meet It*, Helper's book showed that slave labor in the South was wasteful, inefficient, and an obstacle to increased production and prosperity; and by projecting his graphs he was able to foretell accurately the rate at which the slave states would fall further and further behind the progressive, free-labor North in economic development. Naturally these dismal prophecies were howled down by the slaveholders, and Helper's book was banned in the South, while he personally was excoriated as another example of that most despicable type of traitor, a Southerner (like Andy Johnson) who went back on his kind. "Helperite" became an epithet of loathing. In the North, Helper's book was circulated as a Republican campaign document in 1859, bearing the endorsement of sixty-eight members of Congress.

Economy and efficiency were among Johnson's concerns also, and as the first order of business in the Senate's new hall he introduced a resolution calling for a survey to determine ways of reducing federal spending. From 1790 to 1859, he pointed out, the population of the nation had increased sevenfold, but government spending had increased thirty-five times. Offered the chairmanship of a subcommittee to carry out this study, he declined, believing the matter could be handled better by the judiciary committee. This was another act of self-abnegation which confirmed his reputation for being a "loner" and unpredictable; every senator knew that identification with a special cause—especially one that promised sensational and even scandalous disclosures—was the best possible means of "image-making" to build a political reputation.

Just as he wished the finances of the government to be conducted in a businesslike manner, so Johnson handled his own money transactions. A man of some wealth, he was in a position to oblige associates in Washington or at home with loans now and then, though there is no record of his borrowing. These loans he expected to be repaid; and should a borrower prove remiss or unduly dilatory, he would not hesitate to take steps to collect. On April 8, 1859, he wrote from Greeneville to one Robert Hagen, at Memphis:

"I have this day forwarded to Messrs. Gallaway & Campbell of Memphis an order on you for the amount loaned while in Washington now more than a year ago. The amount was one hundred dollars. I hope it will be convenient for you to call and pay it over to them at an early date."

Nor did Johnson relax his watchfulness over family affairs while he was in Washington. Just before the adjournment of the first session of the Thirty-fifth Congress, in June, 1858, he wrote to Robert from the Senate chamber, using a vile pen and with a shaky hand, saying that he would be delayed in reaching Greeneville because he was going to Philadelphia to consult a physician about a possible operation on his injured arm, and then he planned to "stop and see Mary" at the Stover farm in Carter county. As for politics:

"The administration is at present flat. I hope something will turn up that will give it some vitality.

"I hope that you have been attending to those money matters and that they are all in proper train. I want you to begin thinking about your future and take some definite course this summer and fall . . . that will suit you whether it suits me or not. I will help you all I can when I get home. Tell your mother what it is that causes my detention . . . I hope that Charles has been doing well."

Robert, now admitted to the bar, was considering entering politics, and in the next election he would win a seat in the state Assembly. But Charles was not doing well: his old trouble, insobriety.

Six months later, in a long letter crowded into four full pages, Johnson wrote again to Robert, from the new Senate chamber: "I do hope that Charles is at his business & sober." And a couple of months after that, on Washington's birthday, 1859, in a letter to "my dear son": "Your letter & that of your mother were received by the same mail. I was more than rejoiced to hear that Charles had recovered & was one time more attending to his business . . . I will be at home in a short time when I can see and talk with you freely in reference to your own course." This letter carried a scribbled postscript saying that it had been written "in great confusion while the Senate is in session."

The Senate was in upheaval for weeks after the convening of the Thirty-sixth Congress on December 5, 1859, for John Brown's raid on Harper's Ferry the previous October had raised the sectional bitterness to fever pitch. The avowed purpose of the raid had been to incite the Negroes of the area to rebel and instigate a slave insurrection that would sweep the South. The act induced hysteria in both North and South. The South cried that Northern abolitionists were plotting to plunge the slave states into a bloodbath more horrible than that which had drenched Haiti under Dessalines, that Brown's attack was a forerunner of a planned campaign of arson, murder, and devastation. In the North, abolitionists venerated Brown as a martyr, whose swift hanging by the state of Virginia called for vengeance.

In the Senate, Mason of Virginia demanded that the instigators

of Brown's treason be sought out and punished. Who had furnished Brown's band with arms, with money? Who, from some
secure control point, probably in Boston, had directed the mur-
derous affair? The debate on his resolution for an investigation
ran the gamut of appeals and accusations on both sides; yet amid
the frenzy, some senators retained their calm. One of these, surprisingly, was Ben Wade; but "Bluff Ben" now and then confounded the wiseacres by acting contrarily to expectation. When
the Southern spokesmen flung at their Northern colleagues the
charge of "criminal countenancing" of lawlessness, Wade asked
Mason reasonably:

"Do I stand here to accuse a gentleman who is a slaveholder
with *crime?* I have never done so. You may say that if we regard
slavery as wrong, and as a robbery of the rights of man, we
should accuse you of being criminal. Well, sir, the logic would
seem to be good enough, were it not modified by the fact that
with you it is deemed a necessity. I do not know what you can do
with [slavery]; I was almost about to say I do not care what you
do with it; I will say it is none of my business what you do with it,
and I undertake never to interfere with it.

"To be sure, believing it to be wrong—wrong to yourselves
and wrong to those whom you hold in this abject condition—I
wish you could see the light as I see it; but if you do not, it is a
matter of your own concern, and not mine."

This sweet reasonableness on the part of "Bluff Ben" caused
some of the opposition party to doubt their ears. But more was
to come, as he reassured the chivalry:

"I can very well have charity towards you, because with all my
opposition to your institution, I can hardly doubt that if we had
changed places, and my lot had been cast among you, under like
circumstances, my opinions on this subject might be different,
and I might be here, perhaps, as fierce a fire-eater as I am now
defending against fire. I can understand these things, and I accuse no man."

This mood was the more impressive because Wade, who ex-
temporized his speeches, never using notes, notoriously spoke the
thoughts that arose spontaneously in his mind. That he had not
abandoned his own position in regard to slavery and its extension,

merely because he comprehended the rationality of the Southerners' views, he made plain as he proceeded. The slaveholders had
repeatedly warned that the election of a Republican—that is, a
sectional—President in 1860 would be followed by the immediate
withdrawal of their states from the Union. To this threat Wade
opposed defiance, informing the other side of the chamber:

"These are very harsh doctrines to preach in our ears. What,
sir, are you going . . . to go into the election with us, with a settled
purpose and design, that if you win you will take all the honors
and emoluments and offices of the government into your own
clutches; but if we win, you will break up the establishment and
turn your back upon us? Is that the fair dealing to which we are
invited? . . .

"But if it should turn out so—and heaven only knows whether
it will or not—I give gentlemen now to understand, this Union
will not be easily disrupted. Gentlemen talk about it in a very
businesslike way, as though it were a magazine to be blown up
whenever you touch the fire to it . . . on a given day, at a moment's warning, at any time and in any event . . . Do you not
know, sir, that this government fabric has been eighty years in
building, and do you believe you can destroy it in a day?"

Andrew Johnson took different ground. Although he defended
the constitutional rights of the slave states, it was without raising
the bogey of secession. He could not conceive of an action so
heinous, so suicidal, as the willful breakup of the most beneficent
government man had devised.

"I am no disunionist," he said candidly. "Because we cannot get
our constitutional rights, I do not intend to be one of those who
violate the Constitution . . . I intend to place myself on the Constitution which I have sworn to support, and to stand there and
battle for all its guarantees."

The idol and mentor of the extreme South, John C. Calhoun,
was a dangerous guide, Johnson warned—"more of a politician
than a statesman"—a relentless logician who could reason infallibly from premise to conclusion, but who was "as often wrong
in his premises as any man." Calhoun, he said, turning towards
Jefferson Davis, upon whom Calhoun's mantle had fallen, was
"the founder of a sect, not of a great national party."

This was heresy to the fire-eaters, and Johnson not only stood alone among the Southern Democrats, but his apparent alignment with such hated Northern extremists as Wade and Seward further isolated him.

The excitement in the Senate, however, was mild compared with the turbulence that gripped the House of Representatives. Fist fights, brandishing of knives and pistols, and the hurling of bloodthirsty threats produced near riots again and again in a two-month struggle to agree on a Speaker. Southern congressmen stood firm for their "rights," while Northern leaders like Thaddeus Stevens met them with wit, stubbornness, and parliamentary ruse.

Stevens had returned to Congress as a Republican, armed with all the pithiness and puckish humor distilled from his embattled sixty-six years. The fire-eaters time and again were doused by his extinguishing raillery. When Lawrence M. Keitt, a hothead from South Carolina, shouted that his state demanded its rights, and "as God is my judge, I would shatter this republic from turret to foundation before I would take a tittle less," Stevens sardonically cheered him on. Quite right, he commended the excited Keitt, to rely on the methods that had intimidated Northern members for years—threatening to sunder the nation "from turret to foundation." The droll manner in which he imitated Keitt's bombast caused even Southerners to laugh.

Another time, having been taken to task for flouting a party directive, Stevens announced that the explanation might be found in the paper he had sent to the clerk to read, and which he asked the clerk to read.

"The paper is printed in German and the clerk cannot read it," that official protested.

"Then," said Stevens solemnly, "I postpone my remarks till the clerk can read it."

At a tense moment when bloodshed seemed imminent (during a scrimmage in which a Northern member swung a cuspidor over the head of Representative William Barksdale of Mississippi, who was advancing with Bowie knife in fist—and then simply could not bring the spittoon down when Barksdale's luxuriant wig fell off, revealing a shiny bald dome), Stevens diverted the danger by blaming President Buchanan for all the turmoil.

This brought an administration Democrat to his feet with a

demand to know how a black Republican could be so deep in the intentions of the White House. With sly modesty (alluding to the fact that Buchanan lived in Stevens' Congressional district in Pennsylvania), the old man replied demurely: "The gentleman must remember that the President is one of my constituents."

On the main issue, Stevens made his own stand as plain as did Ben Wade. As an acknowledged leader of the Republicans in the House (by force of character and not by seniority), he laid down the principles of his party as he understood them, in a "plain, temperate, and true" statement. He wished, he said, to avoid all ambiguity: "I would have no man vote under false pretenses."

"In my judgment, Republicanism is founded in love of universal liberty, and in hostility to slavery and oppression throughout the world," he said. It was true that had they the power, the Republicans would gladly abolish slavery and overthrow despotism everywhere; but they claimed no such right. Where slavery existed lawfully, they would not interfere. "It is a stern, an inflexible, a well-recognized principle of the Republican party that every law must be obeyed till it is either repealed or becomes so intolerable as to justify rebellion. But . . . there is no law to prevent our sympathizing with the oppressed of Italy, Turkey, or with the crushed souls of America; and . . . no earthly power shall prevent our . . . denouncing such wrongs whenever we deem proper. We claim no power to interfere with any institution in the states, yet where the law of no state operates . . . we do claim the power to regulate and the right to abolish slavery."

This point he drove home with unimpeachable clarity:

"I do not found this remark on exclusion by climate, or latitude, or soil. My hostility to slavery is of a higher character, I trust, than that. If it was not, there would be no kind of necessity for the existence of the Republican party at all. If I believed that slavery was right in itself, and it might be permitted in places where certain labor was or was not useful, I cannot see what principle the Republican party could stand upon. The whole ground is yielded, and this Republican party is a nuisance, and this agitation is a crime, in my judgment . . .

"Now, sir, these are the principles of the Republican party. Let those who approve them aid in their propagation. Let those who

condemn these principles oppose us. For ourselves, we have resolved to stand by them until they shall become triumphant; and
we cheerfully submit them to the judgment of our fellow countrymen, to the civilized nations of the earth, and to posterity."

Such high ground was not taken by all who adhered to the
Republicans as the rising party. Thaddeus Stevens hated slavery
with a virulence as great as that with which "Parson" Brownlow
hated Democrats and sin. But Stevens enjoyed being gay in his
detesting. With Owen Lovejoy, abolitionist of fanatical stridency
(with cause, for his brother, Elijah, had been murdered by a pro-
slavery mob in Illinois), Stevens agreed that "the principle of
slavery is the doctrine of devils"; but the old man took perverse
pleasure in playing merry hell with the devils, to see them cavort
before cutting them down with his lacerating wit.

In the midst of this upheaval, Andrew Johnson pressed his
Homestead Bill to a new test of strength. The Republican up-
surge in the 1858 elections, when every Northern state except
California returned Republican majorities, worked in favor of the
measure, and the bill was passed by the House, one hundred and
fifteen votes to ninety.

In the Senate, the opposition remained impregnable. Again
Johnson came under a concentrated fire of abuse from members
of his own party. The feeling of the slave state senators was
summed up by Arkansas's Robert W. Johnson, who denounced
the homestead plan as "so tinctured with abolition that no
Southern man could vote for it." On the other hand, Seward,
Wade, and Senator James R. Doolittle of Wisconsin strongly supported the measure, seeing in it a vital blow at slavery. Their very
candor in this respect sometimes disconcerted Tennessean Johnson, but he did not reject their help.

Senator Wigfall, the Texas terror, jeered at these Northerners
who wished to interfere with Southern institutions. Where among
the lot of them was one real fighting man, he demanded. "Who
among you is a soldier or a fighter? . . . An irrepressible conflict
indeed! The North would be a barren waste without the South!"
And Hammond of South Carolina complacently assured Seward:
"You dare not make war on cotton. No power on earth dares to
make war upon it. Cotton is king!"

But on May 10, 1860, when the Homestead Bill, in a slightly amended form, came to a vote, surprisingly it passed, forty-eight senators voting for it and only eight against. Among those voting "aye" were some who had assailed the measure most immoderately, and their sudden conversion stunned Johnson.

The bill went back to the House, which substituted its version, and on June 19, 1860, the Senate concurred and sent the measure to the White House. Now Johnson could "die content"; the fight that started in 1846 had been won.

Then on June 23 President Buchanan vetoed the bill. And in the Senate, enough Southerners, including Jefferson Davis, changed sides again to sustain the veto. Johnson's fourteen years of effort were thrown into the dust bin.

At this betrayal—by the President whom he had helped to elect—Johnson was beside himself with rage. He had been given to understand that Buchanan approved the bill. Had it been a plot by his opponents to appear to be won over, and then, by underhanded agreement, allow the White House to scuttle the bill by a veto?

"If there were forty Presidents, with forty assistants to write out vetoes, I should stand by this bill!" he cried wrathfully.

Two days after sustaining the veto, Congress adjourned until December, and Johnson headed back to Tennessee, sore at heart, burdened with another failure.

FOUR

"THE UNBELIEVABLE HAS HAPPENED"

ANDREW JOHNSON'S fight for a homestead law was bringing him wider recognition. As the only consistent spokesman the South had produced for the rank and file and the labor element, he was becoming an object of curiosity and commendation in many quarters. Workingmen's societies passed resolutions of approval, and a labor convention gave "Andy" (as he was everywhere known) complimentary votes for President of the United States. Already he had visited New York City at the invitation of Horace Greeley, and addressed a land reform rally there, earning praise in Greeley's *Tribune*.

But these gestures carried no political weight. More significant were the letters from strangers that were beginning to dot his mail. People were curious about him. From Camden, Kentucky, for example, a man who was weak on grammar but of an inquiring mind wrote seeking "some facts about your early history, etc. I have within the last year read so many conflicting accounts concerning your early life that I now feel a deep interest to learn the whole truth, and nothing else . . . Various papers that I have seen of late state that you were in early life a journeyman tailor, and was fully twenty-five years old before you were able to read or write. This item has struck me with great surprise, and the truth of it I should like very much . . ."

With this widening public interest came a growing realization, inside the Democratic party, of Johnson's broad-based strength. His power in Tennessee was undoubted, and in other states voters were being attracted to this champion of the common man's interests. Ballyrag and bully him as other Southerners might, they felt his force. Their anger against him was as much irritation over his being different from them, as disagreement with his principles, though some of these they feared and detested; but his unshakable independence jarred them. In his state, politicians who did not like him bowed to his strength, and already in 1856 the state Democratic convention had endorsed Andrew Johnson as Tennessee's "favorite son" choice for the Presidential nomination.

As the time for the 1860 nominations drew near, there was again sentiment for presenting Johnson's name to the national convention which was due to meet in Charleston, South Carolina, in April. Sounded out by friends, Johnson was pessimistic. The Democratic party was split wide open, he pointed out. Front-runner in the race for the nomination was Douglas, the hero of the Northwest and attractive to Northern Democrats generally. In the South, however, Douglas was execrated for having promulgated the doctrine of "squatter sovereignty," that is, letting the people living in a territory decide for themselves whether to permit or to exclude slavery. This heresy the South repudiated, and Douglas, long popular in the slave states, was now hated there.

During the long argument the attitude of the slave-state leaders had changed and hardened. Previously their contention had been that the national government had no authority to interfere for or against slavery in the territories; now the extreme clique, led by Jefferson Davis, insisted that the federal government was obliged by the Constitution actively to *protect* slavery everywhere, even in free states.

The North's reaction to this militancy had been the enactment by several legislatures of so-called personal liberty laws. These made obedience to the federal law known as the Fugitive Slave Act a crime punishable by imprisonment. In Vermont, a person convicted of helping to recover a runaway slave (a duty that the federal law *required* of every citizen) was liable to be sentenced to twenty years in prison and fined ten thousand dollars.

The situation was sheer anarchy, and Johnson was only one of many Southerners who resented the flouting of Constitutional authority by state whim.

With a Presidential election coming up, the burning question was which candidate the Democrats would put forward to meet the still unnamed Republican contender. The Northwest maintained that Douglas was the only Democrat who could carry the free states. Southern leaders said he would draw hardly a vote in their section, that only a definitely pro-slavery candidate could carry the South.

To Andrew Johnson the dilemma was severe. The clamor for secession being raised by the fire-eaters he still considered a bluff; when the decisive moment arrived, he insisted, the most violent would back down. But how the party might be drawn together he did not see. On January 12, 1860, he informed Blackston Mc-Dannel from Washington:

"All seems to be confusion and doubt. And unless there is some straiting [sic] up with the democratic party and the introduction of harmony, defeat will follow as certainly as the nomination is made. I fear the chances are against us under the most favorable circumstances, and with distraction and a bitter contest among our own [friends] it makes defeat absolutely certain."

To his son Robert, that same day, Johnson acknowledged the receipt of "four phials of Arnold's pills," of which he "at once took two . . . and this morning feel somewhat relieved and hope to be entirely so in a few days." Turning to the political outlook, he said that as regarded a "favorite son" endorsement of himself by the state Democratic convention, which would meet in five days, "I do not care one fig about it, and will take no steps to procure such an expression at this time."

"There are some persons, it is true," he went on, "to gratify their personal envy and jealousy would like to defeat anything that might be calculated to give me standing and consequence, either here in the Senate or before the Charleston convention. On this account, if none other, it would be a source of some personal pride and satisfaction. But I intend to let matters take their course."

For Robert himself, since he was going to attend the state convention, his father counseled moderation:

"I do not want you to place yourself in any position that would subject you to the charge of being wanting in delicacy in reference to your relation to me. I would be prudent and discreet in all that I did or said in reference to my position. You have already acquired some credit for discretion and good common sense in going over the state, and would now do nothing to lose it."

Warmly for his undemonstrative nature, Johnson signed this

letter, "Accept assurances of the best wishes of a devoted father's heart, *Andrew Johnson.*"

When the state convention met, the Douglas forces attempted to secure the endorsement, but realizing that they could not succeed, they joined the Johnson backers and the convention named the latter as their state's choice for the Presidential nomination.

Johnson's aversion to Douglas had not lessened, but it was personal. On political issues he was not entirely hostile, and as a politician he understood the wisdom of aligning one's self with strength. During the state convention he had advised Robert Johnson, who was on the ground, to remain noncommittal regarding Douglas:

"I would not say any hard things at present, for it might so turn out that he might be the nominee, and as against a B[lack] Republican we might be compelled to go for him, for at present he is the strong man in the free states and will go into the [national] convention the strong man of the party. What will be done there no one at this time can tell."

But he gave no indication of endorsing Douglas himself, and the outcome at Charleston he awaited without absorbing interest. The Homestead Bill, then still being debated, was at a crucial stage, and he wished to avoid taking sides in the struggle.

As a representative of a slave state, and expressing the undoubted sentiments of the great majority of his constituents, he had voted for the Jefferson Davis resolutions in February, which spelled out the duty of the national government to enforce the claims of slaveholders everywhere. These resolutions, embodying the most extreme Southern demands, were regarded in most quarters as of little except theoretical value, and as a strategical device on Davis' part to undercut the position of Douglas, the apostle of "squatter sovereignty." Johnson's support of them had been perfunctory.

But the intrusion of this issue upon what he deemed more important matters had exasperated him, and at one point he had exclaimed that if he had the power he would "punish Southern fire-eater and Northern abolitionist" in the same way:

"I would chain Massachusetts and South Carolina together, and I would transport them to some island in the Arctic Ocean, the colder the better, till they cool off and come to their senses."

On the day the state convention met in Nashville, Sam Milligan wrote from Greeneville, disclosing his own answer to the riddle.

Addressing his old friend as "Dear Governor," Milligan explained that he was not attending the convention: "the weather has been bad, the trains irregular, and my funds low." But having "a notion to write a letter on the slavery question," he reviewed the situation. The "Old Public Functionary" (President Buchanan's description of himself), said Milligan, "thinks the agitation will burn out, or be displaced by other questions less threatening in their character. I can see no just grounds for such a hope."

The "fanaticism of the North" was relentless. "Nearly or quite all the Protestant churches have separated and organized separate polities; and the affection of one section is thoroughly alienated from the other. What, under such circumstances, can we expect from delay? The answer must be—Nothing! Nothing! But what is the remedy? Will empty eulogies on the Union—the glorious Union—save the Union? That is nonsense and generally hypocritical twaddle. What then must be done?"

The only way out that he could see was to "restore the equilibrium of political power" between the North and the South as it "was incorporated by the fathers of the republic . . . I know the South has not the power to enforce any such demand. But it is equally obvious, unless the North grants it, the South can not maintain the institution of slavery ten years longer. Already the North has the power in a large majority of the states, the House of Representatives, the Electoral College, and soon will have it in all probability in the Senate. And by the admission of a few more free states, which must come in, she can alter and amend the Constitution at her pleasure."

But how was the balance of power to be regained? "It must be done either by an amendment of the Constitution, or by cutting up the Southern states so as at least to secure in the Senate that equilibrium . . . which the South originally had. Nothing else will do it . . .

"I am not for dissolution of the Union, because that would end in revolution, and in no wise secure the South against Northern aggression. But it matters but little what we are for, we have no power in the South to do anything, and can gain none by longer indulging the North . . ."

The letter voiced the despair of a good and thoughtful man, who could see no practical way out of the impasse. Johnson pondered it. To a certain extent he shared his friend's views; but his nature was not one to lie down before an obstacle and sigh, "not possible." And at the moment all his energies were directed towards winning the homestead fight.

The Tennessee delegation to the Charleston convention was instructed to vote for Johnson for President, and the Democratic press of the state pushed his claims vigorously. Making a virtue of what his enemies decried as a deficiency, the *Nashville Union* & *American* termed Johnson "a people's man . . . unafflicted with the crude learning of schools." He was "the favorite son of the toiling millions," a "lion of the tribe of Jackson." No "pampered son of wealth," but "a real homemade man, standing head and shoulders taller than those who have rubbed their backs against a college wall."

It was a class appeal, and crass even on that basis, but it found a response in Tennessee, where the "homemade man" was measured by homemade standards that would have filled historic ghosts with amazement. The small-town *Lebanon Democrat*, for example, concluded a eulogy on Johnson with the startling announcement:

"We believe that he comes nearer combining the executive ability of Jackson, the profound statesmanship of Calhoun, and the diplomatic sagacity of Talleyrand than any man that our country has produced."

Talleyrand would have been amused.

As convention time neared, the hopes of Johnson's friends grew bright, though his did not. On March 4, 1860, Milligan wrote again from Greeneville:

"At home, Sunday evening. This is the 4th of March. I wonder what the 4th of March 1861 will develop? I hope it will witness your inauguration as President of the United States!! But about that no one can possibly foretell. I think your prospects are brightening. Douglas is not making any headway with the masses in the South."

On March 19 an old associate wrote to Johnson from San Francisco, California: "I don't know why it is, but I have a sort of presentiment that you will be nominated at Charleston for V. P. I hope so."

Johnson had no confidence in these "presentiments." On the eve of the Charleston convention he watched the fever of expectancy in the Senate, and assured a Tennessee friend that "the whole Senate" seemed to be in hopes of getting a nomination, on one ticket or the other, especially Jefferson Davis, who he said was "burning up with ambition, [and] is nearer consumed by an internal heat than any man I ever saw . . . What Jeff will do if he is not nominated, *God* only knows."

Robert Johnson was eager to attend the Charleston gathering, and the senator offered to pay his son's and Sam Milligan's expenses, if they would go together. On April 8 he wrote to Robert his lack of enthusiasm, saying:

"As to my nomination at Charleston there is little or no hope, if I even desired it, which I do not unless it can be attained in a proper manner, which is a thing that cannot be done in my opinion. There will be every possible appliance brought to bear on the convention, foul or fair, that is believed will have any influence whatever."

Two days later, Robert, preparing to leave Greeneville, wrote in high good humor:

"I will leave at one o'clock for Carter county, as I have not been to Mary's for over two years. Milligan and myself will start to Charleston Wednesday or Thursday week. I have an abiding faith and presentiment that the convention will nominate you . . . *Mark it down—'The Stars have said it.'* "

The convention opened on April 23, and from the first it was evident that the delegates had not come together to unite, but to divide the party. Each faction was determined to rule, be the consequences what they might. The inevitable—the planned result, in fact—came to pass. Douglas could command a majority in the voting, but in ballot after ballot could not reach the two-thirds required under the rules. The delegates from the cotton states marched out of the hall and met in a rival convention a few doors away. Each faction called the other the "rump" convention, and the asperity was mutual. The Southerners demanded a can-

didate who would espouse their pro-slavery demands; the Northerners knew that such a candidate would cost them the vote of
the North. Douglas could not afford to compromise, and the
Southerners were determined to perish, rather than commit themselves to his policy.

For days the deadlock held, while Washington watched in suspense. News came fragmentarily through the faulty telegraphic
connections, and fresh rumors were brought by every gust of
breeze. Johnson, viewing the happenings from afar and dimly,
like others personally interested, foresaw accurately that Douglas
would continue to be the front-runner; and at one point he wrote
tentatively to Robert (marking the letter "Private"):

"Since my last letter to you I have become satisfied that Douglas must be nominated, and Tennessee should take that position
which will contribute most to her present and future success. If
she is defeated for the first, the query comes up, if it would not be
better to take that position which would give her the inside track
four years hence?" In other words, should not the Tennessee
delegation try to secure the Vice-Presidential nomination, since
the top place was not available? He continued:

"There would be no safer position to secure the first place four
years hence than second place on the ticket now. It would in fact
say to the country that the second man now must be the first
four years hence. This I say to you and no one else. You see the
force of the position." In the event of securing the first place
four years later, Tennessee, he pointed out, "at the same time
would be passing one of her citizens through all the gradations of
office from the lowest, which would be a very memorable fact to
record in history."

The unique prospect was tempting, and Johnson elaborated on
it. But he cautioned Robert again to "be prudent and say no
foolish things which can be used against you or me. There will be
much importance attached to anything you may say . . . If the
whole affair is managed right, if Tennessee is not first now, she
can be second, and first next time without a doubt."

But the affair was not "managed right." The Tennessee delegation cast its twelve votes for Andrew Johnson on thirty-six ballots,
and when the fight became hopeless, sought and obtained from

the senator authorization to scatter their votes elsewhere. Still the deadlock held, and finally the convention adjourned for six weeks, to meet again in Baltimore.

In June the "loyal" delegates gathered at Baltimore, and some Southerners walked out again. Johnson insisted that his name be withdrawn, to preserve harmony in the only national political group remaining, and in order that "the Union, with the blessings, guarantees, and protection of its Constitution, be perpetuated forever." Milligan hoped to the last, but his hopes were foredoomed. Douglas was nominated by the Northern Democrats. The Southern wing nominated John C. Breckinridge of Kentucky, Buchanan's Vice-President, and Senator Joe Lane, a fire-eater originally from Virginia but representing Oregon in the Senate. A splinter group, mostly of old-line Whigs, formed the Constitutional Union party and nominated John Bell of Tennessee its candidate. The Democratic party was split beyond redemption, and perceptive politicians conceded the election in advance to the Republicans.

That party, in May, had met in Chicago, and to the surprise of many, and the chagrin of the Eastern branch, had nominated Abraham Lincoln of Illinois for President, and Hannibal C. Hamlin of Maine (a man so swarthy that in the South he was believed to be part Negro) for Vice-President. William Seward, who before the convention had been regarded everywhere as the likely choice, was passed over; but after the momentary shock, he took his defeat in good spirit and entered into the campaign on behalf of his victorious rival loyally.

Behind the tangle of interests and issues, a few men saw what had been done at Charleston. One of these was Edmund Ruffin of Virginia, a dedicated secessionist. Ruffin (who would fire the first and last shots in the coming war, the first at Fort Sumter and the last into his own brain), with a few other Southern extremists, had known that the objective of the fire-eaters at Charleston had been to wreck the Democratic party, for only by doing so could they make secession possible. As he put it: "You can't smash the United States until you smash the Democratic party."

Political insight lay behind that statement, for in 1860 the Democrats were the only national party, organized in every section of the country and strong in all. The Republican party was sectional, as the South constantly emphasized. In the coming election, several Southern states, Tennessee among them, would not even have a Republican ticket in the field. The Whig party, except in pockets, was almost nonexistent. The Douglas wing of the Democrats was also sectional, with that candidate anathema to the South.

The overriding issue, therefore, to many earnest men appeared to be sectionalism versus nationalism, and Andrew Johnson, with his strong sense of the Union, cast his lot with the only branch of the Democrats pretending to appeal to every portion of the country—the branch backing Breckinridge and Lane. They avowed their devotion to the Union, and Johnson had not forgotten Breckinridge's moving apostrophe to the Constitution on the occasion of the Senate's leaving its historic old chamber. Still, it was with a heavy heart that he entered the campaign.

"The blood of secession at the Charleston convention is not on my head," he told friends. "The Democratic party has made a fearful mistake."

Charles Johnson, who had accompanied Robert to Charleston (and had worried the family by going on a spree), wrote upon returning home that Douglas' nomination was "the signal of defeat," and the senator could not disagree.

Returning to Tennessee upon the adjournment of Congress in June—smarting from Buchanan's last-minute annulment of the homestead victory—Johnson canvassed the state on behalf of the Breckinridge-Lane ticket. But his speeches were lackluster, and nationally he found himself in odd company.

In Massachusetts, beating the bushes on behalf of Breckinridge, was that mixture of political shoddy and the real wool of practical ability, Ben Butler. After bulldozing his way into the state legislature, Butler had voted fifty-seven times for Jefferson Davis at Charleston; then had helped to nominate Breckinridge, and was leading that candidate's hopeless cause in Tennessee— because the Kentuckian was the only Democrat who seemed to offer any national appeal.

Promoting the interests of Breckinridge among Ohio friends was that good Democrat, Edwin M. Stanton. After a sojourn in

California, where he had straightened out a snarl of land titles with callous efficiency, Stanton had returned to Washington and was high in the counsels of the Buchananites, or "Buchaneers," as their rivals called them. He, too, stuck with Breckinridge as the only national candidate.

Another potent speaker on the behalf of Breckinridge was perhaps the foremost plotter of Southern secession, the spokesman of the most extreme fire-eater section in the South, suave, eloquent, mild-speaking but ferocious William L. Yancey of Alabama. Because Bell had much strength in Tennessee, Yancey was sent into that state to campaign for Breckinridge, and at Knoxville, in East Tennessee, he encountered an antagonist whom his ferocity could not fluster.

A written question having been passed up to the speaker's stand, Yancey read it aloud. It was the question uppermost in everybody's mind: "What do you advise, if Lincoln is elected?"

Yancey called for the propounder of the question, and a man stepped forward. Who had prompted him to ask it, Yancey asked. The answer was Oliver P. Temple and the Reverend William G. Brownlow, two ardent campaigners for Bell. Yancey wondered whether these men were present, and Brownlow strode into sight, propelling Temple before him. Eyeing the two with deceptive mildness, Yancey inquired:

"Have you the honor of John Bell's acquaintance?"

They had.

"Is he a man to be trusted and followed?"

He was.

Whereupon the Alabamian drew from his pocket a letter written by Bell, in which the latter in effect urged secession in the case of Lincoln's election.

Temple was taken aback, but the "Parson" not a whit. Drawing himself up, he croaked in his rasp of a voice:

"If a passel of secessionists should march to Washington to dethrone Lincoln, after he has been lawfully elected, I am for seizing a bayonet and resisting such an attack, and they shall walk over my dead body on the way."

To which the Alabama secessionist replied:

"If my state secedes, I shall go with her, and if I meet this

gentleman," pointing to Brownlow, "marshaled with his bayonet
to oppose us, I will plunge my bayonet to the hilt through and
through his heart, and feel no compunction for the act, and thank
my God that my country has been freed from such a foe."

On that note the meeting ended. Such were the amenities of
electioneering in Tennessee in 1860.

Johnson regretted the episode, calling it "a bad day's work." At
the same time he admitted to a friend that "the slavery agitation
has become nauseating to my stomach." In fact, as the campaign
progressed and the intentions of the secessionists became clearer,
he became deeply troubled. The cry throughout the South was
that in the event of a Republican victory, secession would surely
follow. Hitherto he had refused to take such vaporings seriously;
but around him now old party associates were succumbing to the
disunion fever. Governor Isham Harris was all for defying the
North, and A. O. P. Nicholson, Johnson's Senate colleague,
thought that the border states should form their own confederacy, independent of both North and South.

To Johnson, disruption of the Union seemed worse than foolish,
it seemed sacrilegious. So worried did he become that halfway
through the campaign he retired to Greeneville to think things
over. There, in solitary wrestling with his doubts, and in long,
earnest consultations with Sam Milligan, Blackston McDannel,
and others of the "real people," he groped his way to a decision.
Characteristically, the course he embraced ran counter to the
sentiment of his party.

November 6 was election day. On November 5 Johnson spoke at
Gallatin, in company with Colonel J. J. Turner, a prominent
Democrat. After the meeting the colonel invited the senator to
tea, and the talk was about the election the next day, and what
would happen if Lincoln should win. Johnson was convinced that
he would win, and he also believed that the South would seize
upon the Republican victory as a pretext to secede. For his part,
he did not believe any state had a right to secede and break up
the Union. Rising from his chair, and speaking with utmost
solemnity, he then announced:

"When the crisis comes, I will be found standing by the
Union."

Furthermore, he said, he intended to return to Washington and there "come out distinctly in opposition to a dissolution of the Union . . . The attempt to secede will fail, as the South has no resources, cannot manufacture arms, and will probably be cut off from the whole world . . . Slavery will find no friends anywhere."

Turner was shocked by this avowal, and hastily telegraphed to Governor Harris a request to meet him and Johnson in Nashville the next day. Harris, in turn, wired to Senator Nicholson to join them; and the three men, in heated conference, tried to dissuade Johnson from his proposed course. But in Turner's words, "Nothing could be done with him."

Abraham Lincoln was elected President of the United States. In the eyes of the South he had been chosen President of only a fragment of the United States, not of the whole.

When the result became known, "Parson" Brownlow, who had battled valiantly on behalf of that virtuous Whig, John Bell, was thunderstruck.

"The unbelievable has happened!" he gasped. "The Democrats are the cause of it all!"

FIVE

THE SOUTH IS SPLIT

JOHNSON did not linger in Tennessee. Directly after the election he returned to Washington, where the momentous drama was about to unfold. The capital he found tense, with Southerners swaggering and claiming that the issue was all settled: the South must and would "go out."

On December 3 the second session of the Thirty-sixth Congress was called to order. The Senate chamber was somber. Across the dividing aisle men of the North and men of the South glowered. Anxiety showed on some faces, defiance on others. The geniality usually marking such reunions—the handclasps, the good-natured joshing—were missing; Democrats huddled with Democrats, and Republicans stayed by themselves. Johnson took his seat, grim and silent. The seats of South Carolina's two senators were vacant; they had not even returned for the session.

President Buchanan sent in his message, and so taut were tempers that the routine resolution authorizing the printing of the usual number of copies touched off an acrimonious debate. Senator Clingman of North Carolina, in presenting the motion, disclosed the object of the Southern attack: it was the Constitution of the United States. "If the federal Constitution were out of the way," Clingman cried, the Republican minority that had elected Lincoln could be resisted and checked. It was the "accursed Constitution" that stood in the way of the South's obtaining its rights.

Senator Hale of New Hampshire turned his attention to Buchanan's message, and said that if he understood it at all, it set forth three propositions, namely: "South Carolina has just cause for seceding from the Union . . . she has no right to secede . . . we have no right to prevent her from seceding." What sense did that rigmarole make? Here was the President, mocked Hale, rep-

154

resenting the United States "as a great and powerful country . . . but the power of the country consists in . . . a power to do nothing at all."

All Buchanan had to offer was a policy of drift and deplore, and that policy he pursued, with tears and breast-beating, bewailing that he was so bedeviled by demands for action from North and South, he "did not have time to say his prayers." Seeking a refuge, one intolerable day, he burst into the office of General Winfield Scott, flung himself despairingly into a chair, and exclaimed, "The office of President of the United States is not fit for a gentleman!"

During this word-spinning, South Carolina went forward with her intention to pull out of the Union, rather than submit to a sectional, Northern, "Black Republican" administration, and a convention had been convoked to take the overt step of separation. That convention began its work the day after Congress reassembled. While the senators wrangled, the Union was disintegrating around them, for it was generally understood—indeed their representatives boasted—that in South Carolina's wake the other cotton states would "go out."

"Iverson the Terrible" was predicting that by the next March 4, five states would be out of the Union. Only Texas was hanging fire, thanks to the determined efforts of Sam Houston, who had retired from the Senate to return home and fight against secession. But Iverson had no doubt of what would happen in Texas, too. "Texas's secession is now clogged by Governor Houston," he declared, "and if he does not yield, some Texas Brutus will rise to rid his country of the hoary-headed incubus."

Amid such talk Andrew Johnson prepared himself for his decisive step. He read and studied much, assembling authorities, delving into historical precedents, and ransacking the background of the events that had culminated in the Constitution. He did not seek breadth of vision; instead, he wished to focus every available ray of light on the one vital principle, the pivot upon which the whole crisis hinged. Despite the outcry about slavery, that, he suspected, was a secondary cause, a cover-up for deeper motives prompting the Southern oligarchy to their rash determination. That motive, he believed, was rage at seeing their long-held su-

premacy in the government slipping away. In the house of Union
they would either rule or perish. Personally, he was incensed at
the deceit which he felt had been practiced upon him by the
Breckinridge wing of the Democratic party in the campaign; he
resented having been, as he saw it, hoodwinked and used.

Still, though without hope, he would make a final, desperate
attempt to restore that equilibrium of political responsibility
about which Sam Milligan talked, in a way to insure for the South
the continuation of its constitutional influence.

On December 13, therefore, he proposed three amendments
to the Constitution. These provided for the election of the President, Vice-President, and senators by popular vote, with the stipulation that the President and Vice-President must come from
opposite sections, one from a slave state, the other from a free
state, alternately. Also, the federal judiciary would be appointed
for twelve-year terms, under a system of rotation, and they also
must be drawn equally from slave and free states. In addition, he
called for the naming of a committee that would draw a fixed line
east and west, north of which slavery should be permanently prohibited, and south of which slavery should be sanctioned permanently. He did not speak in support of these reforms at once,
but reserved his fire while the debate rambled on.

The word being heard constantly—the "bogey," the North
called it, the key to the situation, the Southerners insisted—was
"coercion." Iverson, with his usual forthrightness, put the issue in
a nutshell: did the federal government possess the right, under
the Constitution, to "enforce or coerce" a seceding state "back
into the Union"? He maintained that it had no such right, and all
his Southern colleagues backed him. Nor were his Southern
friends alone: throughout the North, large segments of public
opinion held that coercion would be as flagrant a violation of the
Constitution as secession. In taking this stand they echoed the
helpless, hopeless quandary of President Buchanan. Meetings
were called and resolutions were passed in Northern cities condemning the doctrine of coercion, while in the Senate fire-eater
after fire-eater flung defiance at the "coercionists."

True, a few senators who had been profligate of threats did
draw back from the precipice now that the moment of truth was

at hand. Toombs of Georgia, for example, proposed that the dis-affected states be allowed to secede and play at the independence game until their ardor cooled; then, at their instigation, they could be welcomed back into the national fold. Senator Seward publicly was for much the same policy of benevolent do-nothing-ism, though privately he was not sanguine. If left alone, he con-tended, the specter of dissolution would evaporate. "Why," he brushed aside impatient objections, "my sisters and brothers and I seceded from home when we were young, but we came back again."

Such remarks led Iverson to sneer that there would be no war, nor even danger of war, because, "like Senator Seward, the North has too much *common sense* for that."

When the truculent Wigfall declared that "the blood-bought Union cannot be held together with hemp," spectators in the Sen-ate gallery burst into applause. Such demonstrations of Southern sympathies were frequent when the fire-eaters ranted, and they were only mildly rebuked. Wigfall and Lane of Oregon repeat-edly taunted their opponents with hypocrisy, with helplessness, with cowardice. Jefferson Davis, more fastidious, found that the sweet smell of Union had evaporated; and who, he asked, "would keep a flower that has lost its beauty and fragrance and in their stead has formed a seedpod containing the deadliest poison?"

Outside of Congress opinion was no less divided and men's minds were no less confused. The manufacturing and commercial interests of the North trembled for their markets in the South, and urged conciliation. A panic was feared. Money was hard to borrow even at twelve percent interest, and in the *New York Tribune*, an organ even more powerful throughout the Northwest than in its own city, Horace Greeley was counseling, "Let the erring sisters go." Abolitionists were as hell-bent to part from the sinful South as the fire-eaters were to be quit of the hateful North. Abraham Lincoln's election meant next to nothing to Northern extremists. Because Lincoln refused to say that he would ignore the Fugitive Slave Law, William Lloyd Garrison posted him as "the Slave Hound of Illinois"; while the lofty Wendell Phillips contemptuously demanded, "Who is this huck-ster in politics?"

Stout Ben Wade showed signs of wearying of the perpetual debate. A year before, during the John Brown furor, he had told the Southerners flatly that there was no way by which they could get out of the Union: "We are found in one ship; we are married forever, for better or for worse. We may make our condition very uncomfortable by bickerings if we will, but nevertheless there can be no divorcement between us."

But on December 17, 1860, in an elaborate statement of his latest conclusions, he all but offered to let the South go it alone, and see which section would thrive more. He had not changed his opinion of slavery, he made clear, nor had his party, in view of their imminent assumption of power.

"The Republican party of the Northern states," he said, "holds the same opinion of this peculiar institution of yours that is held by all the civilized nations of the world. We do not differ from the public sentiment of England, of France, of Germany, of Italy, and every other civilized nation on God's earth." But there must be an end of indecision.

The galleries, the lobbies, and the anterooms were crowded while Wade spoke, and members of the House filled every inch of space on the Senate floor. It was the impression that he was appearing more or less on behalf of the incoming administration, and the excitement mounted as he went on to deliver what *The New York Times* called "a regular war speech."

"In my judgment this long, chronic controversy that has existed between us must be met, and met upon the principles of the Constitution and laws, and met now. As for South Carolina," he allowed his harsh sarcasm to digress, "I will say that she is a small state; and probably, if she were sunk by an earthquake today, we should hardly ever find it out, except by the unwonted harmony that might prevail in this chamber."

A wave of laughter swept the hall.

Wade went grimly on. Let the Southern states, with their slave labor, set up for themselves, he challenged, and the North would "invite the poor, the destitute, industrious white man from every clime under heaven to come here and make his fortune . . . We shall very soon see whether your principles or state of society, or ours, are the most prosperous and vigorous."

Lest the fire-eaters be unmindful of the fate they were inviting, he admitted the right of a people to throw off oppressors; but that was the right of revolution; and a revolution must succeed, or its leaders suffer. If they win, "then all is right and they are heroes; if they are defeated, they are rebels . . . the government from which they have rebelled treats them as traitors. The senator from Texas [Wigfall] says . . . 'we will force you to an ignominious treaty up in Faneuil Hall.' Well, sir you may . . . [but] if you are the weakest, you must go to the wall, and that is all there is about it." His foes would know where to find him, when the test came. They might make good their brag that they would capture the Capitol and use it for their government, but "although it be assailed by traitors on every side, by the grace of God, under its shadow I will die!"

Amid applause from the galleries at this counterdefiance, Senator Johnson got the floor. But an immediate adjournment blocked his speaking until the Senate resumed, the next day.

Again the galleries were crowded, because Johnson had not yet declared himself. He had supported Breckinridge, the candidate of the Southern Democrats, and he had worked actively to defeat Lincoln. Presumably he would side with his section, being the representative of a Southern state and himself a slaveholder. The pressures for secession were enormous; yet Johnson had shown maverick tendencies, and both sides of the Senate listened with more than perfunctory attention as he began.

Technically he arose to speak on behalf of his proposed amendments to the Constitution, but he soon disposed of that subject in order to come to grips with the chief issue: the right and necessity of secession. It was nearly two o'clock when he finally got going, and his opening sent a thrill through the chamber:

"We are now involved in a revolution," he said gravely. "I think it behooves every man . . . to indicate, in some manner, his opinions and sentiments in reference to the questions that agitate and distract the public mind. I shall be very frank . . . I am opposed to secession. I believe it is no remedy for the evils complained of . . . I believe that this battle should be fought not outside, but inside of the Union, and upon the battlements of the Constitution itself."

A stir swept the galleries. Even his political enemies conceded Johnson's influence in Tennessee. He now had the full attention of the Senate. Proceeding, making few gestures, speaking in his quiet voice but with convincing earnestness, he said:

"I believe it is the imperative duty of Congress to make some effort to save the country from impending dissolution; and he that is unwilling to make an effort to preserve the Constitution and the Union . . . I think is unworthy of public confidence and the respect . . . of the American people."

This was a gage of battle thrown at the feet of his fellow Southerners, and their faces showed their displeasure. But Johnson served notice, on both North and South alike, that neither he nor the people of Tennessee would be forced out of the Union by threats or violations of law. "We do not intend to go out. It is our Constitution; it is our Union; . . . and we do not intend to be driven from it."

He then launched into a closely reasoned, heavily documented attack upon the whole theory of secession, finding it utterly at variance with the expressed intentions of the framers of the Constitution.

"If the doctrine of secession is to be carried out upon the mere whim of a state, this government is at an end," he said; "it is not stronger than a rope of sand; its own weight will tumble it to pieces . . . If a state may secede at will and pleasure, why, I ask you, on the other hand, as Madison [asks], cannot a majority of the states combine and reject a state out of the Confederacy? . . . There is but one way to get out of [the Union] without the consent of the parties, and that is by revolution."

Northern states had trampled upon the Constitution by enacting their personal liberty laws, he went on. Congress possessed the right to enact laws and the Constitution gave the federal government power to enforce them. Therefore, "if anybody must go out of the Union, it must be those who violate its Constitution."

Senator Collamer of Vermont interposed a rambling defense of his state's legislation, but soon subsided, because the plain fact he could not deny. Other interruptions arose from the Southern side, breaking into Johnson's train of thought, drowning out his words by angry objections, until in disgust Wigfall exclaimed, "Let him alone!" But these tactics used up time, and soon after three o'clock the Senate adjourned, to resume with Johnson the next day.

That night there was talk all over Washington about the Tennessee senator's extraordinary stand. The secessionist element was furious, and damned Johnson as an "apostate" and "traitor to his section." This break in their ranks shocked them, and Johnson's "obstinacy," his "pigheadedness" in going against the expressed determination of the leaders of his party were denounced. Northern senators, too, were smarting under his castigation of their breaching of the Constitution to which they were constantly appealing. Johnson was calling a spade a spade, and neither side liked it.

The next day the galleries again were crowded, and the tension increased as Johnson took up where he had left off. He now cited the writings and actions of Washington, Jefferson, Madison, Monroe, Webster, Clay, and Marshall in opposition to secession, and drew parallels with the Whisky Insurrection of 1794 and the Nullification crisis of 1832. The legal difficulties alone would be insurmountable, he contended. For instance, suppose Florida and Louisiana did secede; what would their status be then? They had been bought and paid for by the United States of America; they had been territories before they became states; would they become territories again, if they renounced their statehood within the Union? Would Florida go back to the Seminoles? And would not Mississippi and Louisiana, as foreign powers, close the mouth of the Mississippi River to our commerce? Where would the Northwest be then?

Using the method he had used for years—driving home each point by repetition and overwhelming supporting evidence—he ridiculed the "absurdity of the pretension that there is a right to secede." Why, South Carolina was acting with the logic of the madman who, because mankind had been given dominion over the beasts of the forest, asserted his right to shear a wolf. Never mind the risks and dangers involved; he had a right and he was going to exercise it.

Again Southern senators heckled. At one point Wigfall protested that he was being misquoted, and insolently added, "I corrected this the other day."

"Well," retorted Johnson, reading from the record, "you just corrected it the way it was not, that is all."

The laugh was on the Texan, who shrugged sourly as he

slouched into his seat: "Well, if the senator from Tennessee wishes to pervert the facts, I have nothing to say."

"I will publish them as the records show them to be," replied Johnson doggedly, and Wigfall became silent.

Next Johnson assailed another "absurdity": while the Southern states were decrying the right of the federal government to "coerce" them, South Carolina already was threatening to force the border states into following her insane course—threatening Tennessee with economic sanctions, if nothing worse, unless she joined the secession. Johnson flung back this threat:

"I say to you of the South, we are not to be frightened or coerced. Oh, when one talks about coercing a state, how maddening and insulting to the state! But when you want to bring other states to your terms, how easy it is to point out a way to coerce them!"

"What is the issue?" he demanded. Not slavery, but "this and this only: we have not got our man. If we had got our man we should not be for breaking up the Union." Everybody knew that if Breckinridge and Lane had been elected there would be no talk of secession. But "how has Mr. Lincoln been elected, and how have Mr. Breckinridge and Mr. Douglas been defeated? By the vote of the American people, cast according to the Constitution and force of law, though it has been upon a sectional issue. It is not the first time in our history that the two candidates have been elected from the same section of the country. General Jackson and Mr. Calhoun were elected on the same ticket, and nobody considered that cause for dissolution. *They* were both from the South."

True, Lincoln had been elected by a minority vote, and his was a minority, sectional party; but they presented no insuperable danger. Johnson proposed to stay in the Senate and "put down Mr. Lincoln and drive back his advances upon Southern institutions, if he designs to make any. Have we not got the power? We have."

Ben Wade had taunted the South by asking "Why is she kicking? She controls the nation, including Congress and the courts. As for the President [Buchanan], why, you own him as much as you do the servant on your plantation!"

This control had not been forfeited, Johnson pointed out.

"Let South Carolina send her senators back . . . and on the fourth of March next we will have a majority of six in this body . . . Mr. Lincoln cannot make his cabinet . . . unless the Senate will permit him. He cannot send a foreign minister, or even a consul, abroad, if the Senate be unwilling. He cannot even appoint a [first-class] postmaster . . . I voted against him; I spoke against him; I spent my money to defeat him; but still I love my country; I love the Constitution; I intend to insist upon its guarantees. There, and there alone, I intend to plant myself."

Were the Democrats of the South so "cowardly" that they would let the enemy take over?

"I say no! Let us show ourselves men, and men of courage . . . We have it in our power—yes, this Congress today has it in its power to save the Union, even after South Carolina has gone out . . . Shall we shrink from our duty, and desert the government as a sinking ship, or shall we stand by it? . . . The time has come when men should speak out. Duties are mine; consequences are God's. I intend to do my duty . . .

"The Constitution declares and defines what is treason. Let us talk about things by their right name! . . . If anything be treason . . . is not levying war upon the United States treason? Is not attempt to take its property treason? . . . It is treason and nothing but treason; and if one state, upon its own volition, can go out of this Confederacy without regard to the effect it is to have upon the remaining parties to the compact, what is your government worth? . . . It is no government at all!"

Let those Southerners who conceived that only by secession could they preserve slavery beware, he went on, for "I believe that the continuance of slavery depends upon the preservation of this Union . . . I avow here, today, that if I were an abolitionist, and wanted to accomplish the overthrow and abolition of slavery in the Southern states, the first step that I would take would be to break the bonds of this Union and dissolve this government."

The people would soon settle the matter, in his view.

"I believe there is too much good sense, too much intelligence, too much patriotism, too much capability, too much virtue in the great mass of people to permit this government to be overthrown.

I have an abiding faith, I have an unshaken confidence, in man's capability to govern himself. I will not give up this government . . . No, I intend to stand by it, and I entreat every man throughout the nation who is a patriot . . . to rally around the altar of our common country . . . and swear by our God . . . that the Constitution shall be saved and the Union preserved . . .

"Sir, I intend to stand by the Constitution as it is, insisting upon a compliance with its guarantees. I intend to stand by it as the sheet anchor of the government; and I trust and hope, though it seems to be now in the very vortex of ruin . . . that it will be preserved, and will remain a beacon to guide, and an example to be imitated by all the nations of the earth. Yes, I intend to hold on to it as the chief ark of our safety, as the palladium of our civil and our religious liberty. I intend to cling to it as the shipwrecked mariner clings to the last plank, when the night and the tempest close around him. It is the last hope of human freedom."

His strength about exhausted, for he had not been well and the preparation of his speech had drained his vitality, he concluded quietly, with moving sincerity:

"In saying what I have said, Mr. President, I have done it in view of the duty that I felt I owed to my constituents, to my children, to myself. Without regard to consequences, I have taken my position; and when the tug comes . . . then it is that I will perish in the last breach; yes, in the language of the patriot Emmet, 'I will dispute every inch of ground; I will burn every blade of grass; and the last entrenchment of freedom shall be my grave.' Then let us stand by the Constitution; and, in saving the Union, save this, the greatest government on earth."

That evening, as he walked down Pennsylvania Avenue from the Capitol to his rooms in the Kirkwood House, he was met with scowls, insults, jeers, and curses; while to every corner of the nation the telegraph wires spread word of Andy Johnson's startling "declaration of independence" from secession.

SIX

TORCHES TO LIGHT THE WAY

THE sensation produced by Johnson's speech had been made clear even before the Senate adjourned on that December 19, 1860. Hardly had he resumed his seat when Senator Lane of Oregon opened a scathing attack on the address and the man who made it. He would not "march under the bloody standard of the senator from Tennessee to trample South Carolina underfoot," cried Lane. "Sir, you will not subjugate a gallant state struggling for her rights—rights denied to her in the Union!" As for Johnson's contention that the federal government could not be barred from executing simple laws, such as collecting the revenue, in any state, Lane ventured to predict that there would be hardly a man "so hardy as to try it in South Carolina," after that state "went out."

"Sir," he shouted, "you must meet your humble servant and walk over his dead body before you can do it!"

The galleries applauded and there were cries of "Good!" and as Lane went on the applause was repeated.

South Carolina's answer came swiftly: on the next day, December 20, she seceded, and the day before Christmas Governor Pickens proclaimed her a sovereign and independent nation. True, there were a few even in South Carolina who persisted in the belief that the step was madness. James Louis Petigru, revered citizen of Charleston and a wit as well as a staunch Unionist, shook his head dolefully.

"It won't work," he said. "South Carolina is too small for a nation and too large for a lunatic asylum."

But wit was powerless before the excited passions of the jubilating crowds.

In Washington the talk was for war as well as for peace, and not only Southerners were bellicose. Coarse-grained Zach Chandler thought a little bloodletting would be just the thing to tone up the country. At a White House dinner—sitting at Buchanan's table, in the midst of Southern sympathizers—Chandler muttered to the army officer beside him that "before the rebels get to Washington they will have to kill Western men enough to cover up the dome of the Capitol with their dead bodies." Everywhere defiance and "dead bodies" was the refrain.

There were areas in the South where secession sentiment was at best lukewarm. But the fire-eaters had their remedy for that: "throw a little blood in their faces"; that would arouse the fighting spirit.

The advantage, of course, lay on the side of those who were calling for *positive* action—the secessionists and their counterparts in the North, the warmongers. Advocates of peace and moderation fumbled with *negative* appeals: "don't go out"; "wait and see"; "think twice"; "find some compromise." But the time for compromises had passed, and leaders on both sides prevented fresh proposals from even coming to a vote in Congress. The mass of Unionists were confused, disheartened, frightened; and when Johnson spoke out, positively and forcefully, in plain language, reducing the case for the preservation of the Union to simple emotional terms and taking his stand unalterably on that issue, his words met an instant, grateful response in the North, and to some extent in the South.

His mailbag suddenly ballooned. Up to then it had contained the ordinary correspondence of a congressman; now it bulged with praises of his bold action. The letters came from every state in the North, and from several in the South.

"God bless you!" was the predominant sentiment, coupled with congratulations on "your patriotic and sensible remarks," "your true doctrine," "your proud, patriotic, and statesmanlike position," "your noble, manly, and eloquent appeal on behalf of our Union." The wavering Union ranks stiffened.

"Though the office seekers and politicians will decry you, the people will rally around you and sustain you as in other days," wrote a Tennessee admirer.

Another, in Richmond, Virginia, urged Johnson to persist, "you are on the right track."

"Your speech is in the mouths and minds of *every* one," came an endorsement from Philadelphia.

"You have won golden opinions in the Hyperborean regions," wrote a Wisconsin Democrat.

"Keep on talking and send your speeches to the people," advised "your fellow citizen" from Alabama.

Letters of approval came from New Orleans, from Memphis, and from Corinth, Mississippi, where one enthusiast wrote that Johnson was being denounced there "for saying less than Andrew Jackson was immortalized for saying."

In New York the Working Men's Association voted a resolution of thanks. So did the Minnesota legislature. A Baltimore laborer expressed his belief that Johnson had simply told the truth, and "the poor workingman will no doubt be called on to fight the battles of the rich."

The *New York Herald* said the speech was "the talk of every circle in Washington and was uniformly condemned by Southern men." *The New York Times* spoke of Johnson's "great Union speech," and the *Cincinnati Times* praised it with thanksgiving that at last one Southern loyalist had been found.

Requests for copies of the speech poured in—a dozen here, five hundred there, a thousand yonder. The *Chattanooga Gazette* wired that it had received orders for a thousand copies, and before the furor settled Southern spokesmen would be asserting that the speech had been circulated "in hundreds of thousands of copies" to "inflame Northern sentiment."

The expense of providing copies Johnson bore in large part himself. One receipted bill rendered by a job printer showed him paying two hundred and twenty-five dollars for fifteen thousand copies; although with characteristic shrewdness, he had secured a fifteen-dollar rebate "after consulation with the *Globe* office." Friendly government clerks volunteered help in addressing labels and compiling lists of voters who might benefit by a copy.

Why did the speech produce such a reaction? Northern senators had said much the same, and even more belligerently. But the Southern fire-eaters knew that so conspicuous a break in their solid front was a setback. Not only had Johnson announced his intention to stand by the Union, he had torn to shreds the specious arguments they had been advancing to justify their action. Had a Northerner given the speech, the effect would have been negligible. But Johnson's position gave weight to his language, and his fearlessness made him a redoubtable opponent. How the Southern hotheads gauged the impact of the December 19 speech was fully avowed only years later, after the dust had settled.

Senator Clingman believed that speech "caused the Civil War."

Alexander H. Stephens, who was to become Vice-President of the Confederate States of America, rated the December 19 speech as "one of the most notable, as it certainly was one of the most effective, ever delivered by any man on any occasion. I know of no instance in history when one speech effected such results, immediate and remote, as this one did.

"Characterized by extraordinary fervor and eloquence," Stephens went on in his considered estimate, "it did more to strengthen and arouse the . . . people at the North than everything else combined, its power and influence springing from the very source from which it emanated. The author stood solitary and alone—isolated from every public man throughout the Southern states, and from nearly every public man throughout the Northern states attached to the same political party to which he belonged, upon the questions involved."

Johnson was not alone among Tennesseans declaring for the Union. In 1859, T. A. R. Nelson, East Tennessee's most popular Whig orator, had entered Congress, and within two days had taken on Roger Pryor, fiery Virginia secessionist, with a ringing declaration in favor of the Union. Horace Maynard, the sinister-looking former schoolmaster of Knoxville, had entered Congress as a Whig and a Unionist; his party had been consistently against any form of secession or disunion. The Whigs were still strong in Tennessee; the party had not disintegrated in that state to the extent it had elsewhere; and rejection of disunion on the part of Nelson and Maynard was expected.

But the Democrats of Tennessee were the ultra states'-rights, secessionist party, and this gave significance to Johnson's defiance of the party's stand. The reaction in Tennessee generally was one of wrath and hatred. He was hanged and burned in effigy in

Memphis, in Nashville, and elsewhere; indignation meetings passed resolutions branding him a "traitor"; the state legislature voted censure of his speech; leaders of his party cast him out; he was reviled on the streets of his own town, Greeneville, and former friends spat at mention of his name.

But there were loyal friends, too. In the first flurry of excitement, before the text of the speech had become available, Sam Milligan had hastened to write his approval of the tenor of the address, so far as he could judge it by the telegraphed summaries.

"If secession is revolution, there must be an *inherent* right in the government to suppress it," his judicial mind concluded. And if a state breaks faith with the government, violates its laws, cuts off its revenues, and imperils the peace and security of all the other states, "it is not the duty of the President to exercise any discretion about it; he is *bound* to vindicate the law, protect the revenue, and secure the rights of the people under the Constitution. The law is one thing, and the consequences another. The President should attend to the one, and God will look after the other."

(The recurrence of this phrase was evidence of the close working of the two friends' minds; under even more dramatic circumstances, the phrase would recur again.)

Milligan was not hopeful that bloodshed could be avoided. No revolution had ever succeeded without spilling blood, he pointed out, "and I believe we will not be an exception to the general rule."

Blackston McDannel wrote enthusiastically from Knoxville asking for copies.

"You are being denounced here by a little clique calling themselves Democrats," he reported. "They have been trying for several days to burn you in effigy, but as yet have not been able to raise a crowd. If they do, I prophecy it will be a sore job for them."

Then came a disclosure of startling significance, as Blackston went on:

"Your worst political enemies, Brownlow for instance, now speak of you in the highest terms. Brownlow said to me yesterday, 'Johnson is right. He is a true Democrat, and occupies the same position now that he did in 1832, and I will defend him to the last.' There is many others here of the same kind, but I mention this one because I know he has been your most bitter enemy. The people of Tenn. are with you and no mistake . . . I am still a Johnson Democrat, and for the Union all the time. Be sure to send your speech."

Best of all, Johnson had the entire support of his family. On New Year's Day, Robert wrote that "the *Nashville Banner* endorses [your speech] out and out . . . Milligan approves it and is very bitter on those that denounce it . . . I suppose you have heard of the burning of your effigy, etc. As John Tyler once said, they merely give light for a man to walk by . . . We are all well—Charles all straight."

Charles sent his congratulations. He had been hunting in Carter county, he said, and had "killed seven bear—thirty killed in those mountains this winter." He hadn't met a single man who did not approve Johnson's stand.

And all the way from Texas, brother Bill wrote "as a brother to a brother," saying that he was against secession, "but am going to vote for it and let the slaveowners fight it out."

The climax was the arrival in Washington of Eliza Johnson. Although a semi-invalid, she knew the pressures to which Andrew would be subjected, and she insisted in taking her place at his side. In spite of bitter weather (Robert, writing from home during a snowfall, begged to "excuse this writing, for my ink freezes almost as fast as I can write"), she made the journey, and she would remain at the capital throughout that hectic spring.

Even yet, it was not too late for Johnson to pull back and swing with the trend of Southern feeling. But once embarked upon a course, it was not in his nature to retreat.

SEVEN

"A BLOW STRUCK AT TREASON"

EVENTS did not wait upon wishes, but came crashing around the wrangling senators and representatives of Congress. Having declared herself independent, South Carolina demanded the surrender of all federal property within her borders, seized post offices and custom houses, and moved to take possession of the coastal forts, notably Fort Sumter in Charleston harbor. To enforce the demand, batteries of heavy guns were emplaced, bearing on the fort; and when, on December 26, by stealth and in darkness, Major Robert Anderson succeeded in transferring his little garrison from a defenseless sandspit to Sumter, on an island, the cry went up that he had committed an act of aggression. The Carolinians were undecided whether to blast Anderson out of his fortress or to starve him out; they took the latter course, while Buchanan's cabinet wrestled with the question of surrendering without firing a shot or putting up a foredoomed resistance.

The cabinet was at sixes and sevens, until the President could hardly tell the time. Four members resigned—Secretary of State Cass, because Buchanan was subservient to the South, Secretary of the Treasury Howell Cobb, and, a month later, his replacement, Philip Thomas, because the President was too submissive to Northern demands, and Secretary of War Floyd, in a flurry of financial scandals and under suspicion of secretly arming the secessionists. When Secretary of the Interior Jacob Thompson of Mississippi also walked out, the Southerners had deserted the President in a body. In the attendant cabinet shuffle, Edwin Stanton, that pushing lawyer, became Attorney General, and dug in to push some more.

Buchanan would later claim that Stanton flattered him ad nauseam, then betrayed him; be that as it may (and it may be), this was for the future. Now, while counseling Buchanan, Stanton shared confidences with Senator Seward and other Republican leaders, simultaneously and sub rosa expressing contempt for President-elect Lincoln. Did he not know the fellow—an uncouth country lawyer who had been Stanton's legal drudge as associate counsel in a celebrated law suit four years before? Then Stanton had snubbed, sidetracked, and humiliated the Springfield lout, and he considered the man vacuous if not a cretin now. Stanton was sly and capable, a lawyer who respected and excelled in his craft, an intractable and vigorous administrator, bullying towards inferiors, obsequious towards superiors who might help or hinder him; and at all times, under all conditions, out to enhance Stanton. Yet he was not a villain. A man who is constructed with an overpowering urge to exhibit himself in contradictory guises, concurrently or consecutively, is not necessarily for that reason inherently evil. Such was the case with Stanton. He was as God made him; and God knows why.

January of '61 produced a series of blows to Union hopes.

On January 5, the *Star of the West*, an unarmed transport carrying provisions to the men in Fort Sumter, attempted to enter Charleston harbor and was driven off by a cannonade. The defenders of the fort watched their last hope of succor sail away and dug in for a forlorn finish.

On January 9 Mississippi seceded; on January 10, Florida; Alabama on January 11; and on January 19, Georgia.

On January 21, Jefferson Davis, Clement C. Clay, Jr., and other senators from the seceded states took stately farewell of the United States. The scene was emotional; Davis' valedictory brought tears to the eyes of susceptible senators, while in the gallery ladies sobbed into scented handkerchiefs. They were witnessing, they felt, the solemn obsequies of a nation. In his remarks Davis managed to couple Senator Johnson with the abominated Wade as partners in nefariousness, and again, without naming the Tennessean, lumped him with other "miserable recreants nailed to the cross."

Five days later, on January 26, Louisiana joined the exiting parade.

On February 1, some fifty women and children of all ages, dependents of enlisted men in Sumter, were ferried out of the fort under a flag of truce. Spunky for the most part, they came away reluctantly and full of fight. Charleston did not tender them a welcome, and on February 6 thirty-six of these refugees reached New York aboard the steamer *Marion*. Their reports were ominous for peace.

Two days earlier, at Montgomery, Alabama, the Confederate States of America had been organized, and Jefferson Davis—already created a major general in command of Mississippi's troops—was elected provisional President, and the wizened Alexander H. Stephens of Georgia, provisional Vice-President.

Meanwhile, in Tennessee, sensational happenings portended. Governor Isham Harris, turned ultra secessionist, on January 7 had called the legislature into secret session "to consider the present condition of the country." This was a blind to mask his real purpose—to take Tennessee out of the Union. Harris was in communication with Southern fire-eaters, and agitators for secession swarmed in Nashville. The legislature ordered a state-wide election of delegates to a convention that would cut the state's ties with the United States. The election date was February 9.

Governor Harris, writing to a friend in Paris, foresaw "a most spirited & bitter canvass," with the outcome doubtful. The loss of Johnson's support he especially regretted, but most Democrats, he said, were for separation despite Johnson's apostasy.

Proponents of both sides swung into action. Unionist sympathizers in East Tennessee, throwing caution to the winds, invaded the western sections of the state, denouncing the convention as an invitation to disaster.

From Washington Johnson watched anxiously. The plebiscite would mark the first time that the question of seceding had been submitted to the people of any state. All previous action had been taken through conventions, whose decisions had not been referred to the voters for ratification or rejection. To Johnson this was iniquitous. He retained religious confidence in the ability of the common people, in the long run, to reach just conclusions; they might be misled for a while, but that they would always come right in the end he never doubted, and he prepared to lend his voice to the Union cause in the referendum, at the right moment.

The atmosphere in Washington was heavy with foreboding. Captain Erasmus Darwin Keyes, confidential secretary to General Scott, lived through those tempestuous weeks as an "insider"; and he would always maintain that to a person who had not experienced the shocks of that critical interval it was impossible to convey any adequate idea of their intensity. Keyes, a Northerner, kept a journal, and on December 23, 1860, he recorded that he had just returned from a dinner given by the Speaker of the House, William Pennington, of Pennsylvania. The other guests had been Senators Trumbull of Illinois, Chandler of Michigan, Crittenden of Kentucky, and Dixon of Connecticut, and Representatives Henry Winter Davis of Maryland and Charles Francis Adams of Massachusetts, all leading Unionists. Keyes remarked that "all gave little hope" when the state of the Union was discussed. "Mr. Dixon appeared uneasy and uncertain. Mr. Adams was calm but said little . . . Senator Chandler, as usual, was defiant, and declared that the slightest violence in Washington done to any Republican would bring down from the Northwest 500,000 armed men, and they were fond of fighting."

On Christmas Day, at another dinner, Keyes found himself the only Northerner at the table, and "the vein of conversation was Southern entirely . . . I was careful not to express any very decided Northern sentiments."

On January 9 (the day Mississippi seceded), Keyes was startled by General Scott's explosion of indignation, upon returning from dinner at the home of banker William W. Corcoran, a Southern sympathizer. Exclaimed Scott, Toombs and Cobb of Georgia had "given way to such violent outbursts of passion" as he had never before witnessed. "They cursed the Union as it is, as it has been, and they cursed its founders. They abused the President and other high functionaries. They abused Major Anderson, and behaved in their discourse like madmen."

Five days after this, Keyes put down his own disgusted comment on Seward's Senate speech on the crisis: that he "stated in effect that the Union was not worth preserving at the expense of civil war."

Disaffection in the army was rampant. There was constant anxiety regarding the safety of Washington. Mysterious "volunteers" were drilling, often at night and under the instruction of regular army officers. Nearly all the important commands were held by Southern men, or officers with Southern affiliations. A letter to Scott from Nashville reflected the nervousness felt outside the city; the writer warned that "the rebels will prevent the inauguration of Mr. Lincoln." In the seceded states federal arsenals were being surrendered without a struggle. "Rumors of peril to the capital thicken," Keyes noted.

In this superheated atmosphere, on February 5, 1861, Johnson spoke again in the Senate, in reply to the steady fire of invective that had been directed at him ever since his December speech. And he stated why he had been chosen as a special target of Southern animosity.

"I have been denounced," he said, "because I happened to be the first man south of Mason and Dixon's line who entered a protest or made an argument [here] against this political heresy [secession] . . . the prolific mother of political sin . . . productive of anarchy . . .

"Mr. President, I never do things by halves. I am against this doctrine entirely. I commenced making war upon it—a war for the Constitution and the Union—and I intend to sink or swim upon it."

The galleries broke into applause, and were sternly rebuked by the chair.

"Now, sir," continued Johnson, "what is treason? The Constitution of the United States defines it, and narrows it down to a very small compass. The Constitution declares that treason against the United States shall consist only in levying war against them, or in adhering to their enemies, giving them aid and comfort." Well, five states had seceded, and were seizing the property of the United States, raising armies to levy war upon the United States. "Does it require a man to take the lantern of Diogenes and make a diligent search to find those who are levying war upon the United States? . . . If there are any such in the United States they ought to be punished according to the law and the Constitution. For myself, I care not whether treason be committed North or South; he that is guilty of treason is entitled to a traitor's fate!"

The galleries applauded again, more vigorously, and again

were warned. Texan Wigfall, a waspish heckler, broke in to correct a date, as he said, sneering, "If you will read history and inform yourself, you will not fall into so many errors." With a side explanation he told the Senate he was offering the correction "out of kindness to the senator."

"I do not accept the correction nor have I very much respect for the spirit that prompted it," retorted Johnson; and he read the date as printed in the document he had been accused of misquoting.

Then Johnson directed his wrath towards Lane. The previous summer, he reminded that senator, he had campaigned for him, going up and down Tennessee refuting the charge that Lane and Breckinridge were disloyal. "You deceived me then; that was your fault. The next time it will be mine!"

He pitched into Lane's jumping from side to side of the main issue, and read from the record that on May 25, Lane had voted against a resolution declaring that slavery required protection in the territories. "Yes, Lane of Oregon," he read, "voted . . . that slavery did *not* need protection in the territories. Now he will get up and tell the American people and the Senate that he is for a state seceding, and for breaking up the government, because they cannot get what he swore they did not need."

The laughter was at Lane's expense as Johnson exclaimed, "That's what I call putting the nail through!"

Lane tried vainly to interrupt, until Senator Hemphill of Texas came to his rescue and moved to adjourn. But Johnson still held the floor, and the next day, with Vice-President Breckinridge in the chair, he went after Lane again.

"Human nature deplores the folly of disunion," he insisted, and offered his remedy again:

"If the question could be taken away from the politicians; if it could be taken away from the Congress of the United States, and referred to the great mass of the intelligent voting population of the United States, they would settle it without the slightest difficulty . . . and bid defiance to the secessionists and disunionists."

The Vice-President was forced to warn the galleries repeatedly to cease applauding as Johnson took up the parting sneer of Jefferson Davis, who had made the Tennessean an *ally* of Senator Wade, a "Black Republican." Well, "if Senator Wade, or senator anybody else, is willing to come up to this great work . . . and perpetuate this Union, I am his ally and he is mine."

All this outcry over "coercion" of a state—this dread of "the power of this federal government to secure obedience to its laws," was idiotic. "The public property can be taken, your flag fired upon, your ships driven out of port, your gallant officer, with a few men, penned up in a little fort to subsist as best they may . . . and still you are alarmed at 'coercion'!"

The ingratitude of Davis revolted him. "When I consider his early associations, when I remember that he was nurtured by this government, that he fought for this government . . . I cannot understand how he can be willing to hail another banner . . . It seems to me that if I could not unsheath my sword in vindication of the flag of my country . . . I would return the sword to its scabbard. I would never sheathe it in the bosom of my mother! Never! Never!"

As for the threats being made against the border states by truculent Carolinians:

"Will Tennessee consent to be lashed to the car of South Carolina? . . . I cannot believe it; I will never believe it. And if an ordinance of secession should be passed by that state . . . and an attempt should be made to force the people out of the Union . . . I tell the American people that there are many in Tennessee whose dead bodies will have to be trampled over before it can be consummated."

Again the galleries broke into applause, and were rebuked. Carried away by his emotions, Johnson went on, defying his opponents:

"I care not for the number that have attacked me! . . . I care not how many may come hereafter! Come one, come all! . . . I have been told . . . that the Union is gone . . . If this be so . . . and that glorious flag, the emblem of the Union, which was borne by Washington through a seven years' struggle, shall be struck from the Capitol and trailed in the dust—when this Union is interred, I want no more honorable winding sheet than that brave old flag, and no more glorious grave than to be interred in the tomb of the Union! . . . God preserve my country from the desolation that is threatening her, from treason and traitors!"

A storm of applause swept the galleries as Johnson sat down.

Beyond the limits of the Capitol, this "scathing anti-secession speech," as *The New York Times* called it, created a sensation. "The secessionists winced visibly under his lash, and manifested almost uncontrollable rage," reported the *Times*. And the next day Wigfall gave vent to their wrath in an attack that for scurrility was without precedent in the Senate. The day before Texas had at last seceded, though Wigfall would protract his stay in Washington for nearly two months, in order to act as on-the-ground observer for the Montgomery government.

Repeating Johnson's statement that Louisiana, Florida, and Texas had been "bought and paid for," the Texan stormed, "Shame, where is thy blush!" What impudence to try to palm off "this fraud on the people I represent!" Why, even the infamous Helper in his infamous book had never uttered anything "so slanderous against the South as the sentiments uttered by a renegade Southerner on this floor." He complained that nobody had answered his argument. What argument? Wigfall had heard none. And after thinking the matter over for six weeks, the senator from Tennessee cried out that he was misrepresented, and said he had been the object of attack!

"Oh," groaned Wigfall, "how it maddens me to see a popinjay speak of guns and drums and wounds! After six weeks he attacks the noble Davis, no longer here to reply!" Like the jackal, "he preys on the carcass his royal master left. If he had dared to vilify the senator from Mississippi to his face, the reply would have been, 'Lord Angus, thou hast lied!'"

Cries of "Shame!" "Shame" came from the galleries, and amid general disorder one gallery was cleared, while Wigfall ranted on.

Johnson he called "a mousing owl, striking at a proud eagle . . . the vilest of Republicans, the reddest of reds, a sans-culotte! For four years past he has been trying to please the North with his homestead and other bills. When war comes, he'll not be in the breach, he'll not take up arms! When Tennessee adopts the ordinance of secession, he will have sworn to support any constitution for the last time in his natural life!"

The Senate adjourned that day in a hush, and the *New York Herald* reported that a duel was certain to follow such insults.

Johnson had not uttered a word during the tirade. He had no need to reply, for on the day after Wigfall spoke, Tennessee answered for him. The people there went to the polls and rejected the convention call by a rousing majority. That was an answer that the politicians of the South could comprehend. For the time being, Tennessee was saved for the Union, and Andrew Johnson's name was on every lip as that of the man who, more than any other person, had turned back the tide.

EIGHT

"BUT FOR THIS SPEECH"

REQUESTS for copies of Johnson's speeches, in batches of hundreds at a time, kept snowballing. The effect his words were producing was the more significant because Andrew Johnson's speeches, when read in print, conveyed only a glimmer of the fire they radiated when heard. This was remarked by numerous commentators, one of whom said the difference was like that between reading a musical score and hearing it played by a fine musician. The "magnetic voice, the action, the earnestness, the fire, the subtle contagion of sympathy and enthusiasm" flowing from speaker to listener—all these were lacking when the words were read in print. Yet even in that form, Johnson's stand for the Union was being echoed in all quarters. The response in Washington became manifest in a demonstration that occurred in the Senate chamber on March 2. The scene was unique in the annals of Congress.

It was the last day of the Thirty-sixth Congress; on Monday, March 4, Abraham Lincoln was to be sworn in as President and a new Congress would take over. Washington was beset by alarms. One rumor had it that Ben McCulloch, Indian fighter of the Southwest, was poised with five hundred of his Texas raiders, prepared to swoop down on the inaugural parade and seize the new President before he could get from the Capitol to the White House.

In the Senate, the seats of six seceded states stood empty, while senators from the border states—Virginia, North Carolina, Maryland, Kentucky, Missouri, Arkansas—expected to depart soon. The usual last-minute logjam of bills was waiting to be acted upon when Lane of Oregon arose to make a fresh attack upon Johnson. Lane was on his way out of public life; this was his last Senate speech, and his vindictive wrath boiled over.

"The senator from Tennessee," he spat out spitefully, "is so entirely devoted to the interests of the 'dear people'! . . . I have had the *honor* of knowing the *honorable* senator for ten years, and I have never known him to try to do anything but to give away the public lands, and he has not even succeeded in doing that! . . ."

Lane read from manuscript; the speech was not impromptu.

"The senator is surprised that I, as a Northern senator, should have replied to him at all. It was because I was astonished that he, as a Southern senator, should make the speech he did. He is surprised that I, as a Democrat, should reply to him. It was because I was mortified that he, as a Democrat, should make the speech he did . . . Sir, I thought no time was to be lost in giving him and the country notice that we . . . would not be the tools, the hangmen, or the executioners of brethren for the gratification of fanatics; that we would not be their allies, or his allies, in the incendiary and unnatural scheme of desolating the South, our fellow men and fellow Democrats."

Referring to Johnson's denunciation of Jefferson Davis and the other seceding senators, Lane cried that anybody who called such patriots traitors was a coward. "The senator . . . looked at me, pointed in my direction, and made remarks . . . that no gentleman would ever make. He said he had struck treason a blow. The mighty senator from Tennessee struck treason a blow!" Lane's voice dripped scorn. "Sir, I cannot express my contempt for [such] a man! . . . Does the senator dare charge treason upon me?"

Unwittingly Lane then paid a compliment to the effectiveness of Johnson's December speech:

"It was an unnatural speech; it was a bad speech; and it did more to strengthen the Black Republican party than all the speeches of all the senators on the other side of the chamber . . . But for that speech, we should have had a settlement of the difficulty before this. It went to the country, and made the people believe that the 'giant' senator from Tennessee was for coercion. It was complimented and eulogized by the Republican press, and in pamphlet form circulated by the hundreds of thousands throughout the North, and the distinguished senator from New

York [Seward] speaks of him as the 'noble' senator from Tennessee! Noble for what! . . . God save the country from such speeches! . . .

"There stood the senator from Tennessee . . . with an air of triumphant ignorance and exulting stupidity, boiling with patriotic rage, rising up and declaring that 'this treason must be punished; the laws must be enforced.'" George III and Lord North had said the same thing, but the one was a lunatic and the other of low mentality. "What a pageant—what a ridiculous pageant—has the senator made by stuffing himself (and it only took six weeks!) with . . . scraps of law of learned length . . . to prove nothing, and to fit nothing! . . . And with this remark I part with him, who, in imitation of Esau, seeks to sell his birthright."

Johnson at once took the floor to reply to this vituperation, which had found little favor even among Lane's Southern friends. This was the sort of personal attack that Johnson had met innumerable times on the stump in Tennessee, and his reply took on the tone of one of his stump speeches. This time the galleries were packed with Union supporters, eager to applaud Northern sentiments; Southerners generally had left Washington, and the atmosphere of the Senate chamber was altogether changed.

Starting quietly, as was his wont, Johnson observed that personalities were not arguments, and he would have refrained from occupying the time of the Senate with any reply, "if I did not feel it was a duty to myself, and a duty to the country."

Encouraged by exclamations of "Go on!" emanating from the floor, he then asked why it was "that no one, in the Senate or out of it, who is in favor of the Union of these states, has made an attack upon me?" And why had there been a "concerted attack" upon him especially, "from the beginning of the discussion to the present moment, not even confined to the ordinary courtesies?" The questions at stake transcended personalities, which were "the resort of men whose minds are low and coarse. I care not from what direction the senator comes who indulges in personalities towards me; I feel that I am above him and that he is my inferior."

This he said looking directly at Lane, and the galleries applauded. Senator Trusten Polk of Missouri, presiding, rapped for order, and Johnson went on.

"It is very easy to talk about 'cowards' . . . and in this connection I want to say . . ." Here he drew himself erect, and with one
of his rare, abrupt gestures shot out his right hand with two
fingers pointing at Lane, ". . . that these two eyes of mine have
never looked upon anything in the shape of mortal men that this
heart feared."

Johnson's blood was up, and he ripped into a Tennessee-style,
savage attack.

"Sir," he cried, "have we reached a point at which we cannot
talk about treason? . . . Who is it that has been engaged in conspiracies?" Yes, on the very floor of the Senate. "Who is it that has
been engaged in making war upon the United States? Who is it
that has fired upon our flag? Who is it that has given instructions
to take our arsenals, to take our forts, to take our dockyards, to
take the public property? . . . Show me who has been engaged in
these conspiracies, who has fired upon our flag, who has given
instructions to take our forts and our custom houses, our arsenals
and our dockyards, and I will show you a traitor!"

Again the galleries burst into applause, and the chair ordered
one gallery cleared, while the Senate degenerated into incoherence.

Senator Clingman urged that the order be rescinded, arguing
that applause had been tolerated forty or fifty times during the
session, and "if you allow an audience to applaud, you have no
right to punish them for applauding in the wrong place."

Senator Douglas moved that the order be revoked, but the
chair refused to entertain the motion. Senators in the cloakrooms,
hearing the commotion, hurried in and added their voices to the
gabble of objections and counterobjections, the calls for the
"yeas" and "nays," readings of rules, and disputes over the meaning of words.

Stubbornly the chair repeated: "The sergeant at arms will clear
the gallery immediately."

Senator Hale remarked that it was something new when Union
speakers were applauded. Southern senators took exception to
this, and above the tumult Senator Thompson of New Jersey
moved to adjourn.

This brought a chorus of groans and "Oh, no!" because to adjourn then would be to adjourn permanently, and much business remained to be wound up.

In disgust, Senator Wade moved to "lay the whole subject on the table; let's get rid of it." But Mason of Virginia insisted there was nothing to lay on the table, the chair must be upheld. The hubbub became unintelligible to the reporters, who could catch only phrases—"I object"—"I take occasion to say"—"out of order" —"let's have a vote"—"may I have the ear of the chair"—"the question is"—"I appeal"—"withdraw the motion"—"I insist"— "suspend the order"—"I object"—"I object even to that."

Senator Bayard of Delaware snapped that the Senate had been turned into a theater, and Wade suggested that the inane debate be kept up a little longer and the galleries would clear themselves.

Throughout the tumult Johnson waited, his eyes smoldering, while Lane paced the aisle, sputtering that people might applaud as much as they wished; he would not be intimidated, even if the galleries were armed. The disorder continued for twenty minutes, until at last the presiding officer suspended his order, after Johnson had offered to go surety for the respectful behavior of the audience.

Resuming his arraignment of traitors, he then said:

"Show me the individuals who are engaged in nightly conspiracies, in secret conclaves, and issuing orders directing the capture of our forts, and the taking of our custom houses, and I will show who are the traitors; and that being done, and the persons pointed out . . . were I the President of the United States, I would do as Thomas Jefferson did in 1806 with Aaron Burr: I would have them arrested, and if convicted . . . by the eternal God, I would execute them!"

In the men's gallery one spectator shouted, "Arrest and be damned!" The man was hustled out; and Johnson went on in a voice vibrant with earnestness:

"Sir, I alluded to treason and traitors, and while I was speaking, Tennessee sent an echo back . . . that has carried terror and dismay through the whole camp of traitors! . . . I have been held up, and indirectly censured, because I have stood by the people . . . I have advocated those measures that are sometimes called demagogical. I would to God that we had a few more men here who were for the people, and who would legislate in conformity with their will and wishes! . . .

"During the last forty days, six states . . . have been taken out of the Union. How? By the voice of the people? No; it is demagogism to talk of the people . . . Have the people of South Carolina passed upon the ordinance of secession adopted by their convention? No; but a system of usurpation was instituted, and reign of terror . . . So with Louisiana; so with Mississippi; so with all the states that have undertaken to form a new confederacy. Have the people been consulted? Not in a single instance!

"In some of these states even our Stars and Stripes have been changed. One state has a palmetto, another has a pelican; and . . . one has a rattlesnake run up as its emblem . . . Yes, sir, the wily serpent, the rattlesnake, has been substituted . . . Will Tennessee desert the flag that [Jackson] waved with success? No! We were in the Union before some of these states were spoken into existence; and we intend to remain in it, and insist upon—as we have the confident belief we shall get—all our constitutional rights and protection in the Union, and under the Constitution of the country!"

Here the galleries again erupted in applause, and the chair ordered them to be cleared without exception.

With a simple gesture, Johnson said, "I have done." But before he could sit down, one spectator (Joseph Bushnell Grinnell, of Grinnell, Iowa) jumped up on his seat, swung his hat in the air and called for "three cheers for the Union" and "three for Andy Johnson." The cheers were given, to the indignation of the senators. Above the din the presiding officer shouted to arrest every man "guilty of this disorder," and after the galleries were cleared to lock the doors. Senators joined in the outcry, while the men and women who were being pushed through the doors "hissed and clapped, stamped their feet, and indulged in other expressions of feelings." (This is the wording of the official transcript.)

It took the sergeant at arms and his deputies ten minutes to herd the audience outside. Then the doors were locked and the Senate resumed, more or less, its business.

The next day, *The New York Times* expressed the amazement

of the country at the outbreak, but pointed out that while it "disgraced the Senate and insulted the senators outrageously, it gave evidence of a feeling deep and strong for the Union . . . Andy Johnson in his castigation of Lane eclipsed all his former efforts. His name is in every mouth today, and he is freely applauded as the greatest man of the age."

Then came March 4, hailed by the *Times* as the day of "happy deliverance," when James Buchanan ceased to be President and Abraham Lincoln and the Republicans took the helm.

With the inauguration terminated a period of leaderless drift and febrile inaction. During the final three months of Buchanan's defeatist control, Union men and women had waited for some word of assurance from the incoming leaders; but Lincoln and his associates had nothing to say. They had no fixed policy yet; nobody (least of all themselves) knew what their course would be.

In this critical juncture, when the forces of secession seemed sweeping on almost unopposed, Andrew Johnson's indomitable Senate speeches kept alive the faith and courage of thousands who clung to the Union in spite of all. Battles may be decided by words as well as blows; and Senator Lane, in a moment of unguarded candor, had divulged that Johnson, acting almost alone, had managed to throw up a roadblock in the path of disunion that had prevented the swift consummation of a breakup of the nation.

NINE

DEFEAT AND EXILE

ALREADY the newly instituted Confederate government had its "commissioners" in Washington, threatening instant war unless the forts in their territories were yielded without palaver. Lincoln's inaugural address, mild in tone, was viewed in the North as disavowing any aggressive intentions; but in the South it was cried up as clear evidence of a design to put the Confederacy to the torch and sword.

"Parson" Brownlow had no hesitation in approving Lincoln's start.

"I endorse the inaugural address of Mr. Lincoln and I commend it for its temperance and conservatism and for its nationality of sentiment," he declared in the *Whig:* and when South Carolina readers indignantly canceled their subscriptions, he pilloried their state as a nest of hereditary traitors.

March passed, and Johnson was kept busy with his ever mounting mail. Copies of his speeches were in constant request, and with the change of administrations and the federal patronage being redistributed, many letter writers assumed that he, though a Democrat, would have influence. "Hearing yesterday that you controlled the appointments in Tennessee," one of scores of similar letters began. Even Blackston McDannel applied for the office of United States marshal of East Tennessee through Johnson, deeming that a more effective route than the customary petition addressed to the President.

"You will therefore confer a favor by calling on the President and communicate to him my wishes in such manner as may best suit you," McDannel wrote. "For thirty years you have known me intimately, and I leave it with you to give me such a recommendation as you think I deserve."

Not then, but later, McDannel would get the job.

In April President Lincoln informed South Carolina authorities that he was sending food to Major Anderson's starving garrison. Immediate surrender of the fort was thereupon demanded by the Confederates. Anderson refused, and at 4:30 A.M., on April 12, the bombardment of the fort began. On the afternoon of April 13, after thirty-four hours of incessant shelling, the garrison capitulated. The war had begun.

President Lincoln proclaimed the seceded states in insurrection and called for seventy-five thousand volunteers to suppress the uprising. Thereupon Virginia seceded at once, crying "invasion," and North Carolina and Arkansas followed. From Tennessee, Governor Isham Harris wired to the White House:

"Tennessee will not furnish a single man for coercion, but fifty thousand, if necessary, for the defense of our rights and those of our Southern brothers."

On April 25 Harris called the legislature to meet and take the state out of the Union.

Meanwhile, in the East, for six suspenseful days Washington had been cut off from the rest of the country, when mobs of Baltimore "plug-uglies" destroyed the railroad tracks and cut telegraph wires around the capital. Communication was restored with the arrival of Northern troops on the day the Tennessee legislature assembled, and the fear that had been felt everywhere in the North for the safety of the government was dissipated.

Chief credit for this prompt breaking of the blockade was due to plucky, bold, brassy Benjamin Butler of Massachusetts. The former booster of Jefferson Davis and John C. Breckinridge was now a red-hot Unionist and brigadier general of militia. Already he was exhibiting his cleverness at securing practical results by unorthodox means, and also his positive genius for embroiling himself in every controversy that the times, the personalities, and his own immodestly immoderate demands could engender. Butler always demanded immoderately on principle; as a consequence he got much.*

---

* Butler's energy was phenomenal. After having bulldozed his way into the Massachusetts legislature, at the first news of Sumter he had morally blackjacked Governor John Andrew into commissioning him a general of militia; and when Lincoln called for troops, Butler got his into motion so speedily that as the companies lined up on Boston Common to receive the governor's oratorical Godspeed,

The alarm felt for Washington outside the city had been even greater than that experienced by its residents. When Robert Johnson wrote his father anxiously, he received assurances that all was serene at the seat of government.

"We are all well, & I believe as safe, if not safer here, than in any other place to which we could remove," Johnson wrote. "Many exaggerated and sensational reports are circulated as to the condition of Washington, the whole entirely groundless. We have between eighteen & twenty thousand good true men in this city, who are enabled to hold in check any number of men that may be sent by Jeff Davis for our subjugation. This was doubtless the design of the traitors, but they have been completely foiled . . . The old Stars and Stripes are safe, and I believe our government will pass through the ordeal safely . . . The regiments that have already reached the city . . . are a fine body of men, quiet, unobtrusive, but determined; you never see the least intoxication . . ."

Robert's inquiry, and other letters he had received, Johnson added impassively, "convinced me that you have heard shocking accounts of our condition, not one word of which is true. Our business has proceeded uninterruptedly, & with the exception of a little interruption of the railroad facilities, you would hardly see a different scene from our accustomed every-day life."

This calm appraisal contrasted sharply with reports that were being sent South by rebel sympathizers. One Southern spitfire, Mrs. Philip Phillips, wife of a former congressman from Alabama, wrote to a friend in wails of anguish about "our once honored Capitol . . . desecrated, disgraced by Lincoln's low soldiery . . . They go about the avenue insulting women and taking property without paying for it." It is understandable that General Butler should feel justified, at New Orleans some time later, in jailing Eugenia Phillips as an "uncommonly vulgar" scold.

With secession spreading, and the course of Tennessee in doubt, appeals to return home and resist Governor Harris' intentions spilled from Johnson's mailbag. From Nashville came a plea:

---

tailors were between the rows sewing the buttons on the backs of the men's overcoats. The overcoats, with Ben Butler's foresight for patriotism and profit, had been purchased from Butler textile mills.

"Are you coming home soon? The state needs your services and advice and I beg of you to hasten home . . . You, my dear sir, have been posted here as sending traitorous dispatches . . . Please hasten home and God bless and protect you."

Twenty-four citizens of Jacksborough, both Whigs and Democrats, signed an appeal of the greatest possible urgency:

"Come to Jacksboro and address the people on the great question of Union and Liberty, or Disunion and Despotism. We ask you to come with all the power and force of the English language, with super added emphasis to the word COME." Not only was "COME" in capital letters, it was triply underlined.

Lincoln's call for troops had changed the feeling in Tennessee, and the state now was filled with secession enthusiasm. John Bell, who had carried Tennessee in November on the sole issue of standing by the Union, declared for "going out," and he took most of his followers with him. Middle and West Tennessee were solidly for secession, but East Tennessee's former Whigs clung to their traditional loyalty. Democrats everywhere were whooping it up to join the Confederacy.

In his own party, Johnson had become an object of hatred. His protest that he had not been aware of the intention of the Breckinridge wing to pull out of the Union was not accepted, and he was denounced bitterly as a traitor to both party and state. Should he return to Tennessee his life would be in peril, both friends and enemies warned.

Nevertheless, towards the end of April, 1861, he set out. Presumably Eliza Johnson traveled with him.

The closeness of the war was brought home by the sight of Confederate pickets patrolling the Virginia end of the Long Bridge, which Johnson crossed to take the train at Alexandria. He was not challenged, however.

By coincidence, another passenger on the train was ex-Senator Wigfall, heading back to Texas after having taken part in the assault on Fort Sumter. At every station, crowds cheered the Texas hero, and directed groans and hisses at Johnson.

The demonstrations grew more threatening when the train reached the western part of the state. At Liberty, an armed mob rushed into the car where Johnson sat, and one man, thrusting his face close to Johnson's, demanded:

"Are you Andy Johnson?"

"I am."

"Then I am going to pull your nose!"

The assailant reached out to do so, but Johnson drew his revolver. The mob yelled and clutched his coat, trying to drag him out. Women screamed, and the conductor ran in shouting, "No shooting, gentlemen, please! There are ladies in the car!"

The crowd slowly drew back, Johnson, with drawn pistol, pressing them step by step; and as the train pulled out, he held them at bay from the platform, to their yells returning his defiant shout:

"I am a Union man!"

Another crowd assembled at Lynchburg, and though there were cries of "Hang him!" "Here's the rope!" Johnson stood on the steps of the car challenging them, and no serious violence was attempted.

Word of his coming flashed along the line, and at Bristol, on the border between Virginia and Tennessee, a sullen crowd gathered at the depot, bent on a lynching. Their design was foiled by the intervention of the Confederate authorities at Montgomery, as was revealed years later.

Just before Johnson's train was due to reach Bristol, the Virginia military officer in command there received a telegraphic order signed by Jefferson Davis, commanding that the train should not stop, and stating why; namely, that Andrew Johnson was aboard, and his life would be in extreme danger if a halt were made. The order was explicit and peremptory, and the officer obeyed it, forcing the engineer to keep the cars rolling past the depot and through Bristol without stopping.

How the Montgomery authorities knew of Johnson's presence on the train, or of the intentions of the mob at Bristol, the officer made no attempt to find out, and he disclosed the story only after the war. The mystery, however, may not have been impenetrable, even at that time. Tennessee had not yet seceded, and the Confederates were desperately anxious to carry the border states with them. They were at all times fully informed regarding events and personalities at Washington through a network of spies, professional and volunteer, and they would have been at once alerted regarding Johnson's heading back to his home state. Had he been lynched on the way, and thereby made a martyr to the Union cause, the reaction among Tennesseans might have destroyed the secessionists' hopes. It was urgent that Andrew Johnson be kept alive, at least at that moment, and it behooved the Confederate authorities to invoke the highest authority to accomplish that end.

Much as the secession leaders disliked Johnson, all during the bitter Senate debates they never entirely relinquished the thought that he might be induced, or driven, to go along with his section. Other Southern Unionists were giving in, and had that occurred in Johnson's case, he might (so Jefferson Davis himself stated later on) have been offered the Vice-Presidency of the Confederate States of America. That Johnson's attachment to the Union was greater than that of Robert E. Lee and many other sincere Southerners was the Confederates' loss, and even after hostilities had commenced, they did not give up hope of winning his acquiescence, or neutrality at least.

Reaching Greeneville safely, Johnson found the state in turmoil. He spent a few days attending to home business and consulting with trusted advisers. Spring in Tennessee had never been lovelier than it was that year. The Homestead, as Johnson affectionately called the house on Main Street, and his other property never appeared more attractive or thriving. A two-room building on the grounds of the hotel he owned he had fitted up as an office, where he received visitors; one room was filled with records of his public service—scrapbooks, files of letters, reports, all arranged in order. These contained the story of his struggles and his achievements. Now all this—the fruits of a lifetime of hard labor, thrift, and integrity—was in jeopardy, and he knew it. But that did not deter him from doing his best to hold Tennessee in the United States.

The program of the secessionists was being carried out systematically. The legislature had convened at the governor's summons and had gone into secret session. Robert Johnson, an Assemblyman, wrote to his father from Nashville that an ordinance of secession would surely be passed. The few Union members were afraid to speak on the streets. They held a meeting in Robert's hotel room, and agreed that when the ordinance came up, they would vote against it and then leave.

In rapid succession, the legislature authorized Governor Harris to raise fifty-five thousand troops, and listened to a persuasive speech by a Confederate agent, telling the advantage of adhering to the Southern cause. On May 7, with the concurrence of the legislators, Harris entered into a military alliance with the Montgomery government and placed Tennessee's entire military resources under the control of Jefferson Davis. At the same time, Nashville was offered as the permanent capital of the Confederacy.

After—and only after—this had been done, a date was set on which the people might signify their approval or rejection of an ordinance of secession. The date for the election was June 8.

This coup d'état stirred up scathing condemnation. The influential *Louisville Journal*, edited by the widely respected George D. Prentice, excoriated the action, calling it "as bitter and insolent a mockery of popular rights as the human mind could invent."

To prevent the consummation of this betrayal, Johnson set out to stump every county in East Tennessee.

He did not go alone. Around him rallied a coterie of prominent East Tennesseans, most of them Whigs, who had fought him relentlessly for a third of a century.

Foremost, and terrible in his denunciations of "this hell-born and hell-bound rebellion," was "Parson" Brownlow. His *Whig* had echoed Johnson's appeals in Congress stage by stage; indeed, often the "Parson" had been in advance of the senator, voicing the same arguments, expressing the same horror of disloyalty, but with greater verbal agility. Alternately he laid on the lash and pleaded with the people to turn from certain disaster. "Revolution, or civil war, is no *holiday affair*," he preached; and he warned that the "honest yeomanry" of the border states, "whose families live by their hard licks, four-fifths of whom own no Negroes and never expect to own any, are to be drafted . . . [to] fight for the purse-proud aristocrats of the cotton states."

"I am for my country," he served notice, "and on the side of the general government; and in every contest, either at sea or on land,

I shall rejoice in the triumph of government troops fighting under the Stars and Stripes. Should Tennessee go out of the Union, I shall continue to denounce Secessionism, and war against . . . the assaults of demagogues and traitors at the South, though their number be legion . . . Come what may, through weal or woe, in peace or war, no earthly power shall keep me from denouncing the enemies of my country until my tongue and pen are paralyzed in death!''

That Brownlow and Johnson should be fighting side by side, and should be linked as "twin brothers," was typical of the anomalies of the troubled times. For years they had carried on a remorseless vendetta; they had said terrible things about each other; for years they had not spoken to each other. But now, in the cause of the Union, animosities were buried, and they were inseparable. Other leading East Tennesseans were with them: Horace Maynard, T. A. R. Nelson, Oliver P. Temple—all Whigs, all hitherto militant enemies of Andrew Johnson.

The Democrats, almost to a man, were for secession. Just after Johnson reached home, Gideon J. Pillow, one of the party leaders who had always resented and detested the upstart tailor, wrote to Leroy P. Walker, Confederate Secretary of War:

"We are now united in Mid. and West Tenn., and we think East Tenn. will soon be so . . . Johnson has at last returned to East Tenn., and had his nose pulled on the way; was hissed and hooted at all points along his route . . . His power is gone, and henceforth there will be nothing left but the stench of the traitor."

How far his power was gone Johnson proceeded to find out. He teamed with Nelson, the most effective Whig orator in East Tennessee, and they addressed crowds day after day. Johnson appealed to the Democrats and Nelson to the Whigs, and men were lifted out of themselves by their combined eloquence. Threats of death were of daily occurrence; Johnson's life was in constant danger. Among the thousands who turned out to hear him, many were savagely hostile.

The rallies were held wherever accommodations could be found, indoors and out of doors. At Kingsport, where atrocious threats had been circulated, the meeting was in a church, and Johnson prefaced his remarks by taking out his revolver, laying it on the pulpit and covering it with a handkerchief, in plain sight. No violence occurred.

At Rogersville, in Hawkins county, the meeting was in the court house, and while Johnson was speaking a company of "Hawkins Boys," all armed, marched in. Their leader, Captain Fulkerson, ordered that the meeting disband.

Holding up his hand for silence, Johnson pointed at Fulkerson and said:

"I have been a Democrat all my life and accustomed to the rule of the majority. If a majority of this crowd want me to stop speaking, I will stop. If a majority want me to continue, I will speak on, regardless of you and your company."

Without giving Fulkerson a chance to reply, he requested all who wished him to continue to step to the right side of the room, and those who were opposed to the left. Nearly everybody pushed toward the right, and without another word Fulkerson and his bravos marched out.

But the tide was against the Unionists. Secession was sweeping the state, Governor Harris was raising troops, and the terrorizing of Unionists became popular. Men changed their opinions for no reason at all. Colonel Gentry, Johnson's whilom rival for the governorship, looking back could not account for his conversion.

"I was always a Union man," he said, "but one day a wheezy old side-wheel steamer, labeled *Secession,* came puffing along and *hove* up to the wharf. As everyone else was jumping aboard, I jumped too; and all hands went to hell together."

"It is nothing to know that a particular man was a Union man last night," ran Brownlow's clinical notes. "Men rise up and dress as Union men, and turn Secessionist before breakfast is over . . . The disease is contagious," he warned, "and a clever man will contract it by drinking mean whisky out of the same tumbler with one afflicted with it."

At times Johnson seemed to those around him to be transfigured. Temple, who had known him for thirty years and never liked him, was one of those who were deeply moved. Describing the speech at Knoxville, Temple recalled:

"I had never seen him so cool, so determined, so eloquent, and so impressive in bearing . . . As he appeared before the large as-

semblage . . . and appealed with burning words for the preservation of the Union, my heart—all hearts—turned towards him . . .
It seemed as if his lips had been touched by a live coal off the
very altar of patriotism . . . Deeply conscious of the awfulness of
the crisis, with thick clouds around him, he rose to the full height
of the occasion. A disinterested love of country seemed to glow in
his heart, flame out in his countenance, and burn on his tongue.
As with outstretched arms and melting voice he stood that day
pleading so persuasively, so kindly, so powerfully for his dis-
tracted country, he rose to the very heights of splendid eloquence."

Andrew Johnson had found his cause.

The day of voting neared. Johnson and his friends had not
ventured into Middle or West Tennessee, for they knew that they
would not be permitted to speak. Union men there were being
murdered, and on one occasion Brownlow narrowly saved Johnson's life. The latter had spoken at Loudon, where there was no
railroad, and had arranged to drive to the nearest railroad point
in time at catch the train for Knoxville. Brownlow got word that
aboard the train were two thousand Louisiana troops, on their
way to Virginia, who had vowed to "deal with the traitor Andy
Johnson."

Brownlow dispatched his son with the warning. At first Johnson swore that he would ride that train in spite of every man in
Louisiana; but friends prevailed, and with young Brownlow he
drove forty miles over rutted country roads to keep his next
speaking engagement.

On the eve of the balloting, Brownlow again became alarmed,
and on June 3 he sent Blackston McDannel word that Johnson
must be induced to leave the state at once, because the Nashville
authorities had determined to have him arrested and summarily
shot.

"There is no humbug in it," Brownlow stressed. "He will be
assassinated in less than ten days if he does not get out of the
way."

Five days after this warning was given, Tennessee voted, and
the state that in February had overwhelmingly rejected secession
this time overwhelmingly embraced it. The majority in favor of

Charles Johnson, Andrew's eldest son, killed by a fall from a horse during the war. He was the sunny-dispositioned member of the family, and Eliza's favorite. *Credit: Mrs. Margaret Johnson Patterson Bartlett.*

Robert Johnson, the second son. He died in Greeneville just after the return of the family from Washington in 1869. *Credit: Mrs. Margaret Johnson Patterson Bartlett.*

Andrew Johnson, Jr., called "Frank" by the family because of the profusion of Andrews. This photograph was taken during White House days. *Credit: Mrs. Margaret Johnson Patterson Bartlett.*

Martha Johnson Patterson, White House hostess. *Credit: Mrs. Margaret Johnson Patterson Bartlett.*

Mary Johnson Stover in White House days. *Credit: Mrs. Margaret Johnson Patterson Bartlett.*

The fine portrait photograph of Andrew Johnson by Brady. Probably 1865, just after Johnson's succession to the Presidency. *Credit: Library of Congress.*

Andrew Johnson Patterson and Belle Patterson, children of Martha and Senator Judge Patterson, and grandchildren of the President, during White House days. *Credit: Mrs. Margaret Johnson Patterson Bartlett.*

President Johnson's first meeting with his cabinet, in the room at the Treasury temporarily converted into an executive office. The center pillar is wrapped in mourning band. Stanton is presenting the first Reconstruction plan. *Credit: Library of Congress.*

Seward as he appeared during Andrew Johnson's administration — old and worn by the strain of years of crisis. The right side of his face was badly disfigured by the scars left by the assassin Paine's knife, and he never allowed that side of his face to be photographed after 1865. *Credit: Library of Congress.*

Edwin M. Stanton. *Credit: Library of Congress.*

joining the Confederacy was roughly sixty thousand out of a total of one hundred and fifty-six thousand. West Tennessee voted for secession, twenty-nine thousand to six thousand; Middle Tennessee, fifty-eight thousand to eight thousand; but East Tennessee heeded Johnson and the other Unionist leaders and rejected secession by thirty-three thousand to fourteen thousand. The state as a whole went for secession by better than two to one; East Tennessee went for the Union by the same ratio.

It was the swing-over of Democrats that produced this startling result in East Tennessee. The Whig vote there was just about the same as it had been in February. Political observers considered this demonstration of power the greatest in Johnson's career. A few months earlier he had urged the Democrats of his region to support the party of secession, and they had heeded him. In June he asked them to vote against that party; he asked them to abandon lifelong loyalties, and line up not only with the Whigs, whom they despised, but with Free Soilers and abolitionists, whom they had been taught to hate and fear. Largely at Johnson's behest, they had made the change, and it was lasting. No other Democratic leader had helped; Johnson had accomplished the feat alone.

On June 24 Governor Harris proclaimed Tennessee out of the Union and in the Confederacy.

Before that time, bowing to necessity, Andrew Johnson had left the state. Scorning to slink away, he had set out openly, in a light carriage, accompanied by three trustworthy friends, heading for the Cumberland Gap. To travel by rail would have been suicidal. The road lay through passes and narrow valleys suited to ambush, and several times the party was fired upon. A militia colonel sent out an order to stop the "traitor Andrew Johnson," but not a militiaman responded. And eventually, passing safely through the mountains, Johnson was set down in neutral Kentucky.

Behind him he had left everything—family, friends, home, possessions. Not for eight years would he again see the hills of East Tennessee, or drink again from the "Gum Spring" in Greeneville.

TEN

"ERECT AMONG THE NATIONS
OF THE EARTH"

JOHNSON came out of Tennessee carrying word of what he had left behind—proscription of Unionists, terrorizing, and confiscation. At every step he was spied upon by Confederate sympathizers, and his words were sedulously reported to rebel authorities. In Lexington, Kentucky, a spy composed a scandalized account of the "extraordinary speech of three hours" made there by the senator, filled with "the most vindictive hatred towards the South & all men who are for the South . . . He contemplates the blackest treason against the sovereignty of Tennessee . . . [He] openly charged . . . that the vote in Tennessee was controll'd by armed bands of soldiers & that a reign of terror was in force—that E. Tennessee would resist the State & fight for the Union, if they could procure arms. Arms was all he wanted."

In Cincinnati, Johnson sharply corrected those secessionists who were crowing that he had run away. He knew that warrants had been issued for his arrest, but "I am no fugitive, especially a fugitive from justice . . . Thank God, the county in which I live gave a majority of two thousand and seven against this odious, nefarious disunion doctrine."

Northern newspapers rejoiced at his escape. At Washington reporters besieged him for news from his state, and Lincoln got a detailed briefing on the distress in East Tennessee. The collapse of the government there, following secession, had produced an interval of anarchy, concerning which the Confederate officer in charge at Knoxville reported feelingly:

"Marauding bands of armed men go through the country, representing themselves to be the authorized agents of the state or

Confederate governments; they 'impress' into 'service' horses and men; they plunder the helpless, and especially those quondam supporters of Johnson, Maynard, and Brownlow; they force men to [join them] by representing that otherwise they will be incarcerated at Tuscaloosa; they force the people to feed and care for themselves and horses without compensation."

The strategic importance of East Tennessee both sides in the conflict recognized. By the Confederates East Tennessee was considered "the keystone of the Southern arch," for through it ran the railroad into Virginia, the supply line for men and supplies from the Gulf states. The alternative route was slow and roundabout: east into Georgia, and thence by a patchwork of connecting lines north through the Carolinas. East Tennessee also was a major source of foodstuffs for the Confederates; its loss would be a severe blow to the armies operating in Virginia.

Lincoln and Johnson pressed for quick action to hold this vital area, but reasons were advanced for delaying. Meanwhile, the Confederate military overran the area almost without opposition. They found that occupying it was easy, but subduing its stiff-necked Unionists was difficult. Governor Harris poured troops into East Tennessee, and called on Richmond for help from that end.

The rigor shown to Union sympathizers was relentless; "agitators" were arrested and transported south to prisons, or forcibly "enlisted" in the Southern army. They were beaten, shot, and hanged. Their farms were pillaged, their cattle driven off, their crops confiscated, their fences destroyed, buildings burned, their families turned into the fields. From the Confederate point of view, the area seethed with sedition. General Felix Zollicoffer was given the command in the hope that he, as a Tennessean, could persuade the stubborn inhabitants to accept the inevitable. Zollicoffer had been a staunch Unionist until Sumter and Lincoln's call for troops; in fact, he had been in the midst of a speech for the Union when the news of Lincoln's action reached Nashville; he had changed his allegiance on the spot.

His presence did nothing to allay the bitterness. An underground resistance grew up, aimed at hampering the Confederate authorities, and many loyalists, rather than submit to the hated

"Sesech," melted away into the mountains, whence they made their way by stealth past the pickets that patrolled the passes into Kentucky, and there joined the regiments of Tennesseans in the Union army.

For the relief of this hard-pressed people Senator Johnson bestirred himself in Washington. He procured arms and directed their smuggling into East Tennessee from Kentucky. He collected money for destitute refugees, and kept everlastingly after the army to speed a rescue expedition. But this failed to materialize.

In the midst of his activity, he remained in constant anxiety regarding his family. News came infrequently, often through devious channels. A letter written by one of Brownlow's sons was smuggled out of Knoxville by a woman sympathizer; it brought word that Robert Johnson had "bade me say that your family are well." That was all; and this letter, dated June 26, had taken two weeks to reach Washington. From time to time there were further scraps of news, mostly bleak: Robert, Charles, and Daniel Stover had disappeared into the hills and were with the resistance; Judge Patterson was in jail; Eliza Johnson and little "Frank" were with Martha and her children at the Patterson home near Greeneville; Johnson's property had been confiscated.

Eliza, on her side, was distressed by the lack of reliable information about her husband. One report said he had been murdered in Kentucky; another said he was in Washington; a third had him about to lead an army into East Tennessee.

News of "Parson" Brownlow did reach Washington through the newspaper exchanges, which the war had not interrupted: Northern and Southern editors continued to copy from each other's columns, and through this medium Washington ascertained that the "Fighting Parson" was still scorching with his brimstone vocabulary the whole secession movement on principle, and its authors by name.

Not a day passed but the fighting editor's life was endangered. After the February election he had raised a United States flag over his house, and had defied hostile crowds of both civilians and soldiers, again and again, to haul it down. After the June debacle for his cause he did lower the flag, because, as he said, it had ceased to be the banner of the region where he lived, and as a

peaceful, law-abiding Christian he was obliged to render unto
Caesar the things that are Caesar's. But in the *Whig* he never
ceased to express his chagrin at the temporary overthrow of the
real government, or to predict the downfall of secession. And in
spite of cancellations, the subscription list of the *Whig* (as its
editor aggressively advertised) continued to exceed that of the
other twelve newspapers published in East Tennessee *combined*.

Governor "Eye-sham G. Harris" and the rebel establishment in
Tennessee came under Brownlow's special lash when an attempt
was made to blacken Andrew Johnson's reputation by forged evidence purporting to show that the senator was hand in glove with
the most detested Northern slavery haters.

The conspiracy came to light after Johnson had left Tennessee.
The *Knoxville Register* (a secession sheet edited by a man whom
Brownlow called "a corrupt liar, low-down drunkard, irresponsible vagabond, and infamous coward") published asserted correspondence that had passed between Johnson and Amos A. Lawrence, Boston philanthropist known to have been a financial
backer of John Brown, of Harper's Ferry infamy. The letters were
dated before the June election, and contained solicitations of
money from Lawrence for the purpose of covertly arming Unionists in East Tennessee; Lawrence had sent a draft for one thousand dollars drawn on a Boston bank; but Johnson had been
afraid to cash the draft, the letters said, and he had asked Lawrence instead to send five or ten thousand dollars "in New England currency, in large bills, to me by mail, via Cincinnati. I can
purchase a lot of arms if I had the means."

The letters had been mailed in Knoxville, it was said, and they
"proved" Johnson's treacherous alliance with a black abolitionist.
The *Richmond Enquirer*, a mouthpiece of the Confederate government, also published the correspondence, and drew the inference that Johnson had not only plotted against the peace of his
state, but that he was a thief—for where had the money gone?

Johnson exposed the forgeries, made clear that he had never
communicated with Amos Lawrence on any subject until he had
queried him about the letters, and demonstrated further that on
the day when one of the letters was mailed in Knoxville, under his

Congressional frank, he had been more than one hundred miles away, in Elizabethton, making a speech.

Brownlow pushed the matter home. He nailed the "hellhounds, letter-forgers, and thieves" who were seeking to ruin Johnson "by means as foul as the parties are corrupt, and as wicked as the deeds of the infernal regions," saying they were "the Secession clique in Knoxville." Postal officials were in the plot, he claimed, because they were perfectly familiar with Andrew Johnson's signature—a signature "as peculiar as that of Andrew Jackson: it is coarse, heavy, and bold, and cannot be mistaken." So the men in the post office at Knoxville were at the bottom of this "base, dark, and infinitely infernal transaction," the "Parson" published, while the collusion of the Confederate authorities at Richmond he pointed to as a fitting commentary upon the "morality and integrity of this bogus Confederacy!"

How long could this verbal war-to-the-death go on? The "Parson's" friends lived in hourly expectation of hearing that he had been assassinated, but he gave no sign of turning from his course by a hair's breadth, come good news or come bad. And bad did come.

When the Confederacy moved its capital to Richmond, and word was published that the rebel Congress would assemble there on July 20, people in the North flew into a frenzy of war fever. "On to Richmond!" shrieked Greeley's *New York Tribune*, and the clamor for an attack that would crush, disperse, dispel, and annihilate the rebels became deafening. One brilliant, knockout blow would do it, was the belief; in fact, men who intimated that the South would fight well and long were knocked down in the streets of Northern cities. Bowing to the storm, President Lincoln ordered an advance. The Union commander, General Irwin Mc-Dowell was reluctant to risk his amateur soldiers in a real fight, but he was overruled. The Confederates, under General Pierre Gustav Toutant Beauregard of New Orleans, were massed at Manassas, in Northern Virginia, and the collision occurred on July 21.

The weather was fine, although hot, and Congress (which Lincoln had called into extra session on July 4 to ratify his actions against the rebels) took a recess to ride out on a pleasant Sunday morning and enjoy the invigorating spectacle of a battle. Among the junketeers, well armed, was Ben Wade, in a carriage with Senator Chandler and the Senate's sergeant at arms, George T. Brown.

Northern cockiness that day was drowned in the little stream called Bull Run, and before nightfall, Congressional holiday-makers and troops alike were fleeing pell-mell back to Washington, spreading the alarm that the "Rebs" were at their heels.

There was no panicking Wade. Having come out to see the show, he was not indisposed to take a hand in it himself. When raw troops ahead of his party broke and ran like rabbits, Wade swung the carriage across the road, and standing up with his rifle, his hat pushed well back on his head, yelled, "Boys, we'll stop this runaway!" And for a quarter of an hour he did, until rescued by a detachment of infantry hurrying towards the firing.

Out of the confusion of that Union defeat two positive results emerged: the North was shocked into realizing that the war was going to be no picnic; and a recent master of mathematics, named Thomas Jonathan Jackson, took a lien on immortality with the title "Stonewall."

The fright felt in Washington was imparted to Edwin Stanton, Buchanan's ex-Attorney General, who was posting regular bulletins to the ex-President, on his farm in Pennsylvania. Stanton wrote of the "imbecility of the administration" and the "dreadful disaster" that had resulted from "Lincoln's 'running the machine' . . . The rout, overthrow, and utter demoralization of the whole army is complete . . . The capture of Washington seems now to be inevitable." Stanton's words for the current occupant of the White House were "gorilla" and "ape."

Horace Greeley was undone by Bull Run. He could not sleep, and after seven consecutive nights of insomniac horrors he appealed to Lincoln to consider whether, "if the rebels *cannot* be beaten . . . if the Union is irretrievably gone, an armistice for thirty, sixty, ninety, one hundred and twenty days—better still, for a year—ought at once to be proposed, with a view to a peaceful settlement? . . . The gloom in this city is funereal," he desponded. "On every brow sits sullen, scorching, black despair."

Not on the brow of "Parson" Brownlow. Though he was surrounded by exulting rebels in Knoxville, he spoke his feeling in the next issue of the *Whig:* Let the war continue for three, four years, if need be; he was not yet convinced that one Southerner could lick five Yankees, and "though I have studied the character of God for twenty years past, I have found no indications of his being on the side of the South."

Senator Johnson had not joined the Congressional sightseers, and his reaction to the disaster was not one of dismay. With a Kentuckian who wrote, "we were not yet whipped, not by a damned sight," Johnson agreed. But he believed that the real aims of the war, which now promised to be prolonged, should be clarified. What was the North fighting for?

With this in mind, he introduced in the Senate a resolution that stated that the war would be prosecuted not "in any spirit of oppression, nor for the purpose of conquest or subjugation, nor for the purpose of overthrowing or interfering with the rights or established institutions of these states, but to defend and maintain the supremacy of the Constitution and all laws made in pursuance thereof, and to preserve the Union, with all the dignity, equality, and rights of the several states unimpaired."

This did not agree with the ideas of the abolitionists, or with those of the ultra Republicans who were beginning to be called radicals. The God-given opportunity which the war offered, in their view, was the chance to extirpate slavery, and not to coddle the slaveholding border states whose devotion to the Union was at best lukewarm and must be bought with bribes. Cried Indiana's George W. Julian in the House, "A Union with slavery spared and reinstated would not be worth the cost of saving it!" And as for the "never-ending gabble about the sacredness of the Constitution," Julian's constituents were sick of it. "It will never be forgotten that the red-handed murderers and thieves who set this rebellion on foot went out of the Union yelping for the Constitution which they had conspired to overthrow by the blackest perjury and treason that ever confronted the Almighty!"

Senator Johnson did not subscribe to this. His creed was, and would continue to be, "the Union as it was, the Constitution as it is"; and under his spurring the Senate passed his resolution almost unanimously; the disapproving Sumner held aloof.

In the House, John J. Crittenden of Kentucky (former senator, former governor, former Attorney General, former Secretary of State) introduced an almost identical resolution, which also passed with only two contrary votes. Thad Stevens abstained from dignifying such namby-pamby talk by a vote; his advice was to "ask those who made the war what its object is. Do not ask us. Our object is to subdue the rebels."

In a speech shortly afterwards he made his stand clear:

"It is said that the South will never submit—that we cannot conquer the rebels—that they will suffer themselves to be slaughtered, and their whole country to be laid waste. Sir, war is a grievous thing at best, and civil war more than any other; but if they hold this language . . . if their whole country must be laid waste, and made a desert, in order to save this Union from destruction, so let it be . . . There will be no bargaining, there will be no negotiation, there will be no truces with the rebels, except to bury the dead, until every man shall have laid down his arms, disbanded his organization, submitted himself to the government, and sued for mercy . . . That is my doctrine, and that will be the doctrine of the whole free people of the North before two years roll round."

But though Stevens would not dignify the resolutions by voting against them, they expressed the general sentiment of Congress. The radicals were in disfavor; they were blamed for the humiliation of Bull Run. And passage of the resolutions upheld Lincoln's hands in his endeavor to keep the remaining border states from seceding. This he believed to be indispensable for winning the war. Not only were they strategically valuable, as their resources and manpower represented a much-needed addition to Northern strength, but they possessed a political importance that could hardly be overestimated. As long as these border states remained in the Union, they advertised to the world that the United States was not irretrievably split, that the doctrine of secession was rejected by slave states as well as free. To retain the loyalty of the border states, therefore, Lincoln was willing to make concessions and give repeated assurances that their interests would not be sacrificed, or their local institutions tampered with.

This political aspect of Lincoln's border-state policy no one

understood better than Tennessean Johnson. The radicals abominated it. To them it was shameful; it was truckling to slaveholders.
It was contemptuously said that Lincoln "would like to have God
on his side, but he *must* have Kentucky."

Senator Johnson followed his war-aims resolution with a speech
in support of Lincoln's war measures that in some ways produced
a greater effect than any other he ever made. It came at a crucial
moment. Bull Run was not a week in the past. The Senate was
debating the legalizing of emergency actions which the President
had taken. These included the suspension of the writ of habeas
corpus in Maryland and the jailing of suspected disloyalists without trial. There also followed the President's proclamation of a
blockade of Confederate ports.

The fight against confirming these actions was led by John C.
Breckinridge, the former Vice-President, now a senator from Kentucky. Breckinridge assailed Lincoln's "usurpations," denouncing
them as unconstitutional, the acts of a dictator. The North's most
eloquent and learned speakers had expended their energies in
replying to Breckinridge's assault (stigmatized by Senator Baker
of Oregon as "polished treason") when on July 27 Senator Johnson gained recognition by the chair.

Every nation, he began, must pass through three phases before
it can attain stability. The first phase is gaining independence,
and in the Revolutionary War this nation had successfully passed
through that ordeal. The second phase was demonstrating that
the nation could maintain itself against foreign foes. That phase
in the United States had occurred in 1812–14. In the third phase,
the nation must show its ability to subdue internal enemies—
those who had no confidence in its institutions or its integrity.
The United States was in the midst of that ordeal, and upon its
outcome hung not only the fate of the nation, but the hopes of
freedom-hungry people everywhere.

Quoting Lincoln's recent message, that "this is essentially a
people's war," Johnson contrasted this with Toombs's remark that
"when traitors become numerous enough, treason becomes respectable." Traitors had become numerous, surely, and treason
may have become respectable; but, "God being willing . . . I have
hitherto warred against traitors and treason, and in behalf of the

government which was constructed by our fathers, [and] I intend to continue to the end."

Violations of the Constitution had occurred; first of all, the great violation of the South's secession. But, he asked, "are not violations of the Constitution necessary for its protection and vindication more tolerable than violations of that sacred instrument aimed at the overthrow and destruction of the government? A great deal has been said here about searches and seizures. I reckon it is equally important to protect a government from seizure as an individual."

Then he ripped into the hairsplitting arguments over whether the President had any "war powers," inasmuch as Congress had not declared war.

"Mr. President," he said, "we are in the midst of a civil war . . . Traitors and rebels are standing with arms in their hands, and it is said that we must . . . compromise with them . . . All the compromise I have to make is the compromise of the Constitution of the United States!"

No cry about violations of the Constitution had been raised while the South controlled the government, he pointed out; and again he excoriated Jefferson Davis for ingratitude to the government in whose service he had "got all his distinction, civil and military . . . Such men have their apologists here. But you never hear from them of the law being violated *down there*. Oh, no! That is never mentioned."

Tyranny and anarchy were the legitimate offspring of secession, he declared, and in evidence he read from the *Memphis Bulletin* an account of the chaos prevailing in that seceded city, concluding with the editor's cry for deliverance at any price: "Let Governor Harris be king if need be, and Baugh a despot!

"Who is Baugh? The mayor of Memphis. The mob reign of terror gotten up under this doctrine of secession is so great that we find that they are appealing to one-man power. They are even willing to make the mayor of the city a despot, and Isham G. Harris, a little, petty governor of Tennessee, a king! Isham G. Harris a king! . . . He, a king over the free and patriotic people of Tennessee! Isham G. Harris to be my king! Yes, sir, my king! I know the man . . . I know the ingredients that constitute the compound called Isham G. Harris! King Harris to be my master, and the master of the people I have the proud and conscious satisfaction of representing on this floor! Mr. President, he should not be my slave!"

Here applause from the galleries broke through the decorum of the Senate. After order had been restored, Johnson went on, lifted out of himself by his theme and the remembrance of the sufferings of East Tennessee.

"*We* claim to be the state! The other division may have seceded and gone off . . . we still claim to be the state. We ask the government to come to our aid . . . We have lived entertaining these opinions; we intend to die entertaining them. We have commenced the battle of freedom. It is freedom's cause. We will triumph. We must triumph. Right is with us. A great and fundamental principle of right, that lies at the foundation of all things, is with us. We may meet with impediments, and may meet with disasters, and here and there a defeat; but ultimately freedom's cause must triumph . . .

"Though sometimes I cannot see my way clear, when my facts give out, when my reason fails me, I draw largely upon my faith. My faith is strong . . . that a thing so monstrously wrong as this rebellion cannot triumph."

Let partisan politics be forgotten.

"I am a Democrat today; I expect to die one. But do not talk about Republicans now; do not talk about Democrats; do not talk about Whigs or Americans [Know-Nothings] now; talk about your country, and the Constitution and the Union. Save that; preserve the integrity of the government; once more place it erect among the nations of the earth; and then, if we want to divide about questions that may arise in our midst, we have a government to divide in.

"Though the government has met with a little reverse within a short distance of this city, no one should be discouraged. Let the energies of the government be redoubled and let it go on with the war . . . not a war upon sections, not a war upon peculiar institutions anywhere; but let the Constitution be its frontispiece and the supremacy and enforcement of the laws its watchword. Then it can, it will, go on triumphantly.

"We must succeed. This government must not, cannot fail. Though your flag may have trailed in the dust; though a retrograde movement may have been made; though the banner of our country may have been sullied, let it be borne onward. And if, for the prosecution of this war in behalf of the government and the Constitution, it is necessary to cleanse and purify that banner, I say let it be baptized in fire from the sun and bathed in a nation's blood! The nation must be redeemed; it must be triumphant! The Constitution—which is based upon principles immutable and upon which rest the rights of men and the hopes and expectations of those who love freedom throughout the civilized world—must be maintained!"

This speech lifted the war above a contest between factions, above sectarian causes and personal animosities, and placed it on the high plane of principle and of vindicating the aspirations of humanity. Its practical effect was far-reaching. In the judgment of Alexander H. Stephens, this speech "gave the war a vigor and real life it had not before, and would not have had without it, on the Northern side." Stephens estimated that it put one hundred thousand men into Union uniforms.

ELEVEN

EVENTS IN TENNESSEE

THE news from home was meager and most of it was bad. Regarding his family Senator Johnson learned little, except that Charles was recruiting for the Union regiments drilling in Kentucky, and that Dan Stover was a leader of the mountain commandos who harried the Confederate lines.

Union sentiment had not slackened in East Tennessee. After the June election a convention of Unionists met at Knoxville and rejected the illegal acts of Governor Harris and the legislature. The rejection was met with contemptuous silence, except for newspaper comment, as that in the *Memphis Appeal,* which dismissed the convention as "that little batch of disaffected traitors who hover around the noxious atmosphere of Andrew Johnson's home."

Another Unionist convention met at Greeneville and petitioned the legislature for permission to erect a separate state out of the eastern counties. The petition was pigeonholed, and the convention adjourned subject to recall by its president.

In August of '61 elections for Congress were held in Tennessee, with two slates in some districts—one open and aboveboard, of candidates for the Confederate Congress at Richmond, the other unannounced but known, of candidates for the Congress of the United States at Washington. In the First and Second Districts of East Tennessee, T. A. R. Nelson and Horace Maynard were sent back to Washington overwhelmingly, in spite of poll-watching by the secessionist authorities. The results marked the two men for immediate arrest, and on election day Maynard rode into Kentucky. Thence he made his way to Washington and took his seat in the House of Representatives, not on the certificate of the governor of his state, but on the certificates of the loyal sheriffs of the counties in the district, stating that he had received a majority of the votes cast.

Maynard's presence in Congress was of inestimable help to Lincoln, for it advised the nation and the world that Tennessee was still a member of the Union, with its representatives in the national legislative body. Johnson, also, was helped by Maynard's return, as they joined forces to bring relief to their friends in East Tennessee. But the military situation was inauspicious; the Confederates, holding all Tennessee, were extending their lines into Kentucky, and the need of the hour was to hold that state; a thrust into East Tennessee must wait.

T. A. R. Nelson was not as fortunate as Maynard. While attempting to get through to Washington, he was captured and taken to Richmond. There pressure was brought to bear upon him, by mingled threats and blandishments, to cease resistance to Confederate rule. His influence could do much to bring peace to his region, he was told; and finally, in an exchange of letters with Jefferson Davis, Nelson pledged himself to make no speeches and remain neutral throughout the war. He then was allowed to return home. There he published the correspondence, without comment, and lapsed into silence. But the bitterness with which he witnessed the oppression around him came to light in later years with publication of his privately jotted notes during that period. In one passage he described how the conscription law was enforced in East Tennessee:

"Men and women were whipped, and the latter sometimes hanged, to make them tell where the conscripts were secreted. Many were shot, and nothing was more common than to bring them tied and handcuffed into the little towns. At Knoxville conscripts were whipped, compelled to wear the ball and chain, and, in some instances, hanged for desertion."

Amid this terrorism, one man would not be silenced: the indomitable Brownlow. His friends watched in wonderment as, in spite of his associates' flight and the hatred vented on him by the Confederates, he continued to publish his detestation of "this hell-born and hell-bound rebellion." The *Whig* was banned in West Tennessee, but circulated heavily in the eastern counties.

Rebel boasts of military feats he delighted in deflating. When a communiqué announced that after what the "Parson" called "some scouting party skirmish" the rebels had "retired to strong defensive positions," Brownlow published that they had been "whipped, *whipped*, WHIPPED." He was constantly searching for that one Southern man who could whip five Yankees. Southern preachers who prayed for the triumph of Southern arms moved him to derision. "The idea of a Secession preacher heaving and setting at the throne of grace—like a ram at a gate-post!"

The marvel was that he stayed alive. Mississippi and Louisiana troops passing through Knoxville were incited to murder him, but he escaped. He was continually threatened with arrest and summary dispatch as a traitor. After months of defiance, becoming convinced that the suppression of his paper and of himself by drastic means was imminent, he published the last issue of the *Whig* on October 24, 1861. In a dignified farewell to his readers he revealed that he had been told he might live in peace if he would give a bond to cease his vendetta. That he would never do. "I will submit to imprisonment for life, or die at the end of a rope, before I will make any humiliating concession to any power on earth!"

He fully believed he would be arrested, and was prepared for it. "I shall feel in no degree humbled by being cast into prison. I shall go because I failed to recognize the hand of God in the work of breaking up the American government, and the inauguration of the most wicked, cruel, unnatural, and uncalled-for war ever recorded in history . . ."

Retiring to his home, he awaited arrest, but this did not take place as speedily as he had expected. He was, however, treated to daily abuse by drunken soldiers who flourished knives and pointed their guns at the windows. His family, terrified lest one of those guns go off, beseeched him to seek safety, and consequently, early in November the "Parson" set out with another preacher to collect, as he said, advertising debts owed him in the adjoining counties.

Hardly had he left home when during the night every railroad bridge in East Tennessee mysteriously burst into flames and was destroyed. The action was carried out by Union commandos under Dan Stover, Andrew Johnson's son-in-law. Immediately a hue and cry was raised to apprehend Brownlow, his departure from home just before the outrage seeming to indicate complicity on his part. This accusation he strenuously denied, and he was notoriously truthful. But in view of the fury of the Confederates at the interruption of their vital rail link with Virginia, he and a number of real bridge burners took refuge in a cave in an inaccessible ravine in the Great Smokies, on the North Carolina border. Friendly mountain folk fed them, but the exposure was hard on the older men. Scouts brought word that martial law had been proclaimed in Knoxville, and cavalry patrols were scouring the countryside in search of bridge burners.

The fugitives decided it would be safer to scatter. Brownlow determined to reconnoiter, and riding through rocky gorges, in the dark of night, reached the home of a trusty friend, six miles outside Knoxville. From there Brownlow sent to the general commanding the area, Brigadier General W. H. Carroll, a statement explaining his departure from home, denying any knowledge of the bridge burning, and declaring his readiness to face trial "before any *civil* tribunal; but I protest against being turned over to *any infuriated mob of armed men* filled with prejudice by my bitterest enemies."

Then followed a series of maneuvers that left everybody confused. General Carroll reassured Brownlow that he would suffer no violence by the military if he returned, and need fear nothing if he could prove his innocence, as he asserted he could. Brownlow disliked the ambiguity in the general's promise, and submitted an affidavit to reinforce his previous statement.

Meanwhile, Judah P. Benjamin, late United States senator and now confederate Secretary of War, at the instance of a friend of Brownlow in the Confederate Congress, had written to the top commander at Knoxville, Major General George B. Crittenden (a son of John J. Crittenden, who had introduced the war-aims resolution in Congress), saying that he had been requested to give the "Parson" a passport to leave Tennessee.

"I cannot give him a formal passport," Benjamin wrote, "though I would greatly prefer seeing him on the other side of our lines, *as an avowed enemy* . . . I would be glad to learn that he has left Tennessee; and I have no objection to interpose to his leaving, if you are willing to let him pass."

This hint was sufficient for General Crittenden, who wrote to Brownlow that if the latter would call at headquarters in Knoxville within twenty-four hours, he would be issued a pass to go into Kentucky.

Brownlow reported as directed, and was informed that his pass would be ready in two days, and he could set out then.

But before that time, the "Parson" was arrested on a civil warrant charging treason. The warrant was issued by the Confederate commissioner, Robert B. Reynolds—whom Brownlow instantly stigmatized as "a third-rate county-court lawyer, a drunken and corrupt *sot*, who had been kicked out of a grocery a few days before by a mechanic, and who was afterwards taken up from the pavements of the street, in a beastly state of intoxication, by rebel troops, and lodged in the guardhouse."

Brownlow was lodged in the Knoxville jail, and his tussle with the powers that be in Secessia continued.

TWELVE

WAITING AND WORKING

THAT autumn had continued to be bleak for Johnson. No more news came from his family, but only rumors that added to his anxiety. No relief was sent to East Tennessee. Brownlow was silenced, Nelson silenced, Temple silenced. Other recent Unionists had defected, and some were now occupying seats in the Congress of the Confederate States of America. Union armies were bogged down in seeming helplessness and indecision. Johnson strove against despair.

Harrowing reports of the suffering in East Tennessee continued to come over the grapevine, and he and Maynard did their utmost to stir the Union commanders into sending a relieving army there. Promises were made; Lincoln begged for action; but reasons were found by the generals for postponing such an advance.

In June, when Congress adjourned, Johnson had been urged by numerous admirers in the North to spend the summer with them, since he could not return to Tennessee. But he could not rest; he went on speaking tours, to stoke the fires of resistance wherever they were low. In October he paid a visit to Camp Robinson, in Kentucky, where two regiments of Tennessee infantry—East Tennesseans for the main part—were training. Asked to say a few words to them, he was so shaken by emotion that he could not utter a sound.

The next day, at Columbus, Ohio, appearing before an immense crowd, he described that experience:

"There they were, my friends and fellow citizens of my beloved state . . . from the tender stripling of sixteen to the gray-haired father of sixty, all mourning the evil that has befallen our land and our homes, but all seeking for arms wherewith to go back and drive the invader from our fields and hearthstones . . . Speech was denied me. I stood before them as one dumb . . . Two thousand of us exiled Tennesseans, and all silent as a city of the dead!

"Each of that throng of exiles, who had wandered among the mountains and hid in their caverns, who had slept in the forest and squeezed themselves, one by one, through the pickets of the invader, each one was now offering comfort and pledging fidelity to the other . . . There were their homes, and there, too, is mine— right over there! And yet we were homeless, exiled! Was it for crime? No, our only fault was loving our country too well to permit its betrayal. And for this the remorseless agents of that 'sum of villainies,' secession, drove us from our families and firesides, and made us exiled wanderers! But the time will soon come when we wanderers will go home! This monstrous iniquity cannot long exist! . . . Whatever they do—though they may ravage our state and make desolate our homes—they can never, while God reigns, make East Tennessee a land of slaves!"

On December 2, 1862 (four days before "Parson" Brownlow entered the Knoxville jail), Congress reconvened, and Johnson plunged into the work of the session. The main business was upholding the war effort, and in the House of Representatives Thad Stevens was proving invaluable in lending every possible support to the President for prosecuting the war. As chairman of the Ways and Means Committee, Stevens was in a key spot to help or hinder the administration, and he developed aptitude in devising ways to pay the staggering costs of the conflict. But on the issue of slavery, he mistrusted Lincoln and all moderates.

Already Congress was divided into two factions—the moderates, or constitutionalists, and the radicals. The former, among whom Johnson, Trumbull, Fessenden, Collamer, and Orville H. Browning of Illinois (a newcomer to the Senate, appointed to fill out the term of Stephen A. Douglas upon the latter's death at the start of the war) were the leaders in the upper house, were bent on preserving the Union within the limitations of the Constitution; the radicals, and their extreme wing, the abolitionists, were equally determined to save the Union, but were prepared, if necessary, to scrap the Constitution in order to stamp out slavery. Between the groups friction was continual; but the day-to-day demands of the fighting forces kept the antagonism within bounds.

Changes had occurred in the military setup. George Brinton McClellan, young, dashing, and endowed with brilliant organizing ability but handicapped by an itch to play politics, had been given command of Union forces, upon General Scott's retirement. He had set about forming an army out of the disjointed commands and had done a magnificent job; but his apparent reluctance to send that army into battle was playing hob with the radicals' small stock of patience. Time and again pressure had been put on McClellan to order an advance, and attempts were made to force President Lincoln to insist on some show of fighting, without success. The handsome "Mac" dawdled in Washington and filled the newspapers with glowing accounts of his social triumphs, rather than triumphs in the field.

Already, while Congress had been in recess, three radical senators, Wade, Campbell, and Trumbull, had come to Washington to induce the commanding general to move. They had tracked McClellan to Silver Spring, the home of Montgomery Blair, just north of Washington, and in a discussion lasting until 3 A.M. they exhorted him to launch an attack. At least, as Wade put it, "for God's sake push back the defiant traitors from around Washington." McClellan had demurred, blamed others, insinuated that he lacked cooperation. Risk a battle, the senators urged; defeat would be better than inaction. McClellan protested that he would require more troops. The senators laughed derisively at this; but the only result of the interview was that the three senators thereafter were excluded from the general's dinner parties.

The apparent favoritism Lincoln was showing to Democratic generals further aroused the radicals' suspicions; they sniffed treachery. The War Democrats of the North (those who supported the war as necessary to preserve the Union) were viewed by extreme Republicans with only a little less aversion than they had for the Peace Democrats (those who deplored all the bloodshed, and urged immediate negotiations with the rebels). Yet Democrats of all sorts swarmed around McClellan's headquarters.

But Lincoln was convinced that without the support of the Northern Democrats the war could not be won. His own party was a minority; it commanded only a segment of the North's resources. Therefore he employed every stratagem, every device and trick of politics, to bind the Democrats to the administration, and many members of that party were given important posts, military and civilian. McClellan was a Democrat, and he appointed Democratic friends to subsidiary commands, like his fellow West Pointer, General Don Carlos Buell, who was given the command of the Cumberland district in Tennessee. From the failure of any of these generals to hit the rebels hard, the radicals drew a direct line to the cause, they believed, of the stagnation of the Union armies: Democratic generals who sympathized with the South simply did not want to fight, was the deduction.

Johnson and Maynard had lost no time in importuning General Buell to strike into East Tennessee and relieve the Unionists there. "Our people are oppressed and pursued as beasts of the forest; the government must come to their relief," they telegraphed. Back came assurance that Buell would "recognize no more imperative duty, and crave no higher honor, than that of rescuing our loyal friends in Tennessee." But he did not move, even when reprimanded by both Lincoln and McClellan.

Galled by their impotence, the frustrated radicals now were taking out their anger at the administration by social snubs. Their choice for commanding general, to supersede McClellan, was General John Charles Frémont, an abolitionist and fervent Republican. Frémont and his wife coming to Washington, they were tendered a dinner and reception at the White House, but Mrs. Lincoln had eighty of her invitations returned with "regrets." Wade even replied:

"Are the President and Mrs. Lincoln aware that there is a civil war? If they are not, Mr. and Mrs. Wade are, and for that reason decline to participate in feasting and dancing."

The reception was torture for Mary Lincoln, because the guests, ignoring their host and hostess, clustered obsequiously around the Frémonts.

Andrew Johnson had nothing to do with this social skirmishing, although he was as eager as the most extreme radical for a Union advance that would deliver East Tennessee. His eagerness won for him, at this moment, a position that gave him much inside information regarding the functioning of the military machine.

This came about when Congress, on December 10, 1861, took action to learn, if possible, the army's real intentions, and to assume an overall supervision of the war effort. The Joint Committee on the Conduct of the War was created, with Ben Wade as chairman. The other members were four Republicans—Senator Chandler, Representatives Julian of Indiana, John Covode of Pennsylvania, and Daniel W. Gooch of Massachusetts—and two Democrats—Senator Andrew Johnson and Representative Moses Odell of Brooklyn, New York. Johnson and Chandler were the only non-lawyers in the group. The feeling of all the members was expressed by the benign, bespectacled, bearded Gooch when he said that he was willing to employ "all the power human ingenuity can devise or human agency execute" to put down the rebellion.

The digging by the committee bore fruit within a few weeks when Simon Cameron was eased out of the cabinet and replaced by Edwin M. Stanton. The War Department under Cameron had become infested with profiteers, and Ben Wade and Thad Stevens had both told Lincoln to get rid of the inefficient, venal Cameron and install a man of force. Stevens became so disgusted with the mess at the War Department that he went to Lincoln and personally exposed Cameron's shady reputation in Pennsylvania. The things he said about his fellow Pennsylvanian caused the President to interject:

"Why, you don't think the Secretary would steal, do you?"

"Well, Mr. President," replied the laconic Stevens, "I don't think he would steal a red-hot stove."

This was humor of the sort Lincoln relished, and too good not to be passed along. Inevitably it got back to Cameron, who demanded that Stevens go with him to the White House and take back the slander. Stevens was agreeable, and off they started. Once in Lincoln's presence, Stevens said:

"Mr. President, the other day I told you that Mr. Cameron would not steal a red-hot stove. I now take that back."

Stanton buckled down to his job. All was forgiven, if not forgotten, between him and Lincoln, as he set about winning the war with the energy and cleverness he had shown when fighting to win a law suit. Of Stanton it might have been said what Montgomery Blair, Lincoln's political-minded Postmaster General, said of his famous family: "When the Blairs go in for a fight, they go in for a funeral."

Stanton's methods of fighting at times tended to resemble those of the guileful Indian, to whom stealth was as praiseworthy as courage, and frequently more serviceable; to Stanton, as to the Indian, an arrow shot from ambush was a perfectly legitimate weapon of war. It may have been this trait that moved former Senator Gwin of California—a practiced politician, well acquainted with Stanton's ways—to relay a warning to his friend, Secretary of State Seward, that, unless strictly watched, the new Secretary of War, "a bloodhound sort of man," would "tomahawk them all."

Stanton and Johnson did see eye to eye on the question of pressing ahead with the war. Just before Stanton took over, there had been a flurry of activity in the Tennessee area, when General Zollicoffer made a feint into Kentucky and was repulsed by Buell. In the skirmishing Zollicoffer was killed, and Lincoln had rushed the news to Johnson through John Hay, the presidential secretary. "Heavy losses on both sides," the dispatch read, but the Confederates had been driven back.

"Thank the Lord!" a friend had written to Johnson from Cincinnati. "The signs begin to look a little more favorable for *East Tennessee!* Shall it not be followed up? . . . Can you not see to this and *have it done?* Now is the time, before the rebels get over their panic and rally, to push right on to Knoxville and take possession of all that great railroad."

Johnson tried to bring about this action. In examining witnesses before the Committee on the Conduct of the War, meeting in the dingy basement room of the Committee on the Territories (of which also Wade was chairman), Johnson sought repeatedly to draw from the military men admissions that would support his recommendations. Sometimes he elicited them, more often not. He also submitted to the generals his own grand strategy, which he maintained would "wind up the rebellion in six months," but the experts brushed this aside without ceremony.

The hostility that the committee felt unanimously for General McClellan became almost pathological, and in frequent consultations with the new Secretary of War, Stanton professed to concur. One day in mid-February, Wade and Johnson called on Stanton to demand that McClellan exert himself to destroy the batteries which the Confederates had thrown up along the Potomac. The general happening to be in the War Department building, Stanton called him in to hear the senators. McClellan gave his usual excuses: not enough troops, preparations for taking the offensive still incomplete, "lines of retreat" vulnerable.

"Retreat!" exploded Wade. An army like McClellan's would need no "lines of retreat" if somebody would just let it fight! Take the men across the Potomac, and if they couldn't win, "let them come back in their coffins!"

Johnson wrote up the report of this interview for the committee's journal, and described the talk as highly satisfactory. "Although the chairman sometimes made his statements in pretty strong and emphatic language, the secretary endorsed every sentiment he uttered."

This scene took place two days after an obscure general out West, named U. S. (whatever those initials stood for) Grant had captured two Confederate strongholds in Tennessee, Forts Henry and Donelson, bagging an entire rebel army of fifteen thousand men. The press decided that the "U. S." in the winner's name meant "Unconditional Surrender," and this Western feat did nothing to lessen the indignation of radicals fretting at the inaction in the East. Behind McClellan, it was surmised, lay a more potent influence; and that sinister influence, the impression grew, was the wily little Secretary of State, Seward. "Serpentine Seward" had always been a compromiser and a schemer, the radicals complained, and now their accumulated venom against the "sharper" overflowed.

A caucus of the Republican members of Congress was called to consider a resolution of no confidence in Seward. The debate grew heated. Senator Browning, able lawyer and intimate associate of Lincoln, recorded the discussion in his diary. Attacks on the administration were made by Senator Trumbull ("very bitterly") and several House members, blasting Seward "for all the disasters that had come upon our arms . . . [Senator] Grimes [of Iowa] followed in a similar strain, and then old Ben Wade made a long speech in which he declared that the Senate should go in a body and demand of the President the dismissal of Mr. Seward. He . . . said he would never be satisfied until there was a Republican at the head of our armies."

"Why," Wade cried, "if we follow such leadership, we will be in the wilderness longer than the children of Israel under Moses!"

The resolution of no confidence was voted. None concurred in it more heartily than Indiana's principal slavery hater, Julian. In his own journal, he applauded Wade's prediction that "the country was going to hell, and the scenes witnessed in the French Revolution were nothing in comparison with what we should soon see here." That revolution Julian lusted for. As an abolitionist he had worked for a quarter of a century to bring it about. Astute as a politician, he appreciated that the nation was not ready; but he contended that the government had "no right to take shelter behind a debauched and sickly public sentiment." From "angry young man of the fifties," Julian had grown into an implacable and single-minded zealot, determined that come what might, slavery must be crushed out of existence. His very appearance, with a fanatic's eyes and a stern, rigid mouth, challenged disagreement.

He reposed little confidence in Andrew Johnson, despite the Tennessean's enthusiasm for hitting the rebels. Johnson was fatally tainted, in Julian's eyes, for three reasons: he owned slaves, he was a Southerner, and he worked for the success of the President's culpable border state policy. Privately Julian would comment on Johnson's "habit of bad English" and "incoherence of thought."

Johnson might have been forgiven for some incoherence in the midst of his many anxieties, complicated by intense concern for his family. In January of '62 he had got the first direct, clear news of them; this came when a young relative of Judge Patterson wrote to the senator from Greensburg, Indiana:

"I having just arrived at this place—direct from home—I left home on the 15th inst. and have been some 2 weeks on the rout. I run the lines of the rebels. When I left home Judge Patterson requested me to go (if I got through) and see you. But I am very unwell and will be compelled to lay over a day or two till I get

better. Mrs. Johnson is in Carter county with Mrs. Stover. Frank
[Andrew, Jr.] is with her. She was a little unwell when I left.
Charles has come in out of the brush and taken the oath. Robert
is still in the bushes. Mr. Stover also is in the bushes, or on his
way to Ky. Judge Patterson has been arrested twice, but released.
Mrs. Patterson is well. Your house is now a Rebel *hospital* and the
Rebels are cutting up Greeneville."

Johnson's Greeneville property had been seized after the Tennessee legislature declared the senator, Horace Maynard, "and
such others of our public men as have expatriated themselves
from our state" to be "alien enemies of our people," and subject to
"the just punishment of the law in such cases made and provided."

The Confederate commander at Greeneville, Colonel Danville
Leadbetter (Brownlow described him as "a native of Maine, who,
after serving fifteen years in the United States Army, married a
gang of Negroes at Mobile, and has become the greatest champion of Southern rights"), on November 29 had found time to
acknowledge receipt of a letter from Martha Patterson saying,
"My mother's house is now ready for the reception of your pa-
tients." Leadbetter had subjoined the unctuous reflection:
"Would it be too uncivil to suggest that had that house continued
to shelter its owner, this military would now have been elsewhere
and engaged in more congenial duties?"

More news of the family reached Johnson in mid-February,
when Robert wrote from a Union camp in Kentucky. He had left
Greene county nine days before, he reported, and "traveled by
night through Hawkins, Hancock, and Lee counties.

"I am almost broke down, but will leave here in a day or two,
and hope to meet you in Washington in good health. Mother is in
Carter county, her health is very much improved. All the family
are well. Stover's and Patterson's family are well. Patterson has
been arrested, but finally released. Stover is out on the scout. I
tried to get him to come with me but he declined. I have been out
on the scout since 9th December. If they had arrested me, I have
no doubt but what they would have hung me . . . It is impossible to put on paper, the scenes that have taken place in
East Tennessee since you left. I will . . . give you full particulars

on sight . . . Charles is at Stevens & is doing well, attending to Stevens farm. Our Negroes were taken [confiscated] some three weeks since & taken to Knoxville, but finally sent them all back. I do not think they will now confiscate them."

Two weeks later Robert Johnson was in Washington, and on February 27 Stanton signed his commission as "Colonel of the Regiment of Volunteers which you are authorized to raise in Tennessee."

Robert brought word of other developments in Tennessee. "Parson" Brownlow, even in jail, was proving as much a match for the Confederate authorities as he had been when at liberty. The more level-headed were determined not to make him a martyr by the summary execution that he expected and would have gloried in, and he could not be cowed by any milder treatment.

His ordeal was terrible enough. Herded into a building so crowded that only half the inmates could lie down to sleep at one time, the "Parson" was ill almost from the time of his arrest. He refused to be transferred to a hospital, saying that he did not "want passports to where I would likely be poisoned in twenty-four hours." When General Carroll (whom Brownlow denounced as habitually drunk, "a walking groggery") offered to release him if he would swear allegiance to the Confederate government, he told the general:

"I do not consider that you have a government; I regard it as a big Southern mob. It has never been recognized by any government on earth, and never will be!"

Men implicated in the burning of railroad bridges were taken from the jail and hanged. The "Parson" himself expected to be hanged, and composed a farewell speech to make from the gallows, consigning the rebels to the hottest hell he could imagine and predicting their eventual overthrow. (He thought he would be permitted to make it because his executioners would be curious to hear his last word.) The duplicity by which he had been lured into a trap he denounced in letters to military authorities right and left, but General Crittenden disclaimed having pledged blanket immunity. Whereupon Brownlow sent a letter to Confederate Secretary of War Benjamin at Richmond, of a sort seldom read by cabinet ministers:

"Hon. J. P. Benjamin:

"You authorized General Crittenden to give me a passport and an escort to send me into the old Government, and he invited me here for that purpose; but a third-rate, county-court lawyer, acting as your Confederate attorney, took me out of his hands and cast me into this prison. I am anxious to learn which is your highest authority—the Secretary of War, a major general, or a dirty little drunken attorney . . .

"You are reported to have said to a gentleman in Richmond that I am a bad man, dangerous to the Confederacy, and that you desire me out of it. Just give me my passports, and I will do for your Confederacy more than the devil has ever done—I will quit the country!"

By now his illness had become alarming, and a doctor insisted that he be released to his home. There he lay ill during January and February of 1862, under surveillance day and night. At length, friends at Richmond (for the "Parson's" private generosity had won and held many such, in spite of political embitterments) obtained an order from Benjamin to the Knoxville commander to send him out of Tennessee by any safe road.

Feeble as he was, the "Parson" set out for Nashville, which had just been captured by Union forces. On March 15, ailing and weary, he neared the city, looking "all wrinkled and drawn up" in the carriage. But at sight of the first Union picket, "he seemed to swell out and his wrinkles to disappear," his escort said, and springing nimbly to the ground he exclaimed:

"Glory to God in the highest, and on earth peace, good will towards all men, except a few hell-born and hell-bound rebels in Knoxville!"

His arrival in the city—after five months of concealment, wandering, imprisonment, and illness, which Andrew Johnson had observed from Washington with intense sympathy—caused a sensation. Hurrying from the St. Cloud Hotel to the Capitol, he met there Johnson himself, just arrived from Washington as newly appointed military governor of Tennessee.

When these two strong men saw each other, after so many trials—both exiles, driven from their homes, separated from their families, proscribed and execrated as traitors in their own Tennessee—all animosity between them was wiped out, and they fell into each other's arms and wept.

Returning to the hotel, Brownlow found a crowd waiting for a speech; and although pleading feebleness and loss of voice, he croaked out a few phrases, concluding:

"Grape for the rebel masses, and hemp for their leaders!"

THIRTEEN

"TREASON MUST BE MADE ODIOUS"

MILITARY governor of a state claiming not even to belong to the Union—what was Johnson's new position? As governor, the only portion of Tennessee over which he could exercise any authority was a narrow strip around Nashville. Lincoln had sought him for the job almost before Union troops entered the city as Confederate General Albert Sidney Johnston retired. Always sensitive to political implications, Lincoln realized that the presence on Tennessee soil of a federally appointed governor would give a boost to Union loyalty everywhere. Johnson's fearlessness was proverbial; he knew both the conditions and the personalities involved, and he was willing to assume responsibility. He yielded at once to the President's request, consenting without hesitation to give up safety and comfort in Washington for grave personal risks and the burden of an almost impossible task.

The appointment was made on March 3, and at the same time Johnson was given the commission of a brigadier general, to lend standing in dealing with rank-conscious military men, and to enable him to command troops. His instructions gave him the widest latitude of action; in fact, he was made the virtual dictator of Tennessee until a civil government should be reestablished. He could appoint officials, organize courts, suspend the writ of habeas corpus, make arrests, raise troops, tax, seize property, call elections, and exercise "all and singular the powers, duties, and functions" pertaining to his office, relying on his own "wisdom and energetic action." He was to adopt whatever measures circumstances might require to reestablish United States authority and bring Tennessee back into normal relations with the rest of the Union.

Johnson was aware that he incurred personal risk by venturing back into Tennessee. Perhaps three-quarters of the people of the state were ardent secessionists, many of them bigoted in their hatred of his supposed apostasy; these would attribute his return, armed with Draconian authority, to a thirst for revenge against those who had calumniated him and impugned his motives for a generation. Confederate fury had become focused on Andrew Johnson as the "arch traitor." His mail teemed with venomous letters, some written by semi-literates, others couched in courtly, stinging prose.

General Buell was apprehensive for Johnson's safety, and telegraphed:

"You must not expect to be received with enthusiasm, rather the reverse, and I would suggest to you to enter without any display."

A plot to kidnap him on the way to Tennessee was sanctioned by Confederate General Braxton Bragg, while the legality of his position was denied North and South. Thaddeus Stevens asserted that there existed no constitutional basis for such an office. Jefferson Davis pointed to the fact that Johnson in no way represented the will of a majority of Tennesseans, and asked sarcastically who was breaking the "sacred Constitution" now.

For Johnson, theoretical subtleties were overborne by the practical necessities of the emergency. In his mind a concept took shape that would govern all his future course. First, he believed that a state could not unilaterally absolve itself of membership in the Union. The renunciation, therefore, of a state's duties towards the other members of the Union could only be the action of individuals, in their private capacity; they were not the action of that abstract entity, the state. The state, in his view, consisted of the loyal citizens within its borders—those who honored and fulfilled their reciprocal duties within the Union—be their number few or many. Those flouting those duties were in rebellion—lawbreakers, subject to coercion and repression, just like the breakers of criminal laws; and such repression was requisite in order to preserve the peace and security of all the law-abiding, that is, the loyal, states of the Union.

By this reasoning Johnson justified the use of extreme force against the secessionists in their capacity as rebellious individuals defying the collective will of all the states, expressed in federal law; at the same time, this concept, while admitting states' rights, supported his contention that no state was or ever could be out of the Union, so long as it contained one loyal citizen.

But theorizing played little part in determining his course of action when Lincoln called him to this opportunity for unique and dangerous service. He set out promptly for Nashville, traveling by way of Cincinnati, and despite the portents, arrived safely about March 12. He found conditions there chaotic. Many of the city's leading citizens had fled before the approaching Northern army. Governor Harris and the legislature had decamped with the archives and all the state's funds. Civil government was suspended, and the military commander, Don Carlos Buell, was irritated by the intrusion of a civilian with nebulous authority, who might be expected to interfere with the prerogatives of the army and at best be a nuisance.

Johnson's first official action was to issue a proclamation, on March 18, assuring the people that he came as a peacemaker, not as an avenger. He recited the ruin and disorder surrounding them —the state government abdicated, the legislature as good as dissolved, the judiciary in abeyance—and he begged all loyal citizens to join with him in restoring orderly government. No harsh reprisals need be feared. "Those who through the dark and weary nights of the rebellion have retained their allegiance to the federal government will be honored. The erring and misguided will be welcomed on their return." Though it might become necessary to "punish intelligent and conscious treason in high places," to all who "in private, unofficial capacity have assumed an attitude of hostility to the government," an offer of "full and complete amnesty" was extended.

The reaction to this olive branch was anxiously awaited.

After an interval of two days, the fugitive legislature at Memphis seemed to throw in the sponge: it adjourned *sine die*. Governor Harris faded into Mississippi, taking the state's treasure with him. In a Parthian shot, he said perhaps the bitterest thing that ever was said about Andrew Johnson:

"If Andy Johnson were a snake, he would hide in the grass and bite the heels of rich men's children."

Nevertheless, the departure of Harris left Johnson the only governor in the field.

The Confederate cause in the Western theater suffered reverse after reverse during April, and this strengthened Johnson's position. On the 6th and 7th, Grant won the Battle of Shiloh—barely, it is true; but Albert Sidney Johnston was killed, and the Confederate army drew back under Beauregard to Corinth, in Mississippi, clear out of Tennessee. On April 8, federals under General John Pope captured Island No. 10 in the Mississippi, and compelled rebel forces to pull out of western Kentucky. On April 24, Admiral Farragut forced the mouth of the Mississippi, and the next day Union troops, under that brassbound man of talent and presumptuousness, General Ben Butler, occupied New Orleans. By the end of April, all Tennessee had been rid of Confederates except in the eastern end of the state, where General E. Kirby Smith was enforcing martial law.

One of Kirby Smith's actions had been to order expelled the families of Union men who had fled to the North, with special attention paid to the families of Johnson, Maynard, and Brownlow. These were given thirty-six hours to clear out.

On April 24, Eliza Johnson, too ill to travel, informed General Smith, "I cannot comply with the requirement," and the provost marshal at Knoxville, Colonel William M. Churchwell, extended the time limit. In the end, the order against Mrs. Johnson was held up for months; but no reprieve was allowed to the Maynards and Brownlows. Eventually they got through to the North, with what baggage they could carry.

Maynard had been named state Attorney General by Governor Johnson, but he remained in Washington, trying to get help to East Tennessee. Unionists there, he wrote the governor, were "cursing Johnson and Maynard for having utterly neglected them. O heaven, if they only knew what we know, they would curse, but not us. Perhaps it is better that they should blame us than their government."

The difficulty, as Johnson and Maynard saw it, was the obstinacy of the generals, whose strategic plans relegated East Tennessee to minor consideration. The need for an immediate invasion of that area was the topic of a running dispute between the military and the governor, and when Johnson took his complaints to the White House, he was sustained by President Lincoln and Secretary of War Stanton.

Johnson was especially outraged when the Minnesota regiments guarding Nashville were ordered south to Corinth, where General Henry Wager Halleck was inching his way towards Beauregard's emplacements. The effect of ordering away these troops, Johnson told Maynard, "is visible on the face of every secessionist . . . My understanding was that I was sent here to accomplish a certain purpose. If the means are withheld, it is better to desist from any further effort."

Lincoln intervened, and Halleck modified the order, conceding that there was a political as well as a military aspect to the operations in Tennessee. In expectation of soon bagging Beauregard, Halleck reassured Johnson:

"East Tennessee will very soon be attended to. We must drive off the main body of the enemy before we can approach his other corps. The head must be attended to and the toenails afterwards. Everything is working well."

But things were not working well. Beauregard got away, leaving Halleck with a hollow victory, and East Tennessee was not relieved.

In April Johnson reopened the county courts in the parts of Middle Tennessee that were controlled by the army. Trade revived somewhat when Northern cotton buyers swarmed after the army, bringing in money. Unionist meetings were organized in the area, and Johnson addressed them in a conciliatory vein. Apparently disillusionment with the faltering Confederate cause was gaining headway. Impatient to make a start on civil restoration, the governor decided to risk an election for a judge of the circuit court of the Nashville district. Lincoln had high hopes of the outcome, and his disappointment was severe when a man with an open record of disloyalty received a majority of the votes. Observing the letter of the law, Johnson issued a commission to the winner, then arrested him and appointed the defeated candidate to the vacancy. Chagrined by this setback, the governor became wary of duplicating the mistake.

This rebuff encouraged Nashville's disloyal population, which was extensive, to make Johnson feel their scorn by every means that malice could invent. A few homes of distinction opened their doors to the governor, but most of the city's elite remained hostile. He was subjected to snubs, pinpricks, and covert insults, and hampered by systematic noncooperation. Yet obstructive as the Southern sympathizers were, a greater obstacle for Johnson was the military establishment. In bitterness he turned to Lincoln for help:

"Petty jealousy and contest between commanding generals wholly incompetent to discharge the duties assigned to them have contributed more to the defeat and embarrassment of the government than all other causes combined. If I can be sustained in carrying out the objects of the administration in restoring Tennessee to her former status in the Union, and in not being dependent upon staff officers and brigadier generals, it can be accomplished in less than three months. I want a reply from the President."

Lincoln was tactful, but backed up Johnson; and so, without tact, did the Secretary of War. But military requirements were bound to take precedence over the civil administration as long as the enemy remained menacing. Friction between two executive staffs in Tennessee would have been certain even if good will had animated both parties, and it did not. The military chiefs were tenacious of their prerogatives, and Johnson stubbornly resisted encroachment upon his.

A further source of frustration for the governor was contained in the mass of all but unanswerable mail that poured across his desk. A soldier from East Tennessee, sick and despondent, relayed bits of gossip about home folks whom they both knew, and implored the governor to come to their rescue. Troubled mothers of Tennesseans who were held prisoners of war at Camp Douglas, in Illinois, pleaded with the governor to keep them from being exchanged and sent back South. They had been forced into the rebel ranks, although they really wanted to serve the Union. In countless cases, Johnson knew this was true; but the problem was one for the military to act upon; he could only advise.

There were letters daily from people inside the rebel lines, giving tips on troop movements and advising whom to trust; but were these informants trustworthy? There were appeals from destitute refugees who needed everything except faith; that they had preserved in spite of all.

These reachings-out for sympathy harrowed the governor, and the thought of the accumulated suffering produced and being prolonged by this terrible war drove him to feverish activity. By temperament a man of one purpose at a time, his whole being became absorbed in the task of regenerating his state, bringing Tennessee back into its proper, peaceful position in the Union, and ending the carnage. Under the pressures beating upon him a man of less durable fiber and less stubbornness might have cracked, but Johnson held firm.

Threats against his life were of common occurrence. They came from far and near. A well-wisher in Boston warned of danger that might be expected "from the direction of Augusta, Georgia." A friend in Knoxville smuggled out word of the departure from there of three rowdies who had announced their intention of assassinating "the traitor Andy."

His multifariousness extended into any needful field. He reopened post offices where service had ceased, hurried along the soldiers' mail, helped his son Robert procure horses and equipment for the latter's regiment in Kentucky; he acted as Lincoln's adviser on arrests and pardons; he issued passes to men and women having legitimate business across the lines; he organized the care of hundreds of runaway Negro slaves who were wandering about the city; he spurred the recruiting of troops, and conferred constantly with Washington and the governors of Ohio, Indiana, and Illinois on problems of mutual defense. And unremittingly he fought against the obstruction offered by the petty brass of the army.

Covert enemies of the government had to be ferreted out and rendered harmless. The mayor and city council of Nashville refused to take the oath of allegiance, whereupon Governor Johnson arrested them and appointed reliable replacements. Retribution was meted out to preachers whom Johnson found "praying up the rebellion." Seven such pulpit agitators he peremptorily jailed, with orders that they be allowed no visitors to lionize them, or receive dainties sent in by their women parishioners.

"These assumed ministers of Christ," he wrote, "have done more to poison and corrupt the female mind of this community than all others."

When the recalcitrant parsons (except one, who was ill) were shipped to a prison camp in Kentucky, and there got up a petition alleging that they were being held without charges, Johnson exploded. They certainly had been told, "in express and distinct terms," he answered, that they had been seized "not as ministers of the Gospel," but as advocates of treason.

"I concur with you most fully," he informed the general in charge of the batch, "in regard to expelling and putting to the sword all traitors who continue to occupy a hostile attitude to the government. There must be a vigorous and efficient prosecution of this war. The burdens and penalties resulting from it must be made to rest upon the rebels, and they to feel it. *Treason must be made odious, traitors punished and impoverished.*"

Still no definite word came through regarding his wife and children, isolated behind the Confederate lines. "No news from home," Robert telegraphed repeatedly in answer to his father's anxious instructions: "If your mother and Charles get through, telegraph me immediately." Robert was at Cumberland Gap, where most of the refugees from East Tennessee were arriving. Although the main Confederate army had been pushed out of the state, cavalry raiders under the debonair John Hunt Morgan and more fearsome General Nathan Bedford Forrest were roaming the counties. Their sudden attacks could not be guarded against; they struck and vanished, terrorizing Union sympathizers, robbing and pillaging, immune because they found friends everywhere. In their shadow roved guerrillas, mere outlaws, who cruelly plundered and murdered without allegiance to either side.

Persisting in his efforts to reawaken Union loyalty in the population of Middle Tennessee, the governor resorted to his proven powers as a stump speaker. On May 24 he spoke at Murfreesboro, a center of secessionist sentiment. A reporter, Samuel R. Glenn, former editor of a Boston paper, now the *New York Herald*'s Washington correspondent, was on hand; he never forgot the scene.

In front of the courthouse a few boards laid across barrels made a platform. Edmund Cooper, Johnson's confidential secretary, spoke first.

"The audience," said Glenn, "was a queer mixture of 'bluecoats'

and 'butternuts' [Northern and Southern sympathizers]. The latter stood listlessly inside the railing of the courthouse yard, and
even the spirited . . . remarks of Mr. Cooper could not arouse
them . . . But as Governor Johnson proceeded, they began to
exhibit more interest and attention." He spoke for three hours,
and "it was a sight to observe the sway he seemed to have over
them . . . Now they lent silent and immovable attention; again . . .
they would burst into a laugh, and applaud with . . . 'Good for
Andy!' 'That's the talk!' etc., and when he particularly alluded to
his sufferings and to those of others, and to the horrors that encompassed a continuance of the rebellion, tears were shed by
more than one stout and stalwart Tennessean."

But the crowd was sparse. After the meeting the governor and
his party were entertained at the nearby home of a Unionist;
there was tea, with strawberries and cream, and music in the
evening. After Johnson had gone to bed, an alarm was given
about an attempt to seize the governor: six hundred men, said to
be Morgan's, were reported to be converging on the house. A
regiment of Union troops was brought hastily from the town to
defend the house, but no attack ensued.

The next afternoon, the bodies of several Union men, murdered
by guerrillas just outside Murfreesboro, were brought into town,
and the Union commander urged Johnson not to take the train to
Nashville that evening, for it was sure to be attacked.

Thanking the colonel for his solicitude, Johnson said, "My duty
calls me to Nashville and I am going there tonight."

Some of the other passengers were undecided, and a number
stayed behind; the rest elected to "stick with Andy Johnson," and
boarded the train. The reporter Glenn saw the governor take his
seat "looking as calm and unconcerned as if going to a picnic."
Night was closing in; it was a thirty-mile trip, and guerrillas were
all around. "Governor Johnson exhibited no signs whatever of
alarm. He conversed as pleasantly and composedly as he ever did.
He had made up his mind to one thing—never to be taken alive
by the rebels."

The train reached Nashville safely, although the rebels tore up
the tracks behind it.

The matter of the murdered Union men received the governor's attention immediately. He wired to the colonel at Murfreesboro:

"You will arrest as many persons as you in your judgment may believe will have a proper effect upon the spirit of insubordination [that] seems to prevail in that community . . . Act out your judgment and you will be sustained . . . Teach them a lesson that they will not forget."

This procedure he submitted to Lincoln for confirmation, together with a proposal to arrest "seventy vile secessionists" and offer them in exchange for seventy East Tennesseans who were being held imprisoned and maltreated at Mobile. If the exchange should be refused, let the seventy be sent South with the warning that if they reappeared inside the Union lines, they would be dealt with as spies.

"Does this meet your approval?" Johnson asked the White House. "It is no punishment now to send secessionists North. In most instances they would rather go to the infernal regions than to be sent South at this time."

Lincoln wired back, "I certainly do not disapprove," and Stanton added his own hearty concurrence.

Undaunted by the near squeak at Murfreesboro, Johnson risked other forays to speaking dates in the central portion of the state. At Columbia, in the heart of the patrician bluegrass country, he addressed a slim crowd from the stump of a large tree. On June 7 he spoke at Shelbyville, where some remains of Unionist sentiment still flickered, and drew a crowd of nearly four hundred. This was the largest turnout to date, and he was encouraged. There were constant guerrilla alarms and reports of schemes to waylay him, but seemingly miraculously he escaped each time.

Then the situation changed when a subordinate of Buell's, who was pushing Bragg in northern Alabama, got into trouble and called for help. In rushing reinforcements, Buell almost stripped Nashville, and the quarrel between the military and civil leaders flared dangerously, Johnson complaining to Lincoln and Buell retorting furiously that his disposition of troops was necessary to hold Middle Tennessee—an objective that he believed to be of "far greater moment than the gratification of Governor Johnson, whose views upon the matter are absurd."

Then in July Forrest lunged towards Nashville, and Morgan

swept north of the city and cut the rail connection with Louisville. On July 3 Forrest captured Lebanon, and on July 13 Murfreesboro. Panic gripped the capital. On the night of July 21 the
streets of Nashville were barricaded in expectation of an attack.
Johnson supervised the preparations, and embroiled himself further with Buell and Halleck. In a stream of telegrams to Washington he cast doubt on their bravery and hinted at a secret understanding with the enemy. The generals reacted to this with
acerbity, and Lincoln was forced to use all his tactfulness to calm
both sides. To Halleck the President wired: "The governor is a
true and valuable man—indispensable to us in Tennessee." Halleck grudgingly conceded that such was the case; Buell did not.

On July 15, Forrest was only six miles outside Nashville, and in
response to Johnson's frantic pleading several regiments were returned to the city.

On the 16th, Glenn, the news man, recorded in the diary he
was keeping:

"Three respectable Union men were hanged twenty-five miles
from Nashville yesterday for entertaining men engaged in con-
structing telegraph lines."

Three days later he set down:

"Governor Johnson has been in constant consultation . . . preparing for the defense of the city."

On July 23 Glenn recorded:

"On duty with Governor Johnson and staff for four consecutive
nights at the Capitol, anticipating an attack . . . [Forrest's] path
tonight is lighted by the burning houses of Union people. A courier reported him at 4 o'clock this morning within 1½ miles of
Nashville. Slept an hour or two during the night in the Capitol,
with the back of a chair for a pillow . . . Governor Johnson slept
several hours during the night . . . quietly . . ."

The calmness of the governor's slumber was remarkable because during those hours his ultimatum was being considered at
Forrest's headquarters. Several days before, he had called in some
of the more prominent Southern sympathizers and told them to
get word to the Confederate commander (he was sure they had
means of communicating with the rebels) that rather than let
Nashville be taken, he would burn it to the ground. Glenn's diary

related the sequel. On the day after the midnight siesta, the entry read:

"The enemy have withdrawn from our front, and departed in haste, frightened off, no doubt, by Governor Johnson's declaration that the first shot fired at the capital would be the signal for the demolition of the houses of every prominent secessionist in town. They know him to be a man who will keep his word. It has been made known that at an inteview between Forrest and some secessionists at The Hermitage . . . Forrest was implored not to attempt to take the city, as it would inevitably involve the destruction of their property . . . Forrest has fallen back to Carthage."

For the time being, Nashville had been saved, and the Stars and Stripes still waved over the Capitol of Tennessee.

Almost as a reward, came a message containing some good news from Robert Johnson, at Cumberland Gap:

"Boys just in from Greeneville. Mother's health improving. Rebels have our house for barracks."

But no further word arrived, and the governor's worry deepened.

Commendation of Johnson's conduct came from Washington. Maynard wrote that the President had expressed himself "gratified in the highest degree . . . Your administration so far has commended the approval, I might add the admiration, of the whole country."

Even more significantly, Schuyler Colfax, Speaker of the House of Representatives, in a letter seeking Johnson's help in a bid for reelection, reported that "the President has told me twice that while he has had troublesome questions to settle from other military governors and officers, as in North Carolina, New Orleans, and so forth, 'Andy Johnson has never embarrassed me in the slightest degree.' You enjoy his fullest confidence, as you so rightly deserve."

That the pliant Colfax ("Smiler" was his nickname), an extreme Republican, should consider the endorsement of Andrew Johnson an asset indicated the esteem in which the Tennessean was held. Before leaving Washington, Johnson had done Ben Wade a political service by urging the Democrats of Ohio to support the senator in his campaign for a third term—to the bewilderment of Ohio's Democrats, but to Wade's advantage.

Among the majority of the people of his own rebellious state, however, Johnson's stock was low.

Then in August the situation changed again, precluding any fresh step on Johnson's part towards restoring civil government. General Bragg struck north from Alabama, and simultaneously Kirby Smith invaded Kentucky from East Tennessee. Buell became confused, uncertain what objective the two-pronged offensive was aimed at. Gradually it became apparent that the target was Louisville, four hundred miles north of Nashville, and to save that important center from capture Buell decided to abandon Nashville and send every available man north on the double in a race to reach Louisville first. On August 21 he notified Governor Johnson that strategic considerations were forcing him to bypass Nashville, and the governor had better pull out with the army.

Johnson was dumbfounded. Glenn, the reporter, again told the story in his diary. When the first rumor of Buell's decision reached Johnson, the governor exclaimed:

" 'What, evacuate Nashville and leave our Union friends to the mercy of these infernal hell-hounds? Why, there is not a secessionist in town who would not laugh to see every Union man shot down in cold blood by rebel soldiers if they come here!' The governor protests against an evacuation or a surrender without a fight. He would destroy the city rather than leave it to the enemy. General [George] Thomas arrives at a critical period and takes command. He sustains Governor Johnson, and Nashville is neither evacuated nor destroyed.

"Thus for the second time Governor Johnson [has] saved the city by his . . . firmness and indomitable decision of character. Not only has he again saved the city, but the lives of hundreds of Union men and millions of government property. Union refugees in the most sickening plight are arriving from the South. They report the most horrible outrages by guerrillas."

In a long, bitter letter to Lincoln, Johnson poured out his accumulated dislike of Buell, saying that the general never intended to relieve East Tennessee, and cared for nothing but his own safety, using the army as "a kind of bodyguard." Worse still:

"General Buell is very popular with the rebels and the impression is that he is more partial to them than to Union men, and that he favors the establishment of a Southern Confederacy. [If he] had designed to do so, he could not have laid down or pursued a policy that would have been more successful in the accomplishment of these objects . . . East Tennessee seems doomed . . . May God save my country from some of the generals that have been conducting this war!"

That prayer Lincoln, beset by his own troubles with McClellan and his "slows," and other laggard generals who seemed disinclined to fight, might have echoed.

There was prayer in Nashville. On the day Buell decided to abandon the city, Granville Moody, a Methodist evangelist, arrived there. Going to the Capitol, Moody asked:

"Well, governor, how are matters going?"

"Going? Moody, we are sold! Buell has resolved to evacuate, and he is requesting me to leave also. But I am staying."

Well, responded Moody, after a moment's reflection, he thought he would stay with Andy. "I have faith in God that He will deliver us from falling into the hands of the enemy."

"I am glad to hear you talk of faith in God," said Johnson. Then, "Moody, can you pray?"

There was none more eloquent, and in a moment governor and evangelist were on their knees, on opposite sides of the room, and Moody was praying with fervor. "Amen!" "Amen!" responded the governor. Gradually he inched his way across the room to Moody's side, and throwing his arms around the preacher's neck, cried loudly, "Amen! Amen! God, hear Moody's prayer!"

When the men arose, Johnson seemed fortified.

"Moody," he said, "I feel better. I believe that God Almighty sent you here, and that Nashville will be saved. That prayer has been answered. I feel it. I know it. Buell can go. I stay right here."

The talk shifted to immediate necessities, but suddenly Johnson interrupted.

"Moody," he said sternly, "I don't want you to think that I have become religious because I asked you to pray. But Moody, there is one thing that I do believe: I believe in Almighty God; and I also believe in the Bible; and I say, *I'll be damned if Nashville shall be surrendered!*"

In that grim spirit he set about fulfilling the divine plan.

FOURTEEN

THE SIEGE OF NASHVILLE

DENIED sufficient troops, denied adequate supplies, denied even the moral support of Buell's encouragement, Johnson's resolve to hold Nashville indeed seemed hopeless. For weeks Confederate raiders had been spreading alarm. Generals Morgan and Forrest were reported to be closing in on the city with several thousand men, and Morgan was said to have remarked that if he only captured Andy Johnson, he would take a chance on Nashville's being destroyed. Reporter Glenn noted that the elusive cavalry leader was "the terror of the country, and, it is said, has recently been in Nashville, disguised. He is the enemy most talked of now, and has many warm sympathizers here."

The capture of Union couriers within a few miles of the city was frequent, while Buell was heading four hundred miles north; not, in Glenn's words, "because an enemy pressed him in front, but because Bragg has flanked him . . . Governor Johnson deplores this wholesale desertion of the country."

By September 15 Nashville was under siege by Forrest. Connections with the outside world were cut off, and the *Herald* reporter, caught inside the beleaguered city, noted on September 30:

"We are surrounded by the enemy. Things look gloomy. The work of fortifying goes on briskly, and if the enemy gives us two weeks more we can defy them."

Johnson had a small military force, part of it his expanded governor's guard, under his direct command. In addition, every Unionist willing to fight was given some post to man or task to perform.

On October 8, Glenn jotted down:

"No communications for a month. Parties attempt to leave in flatboats and canoes, but are captured by guerrillas before they get fairly out of the city. Rations getting scarce. People getting uneasy. Hotels closed for want of supplies. Correspondence captured by guerrillas. No one writing. Governor Johnson takes everything coolly."

Four days later he reported:

"Quite a sensation has been produced by the arrival in Nashville of Governor Johnson's family, after incurring and escaping numerous perils while making their exodus from East Tennessee."

The party included Eliza Johnson, eight-year-old Andrew, Jr. ("Frank"), the Stovers and their three small children, and Charles Johnson. Just this moment, with Nashville invested and the head of the family in imminent peril, the Confederate authorities had chosen to expel the brood. On September 20, Mrs. Johnson had been served with notice that arrangements for their departure had been made, and although she was far from well, and little Frank was showing signs of having contracted consumption, she marshaled the group and they set out. A few miles outside of town they were overtaken by an order to return. Straightening out this tangle consumed one day. Then they started again, and after a long, torturous ride reached Murfreesboro, where General Forrest refused to let them proceed. Night had fallen, and the group trudged from house to house seeking shelter. One woman at last consented to let them come in, on the condition that they leave at dawn.

The next day they were ordered back fifty miles to Tullahoma. There a telegram was waiting, countermanding the retreat and authorizing them to go forward. For this reprieve they were indebted to Isham G. Harris and Andrew Ewing, both onetime friends of the Johnsons, who had wired to Richmond and obtained a peremptory order to let the party pass. Nightfall prevented immediate compliance, and camp was made in a vacant house beside the railroad tracks. Forehandedly, Eliza had brought candles and matches, and there were scraps of food for the children; otherwise they would have passed the night hungry and in darkness. As things were, they suffered from the cold.

The next morning they set out again, running through numerous blockades, challenged every few miles, and constantly subjected to abusive scrutiny, and the men to threats. Mrs. Johnson was the mainstay of the party, and insisted that they push forward in spite of obstacles. On October 12, at long last, they entered Nashville.

"The great joy of this long and sorrowfully separated family may be imagined. I shall not attempt to describe it," commented Glenn. "Even the governor's Roman sternness was overcome, and he wept tears of thankfulness."

One daughter, Martha, was still marooned in Greeneville with her husband, Judge Patterson, and their two children.

With his family sharing the danger, Johnson's will to defend the city to the utmost was strengthened, and on October 21 Glenn recorded:

"Days, weeks, nay months roll round, and there seems to be no change for the better in this important city . . . Our supplies become exhausted. Deprived of almost all articles of luxury and even comfort, and subject to the ill-disguised sneers and taunts of Union-haters, our lot is a hard one."

Those in the city did not know that relief was on the way. Buell had succeeded in reaching Louisville before the Confederates, and then turning on the invading force, had defeated them at Perryville, Kentucky, on October 8. Stung by accusations of treasonable intent, Buell then demanded a court of inquiry, and on October 24 he was replaced by General William S. Rosecrans, who immediately pushed southwards toward Nashville.

As the siege tightened, the indomitability of Governor Johnson inspired the city's defenders. General John C. Breckinridge (the same who had been Vice-President, and was now a Confederate commander) was reported to be close at hand with fifty thousand men, and Forrest was said to have sworn that he would have Nashville at any cost.

"But those in the confidence of Governor Johnson," Glenn wrote, "know that the enemy, if they should capture the city, will achieve an empty triumph amid blackened and crumbling ruins. The coolness and calmness of the governor amid these trying scenes are beyond all praise. He does all he can to preserve order; but notwithstanding this, midnight assassinations are frequent. There were six murders one night recently."

Early in November, alerted that Rosecrans was approaching,

the Confederates launched an attack. Glenn reported on November 4:

"Great activity prevails in the city. Governor Johnson [and his military aides] are on duty night and day in the governor's room . . . All hands are engaged in cleaning firearms, sharpening cutlasses, etc. Four Rodman guns have been placed in position to defend the Capitol, which is also protected by lines of earthworks and breastworks of cotton bales. The Capitol will be defended to the last extremity. The cool and determined demeanor of Governor Johnson is the admiration of all."

The next day, Forrest and Morgan attacked at four points. The governor and his staff took position in the cupola of the Capitol, where they could observe the battle two miles away. Once it appeared that the Union line had been smashed and the men were fleeing back into the city. At this crisis, Johnson looked around and said ("in the forcible manner he is accustomed to use when he means a thing"):

"I am no military man, but anyone who talks of surrendering I will shoot!"

The apparent repulse, however, was a feint; the Union line wheeled about and drove the rebels before them. The rout was decisive, and with Rosecrans near, the Confederates withdrew. On November 14 Rosecrans entered the city and the siege was ended.

"Thus was raised the siege of Nashville, and the city for the third time saved by the inflexible firmness of Governor Johnson, aided by the bayonets of the flower of American soldiery," Glenn concluded his narrative.

The ordeal had deepened the governor's detestation of war, and he declined to accept military honors. The chief engineer of the defending forces, in naming the fortifications hastily thrown up, had called the bastion at the Capitol "Fort Johnson." The governor asked that the name be changed. In a letter to the officer in charge—a letter not intended for public perusal, and in fact not published until nearly a century later—he wrote that while appreciative of the compliment intended, he merited it neither as a citizen nor as a public man. Tennessee, he said, had given him "every honor that a state can confer upon one of her citizens, and in this the measure of my ambition has now been fulfilled.

"I am certainly not entitled to [the honor] for any military service or prowess," he went on. "I had rather an inquiring public would ask why my name was *not* given than why it was." Then, in an aside: "It is not safe at all times . . . to name children, cities, forts, after the living, for the bestowal is often regretted and repented.

"War is not the natural element of my mind . . . For my part, I would rather wear upon my garment the dust of the field and the dinge of the shop as badges of the pursuits of peace, than all the insignia of honorable and glorious war . . . I feel more than flattered at the compliment conferred, but a consciousness of duty performed is my present remuneration; and the only reward I ask in the future is the lowly inscription of my name with those who loved and toiled for the people."

The governor's mood seemed to have undergone a change with the passing of the immediate crisis, for he instructed his subordinates to try kindliness in dealing with Southern sympathizers, in spite of the latter's snubs and occasional downright insolence. Towards "Secesh" women especially he urged forbearance. Eliza's influence may have brought about this softer policy, for she had always been able to control him when in a passion. Her hand on his shoulder, and the single word, "Andy!" would instantly calm him. In his files the governor had copies of General Ben Butler's notorious General Order No. 28, which had raised a hullabaloo in New Orleans—the order stating that any lady showing contempt for Union soldiers would be considered "a woman of the town plying her avocation," and treated accordingly. The outcry against this "brutality" had earned the general his sobriquet, "Beast Butler," but the order produced the desired results. Johnson never made use of such measures, but on the contrary did his best to placate the spitfires of Nashville.

A rich widow whose plantation lay near Franklin, south of the city, wanted a permit to carry out six barrels of salt, a scarce commodity in the Confederacy. She got the permit, and a couple of weeks later applied for permission to take out twelve barrels, explaining that she had nearly a hundred slaves to feed and was salting down meat for them.

The widow was a renowned beauty; but despite her loveliness, Johnson held her to six barrels, suggesting to his secretary that the lady be told gently that she would not be obliged to feed her slaves much longer. The secretary was more susceptible, surreptitiously wrote out *two* permits, for six barrels each, and was rewarded with a smile.

Another incident that brought out Johnson's less severe side occurred at the St. Cloud Hotel, where the governor boarded. The hotel was kept by a Union man, whose daughter, Laura, pretty and twenty, was an uncompromising rebel. When she spat on Union officers from the hotel porch, the provost marshal arrested her.

Explaining to the governor, he said that he had hated to make the arrest on account of Laura's father, and also because of the governor.

"I told her that she ought to behave herself while you were a guest in the hotel," the officer complained, "but she defied you, and said she would dance on your grave."

"Oh, you mustn't mind these little rebels," Johnson replied. "There is no harm in Laura. Dance on my grave, will she? She'll plant flowers instead. I'll take care of her. Let her go."

Laura was released, and within a year she became the wife of a captain in the Union army.

FIFTEEN

TIDES OF WAR AND POLITICS

THE year 1863 had opened with a Union gain of sorts in the West, and a Union defeat in the East. In Virginia, General Burnside's veterans, bloodily repulsed at Fredericksburg, floundered to nowhere in the celebrated "Mud March" that brought his Virginia command to an end. In Tennessee, General Rosecrans, after having relieved Nashville, pursued Bragg and met him in an indecisive battle at Stone River (Murfreesboro). Union forces thus were put a bit deeper into central Tennessee; but the drawn battle proved so costly to both antagonists that they were forced to take a lull of several months. Meanwhile, in the extreme west of the state, and farther south in Mississippi, General Grant was trying method after method in his so far unsuccessful attempt to knock out the Confederate fortress at Vicksburg.

Governor Johnson had met the hero of Donelson shortly after Shiloh, at a moment when Grant was contemplating resigning from the army. Halleck had supplanted him, and W. T. Sherman had a hard time persuading him not to throw up his commission in disgust.

Had Grant yielded to that impulse, it would have been for him a second inglorious close of his military career. The first had occurred in 1854 on the Pacific coast, where he had been assigned after the Mexican War. The boredom of garrison life, the monotony and loneliness resulting from separation from his family, and the persistent dreariness of the surroundings had driven him to heavy drinking, and his commanding officer had accepted his resignation with relief.

In 1854, by contrast, Andrew Johnson already had been governor of Tennessee, and since then he had served in the United States Senate and become a national figure.

Grant, until the war, had shown consistent incapacity to cope with every occupation he had tried, whether farming or clerking in his father's store. Now Johnson, military governor of Tennessee, looked over the apparent flash-in-the-pan general and was impressed with the man's "air of obstinate determination." That quality was well developed in Johnson, too. A contest between their two wills might become a contest of bulldogs.

With armies marching and countermarching through Tennessee, and Morgan's raiders keeping even the relatively pacified counties stirred up, no progress was possible towards restoring civil government. In almost daily communication with President Lincoln, Johnson took out his frustrations, and Lincoln sympathized.

The President was having troubles, also, with his political opposition, the radicals in Congress. Impatient to apply their cure-all for the miseries of the war—universal freeing of the slaves—they had jockeyed the President into reluctant acceptance of their thesis that emancipation must go hand in hand with military conquest. He had tried to stave off interference with slavery, fearing the effect upon the critical border states, and believing that emancipation, if carried out suddenly, would work immense hardship on the Negroes as well as on the white population of the slave states. He had proposed gradual, compensated emancipation, and at one point Thaddeus Stevens had offered to go along with the payment of compensation to loyal slaveholders, though nothing to rebels. Not that Stevens would concede that compensation was right in principle, but he was ready to support it as politic, if the slaveholders would agree. The slaveholders would not, and on September 22, 1862, directly after the battle of Antietam, Lincoln had issued his preliminary proclamation warning that emancipation would be imposed upon the rebellious states. On January 1, 1863, he promulgated the final proclamation.

The measure did not apply to all slaves in the country, but only to those in the seceded states. Kentucky, Maryland, Missouri, for instance, were not affected; nor were Tennessee and portions of Virginia and Louisiana that the Union armies already controlled. Lincoln's purpose was to disrupt the Southern economy more than to liberate the Negroes, and the action was based on a rather strained interpretation of the President's wartime powers as commander-in-chief. Lincoln himself doubted whether the proclamation could withstand a constitutional test, upon the return of peace.

The effect on the Republican party had been damaging. The radicals were contemptuous of the halfway measure, and in the 1862 autumn elections the Democrats had made extraordinary gains in most of the free states. They had captured Illinois and New York outright, elected a Democratic legislature in Ohio, and wrested eight seats in Congress from Indiana's Republicans. But the border states had repaid Lincoln for his placative policy toward them, the entire tier, from Missouri to Delaware, going strongly Republican.

In Tennessee the administration's emancipation policy split the ranks of Unionists, and confronted Johnson with a determined opposition within the minority that had supported him at the start of his military governorship. Tennessee's exemption from the proclamation had been at his request, for while he recognized that slavery would have to go, he wished his state to take the step voluntarily. To do that was impossible until a government should be installed; meanwhile, he made known his views on the vexing problem of the Negro. He put his stand plainly:

"I am for a government based on and ruled by industrious, free white citizens, and conducted in conformity with their wants, and not a slave aristocracy. I am for this government above all earthly possessions, and if it perish I do not want to survive it. I am for it though slavery be struck from existence and Africa be swept from the balance of the world. . . . If you persist in forcing this issue of slavery against the government, I say, in the face of heaven, give me my government and let the Negro go!"

As for the freed Negro's new relation to society, that must be governed by the same laws that governed others.

"Political freedom means the liberty to work and at the same time to enjoy the products of one's labor. If he [the Negro] can rise by his own energies, in the name of God, let him rise!"

As an auxiliary step in the integration process, Johnson considered the advisability of raising Negro troops. This was one of the demands the radicals were making, and one strenuously opposed by the conservatives.

Lincoln was pleased when the report reached him.

"I am told that you have at least thought of raising a Negro military force," he wired the governor. "In my opinion the country needs no specific thing so much as some man of your ability and position, to go to this work. When I speak of your position, I mean that of an eminent citizen of a slave state, and himself a slaveholder."

Putting "fifty thousand armed and drilled black soldiers on the banks of the Mississippi" would end the rebellion at once, Lincoln believed.

Clashes between the civil and military authorities aborted this scheme. When the army arrogated to itself control of the recruiting, Johnson shot angry protests to Stanton, and was sustained. "Upon your judgment," Stanton wired back, "the [War] Department relies, in respect to whatever relates to the people, whether white or black, bond or free." The disagreements remaining unresolved, recruiting halted.

General Rosecrans ran afoul of the governor over the leaking of war plans. The *Nashville Daily Union* was the organ of the administration, and when a Louisville paper published some highly sensitive information about Union troop movements, Rosecrans flared out at what he charged had been the indiscretion, if nothing worse, of a *Union* reporter.

"For God's sake stop that!" he lectured the governor. "Such information is the very worst injury that a spy could inflict. I would give a thousand dollars to know as much of the rebels."

The governor on his side had complaints against Rosecrans. A "pet" of the general, a Colonel Truesdale, chief of the army police, was spreading bitterness by ruthless confiscations, and bribery was rumored. Rosecrans stood by his man; whereupon Johnson denounced Truesdale as "a base and unmitigated Jesuitical parasite . . . I have refused and rejected the applications for release of fifty convicts, confined in the cells of our state prison, who are better and more worthy men than he is."

Johnson won that round, and General Halleck, now in supreme command at Washington, instructed Rosecrans "not to interfere with the loyal officials of the state government, except in cases of urgent and pressing necessity." Rosecrans wisely gave in.

During the siege of Nashville, a reporter for the *Washington Chronicle* had managed to slip through the rebel lines with confidential messages for the owner of the *Chronicle*, John W. Forney, Secretary of the Senate. Forney was deep in the political intrigues of the capital, and during the Buchanan administration he had formed a working alliance with Johnson in the Senate.

The reporter, Benjamin C. Truman, reached Washington safely, and wrote back a full account of his reception by Lincoln and Stanton, to whom he had unfolded the desperate situation in Tennessee.

"Well, I had a long conversation with Mr. Forney," Truman wrote. "I gave him a detailed account of matters . . . told him how your authority had been put to nought by everybody . . . We went to see the President today. At first he seemed to be disposed to be more than indifferent, when Mr. Forney jumped up and told him that any request of yours should be promptly acceded to. Mr. Lincoln himself then took the [reports], endorsed them and wrote me a letter to Mr. Stanton and Gen. Halleck."

The President's endorsement on the Johnson reports ran: "Please give the enclosed papers and statements of the bearer immediate notice. Gov. Johnson is our great reliance in Tennessee."

"If I had not seen Mr. Forney I would have made out bad with the President," Truman continued. "Mr. Forney told me that Stanton was gruff, etc., but told me to be brief, and touch on all subjects, and in a semi-authoritative manner. I did so, and he treated me well . . . The President wouldn't listen to me about the railroad."

The railroad was a line that Johnson proposed to build connecting Nashville with the Tennessee River at Johnsonville, to facilitate the transport of supplies; later he did obtain Stanton's endorsement of the project, and carried it through, only to have the docks at Johnsonville and an immense quality of stores in transit wiped out by Forrest.

With White House backing, the governor, at the start of 1863, adopted a more rigid attitude towards disloyalists who resisted all inducements to recant. Confiscation of the property of disloyal persons to compensate loyalists for losses inflicted by rebel raiders was decreed. The governor's order to field commanders read:

"Where secessionists have robbed and plundered Union men of their property, you will out of the property of secessionists compensate them to the full extent of the losses and damage sustained. In making arrests, you will make them to the extent that the public interest requires, let them be many or few."

In May, with the purpose of stopping the maltreatment of Unionists and their families by enemy cavalry, the governor issued a proclamation directing that in every case where a Unionist was molested, five or more of the most prominent rebels in the vicinity should be imprisoned "or otherwise dealt with"; and whenever property was taken or destroyed, the victims should be reimbursed out of the property of those in the vicinity who had given "aid, comfort, information, or encouragement" to the raiders. This order was carried out sternly, and "Parson" Brownlow heard from refugees that the governor's "threat to send rebel families out of Middle Tennessee, if other Union families were sent out of East Tennessee," had halted the deportations.

At Johnson's order, suspected disloyalists who refused to take the oath of allegiance were shipped to Northern prisons. Again and again the refrain occurred in his correspondence with Stanton and others, that foes of the government "must be made to feel the weight and ravages of the war they have brought upon the country; *treason must be made odious and traitors impoverished.*" The *Nashville Union* explained the governor's new policy as a determination "to draw a line between [the government's] friends and its enemies, and give protection where it finds allegiance."

With all his anxieties over public affairs, Johnson was not spared family grief. Early in April Charles Johnson had been killed accidentally. Attempting to ride a fractious horse, he was thrown to the ground and his skull fractured. The undertaker's bill for "caskett for son, winding sheet, 8 yards of crape, and use of hearse" was paid by the grieving father on April 9.

The death of her best-loved child prostrated Eliza Johnson; she would never fully recover from the shock. Robert Johnson was doubly dear thereafter, yet he was causing his parents sorrow,

also. Although his regiment was not yet in service, he was pestering his father to get him a brigadier general's commission, with
authority to raise an entire brigade of cavalry. He was sure he
could do it, although thus far he had been unable to find saddles
for the men he had, and he had seen no service. Then he became
involved in a squabble with another Tennessee colonel, each accusing the other of luring away recruits, and one day the governor was startled to receive notification that his son was under
arrest. Daniel Stover, Mary's husband, intervened (Stover himself
had been commissioned a colonel, though he was so ill with
tuberculosis he could render little effective service), and between
his efforts and those of Brownlow, whose son was Robert's lieutenant colonel, the matter was straightened out and Robert was
released.

Then Robert made himself objectionable to his superiors by
presuming on influence and absenting himself without leave. To
top all, he was drinking heavily. High-spirited and convivial, he
indicated by his actions that sudden authority had gone to his
head.

In hope of recalling the young man to a sense of duty, Eliza
made a trip to Cincinnati, and the governor became further
alarmed when Robert sent back bulletins from there reading,
"Mother quite feeble," "Mother is very low." But she rallied, and
the bulletins changed to, "Mother improving," "Mother better."

Johnson himself cautioned Robert against associating with
dangerous companions (whom he named), and exhorted, "Do
your duty and all will end right." But though Robert did at length
bring his regiment into Tennessee, his irresponsible behavior continued, and Eliza's condition, after she returned to Nashville, was
perturbing. Little Frank was now definitely ill with tuberculosis,
and from time to time acute alarm was felt for him.

Johnson had taken time in the previous February to make a
tour of Indiana and Ohio, speaking at patriotic rallies. The people
in the North, who were being spared the agony gripping Tennessee, he urged to greater efforts in the war.

"Never ground your arms until the Constitution is enforced and
its enemies put down!" he exhorted. "I say you dishonor your-

selves and the graves of your offspring, if you let them sleep upon the confines of a Confederacy established upon the remains of this government!"

At last General Burnside, who had been transferred west, began preparations to enter East Tennessee, and in June, 1863, Johnson was called to Washington to assist in the planning. Lincoln expressed his concern about the delay in organizing civil government in Tennessee, but Johnson convinced him that as long as parts of the state were still in Confederate hands, and the remainder exposed to Morgan's and Forrest's depredations, elections were impossible. By now Johnson was resolved that when elections should be held, only loyal men should vote; both he and Lincoln dreaded that the result of any election should favor the Confederates and in effect stamp the military governor an interloper.

While in Washington, Johnson renewed his association with the Committee on the Conduct of the War, and helped to compile the interim report the committee was about to issue. The purpose of this report was to destroy the last trace of public confidence in General McClellan. The hatred of the committee for the former commander had become completely irrational, and their excitability was worked upon by the talk that the Democrats would make McClellan their candidate for the Presidency in 1864. This must be prevented at any hazard, the committee decided, and their grossly biased report was aimed at doing just that.

Johnson mistrusted McClellan as much as did any member of the committee. He had no faith in his military capacity, he suspected his devotion to the Union, and he was repelled by McClellan's familiarity with Peace Democrats. In addition, Johnson himself was considered in some quarters to be the nation's leading Democrat and available for the presidential nomination. This last consideration may have been a factor in Johnson's estimate of McClellan, but there is no indication that it was the determining factor. Until the war was won, he put aside party labels and party advantage—a sacrifice which the radical Republicans never made. For them, party, principle, and patriotism were indivisible.

Nor had partisan politics been laid aside for the duration by former Whigs and Democrats in Tennessee, who, though Unionists all, were in bitter opposition to the radicals there over the question of how civil rule should be restored in the state. By August, when he returned from Washington, Johnson found a formidable clique arrayed against him in the Unionist ranks. His harsh treatment of rebel sympathizers had alienated many moderates—so had Lincoln's emancipation proclamation. Old-line Whigs favored a hands-off policy as regards slavery, and they were insistent that the rebellious should be enticed and led back gently to their old loyalties, rather than coerced.

Johnson was tougher and more realistic. The policy of leniency had been tried and had failed, and disaffection was more widespread and deep-seated than ever in many districts of the state. Every Confederate victory brought smiles to a majority of the populace, and there was no doubt that Tennesseans generally were living for the day when the last Yankee troops should be driven out of their state.

But once more, in that summer and autumn of '63, political preoccupations were overshadowed by military events. Grant, having crossed the Mississippi River and laid siege to Vicksburg from the rear, on July 4 accepted the surrender of that fortress with its thirty thousand men. On the same day, at Gettysburg, in Pennsylvania, Lee's northmost offensive was blunted and turned back. A few days later John Hunt Morgan led his cavalry across the Ohio into Indiana on a raid that spread panic.

The governors of Indiana and Ohio, Oliver P. Morton and David Tod, frantically called for help; both these executives were more excitable under an invasion threat than Governor Johnson, who lived in the center of such alarms. There was justification for their fears in this instance, inasmuch as the southern tier of counties in Ohio, Indiana, and Illinois had been settled largely by people from Kentucky and Tennessee, and contained many "Secesh" sympathizers.

Congressman Julian, the valiant fighter against slavery, got his only taste of military life during this emergency, through an eight-day call-up of the Indiana militia, to which he belonged. He was disgusted by the "profanity, obscenity, and moral recklessness" of both officers and men, and loathed the drunkenness on all sides.

The thought of the numbers of men who had perished in the war under the influence of liquor caused him to shudder.

(It is difficult today to recapture the intensity of the repugnance which "temperance" advocates of the last century entertained for spiritous liquors. To them what "Parson" Brownlow called "mean whisky" was not an inanimate liquid, but deviltry distilled—a living spirit, malignant, sinister—the draught of Circe that turned men into beasts. "Temperance" writers of the period did not hesitate to depict Satan and his imps as carousing in hell, all roaring drunk. A drunkard, or even a moderate consumer of the sinful potions was one to be sorrowed over, and if not positively shunned, certainly one to be denied all trust.)

Julian was filled with gloom that summer. At the adjournment of the last Congress, he and his radical associates had told each other despairingly that they would probably never meet in another session in Washington. Ben Wade had expressed their feeling when he said that the country was on its way to hell, and Lincoln was clinching its doom. These extremists were further discouraged, when they returned to their districts, by the apathy of their constituents, who did not feel the same bitterness towards the President, and who, although war-weary, were not conceding yet that the nation was past saving.

While Julian was glooming among the whisky-reeking home guards of his state, the raider Morgan was brought to bay at New Lisbon, Ohio, captured, and locked in the Ohio State prison. Unionists in East Tennessee breathed more easily.

Then Burnside made his move, and on September 2 he entered Knoxville in triumph.

Johnson rejoiced, though the letters he received from the liberated region, telling the sufferings that friends and others had experienced there, were poignant. One friend wrote from Greeneville, sending "love to Mrs. Johnson, Col. Stover, & all the family," and revealing how insecure the people still felt. The letter, dated October 21, bridged a gap of years:

"Many fearful events have swept over our once peaceful, happy, and prosperous country since I saw you. Thank God my faith in the ultimate triumph of *truth*, and the power of the government, tho' often blind . . . has not for one moment failed me. I am still here as you left me, tho' broken in my profession, and nearly all my little means of life gone—*an unyielding Union man* . . . Judge Patterson can give you all the ups & downs, and the miserable triggerings going on here." Even now they could not feel safe. "We have had once to 'fall back' and how soon that may again occur none of us knows . . . Well, Johnson, I feel curious even while I write. It seems even yet contraband to mention your name, and I instinctively look around me to see if any 'gray-back' is not watching me."

This letter had been signed, then the signature painstakingly obliterated. Perhaps Johnson was able to guess the identity of the sender.

Organizing relief for these people required immediate attention, and Johnson spurred the work forward. Soon money and supplies were arriving from generous Northerners, and this relief saved many of the mountain folk from starvation.

The Patterson family—the judge, Martha, and their two children, Belle and Andrew—hurried to Nashville. And Blackston McDannel, who had been in Nashville, set out for Greeneville, hoping to get past the guerrillas along the route.

Immediately behind Burnside entering Knoxville was "Parson" Brownlow, who had been carrying on the war in his fashion ever since his exile from Tennessee. In morale-building appearances in Northern cities, he had been received with cordiality and curiosity, his unique personality and heroic adventures making him a celebrity. In Cincinnati he spoke before some four thousand persons and candidly avowed his position: he was a Southerner and he supported slavery, but he was for the Union "though every institution in the country perish."

"I am," he informed the eager audience, "perhaps the only man who ever did, or ever will, appear before a Cincinnati audience confessing that he descended from one of the second families of Virginia. All others are descended from the F.F.V.'s which, since their recent retreats, before Rosecrans and others, signifies, Fleet-Footed Virginians."

His mingled drollery and invective were applauded, and from the fifty-cent admission fee charged he realized over eleven hundred dollars to start a "revive-the-*Whig*" fund, as soon as the rebels should be chased out of Knoxville and he could return home.

Chicago gave the "Fighting Parson of the Southern Highlands" a municipal welcome. At Columbus, Ohio, he addressed the state legislature. He had teamed up with an officer of the recruiting service, "General" S. F. Carey, and after Brownlow warmed up a crowd, Carey would strike a blow for volunteers. The method was effective. From Pittsburgh, and another civic reception, to Harrisburg, Pennsylvania, the "Parson" rode on the cowcatcher of the locomotive in order to enjoy the scenery. An enterprising Philadelphia publisher signed him to turn out an account of his exploits among the rebels, a job that required only a few weeks, and the book sold more than one hundred thousand copies.

Brownlow stunned New York City. *The New York Times* thought he could "safely be pitted against the whole Confederacy"; while Theodore Tilton, writing in the religious weekly, the *Independent*, marveled at such a strange combination of "high moral and intellectual qualities with an almost unaccountable deficiency in that sense of the fitness of things which is called good taste." His language, Tilton said, was "so grating to polite ears" that it kept "sensitive listeners from blushes only because it irresistibly provokes to laughter." The "Parson" was a rare show, and Judge David Davis, about to take his seat on the United States Supreme Court bench, observed after hearing him in Bloomington, Illinois, that "the wind was so high he could not speak longer than an hour and a half," but the "two thousand persons present went away disappointed when he quit."

Entering Knoxville almost on Burnside's heels, Brownlow hauled in from Louisville and Cincinnati paper, ink, and presses, and reissued the *Whig* two years after its suspension. It bore a new and ominous title, the *Knoxville Whig and Rebel Ventilator*; for Brownlow had returned a thoroughgoing radical Republican, dedicated to wreaking vengeance upon rebels. He had given up on the Lincoln government because of its long delay in redeeming East Tennessee, and was prepared to practice the ferocity that had marked his speech.

His first public action was to meddle with Governor Johnson's system of dispensing the relief supplies coming from the

North; the "Parson" wanted to give these only to Unionists and their families; let the rebels and their ilk scratch for themselves. More humane counsels prevailed; but Brownlow kept grumbling about the tenderness shown to Confederate prisoners of war, especially the wounded. "Shoot 'em down like dogs!" had become his motto—a motto that was to prove disastrous to Tennessee and to Johnson alike.

SIXTEEN

"WE MUST HOLD OUT . . .
IT IS OUR FATE"

BURNSIDE held Knoxville, but Bragg and his restrengthened army were at Tullahoma, in Middle Tennessee, and the state was still not delivered from Confederate raiders. In mid-August Rosecrans resumed his advance, and in September succeeded in forcing Bragg out of Chattanooga, a key position. Then Rosecrans divided his force into three columns, to pursue Bragg through narrow mountain defiles, and at Chickamauga the Union forces were caught in a trap and sent fleeing. But for the last-ditch stand of General Thomas, Rosecrans' army would have been annihilated. As it was, the troops swarmed in panic back to Chattanooga, and were besieged there by the victorious Confederates. Rosecrans was relieved and General Thomas took command.

Governor Johnson, watching tensely from Nashville, again fumed at the incapacity of the generals; only Thomas, a fighting man who could not be budged from a position once taken, aroused his admiration; Thomas the governor trusted.

Shaken by the disaster, Washington at last consolidated its efforts, put Grant in supreme command in the West, hurried reinforcements there, improvised a supply line to keep the troops shut up in Chattanooga alive; and on November 23–25 the Confederate vise was pried open. Missionary Ridge and Lookout Mountain were inscribed on the roll of fame, and the Confederates were hurled into Georgia.

At last Tennessee was cleared of any main body of the enemy, and the way was opened for action to set up a civil government. Johnson and Lincoln perceived the opportunity simultaneously.

"You need not be reminded that it is the nick of time for re-inaugurating the loyal state government," the President telegraphed. Of course, precautions must be taken to insure the desired outcome, for "the whole struggle for East Tennessee will have been fruitless to both the state and nation if it so ends that Governor Johnson is put down and Governor Harris is put up."

The warning coincided with Johnson's own analysis of the risks. Nevertheless, he prepared to go ahead. Then a spurt of political bickering between the rival elements of Tennessee's Unionist party temporarily stymied him.

Meanwhile, domestic anguish was added to his public perplexities by his son Robert. The young colonel, undisciplined and dissatisfied, was not distinguishing himself in the army, and repeated pleas by his father to straighten up and be a man had been disregarded. On the eve of the Battle of Chattanooga—at a moment when Union hopes hung in the balance and Johnson was in cruel suspense—Robert threw up his commission, alleging that his father had required it.

Taking time from the press of his official duties, in the midst of the military crisis, the governor wrote one of the few letters dealing exclusively with a family involvement that he ever committed to paper. All letter writing was against the grain for Johnson, and to write demonstratively was impossible. He was not articulate except in public and in impersonal discussion; he shrank from any display of strong personal affection. Often his secretaries would observe him begin a letter, and halfway through tear it up, the difficulty becoming too great. Eliza had tried to help him in this respect, but to little effect. Family troubles and private emotions seldom found expression, even in his most intimate letters, except in conventional terms. Now, at a moment decisive for himself, for Tennessee, and perhaps for the outcome of the war, he took up a pencil (he seldom used a pen any more) and on official "Executive Department" stationery forced himself to be blunt:
"My dear son,

Your note of the 17th is now before me. My [measure] of grief and love [has] been enough without your adding to them at this time. I have been determined that no act of mine should be an excuse for your recent course of conduct and do not now [mean] to depart from it. You tender your resignation predicated upon my wish for you to do so, and as I obtained the commission for you, [I] have the right to require you to resign and therefore you do resign.

"I have not indicated to you by word or deed any desire on my part that you should resign your commission as Col. of the regiment; but on the contrary have expressed myself in the most emphatic terms that I would rather see you once more yourself again and at the head of your regiment going to your own native home than be possessed of the highest honor that could be conferred upon me. In this so far I have been doomed to deep disappointment. I have said and now repeat that I feared you would be dismissed from the army unless you reformed and took command of your regiment, and gave some evidence of a determination to serve the country as a sober, upright, and honorable man.

"I have also said further, that your own reputation and that of an exiled family required one of two things, reformation in your habits and attention to business, or to withdraw from the Army. One or the other is due yourself, the regiment, and the Government . . . This is what I have said. It is what I now feel and think. Though [you are] my son, I feel I am not discharging the duty of a father who has devoted his whole life to the elevation of those he expected to leave behind him.

"In your letter you say my will is the law with you in reference to the resignation. I do most sincerely wish that my will was the law in regard to your future course. I would be willing this night [to] resign my existence into the hands of Him who gave it. Your devoted father . . ."

The writing was crabbed, for the injury to his arm suffered years before made holding a pencil awkward. Having written this call to simple duty, he turned his attention to the public complications in which he was struggling to hold his own course straight.

A reply from the repentant, contrite Robert came on the day the Battle of Chattanooga opened. With thankfulness the governor acknowledged this, again in his own hand:
"My son,

"Your note was handed to me by your sister and was read with pleasure. My heart more than rejoiced to find that you had determined [to] reform your course and become a sober man. Whenever you are sufficiently restored to do business it will be most gratifying to me to place you in the office or anywhere else within my control. But I must add that promises do not amount to much without performance. You have made the promise, that is done, the next thing is compliance with it. You certainly can control your appetites until reason and self-respect once more get the ascendancy. I shall wait with anxious hope for the result. Your affectionate father, *Andrew Johnson*."

This time beneath the bold signature was a flourish, graphically expressive of the writer's relief.

Relief of brief duration, however, for hard upon the Union victory at Chattanooga came the depressing news that Morgan had escaped from prison in Ohio, and that General James Longstreet, dispatched by Bragg to dislodge Burnside from East Tennessee, was pounding at the defenses of Knoxville, and that the ravaged countryside was undergoing a fresh ordeal of pillage, destruction, and bloodshed.

As soon as possible, Grant detached Sherman to push back this new assault, and Longstreet was forced to retreat towards Virginia, stripping the land as he passed.

This fresh setback had hit Johnson hard. Yet he would not be daunted. As he had said in the Senate, when facts failed him, when reason gave out, he drew on his faith. In a dark hour he had written to his wife, who suffered through these crises with him:

"I feel sometimes like giving up all in despare [sic]; but this will not do. We must hold out to the end. This rebellion is wrong and must be put down, let cost what it may in life and treasure. I intend to appropriate the rest of my life to the redemption of my adopted home in East Tennessee, and you and Mary must not weary. It is our fate and we should be willing to bear it cheerfully. Impatience and dissatisfaction will not better it or shorten the time of our suffering."

Tortured in mind by uncertainty, his body drained of energy, as he had assured Eliza, he would hold on. No matter that all the hostility to the Union cause in the state seemed to have become concentrated upon him individually; no matter that his very determination at times worked against him; he was carrying on.

Union generals were reporting astonishment at the virulence of the hatred against the governor that they encountered personally. Wrote one: "In questioning many people they cannot point to an act that he has not been warranted in doing by their own showing; but still, either in his manner of doing it, or that it should be done by *him*, or from some indefinable cause touching him, their resentment is fierce and vindictive." He had undertaken to do what no man had yet succeeded in doing—restore his state to its proper, proud position as a fully participating, fully privileged member of an imperishable Union. For two years he had been frustrated and mortifyingly defeated. Still he would carry on. Sustaining him were three great assets—singleness of mind, tenacity of purpose, and fearless indomitability.

SEVENTEEN

"GOD SAVE THE REPUBLIC!"

IN war men may live years in a brief span of time, and after two years in that cockpit of battles, Tennessee, Andrew Johnson was toughened, but he was also tired. No state, not even Virginia, was so fought over as was his state. During the four years of conflict, more than seven hundred engagements took place on Tennessee soil, at least one hundred of them pitched battles, including some of the bloodiest of all. No portion of the state was untouched as the opposing armies swayed back and forth; what one left, the other seized or destroyed. And there was the scourge of guerrillas, who spared nothing and nobody. In the confusion it was difficult to tell regular cavalry from irregular, and both kinds behaved much alike. For this reason, upon receiving word that Morgan had escaped and was on the prowl again, East Tennessee became filled with apprehension.

Unable to command armies for its relief, and leaving the military to continue trying to knock out their opponents finally, as 1864 arrived, Johnson was striving to make progress politically. Lincoln had given an impetus to reconstruction by his December proclamation offering amnesty to all Confederates, barring a few exceptions, who would lay down their arms and pledge allegiance to the national government, and also offering to recognize civil governments in the seceded states that might be set up by at least ten percent of the voters registered in 1860. Under this plan, reorganization had been started in Louisiana and Arkansas. In Tennessee Johnson took his own measures.

Organization at the county level was the first step, and he prepared to hold an election in March for county offices. The oath of loyalty bothered him. In January he had telegraphed to Washington for clarification and guidance. Would persons "notoriously loyal" have to take the oath in order to vote? Who would administer the oath—election officials or the army? And what about using the governor's appointive powers to name two United States senators immediately? Would the Senate admit them? Looking to the future (for 1864 was a presidential election year), he added, in a message to Maynard:

"I would give some of the faultfinders to understand that the real Union men will be for Abraham Lincoln for President. The war must be closed under Lincoln's administration. I desire you to see the President in person and talk with him in regard to these matters."

Maynard checked, and returned the necessary instructions to Nashville:

"Loyal as well as disloyal should take the oath because it does not hurt them and clears all questions as to their right to vote and swells the aggregate number who take it, which is an important object. This is the President's reply to your question."

Not satisfied, Johnson made a quick trip to Washington. The voters, he pointed out, should be required to pass the severest test in order to prevent the polls from being taken over by disloyalists, and to that end he had prescribed a more stringent oath. This oath Lincoln read and approved.

While in Washington, the governor had a fresh occasion for anxiety about his son Robert, who wrote that he had decided to pull up stakes and go west.

"Taking everything into consideration, after mature reflection, I believe I will resign and try my future in some of the new territories," his letter read. "Next Sunday is my birthday, and I have, in anticipation thereof, cast away forever my past conduct . . . I *will* succeed . . . *the intoxicating bowl goes to my lips no more.*"

Robert's departure, Johnson realized, would be a blow to his mother, already stricken by the loss of one son; the thought almost nullified the news that Robert's letter brought about other members of the family. Stover, although sinking under his illness, "seems better the last few days . . . Frank wrote to you today and done very well. With a little pains taken with him, and a little practice, he will learn to write an excellent hand. I think he is improving rapid [ly]. Frank and Andrew Patterson are sleeping in [the secretary's] room, a great thing with them."

There was a postscript:

"It is rumored at Knoxville that the rebels have taken possession of all our books, papers, etc., at Greeneville."

This was true; Johnson's library and accumulation of records, covering his career up to the war, had been scattered to the wind by Confederate soldiers.

In the end Robert Johnson did not go west, but resigned from the army and joined his father's staff as a special aide.

The March elections were held, and proved a fiasco; in fact, they were admitted by the dismayed Unionists to be a farce. The vote was so light as to be meaningless. In some counties no election was held. The military officer in charge of one district reported that he could find no citizen "with *manhood* enough" to accept the job of supervising the voting. "With scarce an exception the citizens profess anxiety for the restoration of civil government, but lack the nerve to face the music." Unionists everywhere were wary; the tide of war had turned too often to give them confidence. Many loyalists stayed away from the polls in protest against their being required to take the oath; it seemed degrading.

So this election was another setback for Johnson. Nevertheless, he returned to Nashville resolved to try a fresh approach.

The national convention of the Republican party (renamed in a gesture of solidarity the National Union party) was to be held in Baltimore in June. Should Tennessee send a delegation that was recognized, the party's seal of agreement would be placed on Johnson's contention that the state had never left the Union. A call was issued for meetings in the three divisions of the state to select delegates, and ten were chosen. The proceedings were highly irregular, but no procedure that would satisfy every challenge was possible.

These meetings endorsed the war policy of Lincoln, and recommended Andrew Johnson for the Vice-Presidency. Johnson himself did nothing to invite the nomination, and his "favorite son" candidacy was not considered significant. Backstage, however, the wheels were turning.

Hannibal Hamlin, the current Vice-President, was a radical Republican from Maine; and as a stroke of policy, Lincoln wished to replace Hamlin with a War Democrat of vote-getting appeal.

It was a gesture, like the party's change of name, aimed at attract-
ing Democratic support.

Lincoln's first choice was Ben Butler, a former Democrat who
had real strength at the ballot box. The story of what happened
next might be entitled "Butler's Biggest Bungle."

Confiding his plan to Simon Cameron, the onetime Secretary of
War—a dextrous political manipulator who had just returned
from Russia—Lincoln asked him to go to Fortress Monroe, where
Butler was stationed, and sound out the general. Butler was busy
with a plan to forestall Grant in capturing Richmond by some
unorthodox strategy, and Cameron found him bubbling with
anticipated glory. In Lincoln's name, Cameron proffered the Vice-
Presidential nomination, so far as Lincoln could swing it. Butler
was not to be caught.

"There is nothing in the Vice-President," he answered offhand.
"I prefer to stay in the army. Please say to Mr. Lincoln that while
I appreciate . . . this act of friendship and the compliment he pays
me, yet I must decline."

Then with a laugh, rolling his walrus form in the chair until the
saber at his side clanked, he chuckled ironically:

"Tell him, with the prospects of the [Richmond] campaign, I
would not quit the field to be Vice-President, even with himself as
President, unless he will give me bond with sureties, in the full
sum of his four years' salary, that he will die or resign within
three months after his inauguration."

Butler did not believe that Lincoln could be reelected—an
opinion which, as the summer rolled along, many astute politicians shared.

Rebuffed by Butler, Lincoln turned to Andrew Johnson, who
was a Democrat, a vote-getter, and of unquestionable loyalty. His
services in Tennessee had won the enthusiastic approval of both
the President and Stanton, and he was due to receive some reward. But disquieting rumors about Johnson had come to the
President's attention, and he desired to look into the facts closely
before committing himself. It was rumored that the military governor of Tennessee had been abusing his power, playing the petty
tyrant, and also that he had taken to drink. (Robert's reputation
was becoming confused with his father's.)

Secretary Stanton had conducted his own quiet investigation of

Johnson some time previously. The investigator had been
Charles A. Dana, Assistant Secretary of War, who had undertaken a similar mission in respect to General Grant, after the
Battle of Shiloh. Dana traveled to Nashville and called at the
Capitol, where Johnson by way of welcome immediately brought
out a bottle of whisky and poured drinks for them both. After
several days of inquiry and observation, Dana concluded that
perhaps Johnson did drink more than a gentleman strictly should
(though the notions of a Bostonian like Dana as to what constituted a gentleman's capacity would hardly have met Southern
standards), but he saw nothing to indicate that the governor was
not at all times sober and responsible.

Ben Truman, the correspondent for Forney's *Washington
Chronicle*, had remarked on Johnson's abstemiousness long before, during his stay in Tennessee, because it was so exceptional
in that hard-drinking region. For eighteen months Truman had
taken his meals at the same table with the governor, and had
never seen him drink a cocktail, and never saw him in a barroom.
Champagne Johnson positively disliked, and although on some
days he did take "two or three glasses of Tennessee whisky,"
Truman said, "there were times when for days and weeks he
would take nothing at all." As drinking went in Tennessee,
Truman thought, Johnson was a curiously temperate man.

The same observation had been made by the *Herald* reporter
Glenn, during the siege of Nashville. Despite the tremendous
strain of those weeks, the governor, said Glenn, had been "a
model of abstemiousness. He never played cards, for amusement
or gain. He never indulged on any single occasion to a greater
extent than possibly a clergyman would at a sacrament, and as for
the smaller vices, he was free from them all. His whole aim and
object, his entire aspirations, seemed to center in the reestablish-
ment of the authority of the federal government over his state,
her speedy return to the Union, protection of loyal citizens in all
parts of the state, and "punishment of 'conscious and intelligent
traitors' wherever found."

Johnson's indifference to amusements had puzzled Truman. He
tried to persuade the governor to attend the theater, but Johnson
was always too busy. He had never seen a play, he said, although
he had gone to a minstrel show, and liked it, and he had attended

the circus. When he was young, he explained, he had been too poor to afford amusements, and by the time he could afford them, there was always something else to do—study, reading, work.

The troubleshooter whom Lincoln sent in 1864 to check on Johnson was General Daniel E. Sickles, a *bon vivant* of New York, London, and Paris, well qualified to judge a man's drinking habits. He came to Nashville in mid-May, and by chance Ben Truman, who also was in town, ran across an old newspaper associate in the street. This man was acting as aide to Sickles, and during their chat he confided that the general was on an "important mission"; in fact, had been sent by Lincoln personally to "look into Governor Johnson's habits." The President wanted Johnson on the ticket "if his habits would permit." The general was there to find out.

Although it was nearly midnight, Truman hurried to Johnson's quarters, awakened him, and repeated the conversation. Sitting up in bed, the governor said tersely:

"I want you to leave for Washington tomorrow, and go direct to Forney and repeat to him what you said to me and ask him to look out for my interests."

Then Johnson went back to sleep.

Sickles's report—favorable to the governor—was in Lincoln's hands before the National Union Convention opened in Baltimore on June 7.

Immediately the question arose as to whether Tennessee's delegation should be seated. The state had sent ten delegates, among them Horace Maynard and "Parson" Brownlow. Maynard made a moving appeal for recognition:

"For you who drink in the cool breezes of the Northern air, it is easy to rally to the flag . . . but we represent those who have stood in the very furnace of the rebellion, those who have met treason eye to eye and face to face, and fought from the beginning for the support of the flag and the honor of our country."

Then Brownlow was called upon, and although just out of a sickbed, he gave the convention his rattling best. "So rash an act" as excluding the Tennesseans, he warned, would proclaim to the world that their state was out of the Union.

"We don't recognize it in Tennessee," he said. "We deny that we are out. We deny that we ever have been out. We maintain that a minority first voted us out, and then a majority whipped the minority out of the state with bayonets." Then he introduced Johnson's name:

"We may take it into our heads, before the thing is over, to present a candidate from that state in rebellion for the second highest office in the gift of the people. We have a man down there whom it has been my good luck and bad fortune to fight untiringly and perseveringly for the last twenty-five years—Andrew Johnson." Here the galleries burst into applause, and when it ended the "Parson" got another round with the exclamation: "For the first time, in the providence of God, three years ago we got together on the same platform, and we are fighting the devil and Jeff Davis side by side!"

The next day the convention seated the Tennesseans, nominated Lincoln for President, although grumpily, and Andrew Johnson for Vice-President, thereby causing numerous seers and prophets to eat crow.

The *New York Herald*, three days before the convention, had been sure that the practical politicians at Baltimore would ditch Lincoln. And if, by unlucky chance, Lincoln and "his shoddy men" should be nominated, they would be "terribly defeated," the *Herald* predicted. "We would not be surprised if Old Abe . . . is voted on the retired list with Fillmore, poor Pierce, and poor old Buchanan, which will be just the thing, exactly," was its feeling.

The *New York Tribune* had urged indefinite postponement of the convention, believing the war at too critical a stage for political discussions. Sherman was before Atlanta, Grant, the "butcher," was at Cold Harbor, and there were operations along the Gulf; news from the battlefronts filled page after page in the newspapers.

The *New York World*, the leading copperhead journal of the nation, had conceded Lincoln's nomination in advance, and had given this character sketch of the "Honest Ape" in the White House:

"As a *man*, his instincts are vulgar, his education narrow, his manners a cross between a boor and a buffoon. As a *statesman*, he

selects the unfittest instruments for the most important functions
. . . His Secretary of State is shallow and pretentious; his Secretary
of War, wrong-headed and impetuous; his Secretary of the Navy,
a noodle; his Secretary of the Interior, a nobody . . ."

The nominations brought a repetition of this castigation, with
Andrew Johnson included. The *World*'s leading editorial after the
convention adjourned read:

"LINCOLN AND JOHNSON"

"The age of statesmen is gone; the age of railsplitters and tailors, of buffoons, boors, and fanatics, has succeeded . . . Mr. Lincoln and Mr. Johnson are both men of mediocre talents, narrow
views, deficient education, and coarse, vulgar manners . . . The
only merit we can discover in the Baltimore ticket is the merit of
consistency; it is all of a piece; the tail does not shame the head,
nor the head the tail. A railsplitting buffoon and a boorish tailor,
both from the backwoods, both growing up in uncouth ignorance,
they afford a grotesque sight for a satiric poet . . . In a crisis of the
most appalling magnitude, requiring statesmanship of the highest
order, the country is asked to consider the claims of two ignorant,
boorish, third-rate backwoods lawyers, and to the highest stations
in the government! Such nominations are . . . an insult to the
common sense of the people. God save the Republic!"

The *Herald* commented upon the outcome scarcely less caus-
tically:

"We do not object to Mr. Lincoln because he was once a railsplitter, nor because his associate nominee was once a tailor. We
know that some of the greatest men in the world have risen from
a low origin, and in a nation like this, a man's occupation, provided it be honest, is no bar to his future advancement.

"We object to Mr. Lincoln because he has been tried and found
wanting, and because his reelection would, in all probabilities,
seal the fate of republican institutions . . . President Lincoln has
protracted the war for four years, when he could have ended it in
one . . . He has surrounded himself with a cabinet notorious for
incapacity and containing some of the most imbecile men in the
country, as an example of whom we may instance [Secretary of
the Navy] Gideon Welles . . . He has allowed thousands of brave

men to be slaughtered in vain . . . This Presidential pygmy . . ."
And so on and on.

Not all reaction was adverse. A letter to the editor, published in
the *Herald*, praised Andrew Johnson as a man of "great executive
ability . . . a will inflexible as iron . . . quick perception of the
right . . . of decision and energy . . . patient to bear . . . It is a
satisfaction to know that God has given us such a man to be the
associate of him we delight to call 'Honest,' and that, should he
be taken away, there is another of equal ability and patriotism
who will worthily fill his place and be to us all that the nation will
require."

Ben Butler dashed off a hasty jeer to his wife:

"Hurrah for Lincoln and Johnson! That's the ticket! This country has more vitality than any other on earth if it can stand this
sort of administration for another four years!"

EIGHTEEN

"AND ALL THE PEOPLE
WILL SAY 'AMEN'"

THADDEUS STEVENS, as a delegate to the convention from Pennsylvania, had roughly opposed Andrew Johnson's nomination. Stevens denied the right of the Tennesseans to a place in the convention on the ground that they were not citizens of the United States, and in a fiery speech maintained that Southerners had no rights in the Union that they had deserted; that they had gone out by their own choice, had renounced their rights, and were no more citizens of the United States than were the Hottentots. "Can't you get a candidate for Vice-President without going down into a damned rebel province for one?" he growled; and in the heat of passion he called Andrew Johnson "a damned scoundrel," particulars not specified.

There was opposition from other quarters, too. Just before the Baltimore convention, some four hundred extreme radicals—abolitionists, cranks, and well-known fanatics among them—had assembled in Cleveland and nominated John Charles Frémont for President. And in August the Democrats, who were Andrew Johnson's party, met at Chicago and nominated General McClellan. Lincoln by an adroit power play managed to get Frémont to withdraw (at the price of Montgomery Blair's retirement as Postmaster General), and then faced McClellan alone.

The general had been nominated on a "peace plank" platform, which denounced the war as a failure and called for a peaceful settlement with the Confederates. This was what Lincoln and Johnson feared most—a negotiated peace that would recognize the Confederacy. The country was sick of slaughter, and the suspicion was strong in the North that the South could not be whipped. The slow progress of the Union armies seemed to show this; Grant's losses in Virginia were sending a chill of death through tens of thousands of homes. In Georgia Sherman seemed to be making little headway. Lincoln's whole being was absorbed in the effort to end the war victoriously and restore the Union; Johnson's, no less. When the official committee from the Baltimore convention called at the White House to notify the President of his nomination, there was talk about Johnson's reaction; would he *do?* With a chuckle, Lincoln assured the delegation that "Andy" would be radical enough to suit any of them.

"Don't be concerned," he said. "When Andy was here last, he said if it were necessary to carry on the war for thirty years, he was for carrying it on."

Johnson's acceptance remarks were a plea for unity:

"This is not the hour for strife and division among ourselves. Such differences of opinion only encourage the enemy, prolong the war, and waste the country."

In Tennessee, unity was the foremost need, and there seemed to be less and less of it. The Unionist elements were irreconcilably divided into "unconditionals" and "moderates," and their councils had become mere wrangles over theoretical details.

After the March election blunder, some of the governor's staunchest friends begged him not to risk another humiliation. But without an expression of the popular will—or the will of the loyal portion of the population—civil government could not be resuscitated; and most certainly the governor was in duty bound to carry his state for the Republican ticket in November. The way must be found.

The main obstacle blocking effective action was uncertainty about the ultimate fate of Tennessee. So long as the Army of the Cumberland under General Thomas was confronted by a vigilant and powerful foe, final domination of the state by either Union or Confederate forces was in doubt; and bitter experience had schooled the civilian population to "lie low" and for their self-preservation observe a judicious inaction. This applied to Unionists as well as to Southern sympathizers. Throughout the summer of 1864 this paralysis prevailed, and Johnson's correspondence teemed with advice not to risk another political defeat.

Nevertheless, at the governor's prompting, the executive committee of the Greeneville Unionist convention (which had met in 1861 and adjourned subject to recall by its chairman), on August 4 sent out a call for "unconditional Union men" to gather at Nashville on September 5 for a threefold purpose. This was defined as (1) to consider "the general condition of the country"; (2) to decide on means of "reorganizing the civil government and restoring order"; (3) to discuss the expediency of holding an election for President and Vice-President in November.

The "delegates" attending this convention were a mixed lot. Few had been chosen by regular county organizations. Some counties were not represented at all, because of raiding Confederate cavalry. Some delegates came on their own volition and responsibility, representing themselves. Any soldier was admitted, if he gave evidence of being strongly Unionist. Sam Milligan was chosen president of the convention, and behind him, as everyone understood, was the guiding hand of Governor Johnson.

The day before the convention was called to order, Nashville was excited by the news that John Hunt Morgan had been killed. The dreaded—and on the Southern side, adored—raider, since his escape from Ohio, had been in command in southwest Virginia, and even the Richmond authorities had been deploring the "excesses" committed there by his troopers. Early on the morning of September 4, a Union advance force surprised him in Greeneville, Tennessee, and as he attempted to flee he was shot down two blocks from the Andrew Johnson tailor shop.

This good news for the Northern side seemed to give the Nashville convention an auspicious start; but within two days the meeting had taken on the aspect of a free-for-all brawl, with the radical Unionists trying to drown the moderates out. When one "strict constructionist" offered a resolution deploring the disregard of constitutional procedures, he was howled down. A rival delegate moved that the resolution be laid on the table, "or better still, thrown under the table." A colonel (the convention bristled with military titles) cried that "in every convention of Unionists, some members are sure to show the cloven hoof," and another shouted, to a chorus of applause, whoops, and catcalls, "Show me a stickler for constitutions, and I'll show you a none too good Union man!" That session broke up in disorder.

The next day the delegates took up the problem of devising an oath that would keep copperheads and McClellanites from voting.

Lincoln's amnesty program had proved a failure in Tennessee. Southern sympathizers did not scruple to take the oath of fealty for the sake of trading privileges, or personal protection, without the slightest intention of honoring it. Bushwhackers were captured with amnesty certificates in their pockets. Johnson had been forced to ask the President to take Tennessee out of the scope of the amnesty, and instead require every Tennessean desiring a pardon to apply individually and directly to the President. This, he believed, might impress upon the applicant the gravity of his oath and the extent of his obligation to the government. "As it now operates," he told Lincoln, "its main tendency is to keep alive the rebel spirit, in fact reconciling none. This is the opinion of every real Union man here."

Some stronger device would be needed to safeguard the election. One member of the convention gave his opinion that "even if all the copperheads and traitors were to take an *oath to vote for Lincoln and Johnson*, McClellan would still beat them" because of disregard of the oath.

A moderate delegate who urged tolerance was assailed with fury, a captain exclaiming that copperheads like that fellow ought to be "invited out."

"Kick 'em out!" a colonel agreed. "Point 'em out, and by God, I'll lead the charge!"

Timorous conservatives took the hint and left the hall. The remaining delegates thereupon unanimously voted that an election be held on November 8, and stipulated the oath that each voter would be required to take before he could cast his ballot. This was a stricter test than was applied in any other state, and it had unique features.

First, the applicant had to swear that he was "an active friend of the government of the United States," and would henceforth support and defend the Constitution of the United States. Then came the "stinger." The would-be voter was required to swear as follows:

"I sincerely rejoice in the triumph of the [United States]

armies and navies and in the defeat and overthrow of the armies, navies, and all armed combinations in the interest of the so-called Confederate states"; and "I will cordially oppose all armistices or negotiations for peace with rebels in arms, until the Constitution of the United States and all laws and proclamations made in pursuance thereof shall be established over all the people of every state and territory embraced within the National Union."

Even this solemn declaration was made subject to disproof by incredulous registrars.

McClellan had been nominated by the Democrats on a platform deploring the war and calling for a negotiated peace; hence no Democrat, however strongly attached to the Union, could vote for McClellan under that oath without perjuring himself.

On the day the convention approved this means for excluding everybody except Lincoln-Johnson voters from the polls, Governor Johnson issued a proclamation warning that the period of clemency was at an end. Henceforth, "those who still continue to adhere to traitors and treason can no longer expect the protection of the government they daily revile and seek to destroy. They must yield their opposition (male and female) or they will be removed beyond the reach of harm to the government and authority of the United States."

Unionist Democrats were outraged by their disfranchisement, and a delegation of their most respected leaders carried a protest to Lincoln. But the President was standing by Governor Johnson. After reading the petition, he asked with unconcealed sarcasm:

"May I inquire how long it took you and the New York politicians to concoct that paper?"

New York City was a nest of copperheads, and the Tennesseans indignantly spurned the suggestion that they were associated with Tammany Hall. None but they themselves had had a hand in drawing up the protest, they replied. Whereupon Lincoln said coldly:

"I expect to let the friends of George B. McClellan manage their side of this contest in their own way, and I will manage my side of it in my way."

In spite of every precaution, the outcome of the election was doubtful. On August 28 Lincoln wrote a memorandum to himself, conceding that as of that date his reelection appeared unlikely. In Tennessee, Johnson was besieged with appeals to speak in Northern states, especially in Indiana, where the prospect for beating the Democrats seemed gloomy. Henry J. Raymond, editor of *The New York Times* and the Republican campaign manager, who had been largely instrumental in obtaining Johnson's nomination, beseeched the governor to tour Ohio and Pennsylvania, at least; while from Illinois came assurances that one speech there by Johnson would bring twenty thousand votes for the ticket. Harassed though he was by problems at home, Johnson did make a swing around Indiana to great acclaim.

The campaign in Tennessee wound up with a rally of Negroes before the Capitol in Nashville. The turnout was large, and the atmosphere was highly emotional. Always susceptible to the mood of the crowd he was addressing, the governor lashed out at slaveholders as oppressors of the poor and humble, black and white alike. He cited the planter-aristocrats' notorious concubinage with their female slaves, "compared to which polygamy is a virtue."

"The representatives of this corrupt and damnable aristocracy taunt us with our desire to see justice done, and charge us with favoring Negro equality," he cried. "Of all living men, they should be the last to mouth that phrase. Negro equality, indeed! Why, pass any day along High Street, where these aristocrats more particularly dwell—these aristocrats whose sons are now in the bands of guerrillas and cutthroats who prowl and rob and murder around our city—pass by their dwellings, and you will see as many mulatto as Negro children, the former bearing an unmistakable resemblance to their aristocratic owners! Thank God, the war has ended all that!"

This "damnable aristocracy" must be pulled down, he shouted, and as in days of old, some Moses would arise to lead the Negroes out of bondage into a Promised Land of freedom and happiness.

Back came a chant, "You be our Moses!" and in an access of enthusiasm Johnson responded:

"Humble and unworthy as I am, if no better shall be found, I will indeed be your Moses, and lead you through the Red Sea of war and bondage to a fairer future of liberty and peace!"

The ecstatic spirit of a Southern camp meeting worked upon

both speaker and crowd, and in the fervor of the moment the exclamation came naturally; though later, in cold retrospect, the speech would seem a little silly.

November 8 arrived, and despite every effort, the election in Tennessee was another fiasco. Forrest's cavalry kept many polls from opening; Peace Democrats abstained; and although the Lincoln-Johnson ticket won, so unreliable were the returns, Tennessee's electoral vote was disallowed, with Lincoln's sanction.

Now time was running out. As Vice-President-elect, Johnson had only a few more weeks in which to achieve the purpose that had impelled him for nearly three years: the return of his state to its loyalty within the Union. There was no doubt that the majority of the population was against this, but the Confederates were losing hope in the struggle. And what constituted the state? The loyal citizens in it; that was Johnson's thesis, from which he never deviated. One more attempt should be made to enable the loyal Unionists of Tennessee to take the necessary steps for restoring civil government. This time the strategy was worked out with precision in advance.

Four days after the Presidential election, a call was issued by the Greeneville convention executive committee for loyalists to gather in Nashville on December 19, for the purpose of nominating delegates to a constitutional convention that would start the machinery turning to restore civil government.

Hardly had the call been promulgated when the state again was shaken by invasion. In the East, General Breckinridge led an army of Confederates towards Knoxville. The "governor's guard" protecting that city, commanded by General A. C. Gillem, a military novice, was routed at Bull's Gap.

Terror-stricken Unionists stampeded into Knoxville, thirty-four hundred refugees (half of them children) pouring into the city during the week after Gillem's defeat. The weather was freezing cold, with rain and sleet, and mud knee-deep. "Parson" Brownlow wrote to Johnson:

"It is sickening . . . to stand here and look at one thousand men, women, and children coming in through the mud and rain, leading their stock, driving cows and stock, to save what they can, as they are driven from their homes—no shanties, no anything else to give them shelter. The picture is worse than I make it. You can imagine the rest . . . Men and women are weeping, and coming in, in whose statements we can place reliance, and the tales they tell are heart-rending. Robbed of all but *their clothes* . . . Union men are shot down, and the reason assigned for these acts of violence—they 'voted for Lincoln and Johnson.' "

But no help could be given, for simultaneously, General Hood had swept into Middle Tennessee from Georgia with the main Confederate army. Having replaced General Joseph Johnston in opposing Sherman, Hood had decided to throw his army into Sherman's rear, threaten Nashville, and cut Sherman's supply line, forcing the Union commander to turn back.

General Thomas, commanding in Tennessee, refused to be drawn into battle prematurely, but retired northward through the state in what to Governor Johnson ominously resembled Buell's disastrous retreat. Nevertheless, in Thomas he still reposed faith, and his hopes rose slightly when, on the last day of November, General Schofield checked Hood at Franklin in a bloody encounter, then fell back and joined Thomas at Nashville. There, on December 15–16, Thomas fell like a thunderbolt on Hood's army and pulverized it. That victory was the most crushing of the war; nothing was left of the Confederate force except fragments, fleeing for their lives to find sanctuary in Alabama.

With Hood disposed of, Breckinridge was speedily driven out of East Tennessee, and for the first time the state could feel secure. On December 30, General Thomas made his report on a job done with thoroughness and finality, ceremoniously addressing it to "Hon. Andrew Johnson, Vice-President-elect of the United States":

"As the enemy is now entirely driven out of the state of Tennessee, I would respectfully suggest that immediate measures be taken for the reorganization of the civil government of the state . . . All should certainly now feel that the establishment of rebel authority in the state of Tennessee is hopeless, and their own interest should induce them to return to their allegiance to the United States without further quibbling."

The Battle of Nashville (during which Daniel Stover, Johnson's son-in-law, died of the disease induced by the hardships of his resistance fighting in the early days of the war) had prevented the assembling of the announced convention on December 19. A notice in the newspapers had advanced the date until January 8, 1865—a date hallowed in Tennessee tradition as the anniversary of the Battle of New Orleans. Under the circumstances, it was decided to throw the convention open to all Union men, without formalities. "If you cannot meet in your counties, come on your own responsibility," read the summons.

January 8 falling on Sunday, the convention came together on the 9th. At once the radicals, jettisoning the announced purpose of the meeting, made clear that they intended to draw up constitutional amendments on the spot, dispensing with a later constitutional convention regularly elected. This disregard of the announced purpose of the assemblage was denounced by the moderates; the minimum of irregularity should attach to the process by which the state was brought back to its allegiance, they urged, for the trickery by which Tennessee had been hustled out of the Union in '61 had rankled.

But there was no time for nice observances, and from Washington came pressure for swift action. The Thirteenth Amendment, writing the abolition of slavery into the Constitution, was before Congress, and its passage seemed in jeopardy. If Tennessee were represented in Congress by an anti-slavery delegation, the amendment would be saved, and its proponents appealed to Johnson to make haste.

Thereupon, with the governor calling the shots, though not appearing openly, the radicals jammed their program through despite protests and submitted to the convention four amendments to the state constitution.

The first abolished slavery, and the second forbade the legislature ever to revive it. The remaining two provided for a change in the selection of the judiciary, and set up voting requirements, including extension of the franchise to Negroes who had served in the war, and disfranchisement of certain classes of Confederate leaders.

On January 12 the moderates presented their demand that they return to the original, announced program and order an election of delegates to a regular constitutional convention, which would meet on March 4 and take action on the proposed changes. Exerting all their strength, the conservatives seemed headed towards victory.

Then Governor Johnson presented himself for a speech, and as one commentator put it: "The stage was set for him, and before he had finished, he seemed to be the only actor on it." Where others were confused, he saw the central issue, and he struck home.

The stumbling block, for the moderates, was the irregular process urged by the radicals. Well, said Johnson, suppose it did go against the letter of the law. "If by so doing you restore the law and the Constitution, your consciences will approve your course, and all the people will say 'Amen!'

"You are without law and without a constitution, and it is your duty to get it back for the people. If you do boldly what the hour demands, you . . . may hold up your hands when the struggle is ended and swear that you have saved your state and the republic . . . This is the most favorable opportunity that has presented itself . . . Why not agree on two or three simple propositions, and get back your state government?"

If the question were left to him, he advised, he would simply forbid slavery now and hereafter, and leave the other issues to be settled later. How the action was taken was immaterial, because before any action could become valid, it would have to be approved by the sovereign people.

"Any man can draw up a few 'whereases,' submit them to his friends, and they recommend them to the people of the state, and if the people ratify them, the subject matter becomes law—it is constitutional, and the procedure consonant with the spirit of free government."

The argument was unanswerable.

"If you call a convention, involving expense, delay, and vexation, their action must, after all, go to the people to be sanctioned before it can become part of the constitution. Then let *the people* act. The important thing is to restore the civil government at once, free from the encumbrances that brought on the rebellion. As for the elective franchise, get a legislature, and let it act on that."

When Johnson concluded, the result was foregone. Many moderates went home, passing up the session the next day, which passed the amendments ending slavery in Tennessee forever, and added provisions annulling the ordinance of secession and all acts of the secession legislature, and repudiating the debts incurred by the rebel government. Brownlow was nominated for governor by acclamation, and in a tense, bitter acceptance speech he promised:

"God being my helper, if you will send up a legislature to reorganize the militia and pass other necessary laws, I will put an end to this infernal system of guerrilla fighting in Tennessee, if we have to shoot and hang every man concerned."

The convention cheered this declaration wildly.

On February 22 the plebiscite was held under the strictest controls to shut out all but radicals, and the convention's proposals were ratified with only forty-eight dissenting votes, against twenty-five thousand in favor.

"Thank God the tyrant's rod is broken!" Johnson jubilantly telegraphed to President Lincoln. "All is now working well, and if Tennessee is let alone, [she] will soon resume all the functions of a state according to the genius and theory of the government."

March 4 was set as the date for election of state officials, and on that day Brownlow was elected governor with only a demisemiquaver of objection—twenty-three thousand votes for him, and thirty-five against. With the new legislature, he would take office one month later.

In anticipation of the turnover of authority, the retiring military governor addressed a proclamation of felicitation to the citizens of Tennessee:

"The folly of destroying their government and sacrificing their sons to gratify the mad ambition of political leaders needs no longer to be told to the laboring masses. The wasted estates, ruined and dilapidated farms, vacant seats around the hearthstones, prostrate business . . . everywhere proclaim it. But all is not lost. A new era dawns upon the people of Tennessee."

In idyllic hues he pictured this coming commonwealth of the common man:

"The unjust distinctions in society, fostered by an arrogant aristocracy, based upon human bondage, have been overthrown, and

our whole social system reconstructed on the basis of honest industry and personal worth. Labor now shall receive its merited
reward, and honesty, energy, and enterprise their just appreciation . . . If the people are true to themselves . . . they will rapidly
. . . raise the state to a power and grandeur not heretofore even
anticipated . . ."

About realizing this alluring prospect, Governor Brownlow
would have much to say. But by that time Andrew Johnson
would be beyond the borders of Tennessee, caught up in a different world, and embarked upon a different and wider life.

INTERLUDE

*Six Weeks Suspended Between
Two Worlds*

ONE

"REPUTATION, REPUTATION, REPUTATION!"

ANDREW JOHNSON returned to Washington on March 1, 1864, a changed man.

After the January convention, he had succumbed to a fever, and his doctor had kept him in bed for several weeks. The fever was variously described as typhoid and malarial. Whichever the diagnosis, it was severe, and it left him debilitated.

This was not surprising. For years he had been under constant strain, fighting for survival in the maelstrom of war and hatred that Tennessee had become. He had been obliged to fight to retain a foothold in the state, when military men abandoned it. He had fought the open and furtive hostility of rival elements in the wartime alliance of Unionists who, except on that one issue, were antagonistic to him. Hardly a day had passed without bringing danger. All his tenacity had been required to make headway against heartsickening setbacks and dashing-down of hopes prematurely raised high. For months he had poured the last reserves of his nerve and will power into the determination to end rebellion in his state and bring it back into the Union on an acceptable basis. There had been no slackening in this endeavor; the tension had been unrelaxed right through his carrying to success the January convention. Then, in a surge of physical and emotional release, he had fallen prey to the fever.

The truth was that for the time being Andrew Johnson was worn out, and the prospect of a journey to Washington, and plunging into the turmoil of politics there, in an arena grown unfamiliar, oppressed him. His mail was filled with letters broaching subjects that had occupied little space in his recent thoughts. John W. Forney, the Secretary of the Senate, was cultivating good relations with his future chief, attempting to make him assume the burden of insuring that the War Democrats should not be slighted by Lincoln when the awards for good behavior were being distributed.

"No man in the Union is more concerned in this than Andrew Johnson," Forney urged, speaking as a former Democrat himself to the man who had never disavowed or forsworn his Democratic principles even when running on the National Union ticket with Abraham Lincoln.

The President wired on January 14:

"When do you expect to be here? Would be glad to have your suggestions as to supplying your place as military governor."

But Johnson shrank from undertaking the trip. There were loose ends to tie up in terminating his governorship, and the civil government to be chosen on March 4 would not take office until a month later. Hoping that his presence in Washington on inauguration day would not be mandatory, he asked Forney to look up the precedents. The latter found that five Vice-Presidents had been sworn in after the Presidential inauguration; but still he wanted Johnson to be on hand, for political reasons.

"All our friends," he wrote, "would be greatly disappointed if the Vice-President failed to appear . . . Not alone your interests, but the interests of the country, demand your presence. You are in fact the representative of the Democratic element, without which neither Abraham Lincoln nor yourself could have been chosen. The present partisans of Mr. Lincoln will be on the ground, and I think you should be here, if only for a few days, to see the people who look to you in shaping generous, magnanimous policies. If this is not done, my dear sir, the great Union party will be a failure."

Forney did not need to point out that if the National Union party should fail, his political fortunes would probably fail with it. As proprietor of two newspapers—the *Chronicle* in Washington, and the *Press* in Philadelphia—in line for lush printing and advertising contracts, Forney had an interest at stake.

Informed of Johnson's hesitation, Lincoln on January 24 wired peremptorily:

"Several members of the cabinet with myself considered the

question today as to the time of your coming here. While we fully appreciate your wish to remain in Tennessee until your state government shall be inaugurated, it is our unanimous conclusion that it is unsafe for you not to be here on the 4th of March. Be sure to reach here by that time."

This was an order from the commander-in-chief, and Johnson, a general in the army, could only obey. With misgivings, therefore, and despite great lassitude, he set out from Nashville on February 25th. He was warned that bushwhackers planned to waylay the train in Kentucky, but this warning, like innumerable others, was waved aside; threats had ceased to make an impression.

His family Johnson left at Nashville, waiting until it should be safe to return to Greeneville; the war was still on, and marauders were active.

The Vice-President-elect reached Washington on the first day of March. He looked ill. His face showed traces of the ordeal he had passed through. His dark hair, still abundant and worn long on the neck in an old-fashioned style, now had gray streaks, and his mouth had taken a grim downward curve. Carl Schurz, liedersinging German liberal who, as a political major general, had failed to distinguish himself for much besides enthusiasm and a faculty for quarreling with superior officers, thought Johnson's countenance "sullen"; others saw in it only determination.

Something of the frankness that had lightened his features in the old Senate days was gone, and the direct, piercing gaze of the intensely black eyes could be disconcerting. In moments of excitement those eyes would flash with flickerings of banked-down fires which Schurz guessed correctly underlay the stern exterior. And behind Johnson's well-known taciturnity, there now seemed to be an added lethargy suggesting disinclination to speak at all.

Washington had changed much in the four years of war. During his hasty visits while military governor, Johnson had been too preoccupied to observe it closely; now he found it a Northern city, animated by a spirit uncongenial to the easygoing, Southern-type semivillage it had been before. He reached the capital in wretched weather. On March 2 and 3 the rain came down in torrents, and he remained in his rooms at the Kirkwood House, a modest hotel at Twelfth Street on Pennsylvania Avenue. His second-floor suite of parlor and bedroom overlooked the Avenue, and streaming gutters and quagmire roadway proved a sufficient deterrent against venturing out in his weakened condition.

One piece of official business remained to be transacted—his resignation as military governor of Tennessee, and the surrender of his commission as a brigadier general. With the help of his secretary, Colonel William A. Browning, he prepared the requisite documents and on March 3 sent them to Secretary of War Stanton. A covering letter expressed Johnson's high regard for the Secretary, and thanked him for "the uniform kindness which you have been pleased to extend to me personally and officially during my service under the War Department."

In accepting the resignations, Stanton piled praise upon praise for the governor's "patriotic and able" services.

"In one of the darkest hours of the great struggle," ran the official testimonial, "the government called you from the Senate and from the comparatively safe and easy duties of civil life, to place you in the front of the enemy, and in a position of personal toil and danger perhaps more hazardous than was encountered by any other civil or military officer of the United States. With patriotic promptness you assumed the post, and maintained it under circumstances of unparalleled trials, until recent events have brought safety and deliverance to your state and to the integrity of that constitutional Union for which you so long and so gallantly periled all that is dear to man on earth."

Praise so spontaneous and emphatic seldom emanated from the temperamentally noncommendatory Stanton.

In spite of the weather, Washington was crowded for the inauguration, and the newspapers daily listed the celebrities who were arriving. One whose presence stirred a shoal of memories was Miss Harriet Lane, ex-President Buchanan's niece, who just four years previously had been relinquishing her role as White House hostess. Miss Lane was to stay at the Belgian legation, it was announced.

On inauguration eve, March 3, during the closing hours of Congress, the Capitol was thronged. Lincoln and the cabinet

CONSTANCY.

Johnson and the Constitution. *Credit: Library of Congress.*

Mother Seward Rubs on Russian Salve. A Nast cartoon from *Harper's Weekly. Credit: Library of Congress.*

Sketch of Johnson's arrival at Delmonico's, Fifth Avenue and 14th Street, New York, at start of the "Swing Around the Circle" tour of 1866—pomp and splendor, glittering military escort, and cheers. *Credit: Library of Congress.*

Nast cartoon from *Harper's Weekly* for March 30, 1867, on the New Orleans riot, June 30, 1866 — Seward behind Emperor Andy; Gideon Welles peering over the parapet; Stanton looking the other way; Grant staying Sheridan's hand on the sword, declining to interfere. *Credit: Library of Congress.*

Cartoon of November 1866 (Frank Leslie's *Bucket of Fun*) on the head-on clash between Johnson and Thaddeus Stevens. *Credit: Library of Congress.*

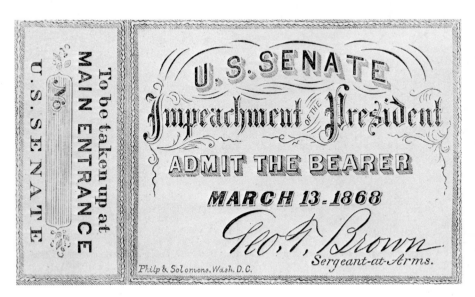

Coveted ticket of admission to the impeachment trial. *Credit: Library of Congress.*

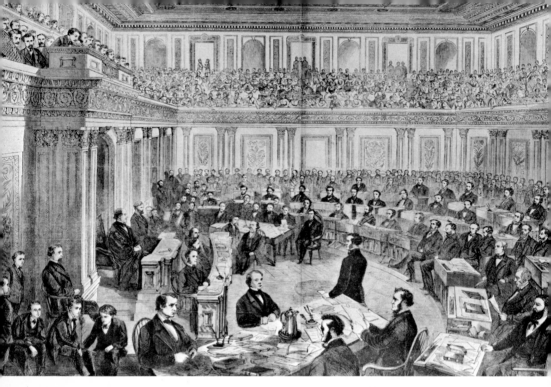

Opening of the impeachment trial, Chase presiding. The defense lawyers are at near table and the impeachment managers at far table. Members of the House of Representatives are standing in rear. Wood engraving from *Harper's Weekly*, April 11, 1868. *Credit: Library of Congress.*

Below, managers of the impeachment trial, 1868. Back row, left to right, Wilson of Iowa, Boutwell of Massachusetts, and Logan of Illinois. Front row, Butler of Massachusetts, Stevens of Pennsylvania, Williams of Pennsylvania, and Bingham of Ohio. *Credit: Library of Congress.*

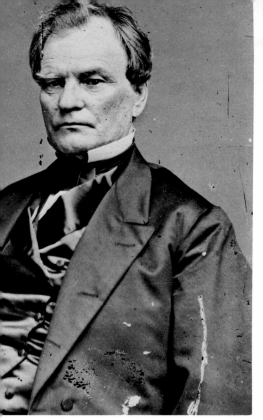

Companion photographs of Senator Benjamin F. Wade of Ohio: at left, as the fighting, indomitable abolitionist of the Senate, defying the Southern fireeaters before the war. At right, old and worn, yet still tough and implacable, presiding as president pro tem of the Senate during the struggle with Johnson and the impeachment. *Credit: Library of Congress.*

Ben Butler making open speech of the prosecution in trial. Nearsighted, Butler read from paper held close to his eyes and generally made a poor impression. Wood engraving from *Leslie's Illustrated Weekly*, issue of April 18, 1868. *Credit: Library of Congress.*

Portrait of President Johnson, probably about 1868, showing the marks
of his ordeal in office. *Credit: Library
of Congress.*

Senator Edmund G. Ross of Kansas,
at the time of the impeachment trial.
Credit: Library of Congress.

Harper's Weekly (March 21, 1868) version of the intent scene in the House
when Thad Stevens wound up the impeachment debate, March 2, 1868. *Credit:
Library of Congress.*

An exclusive portrait of Andrew Johnson circa 1875, when he returned to the U.S. Senate. *Credit: Mrs. Margaret Johnson Patterson Bartlett.*

This French coffee-maker was brought from France on a blockade runner during the war and presented to Jefferson Davis, President of the Confederacy. It was intended to brew coffee: the lamp under the boiler heated water which, when boiling, rose in the glass tube and dripped down on coffee in smokestack, the brew being drawn off through the petcock in front. (Cups and cigars were added without warrant for this photograph.) When Davis fled Richmond hurriedly, his home (the White House of the Confederacy) was seized and looted by Union soldiers. Just after Johnson became President by Lincoln's assassination, this souvenir was presented to him by a Union officer, and during his temporary stay at the Treasury, while waiting for Mrs. Lincoln to vacate the White House, Johnson used it to brew tea in his office. *Credit: Smithsonian Institution.*

Steinway piano in Homestead, Greeneville. When Johnson left the White House in 1869, he purchased furniture for the Greeneville home, stripped and vandalized by Confederates during the war, including two identical Steinway square pianos for his two daughters. This was Martha Patterson's. *Credit: Mrs. Margaret Johnson Patterson Bartlett.*

The Andrew Johnson National Monument, Greeneville, Tennessee. The grave site is at the apex of a high, steep conical hill outside Greeneville. The members of his family also are buried within the enclosure. *Credit: Mrs. Margaret Johnson Patterson Bartlett.*

were on hand, socially and officially, and former Treasury Secretary Chase, now doubly dignified as Chief Justice, dropped by for half an hour. Forney was staging a jollification in his office, which Johnson had been persuaded to attend despite his indifferent health. The party, Forney had stressed, was a sort of "victory celebration" by the Democratic wing of the incoming administration, and his absence might be resented. The hours passed pleasantly, as Gideon Welles, the patriarchal Navy Secretary, noted; so pleasantly that it was midnight before Welles bade good night and rode home with Secretary of State Seward, the two congenially tearing to rags the obvious and quite hopeless political yearnings of the Chief Justice, who felt sidetracked in his exalted post. In Forney's quarters the corks were still popping.

Ben Truman, Johnson's companion in Tennessee, was at the party; and the next morning he would bear witness to Johnson's chagrin when he awoke in the throes of a sick hangover. He was still shaky when Senator James R. Doolittle, of Wisconsin, a member of the committee to escort the Vice-President-elect to the Capitol, arrived at half past ten o'clock; but pulling himself together, he was steady when the outgoing Vice-President, Hamlin, called shortly afterwards in his carriage. Together the three men rode to the Capitol. The rain had slackened, though it had not entirely stopped; Pennsylvania Avenue was a sluice of mud.

At the Capitol, Johnson and his escorts went directly to the Vice-President's room to await the signal to enter the Senate chamber, where the Vice-Presidential inauguration was to take place.

The Senate galleries were filling up, although the ceremony would not take place until noon. Because of the uncertain weather, alternative programs had been worked out for Lincoln's inauguration: should the rain keep up, he would be sworn in the Senate chamber; should it stop, the formality would take place on the Capitol steps. In view of this, there had been a rush by spectators to secure seats in the Senate as soon as the doors opened at ten o'clock.

The press gallery was crowded with reporters from out of town; sandwiched in between the newsmen were excited women guests. The ladies' gallery filled almost at once, with much jostling and crushing of mud-spattered skirts. An incessant chatter was kept up. On the floor senators visited with distinguished guests; among these were Admiral Farragut and General Joseph Hooker. In a semicircle before the presiding officer's desk were ranged the seats assigned to members of the cabinet and the Supreme Court; the center seat was reserved for the President.

As noon approached, the air grew dank and stifling. The clanking ventilating system of the Capitol, never very efficient, was inadequate to cope with the reek of rain-soaked garments, and the temperature rose.

The diplomatic gallery drew attention by its brilliance, the representatives of the legations (in the words of the *New York Herald* reporter) "presenting an array of chapeaux and feathers, gold and silver lace, and sparkling decorations of honor." A commotion was caused when the representative of a South American nation got his feet tangled in a crinoline and rolled down the aisle.

A few minutes before twelve, the procession began to file into the chamber, the Vice-President-elect leaning on the arm of Vice-President Hamlin. The *Herald* reporter noticed that Johnson walked unsteadily, and concluded it was because of excitement.

No one in the galleries was aware of what had occurred in the Vice-President's room shortly before. While waiting with Hamlin, Doolittle, and others, Johnson had suffered an attack of nausea that left him faint. The men with him saw his distress, and thought to themselves that he looked ghastly. Like an actor seized by uncontrollable stage fright, he felt incapable of "going on," and he asked Hamlin whether he had any whisky. The Vice-President, a teetotaller (he had banished liquor from the Senate restaurant during his term), had none, but sent a page to fetch a bottle. When it came, Johnson poured a stiff drink and downed it gratefully. It seemed to steady him.

Two factors were contributing to this sudden loss of nerve: first, the momentousness of the impending ceremony, by which he, the once friendless "bound boy," would be invested with the second highest honor that could be bestowed by that mystic "people" for whom he had always entertained a devotion bordering on reverence; and second, his physical debility, aggravated by the late hours and jollification of the evening before.

The time came to enter the Senate; but at the door Johnson, again seized by panic, turned back, and pouring another half-tumblerful, gulped it down. Then, gripping the Vice-President's arm, he walked into the buzzing, superheated Senate chamber, where everybody craned to get a good look at Andy Johnson of Tennessee.

The Vice-President assumed his place on the rostrum, and Johnson took his at the clerk's desk, directly below Hamlin. Lincoln, in the President's room nearby, was signing last-minute bills.

At twelve o'clock precisely, Hamlin began his graceful farewell speech, but was interrupted by the filing in of the cabinet, led by the venerable, wispy Secretary of State Seward. Next came the robed justices of the Supreme Court. Hamlin resumed, but was interrupted again when Mrs. Lincoln appeared in the diplomatic box, escorted by two senators, and took a front seat. There were audible comments upon the First Lady's costume, "a black velvet trimmed with ermine." Then more diplomats came in, glittering with braid and plumage, and Hamlin struggled to a close amid much confusion.

It was Johnson's cue to make the customary short induction speech. He began, and had been talking about five minutes when Lincoln entered and took his assigned place facing the new Vice-President.

"During all this time," reported the *Herald*, "Andrew Johnson —for such he simply was then, not having taken the oath of office (would to Heaven that it could still be said in behalf of the country that he was still Andrew Johnson!)—continued his speech. Such a speech! It might have been appropriate at some hustings in Tennessee, but it certainly was far from being appropriate upon this occasion. It was not only a ninety-ninth-rate stump speech, but disgraceful in the extreme. He had not proceeded far when senators on the Republican side began to hang their heads, sink down in their seats, and look at each other as much as to say, 'Is he crazy, or what is the matter?'

"The Democratic senators leaned forward and appeared to be chuckling with each other over the figure made by the Republican party with their Vice-President-elect. The foreign ministers showed unmistakable signs of amazement as the incoherent sentences came from Mr. Johnson's lips. Republican senators moved around in their seats, unable to sit still under the exhibition before them. Some of the senators sat sidewise, others turned their backs, as if anxious to hide themselves."

Senator Sumner covered his face with his hands and bowed his head on the desk. The members of the cabinet whispered together. Attorney General Speed, sitting at Welles's left, muttered, "All this is in wretched bad taste," and a moment later groaned, "The man is certainly deranged." To Stanton, sitting on his right, Welles protested, "Johnson is either drunk or crazy," and Stanton, "petrified" with astonishment, nodded that "there is evidently something wrong." Seward put a good face on the situation and said it was probably the effect of emotion, upon returning to the Senate under such circumstances; the secretary felt rather emotional himself. Forney, facing the President, observed Lincoln's head droop and an expression of sadness and humiliation cross his face. Johnson rambled on, while the members of the House of Representatives trooped in, coming from their adjournment.

Reporters were unable to catch the drift of the discourse, so disjointed it was, and so drowned out by exclamations in the galleries.

"Has he no friends?" "Is there no person who will have mercy upon him?" "Tell him to stop and save the country from further disgrace!" These were plainly heard.

At one point Hamlin leaned over and yanked Johnson's coat, hissing, "Stop, Johnson! Stop!" There was no stopping Andy. Scheduled to speak seven minutes, he kept on for nearly seventeen.

What he said, as far as it could be caught at all, was reported in widely different versions, depending upon the political slant of the reporter and his newspaper. A "cleaned-up" version, which preserved the sense, though not the manner, of the address, appeared eventually in the *Globe*. The ideas were those that Johnson had expressed over and over for years past: the sovereignty of the "people"; the marvel of his rise from lowly origins; the benevolence of the government that made such a rise possible; faith in the Constitution; the loyalty of Tennessee.

The *Herald* reporter (without attempting to reproduce the rustic Tennessee vernacular into which Johnson unconsciously dropped, as some newspapers did, maliciously) stated that the speech was so "disconnected, the sentences so incoherent," and the babble of the spectators so distracting, he had heard only snatches of it; the gist, more or less, he gave as follows:

"Your President is a plebeian—I am a plebeian—glory in it—Tennessee has never gone out of the Union—I am going to take two minutes and a half on that point—I want you to hear me—Tennessee always was loyal—we derive our power from the people—you, Mr. Chief Justice Chase, are but a creature of the people—I want you to hear me two minutes on that point," and so on.

He addressed each member of the cabinet by name and title, admonishing each that he derived all his power and authority from the people. "You, Mr. Stanton, Secretary of War and you, Mr. Speed, Attorney General, and you . . ." Here he paused, staring at the white-bearded Welles, and mumbled in a bewildered aside, "Who is the Secretary of the Navy?" "Welles," prompted Forney, and the speaker went on: "You, Mr. Welles, Secretary of the Navy . . ."

The *Herald* reporter refrained from stating positively that Johnson was drunk; he merely averred that the new Vice-President "evidently did not shun Bourbon county, Kentucky, on his way here."

At last, apparently unmindful of the consternation around him, the speaker desisted, and Hamlin quickly administered the oath of office, repeating it sentence by sentence, and (said the *Herald*) "the effort of the Vice-President-elect to go through with the form of repeating the sentences was painful in the extreme. He stumbled, stammered, repeated portions of it several times over." Then he started to make a second speech, but the officials around him halted that.

Having been installed, his duty was to swear in the senators as their names were called. Holding out the Bible, he indicated to each senator to touch it and bow the head in assent, then waved each along without repeating the oath. Halfway through, the omission was noticed, and one by one the senators were called back and Forney, as Senate Secretary, administered the oath properly. Then Forney hurriedly announced that the procession would form to escort the President to the East Portico (the rain having stopped). As Johnson took his place in line, Lincoln whispered to Senator Henderson of Missouri, at his side, "Do not let Johnson speak outside."

The crowd outside, meanwhile, waiting for the inaugural ceremonies to commence, had been puzzled by the sound of a "harsh, shrill voice" coming from the Senate chamber. There had been speculation as to who was orating at such a moment.

"That's a gasbag," said one standee.

"A pretty time to make a stump speech!"

"Why don't he dry up and let Old Abe be sworn in?"

A page came out and said the speaker was Andy Johnson, but nobody believed him. "Andy ain't no such man," said one who claimed to know him personally, and he found general agreement.

Then Lincoln appeared, was sworn in by Chief Justice Chase, and delivered his inaugural address of hope and compassion ("with malice toward none, with charity for all"). After the applause and cheers, there were shouts for the Vice-President, and Johnson stepped into view and waved his arms in acknowledgment. "Speech! Speech!" yelled several voices, but (to quote the *Herald*) "Johnson rubbed his red face with his hands, as if to clear his mind, but did not succeed, and said nothing."

The formalities concluded, the senators straggled back to their chamber by twos and threes, and stood around in knots discussing the indignity that had been inflicted upon them. The Vice-President was supposed to return and adjourn the session, but he did not appear, and after waiting an hour the senators slipped away one by one without taking adjournment.

"It is therefore supposed," concluded the *Herald*, "that legally the Senate is still in session, though not one of the senators is in his seat."

The reaction nationally to Johnson's maudlin performance was one of shock, dismay, and humiliation. Some correspondents candidly told their editors that they had been too ashamed to report the happening. The speech itself, or what purported to have been the Vice-President's remarks, was published in garbled forms, no two of which jibed. Some administration newspapers suppressed the entire scene; the *New York Tribune*, for example, devoted one sentence to the inauguration of Johnson, to the effect that at fifteen minutes past noon the Vice-President was sworn in. In an apparent attempt to gloss over the embarrassment and present an appearance of harmony, the *Tribune* reported gratuitously that Johnson was seen at the White House reception that evening, "paying considerable attention to Mrs. Lincoln." This, had it occurred, would have been another unforgivable faux pas, because Mary Lincoln despised the "tailor," and the exhibition in the Senate had turned her dislike to positive detestation.

The New York Times, another administration supporter, quoted Johnson's speech in a version drastically revised by the Senate reporter, and made no mention of Johnson's condition.

Throughout the country, the humiliation was felt keenly. The United States, in the person of its Vice-President, had been shamed before the world, and the radical *Independent* rebuked the newspapers that tried to hush up the disgrace, boldly saying what everybody was saying privately, namely, that Johnson had "presented himself to take his solemn oath of office in a state of intoxication."

"In the name of an insulted people," the *Independent* demanded, "so great an affront to the dignity of the republic should be made to bear a fit penalty, atonement, and warning." At the least, it said, the Vice-President should apologize and resign.

The copperhead press wept crocodile tears. The *New York World* condemned the Vice-President's speech ("the most incoherent public effort on record") impartially with Lincoln's address, terming them equally disgusting. Duty alone (said the *World*) compelled it to lay before its readers such excrescences of language, "with a blush of shame and wounded pride, as American citizens. But we cannot hide the dishonor done to the country we love by withholding these documents from publication. 'The pity of it, the pity of it,' that this divided, suffering nation should neither be maintained in this crisis of its agony by words of wisdom nor cheered with words of hope, but mocked at in its calamity by a prose parody of 'John Brown's Hymn' from the lips of its chosen chief magistrate.

" 'The pity of it, the pity of it' that the life of this chief magistrate should be made precious to us by the thought that he at least excludes from the most august station in the land the person who defiled our chief council chamber with the spewings of a drunken boor."

So meaty was the opportunity to load with opprobrium the administration it hated, the *World* the next day raised a second ululation of woe, referring to the Vice-President's behavior in such terms as "incoherent indecency," "exhibition of drunken impertinence," "beastly orgie," and "outrageous impertinence." "Unluckily," it moaned, with hypocritical gusto, the speech had been heard by foreign diplomats and the nation's disgrace was being trumpeted around the earth. Warming up to its text, the *World* concluded:

"The drunken and beastly Caligula, the most profligate of the Roman emperors, called his horse to the dignity of consul. The consulship was scarcely more disgraced by that scandalous transaction than is our vice-presidency by the late election . . . And now to see [this office] defiled by this insolent, drunken brute, in comparison with whom even Caligula's horse was respectable! . . . And to think that one frail life stands between this insolent, clownish creature and the presidency! May God bless and spare Abraham Lincoln!"

Well might Andrew Johnson have cried, on March 5, 1865 (to Forney, perhaps?):

"Reputation, reputation, reputation! O, I have lost my reputation! . . . My reputation, Iago, my reputation!"

TWO

A POUNDING ON THE DOOR

THE Vice-President was not a figure in a play, able to redeem himself by a contrite speech in the last act; a speech had been his undoing. Since it could not be expunged, he must live out the consequences. And at what cost! By one flagrant offense, it seemed, he had all but annulled the record of a lifetime of honored and honorable service, and blotted out years of recent sacrifice and striving in Tennessee. How could a man of upright conduct in one day become an object of such derision? What protest or excuse could avail against the ignominy of such a degradation? Could the downfall ever be retrieved? Fortunately there were people, some of them older and more experienced in the world's fickle ways, who believed all would come right under the attrition of time, and they rallied to Johnson's aid.

First to demonstrate unimpaired confidence were the Blairs, old Francis Preston Blair and his son, Montgomery. They whisked the Vice-President directly from the Capitol to Silver Spring, and there shielded him from visitors for about two weeks.

Johnson of course was aware of the shock he had given the nation, but he did not attempt any public explanation. His friends could do that. The *matter* of his dreadful speech he had meant; he had said it many times before; but for the *manner* he was to blame, and that was that. Johnson was never an apologizer.

No immediate business was required of him and he rested in the Blairs' sanctuary. The only letter he is known to have written during the interval was addressed to the chief reporter of the *Congressional Globe*. Much was being made of the fact that the March 4 speech had not yet appeared in the *Globe*'s reports of the transactions of the Senate, although there was nothing remarkable about this. Only so many columns of the proceedings of

Congress were printed by the *Globe* each day, and toward the close of a session a lag of a week or longer often occurred between the delivery of a speech and its publication.

On March 9, Johnson wrote to the *Globe* reporter, M. Sutton:

"I am not well, have been confined to my room for some days past and am unable to call and see you. I see . . . that the proceedings of Saturday, the 4th inst., have not as yet been published, and as I understand there has been some criticism of the address delivered by me in the Senate chamber, will you do me [the] favor to preserve the original notes, and retain them in your possession, and furthermore, at your earliest convenience, *bring* me an accurate copy of your report of what I said on that occasion."

This procedure was not unusual; members of Congress regularly edited and revised their speeches before publication; it was standard practice.

A curt telegram went to Robert Johnson at Nashville on March 12, reminding him that until the civil government should take office in April, the Secretary of State, Edward H. East, would be the acting governor.

Apart from these two communications, Johnson's correspondence during the rest of March, at least on his side, was a blank. Since Congress was not in session, he was not called upon to preside over the Senate. His seclusion was complete.

The senators stewed for days over the scandal. Senator Sumner prepared a resolution demanding that the Vice-President resign, but the Republican caucus failed to adopt it. Johnson was not a member of the Senate, but of the executive branch, so the senators could inflict no punishment; but they took out their mortification by suddenly excluding all alcoholic liquors from the Senate wing of the Capitol, and by dropping from all standing committees two notorious inebriates—Senators James A. McDougall of California, and Willard Saulsbury of Delaware. Inasmuch as both these offenders were Democrats, it is possible that the Republican majority acted more in anger than in sorrow. This belated burst of reform drew ironic congratulations from the skeptical temperance press.

Johnson's friends were not idle about setting the record

straight. Hugh McCulloch, the new Secretary of the Treasury—a prim banker from Indiana—grew so alarmed by the stories reaching him that he went to Lincoln for reassurance, pointing out that the nation now had a larger stake than ever in Lincoln's life.

The President hesitated before replying, and then spoke with unusual seriousness, telling the Secretary not to worry.

"I have known Andrew Johnson for many years," he said impressively. "He made a bad slip the other day, but you need not be scared; Andy ain't a drunkard."

Hamlin defended his successor in an interview and assumed at least part of the blame for the incident, inasmuch as he had supplied the whisky without thought of the effect it might have on a man in Johnson's convalescent condition.

"Andrew Johnson is not an intemperate man," said Hamlin. "He is sober and in his right mind, and is the right man in the right place, and may God keep and preserve him."

Since Hamlin had served in the Senate with Johnson and knew him from long experience, this testimony carried authority.*

Even more convincing was "Parson" Brownlow's emphatic witnessing. Writing to Chief Justice Chase, Brownlow pointed out that during a lifetime of vituperative warfare, the one name he had never applied to Andrew Johnson was "drunkard"; in fact, wrote the "Parson," "nobody in Tennessee ever regarded him as being addicted to the excessive use of whisky."

Under this weight of evidence, even the ultra-radical *Independent* backtracked to the extent of printing that the Vice-President had been "in a shattered condition, resulting from a severe illness and severe labor," and probably would "never have committed the terrible blunder" if he had been well.

"It is asserted that he is determined never again to give offense to the Senate and the country by use of intoxicating liquors," the *Independent* added dubiously. "If he is to keep this noble resolution, he must part company with some of the Senate officials, or they must throw their whisky demijohns out of the window of their official apartments."

---

* Several years later Hamlin would give a different version that was more damaging to Johnson; but by that time they had broken politically.

The dig could not have been more palpably aimed at the Senate secretary, Forney.

But though the record might be corrected, nothing could efface the popular impression of a reeling, whisky-tongued Vice-President; and to the end of his life, Johnson would have to endure the epithet thus placed so temptingly within the reach of any enemy or critic—"drunken tailor."

Passage of time did soften the public's shock, as old Preston Blair had forecast. This Nestor among politicians, who had been a member of President Jackson's "kitchen cabinet" and who still wielded much influence, kept Johnson's mind off the incident by bringing him up-to-date on political developments that had occurred in Washington while he had been immersed in Tennessee affairs.

This coaching by old Blair, who knew as much secret history as any man alive, had a certain disadvantage for Johnson. The Blairs —the father and two sons, Montgomery, who had been Lincoln's Postmaster General until 1864, and Francis Preston, Jr., who as general and congressman during the war had been mainly instrumental in holding Missouri for the Union—were anathema to the Republicans. Not only were the Blairs former Democrats and prominent in that party, they were among the most conspicuously successful political intriguers in the land. The clan stuck together, and Johnson himself would comment upon the fact that no important public office could fall vacant—or even appear about to fall vacant—without the Blairs discovering that the ideal man to fill it was one of themselves. The news that the Vice-President was "in the hands of the Blairs," therefore, sent his stock, already low, plummeting further in the opinion of the radicals in Congress.

But events during late March obscured the scandal of the tipsy Vice-President. The end of the war was in sight, but the North was suffering an attack of nervous jitters brought on by last-minute acts of desperation perpetrated by the rebels—conspiracies hatched in Canada to terrorize the North by liberating thousands of Confederate prisoners of war, and plots to burn down Northern cities. In several New York hotels fires were started by Confederate incendiaries, but the work was done so clumsily that disaster was averted. The North feared more vengeful schemes might be tried by the dying Confederacy.

Johnson had telegraphed to Robert that he would start for Tennessee on March 28, when a series of developments caused him to change his mind.

Lincoln had gone to Grant's headquarters at City Point, below Richmond. Secretary Welles suspected the President had really taken refuge there to escape the horde of office seekers besieging the White House. On March 28 Lincoln held a council of war with Generals Grant and Sherman and Admiral David Porter aboard the steamer *River Queen*. During this talk he outlined the broadly magnanimous terms on which he would accept surrender of the Confederate armies. All three military men took careful note of the President's instructions.

On April 1 the Battle of Five Forks was fought, and on April 2 Lee evacuated Richmond. Jefferson Davis and his disintegrating cabinet fled southward. On April 3 the first contingent of Union troops (a Negro regiment) entered Richmond, and on April 4 Abraham Lincoln walked through the smoking ruins of the Confederate capital without insult or molestation.

News of the fall of Richmond threw Washington into a delirium of joy. Business halted, government clerks poured into the streets, singing, dancing, hugging each other rapturously. A crowd gathered in front of the War Department and cheered for Stanton, and the Secretary emotionally confirmed the glad tidings. Andy Johnson was spotted in the throng, a speech was demanded, and he delivered what the *Washington Star* described as "a few stirring remarks." A salute of eight hundred guns was fired in Lafayette Park.

On that Tuesday evening, April 4, all government buildings were illuminated with tens of thousands of candles and gas jets, and flags, bunting, and transparencies blazing with mottos of thanksgiving. At the Treasury, the District's Chief Justice David K. Cartter invoked vengeance on the rebel leaders, and Vice-President Johnson in a vigorous speech struck the same note. What should be done with Jeff Davis, he asked the crowd, and back came the roar, "Hang him!" Yes, hang him twenty times over,

Johnson cried, amid tremendous cheering. No one thought his stump speaking out of place on that wild night.

On April 5 Lincoln sent word urging the Vice-President to come and see the remains of Richmond.

On the same day, two pieces of major news reached Johnson. In Tennessee, Brownlow was installed as the duly elected governor. In Washington, Secretary of State Seward was injured in a carriage accident so badly that his life was in danger. His horses had bolted, and in attempting to leap out he had been dashed to the ground, fracturing his right arm and jaw and sustaining a severe concussion. He was carried home unconscious, and to hold the broken jaw the doctors rigged a cagelike wire support. This was extremely painful, and the newspapers reported his condition as most grave. Seward's death, Johnson foresaw, would have far-reaching political repercussions.

On April 6 the Vice-President was issued a pass by the provost marshal of the District, authorizing him to travel to Richmond and return with his secretary, Colonel Browning, and a servant. Also going along was Preston King, jolly, rotund former senator from New York, who had attached himself to the Vice-President as a social buffer. The group made the journey on the *Dictator*, a dispatch boat placed at their disposal by Secretary Welles.

By now the Navy Secretary was convinced that Johnson's irrational behavior on March 4 had been a temporary aberration, which would yield to "proper treatment." However, Welles suspected that Seward had turned against the Vice-President, an attitude that would create awkwardness in the event of Seward's recovery.

At Richmond, Johnson and his party put up at the Spottswoode House, one of the few hotels open because of the absolute dearth of provisions. All around him Johnson saw the tragic aftermath of rebellion as it existed all over the shattered South: death, desolation, despair, and ignominy—the social structure smashed into chaos—a generation slain, and bereavement and bitterness the heritage of a generation to come. The once princely province of Virginia and its proud, once thriving people had been reduced to this wreckage of hopes and rubble of material possessions. The haggard persons one encountered in the streets seemed stunned and inert, too dazed even to resent being scrutinized by hated "bluecoats," and passively accepting the rations handed out by Union soldiers.

In Johnson's heart there burned anger against the class of men whom he held to be responsible for the terrible reckoning—the aristocrats, rich, powerful, and blind. *They* had betrayed the South into its treason. Amid the desolation of burned Richmond, he repeated what he had so often said—that "treason must be made odious, and traitors punished."

Although Lincoln and Johnson were in Virginia simultaneously for one day, they did not meet. On Palm Sunday, April 9, the President returned to Washington, and there was met with the wonderful news of Lee's surrender at Appomattox Courthouse. Johnson returned shortly afterwards, and found the capital given over to fresh rejoicing.

Serenading of the President and cabinet was almost continuous. On Tuesday, April 11, Lincoln addressed a gathering at the White House "on the subject of resuming friendly national relations" (as Secretary Welles described the President's intention to achieve a soft peace). Other speakers were shouting for a bloodbath. Ben Butler, recently eased out of his command by Grant, not only demanded that rebels be hanged, but that the boundaries and names of their accursed states be obliterated to wipe out all reminders of their villainy.

Several members of the Committee on the Conduct of the War hastened to Richmond to glut their eyes on the overthrow of their enemies. They found what they had been primed to discover, and gloated accordingly. Congressman Julian filled pages of his diary with unconcealed exulting. The group arrived on a navy craft and slept aboard, on the night of April 11, "lulled by the music of the guitar and the singing of the Negroes below."

The next morning they started out to see the sights, and visited Jefferson Davis' hastily deserted house, and the Confederate Capitol ("not to be compared with our best modern state capitols in size or style of architecture") and Libby prison. There Julian roamed the upper floors, but did not venture into "the more loathsome dungeons below, where our poor boys suffered so much, and which are now occupied by rebel prisoners."

Back to the ship for a peaceful night's rest, only to be greeted the next morning, Thursday, April 13, with an announcement in the *Richmond Whig* that the rebel leaders, including Virginia's rebel legislature, had been invited to assemble in Richmond on the 25th to confer on the restoration of peace. Confer with rebels! ... The committeemen could hardly believe their senses.

"We were all thunderstruck," Julian recounted, "and I never before saw such force and fitness in Ben Wade's swearing. Curses loud and long were uttered by more than one at this infamous proposition to treat with the leading rebels."

Fearing that "this false magnanimity is to be our ruin after all," back to Washington the committee hurried, bent on combatting Lincoln's intended leniency. They did not know that Lincoln had already countermanded the startling order. In an informal conference at Richmond with John A. Campbell, a former justice of the United States Supreme Court and member of the Confederate cabinet, Lincoln had suggested that it might be the simplest way out of a dilemma to let the Virginia legislature revoke its own acts of rebellion. But when he found sentiment at Washington unanimously against this policy, he rescinded the authorization. The indignant committee members did not know this.

Reaching Washington at about 7 p.m. on Friday, April 14, Good Friday, they separated. Julian was in bed by ten o'clock.

Johnson had put in a dull, dispiriting day. As Vice-President, he would play no considerable part—if indeed he played any—in untangling knots of policy. For the next four years his place would be on the sidelines, as a privileged spectator and not a participant in governmental responsibility. Nor was he averse to the prospect. His service in Tennessee had been arduous, and he still felt the lassitude left by recent illness. Most of all he needed to rest for a while, and he renewed his plan to go home to Greeneville. He had spent the day at the Capitol, clearing up accumulated correspondence. Most of his letters were appeals for jobs or favors, filled with requests that he use his influence to promote some cause or obtain something important to the writer. His influence! What influence did a Vice-President have? These letterwriters hardly seemed to understand this. Nevertheless, he made such recommendations as he could, and hoped that Lincoln would follow some.

Chores disposed of, Johnson threaded his way back to the Kirkwood House through the crowds milling along Pennsylvania Avenue. The town had been on a spree for more than a week, and was still randy and rowdy; Johnson was glad to get back to the quiet of his suite.

After dinner, which he ate in the almost deserted dining room downstairs, he had a chat with an acquaintance, Leonard I. Farwell, a former governor of Wisconsin, now employed at the Patent Office. Farwell boarded at the Kirkwood, and often exchanged gossip with the Vice-President. Tonight he was headed for the theater, he said; a friend in town wanted to see the President, and the papers said Lincoln would attend Laura Keene's performance of "Our American Cousin" at Ford's Theater, so Farwell had got two orchestra seats that commanded a fine view of the presidential box. Come along he proposed; the papers said Grant would be on hand, too.

Johnson waved the invitation aside. Never went to the theater, never had time. No, he was going to read a while, then go to bed.

Farwell left, and in a short while the Vice-President retired. He had not been able to shake off that feeling of heaviness, of inertia, since his attack of fever. Turning off the gaslight, he composed himself for sleep.

The next thing he was aware of was that someone was battering on his door.

THE THIRD LIFE

". . . . . The little dogs and all,
Tray, Blanch, and Sweetheart, see, they bark at me."
—*King Lear*

PART ONE

TO THE TOLLING OF BELLS

NO fiddles played when Andrew Johnson was wrenched from sleep and hurled into a new world and a new life.

That night was filled with alarms and eerie dread—"a night of horrors," Chief Justice Chase called it, though he was only on the edge of the nightmare. Having gone to bed at about ten o'clock, Chase had been aroused by a breathless messenger from the Treasury, who gasped that President Lincoln had been shot—in Ford's Theater, a few blocks away. The news was repeated a few minutes later by a second courier, who brought the further report that Secretary of State Seward had been assassinated, with his two sons, as part of a plot to murder the chief officers of the government and seize the city. Guards were being posted at the homes of those believed threatened, and the Chief Justice was implored not to venture out, for murder stalked the streets.

Chase's first impulse was to go immediately to the President, whom he could hardly believe to have been fatally wounded; but "reflecting that I could not possibly be of any service, and should probably be in the way of those who could, I resolved to wait for morning and further intelligence. In a little while the guard came (for it was supposed that I was one of the destined victims), and their heavy tramp, tramp was heard under the window all night."

By remaining at home, Chase displayed a coolness and restraint almost unique in Washington that night. At the first report of the catastrophe, people surged into the streets, impelled by an unreasoning fear—a sense of unknown dangers. Groups ran distractedly through the misty darkness, asking, "What news? What news?" Reports piled calamity upon calamity. Congressman Julian, routed out of a sound sleep by an excited friend, suddenly felt "cold, heartsick, and almost helpless," but hurried into the street with the rest; he found the city "in a blaze of excitement and rage." Soon he heard that the President's assassin was John Wilkes Booth.

In Petersen's boarding house on Tenth Street, opposite Ford's Theater, a lodger was startled by a violent commotion outside, and running to the door he saw people streaming out of the playhouse, acting frantically for no apparent reason. They wept, shouted, fought, struck each other, and shrieked. Then a huddle of men issued from the doors carrying what seemed to be a lifeless person; and purely by reflex the lodger, standing with lighted candle in his hand, called, "Bring him in here!" By the flickering candlelight he led the shuffling bearers along a narrow hallway into his room in the rear of the house. There the unconscious Lincoln—blood oozing from the back of his head—was laid diagonally on the too-short bed, and doctors set to work, but without hope.

Soon Secretary of War Stanton arrived in a hack driven by Judge Cartter (the hackman had been too terrified to hold the reins), and as the head of the military establishment he took charge. He had come from Seward's bedside, and brought the information that the Secretary of State, although horribly gashed in the face and neck by the assassin's knife, was still living; the wounds of one of his sons were probably fatal. Stanton ordered the house cleared of the press of spectators, and induced Mrs. Lincoln, whose self-control had given away completely, to sob in the front parlor. In rapid succession, cabinet members, senators, and generals crowded in, some in an access of grief, others stunned and bewildered, too crushed to think clearly.

Outside the house a crowd seethed in the street, people continually coming and going. From time to time the darkness was punctuated by drums beating the long roll, or the galloping horses of officers dashing away with urgent orders, or the rhythmic tread of troops being hurried to some point of fancied peril. Few people besides Chief Justice Chase behaved rationally that night.

At the Kirkwood House, behind the locked door, Farwell told his story to the Vice-President. From his seat in the orchestra, he said, he had been startled by the crack of a pistol shot, and had seen the President crumple; then a man leaped from the President's box to the stage, brandishing a knife or dagger; he had called out something, then vanished into the wings.

The audience was in an uproar. Men scrambled across seats to reach Lincoln's box, women screamed, and word passed from lip to lip that the President had been killed. Into Farwell's mind flashed the thought that other high government officials might be in danger; he had recently read a call for wholesale assassination of Northern leaders published by a Southern newspaper.

Intending to warn the Vice-President, Farwell had fought clear of the panic-stricken throng, and had run the two and a half blocks to the hotel, dreading that he might be too late. Shouting to the clerk on duty to guard the stairs, he had dashed up to Johnson's door, and after agonized moments of waiting had heard Johnson stirring inside. Let the Vice-President look to his safety, Farwell urged; no one could tell what the enemies of the country planned to do that night.

While Farwell was speaking, friends began to arrive, but none were allowed into the suite except those approved by Johnson himself. Others stood as sentinels on the landing, where they were shortly relieved by city detectives. Each new arrival brought a fresh rumor indicating the existence of a general conspiracy to disrupt the government. The President's wound, by all accounts, was mortal; the end might come at any minute, and it could be delayed only a few hours at the longest.

Gloom and apprehension filled the room. Torn by anxiety, Johnson asked Farwell to go back to Tenth Street and ascertain for himself the true condition of Lincoln. Accept no second- or third-hand conclusion, he instructed, but see Lincoln and form your own judgment. Farwell left, and while waiting for his report, the Vice-President paced the floor, again and again cursing savagely the perpetrators of the bloody deed. When Farwell returned, after having himself observed the dying President, he confirmed that there was no hope, that the doctors had known this from the first.

It was then about two o'clock in the morning of April 15. Rejecting all remonstrances, Johnson set out for his chief's bedside. He muffled himself in a cloak and pulled his hat down over his eyes, and was escorted by Major James R. O'Beirne, commander of the provost guard, who had arrived with a squad of soldiers. The two men went alone, and reached the Petersen house unmolested. There Johnson stood at the bedside and looked down mutely at the expiring President, who was unconscious and breathing raucously. The Vice-President saw the blood-drenched pillow, heard Mary Lincoln's hysterical sobbing in the front parlor. In the back parlor members of the cabinet waited. Now and then Secretary Stanton, seated at the foot of the deathbed, would whisper an order. The only sounds were sobbing and that strained, rasping breathing.

The Vice-President's presence in the crowded room was resented by some of those at the bedside: as the successor, he appeared to be a too-eager harbinger of death. Later Senator Sumner would aver that he had requested the Vice-President not to linger, because the sight of him would aggravate Mrs. Lincoln's distress. In any event, it was plain that he could render no service and would only hamper those who could, and shortly he withdrew. Guarded by Major O'Beirne, he regained the Kirkwood House safely.

There another death watch kept vigil. Conversation went on in constrained tones. It had started to rain, and during pauses of silence a steady drip-drip against the windows was heard. The hours dragged by, and dawn—gray and ominous—crept across the sky.

At about seven-thirty General Halleck entered, having come from Tenth Street. Gravely he informed the Vice-President that henceforth he must under no consideration leave the hotel without a guard.

By that statement, and by the church bells that just then began to toll, Andrew Johnson learned that he had become the seventeenth President of the United States.

Chief Justice Chase was up betimes that morning, and at about eight o'clock he visited Tenth Street, where he was told that Lincoln was dead; the body already had been removed to the White House. The Chief Justice continued his stroll to Seward's house, and there learned the details of the attack upon the Secretary of State: how the wire cage that had been clamped on the Secretary's shattered jaw after the carriage accident had deflected the assassin's knife from the jugular vein. Still, the wounds inflicted were terrible, the right side of his face and throat showing deep gashes, and it seemed unlikely that he could recover.

Chase next went to the Kirkwood House, where he found Johnson "calm, but very grave." Treasury Secretary Hugh McCulloch and Attorney General James Speed came in shortly, bringing official notification from the cabinet of Johnson's succession. They conveyed the cabinet's unanimous recommendation that he take the oath of office as President at once, to avoid any lapse in the national authority. It was agreed that Chase should administer the oath in the hotel at ten o'clock, and the Chief Justice left with Speed to look up the law and precedents.

Returning at the appointed hour, Chase found a hushed group assembled in the hotel parlor. Among them were old Francis Preston Blair and Montgomery Blair, both bitter political antagonists of Chase; but at such a time animosities were buried, and they greeted each other with mutual sympathy. The Attorney General was on hand, with McCulloch to represent the cabinet, and the oath was administered amid tense silence.

Johnson repeated the prescribed words "very distinctly and impressively"—swearing to "faithfully execute the office of President of the United States, and, to the best of my ability, preserve, protect, and defend the Constitution of the United States." At the close, he kissed the Bible reverently; Chase noted that his lips touched the open page at the twenty-first verse of the eleventh chapter of Ezekiel:

"But as for them whose heart walketh after the heart of their detestable things and their abominations, I will recompense their way upon their own heads, saith the Lord God."

Extending his hand, the Chief Justice said with great solemnity, "You are now President. May God guide, support, and bless you in your arduous labors."

In a brief response Johnson confessed that he felt "almost overwhelmed" by the sudden call to perform unexpected duties, and his course of action must speak for itself as it unfolded.

"The only assurance that I can now give of the future is reference to the past," he went on. "The course which I have taken in connection with this rebellion must be regarded as a guarantee for the future."

Then he struck the theme that had dominated his career—devotion to the advancement and welfare of the people:

"I have long labored to ameliorate and elevate the condition of the great mass of the American people. Toil and an honest advocacy of the great principles of free government have been my lot. The duties have been mine—the consequences God's. This has been the foundation of my political creed . . . I want your encouragement and countenance. I shall ask and rely upon you and others in carrying the government through its present perils."

As each witness offered good wishes and departed, the President requested McCulloch and Speed to remain; and when they were alone, he told them that he desired them to continue in office, and bespoke their consideration and support. The cabinet had arranged to meet at noon in McCulloch's office at the Treasury, the Attorney General replied; the President was invited to be present. Johnson promised to be there.

When the members assembled—"weary, shocked, and exhausted" after their sleepless night—there was a mutual self-consciousness, for except for Stanton, Johnson had had little association with any of them, nor did they know much about him. What they did know was colored by recollection of that scene in the Senate on March 4.

Speed and McCulloch opened the session by reporting that Johnson had taken the Presidential oath. The President alluded to the desirability of reassuring and quieting the country, and to that end hoped that they all would carry on their duties without interruption. The possibility of a public inaugural ceremony was discussed. Navy Secretary Welles doubted its propriety under the circumstances, and Johnson believed it was unnecessary; his policy would follow along the lines laid down by Lincoln. It was agreed there should be no inaugural address. As a temporary office for the use of the President, pending availability of the White House, McCulloch offered a room adjoining his own. The meeting broke up, to reassemble at 10 o'clock the next morning, Easter Sunday.

The general reaction of the department heads to this first official consultation was favorable. Welles thought the President bore himself "admirably." McCulloch, who was the most reserved man in the cabinet, was struck by Johnson's poise and dignity. The impression left in the Secretary's mind by the March 4 speech already had undergone considerable change, and now "we all felt as we left him, not entirely relieved of apprehension, but at least hopeful that he would prove to be a popular and judicious President."

The note sounded throughout the North on that grief-laden Saturday was one of retribution—punishment swift and fearful for Lincoln's assassins. Most of the nation had learned about the tragedy that morning, and already Secretary Stanton was intimating that the leaders of the Confederacy, maddened by defeat, had instigated this hideous attempt to demoralize their conquerors. Typical of meetings held in many cities that day was a huge rally in New York's Wall Street. The crowd, tossed between grief and rage, was harangued by Ben Butler, and demands were made for hanging Jefferson Davis, Robert E. Lee, and other prominent rebels. Men holding the most moderate views in ordinary times joined in the hue and cry, and persons who were overheard to speak lightly of Lincoln's removal were attacked by crowds and roughly manhandled; one man was nearly killed before the police could rescue him.

That same day, in Nashville, the new President's family waited anxiously for news. At noon Martha Patterson wrote: "My dear, dear Father:

"The *sad, sad* news has just reached us, announcing the death of President Lincoln. Are you safe and do you feel SECURE? . . . Poor Mother, she is almost deranged fearing you will be assassinated . . . Our city is wild with excitement. It presented a gala appearance this morning but our joy was suddenly turned to grief. The Stars and Stripes have all been taken down, and now nothing but the booming of cannon is heard, and soldiers returning to camp . . . The city now presents a gloomy aspect. Almost everything is draped in *mourning;* and the house we *occupy* is also draped . . . How I long to be with you this sad day that we might weep together."

Mary had gone to Knoxville with young Frank, the letter went on, and "Bob had promised to go with her, but was in his *usual* condition, and could not go. He is here, but not sensible of the *awful calamity* which has befallen a *nation*. How much we would prize a few lines from you . . . We hope to hear from you by telegram *today*."

The telegram was sent, and Johnson in turn was reassured that the family had laid aside their fears for his safety, though the prospect opened up by his succession to the Presidency was not altogether to their liking.

All but the most important business of the government was forced to mark time pending the funeral. This was being planned by public authorities, for Mary Lincoln was unable to assist in any way. Shut in an upstairs room of the White House, she was alternately prostrated and raving—raving at times that Andrew Johnson had been instrumental in her husband's death. Only her dressmaker, Mrs. Elizabeth Keckley, seemed able to control her.

The first ceremony was held in the White House on Wednesday, April 19. The East Room had been transformed into a mortuary chapel, the walls swathed in crepe, the mirrors and chandeliers covered, and a catafalque erected in the center of the room to hold the open coffin. Around three walls ran a triple tier of steps for those attending.

Some six hundred persons, carefully screened, were admitted to the services. President Johnson, the cabinet, the Justices of the Supreme Court, senators, admirals, generals, and other notables were assigned prominent places. Johnson remained impassive throughout, his features expressionless as he stood with hands crossed on his breast.

Two incidents remained vivid in the memory of the diarist George Templeton Strong. He had received a ticket of admission in his capacity as Secretary of the Sanitary Commission, the forerunner of the Red Cross. A Wall Street lawyer of upright, candid views, he had helped to found the commission, and had served it throughout the war. His keen eye took in the diplomatic corps, in "fullest glory of buttons and gold lace," but contrasting to their disadvantage, he thought, with the many men of real ability present. But he was most struck by two unrehearsed actions:

"The Italian minister (who looked like a green and gold scarabaeus on its hind legs) leaving his place to march across the room and shake hands with Grant in a very marked way, and Johnson, stepping quietly up to the side of the coffin, looking down a few moments solemnly and thoughtfully upon the dead face."

After the ceremony, the coffin was carried to the Capitol, where it lay in state over Thursday. On Friday, April 21, another service was held in the rotunda, attended by the new President and high-ranking officers of the government; then the coffin was placed aboard the train that would carry it to Illinois, stopping at intermediate cities for separate tributes along the way.

When the train passed through Lancaster, Thaddeus Stevens stood by the tracks and watched it go by in somber silence. He did not raise his hat.

Lincoln's body left Washington one week after Lincoln's last day alive. But well before his coffin had left the capital, the race to "capture" the incoming President was in full swing.

2.

At about the hour, on Saturday, April 15, when military surgeons in an upper room of the White House were preparing to perform an autopsy upon the body of Abraham Lincoln, Congressman George Washington Julian, Senator Benjamin F. Wade, Senator Zachariah Chandler, John Covode (a former member of the Committee on the Conduct of the War), Judge David K. Cartter of the District Supreme Court, and a reporter for the *New York Tribune*, the great mouthpiece of radical doctrine, met in caucus to congratulate each other upon their good fortune. Booth's bullet, they exulted, had removed the chief obstacle to adoption of their program of harsh punishment for the vanquished South. The death of Lincoln, they agreed, would be accepted by radicals everywhere as a "godsend."

At about the moment when the surgeon opened Lincoln's skull, seeking the lethal bullet—and was startled as the insignificant pellet, smeared with blood and brain matter, dropped into his hand—the fastidious Julian was recoiling from the "intolerably disgusting" cursing of his caucus associates—their curses being directed not against the assassin who had fired the bullet that took Lincoln's life, but against the culpable "weakness" and "policy of conciliation" that had been followed by Booth's victim.

Was there not cause to rejoice? Booth's action was dastardly, of course, but it had struck down "the great leaders in the policy of mercy," Lincoln and Seward, and had put to flight "every vestige of humanitarian weakness" and rendered certain that justice would be done and "the righteous ends of the war made sure." These were Julian's conclusions.

But action had to be taken quickly if they were to benefit from this interposition by Providence, and at about the hour when the undertakers were preparing Lincoln's corpse for burial, the caucus dispatched a note to the new President requesting an interview on behalf of the War Committee; they intimated that, having just returned from Richmond, they had important information to impart. What they really had in mind was to demand a a new cabinet, sympathetic to themselves. They drew up possible slates: Covode might do for Postmaster General, and Ben Butler would be a fine replacement for Seward as Secretary of State.

An answer came back saying the President would receive his former Congressional associates at the Treasury on Sunday morning.

Senator Sumner did not wait to ask for an interview. On Saturday evening he called at the Kirkwood House to counsel the President on the course he should adopt. He found Johnson in the lounge, and then and there treated him to an exposition of his theory that the only policy that could carry the government through this crisis was to confer the vote on the ex-slaves—universally, unconditionally, and at once. This, Sumner maintained, was not only due to the freedmen as simple justice, but (since "a question is never settled until it is settled right") was also the wise policy. Other issues and measures he deemed subsidiary or immaterial; on Negro suffrage he was unalterably fixed. The conversation, as usually happened when Sumner had views to express, developed into a monologue, the senator doing the talking, while the President listened with grave attention.

Easter Sunday brought a rash of sermonizing that was concerned more with the God of wrath than with the Resurrection and the Prince of Peace. Orville H. Browning, former senator from Illinois and a close friend of Lincoln, now practicing law in Washington, at breakfast heard an acquaintance maintain that there was now "but one course to pursue—the entire South must be depopulated and repeopled with another race, and all the copperheads among us must be dragged from their homes and disposed of."

Later, at church, Browning sat through "an inflammatory stump speech" from the pulpit, in which the preacher declared that Providence had called Lincoln home because he was too forgiving, and because his mission was finished. In his successor, it was to be hoped, the nation would find a "revenger who would execute wrath."

Communing with his diary, Browning wrote: "If this shall become the prevailing doctrine, terrible scenes are before us."

While Browning was in church, the cabinet met again with Johnson at the Treasury. All were fagged and oppressed by the thought of the still form in the President's House, across the way. Stanton brought up, as pending business, a subject with which Johnson was not conversant, for he had not been admitted to cabinet discussions and there were many current topics upon which he would have to be briefed.

At the last cabinet meeting held by Lincoln, Stanton had presented the outline of a plan of provisional government for North Carolina and Virginia, at the close of the rebellion. The two states were lumped together in a military district, under the control of the Secretary of War, and the occupying force would be entrusted with the restoration of public services, such as the mails, minor courts, and revenue offices, as speedily as feasible; the police power would rest in a centralized system of provost marshals.

Secretary Welles had objected that entirely different conditions prevailed in Virginia from those in North Carolina, and the two states should be treated separately. Lincoln had upheld the objection, and asked Stanton to rework the outline, dividing the states. This revision Stanton now produced and read to the cabinet.

The subject was immensely complex and filled with difficulties, and Johnson declined to be drawn into discussion of the plan. He merely said that he did not treat treason lightly, and when the time should come for reconstruction, the rebels would be punished. Nobody seemed disposed to press the matter, and the problem was only prospective in any case; in North Carolina the war had not ended; General Sherman was still operating against Confederate General Joseph Johnston there, though word of the latter's capitulation had been expected ever since Lee's surrender.

After discussing details in connection with the forthcoming funeral, the cabinet withdrew, and Johnson admitted the delegation from the Committee on the Conduct of the War.

On their way to the Treasury, the group had stopped at Willard's Hotel to consult Ben Butler, just back from New York. They found him in perfect harmony with their views. Cabinet changes? Why, of course, rumbled Ben, putting the case in lawyer's language: Johnson "must not administer upon the estate of Lincoln, but upon that of the government, and select new men to do it."

The President greeted his former colleagues cordially, and Wade announced the purpose of their call. They had come, he said, to offer him their enthusiastic support.

"Johnson, we have faith in you," he exclaimed. "By the gods, there will be no trouble now in running the government!"

Visibly pleased, the President responded heartily:

"I am very much obliged to you gentlemen. I can only say that you can judge of my policy by the past. Everybody knows what that is. I hold this." Here his voice grew dark with anger. "Robbery is a crime; rape is a crime; murder is a crime; *treason* is a *crime;* and *crime* must be punished. The law provides for it and the courts are open. Treason must be made infamous and traitors must be impoverished."

This statement was applauded, and after setting a time to return the next morning and talk over cabinet changes, the delegation left, completely reassured. Events could not have fallen out better for them, and Julian foresaw that their healthy influence would "powerfully aid the new administration in getting into the right track." Grant's terms to Lee, he thought, were "too easy."

Hundreds of messages were reaching Johnson, expressing rage at Lincoln's murderers and pledging support of the new regime.

The pledges came from public bodies, from religious and political associations, from private citizens, from officeholders and office seekers.

A captain of Missouri volunteers wired:

"I beg to be assigned to most desperate duty in the extermination of traitors, here or elsewhere."

A man signing himself "Sexagenarian" ("One of many Millions who hail you as their countries deliverer") wrote with a tremulous hand:

"May God in his unbounded wisdom guide and protect you in your firm *resolve* . . . to meet out justice to the blood stained murderers of our to forgiving diseased President."

Within hours of Lincoln's passing, a mass meeting of Boston citizens was held in Tremont Temple, and telegraphed their "mutual grief at the violent death of our revered President and their greetings to Andrew Johnson, welcoming him to the post which Providence has so mysteriously assigned him, pledging to him our confidence and our prayers, looking to him to complete the work of subjugating treason."

Resolutions, resolutions, resolutions—they came from every quarter, laden with advice, plentiful, prolific, and sometimes pointed. Numerous correspondents urged that Butler be taken into the cabinet, or named "military Attorney General" to smite the rebels.

Here and there appeared a ripple of doubt or equivocation. A federal officeholder at St. Croix, Wisconsin, hastened to advise the President that recent attempts "to injure your reputation in consequence of alleged indiscretions connected with your inauguration as Vice-President" had produced "no perceptible effect upon the Union masses of the great Northwest."

The editor of the Rock Island, Illinois, *Argus*, a Democratic journal, sent a clipping of his quasi-endorsement of the new chief executive which conveyed more than the words meant literally:

"We confess that the impressions we received by reading his speeches, made perhaps in an unguarded moment, and while he was excited and smarting under persecutions inflicted upon him by the rebels; and also by some of his official acts, the reasons for which, possibly, were not fully understood, lead us to look with deep anxiety to his future course. But the salvation of the country itself, from utter anarchy, is in his hands; and it is to be hoped that, forgetting the gross personal injuries he has himself received," he would prove to be "a patriot, and the man for the hour . . . We shall try to see, in what he may do, only the good of our suffering country."

Such lukewarm endorsements were the exception during that kaleidoscopic week. It was plain that Johnson could count on the nation's goodwill, though the people were more occupied with thoughts of the President they had lost than of the President they had gained.

One message that brought special satisfaction came from the President's companion of Greeneville, Sam Milligan. Immediately on hearing the news, Milligan wired to his friend, elevated with such fearful abruptness to the supreme leadership:

"We want nothing. Can we be of any service to you?"

Sam Milligan was worthy of a President's trust.

Amid the confusion of new demands, new revelations, new anxieties, Johnson strove to get a footing. Echoes of earlier times were stirred by a letter Martha sent soon after April 15, in which she recounted another slight of the sort which the Johnson family had suffered for years. The woman who owned the house they rented in Nashville, Martha wrote, "walked in here the other day, and inspected things, without observing the common *ceremonies* of *entering* a *house*, and then asked to see *no one*. I had a better opinion of her ladyship, but . . . I presume she thinks we are an ignorant *sort* of *people*, half civilized and *refugees* from upper E. Tennessee . . . I will enclose her note, written to Mother, asking 'for her *rooms*, in her own house.' I made no reply."

Would the family of a President continue to be the target of petty malice by that stiff-necked aristocracy who would not understand that the day of their greatness was past? Johnson had no time to mull the question. Events otherwise in Tennessee, apart from social snubs, were occupying his attention at the moment; the legislature there was about to elect two United States senators, and Johnson was backing his son-in-law, Judge Patterson, Martha's husband, for one of the seats. Milligan had wired that the prospects seemed hopeful, "if Maynard influence can be secured." Johnson saw that Maynard's influence was forthcoming.

Meanwhile, the parade of self-anointed redeemers and self-appointed policy-makers wound through the presidential office at the Treasury with hardly a break. The day before the White House funeral services, an Illinois delegation headed by Governor Oglesby had pledged that state's wholehearted support, and Johnson in reply had adverted once more to the punishment due to rebels and traitors. It was his stock speech, and Orville Browning interpreted it as portending a policy strongly inimical to the South.

Politicians of every shade of opinion—cranks and crusaders, ministers of the Gospel and pleaders for vested interests, lobbyists and businessmen, timeservers and idealists—all seemed impelled to inform the President of the course his administration must pursue or infallibly perish. Johnson listened to them all, and replied with the stereotyped phrases—treason must be made odious and traitors punished.

The vigor of some of these impromptu responses led Secretary McCulloch, working in the adjoining room, to suspect that their inspiration was whisky. For six weeks he kept watch, and concluded that the only intoxicant the President was addicted to was the intoxicant of addressing a crowd; any half dozen persons, assembled as an audience, could bring out the stump speaker in him.*

McCulloch was unable to detect the slightest trace of liquor in the President's room. Johnson arrived every morning, Sundays not excepted, before nine o'clock, and seldom left before five in the afternoon, and his lunch was the same as McCulloch's—crackers and a cup of tea. And there was no doubt about the heavy load of work which the President got through day after day.

Wade, Julian, and Gooch, of the War Committee, had called on Johnson the second time, and "talked very frankly," in Julian's opinion. He left feeling that "the symptoms seem favorable." The President was as unrelenting as ever against the leaders of the rebellion, though inclined towards showing leniency to the

---

* As a youth of seventeen, James Ford Rhodes, the future historian, in September, 1865, was present at a conversation between President Johnson and the widow of Stephen A. Douglas. Rhodes remembered that as Johnson grew animated, he "rose to his feet and declaimed as if he were speaking from a platform," although his audience consisted of one woman and one boy.

masses who had been misled. Wade thought that hanging was indicated for ten or twelve of the foremost rebels—"perhaps, for full measure, I'd make it thirteen, just a baker's dozen."

Johnson wondered how he would narrow down the list to that number, when so many were equally guilty, but Wade was confident he could do it.

"I think if you would give me time, I could name thirteen," he said. "We could all agree on Jeff Davis, Toombs, Benjamin, Slidell, Mason, and Howell Cobb."

Yet no impression of a vengeful, bloodthirsty President was conveyed to George Templeton Strong when he and other officers of the Sanitary Commission paid a duty call at the Treasury. The interview took place on the day Lincoln's body was started on its long journey home. Strong remarked the two flags that stood outside the door of room 3636, and was told that they had decorated Lincoln's theater box on the fatal night; one showed a long tear where Booth's spur had ripped it. Such a memento, displayed at the door of Presidential authority, augured ill for expectations of clemency, Strong reflected; yet when he was admitted to the President he saw only a man of kindly manner and heard only words of cordiality and sympathy. Yes, Johnson assured his visitors, he knew all about the work of the commission, and he was prepared to assist it in any way he could.

Strong was "most favorably impressed," and put down "the 'incoherencies' of the 4th of March" to an unfortunate accident. "He looks utterly unlike a free drinker," was the lawyer's verdict. "He seemed dignified, urbane, and self-possessed; a most presentable person."

That evening, at the urgent summons of Stanton, the cabinet assembled again, and Johnson was confronted with the first major crisis of his administration. It concerned the amazing conduct of General Sherman, and it produced a near tragedy of misunderstanding.

3.

When the cabinet assembled at eight o'clock on April 21, Stanton appeared in a tizzy of alarm. He was always emotionally unstable, and news of the sort he had just received threw him into a near frenzy. He scented treachery in high quarters—perhaps a coup d'état.

The news was contained in a dispatch from General Sherman to General Grant, announcing the conclusion of an armistice with General Johnston, on terms which, if ratified by the government, would bring peace "from the Potomac to the Rio Grande." Grant, present by invitation, read the dispatch to the startled cabinet.

Sherman had received news of Lee's surrender at Raleigh, North Carolina, and Johnston, realizing that the Confederate cause was lost, opened negotiations for the surrender of his army. After considerable dickering, and reference of the proposed terms to General Breckinridge (the former Vice-President, now Confederate Secretary of War), an agreement had been signed by both commanders. This provided, among other things, that the rebels should deposit their arms in their respective state armories and disperse to their homes, where they would be unmolested as long as they kept the peace; that political and property rights should be guaranteed; and that the existing (rebel) legislatures should be recognized upon swearing allegiance to the United States. In this way the current governments in the Confederate states would carry along without interruption. Each commander referred the convention to higher authority for ratification, but Sherman was announcing it as effective, seeming to take confirmation for granted.

The cabinet received the development with dismay. In effect, Sherman seemed to propose restoring the rebellious states to their condition of 1861, with none of their rights impaired. It was a political treaty which he had dictated, not a military surrender. After four years of desperate struggle to wreck the United States, the rebels were not to be divested of their means of resuming the war at any time they chose—they would retain their arms in their own armories, under the control of traitorous legislatures whose lawful existence Lincoln had denied throughout the long conflict. Yet Sherman would legitimatize these upstart, irregular legislatures and put them in a position to sustain all their wartime acts of defiance. Guarantee of property rights might mean that ex-rebels could sue the government for compensation for their emancipated slaves. The whole arrangement was preposterous and in violation of express orders, Stanton excitedly exclaimed. Attorney General Speed wanted to have Sherman arrested.

Johnson was as indignant as the others, and it was unanimously agreed that the armistice must be repudiated at once. Grant was to go South with power to remove Sherman, denounce the armistice, and either accept a simple military capitulation, or resume fighting.

What nobody present was aware of was that Sherman had acted in good faith, on the basis of the last instructions he had received from President Lincoln. These had been conveyed personally, during the council of war with Grant, Admiral Porter, and Sherman, on the *River Queen*, and they had authorized the extension of the most lenient terms to surrendering rebels.

Subsequent to that conference, however, Lincoln had reversed himself, and in a new order had forbidden the commanders to touch political questions, but commanded them to confine themselves to negotiating military surrenders only. Political decisions he reserved for himself. Grant had acted under this latest order at Appomattox, but through negligence or oversight at the War Department, Sherman had not received a copy. Knowing Lincoln's intentions as expressed in their last meeting, he had acted accordingly, never doubting that his action would be accepted in Washington.

Next to Grant, Sherman was the nation's most popular hero; the exploits of his Army of the Tennessee were legendary. Easterners pictured these Western fighters as a race of giants, capable of anything, and they were reported to adore their "Uncle Billy." What might be Sherman's intention behind this outrageous armistice agreement? Stanton asked. With such an invincible force at his back, might he not be planning to march to Washington, seize the government, and make himself dictator? Such things had happened. Louis Napoleon, on the throne of France, had attained power by that method.

Stanton suspected some such purpose underlay Sherman's defiance of orders, and the hysterical report that he immediately released to the press placed the general in the most questionable light. Sherman's dispatch was garbled, and there was even an intimation of treason in Stanton's insinuation that Sherman had deliberately provided Jeff Davis with a route of escape. The Confederate President was understood to be fleeing southward with a hoard of gold. Was Sherman expecting to share that loot?

The public, already shaken by sensation after sensation, drew the most incriminating conclusions, and overnight William Tecumseh Sherman became the most denounced man in the United States. Forney telegraphed to the President from Philadelphia:

"Almost unanimous against the Sherman armistice. Feeling tremendous."

Grant set off to convey the cabinet's repudiation of the armistice to Sherman, and in the end Johnston surrendered on the same conditions given to General Lee. But when Sherman read the veiled accusations published by Stanton, just after he had performed the greatest single feat of the war by his march through Georgia and the Carolinas, his fury was unbounded.

Johnson had not been consulted by Stanton before the latter sent his distortions to the press; the President knew nothing about the press release until he saw it in the newspapers. At the earliest opportunity, after the misunderstanding had been corrected, he apologized to Sherman. The War Secretary never retracted.

On that same Friday, prior to the night session of the cabinet, a more harmonious incident had been the reception by the president of a delegation from Indiana, headed by Governor Oliver P. Morton. Congressman Julian was in the group, though he and Morton headed opposing wings of the Republican party in their state. Morton had rendered great services to the Union cause during the war, and on this occasion he outlined in a speech his view of the constitutional situation. No state had ever been out of the Union, but had only been in rebellion against rightful authority, he contended, and with this the President entirely agreed. For Johnson that issue had been settled. Julian utterly denied that theory, and as he listened to Johnson his confidence in the President ebbed, and he began to notice again the Tennessean's "bad grammar, bad pronunciations, and much incoherency of thought." Andrew Johnson, he forecast, would prove untrue to the people who had elected him, and would coddle the slaveholders if he got a chance. After that experience Julian tried to convince his associates on the War Committee that Johnson was already at heart a renegade, but Wade, Chandler, and Sumner scoffed; Andy was in their camp, they insisted and believed.

Meanwhile, the roundup of suspects in the assassination was proceeding. Scores of arrests were made, many on the flimsiest grounds. Stanton was convinced that the plot had originated in Richmond, and repeatedly assured the cabinet that he had conclusive evidence—proof, in fact—implicating Jefferson Davis and other high-ranking Confederate officials.

Puzzling ramifications were being uncovered. One of the men seized was a dull-witted German named George E. Azterodt, who, it appeared, had been deputed to kill Vice-President Johnson on the night of April 14. The evidence seemed plain, though its interpretation was obscure.

The day before the murder, Azterodt had registered at the Kirkwood House, and was given a room not far from the Vice-President's. He had made inquiries about Johnson. But on the fatal night he had drifted from bar to bar, cadging drinks. When he did not return to the hotel, his room was entered, and a revolver was found stuffed under the pillow, a Bowie knife tucked under the mattress, and two articles—a coat and bankbook—belonging to John Wilkes Booth. The assumption was that after caching his weapons, Azterodt had lost his nerve, and the Vice-President's life had been saved by his cowardice.

Later a more sinister hypothesis would be offered to account for the multiplicity of clues that were strewn so negligently around that room.

Another enigma was the message that had been left for Johnson at his hotel, on the afternoon of April 14, by a man who resembled Booth. The man had inquired at the desk whether Johnson was in, and had been told by the clerk the Vice-President was out. The visitor then wrote a message on a card and gave it to the clerk, who dropped it into the box of Johnson's secretary, Colonel Browning. The message read: "Dont want to disturb you are you at home [sic]?" It was signed, "J. Wilkes Booth." A handwriting expert identified the writing definitely as the actor's.

Browning had picked up the card that evening, but gave it little heed; having met Booth in Nashville, he assumed that the actor had called socially. Only when Booth was named as the assassin did the inexplicable message come to his mind.

Azterodt was soon captured, with Lewis Payne, Seward's assailant, and others more or less conclusively linked to the conspiracy—Samuel Arnold, Edward Spangler, Michael O'Laughlin, Dr. Samuel Mudd, who had set Booth's broken leg during the assassin's flight, and Mrs. Mary E. Surratt, a boardinghouse keeper, who was seized after her son, John H. Surratt, a prime suspect, fled the country.

On April 26 Booth was killed in Virginia, and his accomplice, David E. Herold, was taken.

The wrathful mood of the nation demanded swift punishment of the plotters. Stanton had said that he would have the lot tried and convicted before Lincoln was buried, but the time went by and the cabinet was divided on the question of trying them by a civil or a military court. Assignment of the case to the civil courts would open the gate to technicalities that might bring about indefinite delay, and then the prospect of appeals, whereas the judgment of a military court would be summary, and only the President could alter its verdict. Stanton fought doggedly for a military trial, and the President instructed the Attorney General to draw up a legal opinion for his guidance. Speed was reluctant, but at length submitted an opinion sanctioning the military trial on the grounds that at the time of the assassination Washington was an armed camp, the headquarters of the commander-in-chief of the army; therefore the murder had been committed against a military officer in time of war, and the accused must face a court-martial.

Accepting the opinion of his chief legal advisor—an opinion in which Stanton, another able lawyer, eagerly concurred—on May 1 the President ordered a military board of high-ranking army officers to be convened to try the case.

On May 2, yielding to the urgings of the War Secretary, who said again and again that he had proof of the connection of high Confederate officials with the assassination plot, Johnson issued a proclamation offering rewards for the arrest of Jefferson Davis, Jacob Thompson (who had served in President Buchanan's cabinet), and Clement C. Clay, Jr., former United States senator from

Alabama, together with several Confederate agents in Canada.

This action brought protests from many quarters. Stanton's "proofs" seemed suspect (they later were exposed as mere fabrications and perjury), but Johnson trusted his War Secretary. The President did hate the leaders of the Confederacy, and was convinced past all argument that they had willfully betrayed the mass of Southern people into embarking on their ruinous course; he was hot against them, and consulted Grant as to whether Lee might not be arrested and charged with treason. Grant, however, seeing his honor as a soldier impugned, insisted that as long as Lee observed the terms of his parole, he should not be molested; such treatment would be shameful. Grant carried the point, although the popular outcry against Lee was as bitter as that against Jeff Davis.

Many men of independent judgment refused to accept Stanton's arraignment of the Confederate chiefs for complicity in the assassination. Thaddeus Stevens, as relentless an enemy of the rebels as lived, disapproved so thoroughly he was willing to serve as counsel for Davis and Clay, should they be captured.

"These men are no friends of mine," he said. "They are public enemies. But I know these men, sir. They are gentlemen, and not capable of being assassins."

From Canada, Beverly Tucker, a prominent Virginian who was among those named in the Presidential proclamation, flung back the charges as "a living, burning lie," and challenged the President to make a test. From a list of twenty-five Union generals, he invited Johnson to select any nine, lay the evidence before them, and Tucker would engage to make out a better case incriminating Andrew Johnson than could be made against Beverly Tucker. *Who benefited by Lincoln's removal?* This was the question he asked, and the implications began to work in some minds.

The conspirators' trial opened on May 9. In charge was the judge advocate general, Joseph Holt, who during the war had acquired a reputation for credulity and vindictiveness.

The next day Jefferson Davis was caught in Georgia. When told that he was accused by President Johnson of conspiring to murder Lincoln, he retorted: "That is ridiculous. Johnson knows I would prefer Lincoln to him as President." Brought North, he

was held in Fort Monroe. Clement Clay had surrendered voluntarily upon learning that he was named among the conspirators,
and he, too, was held under harsh conditions in Fort Monroe.

Stanton had planned to try the conspirators in secret, but so
loud were the objections by both legal authorities and the press,
the sessions were opened to a limited number of reporters. As the
testimony unfolded, under the browbeating Holt and his assistant
prosecutors, it became evident that the defendants had been
prejudged and the trial was little more than a legal lynching.
Reputable lawyers were sickened by the spectacle. Speed's predecessor as Attorney General, Edward Bates of St. Louis, called
Speed's opinion approving the military proceedings "the most extraordinary" reasoning he had ever heard, "under the name of a
law opinion." So exercised was Henry Winter Davis, Maryland
radical who had strongly opposed Lincoln's policy of leniency to
the South, that on May 13 he appealed directly to the President.

"It is not my habit to give advice unasked," he wrote, "But I
cannot refrain from expressing to you my conviction that the trial
of the persons charged with the conspiracy against President Lincoln & Secretary Seward by Military Commission will prove disastrous to yourself your administration & your supporters who
may attempt to apologize for it . . . I assure you Sir that in all
the circle of my acquaintance I have found *not one* person who
does not deplore this form of trial. The damage it threatens to do
the Republic may possibly be averted, but rest assured it will be
at the cost of the ruin of your administration."

This letter, in the sprawling, vigorous handwriting of a confident and able man, was filed unanswered. Johnson held on the
charted course.

He was living temporarily in improvised quarters, for Mrs.
Lincoln had not yet left the White House. As early as April 25,
Robert Lincoln had explained in a note that his mother felt she
could not possibly be ready to leave before two and a half weeks,
but the weeks stretched into six. The President may have been
mystified by a subsequent note from Robert Lincoln, suggesting
that Johnson purchase the Lincoln carriages, a closed coach and
an open barouche. His mother, young Lincoln explained, was
"desirous that they should become the property of some one

whom we know rather than a stranger." This seemed odd in view of Mary Lincoln's known aversion to Andrew Johnson.

The President declined the offer, and also declined the gift of a handsome equipage—carriage, matched span of horses, silver-mounted harness, blankets, and carriage cover—which a group of New York businessmen shipped to Washington in token of their esteem. He could not, the President told the donors, violate the rule he had "ever held in reference to the acceptance of presents by those occupying high official position." The coach was returned, and a short time later Johnson purchased his own carriages, in New York and Philadelphia, at a cost of several thousand dollars paid with his personal checks. He could afford the outlay because he had transferred from the federal depository at Cincinnati to the First National Bank of Washington a balance of forty-three thousand dollars, part of the capital he had amassed.

Pending the availability of the White House, Johnson had accepted the hospitality of Representative Samuel Hooper of Boston, whose residence on Massachusetts Avenue was vacant. Hooper was accounted one of the richest men of his state, and Johnson therefore was taken aback when, on his first morning as Hooper's guest, he found that there were no provisions in the house, and he had to send to market for supplies before he could breakfast. The President also was obliged during his stay to pay the servants' wages and buy feed for the horses. Hooper visited him for two weeks, and on returning to Boston sent back a small flask of cayenne pepper. Johnson was amused by this instance of Yankee thrift.

Early in May, Horace Maynard wired that Judge Patterson and Joseph S. Fowler, a longtime political associate of Johnson, had been elected by the Tennessee legislature to the United States Senate. But Brownlow, as governor, was running into snags, and in mid-May he appealed to Johnson to do something about whipping the legislature into line. The Senate was all right, he said, but the lower house would "do nothing that strikes a rebel down. I believe they will allow all rebels to vote, and if so we are to be run over, the state controlled by the rebels, the city full of returned rebels, many of them insolent and defiant, cursing you and

I and others by name . . . What are we to do? Put forth something from Washington."

The "Parson" was finding out that "Unionist" had ceased to be a distinctive badge in Tennessee; any rebel who took the oath of allegiance to the government automatically became as much a Unionist as Brownlow himself. And the first thing such Unionist ex-rebels would do if they were allowed to vote would be to turn the "Parson" and his cohorts out of office. Naturally the governor viewed that prospect with disfavor. Throughout May and June he continued to write to the President, breathing fire against bogus Unionists who dared to assert their "rights."

"They ought to be imprisoned," was his opinion; they were all guilty of "infamous crimes."

Robert Johnson sent his father a grim report of conditions in East Tennessee. The situation there, he wrote, was out of hand. "The Union men will not permit the [rebel] leaders, and others who persecuted their families, to live in that section. A few have been killed, and others badly beaten."

On May 23 and 24, the close of the war was celebrated in Washington with splendid pageantry as the President took the salute of the victorious armies, before the regiments disbanded. The first day the Army of the Potomac marched down Pennsylvania Avenue past the White House; the second day, Sherman's Army of the Tennessee paraded. When Sherman, at the head of his columns, reached the reviewing stand in front of the White House, he swung out of line and came up on the platform. In full view of the attentive throng, the hero of the "march to the sea" shook hands with President Johnson and with General Grant, but refused to touch the outstretched hand of Stanton. Only one element was lacking in the glory of that day, and everybody felt it: Lincoln was not there.

Two days later General E. Kirby Smith surrendered the last Confederate Army, in Texas, ending organized resistance west of the Mississippi; the surrender three weeks earlier of General Richard Taylor's force in Alabama had ended it east of the great river.

With General Taylor at the time of the surrender was Isham G. Harris, the governor who had carried Tennessee into the Confederacy in 1861. Harris still kept custody of a considerable portion of the Tennessee state funds, with which he and the secession legislature had decamped in 1862. Taylor arranged to have this money sent back to Nashville under convoy of federal troops; but Harris feared to put himself within the reach of either Brownlow or Johnson and prudently set out for Mexico. From there he would seek an even more remote asylum in England, joining abroad other prominent secessionists who had succeeded in making a getaway, including Benjamin and Slidell.

4.

Five days after the last "bummer" of Sherman's long-striding Westerners had trooped out of sight and into history, the President issued two proclamations, breaking his silence on the policy he proposed to pursue in regard to the states lately in rebellion.

The first proclamation offered amnesty and pardon to all persons who had "directly or indirectly participated in the existing rebellion," with restoration of "all rights of property," except as to slaves, on the condition that they take an oath "henceforth faithfully [to] support, protect, and defend the Constitution of the United States and the Union of the States thereunder," and to abide by all laws and proclamations with reference to the emancipation of slaves.

Fourteen classes of rebels were excluded from this amnesty. They comprised military officers of the Confederacy above the grade of colonel in the army or lieutenant in the navy; civil and diplomatic officers; former members of Congress who had resigned "to aid the rebellion"; governors of the seceded states; all who had mistreated Union prisoners; all Confederate officers who had been educated at West Point or Annapolis; and finally (a very special category), all rebels who owned property valued at twenty thousand dollars or more. This was aimed at the "bloated aristocrats" whom Johnson blamed for precipitating the war.

The excepted classes of persons, however, might apply to the President individually for pardons, and the promise was given that clemency would be "liberally extended."

In the second proclamation, Johnson set up machinery to

start the return of his native state, North Carolina, to its proper relations in the Union. A provisional governor was appointed and ordered to conduct an election of delegates to a state constitutional convention, which would amend the organic law to conform with the changes regarding slavery and take other necessary steps to bring the state back to the coequal membership it had formerly enjoyed in the Union. Voters for delegates must qualify under the election laws in force before secession, and must take the amnesty oath, and only such persons could become delegates. The convention would arrange for the election of a legislature and prescribe the qualifications for voters and officeholders thereafter, this being "a power the people of the several states . . . have rightfully exercised from the origin of the government to the present time."

William W. Holden, a Raleigh editor who had danced on both sides of the secession fence before the war, but had "gone out" with his state, was named provisional governor.

Since the prewar election laws of North Carolina excluded Negroes, there was no provision in the President's proclamation that granted the vote to the state's former slaves.

The North Carolina plan was the model for similar action taken during the next few weeks to restore the other disloyal states. Almost identical proclamations were issued for Mississippi, Georgia, Texas, Alabama, South Carolina, and Florida. The remaining four states of the Confederacy—Virginia, Louisiana, Arkansas, and Tennessee—already had provisional governments in varying degrees of effectiveness, and these were not disturbed.

Johnson's proclamations were the first concrete steps taken towards reestablishing the Union intact, as it had existed before the rebellion, slavery alone excepted. That had been the stated aim of the North, registered by Congress on the threshold of the conflict, and Johnson had not forgotten it. The proclamations imposed no harsh penalties upon the South, they preached no bloody retribution, but opened a path to peace and unity. Generally they were viewed as projections of the program that Lincoln would have implemented, had he lived.

Most important of all, after weeks of successive shocks, of drifting, of uncertainty, and of irresponsible speculation, they cleared the air morally. They set goals that could be understood and attained.

But these proclamations did more. Unsuspected by the President, they signaled the opening of a second War Between the Sections—one that would rage longer and engender more bitterness than the fighting just concluded.

PART TWO

RUMBLES OF THUNDER

WHAT to do with the states of the South after their rebellion had been crushed? That was the perplexing question that faced the victorious North in 1865, and an answer was demanded.

The situation had no precedent. The Constitution contained no provision for its dissolution, and the attempt to dissolve it had been successfully repelled. But what, in consequence, had become the relationship between the defeated states and the rest of the nation? Everybody recognized that the anarchic conditions produced by the collapse of the South's social structure could not be allowed to continue. The reclaimed states must be knitted back into the fabric of the Union. But by what process? And when? On these points opinions differed widely.

There was the view held by both Lincoln and Johnson that since the states were powerless to withdraw from the Union, they never had been out of it; and presumably as soon as their rebellion ceased they would somehow revert to their positions as full partners in the Union.

Charles Sumner had evolved a different theory, one of "state suicide." He contended that by renouncing their duties and privileges under the Constitution, the seceding states had returned to the status of territories, directly under federal control, and Congress alone could breathe the breath of life back into those "dead" entities to revive them as states.

A third view was that held by Thaddeus Stevens, who talked about "conquered territories." Stevens argued that in plain fact the rebel states had seceded from the United States; that they had set themselves up as a foreign power, and had waged war against the United States in that capacity and had attempted to negotiate alliances with other foreign powers as a separate and independent nation. Having been defeated in battle, they now occupied the same position as would any foreign power vanquished in war. Their people were not United States citizens, for they had renounced that citizenship, and their lives, liberties, and property were at the mercy of their conquerors; their estates were forfeited, and they had no right even to live, unless their conquerors willed it.

Besides these main positions there were many variants—in fact, so numerous and diverse were the opinions on the subject that there really was no settled opinion at all.

Lincoln had made a start towards reconstruction in his "ten percent" plan. Launched by proclamation on December 8, 1863, this had been essentially a war measure to create loyal governments in opposition to the Confederate authority in areas which the Union armies had taken over. Amnesty was offered to all rebels who would swear allegiance to the United States, certain classes of leaders being excepted, and the generals commanding in the affected areas were authorized to register as voters those who took the amnesty oath. When a number equal to ten percent of the voter registration of 1860 had been signed up, they could elect state governments that Lincoln would recognize.

The plan had been put into operation in Louisiana and Arkansas, and under it governors and legislatures had been elected. Lincoln had made the experimental nature of the scheme perfectly clear. Towards the close of the 1864 session of Congress, a rival plan had been voted by Congress. It was sponsored by Henry Winter Davis in the House, and Ben Wade in the Senate, and provided for elections to be held to set up state governments whenever fifty percent of the state's 1860 registration had taken the prescribed oath. It disfranchised all who had held major office or military rank in the Confederacy, and required the abolition of slavery and repudiation of the rebel debt. Most important, it laid down the rule that postwar reconstruction must be conducted by Congress, and not by the President.

This bill had come before Lincoln on July 4, 1864, during the last hours of the session, and he had pocket-vetoed it, to the indignation of its authors. The President had stated his objections publicly. The plan, he said, offered one way of dealing with the problem of reconstruction, but it was not the only way, and he believed that to freeze policy at that stage and limit the power of the President to meet conditions as they might develop would be impolitic and even dangerous.

Lincoln had returned to this theme in the last speech of his life, made before a throng of serenaders at the White House on April 11. Referring to criticism of his "ten percent" plan, he said that if it should prove a failure, he would not hesitate to scrap it and try something else.

"Bad promises are better broken than kept," he told the crowd, reading from a prepared manuscript. "I shall treat this as a bad promise, and break it, whenever I shall be convinced that keeping it is adverse to the public interest. But I have not yet been so convinced."

Theorizing on the legal status of the rebel states he scouted as profitless, "a merely pernicious abstraction."

"We all agree," he said, "that the seceded states, so-called, are out of their proper practical relations with the Union, and that the sole object of the government, civil and military, in regard to those states, is to again get them into that proper practical relation. Finding themselves safely at home, it would be utterly immaterial whether they had ever been abroad."

To Sumner, this view was heresy, and he wrote to a friend that the President's speech augured "confusion and uncertainty in the future, and hot controversy. Alas! Alas!" But that Lincoln's refusal to allow Congress to set inflexible terms of restoration for the defeated states at that time had the support of the people had been demonstrated in the 1864 autumn elections. In August, Wade and Davis, furious over Lincoln's rejection of their bill, had published in the *New York Tribune* a "manifesto" assailing the President in unbridled language, calling him a despot and usurper of the powers of Congress. The attack had backfired: Davis had failed to be reelected to the House, and Wade went into eclipse. Had he been up for reelection, Ohio probably would have cast him out.

This was the situation when Johnson was thrust into Lincoln's place and the war ended.

Many crucial events had happened in Washington during the years while he was absent, taken up with the desperate struggle in Tennessee. These events he had observed from a distance, and while about some he was well posted, about others he was poorly informed.

The railroad to the Pacific, which he once had opposed, had been authorized in 1862. But that same year a homestead act was passed, and proved so popular that within a year nearly a million and a half acres of public lands were taken up. Johnson knew the background of these developments thoroughly, and he was well acquainted with the history of an even more revolutionary action taken by Congress—the Thirteenth Amendment, abolishing slavery everywhere in the United States by federal law. A constitutional amendment had been advocated by the abolitionists, for while a state (Tennessee, for example) might abolish slavery within its borders, it might also at any time revive the institution. The vote on the amendment had been taken in the House on January 31, 1865, and Julian recorded the "solemn and impressive" scene:

"The result for a good while remained in doubt, and the suspense produced perfect stillness. When it was certainly known that the measure had carried, the cheering in the hall and densely packed galleries exceeded anything I ever before saw . . . Members joined in the shouting, and kept it up for some minutes. Some embraced one another, others wept like children. I never before felt as I did then, and I thanked God for the blessed opportunity of recording my name where it will be honored as are those of the signers of the Declaration of Independence. What a grand jubilee for the old battle-scarred abolitionists! Glorious fruit of the war! I have felt, ever since the vote, as if I were in a new country. I seem to breathe better, and feel comforted and refreshed."

But such events were like peaks jutting up at intervals in the panorama of Washington's wartime activity; many other changes Johnson had overlooked. Yet little by little, these alterations, reflected in minor legislation, summed up in forgotten reports, had altered the temper of the capital and of Congress in a way with which Johnson was not familiar. His first month as President had been taken up largely with a sort of "cram course," to bring himself in line with the new direction of affairs.

As the wearisome procession of delegations from all parts of the country filed past him, the President listened to their opinions, to their recommendations and requests, with patience and attention. The cabinet, while deploring the diversion of his time and energy from pressing business, saw that the interviews provided a means for introducing the President to the country, in lieu of an inaugural address.

This was needful, for there was widespread curiosity about the new chief executive. For some persons, the first reaction to the news of his elevation had been one of shock. ("A drunken tailor for a President! Good God, are we come to this!" was the ejaculation of one horrified New Yorker, and Senator Grimes of Iowa had written to his wife that although Johnson was loyal enough, he was a man of "low instincts, vindictive, violent, and of bad habits.") Most of the major newspapers had rallied to his support. Even the *New York World* (which had not scrupled in March to call the Vice-President a "drunken boor") expressed its intention to reserve judgment until his policy should become known. The *New York Tribune* welcomed Johnson's Southern background, believing that he would deal with the defeated South understandingly. The *Herald* predicted that Johnson as President would be "as Joshua was to Moses"—a consolidator of his predecessor's achievements.

Word of Lincoln's assassination had trickled slowly through the South, owing to the disruption of telegraphic facilities and newspapers, and had produced an immediate revulsion, most Southerners shuddering at the realization that their destinies now were in the hands of "Andy Johnson—that bloody-minded tailor." One rebel in South Carolina warned ominously:

"Lincoln will not be the last President put to death in the capital, though he is the first!"

The truth was that the nation generally, and the North in particular, knew very little about Andrew Johnson. Before and during the war his name had been a symbol of unflinching courage and diehard loyalty, but the man himself had been little seen outside of Washington and his own state. He had never delivered a major speech in New York City. Philadelphia had never heard him. He had never entered New England. He had made a few campaign speeches in Indiana, Illinois, and Ohio, but not many. His very appearance was unfamiliar; during the 1864 election campaign the political cartoonists had drawn him in hardly recognizable forms.

Nor had the North any real comprehension of Johnson's people, and his personality and the peculiar workings of his mind had puzzled even observers in Washington.

One type of Southerner the North knew well—the rich, cultivated, traveled planter or statesman, possessed of suavity, hauteur, and fascinating manners. The other type of Southerner (which Andrew Johnson typified) was more numerous, but nobody ever called it fascinating. And Johnson's special characteristics were also a bar to the forging of a quick bond of understanding between him and the public at large. He was a politician by occupation, had been in politics most of his adult life; yet though politicians dealt in speech, he was a notably silent man. He had never haunted the cloakrooms and caucuses where political gossip was passed around; except when on the stump, he used words sparingly. Yet his secretaries had to learn that he was not secretive; he simply did not talk much at any time. But he was a famous listener. Whoever addressed him could be sure of receiving complete attention. This habit of listening and not interrupting with his own views (like Lincoln, he hated "an interruptious fellow") had given rise to misunderstandings on the part of interviewers who mistook a mere nod of acknowledgment for a sign of concurrence, or innocuous phrases of encouragement as meaning complete endorsement. Again and again such persons would aggrievedly charge that they had been misled, and that Johnson was insincere. This was not true. In their eagerness to detect agreement they had simply misread a word or a gesture.

In regard to policy decisions, Johnson's reticence sometimes was premeditated. The ability to keep one's counsel he considered a commendable trait, especially in an executive; he had praised President Pierce for that quality.

But after the nation had experienced the warm humanity of Lincoln, Johnson's personality was not engaging. Rugged, earnest, honest—these qualities his callers would grant him, but he lacked geniality. Yet occasionally the light of an inner sympathy was revealed, shining through the profound simplicity of his nature.

One day a deputation of Quakers waited on him to present an address favoring Negro suffrage. To their surprise, the President invited them to "sit down and have a family chat." He told them that he was well acquainted with the Negroes of the South, and wanted to help them. But then he went on with earnest feeling:

"You tell me, friends, of the liberation of the colored people of the South. But have you thought of the millions of Southern white people who have also been liberated by the war?"

He had in mind the "poor whites," those freed from the thralldom of a system based on servility. The welfare of these people was never far from his thoughts. When the delegation withdrew, their sympathies, if not their convictions, had been won by the President's straightforward, unpretentious candor.

Two riddles hung over the nation that spring of peace and yet no peace—how the South should be returned to the Union, and the enigma of the President's intentions. For some six weeks Johnson had pondered his course of action. Then he had spoken, issuing the North Carolina proclamations on May 29. The silence was broken, and the relief of the nation was equal to its surprise at the mildness of the terms set forth.

During the next few weeks, the President moved energetically to restore the federal services in the South—the mails, and federal courts where feasible. He lifted the blockade, opening Southern ports to world commerce again. A military force sufficient to preserve order would remain in the South until civil authority could take over, but the bulk of the huge military establishment was being mustered out and absorbed back into the community.

Informally during this period the President instructed the provisional governors he had appointed that he would require three things of the reconstituted states before military rule would be lifted: they must annul their ordinances of secession, repudiate the Confederate debt, and ratify the Thirteenth Amendment.

The President's course, had observers examined it carefully, was simply a repetition, with modifications, of the course he had followed in bringing his own state back into harmony with the

Union. True, Tennessee's rehabilitation had not been fully consummated yet; her representatives did not sit in Congress; but
that would come about soon.

A devoted believer in the right of each state to regulate its internal affairs, Johnson wanted the repentant rebels to purge
themselves of their treason, state by state, just as they had
seceded; themselves to wipe out their acts of secession, renounce
slavery, and cancel the debts incurred by their spurious legislatures. The word "reconstruction" he rejected; "restoration" was
the correct term, he insisted. The seceded states did not need to
be "made over," they required only to be "brought back" into the
Union. To effect this easily and in the shortest time, the plan that
had worked in Tennessee was applied generally.

But in the meanwhile another decision involving far-reaching
consequences was required of the overburdened President, one
that would reverberate through the future dolorously.

2.

During the fateful weeks of May and June, when elaboration of
a "restoration" policy was only one of the heavy responsibilities
weighing upon the President, the trial of the conspirators in Lincoln's assassination had been pressed forward. The country was
still in angry rebound from the crime, and day after day the
testimony published by the newspapers kept the anger alive.
While the proceedings were accepted uncritically by the gen-
erality of people, in thoughtful circles serious doubts had taken
root. The credulity displayed by Judge Advocate General Holt,
and the evident bloodthirst of his assistants, Representative John
A. Bingham and Colonel H. L. Burnett—a ruthless prosecutor
with a record of convictions under military law—had been noted
with misgiving by fair-minded lawyers the country over.

The attempts made to implicate high Confederate officials in
the assassination were tawdry and unconvincing, and the bias and
officiousness of the seven generals and two colonels who composed the court were plain. In Bingham's summing-up, facts,
rumors, inferences, distortions, speculation, unsupported assumptions, and gross perjury were jumbled together without distinc-

tion, treated as all equally worthy of belief. Obvious gaps in the evidence were glossed over, and pertinent questions were not asked. In legal nostrils the mess smelled rank; but the mood of the public was for revenge upon Lincoln's destroyers, and the eight defendants were foredoomed.

On June 29 the court considered their verdict. The prosecutors sat in as advisers; they sought the death penalty. Although a majority vote could convict, the death sentence required a two-thirds vote.

Harold, Payne, and Azterodt were quickly found guilty and sentenced to death. The court disagreed in the cases of O'Laughlin, Spangler, and Arnold, and they were found guilty but escaped death. Dr. Mudd was convicted and sentenced to life imprisonment. The case of Mrs. Surratt presented a special problem, because while a majority of the court believed her to be guilty, they hesitated about imposing a death sentence. The matter was still undetermined when the court recessed to resume its deliberations the next day.

That evening, Stanton, Bingham, and Holt worked out a compromise. The suggestion would be made that the board find Mrs. Surratt guilty and sentence her to hang, as in the case of the first three. However, to the sentence would be attached a recommendation that the President commute her sentence to life imprisonment. The findings of the court must be reviewed by the President anyway, and Holt argued that Johnson would certainly accept the court's recommendation. But mere announcement of the death sentence, he maintained, would bring John H. Surratt, Mrs. Surratt's fugitive son, out of hiding, so that he could be apprehended and tried.

This way out of their dilemma was accepted by the court, and Mrs. Surratt was voted guilty and sentenced to hang. A recommendation of clemency then was written out and signed by four generals and a colonel—five out of the nine judges. Now it was up to the President to act.

At the moment, Presidential action on any subject was out of the question, for Johnson was sick in bed and denied all visitors. Under the strain of recent weeks, and the succession of emotional shocks, his strength had given way, and for the second time in six months he was gravely ill. Johnson had suffered from kidney stone for years, and was seldom free from pain. Since becoming President he had experienced several severe attacks, and to obtain relief he had taken to working at a high desk, standing up. Weeks of tension and overwork had brought on complications, and his doctor, Surgeon General Barnes, had decreed strict isolation. No cabinet meeting was held during the first week of July, because of Johnson's inability to attend, and no visitors were admitted to his bedroom.

On July 5, Preston King, who had moved into the White House to serve as a confidential companion to the President, informed Holt that Johnson had recovered sufficiently to get up for a while. Holt, eager to conclude the conspirators' trial, hurried to the White House with his docket of the case. This included a digest of the evidence which he had himself drawn up, the findings of the court, and endorsement of the sentences already written out, ready for signature.

Holt was admitted to the President's room, and soon afterward Johnson himself stepped into the hall and told a secretary stationed there, General Reuben D. Mussey, that he did not wish to be disturbed while he was looking over the documents with the judge advocate general.

Two or three hours later, the President came out again and told Mussey that he had confirmed the sentences. Mussey asked what they were, and Johnson repeated them from memory, adding that he had ordered the executions to be carried out in two days, on July 7. Nothing was said by the President—nor subsequently by Holt, or by Stanton, or by any member of the court, or by anyone who was aware of its existence—about a recommendation of clemency for Mrs. Surratt, although the President did tell Mussey that he wished to see no one on "errands of mercy."

On July 6 the public learned the results of the trial, and a wave of sympathy set in on behalf of Mrs. Surratt, whose guilt seemed dubious. Orville Browning was shocked, and in New York, George Templeton Strong thoroughly disapproved of the sentence, expressing unmitigated scorn for the capacity of the judges.

"No justice of the peace in the most benighted rural district has judicial capacity much below that of the average military court," was his opinion. "I have read the testimony as it has been published . . . but I remember nothing that establishes more than a strong suspicion that Mrs. Surratt was privy to the plot . . . The most unusual promptness with which execution follows judgment in this case will shock public feeling . . . It will hurt and weaken the administration."

Ben Wade, himself a lawyer and a former judge, denounced the vindictive action against Mrs. Surratt.

"She has done nothing to justify such punishment," he said. "It would be a lasting slur on our reputation for justice and honor if Johnson allows public sentiment to murder her. A damned outrage, sir! An everlasting disgrace!"

When she was told her fate, Mrs. Surratt became so hysterical it was feared that she would go insane. Washington was swept by "a thrill of consternation," and many persons hastened to the White House to intercede for her life, but the President received none. Let them see Holt, he sent word. "If there is anything new, tell him."

Closeted with the President, it was asserted, Stanton was pouring out arguments against heeding any plea for mercy: Mrs. Surratt must hang; justice must not be thwarted. Johnson, still too ill to transact normal business, listened, shut away from all other counselors.

Anna Surratt, the doomed woman's daughter, begged for an interview, and was rebuffed. When she tried to force her way up the stairs, she was barred by Preston King and Senator James Lane of Kansas, another intimate of the President. Collapsing on the bottom step, the wretched girl sobbed wildly until led away.

As a last resort, Justice Andrew Wylie of the District Supreme Court issued a writ of habeas corpus—an act of courage at that moment. The writ was served on General Hancock, in command, but he returned it accompanied by a Presidential order suspending habeas corpus in the case. Hancock was ordered to carry out the executions at once.

July 7 was piping hot, and Washington sweltered as it waited. The city was strangely silent. At intervals bells tolled, while military patrols tramped stolidly through empty streets. The four gallows victims were led from their cells, still manacled, and mounted the scaffold erected in the prison yard. Mrs. Surratt was so faint she had to be half lifted up the steps. All around, on the walls, stood armed sentinels, watching stonily. At the foot of the scaffold were four freshly dug graves, with four open coffins beside them. The sentences were read, an officer gave the sign, the drop fell. By midafternoon the graves had been leveled off and justice had been done.

But the book was not closed.

In New York, Strong was surprised that the "extras" hawked by the newsboys announcing that the sentences had been carried out produced so little excitement. "The feeling seems general that the four . . . got no more than they deserved," was his comment. "There are a few to whom hanging a woman is rather distasteful, but it troubles them little."

It troubled Andrew Johnson.

Hugh McCulloch, who watched his chief through crisis after crisis, would set down that the President "deeply regretted" the affair, and "especially regretted" that he had ordered the writ of habeas corpus to be disregarded.

For weeks afterwards, Johnson was racked by severe headaches, which Secretary Welles tried to alleviate by organizing boating trips down the Potomac, away from the heat of the city. And Postmaster General Dennison divulged that during Johnson's illness, when no one was allowed to approach him, the President's doctors had feared that he was on the verge of apoplexy.

From this there emanated a rumor—through what channels no one knows, but multiplied by the thousand tongues of slander— that the reason why the President had refused to see Anna Surratt and had remained out of public view was because he had been— once again—drunk.

3.

One stroke of good luck had fallen to Johnson—his daughter, Martha Patterson, was with him during his illness.

He had moved into the White House directly after Mrs. Lincoln left it on May 23. The funeral trappings in the East Room had been dismantled then; Mrs. Lincoln had protested that she could not stand the noise the workmen would make.

The mansion was in woeful condition. For weeks the doors had been left unguarded, and strangers had wandered in and carried off pictures, silverware, ornaments, even heavy pieces of furniture. The wallpaper was in tatters, pieces had been snipped out of the lace curtains, the carpets were slashed, and the upholstery soiled and torn. The East Room, where soldiers had bivouacked, was infested with lice. The state dining room was mouldering; Mary Lincoln had closed it, preferring to spend her money on receptions and soirées where she could better display her gowns and jewelry.

President Johnson, confronted with this disorder, wired to Nashville for help, and Martha had reached Washington on June 19. With her she brought her children, Belle and Andrew Patterson, and the President's twelve-year-old son, Andrew, Jr. For Martha it was a poignant return to the mansion which she had known as a girl, when it had been occupied by that immaculate housekeeper, Mrs. Polk. But she set about bringing the house into at least presentable condition, though a thorough renovation was out of the question, there being no funds for the purpose. Then when her father was stricken, Martha doubled as his devoted nurse.

The President's convalescence was protracted. On July 9 Welles found him "pale and languid," and induced him to take a cruise down the Potomac. The outing marked the first time Johnson had set foot outside the White House for a month. It did some good, and the navy chief repeated the prescription as often as possible. But Johnson had plunged back into a man-killing schedule of work, and twice cabinet meetings had to be canceled because he was too exhausted to attend. Welles noted privately that the President took "no exercise, and confines himself to his duties," but remonstrances had little effect. On August 1 Welles recorded again that the President was "confined every day to the house and his room."

Secretary of State Seward also was becoming alarmed. Still not fully recovered from his wounds, Seward had been absent from Washington since his wife's death in June, and on his return he was startled by Johnson's "ill and oppressed" appearance. The President admitted that he was finding the stream of visiting delegations exhausting, and only a sense of obligation impelled him to receive them. But he told Seward that he "knew not what to do with these people" who crowded the anterooms and halls day after day. Seward thought the Cabinet should intervene. But fortunately a remedy for the President's listlessness was provided.

On August 6 two carriages drove up to the White House door and disgorged the whole Johnson family—Eliza Johnson, Mary Stover and her youngsters, Lillie, Sarah, and Andrew, Judge Patterson, and Robert Johnson. The President was working in his office on the second floor when the family arrived, and he hurried downstairs to be smothered by hugs in the joyful reunion. Eliza was forced to rest a bit before going farther, and while the children romped excitedly through the rooms on the ground floor, the elders sat in one of the parlors. Then all went upstairs to select their rooms. First choice was Eliza's, and she took one of the smallest, in the northwest corner of the house.

Suddenly cheerfulness replaced the gloom that had permeated the mansion, and the tonic effect upon the President was visible. The family had always lived methodically, and a domestic time-table was set up to which everybody conformed. Breakfast was served at eight o'clock, although the President usually had arisen an hour or two earlier, and everybody was expected to be on hand except Mrs. Johnson, who breakfasted in her room. Luncheon was at one o'clock, and dinner at seven. Johnson usually sat a while after breakfast, talking with Judge Patterson, or Robert, or with the grandchildren; then he unfailingly paid a visit to his wife and chatted with her for perhaps half an hour before going to his office.

Eliza spent her days (in fact, she would spend the next four years) on the second floor of the mansion. Only twice would she appear in public, for a social event. Always cheerful and sweet-tempered, though the lines in her face showed her suffering, she occupied herself with sewing, knitting, and reading. After Andrew's morning visit, it was her habit to make a tour of the up-stairs rooms, pausing now and then to rest, paying special attention to her husband's bedroom to make sure that it was in order, just as he liked it. She watched over his wardrobe, and kept Sam the valet up to his duties. She coached Martha on the dishes the President favored and exactly how they should be prepared.

Both Eliza and Andrew reveled in the children. Frank (so called to avoid the confusion of several Andrews) was entered at a school in Georgetown, while a tutor was engaged for the five younger ones, coming to the White House every morning and conducting classes until noon. Then the children would make a beeline for "Grandma's" room, where they would find her seated in a low rocking chair, her hands busy with darning or mending. The children had the run of the house, and thought nothing of bursting in on "Grandpa" whenever they had something to tell him. Johnson enjoyed these interruptions, no matter who might be with him, and he never scolded the intruders, but made much of them. And he expected his visitors to make much of them, too.

Now there was no difficulty about getting the President out of the house. On fine afternoons he would drive with the grandchildren into the country, or to Rock Creek Park, where the small-fry went wading and caught waterbugs, while "Grandpa" skipped stones. Sometimes while they were playing he would pace up and down, hands clasped behind his back, deep in thought; then at a hail he would glance up, and the look of care would disappear from his face. The Presidential carriage, returning from a country drive, overflowing with children and wild flowers, became a common sight in Washington that summer. Sometimes Frank would be seen proudly escorting the carriage on his white pony, which had been sent from Tennessee.

The harmony existing between Johnson and his wife was remarked by everyone. In temperament they were direct opposites —she, patient, gentle, forbearing; he, at heart passionate, ambitious, and belligerent. She was immensely proud of Andy, and his manner toward her was always tender, considerate, and solicitous.

Eliza dressed to please her husband, and her gowns, styled very simply, were always of rich, expensive fabrics. She patronized the best dressmakers. An affectionate colloquy would take place every time she appeared in a new dress that was particularly attractive. Andrew's eyes would light up, and he would compliment her, in his warm, melodious voice; in return, she would smile and reach up (for she was very small, and emaciation made her seem even smaller) and pat his shoulder—just once—as her way of thanking him.

At no time did she conceal her distaste for official life, though she was resigned to it for Andrew's sake. Often she told the President's bodyguard, William Crook, for whom she had a fondness:

"Crook, it is all very well for those who like it, but I don't like this public life at all. I often wish the time would come when we could return to where I feel we best belong."

Martha's unpretentious dignity as hostess of the White House, acting for her mother, surprised and pleased capital society. Her squelching of an officious caller was widely repeated:

"We are plain people from the mountains of Tennessee, called here for a short time by a national calamity. I trust too much will not be expected of us."

Robert Johnson, who was in his thirties, was given a place as one of his father's secretaries, charged especially with the search being conducted to recover Johnson's papers, scattered by vandals at Greeneville during the war. Sam Milligan's help was enlisted in this endeavor, but he could report little success.

"I have hunted over my old papers most diligently, and inquired everywhere for your father's speeches, and can find none," he informed Robert. "They have all been scattered & torn to pieces in such a way as to render them wholly worthless."

Milligan thought conditions at home were improving: "The country is becoming more quiet, and I have more hope of its restoration than I have had since the close of the war."

A federal judgeship falling vacant that summer, Johnson named Milligan to it. And Blackston McDannel, now that patronage was in the hands of his friend, got his appointment as United States marshal for East Tennessee.

Not only was domestic serenity granted to the President during that summer of convalescence; the success of his policy of reunion was a source of gratification. Everywhere the reports were favorable, commendation coming from the press, from political groups, and from thoughtful citizens both North and South. True, there were some expressions of surprise at the mild terms laid down to the lately rebellious states, after Johnson's well-known vows of vengeance upon traitors. All sorts of guesses were hazarded as to the cause of this apparent about-face; though had he explained himself more plainly, less occasion for surprise might have arisen.

Johnson had not changed his views. He had held consistently, and had said over and over again, that secession was brought about by a conspiracy hatched and carried out by a handful of Southern leaders, not by the masses of the Southern people; these latter, he maintained, had been tricked, stampeded, and betrayed by the men whom they had trusted. For the great bulk of the Southern people he had always advocated the widest possible clemency.*

In the Senate, and to their faces, he had denounced the men whom he believed to be the plotters of treason; these fellow sena-

---

* This belief in a deliberate and conscious conspiracy on the part of the prewar agitators for secession to mislead their own people was held widely among Northern statesmen, including President Lincoln. In a special message to the extraordinary session of Congress convening on July 4, 1861, at the outset of the conflict, Lincoln stated this belief with great explicitness, saying:

"It might seem, at first thought, to be of little difference whether the present movement at the South be called 'secession' or 'rebellion.' The movers, however, will understand the difference. At the beginning, they knew they could never raise their treason to any respectable magnitude, by any name which implies *violation* of law. They knew their people possessed as much of moral sense, as much of devotion to law and order, and as much pride in, and reverence for, the history, and government, of their common country, as any other civilized, and patriotic people. They knew they could make no advancement directly in the teeth of these strong and noble sentiments. *Accordingly they commenced by an insidious debauching of the public mind.* [Editor's italics.] They invented an ingenious sophism, which, if conceded, was followed by perfectly logical steps, through all the incidents, to the complete destruction of the Union. The sophism itself is, that any State of the Union, may, *consistently* with the national Constitution, and therefore perfectly *lawfully*, and *peacefully*, withdraw from the Union, without the consent of the Union, or of any other State. The little disguise that the supposed right is to be exercised only for just cause, themselves to be the sole judge of its justice, is too thin to merit any notice."

This apportionment of the relative guilt of the rebel leaders and their hoodwinked followers underlay the entire approach of both Lincoln and Johnson to the question of reconstruction.

tors, he had said in their hearing, were deserving of death. He still held so, and to the end of his life would believe that Jefferson Davis should have been hanged.

Yet in Tennessee, where he had been in a position to exert authority, he had been criticized for extending pardons to those of the plain people who earnestly solicited it, even while he was calling for the condign punishment of traitors.

But Johnson did not explain his views easily, tactfully, or wisely. He was a self-contained man, shaped to taciturnity by the habits of a lifetime.

Now that he was President, he added another article to his basic political faith. The war was over. By solemn action of the Congress, an action for which he had been mainly responsible, the objective of the war had been defined as the preservation of the Union. The rebellion had been put down and the Union had been preserved. The only remaining problem was that of bringing the rebellious states back into their normal function within the Union, which they had never left; and this problem was by way of being solved. Andrew Johnson believed that he was President of all the states, as Lincoln never had been; he was President of the South as well as President of the North. And the people of the South recognized him as President as they had never recognized Lincoln. To endorse or encourage, therefore, a vendetta carried on by one section against another would, in his eyes, be a betrayal of his oath of office.

This attitude was not fully understood by those around him, and his failure, or inability, to explain his mental processes was a defect. Hardly had the North Carolina proclamation been issued when rumblings of dissent were heard, although they struck a minor note in the general chorus of commendation.

The first major critic to assail the President's action was Wendell Phillips, New England's eloquent exponent of a lofty but narrow, impractical, and intolerant idealism. Like Sumner, Phillips was a bigot of righteousness, embodying the most irritating Brahminisms of Brahminical Boston. The President's program Phillips called "a practical surrender to the Confederacy . . . a practical fraud on the North." Better would it have been for the nation, Phillips cried in the accents of virtue betrayed, if Grant had surrendered to Lee at Appomattox, rather than have Negro rights ignored.

Sumner's reaction was almost as violent, although not so original; for him also the touchstone was Negro suffrage. Johnson had made no provision for granting the vote to the former slaves; therefore in Sumner's eyes Johnson's policy stood condemned. Sumner was especially wroth because he had deluded himself into believing that Johnson shared his way of thinking. Johnson had listened to the senator's lectures on the necessity of Negro suffrage, and had simply refrained from expressing explicit disagreement, that was all, but Sumner had mistaken this for concurrence.

Secretary Welles had found the clue to the President's behavior when under strong persuasion. "He listens," was Welles's analysis, "but unless he squarely and emphatically disapproves, is disinclined to controvert."

Thaddeus Stevens had been no less disapproving of the President's action, but the basis of his objection was that the President was usurping the power of Congress. Twice he wrote asking Johnson to stay his hand until Congress should assemble. Congress, he maintained, and not the executive, was entrusted by the Constitution with the responsibility for reconstruction. When Johnson went ahead, Stevens told Sumner that "if something is not done, the President will be crowned King before Congress meets."

By July, Wade also was disgruntled, telling a friend:

"We have in truth already lost the whole moral effect of our victories over the rebellion. The golden opportunity for humiliating and destroying the influence of the Southern aristocracy has gone forever."

But these extremists did not reflect the feeling of the rank and file of Republicans, or of Northern opinion generally. Even in radical circles there was some disposition to go along with the President, at least experimentally, rather than risk party disunity.

The rumbling of opposition did not deter Johnson. He was getting his own reports on conditions in the South from on-the-spot observers, and they were encouraging.

In September Harvey M. Watterson, wealthy Tennessee Unionist, conducted a survey, and assured the President that "nobody
fit to be outside a lunatic asylum" dreamt of further resistance to
the United States; that issue had been laid to rest permanently by
the outcome of the war. Watterson found every leading man with
whom he spoke emphatic on this point.

General Grant, after a trip into the Southern states, reported
that "the mass of thinking men of the South accept the present
situation of affairs in good faith."

A third report came from Ben Truman, who made a swing
through the deep South at Johnson's request. As a newspaper
correspondent during the war, Truman had demonstrated that he
had a knack for getting at the truth. In his report he distinguished
between the "loyalty" of the ex-Confederates, and their "patriotism." They were "loyal" enough, he said, and had no faintest
notion of again defying the national authority; but they could not
be expected to take their recent enemies to their hearts in a glow
of "patriotism." There had been too much disappointment, too
much sacrifice, for that; the crushing of hopes had left a scar.

In some of the Southern conventions being held under Johnson's restoration plan, Truman detected "malignity and meanness
and ineptitude," but these were not peculiar to the South. And he
sent a caution to Johnson that "for some unknown cause, a large
number of persons are engaged in writing and circulating false-
hoods . . . of an incendiary character concerning the Southern
people."

A fourth report was prepared, under equivocal circumstances,
by Carl Schurz. Having thrown up his army commission, Schurz
was seeking employment. In a White House interview, he suggested to the President that it might be useful to send a qualified
observer into the South to sound out sentiment there. Johnson
had agreed that such a move might be wise, and said he might
send Schurz. The latter interpreted this as a commitment, and he
at once wrote confidentially to Sumner that on such a mission,
armed with "official" status, he would be in a good position to
give the North "the true facts." Sumner had insisted that he go,
by all means, and had lent financial assistance. He also arranged
that Schurz should forward interim reports, in the form of news

letters, to the *Boston Daily Advertiser*, a mouthpiece for radical opinions.

Schurz found in the South what he was predisposed to find—conditions good and bad, but rather more of the bad, especially as pertained to the freedmen. He agreed that secession was dead, but believed the vaunted "loyalty" of the ex-Confederates was mere "submission," which would last only as long as it was enforced by Northern bayonets. As for Southern treatment of the former slaves, he saw no inclination to deal humanely or even justly with them; on the contrary, he reported that hatred and fear of the Negroes was more intense than it had been under slavery, and he cited numerous outrages—brutal assaults—that had been committed against freedmen.

Schurz also took it upon himself to meddle in a high-policy dispute involving the President, the provisional governor of Mississippi, and the Union commander there, and was roundly rebuked by Johnson. In the end, he failed to submit a final report to the President, but did send one to Congress—one that was highly pleasing to radicals like Sumner.

Meanwhile, the official reports of eager compliance by the Southern states with Johnson's terms for restoration piled up steadily, and late in September the President told an influential White House visitor:

"We are making very rapid progress—so rapid that I sometimes cannot realize it. It appears like a dream."

Throughout the golden autumn weather the President went about his duties confidently. His drives into the country with the grandchildren had become a regular relaxation. When the children could not go along, he would ride out with Crook, his bodyguard, for companion.

One spot which the President liked to visit on these excursions was Glenwood Cemetery, where he found some somber satisfaction in deciphering the inscriptions on the gravestones. One day, strolling the melancholy aisles, he suddenly burst into laughter—startling Crook, for Andrew Johnson seldom laughed. The President pointed to two gravestones, side by side. On the first was chiseled:

"Sacred to the memory of my beloved wife—by her inconsolable husband."

The second, dated two years later, bore a similar epitaph for the *second* wife.

"It didn't take that fellow long to get over his affliction, did it?" the President chuckled.

Crook and the President left that graveyard in a mood almost jolly.

4.

The Congress that was to assemble on December 4, 1865, was united in few things; but one purpose which the members did share almost unanimously was to throw off the yoke of subserviency to the executive branch which had galled them throughout the war.

Since 1861 the Presidency had taken on dimensions not dreamed of before. Lincoln had grasped that an emergency of such scope as the rebellion could be dealt with successfully only by extraordinary means, and under the spur of necessity he had assumed powers of doubtful constitutionality, and had persuaded Congress to acquiesce, though often grudgingly. As a result, by 1865 the President of the United States had become perhaps the most powerful head of state in the Western world. He was commander-in-chief of the most formidable army on earth, battle-hardened and flushed with victory. He commanded a defensive navy second to none, and the world's largest and most heavily armed ironclad, the *Dunderberg*, was nearing completion in a New York shipyard when the war ended. (In those days ironclads were the accepted measure of a nation's striking power, as intercontinental ballistic missiles would become a century later.)

The President could appoint generals and admirals to lead into action this mighty array. He could name judges of the highest court, from whose decision there was no appeal. His patronage encompassed thousands of jobs, to which he could appoint the men of his choice, and remove appointees at will. With a stroke of the pen he could set aside civil authority, render void judicial sentences, and suspend the writ of habeas corpus—something neither Queen Victoria nor the British cabinet would dare to do. He could make arbitrary arrests, and hold prisoners without trial indefinitely; both Lincoln and Johnson did this, exercising in this respect a power as absolute as that of the czar of Russia. He could confiscate property, and the Emancipation Proclamation, in effect, confiscated the capital of one half of the nation, accumulated over many generations. This sweep of power devolved upon Andrew Johnson when Abraham Lincoln died.

But with the advent of peace, thoughtful men in public life were beset by fears that this trend towards the centralizing of authority in the executive branch had gone too far, and for the survival of constitutional liberty they felt it must be reversed. Senator Trumbull of Illinois arrived in Washington in the autumn of 1865 announcing this reversal as his intention. For years, he said, he had been coming back to Washington periodically to legalize the illegal actions taken by President Lincoln; now that must cease.

A colleague who shared Trumbull's resentment against the subordination of Congress was Senator Fessenden of Maine. Like Trumbull he was honest and independent, but testy and irritable, and he had a high conception of the dignity and responsibilities of a United States senator. He proposed to cut no more constitutional corners when legislating.

Senator James Wilson Grimes of Iowa had much influence with Fessenden, and he, also, was ready to insist upon every prerogative of the Senate. During the war, Grimes had distinguished himself by his zeal in ferreting out disloyalty in the public service, and his suspicions of all things Southern had carried over into the peace. Energetic and active, he knew his own mind and set his course accordingly.

So did Charles Sumner, who, like Uncle Toby, rode his hobbyhorse intrepidly, impervious to criticism and oblivious of natural obstacles.

A younger member of the Senate who was forging into prominence was John Sherman of Ohio, brother of the redoubtable William Tecumseh. Already he was accounted a leader, both because of his ability and because of his family's connection with the politically powerful Ewing clan.

And there was old Ben Wade, about whom traditions clung like ivy on a gnarled oak. At sixty-five a veteran of innumerable political struggles, Wade had been embittered by the war. The whole problem of secession for him had been reduced to personalities; he had fought individuals, traitors whom he could see and defy, not fleshless abstractions. Before the war Wade had warned the Southern firebrands that in whistling up a revolution they must either make it good, or "go to the wall, that is all there is to it." He had himself accepted the risks and would not have whined in defeat, and he expected the rebels to do likewise.

All these senators were veritable prima donnas in defense of their prerogatives, and each one was a leader. This made cohesiveness difficult. They seldom presented a solid front except under pressure of some momentary crisis; since their party majority was strong, they felt at liberty to indulge personal differences.

But these senators did possess one thing in common: they had served in the Senate with Andrew Johnson, and they believed they had fathomed his character. They had listened to his speeches, and being Republicans they usually envisioned him as still seated "on the other side of the aisle," among their enemies the Democrats. For that reason he would always remain to some extent an outsider to them, an intruder in their ranks. Certainly they stood in no awe of Johnson, President or not. And though their party had placed him in power, they were perfectly prepared to call him to account the minute he should infringe upon their cherished privileges.

The situation in the House of Representatives of this new, Thirty-ninth Congress was entirely different. There the unquestioned leader was Thaddeus Stevens of Pennsylvania, now seventy-three years old. His power was all but absolute. A young newspaper correspondent in Washington, Georges Clemenceau (who had traits in common with Stevens), was charmed by the raffish old man who wore his wig askew and with scowls and shafts of sarcasm drove the lethargic to accept his dictation and stiffened the backs of the spineless. Clemenceau grasped that "Old Thad" was concerned with but one aim—to consolidate the victory by making over the South in the image of the North.

His motives were not so much punitive as regenerative. A social revolution had emerged from the cataclysm of war, and it was gathering momentum. In the South it had been destructive, in the North, constructive. Under the impetus of wartime demands, Northern industry had boomed, and the era of vast material expansion was in full stride before the guns became silent.

Stevens heartily approved this trend, believing that in that direction lay the future grandeur of the United States. The South, he realized, must be brought into the general transformation, or it would remain as a canker to drain the vitality of the entire nation. The war had been a conflict between two ways of life, and the South's had been smashed. Now the rubble must be cleared away in order that a better structure, conformable to the progressive pattern being set in the North, might be erected on the site. Such was Stevens's reasoning; and that the process could be carried out successfully only by harsh means did not deter him; he would cauterize the wound in order to save the patient. He had told his constituents that he would not recoil from confiscating the estates of the slaveholders and redistributing the land among veterans of the Union armies, the ex-slaves, and European immigrants. His objective he defined candidly as "a radical reorganization in Southern institutions, habits, and manners," and he was ready to do whatever was necessary.

"This may startle feeble minds and shake weak nerves," he admitted with equanimity. "So do all great improvements in the political and moral world. It requires a heavy impetus to drive forward a sluggish people. When it was first proposed to free the slaves and arm the blacks, did not half the nation tremble? The prim conservatives, the snobs, and the male waiting maids in Congress were in hysterics."

The "progress" that President Johnson discerned was no progress at all to Stevens. Elections of representatives and United States senators had been carried out in most of the Southern states, including Tennessee, under Johnson's program, and the men were crowding into Washington. Whether Congress would seat them was the question, and that issue was out of the President's hands.

The Constitution provided that each house should be the judge of the qualifications of its members, and in 1865 none could qualify who could not or would not take the oath of fealty that Congress had enacted in 1862. This so-called "ironclad" oath differed from the presidential amnesty oath by embracing loyalty in the past as well as in the future. The person must swear that he had never "voluntarily" borne arms against the United States or aided the rebellion, as well as pledge loyalty henceforward. No one could hold any office or commission under the federal government without subscribing to this oath; it did not apply, of course, to state officials.

But who were the men whom the late rebellious states were sending to Congress? The list bristled with the names of those who could not possibly take the "ironclad" oath—four Confederate generals, five colonels, and many members of the Richmond Congress who had voted for secession. It was ridiculous to maintain that such men had accepted their positions in the Confederacy other than voluntarily. The most flagrant example was Alexander H. Stephens, ex-Vice-President of the Confederate States of America, now elected by Georgia to the United States Senate. Until a short while before, Stephens had been a prisoner in Fort Warren, in Boston, charged with treason. He had taken the presidential amnesty oath, but for him, as for most of his associates-elect, to take the Congressional oath would be a plain perjury. By what reasoning, then, had the Southern states expected that such men would be seated? A more arrogant gesture of defiance could scarcely be imagined.

And that was not all. Johnson had been disturbed by the change that visibly came over the South during the months between surrender and Christmas. At first, stunned by their defeat, the Southern people had waited in dull apathy, indifferent to the sentence the victorious North might pass upon them. Then, as the spirit of toleration and magnanimity in the North became manifest (once the flare-up of vengefulness ignited by Lincoln's assassination had burned itself out), and as Johnson's proclamations appeared to open the way to hope, the ex-rebels took heart, shook off their apathy, and since they were human, began to see how far they could go in regaining their former places.

Johnson had been provoked by instances of contumacy. The Mississippi convention had been the first to meet, and it had refused outright to ratify the Thirteenth Amendment. This in spite of a direct appeal from the White House, including a suggestion that the franchise be extended to Negroes who could read the Constitution of the United States and write their names, or who owned property to the value of $250 (the voter qualification for Negroes in New York State). By such action, Johnson telegraphed, the convention would "disarm the adversary and set an example the other states might follow." The appeal went unheeded. Instead of abolishing slavery, the convention noted merely that "the institution of slavery having been destroyed in the state of Mississippi," it could not be reestablished there. And the delegates flatly declined to repudiate the Confederate debt.

The other state conventions proved almost as recalcitrant. In South Carolina, the provisional governor, Benjamin F. Perry, failed even to mention the rebel debt when instructing the convention. The delegates "repealed" the ordinance of secession, instead of declaring it null and void, and recorded the fact that slavery had been abolished "by the action of the United States authority."

Alabama, responding to nudging, measured up to the requirements set out by Johnson, and was rewarded with a telegram of congratulations from the President:

"The proceedings of the convention have met the highest expectations of all who desire the restoration of the Union. All seems now to be working well, and will result, as I believe, in a decided success."

But the Georgia convention quibbled, also merely "repealed" the act of secession, and abolished slavery while retaining the right to claim compensation for their emancipated property. The delegates gagged on repudiation of the rebel debt, until Provisional Governor Lewis E. Parsons wired to Washington for guidance and the President replied:

"It should be made known at once, at home and abroad, that no debt contracted for the purpose of dissolving the Union of the states can or ever will be paid by taxes levied on the people for such purpose."

This warning was effective, and the debt was repudiated, though by a narrow margin.

A similar rap on the knuckles became necessary when the North Carolina convention balked, and the President, whose temper was growing short, wired peremptorily:

"Every dollar of the debt created to aid the rebellion against the United States should be repudiated finally and forever."

Again compliance was obtained, although grudgingly.

On this issue of the debt, Johnson was as much concerned for the "poor whites" of the South as for the taxpayers of the North; he saw no justice in taxing the deluded masses to pay for their leaders' duplicity and folly.

When the new Southern legislatures began to meet, more truculence was exhibited. Far from showing remorse, humility, or even tact, these legislatures began demanding their "rights" under the very Constitution that their members so recently had scorned and flouted. By autumn Secretary Welles believed that "the secession element is becoming vicious and bad in some quarters, and I fear it may be general." And he felt that "at the North there is about as much folly in the other direction."

The action that aroused the greatest indignation in the North was enactment by the Southern legislatures of laws to govern the former slaves. Some four million Negroes, until recently held in servitude—ignorant, destitute, and without comprehension either of the nature of their freedom or of competitive life—posed a stupendous problem. The freedmen's place in the social scheme had to be defined, and to this end laws were adopted. But the severity of these laws stunned and shocked many Northerners.

Mississippi's code was the harshest. While all the states granted the freedmen the right to marry, to sue and be sued, and to testify in lawsuits involving Negroes (but not whites), Mississippi forbade them to own, rent, or lease land except in incorporated towns, severely restricted their movements, ordered Negro orphans to be apprenticed until they became of age, preferably to their former masters, and decreed that all "vagrants" (a class vaguely defined) could be arrested, fined, and leased to employers until they worked out their fines. In addition, there were criminal penalties imposed on Negroes that were not applied to whites.

In South Carolina a farm worker could not leave the premises of his employer without permission, under penalty of losing his wages. The working day was from sunrise to sunset, and workers were required to care for the stock, prepare their meals for the day, and do other personal chores before the rise of sun. No Negro could ply any trade, or engage in any employment except farm labor, unless he obtained a license from the county judge and paid a fee which ranged from ten dollars to one hundred.

Under Florida's "vagrancy" laws, Negroes could be seized and forced into virtual slavery for months at a time, to work off heavy fines.*

These "black codes" constituted to Northerners a thinly disguised attempt to reestablish slavery in fact, if not in name, and the reaction was one of white-hot anger. Had the war, it was asked, been fought in vain? Thundered the *Chicago Tribune*:

"We tell the white men of Mississippi that the men of the North will convert the state of Mississippi into a frog pond before they will allow such laws to disgrace one foot of soil in which the bones of our soldiers sleep and over which the flag of freedom waves."

The *New York Herald*, reviewing the reluctance of the Southern legislatures to ratify the Thirteenth Amendment, wondered whether the South was plotting, by blocking ratification, to hold the door open for reviving slavery by state action at some future time.

There were, of course, two sides to the issue. If the states were indeed autonomous in respect to their internal affairs, the responsibility for governing the freedmen rested with the South, not with the North. And to Southerners the indignation of the *Chicago Tribune* sounded hypocritical in view of the statutes of the *Tribune*'s own state of Illinois.

No Negro was permitted there to testify "in favor of or against any white person," and a free Negro who did not possess a certifi-

---

* Harsh vagrancy laws, capable of being used as instruments of oppression, were not confined to the Reconstruction South. As late as July, 1967, the New York State Court of Appeals set aside a law enacted in 1788 subjecting to arrest any person having "no visible means of support." The court, by a split decision (five to two), upheld the appeal of a man who had been harassed by the New York City police under cover of this law, ruling the statute to be "an unconstitutional overreaching of the police power." This happened in the North, a century after the Reconstruction "black codes."

cate of freedom, and keep on file with the county clerk a bond of one thousand dollars, was liable to arrest and to be hired out to forced labor for one year. Mississippi's code required that all apprentices be taught to read and write; but Illinois law specified that Negro and mulatto apprentices need not be "taught to write, or the knowledge of arithmetic." Only in February of 1865 had Illinois repealed the law fining every free Negro entering the state (including, of course, any slave freed by Lincoln's proclamation) fifty dollars, and if he failed to pay, condemning him to be sold for labor to whoever would pay the fine, until the amount was worked off. A specially ugly feature of this law was that half of the fine went to the informer.

Other Northern states had laws quite as discriminatory and repressive. As for Negro suffrage, only six states in the North allowed Negroes to vote, and one (New York) imposed a property qualification that did not apply to whites. During the first year of Johnson's presidency, the voters of Connecticut, Wisconsin, and Minnesota overwhelmingly defeated proposals to extend the franchise to Negroes, and Minnesota would repeat its refusal the year following. In 1867 both Kansas and Ohio would reject Negro suffrage by large majorities. And as late as April, 1868, Michigan would turn down a new state constitution largely because it embodied Negro suffrage.

Facts like these were cited in the South in rebuttal of criticism of their "black codes." As it turned out, none of the codes were enforced long, and the military authorities set aside most of Mississippi's code and all of South Carolina's. But their enactment, on the eve of Congress, served to inflame Northern sentiment and smoothed the path for such radicals as Sumner and Stevens.

President Johnson took a balanced view of these untoward developments. He had urged qualified suffrage on the Southern states, and some provision had to be made for the ex-slaves, who possessed no legal rights whatever under the laws before emancipation. He did not approve of the worst restrictions; but neither could he forget that the apprentice laws of North Carolina, under which he had been bound out to a cruel taskmaster, were still on the statute books, and no maledictions were being hurled against them by Northerners. The Southern states were doing well, on the whole, he believed, and they must be permitted to learn by mistakes. His feeling was the same as that which Lincoln had expressed at his last cabinet meeting:

"We can't undertake to run state governments in all these Southern states. Their people must do that, though I reckon that at first they may do it badly."

Johnson had warned the South against sending to Congress men who could not take the "ironclad" oath; and when such were elected, he urged them to stay at home, and not thrust themselves upon Washington until Congress should pass on their claims. This advice had been ignored, and the representatives-elect swarmed into the capital. Mrs. Welles began to encounter so many ex-rebels and rebel sympathizers at her receptions that she remarked on it to her husband, and at the White House the President's office was thronged, day after day, by what the newspapers called "distinguished pardon seekers"—distinguished in the South for gallantry in battle, but distinguished in the North for rebellion and treason.

Another irritant for Northerners at this juncture was the suspicious conversion of the Democratic press to the policy of the President. Newspapers that had been notoriously copperhead during the war suddenly blossomed with praise of Johnson, to the resentment of many Republicans. A judge in upstate New York wrote feelingly on this subject. Saying that he was Johnson's "sincere friend and a member of the Union party that elected you," he told the President pungently:

"The masses of the Union party feel as members of a Christian church do when Sabbath breakers, whoremasters, and gamblers praise their preacher."

Amid these angry crosscurrents, on December 2 Alabama ratified the Thirteenth Amendment, completing the necessary two-thirds of all the states. Virginia, Louisiana, Tennessee, North and South Carolina, and Georgia, among the Southern states, already had taken similar action. Mississippi would never ratify.

The curse of slavery thus was removed forever. But the problem of the Negro remained.

5.

Thaddeus Stevens arrived in Washington from his home in Lancaster on November 23, and on November 25 he called at the White House. In a talk of perfect candor, he told the President that unless he changed his policy, the party would not support him. Stevens was adamant that only Congress could dictate the terms of Southern reconstruction.

Johnson replied that he had acted under his powers as commander-in-chief, and in obedience to the constitutional obligation to guarantee to every state "a republican form of government." His program was succeeding beyond expectations, he said, and the former rebel states, having met the conditions laid down for their readmission, were entitled to be admitted.

Stevens departed, prepared to fight.

Johnson was receiving notification from other sources that he must expect serious opposition to his policy. In New England, Wendell Phillips was ceaseless in his phillipics, and although he exercised no official authority, as a bellwether of the old abolitionist flock he was influential. The burden of his carping was, "You can't trust Andy Johnson . . . Andy Johnson may not be a traitor, but he is an enemy . . ."

On December 1, George Bancroft wrote to Johnson from New York, carefully marking his envelope *"Private"* and *"For the President alone."* Sumner, he reported, had stopped in New York on his way to Washington, and they had discussed politics for two or three hours.

"I did all in my power to calm him down on the suffrage question," the historian wrote in haste, "& he admitted that *the President* could not have granted suffrage. I believe he left me bent on making in the Senate some speeches, which he has prepared elaborately, but resolved to cultivate friendly relations with you. He told me he would call on you tomorrow night. I take leave to hint, that on *foreign relations* he agrees with you exactly; & that, as he is chairman of the Committee on foreign relations, a little *freedom of conversation* on your part on our foreign affairs would conciliate him amazingly. He goes in the main well disposed. Public opinion is all with you."

To have so notable a collaborator as George Bancroft, author, scholar, and statesman, was gratifying to Johnson. Both were undeviating Jacksonian Democrats, but Bancroft had held office in the cabinet, under President Polk, at a period when Andrew Johnson was an obscure, fumbling congressman. Bancroft's goodwill was a source of strength to the President at this moment, because of the tragic loss of Preston King, who had been one of the few to whom Johnson was able to open his mind, and his counsels had been on the side of moderation and responsibility. In gratitude, the President had appointed him Collector of the Port of New York, a position carrying extensive patronage powers. Years before, King had suffered a mental breakdown, and under the clamor of place-hunters his reasoning faculties had given way again and he drowned himself off a Hoboken ferryboat. The suicide had shocked the public, and was a heavy bereavement for Johnson. Bancroft had been lending his literary skill to the drafting of the President's forthcoming State of the Union message to Congress, and he was correct in stating that opinion in and around New York, at least, was with the President in his reconstruction program.

Nowhere was the sentiment prevailing among intelligent observers reflected more clearly than in the diary being kept by G. T. Strong, the Wall Street lawyer. Strong had poured all his energy, skill, and wealth into winning the war for the Union, and in consequence would struggle with debts and impaired health for the rest of his days. He rejoiced in that sacrifice, entering in his diary:

"These four years have . . . given me—and my wife and my boys—a country worth living in and living for, and to be proud of. Up to April, 1861, it was a mean, sordid, money-worshipping country, in my judgment at least, and I think I was not far wrong."

Although not personally involved in politics, Strong kept a sharp eye on developments, and as early as June, in '65, he had foreseen that a split was coming in the Union, or Republican, party.

"Advanced Republicans grumble over President Johnson's reconstruction policy, and say he is selling his party, after the manner of dirty old Tyler, twenty-five years ago," he wrote. "I do not 'see it in that light,' and have faith in the President's honesty and judgment . . . Copperheads chuckle over the prospect, to my serious aggravation."

The divisive issue, Strong perceived, was Negro suffrage—"a dark and troublesome question, [which] must be met. That freedmen, who have as a class always helped the national cause to the utmost of their ability, at the risk of their lives, should have political rights at least equal to those of the bitter enemies of the country, who are about to resume those rights, sullenly and under protest, only because they are crushed, coerced, and subjugated, is (abstractly considered) in the highest degree just and right. But the average field hand would use political power as intelligently as would the mule he drives."

To the contention that the ballot should be granted to Negroes who had served in the Union armies, simply because of that service, Strong dissented, saying, "The current phrase that 'those who have helped the country with bullets should be permitted to help it with ballots' is mere nonsense." And when the "black codes" were promulgated, and the Northern press inveighed against "reenslavement" of the Negroes, Strong did not join in the demand for federal intervention. He observed judicially that "perhaps [the Southerners] are right, but I think they are fearfully wrong." Still, "they must work out their own destiny."

This was the thesis of President Johnson when Sumner called at the White House on the evening of December 2. No chance to discuss foreign relations arose because the senator talked for three hours, expounding the iniquity of the President's policy towards the South. Johnson had "thrown away the fruits of the victories of the Union army," Sumner iterated; the rebellion, as a consequence, was not yet subdued. According to a witness who was present, his manner was "arrogant and dictatorial."

Johnson listened patiently, and then "coolly and respectfully," according to the same witness, desired the senator to be specific in his complaints. Sumner replied that "poor freedmen in Georgia and Alabama [were] frequently insulted by rebels," and that former slaves had been murdered there.

Well, asked the President, were murders sometimes committed in Massachusetts?

Unhappily, yes, sometimes, said Sumner.

"Are there no assaults in Boston?" the President continued. "Do men there sometimes knock each other down, so that the police is obliged to interfere?"

"Unhappily, yes."

The Socratic dialogue ended in no agreement, and Sumner left the White House, never to meet Johnson again. To a friend he relayed his painful conclusion that "the President's whole soul is set as a flint against the good cause, and by the assassination of Abraham Lincoln, the rebellion has vaulted into the Presidential chair."

Meanwhile, Thad Stevens was acting, not talking. On Friday, December 1, he called together some twenty-five representatives devoted to him, and outlined his strategy for circumventing the President and preventing a take-over of Congress, should that be attempted by Johnson. The plan rested on the creation of a joint committee of both houses of Congress, to whom should be assigned exclusive jurisdiction over all legislation affecting the Southern states. Bills, resolutions, and other measures dealing with reconstruction would be referred mandatorily to this joint committee, and none of the so-called "Johnson governments" would be recognized, or their representatives seated, until the committee should approve such action.

On Saturday Stevens' "crash squad" fanned out through the city to sell the scheme to other Republicans before the full party caucus, which was scheduled to meet that evening. The response was favorable, inasmuch as the feeling generally was that Congress must reassert its independence of the executive, and reconstruction was the issue on which a showdown seemed inevitable.

On Saturday evening the party caucused, and without preamble Stevens moved that a committee be appointed to draw up resolutions on the subject of reconstruction. The motion was carried and the committee was named, with Stevens as chairman. The resolutions were already in his pocket; and within ten minutes he reported them. They were adopted by acclamation. They called for a joint committee of fifteen—six senators and nine representatives—to whom all measures dealing with reconstruction should be referred without debate, and no representative of any of the rebel states should be seated without this committee's recommendation.

The rapidity with which this maneuver was executed dazzled the Republicans present who favored the Johnson program and might have demurred; but they were swept off their feet by Stevens' timing, careful preparations, and "blitz" tactics. As Senator Doolittle later described the stroke:

"Within three minutes by the clock . . . Thaddeus Stevens had moved his committee on resolutions and was withdrawing with his committee . . . to make his report; and within ten minutes, without any discussion, without any consideration whatever, it was by that cool tact and talent of his pressed through the body and declared to be unanimously adopted."

To complete his triumph, Stevens secured adoption of a rule that party members should be bound by decisions of the caucus. This gave him a whip with which to beat down the rebellious.

When the House of Representatives assembled at noon on Monday, December 4, Stevens was in a mellow mood. His seat was on the aisle, towards the front, and as he entered one correspondent thought the "sardonic smile" about which so much had been written was a "very human and kindly smile after all." Physically the old man was quavering and feeble, a mere wraith in appearance; but in his eyes burned an indomitable will.

The galleries were crowded in expectation of witnessing the close of a chapter of history that had opened with secession in '61. Word of the action of the Republican caucus had leaked out, but its significance was not understood.

President Johnson was not perturbed. He had assured Secretary Welles that if Thad Stevens tried to shut out all duly elected representatives from the Southern states, his scheme would be "knocked on the head" at once, because there were men elected from Tennessee whose loyalty nobody could impugn. Horace Maynard, for example, had been sent back by his old district, and Maynard had risked his life for the Union, suffering danger, hardship, and bitter opprobrium. Who would dare to say that Horace Maynard was not entitled to sit in Congress?

In the House the first order of business was the calling of the temporary roll by the clerk, Edward McPherson. Ordinarily this was a mere formality; but McPherson had intimated that he intended to omit the names of representatives from the rebel states. McPherson was a Pennsylvanian, and he owed his place to Stevens.

He commenced calling the roll, and when the names of the first Southerners were reached, they were passed over.

Springing to his feet, Horace Maynard called out:

"Mr. Clerk, I beg to say that in calling the roll of————"

The clerk broke in to say that the calling of the roll could not be interrupted.

When the last name had been read, Maynard again tried to protest, and again was cut off by the clerk.

James Brooks, the minority leader, asked why some names had been omitted.

McPherson glanced towards "Old Thad" and answered that if the House so directed, he would state the reason.

With a wave of his hand Stevens murmured:

"It is not necessary. We know all."

"If Tennessee is not in the Union, and is not a loyal state," demanded Brooks, "and if the people of Tennessee are aliens and foreigners in the Union, by what right does the President of the United States usurp a place in the White House?"

Nobody offered to answer this riddle, and Brooks asked to be informed "when the matter of admitting Southern members will be taken up."

McPherson appealed mutely to Stevens.

Slowly the gaunt figure stood up, and in a sepulchral voice replied:

"I have no objections to answering the gentlemen. I will press the matter *at the proper time*."

Laughter swept the House and Stevens sat down.

A Republican member moved that "this House do now elect a Speaker," and without ado, Schuyler Colfax, Stevens' mouthpiece, was elected.

Instead of proceeding to take the oath and organize the House, "Schuyler the Smiler" launched into a speech, in which he vibrated between silvery platitudes and cynical disclosures of the line the radicals were prepared to take.

"The attitude of Congress is as plain as the sun's pathway in the heavens," he declaimed. "The door having been shut in the rebels' faces, it is still to be kept bolted," until such time as the South should have been put "anew on such a basis of enduring justice as to guarantee every safeguard and protection to loyal people." Then indeed "the stars in our banner, that paled when the states they represented arrayed themselves in arms against the nation, will shine with a more brilliant light of loyalty than ever before."

Planing down from this empyrean flight, the Speaker addressed himself to the mundane formality of being sworn.

This accomplished, Stevens introduced a resolution to create a Joint Committee on Reconstruction to which all credentials should be submitted. An attempt was made to debate the resolution, but Stevens called for suspension of the rules, and was sustained. The top-heavy Republican majority followed him as docilely as the musicians of an orchestra obey the baton of the leader.

At this point Maynard made a final appeal to Stevens, begging to be heard "for a moment."

Coolly the "Great Commoner" (as the radical press delighted to term him) responded:

"I cannot yield to any gentleman who does not belong to this body—who is an outsider."

Another member wondered whether it was not in order to adjourn pending receipt of the President's message, but this suggestion was ruled out of order by the chair. Stevens' resolution was put to a vote and was thunderously adopted. The House then adjourned.

Shortly afterwards, Sumner introduced a corresponding resolution in the Senate and it was carried, with minor changes. The joint committee was appointed, with Senator Fessenden as chairman. Stevens, a member, controlled the preponderance of votes, there being nine representatives against six senators. Already, by controlling the Speaker of the House, he controlled debate and committee assignments there.

Creation of the committee shifted the initiative in the entire field of reconstruction from Congress at large to a junta of party leaders, of whom Stevens, by reason of his parliamentary deftness, his singleness of purpose, and the wizardry of his personality, was the driving force. On the subject of reconstruction the committee would control Congress, and he would largely control the committee. It was the most daring and thorough take-over of power in the history of the United States.

PART THREE

TWO SIDES OF THE COIN

WHEN Congress assembled, Johnson submitted his first State of the Union message. This contained surprises, and one immediate consequence was a sharp revision of the estimate of the new President that had been held at home and abroad.

The literary style of the message was impeccable, inasmuch as it had been phrased by George Bancroft. But though the words were mainly his, the ideas, almost without exception, were Johnson's. Some passages were mere paraphrases of speeches Johnson had made in the Senate or on the stump in Tennessee, twenty years before.

It was not a departure from custom for a President to employ literary competence to draft his state papers; the practice dated from Washington's time, and very few Presidents had not adhered to it. Andrew Jackson's famous Nullification Proclamation had been written by Edward Livingston, his Secretary of State, and Alexander Hamilton's hand is discernible in Washington's Farewell Address.*

Johnson had been forwarding material to Bancroft in New York since October, and the message was copied out in Bancroft's own hand (to guard against premature disclosure) in mid-November.

The lofty tone came as an initial surprise. The public had heard much about the uncouthness of Andy Johnson, and was not prepared for such generosity of sentiment coupled with wise restraint.

"To express gratitude to God in the name of the people for the

* Two Presidents who dispensed with help were Theodore Roosevelt and Warren Gamaliel Harding. Roosevelt was a skillful writer, and Harding, a former newspaper editor, preened himself on the "correctitude" of his English. Grover Cleveland, of "innocuous desuetude" renown, also wrote many of his messages himself.

preservation of the United States," the President set forth as his first obligation. He then paid homage to his predecessor, and appealed for the support and confidence of both the government and the public in carrying a "heavier weight of cares" than had ever devolved upon any other President. In justification of this appeal, he proceeded "to state with frankness the principles which guide my conduct and their application to the present state of affairs."

His policy, he explained, was based upon the ample foundation of the Constitution, which defined the mutual relationships of the states and the Union. Just as the states had created the Union, so the Union sustained the states. "So long as the Constitution of the United States endures, the states will endure. The destruction of the one is the destruction of the other; the preservation of the one is the preservation of the other."

This led to an exposition of his application of this principle to the mutual obligations involved in winding up the late rebellion. In dealing with the "appalling difficulties" presented by the subject, Johnson said, his aim had been "to escape from the sway of momentary passions, and to derive a healing policy from the fundamental and unchanging principles of the Constitution."

Here, if readers of the message cared to look for it, was a simple statement of the motive that had lain behind his apparent change of front since the days when he was calling for making treason odious and for the punishment of traitors.

The suggestion that the Southern states should be treated as conquered territories, and ruled by force, the President rejected as unjust and self-defeating. Certainly discontent would not be allayed by subjection to protracted military rule, which by its nature must be harsh and arbitrary; rather, hate would be "envenomed," instead of affection restored. The expense of maintaining occupation armies would be "incalculable and exhausting," while the harpies who follow in the train of soldiers would flock to prey upon "their erring fellow citizens." To cap these disadvantages, the patronage created by a military setup would be of a magnitude that, "unless under extreme necessity," the President would be unwilling "to entrust to any man."

This voluntary rejection of opportunities for personal aggran-

dizement at once placed Andrew Johnson in the very small
number of political leaders who have ever deliberately thrust
aside power.

Johnson next elaborated on his conception of the constitutional
enigma presented by the lately rebellious states. Military rule
would imply that these states, by the unlawful actions of some of
their inhabitants, had ceased to exist as political entities. But
"states cannot commit treason," he emphasized, although their
citizens might. The acts of secession were expressions of defiance
of the law, uttered irresponsibly, without legal force, and by their
operation the rebellious states had ceased to honor their obligations as coordinate members of the Union. But this breach of
faith had not extinguished the states; it had only impaired or
suspended their functioning.

Whenever a state ceased to function, it became the duty of the
federal government to bring it back to lawful functioning, Johnson went on, to compel it to discharge its responsibilities as a unit
in the grand partnership of the Union. Upon this theory the war
had been fought, and upon it Johnson had acted, quietly and
gradually ("by almost imperceptible steps"), to revive the lawful
functioning of the state governments. Provisional governors had
been named, conventions had been called, constitutions had been
drafted or revised, and legislatures elected, with governors, senators, and representatives. The federal courts had been opened
again wherever possible, the blockade had been lifted, the mails
reinstated, custom houses reestablished, and a return to normal
social and business intercourse promoted. The record of achievements in so short a time was impressive.

That his policy involved risks the President was aware, but the
risks attendant on any other policy would be greater. And since
its success had been predicated upon "at least the acquiescence"
of the states concerned, the risks had been minimized. The culminating step had been "the clearest recognition [by the South]
of the binding force of the laws of the United States, and an
unqualified acknowledgment" of the changes that had been
wrought by the extinction of slavery. To this end the states had
been invited to ratify the Thirteenth Amendment, and a sufficient
number had done so to incorporate it into the organic law of the
land.

"The adoption of this amendment," read this section of the message, "reunites us beyond all power of disruption. It heals the wound that is still imperfectly closed; it removes forever the element which has so long perplexed and divided the country; it makes of us once more a united people, renewed and strengthened, bound more than ever to mutual affection and support."

The amendment ratified, it remained for the states, "whose powers had been so long in abeyance, to resume their places in the two branches of the national legislature, and thereby complete the work of restoration."

Then, in another key sentence, the President by anticipation hinted at the revolutionary nature of the just-created Joint Committee on Reconstruction, when he reminded the Senate and the House of their duty "to judge each of you for yourselves of the elections, returns, and qualifications of your own members." Under the committee setup, individual members of the Congress were barred from carrying out that duty; bound by the caucus rule, they were pledged to accept the recommendations of the committee.

Throughout the message were scattered allusions to the themes that had always animated Johnson: faith in democracy, the betterment of the lot of the common people, and especially the depressed whites of the South. "Our government springs from, and it was made for the people, not the people for the government." Slavery had been a system of labor monopoly, and all monopolies and class legislation, being "contrary to the genius of a free people . . . ought not to be allowed. When labor was the property of the capitalists, the white man was excluded from employment, or had but the second-best chance of finding it, and the foreign emigrant turned away from a region where his position would be so precarious."

Coming to grips with Negro suffrage, the message pointed out that the states disagreed among themselves on this subject, and the President could no more by executive decree extend the vote to Negroes in the South than he could confer it on Negroes in Northern states. The subject, Johnson reiterated, must be left to the several commonwealths, each of which, for itself, would decide whether Negro suffrage was to be adopted "at once and absolutely, or introduced gradually and with conditions." Even if the federal government had the power to intervene (which Johnson believed it did not), the freedmen in his opinion would win the vote sooner through state action, once they had demonstrated that they were capable of exercising the privilege wisely. Certainly the former slaves should be protected in all their liberties, in the right to work, to possess property, and to receive the just return of their toil. Compulsory colonization schemes he opposed, but should Negroes manifest a desire to emigrate, they should be assisted by every friendly means. Meanwhile, an effort should be made to prove that the two races could live "side by side, in a state of mutual benefit and good will."

With a glance towards impatient reformers, the President observed, "I know that sincere philanthropy is earnest for the immediate realization of its remotest ends, but time is always an element in reform." This lesson, of course, reformers then and since have been conspicuously loath to learn.

In other areas of legislation, Johnson recommended: "sparing economy" in government spending; the speedy scaling down of the army and navy; a gradual reduction of the public debt (which, contrary to the blithe assertion of banker Jay Cooke, was not "a national blessing," but an onerous burden); gradual retirement of the depreciated paper currency; and a tariff and taxation policy that would recognize no favored class, and above all would not bear unfairly upon the poor, but would lean, rather, "on the accumulated wealth of the country."

All in all the President could take pride in the accomplishments of his eight months in office. After all that had happened, he asked, was it not a happy augury for the whole nation that throughout the South, so lately in arms against the authority of all the people, "the return of the general government is known only as a beneficence?"

"Who will not join with me," he concluded, "in the prayer that the invisible hand which has led us through the clouds that gloomed around our path will guide us onward, and in a perfect restoration of fraternal affection that we of this day may be able to transmit our great inheritance of state governments in all their rights, of the general government in its whole constitutional vigor, to our posterity, and they to theirs through countless generations?"

The response to this message—one of the most impressive among the state papers of the nation—was virtually unanimous in approval. Dissent was almost inaudible. A surprise, of course, was the light that the message cast on the character, the stature, aims, and abilities of the still largely unknown, and in personal relationships so uncommunicative, chief executive. The statesmanlike sweep of the document came as a revelation. Crowed courtly, scholarly George Templeton Strong:

"This is what our *tailors* can do! Is it much inferior to the average work of hereditary statesmen, of peers who were the first classmen at their university? It will produce an impression abroad."

And so it did. Charles Francis Adams, United States minister to Great Britain, told a cousin that the document had "raised the character of the nation immensely in Europe. I know nothing better in the annals even when Washington was the chief and Hamilton his financier."

Bancroft, naturally delighted by the outpouring of praise, wrote to Johnson that "the confidence you have inspired in Europe has [cut] the debt of the U.S. ninety millions of dollars." He sent along specimens of comment by leading European publications. The London *Saturday Review*'s statement about "the influence of the message in favor of democracy in Europe" was absolutely true, Bancroft said. "Your enunciation of our success in restoring the republic gives immense strength to the cause of liberty in the Old World."

The Paris *Journal des Débats* saw the message as demolishing "all the prejudice that may exist against Mr. Johnson, and which the enemies of the American Union have endeavored to foster and perpetuate. [It] evinces a rare political knowledge, not belonging to an ordinary man."

The *Époque* of Paris could not contain its astonishment at "the contrast between the President as he appears to us at present, and the man of whom so unfavorable a portrait was formerly traced. He was described as a sort of demagogue, fanatically fond of dictatorial power, greedy of vengeance, ready to involve his country in wild adventures; whereas we find him to be a citizen sustaining, without bending beneath the weight, the burden of a terrible responsibility, having resolutely accepted the inheritance of Abraham Lincoln, and coming freely before the representatives of a free people to render an account of his mission."

The praise at home was equally fervent. Publications and letter writers were reminded of Andrew Jackson, and North and South joined in enthusiastic commendation. From Memphis, Ben Truman reported that "the whole people are determined to do precisely what you want them to do." A Chattanooga Unionist wrote that "the South looks upon you as a pillar of cloud by day and of fire by night." In the same vein, Indiana's Governor Morton, then in New York on his way abroad to be treated for partial paralysis, sent congratulations and stated his belief that "the great body of the people of the North will endorse your doctrine and policy, and this the members of Congress will find out before they are ninety days older. I can't be mistaken." From Albany, New York, came a letter of thankfulness "to our eternal Father for a chief ruler who knows neither North nor South."

The influential press of the North had but one voice—that of amazement and approval. "Frank, dignified, and manly," Park Godwin of the *New York Evening Post* called the message, and he wrote the President that "I trust you will adhere to it in the face of any hostility."

"Full of wisdom," said *The New York Times*. A message that "any Democrat as well as any American may well read with pride," was the *Herald*'s verdict, together with surprise that so much sagacity and insight should emanate from a tailor who was supposed to be rude, unlettered, and unenlightened. The *New York Tribune*, usually excessively radical in its political views, doubted "whether any former message has contained so much that will be generally and justly approved, and so little that will or should provoke dissent." And the publisher of the *Philadelphia Public Ledger* assured Robert Johnson that the President "has the confidence and love of the people, and the politicians cannot injure him."

This was the sort of reassurance that Johnson cherished most—the approbation of "the people." This, and a letter marked "Private" which came to him from Nashville:

"I have read your message with care, and without flattery it is emphatically the paper of the age. You need fear no attack upon it, nor the policy it inculcates. It will triumph in the end, over every man that assails it. And God grant that it may, because it contains the doctrines of an enlightened Statesman, and a Christian philanthropist. All here—every man—so far as I have heard, heartily subscribes to it, except one or two, who still desire military rule. God bless you! *Sam Milligan.*"

Nevertheless, hardly had the voices of the reading clerks died away in the Senate and House of Representatives before a vague uneasiness began to be felt. Not at the White House, but here and there, portended those figurative "straws in the wind," which pass by little heeded, although they announce the presence of some approaching turbulence.

Such was a second letter received from Sam Milligan, in which, after telling of the burden of his court work, he closed pessimistically:

"I am really worn out. I hope you will have a pleasant winter, but I fear you may have trouble."

Such also was the warning coming from a well-wisher in St. Louis:

"Your message is as the *Balm* of *Gilead*. In spite of this however you may expect troubled times."

And a promise of such was an order issued by General Grant, during that December, to the generals commanding at Nashville, Raleigh, Richmond, and Charleston:

"Send to these headquarters as early as possible a report of all known outrages occurring in your command since the surrender of the rebel armies, committed by white people against the blacks, and the reverse. It is desirable to have this information as soon as possible after the meeting of Congress."

As commander of the army, General Grant acted under the authority of the Secretary of War, Edwin M. Stanton.

2.

From the day he assumed the Presidency, Johnson had been subjected to rigid demands and supple suggestions that a cabinet reshuffle was due alike to himself and the nation. These demands emanated from strangely diverse sources, and were prompted by widely different motives. Had he acceded to any of them, he would have inevitably displeased other influential factions, and he would have deprived himself of experienced departmental administrators just at the time when he was compelled to lean on them most heavily. His solution had been simple: inheriting Lincoln's office, he accepted also the inheritance of Lincoln's advisers.

"I took my cabinet as I found them," was his answer to suggestions of a change.

All was not harmony by any means within the cabinet. From the start, years before, there had been friction between Navy Secretary Welles and War Secretary Stanton, caused by Stanton's officious attempts to control naval operations as well as those on land. Welles had called him to order brusquely, and thereafter Stanton's manner towards "Father Neptune" (as Lincoln affectionately termed the bearded, deacon-like old man) had been less caustic than it was towards his other colleagues.

Welles disliked Stanton's excitability and tendency to fly into flutters of alarm at slight provocation. Stanton's obsession with intrigues—both his own and those supposed to be directed against him—also irked Welles, who deemed them "ludicrous and puerile." The elaborate system of spying that the war had spawned had been carried over in Stanton's department, and it was an open secret that eavesdroppers in the White House and at army headquarters regularly reported to the suspicious Secretary. When General Richard Taylor, late of the Confederate army, visited Washington in 1865 to intercede for Jefferson Davis, he called on General Grant, and in a soldierly chat these two former enemies expressed their opinion rather freely that the President would be wise to get rid of both Stanton and Seward. The next day Grant was astonished to receive a visit from Stanton and a calm offer to join Grant and Taylor in easing Seward out of the cabinet. This proof that private conversations were reaching unauthorized ears Grant relayed to the President through Taylor; Johnson seemed not to be surprised.

Shortly afterwards, Johnson described Stanton to his new private secretary, Colonel William G. Moore (Colonel Browning having died), as "the bully of the cabinet." Nevertheless, he respected Stanton's ability; his "eminently legal mind" could study a proposition "with greater balance than any other, all the way through," Johnson thought. Unfortunately, this balance was easily upset, for Stanton was emotionally unstable. Johnson noticed how he liked to catch an opponent at a disadvantage.

Postmaster General Dennison, like Welles, had a poor opinion of the "insolent, sneering" Stanton. After one run-in, Dennison told Welles that he had known Stanton in Ohio for twenty-five years, and he was, then and now, a charlatan and an intriguer who delighted in making bad blood.

Between Stanton and Secretary of State Seward there was a rapport of views which frequently cast them as allies in the divisions within the cabinet. Welles suspected that Stanton used Seward to further his own designs. If so, the sinuous Seward seemed unconscious of it.

Johnson liked Seward, and as time went by grew warmly attached to the suave diplomat who seemed to prefer to hide his principles under a bushel of misleading verbiage. Their having served in the Senate together also was a bond between them.

Closest to the President in their general outlook were Welles and McCulloch, and their loyalty was unshakable. McCulloch's besetting fault, in the President's eyes, was a tendency to make hasty judgments. "He spreads a little piece of butter over a large slice of bread," Johnson put it, adding that that might be "a very good thing if the butter is rancid," but was hardly a safe general rule.

Johnson could always count on Welles; he was "a perfect brick." Politically he was extremely compatible, being a Jacksonian Democrat of the old breed, honest and faithful. He managed his department well, and no one was ever in doubt as to where he stood on crucial issues. The radicals had written him off long ago—ever since, in fact, he had skewered the members of the Committee on the Conduct of the War as "mischievous busybodies, a disgrace to Congress." They had taken out their spite in lampoons which Welles shrugged off.

The two members of the cabinet whom Johnson soon came to regard with disfavor were Secretary of the Interior James Harlan of Iowa and Attorney General Speed of Kentucky. Speed was a holdover from Lincoln's appointments; Harlan had been named to succeed Secretary Usher, in compliance with an intention Lincoln had expressed.

For these men the President had little respect. He considered Speed "nothing much—his wife is the better man of the two." And he thought Harlan "wishy-washy"; he could never "look you in the face." Before many months Johnson was ready to accept both men's resignations, but he did not feel strongly enough about it to dismiss them outright.

The clamor that Stanton and Seward should be eliminated would not cease. Both were obnoxious to Democrats, and Seward's authority in the Republican party had nearly evaporated. The radicals detested him. Stanton, however, they humored. Privately he shared their views, and his office was invaluable as a listening post for overhearing what was being said in the executive department. When Sumner, in the summer of 1865, attacked President Johnson's reconstruction program viciously, and declared that only Congress could fix the terms on which the Southern states would be readmitted, Stanton assured him that the speech, which had offended many Republicans, was not a bit too strong for him. "I approve of every sentiment, every point, and every word of it," he said emphatically. But in cabinet discussions Stanton said no such thing.

This ambiguousness, to put no stronger interpretation upon it, was not of recent date only. Throughout the war, Stanton had maintained a flexible position between Lincoln and his Congressional critics, at times to the detriment of Lincoln's aims. In consequence, the anti-Lincoln faction in Congress had usually spared Stanton when they assailed the administration for mistakes in the war; Lincoln was their scapegoat. All Washington had relished the story of Ben Wade's striding to the White House, during the terrible days of Grant's bloody repulses at Spottsylvania and Cold Harbor, and demanding that Grant be relieved.

"You are the father of every military blunder that has been made during this war," "Bluff Ben" had stormed at "Old Abe." "This government is on the road to hell, sir, by reason of your obstinacy, and you are not a mile from there this minute."

A mile, mused Lincoln . . . Wasn't that about the distance from the White House to the Capitol?

Wade glared, grabbed his hat, and took the road to—the Capitol.

Stanton's dubious bearing towards every President he served ("a spy under Buchanan, a tyrant under Lincoln, a traitor under Johnson," was one characterization) might seem to imply total depravity; but the secret springs of his personality were probably obscure even to Stanton himself. He was never well physically, and again and again was condemned to a diet of "mush and milk." He was tortured by recurrent spasms of asthma and nervous ailments that brought him to the verge of neurosis. Craving to be admired, and driven to dominate if he could, he made himself feared but not liked. He luxuriated in power, and immense power had become concentrated in the War Department, which Stanton reveled in using.

His personal situation at the moment was precarious because the modest fortune he had acquired through law practice had been spent, and he was dependent on his salary of eight thousand dollars. One link between him and Lincoln had been that they both had "difficult" wives, and Stanton was uxorious beyond most husbands. Also, in his own way, he was patriotic, although his "eminently legal mind" seldom failed to discover that what was best for Stanton was also best for the U.S.A.—whether those initials stood for "United States of America" or merely for "United States Army." Johnson found the War Secretary both useful and annoying; but he was not unmindful of the staunch support Stanton had given him in Tennessee, so petty irritations were overlooked.

Political pressure was put on the President from another direction by the suddenly emergent Democratic party, disorganized and dismembered by secession and the war. While Johnson was the Vice-Presidential choice of the Union party, the Democrats had excoriated him; but once installed in the White House, he acquired merit in their eyes. Overtures began to arrive—some overt and others transmitted by deft, discreet emissaries—proposing that the President return to the fold that he avowed he had never spiritually left.

George Bancroft had lost no moment in forwarding his hope that "we may rally to your side the best part of the old Democracy." But the difficulty there was that to most Northerners the "best part" and the "worst part" of the Democracy were indistinguishable. The Democrats had become identified too firmly with secession, with copperheadism, and with the slackers and backbiters who had opposed the war for Republicans to be tolerant of them.

At about the time of Bancroft's feeler, Johnson had received a letter from Duff Green, a prewar Democratic leader in Missouri and ex-Confederate, that offered the President another term, if he would desert the Republicans and placate the South.

"You are now in a situation calling for the sympathy and support of your friends," Duff Green had written. "That extraordinary efforts will be made to organize an unscrupulous opposition to your administration and to your election in 1868 you cannot doubt . . . The vote of the South will control the election in your favor, if you act wisely . . . Do you ask what the South want? They desire to be reinstated as loyal, patriotic members of the Union . . . Throw open the prison doors. Send home the captives to their anxious friends at the public expense—recall the exiles, and rest assured that there will be one unanimous, loyal, gratified response throughout the South, and that no one can compete with you for their confidence and support."

So spoke the Democratic South. And from the North came similar temptations, though more subtly put. New York was a powerful factor in national elections, and the Democratic leaders there held out the lure of their state's support, if Johnson would return —by stages, and diplomatically, of course—to the Democratic ranks. They asked no favors at present, except the expulsion from the cabinet of that renegade Stanton and "serpentine Seward." Shake off these encumbrances, the President was given to understand, and the party would rally around him.

The Blairs were prime movers in this cabal; but Montgomery Blair, after repeated hints, found the President bafflingly "closemouthed." Soon he was telling S. L. M. Barlow, master strategist of the New York Democracy:

"I am getting a little afraid of overdoing this business of *advising* the President. I have flooded him with letters . . . until I am pretty sure he knows my views . . . I think Johnson a hard-headed,

sensible man . . . Still I have come to the conclusion to presume
that he knows what is what—& to abstain from going to the
White House at all for the present."

To a man less scrupulous than Andrew Johnson, or to one more
readily worked upon, the prospect of the united support of North
and South in 1868 might have been irresistible. All that would be
required would be one act of apostasy. But Johnson was incapable of joining hands with a leadership that had gone so far astray
in the last four years, and whose purposes were at complete variance with his own. Reconciliation with the Democrats might be
possible, for by his own definition he was still a Democrat; but
before that could come about, the party leadership must undergo
a decided change of heart, and there was no convincing evidence
of that.

To a White House interviewer the President explained his attitude towards the discredited Democrats. In point of loyalty, he
said, "they must come to us, not we go to them." While he
thought he detected such a trend, it was not conclusive. Meanwhile, he would not reject their professions of goodwill and cooperation, but would welcome association with every friend of
peace and unity, meeting them all on the same plane of trust and
amity.

3.

But such a catholicity of sympathies did the President harm in
the public eye. The problem occupying minds everywhere was
what relationship should be reestablished between the crushed
but still vital South, and the victorious, booming North. Numerous possible solutions were proposed, but until the administration
should announce its course, both sections were kept in anxious
suspense. Reading the President's mind on this issue became a
national guessing game; and since the nature of man recoils from
too-prolonged suspense, Northerners and Southerners sought relief by very different interpretations of Johnson's day-by-day actions.

Towards the close of 1865, Northern visitors to Washington
were repelled by the spectacle of former rebels—including men

who less than a year before had been at the nation's throat—hob-
nobbing at the White House with their "Southern President."
Whitelaw Reid, an Ohio journalist, described the scene in the
anteroom of the President's office:

"A throng of coarsely dressed, bronzed Southerners carrying
heavy cases, tobacco-ruminant and full of political talk . . . One
day I saw two or three rebel generals, and as many members of
the rebel Congress, and at least a score of less noted leaders. In a
corner, occupying the only chair which the room contained, sat a
former Secretary of War of the rebel Confederacy . . .

"From seven until three the President sat in the room adjacent
conversing with one or another as the doorkeeper admitted them.
Pardons were discussed, policies of reconstruction were canvassed. The pardon seekers were the counselors for reorganization; there were none others with whom to consult. Thus the
weary day passed with a stream of rebel callers."

Reid was mistaken in assuming that there were "none others"
proffering advice, good and bad. Others *were* consulted; and they
forced their views on the President with the same fervor as the
pardon seekers, and with a persistence that moved a Boston editor to remark with grim sarcasm:

"It must be a great relief to the President to be told by Mr.
Sumner and others what his duty is and how to do it."

Reid also did not penetrate the President's character. As much as
any man alive, Andrew Johnson, in regard to basic policy, made
up his own mind, irrespective of partisan promptings. He was not
easily persuaded; in fact, intimates surmised that he had never
adopted a course of action as the result of persuasion alone. He
must be convinced, and to that end he listened to advisers of all
shades of opinion and bias before making his decisions.

Reid's description of the daily White House levee went on:

"At three o'clock the doorkeeper's hands were full of cards not
yet presented to the President and the anteroom was thronged;
then the doors were thrown open and the crowd rushed in, as if
scrambling for seats in a railroad car. The President stood by his
desk; to his left at another table stood [two] private secretaries.
On a table in the center of the room lay a pile of pardons a foot
high watched by a young major in uniform."

John T. Trowbridge, a New England reporter, was similarly startled by the daily deluge of Southern petitioners. But he found the swarm on the whole well mannered ("for one so dirty") and the President's air of grave attention to each petitioner impressive.

That pardon seekers made up the bulk of the President's callers was inevitable, in view of the thousands who needed pardons to carry on the ordinary affairs of life. Ex-rebels coming within the property disqualification were the most numerous class, and to these Johnson was by no means complaisant. Orville Browning personally recommended that three Virginia manufacturers be pardoned so they might reestablish their business; but the President replied with asperity that he still was not satisfied of the propriety of pardoning that class of men, and would prefer to leave them for the present "where the law and their rebellion had placed them; new men had better go there and do the manufacturing." He suspected, in fact, that the petitioners were still "rebels at heart, and only anxious to make money that they might make more trouble."

On the same day, Johnson refused an immediate pardon for General George E. Pickett, who had led the spectacular Confederate charge at Gettysburg. Although he received the young general's application kindly, and said that he was "anxious to pursue a policy that would heal the wounds and repair the damages of war," he thought it best "to hold some of the principal leaders in suspense for some time."

Thus the impression in the North that Johnson was scattering pardons promiscuously was not well founded; and equally false was the notion formed in some sections of the South, that the President's clemency proceeded from an easily imposed upon mind.

Johnson considered the daily reception at the White House an obligation developing upon the national executive. A democrat as few men really are, he believed that the people's President should be accessible to any citizen, high or low, great or humble, with or without good reason. Every day at certain hours his office was opened to all who felt they had business with him, and his manner toward each of these callers was the same: a moment of concentrated attention to the visitor's petition or greeting, seldom a handclasp, but a nod, or a sign to a secretary to indicate that the communication had been comprehended, and that the matter would be looked into.

One class of persons who scandalously haunted the White House was the "pardon brokers." The process of applying for a Presidential pardon was cumbersome, deliberately kept so in order to lend weight to the step. Intermediaries sprang up who, for a consideration, would prepare the necessary papers, secure sureties and signatures, and personally press the claim. Some of these brokers were unscrupulous, some flagrantly dishonest; and the scandal became the greater when women entered the business. Andrew Johnson had a weakness for a pretty face, and his secretaries deplored his reluctance to admit that guile might lie in a pair of beseeching eyes suffused with tears real-enough, though produced by mercenary emotion.

Never could Andrew Johnson grasp the depth of the antipathy felt for him by many Southern women. Although by and large the men of the South could accept the outcome of the war without resentment, feeling that they had done all that men could do to vindicate their cause and had acquitted themselves with honor, not so the women. Participation in the fighting seemed to give to the bitter draught of defeat at least a clean aftertaste; but the women of the South were vouchsafed no such alleviation. The immensity of their desolation no Northerner could comprehend. A woman of the North, whose son, brother, father, or husband had fallen in battle, could at least draw on the consolation that his life had not been given in vain, that he had helped to achieve victory. But four years of waiting, of mourning, of privation, of dull ache, while principles and the pattern of existence crumbled around them, and ending in not only bereavement and destitution, but in the annihilation of hope—in the women of the South this experience engendered a hatred of the conquerors that neither time nor reasoning would ever extinguish. They submitted, because they must, to a fate which every sense of justice condemned as wrong, intolerable, and wicked, but never would they cease to hate. It was the story of war's aftermath everywhere and in all ages—the victors forget, but the vanquished remember.

Stripped of everything but their memories, these the women of the South would hug to their hearts with sacred implacability.

The day after news of Lee's surrender reached Columbia, South Carolina, a seventeen-year-old girl, reared in a cultured home, wrote in her diary:

"Hurrah! Old Abe Lincoln has been assassinated! . . . Our hated enemy has met the just reward of his life . . . Andy Johnson will succeed him—the railsplitter will be succeeded by the drunken ass."

While her husband lay in irons in Fort Monroe, Mrs. Jefferson Davis filled the mails with remonstrances and appeals from Georgia, to which state she had been confined by executive order. In October of '65, a South Carolina delegation calling on the President urged that she at least be allowed to visit friends in their state.

Johnson replied that he had received several letters from Mrs. Davis which were "not very commendable," although the tone of the last one was "considerably improved." The others, to his mind, were "not of a character beseeming one asking for leniency."

The chairman of the delegation interposed that Mrs. Davis was a woman of strong feeling.

"Yes, I suppose she is a woman of strong feeling," said the President, "but there is no intention to persecute her. There is as much magnanimity and independence and nobleness of spirit in submitting as in trying to set the government at defiance. Manifestations of temper and defiance do no good."

Yet manifestations of defiance, of which sometimes the persons exhibiting them were oblivious (so conditioned were they by education and the sense of superiority inculcated by a slave society), were commonplace among women of Mrs. Davis' class. She herself, when at length she was permitted to come to Washington to intercede for her husband, so wearied the capital with her supplications, based on "justice" and "right," that Senator Fessenden longed Johnson to let Jeff go and lock up his wife, as a favor to the public. Yet Mrs. Jefferson Davis, when all was over, with the indestructible courtesy of her breeding thanked President Johnson for his consideration during that harrowing period.

The President was constantly subjected to the unconscious arrogance of these women, who labored under a sense of grievous wrong. His attitude towards them was one of patience, and even when he could not help, he listened sympathetically. Tact he did not always display, because tact was missing from his character; the "honest dissembling" in painful situations of which Lincoln was a master was denied to Lincoln's successor; his training had been too blunt and bitter.

How Southern women petitioning for favors from a President they despised really felt was revealed in the account left by Mrs. Clement C. Clay, Jr., of her campaign to secure the release of her husband in 1865–66. The former senator from Alabama, who had served with Johnson, was incarcerated with Jefferson Davis in Fort Monroe. He was accused of atrocious crimes either committed or plotted against the United States, including complicity in Lincoln's assassination. For months Secretary Stanton had been assuring the cabinet that he had irrefutable proofs of Clay's guilt, which he would produce at the proper time.

Before the war, during the Buchanan administration, Mrs. Clay had been one of the belles of the capital's social life, admired and feted at gatherings to which (as she frequently remarked) Senator Andrew Johnson had not been invited. Late in 1865, she succeeded in reaching Washington from her home in Alabama, hoping to obtain her husband's release. She sought an interview with the President, and was given an appointment promptly.

When she entered the White House (where she had been received regally by previous occupants) she encountered the widow of Stephen A. Douglas, the former Adele Cutts, who had been Washington society's beauty of beauties in the fifties. The reunion of the two friends under such circumstances was affecting, and Mrs. Douglas offered to see the President with Mrs. Clay.

Upon stepping into Johnson's presence, Mrs. Clay's impression was (let her tell it herself):

". . . That of a man upon whom greatness, of a truth, had been thrust; a political accident, in fact. His hands were small and soft; his manner was self-contained, it is true, but his face, with 'cheeks as red as June apples,' was not a forceful one."

She presented her plea and requested that she be permitted to visit her husband pending his release. According to her account, the President tried to "shirk responsibility" for the case and "throw it on his Secretary of War." Johnson's "shiftiness" becoming more and more apparent, Mrs. Douglas joined in the plea, and bursting into tears knelt before the President, bidding Mrs. Clay to kneel also. The latter's gorge rose at the suggestion:

"I had no reason to respect the Tennessean before me," she recounted. "That he should have my husband's life in his hands was a monstrous wrong, and a thousand reasons why it was wrong flashed through my mind like lightning . . . My heart was full of indignant protest that such an appeal as Mrs. Douglas's should have been necessary; but that, having been made, Mr. Johnson should refuse it, angered me still more. I would not have knelt to him even to save a precious life!"

Her siege of the President continued for months ("I visited the White House fifty times"), and was marked by hauteur, condescension, defiance, and at times impertinence on her part of which she was unaware.

"Whose bust is that?" she demanded imperiously at one interview, pointing to a marble bust in a corner.

"Mr. Lincoln's," was Johnson's startled reply.

"I know it," she snapped. "But is he not a dead President? And why, may I ask, do you, a living one, stand surrounded by his cabinet? . . . Please tell me who has benefited by Mr. Lincoln's death? Was it Clement C. Clay? What good accrued to him from the murder? . . . You, Mr. Johnson, are the one who benefited! You have succeeded to the highest office in the gift of the people! You through this elevation have become the center of the nation's hope, the arbiter of life and death!"

When Johnson terminated the interview without throwing the woman out, she put this down to a "poor white's" innate deference to social superiors. And her feeling typified the tendency becoming more or less general in her class—willingness to use the tailor President, without according him either personal respect or plain dealing as regards their real intentions.

Mrs. Clay finally obtained her husband's release when Stanton's vaunted "proofs" were exposed as fabrications through and through. Her months-long harassing of the President coincided with a backlash that was building up against the President among Southerners of his own background.

Under the rule of the "chivalry," millions of "poor whites" had been condemned to poverty and inferiority. With the upsetting of the prewar leadership, the more intelligent among these saw a chance to forge into places of prominence and profit. The last thing they wanted was restoration of their states "as they were"; yet Johnson's policy of liberally granting pardons to Confederates in the twenty-thousand-dollar class seemed to threaten to have this effect. The ambitious newcomers, in consequence, were turning against the man who so long had been their champion, and were allying themselves with Republicans who would be glad to see "bottom rail on top" in the defeated states.

The privileged class were not relinquishing their power voluntarily. In North Carolina, seven men were elected to Congress who could not take the required oath, although they had received pardons. Several men were elected to the legislature who had not received their pardons, and who could not vote in their own elections. Johnson had seen the trouble this defiance of Northern opinion and prejudices would foster, and he warned Provisional Governor Holden:

"The results of the elections . . . have damaged the prospects of the state in the restoration of its governmental relations. Should the action and spirit of the legislature be in the same direction, it will greatly increase the mischief done and might be fatal."

By perverse stubbornness, the action and spirit of the legislature were in the same direction, and uneasiness spread throughout the North among even well-wishers of the South.

This was the tense situation on the eve of the assembling of Congress in December '65. Few were as clear-sighted, and fewer would have put the matter so succinctly as Georges Clemenceau, who wrote to his newspaper in Paris:

"In spite of what is said, the North is not hostile to the South. The reverse is true. The South hates the North."

The main concern of the victorious party, in the view of this shrewd Frenchman, was "not to let itself be tricked out of what it has spent so much trouble and perseverance to win." Beyond that, it had no rancor against the South. Amid rising truculence in that area, and acted upon by the growing restiveness of the North, Congress addressed itself to the unsolvable problem.

Between the increasingly contentious elements stood the President.

PART FOUR

"I AM GOING THROUGH
ON THIS LINE"

THE bubbling of the political kettle did not divert Johnson from the social observances incumbent upon him. On New Year's Day, 1866, the administration's first reception was held at the White House, and the jam was unprecedented. Although Secretary and Mrs. Welles arrived ahead of schedule, the driveway already was so densely packed with carriages that it took twenty minutes to progress from the gate to the door. Once inside, the Welleses were shoehorned by an attendant into the Blue Room, where the President was receiving, assisted by his daughters. Mrs. Johnson was too ill to appear, and Mrs. Patterson and Mrs. Stover stood at their father's right, a little behind him, welcoming guests with poise and dignity. Their gowns, in quiet good taste, evoked admiring comment: Martha wore blue velvet, embroidered in white, with a point lace shawl, and Mary Stover, in half-mourning, wore heavy black silk embroidered in purple in a novel pattern of leaves.

The reception rooms had been refurbished, but were still quite bare. Damaged furniture had been removed from the East Room, and the patched, worn carpets had been covered with linen. Flowers masked the austerity and provided color. Nothing more elaborate had been feasible, for though Congress had appropriated thirty thousand dollars to repair and refurnish the mansion, one bill alone—for china and silver stolen during the interregnum —came to twenty-two thousand dollars. A second appropriation of forty-six thousand dollars would be required before redecorating could be attempted.

The President's New Year's manner impressed everyone favorably. To each caller Johnson extended the same cordiality, and he insisted that the children be presented to him individually.

One little girl who had been brought by her father, a clergyman from the Midwest, became frightened and was in tears when at last she stood in front of the President. Johnson reached down, drew her gently to him, and kissed her. Instantly her fright disappeared, and she smiled back. (That child, grown to womanhood, would remember all her life Andrew Johnson's smile and the friendliness in his eyes.)

Yet one thing was lacking from this social reopening of the so long gloomy White House—the warmth and magnetism of Abraham Lincoln. Under that towering shadow other men seemed dwarfed and colorless. Never in Andrew Johnson's time would that tragic shadow be exorcised.

On the political front, no overt hostility appeared at once between Congress and President, nor did moderate-minded Republicans believe that there would be any serious disagreement. Yet to sensitive onlookers the outlook was stormy. On the day after the New Year's reception, Orville Browning called on the President with seventy-six-year-old Thomas Ewing, the patriarch of American politics—former senator, former cabinet member, counselor of Lincoln, elder statesman. Both men were worried. Johnson conversed with them for an hour, giving them an insight into the shaping of his thoughts, and Browning considered the confidence so extraordinary that he hastened to record it in his daybook. The President, he wrote:

"Declared his purpose of adhering to the policy he had thus far pursued, and of doing all in his power to restore harmony and unity. Said the states had never been out of the Union and could not get out—that the authority of the government had been temporarily displaced by a hostile force, but that as fast as that force was pushed back, and the country was reoccupied by us, the Constitution and the laws extended themselves at once, without waiting for further legislation to restore them to their relations to the Union . . .

"He said that we could not have states of different grades—all must stand on a footing of equality—and we could not have states without representation in Congress, and that representation must be by just such senators and representatives as they chose to send.

"But if any individual who presented himself was objectionable

. . . send him back, and say to the people, send us a better or more acceptable man—but not shut out entire states, and require them to apply for admission to a Union of which they were already members."

The two men heard this with relief, and left cheered by Johnson's parting declaration:

"I am going through on this line."

The Committee on Reconstruction, meanwhile, was taking testimony on conditions in the South. Most of the witnesses were adverse to the President's policy, and the picture they painted served to augment the anger of Northerners. Inflammatory reports of the doings of unrepentant rebels appeared profusely in the Northern press, and by mid-January even so level-headed and mild-intentioned an onlooker as New York's patriot lawyer, G. T. Strong, was beginning to wonder whether the radicals, after all, might not be right. On January 25 he set down his perplexity:

"*How* shall we deal with our Southern malignants? What shall we do with them? We cannot afford to let them back into the Congressional seats they left so unceremoniously and defiantly and truculently five years ago. We cannot leave our black soldiers, now mustered out, to the mercy of their late masters. We have the Southern wolf or hyena by the ears. Letting go would be ruinous. Holding on a while is inconvenient. I prefer to hold on a while, as the less of two evils, and belong (I suppose) to the radical party."

For a moment he gave way to gloom:

"It seems clear that no Northern man, no Yankee, can live in the South in any moderate safety yet. Negroes are oppressed, tortured, and murdered by their *ci-devant* owners. We may have to undertake another civil war. If we do, it will be waged in most grim and bitter earnest, with no scruple about the summary hanging of rebels and traitors . . . Woe to the next generation that sets up a rebellion!"

The subject was so intricate that almost any conclusion might be drawn legitimately from the facts. All that was sure was that nothing was sure, that no stability or uniformity existed. Nor could it have been otherwise. When a culture is violently overthrown, its pattern smashed, its population torn from their moral and mental moorings and plunged into social and economic anarchy, a confusion like that of a people suddenly stricken blind is the result. Witnesses before the Reconstruction Committee testified with sincerity and truthfulness to outrages committed by whites against Negroes, and by Negroes against whites; to a widespread spirit of defiance of the national authorities, although no armed resistance; to a quickening of quasi-disloyalty. Other witnesses, just as reliable and sincere, testified to the contrary; but few of that sort were called by the committee.

The President was given a temperate view in a report compiled at his request by General J. S. Fullerton. "By telling only the bad acts that have been committed, and giving them as an index of society, any large community could be pictured as barbarous," the general prefaced his conclusions. He had found that loyalty and good will did exist in the Southern states, side by side with bad faith and contumacy, and he urged that this should be taken into account. But such a conclusion satisfied none of the holders of more extreme opinions, and Fullerton was hooted down by the radical Republicans.

While the Reconstruction Committee slowly evolved its answer to the riddle, Senator Trumbull introduced two bills which he believed were urgently needed to restore the South to a semblance of order, and to guarantee to the freed slaves minimal rights. The first bill extended the life and enlarged the powers of the so-called Freedmen's Bureau. The second was a civil rights bill.

The Bureau of Refugees, Freedmen, and Abandoned Lands had been set up during the closing weeks of the war for the purpose, as Trumbull defined it, of aiding a "helpless, ignorant, unprotected people—four million made free by the acts of war and the [Thirteenth] Amendment—until they could provide for and take care of themselves." It was not designed to be permanent, but had been created to operate for one year, as a wartime expedient.

In May President Johnson had appointed General Oliver O. Howard to administer this bureau, and already his management was under fire.

Because of his rather overpowering piety, General Howard

had become known as the "Christian General." (General Sherman liked to tease him by ostentatiously swearing in his presence.)

Howard's record in the war was spotty. About his personal bravery there was no question; he had lost an arm in the fighting at Fair Oaks. But at Chancellorsville his division, through neglect, ineptitude, or disregard of orders, had been surprised and overrun by Stonewall Jackson. Howard was also blamed by some for the loss of the first day's fighting at Gettysburg. A man of high principles, Howard was devoted to the cause of the Negro. (Howard University, whose charter would be signed by President Andrew Johnson, would be named for him.) Unfortunately, his good qualities were offset by inefficiency as an administrator, extreme credulity, and blindness to the shortcomings of some of the bureau's agents. As a result, he was drawing both praise and censure, and the bureau itself had become a center of controversy.

The bill Trumbull drafted to widen the scope of the Freedmen's Bureau and prolong its life was sweeping in its implications. He had discussed it with the President, and when Johnson had expressed no positive objections, had construed the silence as concurrence. This, of course, was an error into which others would fall, but the President's habits of reticence were not to be changed at this date. The bill was passed by the Senate and House on strict party votes, and being the first action taken by Congress dealing with reconstruction, the President's reaction was awaited with keen interest.

Rumors circulated that Johnson would veto the bill. But other rumors asserted he would sign it. The pressure on him from both sides was intense. Former Attorney General Bates took one look at the measure and branded it a "Bill of Enormities." On the other hand, nasty speeches were made in Congress and elsewhere, attacking the President for his rumored intention to dodge the issue, and whipping up public support for the measure. Wendell Phillips referred to Johnson as "an obstacle to be removed." Senator Sumner had likened the President's State of the Union message to President Franklin Pierce's "whitewashing" of the atrocities in Kansas before the war, and had introduced a series of resolutions looking to constitutional amendments that would at

once confer the vote on the Negroes of the South. Sumner tirelessly urged that step on every level, from the ideal to the expedient, until Welles suspected him of monomania.

Sumner frequently called at the Navy Department, and in
January he told the Secretary that while he would not go so far as
to denounce Johnson's policy towards the South as "the greatest
crime ever committed by a responsible ruler," he would call it
"the greatest mistake which history ever recorded." The President, he insisted, was "worse than Jeff Davis—the evil he has
inflicted upon the country is incalculable." Johnson had violated
the Constitution, he said, by appointing provisional governors, by
putting in office rebels who could not take the test oath, and by
"reestablishing rebellion, odious, flagrant rebellion." At least three
members of the cabinet disapproved of the policy, Sumner said he
had been reliably informed; and when Welles expressed doubt, the
senator exclaimed:

"Why, one of them has advised and urged me to prepare and
bring in a bill which would control the actions of the President
and wipe out his policy. It has got to be done. The President must
change his whole course. If he does not do it, Congress will."

Mentally Welles identified the member alluded to as Stanton,
who every day was making more evident his sympathy with the
radicals.

Trying to reason with his visitor, Welles asked Sumner whether
he believed that Georgia could legislate better for Massachusetts
than Massachusetts could for itself.

"Certainly not," the senator replied.

But Massachusetts could legislate better for Georgians than
they could for themselves?

"We will teach them," was the response. "That is Massachusetts' mission."

Before such Pharisaism ("The Pharisee stood and prayed thus
with himself, God, I thank thee that I am not as other men"),
Welles could only conclude that the "vanity and egotism" of this
blind apostle of righteousness were beyond reckoning, and would
lead to disaster.

Yet the creed of Sumner and Stevens seemed to be gaining

ground with the public. From his vantage point in New York City, Strong noted, at the start of February, 1866:

"Every symptom of Southern temper is bad. It seems to grow worse rather than better . . . Nothing but physical exhaustion keeps the Southern hyena from instantly flying at our throats again. The beast . . . will not be domesticated in our day if ever . . . There is a quarrel among his keepers, much to be regretted. The Republican party is cracked, and the crack is spreading and widening. Andrew Johnson seems more and more inclined toward what is called conservatism . . . The 'Radicals' are firm. I am sure their doctrine is gaining with the people. Every change I notice in anyone's political sympathies is that way. Almost everyone has changed a little during the last six months, and become a little more Radical or Conservative."

At about the same time, Orville Browning, deeply depressed, confided to his diary:

"So much bad feeling [has been] engendered that it is not certain that the country can now be saved at all."

In such an atmosphere of foreboding, President Johnson met with the cabinet on February 10, and read to them a message that he had prepared to be sent to the Capitol with his veto of the Freedmen's Bureau Bill.

The message was transmitted that same day, and the suspense was ended. The President had taken his stand, and it fulfilled his pledge:

"I am going through on this line."

2.

The sensation was immediate and reverberating.

Not that the President's message was bellicose or denunciatory. It was a clearly reasoned, calm appeal to principle, and especially avoided inciting to partisan rashness. By contrast with some of the sulphurous statements recently heard in Congress, it seemed the still, small voice of conscience.

Among Johnson's many able state papers, this was one of the best. Though he had had assistance in the writing, from beginning to end it was pure Johnson, with no admixture of other men's ideas.

Many passages were written entirely by himself, and all bore the stamp of his thought and personality.

Even to the cabinet, the President had not announced his decision to veto the Freedmen's Bureau Bill in advance, although Welles, at least, had guessed that a veto was in preparation. McCulloch had first become concerned over the bill, and had urged Welles to read it before it reached the White House. And the President also had sought Welles's opinion, intimating that he might have difficulty signing it.

The subject had become vaguely tied to the question of readmitting Tennessee. Feelers had been put out that seemed to be attempts to trade Tennessee's restoration in return for Johnson's approval of the pending measure. If any bribe could have been effective with Andrew Johnson, that would have been it. He hotly resented Tennessee's exclusion, and his anger had not been allayed by Thaddeus Stevens' obtaining for the Tennessee delegation the privilege of the House floor. They might sit there, but they could take no part in the proceedings.

Tennessee's case obviously was different from that of the other Southern states, and public opinion favored its admission. The Reconstruction Committee had tried to find a formula while the White House was being sounded out, but Johnson refused to haggle; Tennessee's claim was just, and he would not barter for it. He viewed the exclusion of the state as part of an intrigue by Congressional malcontents to transfer to a dictatorial "central directory" the normal powers of Congress and subvert the government. Always present in his mind was the example of the Committee of Safety in the French Revolution—Robespierre, St. Just, and Couthon—who had carried out the Terror. He was convinced that the designs of Thaddeus Stevens and others were as ruthless, and extended even to getting rid of him by declaring him a noncitizen (Tennessee being outside the Union) and hence ineligible to hold the office of President.

Secretary Welles also believed that a plot was afoot to remodel or scrap the Constitution and transfer the powers of the government to the "central directory" for partisan advantage. In the uncertainty prevailing after the war such fears did not seem farfetched. Judgments had become warped, the standards of political morality had been debased by the harsh necessities of the conflict, spies and intrigue had become commonplace, and so many horrors had been perpetrated that it seemed reasonable to expect more. The successive revolutions racking France and the revolving dictatorships in Latin America reflected the political ferment of the century. The period was marked by upheavals, and most Americans realized that in their own nation the end of disorders was not yet in sight.

When the President, therefore, sought Welles's opinion of the Freedmen's Bureau Bill, the Secretary made a point of reading it carefully, and his reaction was one of consternation. "A terrific engine," he called the measure, reading "more like a decree emanating from a despotic power than a legislative enactment by republican representatives." In a "pretty free interchange of opinion" with the President, Welles stated his objections, and Johnson then intimated that he would veto the bill. Still he did not commit himself; but Welles left convinced that at least no consideration regarding Tennessee would induce the President to "sacrifice his honest convictions by way of compromise," or influence him "to do wrong in order to secure right."

At a special cabinet meeting on the morning of February 19 these expectations were borne out. The President read his message, and for three hours it was thoroughly discussed. Seward, McCulloch, Dennison, and Welles endorsed it fully; Stanton, Harlan, and Speed held back, although they would not enter a flat dissent. Stanton said he was "disappointed," Speed that he was "disturbed," and Harlan that he was "apprehensive." In a speech of nearly twenty minutes Johnson grew "warm to eloquence" in reviewing the machinations of "certain radical leaders in Congress" with their "committee of fifteen, which in secret prescribes legislative action and assumes to dictate the policy of the administration." Though he named no names, there was no doubt whom he meant.

The message was sent to the Capitol shortly after one o'clock, and it produced intense excitement. In dour silence each house heard it read.

At the outset, the President denied the necessity for the bill, inasmuch as the law establishing the Freedmen's Bureau had not expired. He denied the constitutionality of the measure on several grounds, but principally because it extended the military power enormously and invaded the functions of the civil courts. Then, clause by clause, he dissected its proposals.

Under it, he pointed out, military jurisdiction would be established over every part of the nation containing refugees and freedmen. "The source from which this military jurisdiction is to emanate is none other than the President of the United States, acting through the War Department and the Commissioner of the Bureau . . . The number of salaried agents that may be employed may be equal to the number of counties or parishes in all the United States where freedmen and refugees are found."

This raised visions of a huge patronage army and millions of dollars of expense.

In eleven states the bureau's jurisdiction would be extended to "all cases affecting freedmen and refugees discriminated against by 'local law, custom, or prejudice.' " This indefinite phrase was open to the most diverse interpretations. In those eleven states, the President went on, the bill subjected "any white person who may be charged with depriving a freedman of 'any civil rights or immunities belonging to white persons' to imprisonment or fine or both, without, however, defining the 'civil rights and immunities' which are thus to be secured to the freedmen by military law."

That this would open the floodgates to abuses was manifest. "The agent who is thus to exercise the office of a military judge may be a stranger, entirely ignorant of the laws of the place, and exposed to the errors of judgment to which all men are liable. The exercise of a power, over which there is no legal supervision, by so vast a number of agents . . . must, by the very nature of man, be attended by acts of caprice, injustice, and passion."

In consequence, the present confusion in the lately rebellious states, far from being abated, would be multiplied manifold. White persons accused of discrimination under the bill would be tried by the bureau's agents, "without the intervention of a jury, and without fixed rules of evidence." The only guidelines by which these alleged offenses would be "heard and determined" by a multitude of agents would be such regulations as the President should prescribe. "No previous presentment is required, nor any

indictment charging the commission of a crime against the laws . . .
The punishment shall be, not what the law declares, but such as
a court-martial may think proper; and from these arbitrary tribunals there lies no appeal . . . to any of the courts in which the
Constitution of the United States vests exclusively the judicial
power of the country."

Next, since no time limit was set, the bill, if enacted, would
become "a part of the permanent legislation of the country." The
bureau had been created as a wartime expedient; but now the
nation was at peace, and wartime expedients were out of place.
"At present there is no part of our country in which the authority
of the United States is disputed . . . The rebellion is in fact at an
end."

The President quoted the Constitution's Fifth and Sixth Amendments, that "no person shall be held to answer for a capital, or
otherwise infamous, crime, unless on a presentment of a grand
jury," except in cases involving the military "in time of war or
public danger"; and that "in all criminal prosecutions, the accused shall enjoy the right to a speedy and public trial, by an
impartial jury of the state and district wherein the crime shall
have been committed." The bill cavalierly set aside, the President
said, these "safeguards which the experience and wisdom of ages
taught our fathers to establish . . . for the protection of the innocent, the punishment of the guilty, and the equal administration
of justice." In this respect it exposed its own unconstitution-
ality.

"For the sake of a more vigorous interposition in behalf of justice," the message stated, "we are to take the risk of many acts
of injustice that will necessarily follow from an almost countless
number of agents established in every parish or county in nearly
a half of the states of the Union, over whose decision there is to
be no supervision or control by the federal courts.

"The power that would thus be placed in the hands of the
President is such as in time of peace ought never to be entrusted
to any one man."

Next Johnson cited the provisions for "a general and unlimited
support of the destitute and suffering refugees and freedmen,
their wives and children . . . for rent or purchase of estates . . . for
the erection for their benefit of suitable buildings for asylums and

schools, the expenses to be defrayed from the treasury of the whole people. The Congress of the United States," he reminded, "has never heretofore thought itself empowered to establish asylums beyond the limits of the District of Columbia, except for the benefit of our disabled soldiers and sailors. It has never founded schools for any class of our own people, not even the orphans of those who have fallen in the defense of the Union . . . It has never deemed itself authorized to expend the public money for the rent or purchase of homes for the thousands, not to say millions, of the white race, who are honestly toiling from day to day for their subsistence."

The President objected also to the expense involved. To enforce the bureau's jurisdiction, an army of occupation would be required "from the Potomac to the Rio Grande," and this just at a time when government retrenchment was the crying need.

The confiscation provisions of the bill, he pointed out, authorized the taking of land without due process. For example, if any portion of a property was owned by a proscribed person, all the owners were to suffer the loss, even though some of the part owners might be minors, or feebleminded persons, not responsible.

As for the condition of the Negroes, they should be protected in all their rights, Johnson agreed. But their situation was not as bleak as it was being pictured. The regions where the freedmen were most numerous were vitally dependent upon their labor, and the law of supply and demand would regulate wages fairly and enable the ex-slaves, instead of "wasting away," to "establish for themselves a condition of respectability and prosperity through their own merits and exertions." Thus far they had used their freedom "with moderation and discretion"; why anticipate that they would not continue to do so? Certainly no system for the support of indigent persons was contemplated in the Constitution, and any legislation based on the assumption that the freedmen would not attain self-sufficiency would tend to keep their minds "in a state of uncertain expectation and restlessness . . . injurious alike to their character and their prospects," while it would be a "source of constant and vague apprehension" to the whites.

In the final portion of the message, Johnson boldly stated the broad ground on which his conception of his duty was based, the bedrock of his philosophy. It posed a frontal challenge to the claims of Congress.

The bill, he said, was above all dubious as public policy. It would not pacify, but would array section against section and revive the hatreds of the war, because it had been enacted without the participation of the eleven states that it affected most.

"The very fact that reports were and are being made against the good disposition of the people of that portion of the country is an additional reason why they need and should have representatives of their own in Congress to explain their condition, reply to accusations, and assist by their local knowledge in the perfecting of measures immediately affecting themselves," the President held.

While there was no intention on his part to interfere with the right of Congress to pass on the qualifications of its members, the exclusion of eleven states was contrary to the letter and spirit of the Constitution. The right of the House and Senate to exclude individual persons could not be construed as including "the right to shut out in time of peace any state from the representation to which it is entitled by the Constitution." This was especially so, he added, in a direct allusion to the injustice done to Tennessee, when the state "presents itself not only in an attitude of loyalty and harmony, but in the persons of representatives whose loyalty cannot be questioned under any existing constitutional or legal tests."

"The President of the United States," read the conclusion, "stands toward the country in a somewhat different attitude from that of any member of Congress. Each member of Congress is chosen from a single district or state; the President is chosen by the people of all the states. As eleven states are not at this time represented in either branch of Congress, it would seem to be his duty on all proper occasions to present their just claims to Congress."

Here, then, was his fundamental position, from which he would not be moved. He went on:

"It is hardly necessary for me to inform the Congress that in my own judgment most of those states, so far, at least, as depends upon their own action, have already been fully restored, and are to be deemed as entitled to enjoy their constitutional rights as members of the Union."

As Forney, the Senate Secretary, finished reading this statement, mingled applause and hisses broke from the galleries, and they were instantly ordered to be cleared. Debate on overriding the President's veto was set for the next day. As Strong noted in his diary that night, the "more extreme Republicans" in Congress were "furious."

3.

When the Senate assembled the next day, consideration of the veto message was delayed until a question of military honor could be weighed. The day before, when the galleries had hissed and applauded and had been cleared by order of the chair, it happened that a major general, sitting among the demonstrators in the full panoply of his rank, and not opening his mouth to cheer or denounce, had, in spite of his vehement protests, been hustled out unceremoniously by an energetic doorkeeper. This affront to one of the "bravest of the brave," the senators agreed, must not recur; and after some debate they authorized the presiding officer henceforward to instruct the doorkeepers to eject demonstrators individually, instead of en masse.

Then a second obstacle arose to prevent immediate consideration of the veto message when Senator Wade insisted upon introducing a constitutional amendment that would prohibit the reelection of any man who once occupied the office of President of the United States, no matter by what route he had arrived at that destination. Ironically, this was a reform long advocated by Andrew Johnson.

"Bluff Ben" had been smouldering for weeks, and the President's lecture to Congress on its rights and duties had worked him up to the bursting point. Speak he must, and he aimed his shafts at the current occupant of the White House.

Before the war Ben Wade had hated slavery with remorseless hatred; during the war he had transferred his hatred to rebels; and now the idea that he might be compelled to sit in the Senate with "unwashed, unrepentant rebels," by the action of Andy Johnson, drove him to fury. In a blazing attack, he cited Johnson's pledge to "make treason odious and punish rebels," a pledge repeated so often it had become "stereotyped."

"I have no doubt he was perfectly single in his mind, sincere, truthful, and honest in the opinions he entertained [then]," Ben rumbled on. "But how has he performed that pledge? Has he punished anybody? Why, sir, we have the unheard-of spectacle of one of the greatest rebellions that ever cursed mankind, involving more people, more lives, more expense, more disasters, than all the rebellions recorded in history, and yet no man has been punished in consequence of it."

What led Johnson to change his position? "I will not say that the ambition which has tempted all who have gone before him weighed upon his mind to bring it to the conclusions to which he has come; but it is exceedingly singular that far from rendering treason odious by punishment, he has foisted into the highest and most delicate trusts many of the worst traitors, the leading traitors in the Union. Who else at any period of the world ever thought of taking a rebel, red with the blood of his countrymen, and placing him in the position of a governor of a state—yes, sir, placing as governor of a state a man who sought to overturn not only the government of the state, but of the Union? . . . Is that the way to make treason odious?"

The target of this allusion was James L. Orr, once a Speaker of the House of Representatives, who had served as a Confederate senator, and had been elected governor of South Carolina under Johnson's restoration program. Johnson had pardoned him so that he might serve, after Forney, among others, had exerted particular pressure on Orr's behalf. The "best results would flow" from leniency to Orr, the Senate Secretary had warmly insisted at the time.

What had brought about the President's change of heart, demanded Wade. "It all points to this fact, that it will not do to tempt men in this way.

"Sir, the policy of bringing these states into the Union with all their rebellion and treason in their hearts is no better than treason itself. For I lay down the rule here, and defy contradiction, that if there is any man, be he high or low, who is an advocate for bringing unwashed traitors into the councils of the nation, that man is a traitor in his heart! He is an enemy to the nation, to the government, and nothing can wipe it out! He that invokes the aid of an unrepentant rebel to come into the councils of the nation and participate with us in its administration is no better than a rebel, and he *is* a rebel at heart!"

At length Wade desisted, and in the glow induced by his belligerency the senators turned to consideration of the President's veto of a measure that had been deliberately designed to keep "unwashed, unrepentant rebels" within bounds.

Senator Trumbull, as the bill's author, rose to its defense. Trumbull was nettled. An upright, precise man, he nevertheless had his vanities, and one of them was extreme touchiness when his legal ability was impugned. Having served on the bench in Illinois, he was still called "Judge," a title of which he was proud. Welles put him down as "freaky and opinionated," though able and "generally sensible." Now he was annoyed that the President, a mere layman (whose education, heaven knows, had been less than adequate), should presume to find flaws in his workmanship. Also, Trumbull felt personally betrayed because of the impression he had gathered that Johnson would approve the bill. Still, he replied temperately to the message, and yielded to sarcasm only when rebutting the President's claim to represent the eleven seceded states.

"How many votes did he get in those states?" he asked acidly, and was answered by a wave of laughter.

When Senator Cowan of Pennsylvania wished to be told "by what rule the rebel is to be treated after he submits—by what law?" the "Judge" snapped, "He is to hang, if he is a great rebel."

One by one the bill's sponsor answered the President's objections, and then in summary set forth the salient points of difference methodically, just as he would have charged a jury:

"The President believes [the bill] is unconstitutional; I believe it constitutional. He believes it will involve great expense; I believe it will save expense. He believes that the freedman will be protected without it; I believe he will be tyrannized over, abused, and virtually reenslaved without some legislation by the nation for his protection. He believes it unwise; I believe it to be politic. I thought, in advocating it, that I was acting in harmony with the views of the President. I regret exceedingly the antagonism which his message presents to the expressed views of Congress."

Following Trumbull, Senator Fessenden made a strong seconding speech. Welles had crustily described Fessenden as "a good critic or faultfinder," but possessing little executive ability, and lacking in independence, self-reliance, and force. Now, however, Fessenden had an issue upon which he could be wholly independent.

He started by citing the liberality of the Senate's rules, which allowed every member "to speak ad libitum, in season and out of season, in breath and out of breath, in ideas and out of ideas," and made plain that he had no intention of abandoning the "prerogatives, the rights, and the duties" of his position as a senator, "in favor of anybody, however that person or any number of persons may desire it."

In his opinion, the President had lectured the Senate like schoolboys, telling them what they must and must not do. This Fessenden would not allow. While the bill in question did not satisfy him in all respects, and under different circumstances he might vote against it, he refused to put himself "in the position of endorsing, or being supposed for a single instant to give my assent to, the closing parts of the veto message." What did he mean by the closing parts of the message? "Simply that, in the judgment of the President, Congress, as at present organized, has no right to pass any bill affecting the interests of the late Confederate states while they are not represented in Congress."

This was piercing to the core of the controversy, and Fessenden drove home this point by averring that if the President could veto one bill on that ground, "he will and must, for the sake of consistency, veto every other bill we pass on that subject." Congress and the President were in agreement when they said that the excluded states must do certain things before they were to be deemed ready for readmission; but the President was in effect adding, "I am the person to decide upon whether those things have been done."

This Fessenden would never assent to. Irrevocable as was his dissent, he remained studiously courteous in his reference to the President, and said plainly that he was not questioning Andrew Johnson's devotion to the Constitution:

"No man has shown a greater attachment to it than he has . . . But whether he means it or not, when he advances opinions and lays down principles which, in my judgment, strike at the very existence of this body as a power in the government, I cannot but enter my solemn dissent to it, and call upon Congress to assert its own rights and its own position with reference to all these questions."

Other speeches were made in the same vein, but none as able or as authoritative as those of these two senators. Then the vote on overriding the veto was taken, and by the narrow margin of two votes the President was sustained. The bill thereupon died.

When the result was announced, "great applause and hisses" greeted it from the galleries, according to the official reporter, and the doorkeepers went to work selectively but vigorously. If any major general was present in aloof dignity, presumably he was not disturbed.

In the House, less temperateness and more temper was on tap when the veto was put to a vote there and was thunderously overridden by one hundred thirty-six votes to thirty-three. Since the Senate already had killed the bill, the gesture was futile. But Thad Stevens' retaliation was swift and deadly.

Reading to the House a newspaper account of what purported to have been President Johnson's remarks to an unnamed senator, criticizing certain measures pending before Congress, Stevens wished to know by what right the executive dared to lay down the law to the legislative branch. There were several proposals before Congress to amend the Constitution in one way or another, and the President had presumed to sneer at these, calling them "as numerous as preambles and resolutions at town meetings." Furthermore, he had disapproved them, and termed all such tampering with the Constitution pernicious, alleging that it diminished the dignity and prestige of the law.

Why, exclaimed Stevens, this was a proclamation—"the command of the President of the United States, made and put forth by authority in advance" of Congress' action on these proposals.

"Centuries ago, had it been made to Parliament by a British king, it would have cost him his head!" Yet this usurper, Stevens went on, shaking his forefinger in the faces of the House, was no better than "an alien enemy . . . a citizen of a foreign state . . . not legally President."

Then with vindictive relish the old man disclosed that at the very time the President had been consulting with his cabinet on the veto message, the Reconstruction Committee had been approaching agreement on a formula for admitting Tennessee.

"But since yesterday, there arises a state of things which the committee deems puts it out of their power to proceed further without surrendering a great principle, without the loss of all their dignity, without surrendering the rights of this body to the usurpation of another power."

"The Commoner" then cannily introduced a concurrent resolution that would pledge both houses to keep the excluded states knocking at the door indefinitely, by binding the House and the Senate mutually to seat no representative of any of the seceded states without the other's consent. The resolution was adopted, while Tennessee's representatives-elect sat silent. And a little later the Senate heartily concurred.

Across the country, the response to Johnson's veto was lively but mixed. The mail brought letters of praise and blame, the former slightly predominating. Comments coming from "plain people" the President read thoughtfully, for these were the barometer by which he gauged the rise and fall in sentiment of the masses whose interests he had most closely at heart. A friend in Syracuse, New York, wrote:

"Pardon me if I trespass; I must Hur-ra for the blood of 'Old Hickory' or burst. You have thrown down the gauntlet . . . Let Stevens & Co. pick it up if they dare . . . Put your trust in God and the people, and keep the powder dry."

But a California correspondent wrote to Secretary McCulloch that from the moment the veto was announced, "an unaccountable hostility to the President personally" had sprung up, and "in a whirl of excitement" political leaders were denouncing the President and stigmatizing his supporters as "traitors."

America's most popular pulpit orator, Henry Ward Beecher, was moved to exclaim that the spectacle of any man refusing to accept the vast power machine offered to President Johnson by the Freedmen's Bureau bill at last refuted the Preacher of Ecclesiastes, for this really was something new under the sun.

The radical press was violent in its dissent. Forney, who had fawned on Andrew Johnson when he was Vice-President and leader of the Senate, now with his official position and lucrative printing contracts at stake had gone over completely to the side of Congress, and his *Washington Chronicle* was scurrilous in its attacks. The President's demand that the Southern states, "now almost as rebellious as they were a year ago . . . should be at once rehabilitated, will send a thrill of dismay to every loyal heart," the *Chronicle* declared.

Governor Israel Washburn of Maine, in a letter sent from the Capitol, had his attention called to the "President's monstrous and arrogant assumption" that he was "the representative of the whole people, and the peculiar guardian of the rights and interests of the unrepresented states. This is modest," the writer stabbed, "for a man who was chosen [only] to preside over the senate, and was made President by an assassin!"

The middle position taken by many well-wishers appeared in the thoughtful commentary of lawyer Strong, at New York. The veto message he endorsed as:

"A tough paper and not easily to be answered. Johnson states his objections clearly and cogently. Had he contented himself with stating them, all but a few extremists would heartily approve . . . but after giving his sufficient reasons for this veto, in a statesmanlike style, Johnson goes out of his way to lecture Congress for not letting in Southern representatives, wherein I think he shews himself impertinent, and what's worse, radically unsound. I am sorry, for I do not want to lose my faith in Andy Johnson."

When word came that the Senate had refused to override the veto, Strong was as much annoyed as pleased:

"So the radicals are defeated, and you can distinguish a copperhead a hundred yards off by the light that beams from his countenance. Confounded be their breed! The veto was wise, but I wish it did not give these caitiffs so much enjoyment."

4.

Still, support of Johnson was widespread, and it was not inarticulate. To dramatize this sympathy, celebrations were arranged by the President's friends to be held on Washington's Birthday, February 22. In New York a mass meeting convened at Cooper Union, and heard Seward, Dennison, and Henry J. Raymond, Republican congressman and editor of *The New York Times;* resolutions were passed endorsing Johnson's actions. In Washington, a similar mass meeting was announced to be held in a theater, after which the crowd was to proceed to the White House to serenade the President.

To express its displeasure, Congress had arranged its own celebration for the day—an elaborate memorial service in the Capitol in tribute to Henry Winter Davis, radical of radicals, who had recently died. Secretary Welles was scandalized that the program duplicated the service that had been held at the Capitol on February 12 to eulogize the martyred Lincoln.

On the morning of the twenty-second, Senator James Doolittle of Wisconsin, who was warmly attached to the President's cause, and Treasury Secretary McCulloch called separately at the White House and urged Johnson to refrain from speaking extemporaneously to the serenaders. McCulloch had overheard Johnson in too many off-the-cuff speeches to visiting delegations not to be uneasy, and he was relieved when the President assured him that he had no intention of saying anything more than polite greetings.

"I have not thought of making a speech and I shan't make one," Johnson said. "Don't be troubled. If my friends come to see me, I shall thank them, and that is all."

Doolittle received the same assurance and left the White House relieved in mind.

Evening came, and with it the crowd, noisy and rowdy. There was a band and singing and cheers when the President appeared, with yells for "Speech!" "Speech!"

Jumping up on the low wall beside the driveway, Johnson pulled some notes from his pocket and began to read. The dusk was deepening, and an attendant held a lighted candle. As the crowd hurrahed and applauded, a change came over the speaker;

the excitement was transmitted to him, and forgetting his notes he launched into the kind of discourse such an informal, friendly, outdoor assemblage seemed to call for.

For Tennessee's best stump speaker, this reaction was as natural as breathing, and his need to speak out was great. He had been President nearly a year, hemmed in by the isolation that attends that high office. Recently he had been systematically and shamefully reviled, and he had not answered back. His views had been twisted, his motives traduced, his accomplishments maligned, and he had replied only in the formal phrases of carefully composed state documents. Now, swept along by the exhilaration of the crowd, he lashed out at those who were opposing his program to restore national unity.

The war, he pointed out, had vindicated the cause he had given his all to defend during the terrible years of the rebellion. And while treason *was* a crime and traitors *should* be punished, an entire people could not be condemned to death.

"Hang eight million people!" he scoffed. "It is now peace. Let us have peace."

His task as President was to restore the Union to prosperity and harmony, and with that end in view he had used the pardoning power liberally, in this respect following "the example set by the holy founder of our religion . . . Instead of putting the world or a nation to death, he went forth and attested by his blood and his wounds that he would die, and let the nation live."

Warmed by the applause, Johnson turned to the "new rebellion" that he said was being plotted, aimed at keeping the nation divided. The powers of government were being concentrated in the hands of "an irresponsible central directory," which must recommend before either House or Senate could exercise their constitutional right to seat members properly elected. No matter by what name you called it, the aim of this was disunion, and the designs of the disunionists were as treasonable as those of the secessionists. He had opposed "the Davises, the Toombses, the Slidells, and the long list of such," he said; and now, when he found men who were "still opposed to the Union," he was against them and on the side of the people.

A man standing four feet away noticed that Johnson's face

clouded with anger as he drove this point home. The crowd called for the names of the "disunionists" he meant. Johnson paused, then said in that far-carrying voice:

"A gentleman calls for their names. Well, I suppose I should name to you those whom I look upon as being opposed to the fundamental principles of this government, and as now laboring to destroy them. I say, *Thaddeus Stevens of Pennsylvania.*" Tremendous applause greeted this name. "*I say Charles Sumner.*" Again great applause. "I say *Wendell Phillips*, and others of the same stripe are among them."

Someone yelled, "Give it to Forney!"

Contemptuously the President shot back, "I don't waste my fire on dead ducks!"

A roar of laughter came from the throng and brought back old times to the now thoroughly aroused Johnson. The crowd was with him, and after months of repression he spoke his mind for an hour and a half, his audience never finding the time too long. He would not be bullied by pretended friends or by open enemies, he said. "An honest conviction is my sustenance, the Constitution my guide." He had been denounced as a usurper. Well, let the people judge of that.

"I know it has been said in high places that if such 'usurpation of power' had been exercised two hundred years ago, in particular reigns, it would have cost an individual his head. What usurpation has Andrew Johnson been guilty of? . . . I have occupied many positions in the government . . . Some gentleman behind me says, 'and was a tailor.' Now that don't affect me in the least. When I was a tailor I always made a close fit and and was always punctual to my customers and did good work."

The crowd laughed, and a man yelled, "No patchwork!"

"No, I didn't want any patchwork," Johnson retorted, then went on.

"Cost him his head! Usurpation! When and where have I been guilty of this? Where is the man who can say that Andrew Johnson ever made a pledge that he did not redeem, or ever made a promise that he violated, or that he acted with falsity to the people?"

There had been innuendoes that "the 'presidential obstacle'

must be got out of the way." Was assassination intended? "Are those who want to destroy our institutions and change the character of our government not satisfied with the blood that has been shed? Are they not satisfied with one martyr? Does not the blood of Lincoln appease the vengeance and wrath of the opponents of this government? . . . Have they not honor and courage enough to effect the removal of the 'presidential obstacle' otherwise than through the hands of an assassin? I am not afraid of assassins.

"If my blood is to be shed because I vindicate the Union and the preservation of the government in its original purity and character, let it be shed; let an altar to the Union be erected, and then, if it is necessary, take me and lay me upon it, and the blood that now warms and animates my frame shall be poured out as a fit libation to the Union of these states!" Applause broke up the phrases, and for several minutes Johnson could not proceed. "But let the opponents of this government remember that when it is poured out," he concluded, " 'the blood of the martyrs is the seed of the church!' "

In homely phrases the President related the last talk he had had with Lincoln, during which the latter had said that he had in mind an amendment to the Constitution which would *"compel the states to send their senators and representatives to Congress."* Yet now Congress would compel the South to stay out.

"There is not a principle of [Lincoln's], in reference to the restoration of the Union, from which I have departed—not one," Johnson exclaimed. "I tell the opponents of this government, and I care not from what quarter they come—East or West, North or South—you that are engaged in the work of breaking up the government are mistaken. The Constitution and the principles of free government are deeply rooted in the American heart . . . I am your instrument. Who is there I have not toiled and labored for? . . .

"They say Andy Johnson is a lucky man, that no man can defeat him. I will tell you what constitutes luck. It is due to right and being for the people . . . Somehow or other the people will find out and understand who is for and who is against them. I have been placed in as many trying places as any mortal man was ever placed in, but so far I have not deserted the people, and I believe they will not desert me."

Familiar words, familiar convictions. And the closing apostrophe was startlingly familiar:

"I intend to stand by the Constitution, as the chief ark of our safety, as the palladium of our civil and religious liberty. Yes, let us cling to it as the mariner clings to the last plank when the night and the tempest close around him!"

Word for word, he had said this in the Senate in '61, and the nation had been thrilled. Now people were complaining that Andy Johnson had changed, that he had run out on his party, that he had been seduced by the flattery of Southern aristocrats. Well, he had not changed. Nor would he change.

That night the President may have gone to bed with a sense of pleasant exhaustion. In the old fighting style he had branded his enemies and stripped the disguise from their traitorous projects.

But as the telegraph brought to the people of the North this revelation of Andy Johnson as he was, and as they had never before really seen him—in action—a shockwave of nonrecognition, as of meeting a stranger, quivered across the country. One excited Ohioan, writing to Senator John Sherman, put the general reaction in three words:

"Was he drunk?"

5.

If contemporary testimony were needed to answer this question with an emphatic "No," it has been preserved, including the testimony of a listener who stood almost touching the President during the long speech, and who vouched for it that Johnson was not only sober, but in dead earnest. He had always been in earnest; that was his way. But the speech itself refuted any suspicion of maudlinism. From start to finish, it was Andy Johnson, fighting mad, but controlled, defending himself and his principles from slander.

The rumor, however, was circulated and believed. A clerk of the House of Representatives wrote to a friend that "Andy had been drunk for a week, and was when he vetoed the Freedmen's

Bureau bill." Count Gurowski, a capital gossip, spread word that the President had "drunk too much bad whisky to make a good speech." Even so well-intentioned a man as Strong thought the bouquet of the speech was "that of Old Bourbon." And a Columbia University professor of chemistry assured Strong that he could testify, as a professional expert, that the inspiration of the speech "came from alcohol and from no other exciting cause"; his acquaintance with toxicology, he said, satisfied him that "Andrew Johnson was more or less *drunk,* on inspection of what A. Johnson said."

Other New Yorkers were of a different mind. Thurlow Weed, as experienced a politician as the country contained, wrote hearty congratulations on "that glorious speech of yesterday. It vindicates and serves our government and Union . . . Faction is rebuked and traitors will seek hiding places."

In Tennessee, neither the matter nor the manner of the speech occasioned any surprise, and A. O. P. Nicholson wrote approvingly that it was "fully equal to any of your best popular addresses."

In the cabinet, Secretary Seward was immensely pleased, but McCulloch feared the speech had injured the President. Secretary Welles though it overlong, but on the whole "earnest, honest, and strong." Nevertheless, Welles told Johnson that he should not have permitted himself to be "drawn into answering impertinent questions to a promiscuous crowd."

The radical press was delighted for its own reasons. Thad Stevens' barbs were finding their mark, it was felt, and the address was published under scornful headlines, in a variety of garbled and misquoted versions. Wendell Phillips went into action against it with a "terrible array of twenty thousand adjectives," as one newspaper put it; while eager-beaver statisticians counted that the President had used the words "I," "me," "myself," and "mine" two hundred and ten times in six thousand words, which worked out an average of three times a minute.

What really shocked the public, however, was the President's deplorable lack of taste in bandying epithets with the crowd. Presidents of the United States should not make stump speeches, was the feeling. They did not even campaign for their own election. Lincoln had not campaigned in either 1860 or 1864; he had remained at home, encouraging and directing the drumbeaters from afar. And although occasionally he had addressed informal gatherings at the White House, he had carefully avoided controversy.

The *Nation*, a magazine of social responsibility, groaned at the spectacle of a President haranguing a "mob." Such "disregard for decency is, of itself, a scandal and a disgrace," read the *Nation's* rebuke, "and anyone whose moral sense was not offended by it the minute his eye lighted on it was past redemption." Still, the *Nation* advised the country to bear in patience "this terrible mistake," for "Andrew Johnson has in times past been tried and not found wanting in patriotism, in devotion to the Union, and faithfulness to his obligations."

The Maryland legislature adopted a resolution endorsing Johnson's sentiments and his program; but a sense of crisis was felt by men of such different temperaments and background as impulsive General Sherman, and the introspective, judicial-minded Strong.

Sherman wrote to his brother John, the senator, that Stevens and Sumner "would have made another civil war inevitable . . . As I am a peace man, I go for Johnson and the veto . . . You must, sooner or later, allow representation from the South, and the longer it is deferred, the worse will be its effect."

In the privacy of his study, Strong set down:

"War now being declared, I fear it is manifest that the 'Radicals' of Congress first drew the sword. This may result in an impeachment of the President within thirty days!!!"

The idea seemed so farfetched that he scouted it until he heard a politically sagacious friend, who was closely associated with Seward, disclose that "the same possibility, or conceivability . . . has occurred to him. Imagine it!!!!!"

Behind the agitation lurked the bogey of the Republican party —the mathematical certainty that, should the Southern states be readmitted, Northern and Southern Democrats between them would control the nation's affairs. In the face of such a threat, any action that would stave off a party split seemed permissible—in the camp of the radicals, revolution, if necessary, and among other Republicans, any compromise, on any issue.

The threat was magnified by the effect that the abolition of slavery had on the South's numerical representation in Congress. Before the war, the slaves had been counted at three-fifths of their actual number, when apportioning representatives. As free men, they would be counted to their full total, and each slave state would pick up additional seats in Congress as a result. In concert with Northern Democrats, this augmented block would submerge the Republicans in the House while with twenty-two senators back, the Democrats, North and South, would regain their prewar ascendancy in the Senate.

This prospect naturally appalled the Republicans. Few members of the party cared to admit openly that retention of party control was the basis of their policy, but not so Thaddeus Stevens.

"Do you avow the party purpose? exclaims some horror-stricken demagogue," he challenged timid colleagues. "I do. For I believe . . . that on the continued ascendancy of the [Republican] party depends the safety of this great nation."

Fessenden took up the serenade speech and objected to Johnson's calling the Reconstruction Committee "an irresponsible central directory." The committee, said its chairman (who was not, however, its most potent member), was "the mere servant of Congress. Can any member of it, or the whole of it, set up its will for a single day or a single hour or a single minute against the will of the body which constituted it?"

In the House, Stevens made his rebuttal with less dignity but more effect. Gaining the floor for the purpose, he explained, of delivering a speech that he had intended making several days previously, he shuffled through a mass of disorderly manuscript, looking at a loss, to the mirth of the expectant members, who knew that he was seldom at a loss. Then, as if remembering what he wanted to say, he begged the indulgence of the House for "a word that might seem egotistic."

Certain newspapers, he said, had been "attempting to disturb the harmony which existed between the President and myself. In the most polite language and the most flattering epithets, they have denounced me as the enemy of the President, and as having waged successful war against him.

"These journals have, perhaps unintentionally, done me too

much honor. I will say, however, once and for all, that instead of feeling personal enmity to the President, I feel great respect for him."

This brought a ruffle of laughter, and an Iowa representative (who had been rehearsed in the role) rose to inquire whether the Thaddeus Stevens he was addressing were not the same Thaddeus Stevens "referred to in a certain speech at the White House?"

With an air of pained concern, Stevens responded:

"Does the learned gentleman from Iowa suppose for a single moment that that speech, to which he refers as having been made in front of the White House, was a fact? Mr. Speaker, that speech which has imposed upon the gentleman from Iowa, and has made some impression upon the public mind, was one of the grandest hoaxes ever perpetrated . . . It is part of the cunning of the copperhead party, who have been persecuting our President ever since the fourth of March last. Taking advantage of an unfortunate incident which happened on that occasion, they have been constantly denouncing him as addicted to low and degrading vices. To prove the truth of what I say, I send to the clerk's desk to be read a specimen of this system of slander. It is an extract from the *New York World* of March 7, 1865."

The clerk thereupon read the editorial of the notoriously Democratic-copperhead *World* blasting Johnson at the time of his inauguration as Vice-President, starting with "the drunken and beastly Caligula" who made his horse a consul, and continuing through to the ultimate dismissal of Andrew Johnson as "this insolent, drunken brute, in comparison with whom even Caligula's horse was respectable."

At the end, Stevens shook his head in feigned distress, and commented lugubriously:

"That was a serious slander. That party have been persecuting the President with such slanders as that ever since . . . Now, when these slanderers can make the people believe that the President ever uttered that speech, then they have made their case. But we all know that he never did utter it."

"Laughter" and "renewed laughter" and "great laughter" sprinkled the page of the reporter's notes.

"It is not possible," Stevens insisted, "and I am glad of this opportunity to relieve him of that odium. Now, sir, having shown that all this is fallacious, I hope they will permit me to occupy the same friendly relations with the President as I did before. I know the gentleman from Iowa is satisfied now that it is all a hoax."

This was Stevens' answer, and it found its way to the ends of the country.

Privately, Senator Fessenden was less restrained than his public rejoinder indicated. A colleague once described him as "a mixture of statesman and shrew, with the shrew predominating," and in his shrewish vein he told a cousin in Maine:

"As certainty is preferable to surprise, the President's recent exhibitions of folly and wickedness are also a relief. The long agony is over. He has broken the faith, betrayed his trust, and must sink from detestation into contempt . . . I see nothing ahead but a long, indecisive struggle for three years, and . . . perhaps a return to power of this country's worst enemies—Northern copperheads."

6.

The clamoring by the scandalized did not deflect Johnson. Opposition he could take in stride, and his conscience was easy regarding his course. As he told his secretary, Colonel Moore, his policy was right because it was based on principle, and "there is nothing like starting out on principle. When you start out right, with principles clearly defined, you can hardly go astray. I have, during all of my political life, been guided by certain fixed principles. I am guided by them still. They are the principles of the early founders of the republic, and I cannot certainly go far wrong if I adhere to them, as I intend to do."

He knew he had good authority for his stand. A letter from Ward Hill Lamon, who had been Lincoln's law partner, had come to Washington with him, and throughout the war had been marshal of the District of Columbia and one of Lincoln's closest companions, now wrote to Lincoln's successor:

"I had many and free conversations with [Lincoln] on this very subject of restoration. I was made entirely certain by his own repeated declarations to me that he would exert all his authority, power, and influence to bring about an immediate and perfect reconciliation between the two sections of the country. As far as would have depended on him, he would have had the Southern states represented in both houses of Congress within the shortest possible time. All the energies of his nature were given to a 'vigorous prosecution of the war' while the rebellion lasted, but he was equally determined upon a 'vigorous prosecution of the peace' as soon as armed hostility should be ended. He knew the . . . designs of the radicals to keep up the strife for their own advantage and he was determined to thwart them, as he himself told me very often . . . If there is any insult upon his reputation which [his friends] should resent more indignantly than another, it is the assertion that he would have been a tool and an instrument in the hands of such men as those who now lead the heartless and unprincipled contest against you."

Other letters assured the President that he was carrying out Lincoln's intentions. These came heavily from New England, the territory of Sumner and Phillips. "God bless you!" "The people are with you!" "You are a man after my own heart!" Such phrases occurred over and over. Strong guessed that once the initial shock of the February 22 performance had subsided sentiment in New York would be predominantly on the President's side. True, there were politicians like Senator Henry B. Anthony of Rhode Island, who moaned that "the party is broken up," and that no such scenes had been witnessed in the Senate "since Buchanan's time, when senators from the seceding states were going out." But Anthony, in Strong's opinion, was "an easy man to scare." Yet it also seemed clear to Strong that just when moderation and good temper were needed to hold the party together, the radical wing was showing little of either.

As a lawyer Strong pondered one course of action that the President might adopt. Suppose, Strong postulated, Johnson should veto the next bill Congress sent to him on the grounds that it had been passed by senators and representatives of only a portion of "the United States of America," the senators and representatives of another portion being shut out.

He imagined the President telling Congress:

"Had you refused to receive them as colleagues because they had been rebels, I should have no right to take their exclusion into account, for you are sole judges of the qualifications of members of your own houses. But you have undertaken to exclude from his seat in Congress every man who professes to represent Virginia or Alabama, because the state he professes to represent was in rebellion a year ago. This you cannot do. Virginia and Alabama and South Carolina have been whipped into recognition of their proper relation towards the nation. While those states are unrepresented in the national Congress, I hold the acts of the body which calls itself a national Congress to be nullities. I ignore them and I ignore you. Go on with your debating club if you like. Your debates do not concern me. I hold that the nation is for the present without a Congress, and I shall, therefore, proceed to execute my own proper official duties to the best of my ability, acting on the theory that no Congress is now in session."

Strong could find no reason why Johnson would not be bound "in logical consistency" to take this ground, and he believed a majority of Northerners would approve—"so anxious are we to have things settled, however illusory and temporary such settlement may be, and however dangerous and disastrous."

Such action, of course, might spark another war; the radicals, fighting against the popular tide, charged that the President *was* plotting a coup d'état. Accused by *him* of plans to subvert the government, they charged the same to Johnson, and used every medium at their command to disseminate the accusation. This included more than half the newspapers, and the alarms sent up by these journals served to lead even men of cool judgment to wonder. Like the politicians, the radical press labored to manufacture hysteria, and speculation about "another civil war" was rife.

By his successful veto of the Freedmen's Bureau bill, the President had won the opening round in a struggle which his Washington's Birthday speech had brought to white heat. Thereafter the issue was joined, plain for all to see.

Other bills dealing with reconstruction were on their way to the White House, and the radicals moved to make sure that these should not be blocked by executive action. The House, overwhelmingly Republican and radical, presented no difficulty, but the Senate was doubtful. The Freedmen's Bureau veto had been upheld by two votes there. The problem, therefore, was to reduce the President's margin of support so as to give the radicals two-thirds of the votes. With this they could override any future vetoes. Under the supervision of Ben Wade and Zachariah Chandler (that "Xanthippe in pants," who was declaring that the only rights a rebel could claim were "the constitutional right to be hanged, and the divine right to be damned"), action was started on two fronts to bring about this result. One move contemplated adding two Republican senators; the other was aimed at subtracting one Democrat.

An enabling act was introduced to admit Colorado as a state. The territory was radical in politics, and if admitted could be counted on to return two anti-Johnson senators. The catch was that Colorado was so sparsely populated it was not morally entitled to even one representative in the House. The current ratio between population and representatives, all over the country, was one congressman to each one hundred and twenty-seven thousand inhabitants. But the total population of Colorado did not exceed twenty-seven thousand—one hundred thousand short of the national average.

This made the statehood proposal absurd, and under cover of this absurdity Sumner set out to kill the bill. His hostility really was caused by the failure of the Colorado constitution to give the vote to Negroes. Against this enormity he erupted in words that the senators had never heard; and perhaps in retaliation for such a bath of erudition the bill was passed. Then the President vetoed it, pointing out the farce of pretending that Colorado was ready to become a state, and the radicals did not have the votes to override the veto.

The attempt to add two Republican senators having failed, the Senate turned its attention to getting rid of a Democrat. The victim chosen was John P. Stockton of New Jersey.

Stockton had been elected by the New Jersey legislature nearly a year before, under a special rule adopted to overcome a deadlock. When Congress convened in December he presented his credentials and had been seated provisionally, a protest filed by the Republican members of the legislature that had elected him being referred to the Judiciary Committee. On January 30 the committee had submitted its report, disallowing the protest and declaring that Stockton had been properly elected. Six of the seven Republicans on the committee signed this report; the seventh, Daniel Clark of New Hampshire, had not signed it, but he had made no objection. Because the Senate was busy with other matters, the report had not been acted upon, but Stockton had continued to occupy his seat, to take part in debates, and to vote.

After the Freedmen's Bureau veto, however, Clark was induced to call up the report for the Senate's consideration. On March 22, he moved to amend the report in such a way as to read that Stockton was *not* entitled to his seat. This was a parliamentary ruse intended to insure two votes on the proposition—one on the amendment, and then a vote on the original report or resolution, amended or not. Debate on Clark's amendment extended to a second day, Friday, March 23.

The other senator from New Jersey, William Wright, a Democrat, was ill at his home in Newark. Before leaving the capital, he had "paired" with Republican Senator Lot M. Morrill of Maine, Morrill agreeing not to vote on the question until Wright could return and cast his vote. In Wright's absence, the radicals put pressure on Morrill to repudiate his pledge, break his "pair," and vote. Still, when Clark's amendment came to a roll call, Morrill held firm and abstained. The amendment was defeated by twenty-one to nineteen.

Clark then called for a vote on the original report. Passage of this would definitely seat Stockton. In the meantime Morrill, increasingly uneasy under threats of party discipline, had intimated to Stockton that he might break his "pair," and in alarm Stockton telegraphed to Wright. The latter wired back that his doctor forbade his traveling until the middle of the next week, and in view of this the Democrats sought a delay. But the radical majority pressed for an immediate vote, and the committee's report was adopted, twenty-one to twenty, a senator who had abstained before adding his vote. Morrill held aloof, and it appeared that Stockton was securely seated.

But the moment the result was announced, every radical in the chamber began shouting at Morrill to cast his vote. "Vote! Vote! Vote!" was the cry, Sumner's voice heard above the others'. Under this attack Morrill wilted. Pale and trembling, he called to the Secretary, "Call my name!" Forney read his name, and Morrill voted against the report.

This made the result a tie, twenty-one to twenty-one, and there being no Vice-President (the only person who could break a Senate tie) the vote had no effect, and the result on the amendment would become decisive, confirming Stockton in his seat despite Morrill's surrender.

But the latter's treachery caused Stockton to lose his head. Leaping up angrily, he demanded that his name be called also. Forney obliged, and Stockton thereupon voted for himself, making the final result twenty-two to twenty-one in his favor.

Over that weekend there were consultations among the radicals, and on Monday Senator Sumner arose to "redeem the honor of the Senate." He moved that the vote of Friday be set aside on the grounds of impropriety, since no senator had a moral right to vote on anything "in the event of which he is immediately interested," and that then the committee's report be resubmitted to the Senate.

The Democrats fought desperately to forestall a vote on Sumner's motion at least until Wednesday, when Wright had wired he would be on hand despite doctor's orders. In the midst of this debate, Senator William M. Stewart of Nevada, who had voted previously in Stockton's favor, unobtrusively left the Senate chamber. He would stay away for two days.

On Tuesday Sumner's motion for a fresh vote was adopted. The vote was taken, and, Stewart being absent, Stockton was unseated by one vote—the vote cast by Lot M. Morrill.

This radical victory proved abortive, however. The governor of New Jersey refused to call the legislature together to elect a replacement senator for several months, during which Stockton's seat remained vacant. But the radicals had succeeded in eliminating one pro-Johnson Democrat, and they had recruited Stewart, who henceforth would vote consistently against the President.

The radicals needed every vote they could muster, for on the

day Senator Stockton was expelled, a second veto message
reached the Capitol, rejecting the other reconstruction measure
Trumbull had sponsored, the so-called Civil Rights Bill.

7.

Civil rights has been a hope, an ideal, and a battle cry familiar
to Americans for a century. In 1866 the first planned effort was
made to cope with this problem in the South, created there by the
outcome of the war. This much debated and debatable attempt
was contained in the bill Senator Trumbull had produced, which
had reached the executive desk on March 18. The agitation over
the President's Freedmen's Bureau veto had not subsided and
speculation was keen as to his probable action on the new measure. Partisans on both sides predicted that a veto would widen
the split between the legislative and executive branches of the
government, and perhaps would render it permanent. Spokesmen
for each side claimed to know either that the President would
sign or that he would reject the legislation. Johnson had
made no advance disclosure, adhering to his well-known habit of
pondering a question exhaustively before reaching a decision.

Some of the President's supporters, quailing under a storm of
radical abuse, begged Johnson to sign, even if only on the
grounds of expediency, to stave off a rupture with Congress.
Henry Ward Beecher wrote in an imploring vein pointing out
that he had "strongly and to my own personal inconvenience . . .
defended both your wisdom . . . and your motives," and now felt
"most profoundly [that] the signing of this bill will strengthen
the position that I have defended in your behalf." Beecher disliked being unpopular. Senator John Sherman stated positively
that the President would sign the bill, and Governor Jacob D. Cox
of Ohio urged Johnson to do so, despite its objectionable features,
because of a growing fear in the North that the gains of the war
were being frittered away under the mischievous and untimely
policy of leniency to the South. Even sensible men, Cox reported,
seemed unwilling or unable to grasp "the wisdom and necessity of
handling the Southern states kindly as well as firmly." From the
standpoint of practical politics, Cox stressed the vital necessity of

holding the party together in the Midwest. Ohio and Indiana, after teetering on the edge of falling under copperhead control all through the war, were held precariously by the Republicans; and in any event, Cox observed cynically, the Southern legislatures would be able to find ways to get around the worst provisions of the bill and render "the bark of the law . . . worse than its bite."

From the opposite side, the President was told by Senator Cowan of Pennsylvania to hesitate not a minute in vetoing the bill; "to do otherwise would be fatal."

A continuing embarrassment to the President was the alacrity of Democrats to support him. A Union general wrote candidly to his father:

"Whether the difference [between Johnson and Congress] is radical or in degree I don't feel competent to judge yet. But I deplore the breach which puts our President in an attitude . . . with all the copperheads and rebels and all the weak-kneed on his side."

But the President was being forced into a position where he must accept this Democratic support—in default of support by the Republicans who had elected him—or sacrifice his principles. Johnson's dilemma was made clear by the Republican governor of Indiana, Oliver P. Morton, when he visited the White House just before the Civil Rights Bill reached there.

No one had more boldly championed Johnson and his policy of clemency than Governor Morton. But for several weeks he had been abroad, undergoing medical treatment in Paris, and on his return he found the political situation charged with tension. In a long, forthright interview, he told Johnson frankly that a choice must be made: either the President must compose his quarrel with Congress, or there would be a parting of the ways. The pending bill would be the test.

When Johnson, "laboring under great emotion," with beads of perspiration on his brow, raised the alternative of forming a third party, that would be neither Democratic nor radical Republican but truly Union, Morton said the plan would never work, that "all roads out of the Republican party lead into the Democratic party"; there was no other course open.

Johnson insisted he had no desire to break up the Republican party, but he could give no promise, and Morton left to consult with associates on Capitol Hill. It seemed to him that the President had grown "suspicious of everyone," and was drifting towards his "old party relations"—the Democrats.

On Monday, March 26, the President read to the cabinet his message vetoing the Civil Rights Bill. Its tone was temperate. He held the measure to be unconstitutional, and besides, contended that it was filled with absurdities and discriminatory features. Although entitled "A Bill to protect all persons of the United States in their civil rights, and to furnish the means of their vindication," it was aimed solely at the South. An amendment had been tacked on in the House providing that none of its provisions should be construed as affecting "the laws of any state concerning the right of suffrage." This protected the laws discriminating against Negroes in the North, while forbidding discriminatory laws of the South.

Under the bill all persons born in the United States (except Indians not taxed) were declared to be citizens of the United States; and all citizens, "of every race and color, without regard to any previous condition of slavery or involuntary servitude," were to enjoy the same rights in every state and territory of the Union. (As one absurdity, not intended by the bill, this provision took in Chinese laborers on the Pacific coast, to whom Californians of neither party had any intention of granting civil or indeed much of any rights.)

Any person depriving a Negro of rights enjoyed by white persons was to be liable to a fine of one thousand dollars and a year in jail. Federal courts were to have jurisdiction in such cases, and agents of the Freedmen's Bureau, among others, were authorized, "at the expense of the United States," to institute legal proceedings against suspected violators of the law. Any federal official who neglected or refused to enforce the act was subject to a fine of one thousand dollars, half of which would be paid to the person discriminated against.

The rights thus guaranteed to the freedmen in the South included the right to make and enforce contracts, to sue, give evidence, hold and deal in real property, and all other rights enjoyed by white citizens; and all citizens were to be subject to "like punishments, pains, and penalties, and to none other, any law, statute, ordinance, regulation, or custom to the contrary notwithstanding."

In his message the President said that "in all our history, in all our experience as a people living under federal and state law, no such system as that proposed by the details of this bill has ever been proposed or adopted.

"They establish, for the security of the colored race, safeguards which go infinitely beyond any that the general government has ever provided for the white race. It is another step, or rather stride, towards centralization, and the concentration of all legislative power in the national government. The tendency of the bill must be to resuscitate the spirit of rebellion."

The bill, he said, took over for the federal government powers that had always been considered as belonging exclusively to the states—rights relating to "the internal policy and economy of the respective states . . .

"I do not mean to say," he stipulated, "that upon all these subjects there are not federal restraints . . . But where can we find a federal prohibition against the power of any state to discriminate, as do most of them, between aliens and citizens, or between artificial persons, called corporations, and natural persons, in the right to hold real estate?" Several Northern states prohibited the intermarriage of whites and Negroes; would their laws be annulled, or would the states be forced to rescind them, if the bill were enacted? Surely such laws discriminated between the races, denying certain "rights."

The punitive features of the bill were especially repugnant to fair-minded men because of their resemblance to the most hated features of the Fugitive Slave Act. The bill defined as crimes actions that until then had been considered entirely lawful. Should a state official endeavor to enforce a law passed by the legislature of his state that conflicted with the measure, he would incur severe penalties. This was reviving the old contradiction between the Fugitive Slave Act and the "personal liberty" laws passed by Northern legislatures in defiance of the federal act.

The President's objections were many, specific, and lucidly stated. He reiterated that he was not being blindly hostile, for the bill's objectives he concurred in, saying:

"I will cheerfully cooperate with Congress in any measure that may be necessary for the protection of the civil rights of the freedmen, as well as those of all other classes of persons throughout the United States, by judicial process, under equal and impartial laws, in conformity with the provisions of the federal Constitution."

But this bill was not "equal and impartial," and he could not, in the discharge of his constitutional duty, sign it.

The reaction of the cabinet after the President had read his message was cool. All realized that much more than the bill hung on the President's action, and all except Seward advised Johnson to sign. Seward said he had examined the bill carefully and thought it decidedly unconstitutional in many respects; also, "having the mischievous machinery of the Fugitive Slave Act did not help to commend it." He did believe, however, that some legislation should be produced to establish the citizenship of the freed slaves.

Stanton spoke at length and ably, indicating that he, also, had given the bill close study. He, too, was offended by the echoes of the Fugitive Slave Law; but while he would have drafted the measure differently, "under the circumstances" he advised the President to sign.

Since Johnson's mind was obviously made up, no one persisted in these arguments, and the next day at noon the veto was sent to the Capitol.

8.

That the storm did not break instantly was due to the death of Senator Foot of Vermont and the Senate's adjournment until after his funeral. But on Wednesday, April 4, the debate opened, with Senator Trumbull again, as the bill's author, leading off. This time he was more incisive and personal than he had been in refuting the veto of his Freedmen's Bureau bill. Point by point, he tore into the President's message, to the satisfaction of his radical colleagues. After disposing of the legal objections, as he believed, he turned to Johnson personally:

"Would that I could stop here! Gladly would I refrain from speaking of the spirit of the message, of the dangerous doctrines it promulgates, of the inconsistencies and contradictions of its author, of his encroachments upon the constitutional rights of Congress, of his assumption of unwarranted powers, which, if persevered in, and unchecked by the people, must eventually lead to a subversion of the government, and the destruction of liberty!"

Bitingly he recalled the angry outburst of a "certain senator" when President Buchanan had "dared" to veto the Homestead Bill, and Sumner's voice rang out, "Who was the senator?"

"Andrew Johnson of Tennessee," came the answer, and mocking laughter swept the room.

Senator Reverdy Johnson of Maryland undertook to reply to Trumbull. A Democrat, a minority member of the Reconstruction Committee (where the minority was hardly consulted), a distinguished authority on constitutional law, Reverdy Johnson had a long record of public service. Speaking in the deep, organ-like tone that lent weight to his words, he first exposed Trumbull's trick of misrepresenting Andrew Johnson's remarks on the Buchanan veto. The Tennessean had indeed been incensed by that veto; but when Reverdy Johnson read the entire passage of his speech in context, the sense was quite opposite to the one conveyed by Trumbull's sarcastic garbling.

The senator took issue point-blank with Trumbull on the question of the bill's constitutionality, declaring it undoubtedly unconstitutional.* He reproached the majority for failing to produce any reconstruction alternative that would bring the excluded states back into their places in the Union.

"Whose fault is it that there has not been Congressional legislation?" he asked. "Is it the fault of the eleven states? Certainly not. It is our fault . . . Why, in the name of heaven, how long have we been here? We came here early in December, and this is the month of April; and here we may remain until July, or as rumor has it, until next December, and shall we be satisfied that within that time Congressional legislation may be safely adopted? And are those [eleven] states to blame? . . .

"How are they to be judged? By the conduct of individual

* A generation later, the Supreme Court agreed with Reverdy Johnson on this point.

men? I can go, I have no doubt . . . into Illinois and find men there by the hundred who are just as 'disloyal' as the same number of men in any of the states formerly in rebellion . . . 'disloyal' in not having confidence in the powers that be."

Formerly disloyalty had meant "want of confidence in the President. Now, confidence in the President is evidence of disloyalty!"

As for obnoxious Southern laws, there were statutes just as obnoxious in the non-slavery states. In Missouri, for example, it was a criminal offense for a minister to preach or pray in public without taking a certain oath, and clergymen had been pulled out of the pulpit and thrown into prison under that law. Why not legislate to protect them? Crimes were committed daily in the Eastern states, yet no national legislation was thought necessary to combat them.

The senator quoted the oath that Andrew Johnson had taken—to "preserve" as well as to "protect" the Constitution of the United States—and said he was carrying out his sworn duty to resist encroachments upon it. And the personal abuse poured out on the President moved the Marylander to indignant remonstrance:

"As to [the President's] intending or being capable of intending anything that could be tortured into disloyalty, anything that could be construed as an unjust interference with the legislative department of the government, it is sufficient to refer to his whole career."

Reminding Trumbull of other days in the Senate, of the days of '60 and '61, Johnson described the President then:

"I saw him, on that side of the chamber, in words that burned, and in a spirit of indignant eloquence rarely if ever excelled, say to the men who were about to inaugurate an insurrection that they were traitors to their country; standing in the midst of them, face-to-face, periling life for aught he knew . . .

"If the President of the United States, on the floor of this Senate, took the manly and patriotic and bold stand which we know he did; if he ran the hazards which we know he did; if, in returning to his home, because of that speech, his life was in peril; if, after his return to his state of Tennessee, he boldly denounced every effort that treason was engaged in, and day and night exposed himself to all the weapons that treason could use or treason procure; who is bold enough and ungrateful enough to say that he is now not patriotic and true to the Union? . . ."

Such prodding of memories was intolerable to some of the senators, and Nye of Nevada interrupted to ask whether Andrew Johnson had not defended the right of secession? Reverdy Johnson was amazed, and in the jumble of explanations that ensued it developed that Nye was thinking of Alexander H. Stephens, Vice-President of the Confederacy. But he had succeeded in cutting off Johnson's defense of the President, and the speaker's conclusion was robbed of much of its effect:

"The President desires—and who does not—that the Union should be restored as it originally existed. He has a policy which he thinks is best calculated to effect it. He may be mistaken, but he is honest."

Senator Wade then took up the attack on the veto, in fighting trim.

"The President of the United States," he said roundly, "has no more power to interpose his authority here to prescribe the principles upon which these states shall be admitted to the Union than any man of this body has out of it. The Constitution makes him the executive of the laws that we make, and there it leaves him. And what is our condition? We, who are to judge of the forms of government under which states shall exist; we, who are the only power that is charged with this great question, are to be somehow or other wheedled out of it by the President! . . .

"Sir, we cannot abandon [our power] unless we yield to a principle that will unhinge and unsettle the balance of the Constitution itself. If the President can impose his authority upon a question of this character, and can compel Congress to succumb to his dictation, he is an emperor, a despot, and not a President of the United States."

The time dragging on (this was the second day of the debate, and the hour was late), attempts were made to postpone further discussion until the next day, especially since two senators, both Johnson supporters, were absent. Senator Wright, at peril of his life, had been brought from New Jersey, and Senator Dixon of

Connecticut was ill at home. But Wade would listen to no humanitarian pleas.

"Because I believe the great question of Congressional power and authority is at stake here, I yield to no importunities. I will not yield to these appeals," he insisted grimly; "these appeals of comity on a question like this. But I tell the President and everyone else, that if God Almighty has stricken one member so he cannot be here to uphold the dictation of a despot, I thank Him for His interposition, and I will take advantage of it if I can!"

Gallery applause greeted this, although some senators stirred uneasily, shocked and embarrassed. But Wade went on:

"The issue the President has made with Congress, the quarrel he has picked with Congress from the very commencement, is nothing more or less than on the question of recognizing and permitting rebels to occupy their old places on this floor for the utter destruction of the government, in my judgment and belief. What power has he to do it? I care not who your President may be, he is not to be a despot! . . . For one, I am willing to stay here all night and all day tomorrow and as long as my physical powers can hold out, in order to vindicate the great principle of constitutional law that I am entrusted with by the people whom I represent . . . Never, with my consent, will I yield it!"

If his constituents disagreed with him, then let them censure him, but he would accept no censure coming from the South.

Sensing disapproval among even his friends (though Senator Chandler urged him on), the old fighter at length conceded the floor temporarily to Senator McDougall of California, who usually could be relied upon to relieve tension by some bibulous irrelevancy. But McDougall had been shocked sober.

"The senator," he pronounced with startling lucidity, "is in the habit of appealing to his God in vindication of his judgment and conduct. But it may well be asked who and what is his God?" Ormuzd or Ahriman, a god of light and beauty, or a god of darkness and death? "Death is to be one of his angels to redeem the Constitution and the laws and to establish liberty! Sickness, suffering, evil are to be his angels; and he thanks the Almighty, *his* Almighty, that sickness, danger, and evil are about!" Such a faith, he hazarded, would avail the senator from Ohio little when he applied for admission at the crystal doors.

"If my condemnation amounts to a rebuke," McDougall concluded amid profound silence, "I trust it may be a rebuke."

On that chastening note the Senate adjourned. But Wade still held the floor the next day.

"Should Congress recede from the position they have taken to claim jurisdiction over this great question of readmitting these states," he warned, "from that hour they surrender all the power that the Constitution places in their hands and that they are sworn to support, and they are the mere slaves of an accidental executive; of a man who formerly associated with us upon this floor; who was no more infallible than the rest of us poor mortals; and yet, the moment, by death or accident, he is placed in the executive chair, it would seem as if some senators believed him to be endowed with superhuman wisdom, and ought to be invested with all the powers of this government; that Congress ought to get on their knees before him and take his insults and his dictation without resentment and without even an attempt to resist . . .

"Some gentlemen may be patient under the charge of treason; but, sir, I am a little too old-fashioned to be charged by the executive branch of this government as a traitor on the floor of Congress, and not resent it. I will not take it from any mortal man, high or low!"

Rounding on Senator James Lane of Kansas, an old border fighter often seen at the White House as a supporter of Johnson, Wade taunted:

"I fought your fight in Kansas and saved you from worse than slavery, and I would do it again. But I don't wear the President's collar because of that! I say to you, senators," he swept the room with smouldering eyes, while Lane appeared to be struggling against apoplexy, "we the majority, who are stigmatized as traitors, are the only barrier today between this nation and anarchy and despotism! If we give way, the hope of the nation is lost by the recreancy—yes, sir, I will say the treachery of a man who betrayed our confidence, who got into power, and who has gone into the camp of the enemy and joined with those who never breathed a breath of principle in common with us!

"Now, sir," he wound up sardonically, addressing the sputtering senator from Kansas, "if your nerves were unstrung by what I said before, I hope they will be calmed by what I have said now."

Amid laughter, Lane arose, and hurled "in the teeth of the senator from Ohio" the suggestion that he had "taken upon myself the collar of the President of the United States. I wear a collar! *I wear a collar!* Indicted for treason by a pro-slavery jury, hunted from state to state, one hundred thousand dollars offered for my head! *Jim Lane wears a collar!*"

Wade just glared, with unblinking eyes.

Other speeches, pallid by comparison, succeeded, and then the vote was taken.

Despite a heavy rain outside, the galleries were jammed as the roll was called. Should the Civil Rights Bill pass, "the objections of the President notwithstanding?" The votes of three senators were doubtful—former Governor E. D. Morgan of New York, and West Virginia's Peter C. Van Winkle and Waitman T. Willey. When the clerk reached Morgan's name, there was a hush, and he hesitated. Then he voted to override, and the galleries clapped.

Tension built up again as Van Winkle's name was neared. In profound silence he voted to sustain the President. Then Willey's vote to override removed the last doubt. The result stood thirty-three to override, against fifteen to sustain. The radicals had won, the bill having been repassed by the necessary two-thirds, with one vote to spare.

Repassage by the House was accomplished three days later. Speaker Colfax, unable to resist the opportunity of placing himself on the winning side, directed the clerk to call his name, and with gusto voted to override. This action was saluted with enthusiastic whoops from the floor. Then, "by the authority vested in me by the Constitution," Colfax declared the bill a law, and the chamber rang with shouts and the stamping of feet.

For the first time in the nation's history, a President had been overridden on a measure of constitutional significance, and Thaddeus Stevens saw fulfilled the declaration he had made to an aroused House of Representatives:

"Andrew Johnson must learn that he is your servant, and that as Congress shall order he must obey. There is no escape from it. God forbid that he should have one tittle of power except what he derives through Congress and the Constitution . . . He and his minions must learn that this is not a government of kings and satraps, but a government of the people, and that Congress is the people."

Grieved Senator Saulsbury of Delaware:

"Reason is thrown away . . . In my judgment, the passage of this bill is the inauguration of revolution—bloodless as yet . . . but it will lead to revolution in blood."

PART FIVE

INTRIGUE AND BLOODSHED

FROM the demeanor of the President, no crisis could have been guessed. He went about his duties, social and governmental, calmly and with complete propriety. On the evening of the day when the Civil Rights veto was overridden, General and Mrs. Grant gave their last reception of the season, and a crowd turned out, including many radical senators and congressmen; Welles had heard that the radical leaders were maneuvering to "appropriate Grant, or at least his name and influence," for their cause. Thad Stevens showed up, although he seldom graced a reception, and old stager though he was, he was taken aback when the President arrived with his daughters. Johnson was self-contained, pleasant to everyone, shook hands with Stevens and seemed at ease, not appearing to notice the strange mixture of the guests. Montgomery Blair, who was hated like Beelzebub by Stevens and his crowd, attended with ladies of his family, and a still more incongruous guest was Georgia's senator-elect, Alexander Stephens, lately Vice-President of the Confederate States of America. Senator Trumbull did betray embarrassment when he encountered the President, but Johnson smiled and shook hands with his old colleague, seemingly oblivious of the harsh things that had been said elsewhere that day.

This trait of self-containment was a puzzle to the President's staff. Crook, his bodyguard, had been as startled as anyone by the President's outburst on Washington's Birthday, for nothing in Johnson's manner had given any warning. Again and again Crook would be struck by the misleading impression conveyed by the published versions of Johnson's speeches. In print, they seemed to suggest an arm-swinging, bellowing demagogue, whereas in fact the speeches were delivered in Johnson's earnest but singularly pleasing voice, seldom raised unduly, and with its peculiar carry-

449

ing power clearly audible at a great distance. More than once, after hearing the President speak, Crook would doubt his senses upon reading the same speech reported in a newspaper; the two seemed like separate addresses. This, of course, told against Johnson, for only a few people could hear him, while millions read the newspaper accounts.

Though the President seemed calm in the wake of the veto reverse, the air around him was filled with alarms. Many persons reacted to the action of Congress as a call to arms in defense of the Presidency. Three days after Speaker Colfax pronounced the Civil Rights Bill a law, "the objections of the President notwithstanding," John Fisk, a former lieutenant colonel of the 2nd Mounted Rifles, New Hampshire Volunteers, wrote to the man in the White House:

"The radicals . . . have succeeded in passing the civil rights bill so-called over the veto. The next step is to impeach the President, and expel him from the seat in which the People, by the Grace of God, have placed him. The masses are with you. Can you rely upon the military about the capital? If not, call upon those in whom you can trust. The moment Stevens, Sumner, and their fellow conspirators make their first move in their treasonable designs, arrest them the moment they are clear of the Capitol, and have them quietly lodged in the Old Capitol or some other safe place until they can be brought to trial for the crimes they are committing against the American People and the President of the United States—And believe me the people will sustain you and shield you with [their] lives. That you may have about you those in whom you can confide at this trying moment, is the prayer of him who pens these lines."

On second thought, Colonel Fisk did not mail this letter; but he preserved it, and would forward it in a later crisis.

About the same time, a colonel of New York Volunteers, William H. Allen, wrote to the President:

"Information which I have received and of which there can be no doubt, is that a most dangerous conspiracy is in existence in [Washington] to deprive you of your personal liberty, under assumed charges of correspondence with many prominent rebels of North Carolina and other Southern states. In one of these letters written three days after the death of Mr. Lincoln you are made to say, 'I will soon have things my own way. You shall have all you want as before the war, and back in the union as you were.' . . . They have also arranged to surround your house with guards . . . [and] if you attempt to arrest them as they believe you will they have also provided a force at hand east of the Capitol to protect them in debate if required. This arrangement is made by Mr. Stanton with the approval of Gen'l. Grant who has attended one of the *secret* meetings nightly held. The letters in question were obtained by the orders of Mr. Stanton to L. C. Baker and his assistants, who went south and returned with eight or ten in all . . ."

In New York, Strong was repelled by the "loose, reckless denunciations" of the President he heard on the streets and in club rooms. " 'When he dies,' quoth ————, 'there will be one comfort. Judas Iscariot will not be quite so lonesome'!!! Another says, 'It's bad enough to have a tailor for a President, but a drunken tailor, and a drunken Democratic tailor, is beyond endurance.' "

The veto message Strong considered "less strong than that against the Freedmen's Bureau, but very able, perhaps sound, possibly a little disingenuous. I fear these vetoes shew Johnson's sympathies and prejudices to be wrong and dangerous. I am losing my faith in him." By no logical process, he conceded, but by "instinctive distrust" of anyone who was commended by the copperhead and Richmond press. Some copperhead papers, Strong noted, were advising the President "to summon Southern Senators and Representatives to Washington and put them in their seats and keep them there by military force . . . The crack spreads and widens."

Orville Browning told a friend in Illinois that he believed the country stood in greater peril than at any time during the war, and he feared "all might yet be lost." President Johnson, he said, had "done more, periled more, and suffered more for the country than any of his revilers . . . The memory of the past should have protected him from the coarse abuse which has been lavished upon him." As for the President's policy, it found its strongest support in its "inherent wisdom and justice, and its conformity to the Constitution." The policy of Congress, Browning felt, was "the reverse of all this . . . and will lose all the advantages we hope for from the costly victories that have been won."

Already William Tecumseh Sherman had written to the Presi-

dent from St. Louis, where the general was stationed, reporting
that while in Washington he had told members of Congress that
"the extreme radical measures of Sumner & Stevens were calculated to lead to a result that even they ought not to desire, viz.,
the everlasting estrangement of all the people of the South.

"I shall always bear in honorable remembrance," this intel-
lectual-in-uniform assured Johnson, "your personal expression
that you will feel that you have fulfilled your highest ambition
when you complete the entire pacification of our country by restoring all its parts to the enjoyment of its privileges and protection. And add my absolute faith in your success, because you
will be sustained by natural laws that mischievous men may
delay but not prevent."

Such was the surge of emotions as the radicals crowed over
their victory, while their opponents petitioned the President to
stand fast, "the howling of office seekers and radical politicians to
the contrary notwithstanding."

The President himself was not daunted. Just before the Senate's
action, Johnson and Browning had "a good chat" at the White
House, during which the President had confided that it would
neither surprise nor discourage him should the coming spring
elections go against him; in fact, he rather expected reverses. But
his faith in the people and their ultimate judgment was unbounded. "He laughed about his 'family'—meaning his Cabinet,"
Browning noted, taking this as evidence of his unruffled spirit.
"Said he called a meeting the day his veto went in, and that his
law adviser, Speed, sent him word that he had a 'bile on his leg'
and could not come." And at the next cabinet meeting, Speed
"laid his leg up on a chair to prove that he was disabled. The
President talks well and seems firm in his purpose . . . I do not
think he will succumb to radical insolence and despotism."

Johnson ruminated the good and bad counsels reaching him,
and his secretary, Colonel Moore, noticed that he often became
lost in thought. A basic issue had been brought into the open,
perhaps even more forcefully by himself than by the radicals. In
the President's view, the plain mandate of the Constitution required the restoration of the Southern states to their constitutional
representation, now that their rebellion had ceased and they had

reaffirmed their loyalty to the United States; and this restoration must precede reconstruction of their laws and society. On the other hand, the radical-minded Congress was equally firm in its insistence that reconstruction must precede restoration. The difference was absolute and fundamental, and Johnson, according to his habit, wrestled with the problem alone; accepting all advice, from whatever quarter, but groping his own way towards a solution based on principle. Not breath of insight, but profundity, was what he strove for.

One hot afternoon, when the clamor was at its height, Moore and the President were sharing a glass of claret in the President's bedroom. Johnson paced the floor, lost in thought. Suddenly turning towards Moore, "with a firm, determined look," he said:

"Sir, I am right. I know I am right. And I'm damned if I don't adhere to it."

The decision had been made. The attempt by Congress to strip the executive branch of its constitutional independence, to reduce the President to a figurehead, docilely endorsing whatever measures Congress might present—in Thaddeus Stevens's honestly arrogant words, to make the President of the United States a servant of Congress, "who must obey"—this attempt to subvert the constitutional balance of powers which had served the nation so well must be resisted. It was not Andrew Johnson personally, but the office of the presidency that Stevens and his cohorts had declared war against; their purpose was to override the Constitution and substitute party rule by a junta or committee in the name of the people.

Johnson's whole life had been an unending struggle. At first he had fought to vindicate his right to rise above poverty and ignorance and fill a respectable and respected position in society. Then as legislator and governor he had fought to vindicate the right of the common people to have a controlling voice in their government. During the war, as a patriot he had risked everything to vindicate the indestructibility of the Union. Now as President he was being called to vindicate the foundation upon which the nation had been erected, on the strength of which it had risen to greatness, and in defense of which it had suffered the ordeal of civil conflict—the Constitution of the United States. As over and over he once had told his fellow senators, "Save the Constitution and you save everything!"

Andrew Johnson had found his ultimate cause. The decision having been made, the issue for him was settled. Henceforward his mind would be at peace.

2.

Despite Reverdy Johnson's scornful allusion to dallying, the Joint Committee on Reconstruction had not been idle. It had been divided in opinion, but had produced, in the January preceding the furor over the vetoes, a report that stated the terms on which the committee believed the Southern states might be safely readmitted to their places in Congress. Their recommendation was put in the form of an amendment to the Constitution, writing into the organic law both the rights of the freedmen and safeguards for the integrity of the government. A statute, like the Civil Rights Act, could be revoked by a majority of Congress, but a constitutional amendment could be repealed only by the states.

Stevens reported the proposed amendment to the House on January 22. The question the committee had faced, he said, had been:

"Whether conquered rebels may change their theater of operations from the battlefield, where they were defeated and overthrown, to the halls of Congress, and through their representatives seize upon the government which they fought to destroy."

Although it would undergo changes in wording, in its final form (as the Fourteenth Amendment) the recommendation embraced five parts.

The first declared all persons born or naturalized in the United States "citizens of the United States and of the state wherein they reside." This incorporated into the basic law the statutory citizenship bestowed by the Civil Rights Act, and for the first time established that there was such a thing as American citizenship; up to then there had been only citizenship of a state. This section also prohibited any state from denying to a citizen equal protection of the laws, or depriving any person of "life, liberty, or property, without due process of law." This prohibition, originally written into the Bill of Rights appended to the Constitution, had applied only to the federal government; the amendment extended it to the states.

The second section, in its final form, provided that any state denying the vote to any race or class of citizens should have its representation in Congress reduced proportionately. Thus, while the Southern states were not to be compelled to enfranchise their Negroes, if they declined to do so the number of their representatives would be diminished.

The third section barred from holding national or state office any person who before the war had held an office that required an oath of allegiance to the United States and had violated it. Reverdy Johnson pointed out that this would exclude ninety percent of the educated, intelligent, experienced leading men (the "gentlemen") of the South; but that was the intention precisely.

The fourth section outlawed recognition of the Confederate debt, forbade payment of Confederate pensions, and affirmed the validity of the United States public debt, as a burden upon all the states.

The final section authorized Congress to enact legislation to enforce the amendment.

In presenting this measure to the House, Stevens said the problem was whether "the criminal should sit in judgment when the extent of his crime and its proper punishment were under consideration," simply that. The debate ran on until January 31, and in closing it Stevens reviewed the case for immediate enfranchisement of the freedmen, which the amendment did not require. He said he did not favor enfranchisement at once; not because he believed the Negroes were not entitled to vote, but because in their present condition of ignorance and confusion they would easily be manipulated by their former masters to their detriment. Also, imposing impartial suffrage by national law would run counter to public sentiment in the North; he doubted that five states could be found that would willingly consent to such a step.

Under the party lash, wielded by the old man, dubious conservatives were whipped into line, and the amendment was adopted by one hundred and twenty votes to forty-six. Then it went to the Senate, where it ran afoul of Charles Sumner.

Because of the inclusion of one word—the word "white"—in

regard to voting representation, Sumner poured forty columns of verbal lava into the *Congressional Globe,* leaving the Senate stunned and reeling. He loathed the measure as "a disgusting tyranny," and as "nothing less than a mighty house of ill fame, which it is proposed to license constitutionally for a consideration." He repudiated it as "a new sale of indulgences on a larger scale than that of Fetzel . . . a muscipular abortion sent into the world by a parturient mountain."* It was to him "the very Koh-i-noor of blackness . . . a new anathema marantha . . . a wickedness on a larger scale than the crime against Kansas and the Fugitive Slave Law . . . a loathsome stench . . . a disgusting ordure . . . an essential uncleanliness . . . a paragon and masterpiece of ingratitude . . . an abomination." Each and every one of its authors he likened to "Pontius Pilate with Judas Iscariot upon his back."

Before the terrible onslaught of his words the Senate caved in, and the amendment went down to defeat. In March the Reconstruction Committee went back to work again.

Meanwhile, the President had been under pressure less prolix but quite as impassioned to get rid of "disloyal" elements in his cabinet. A cabal, taking in conservative Republicans as well as Democrats, was agitating without cease to secure the dismissal of Secretary Stanton, terming him an obstacle to the President's policy, a sneak, a marplot, and a traitor.

Johnson's attitude undoubtedly had become repugnant to Stanton. His excitable and often morbid imagination was haunted by visions of the three hundred thousand Union dead; was the victory bought with their blood being given away? But haunted also by his insecure personal position, he refrained from expressing his inner thoughts to the President.

He was in trouble on several fronts. In December of '65, a man named Joseph E. Maddox had sued him for thirty thousand dollars, charging unlawful arrest during the war. The case looked bad for Stanton, and it had the corollary effect of spreading panic among army personnel, many of whom had reason to fear that they, too, might be called to account for actions committed during the war. Fifty cases bearing on the subject already were pend-

* By interpretation, a mountain laboring and bringing forth an aborted mouse.

ing in the courts of Vermont, Indiana, New York, and Kentucky, and success of the suit against Stanton threatened to validate all these claims. Undoubtedly injustices had been committed, for many army officers were neither wise nor scrupulous. For Stanton himself, an adverse verdict would mean bankruptcy. And it would create havoc in the army garrisoning the Southern states.

The threat was aggravated when, on April 2, the President proclaimed the rebellion officially at an end everywhere except in Texas, where the restoration process was lagging. Martial law in the South was lifted by this proclamation, and the army's morale was further shaken.

Then, on another front, the Supreme Court took under advisement the appeal of an Indiana man, Lambdin P. Milligan, who had been condemned by a military court, although the civil courts were functioning at the time. Stanton, an astute lawyer, realized that he was ringed with menaces as a result of these actions. As a private citizen he would be in a far less advantageous position to combat them than when backed by the resources available to the Secretary of War; hence he really had no choice but to stay in the cabinet, if he could, for his own salvation; but from this time on his dealings with elements in Congress hostile to Johnson would become continuous.

In order to implement the proclamation ending martial rule in the South and bring army policy into line with the changed conditions, Stanton, through the commander of the army, Grant, had instructed regional commanders to refer all offenses against the Civil Rights Act and similar laws to the state courts for trial, wherever these were functioning. But officers in the field complained that the state courts could not administer justice because the local juries would not convict. This greatly hampered the army, and in a subsequent letter, which Stanton and Grant circulated secretly, the field commanders were told to use their judgment about referring trials to the state courts, and if they were challenged they would be upheld.

This secret countermanding, in effect, of an order issued publicly was unknown to the President, and it set a pattern that would be invoked repeatedly as time went on. While outwardly and ostensibly conforming to the directives of its commander-in-chief, the army thus would more and more tend to act independently, deciding for itself the course of action that would best serve its interests in any given crisis. And this, in turn, would force Congress and the President to compete for the army's support, for without it either party was helpless. The outcome of the constitutional struggle that was in progress, therefore, might depend on the army's future construction of loyalty. This factor would also bear upon the President's retention of Stanton in the cabinet. By now Johnson had become exceedingly suspicious of the Secretary of War, and Stanton certainly was no less objectionable to a host of the President's supporters.

These anti-Stanton advisers mistrusted other cabinet members, too, holding them either partially committed to the opponents of the President's policy, or headed in that direction. Secretary of the Interior Harlan and Attorney General Speed were especially unpopular, as was Seward also, in certain quarters. Postmaster Dennison was considered to be unsure. Orville Browning had remonstrated repeatedly with the President against keeping these men around him. When the welfare of the country demanded "unity at the council board," the President should be surrounded by a cabinet in complete sympathy with his views and with each other, Browning had stressed, and so had Welles.

Johnson had replied that in a cabinet, as in a church, there ought to be unity in essentials, but in nonessentials "the greatest latitude and liberty" should be allowed. That cabinet changes must come was inevitable; but he would not act hastily, above all in an election year, when it would hardly be politic to advertise the administration's internal dissensions.

Warnings of treachery in the departments came frequently. Some of these communications were signed, some were anonymous, but both kinds conveyed the same ominous message. A typical letter, signed simply "L.", read:

"In the name of God Almighty do you intend to let this fellow Harlan remain in your Cabinet? Also Otto, his assistant secretary, who, when the 'Veto' was passed over your head, shook hands with the Radicals [and] made FUN OF YOU . . . Be surrounded by your *friends* or you are gone forever."

By the spring of 1866, Johnson had resolved to put each mem-

ber of the cabinet on record with a clear statement of his feeling
for or against the presidential position. An opportunity occurred
on May 1.

The day before, Thad Stevens had reported to the House the
second attempt by the Reconstruction Committee to frame a constitutional amendment that would effectively shackle the South.
During the intervening weeks the committee had been gathering
evidence on conditions in the South, and most of it was unfavorable to the President. Witness after witness had testified to outrages committed against the freedmen and Unionist whites, and
most of this testimony undoubtedly was true; the mail of Stevens
and Sumner was heavy with reports of persecutions. But the witnesses called by the committee were noticeably one-sided, and
radical newspapers like Forney's *Chronicle* declined to publish
testimony on the other side.

The truth of the situation was all but impossible to ascertain, so
immense was the confusion. The governments of the lately rebellious states were hanging in suspense, recognized for some purposes
and not recognized for others. The public was just as bewildered.
In Washington, diametrically different descriptions of the situation in the South were appearing simultaneously in the *Chronicle*
and the *National Daily Intelligencer*, a Johnson organ. Both
papers carried columns of reports from the South. In the *Chronicle*, more than half of the space was taken up by accounts of
atrocities against Negroes and white Unionists; in the *Intelligencer*, more than half of the space was allotted to crimes committed by Negroes and Unionists against pro-Johnson whites. As
long as the South should remain neither in nor wholly out of the
Union, the chaos was bound to continue.

In its fresh attempt, the Reconstruction Committee had made
several alterations in the wording of the proposed amendment.
One put a term to the period for which violators of national loyalty
oaths would be proscribed, setting it at July 4, 1870—a date beyond the next Presidential election.

In reporting the new version, Stevens scathingly attacked Sumner's fatal verbosity in connection with the first attempt, which he
said had been "slaughtered by a puerile and pedantic criticism,
by a perversion of philological definition . . . Let us try again," he

urged, "and see whether we cannot devise some way to overcome the united forces of self-righteous Republicans and unrighteous copperheads." The amendment as it stood was not perfect, he admitted, but he would accept it "in the cause of humanity and leave it to be perfected by better men in better times."

Discussing the proscription until 1870, he struck at "a morbid sensibility, sometimes called mercy, which affects a few of all classes, from the priest to the clown, which has more sympathy for the murderer than for his victim . . . Here is the mildest of all punishments ever inflicted upon traitors. I might not consent to the extreme severity pronounced upon them by a provisional governor of Tennessee—I mean the late lamented Andrew Johnson— but I would have increased the severity of this section . . .

"Gentlemen tell us it is too strong. Too strong for what? Too strong for their stomachs, but not for the people. It is too lenient for my hard heart. Not only in 1870, but in 18,070, every rebel who shed the blood of loyal men should be prevented from exercising any power in this government. Gentlemen here have said you must not humble these people. Why not? Do they not deserve humiliation? If they do not, who does? What criminal, what felon deserves it more? They have not yet confessed their sins; and He who administers mercy and justice never forgives until the sinner confesses and humbles himself before His footstool. Why should we forgive any more than He?"

This House debate was in progress when, on May 1, Johnson read to his assembled cabinet the text of the amendment, and explained that inasmuch as there was "an impression abroad that they were divided in their counsels, and that some of them did not support him," he desired the opinion of each one on the amendment and on his policy. He added that he intended to make their views public.

Seward, speaking first by precedence, expressed opposition to the amendment and strongly endorsed the President's Southern policy. He was interrupted by Stanton, who, in an agitated manner and a loud, emphatic voice, said that he was relieved that the President had brought up the subject of harmony among them, because he had had it in mind to do so for some time. He had supported the President's policy "from the beginning," he went on, and he opposed the amendment. Then he stopped as abruptly as he had started.

McCulloch, next in line, was against the amendment.

Dennison thought it "premature" to discuss the matter, since Congress had not acted. Johnson thought this reply "wishy-washy."

Harlan, looking ill at ease, expressed no decided opinion, and later Johnson contemptuously described him as having acted like a man who had burst into a room without knocking, and found himself in company he hadn't expected to meet.

Attorney General Speed again was not present; he seemed to have acquired the habit of being absent from cabinet meetings at which matters of importance were to be discussed.

Johnson then spoke at length about conditions in the South and the harmful effect the actions of Congress were having; Welles thought the President labored under great emotion and spoke with sincerity and earnestness. The Navy Secretary also thought there had been too much hedging in the answers given, and turning to Stanton he asked him to state his position more plainly.

The latter then said that though he did not agree with everything in the amendment, it might furnish a means by which "the gap between the President and Congress could be bridged," but he definitely lined up with the President on the latter's policy in general.

The session lasted four hours and was very animated, and the next day a full report appeared in the *Intelligencer*.

The frankness of this statement, and the vigor of the remarks attributed to Stanton in support of the President, caused Orville Browning to seek confirmation at the White House. He found the President in good humor, and was invited to sit down. In a long, confident interview Johnson said that the newspaper had not told "half the story"; that Stanton had expressed himself in "the strongest and most decided terms" as against the proposed amendment and in favor of the presidential policy.

Stanton read the *Intelligencer* report, which placed him solidly behind the President, and left town for the weekend. The radicals were furious, and Welles chuckled that the slippery War Secretary now must either let the published report stand, or repudiate it, come out openly against the President, and resign. Either way, he was committed.

On Stanton's return, attempts were made to draw him out, but all these were unsuccessful until May 26. On that evening some fifteen hundred members of a Johnson club serenaded him for the purpose of forcing him to speak. Stanton was prepared. He stepped out on the porch, bowed to the throng, and then, standing between two men holding lighted candles, read a carefully written response.

In its early stages, he said, the President's policy towards the South had been unanimously approved by the cabinet. As regards Negro suffrage, while at first he had differed with the President on this question, and had favored granting the vote, later he had bowed to the President's conviction that to prescribe voting rights was "not within the limited scope of his power." The speaker then expressed opposition to the third (disqualification) section of the pending amendment, but said he believed that Congress had a right to participate in the process of reconstruction. The speech, couched throughout in a tone of candor, dodged about in such a manner that no firm conclusion could be drawn from it, and Stanton still had not been pinned down.

To intimates, however, he dropped all disguises. He had informed a Congressional friend that he would not resign: "they must muster me out." Now Samuel Shellabarger, a radical congressman from Ohio, assured a political crony that he had talked with Stanton privately, and the Secretary "is heart & soul with us . . . That serenade speech . . . as he said to me is [for] Johnson, but it is the Johnson we nominated and elected and not the apostate who is now in sympathy with the traitors. He loathes the present Johnson movement as much as [we] do and if there is any ambiguity in his position it is owing to the fact that good men demand him to stay in the Cabinet."

During all this, the amendment debate went on, and despite renewed assaults by Sumner it cleared both Senate and House, after the 1870 disqualification date had been knocked out and a provision substituted giving Congress the power to lift the disqualification of any person by a two-thirds vote. This change disgusted Stevens, but he yielded, sardonically explaining:

"Do you ask why . . . I accept so imperfect a proposition? I answer, because I live among men, and not among angels."

Thereupon the Fourteenth Amendment was sent to the states for ratification.

This gave the irrepressible "Parson" Brownlow a chance to take center stage, and he lost not a moment in availing himself of it. As governor of Tennessee, he had suffered frustration after frustration in his war against "rebels" and contumacious Democrats, and his bitterness towards the "apostate" President had become vitriolic. Brownlow determined that Tennessee should become the first Southern state to accept the terms laid down by Congress for readmission, and he called the legislature into special session for that purpose. But "rebel" influence was strong enough to prevent a quorum. Several members refused even to vote on so abject a surrender and sent in their resignations, which Brownlow refused to accept. Others, demanding that the amendment be submitted to their constituents first, stayed away from Nashville; whereupon the governor asked General Thomas to bring them in with United States troops.

The general referred this request to Washington, where Stanton, sensing an opening to embarrass the President, carried it personally to the White House. Johnson's reaction was sharp:

"If General Thomas has nothing better to do than to intermeddle with local controversies, he had better be detached and ordered elsewhere."

Thomas did *not* wish to be ordered elsewhere, as both Johnson and Stanton knew; he was contented in his command, and dreaded being assigned to a post in the deep South.

Stanton caught at the chance to create bad feeling between the general and Johnson, and inquired suavely whether he might transmit the latter's very words.

"My wish is that the answer be emphatic and decisive—not to meddle with local parties and politics," Johnson repeated. "The military are not the masters."

This was just what Stanton wanted, and the dispatch was sent.

Immediately Brownlow screamed that the President was meddling with Tennessee politics.

Luck favored the "Parson." An informer disclosed where two of the holdouts were hiding, and the sergeant-at-arms of the Assembly was dispatched to arrest them and bring them forcibly to the Capitol. This completed the quorum, and the two "rebels" were held in custody while a vote was taken and the amendment ratified.

The exultant Brownlow fired off a telegram to Washington:

"A battle fought and won. We have carried the constitutional amendment in the House. Vote forty-three to eleven, two of Andrew Johnson's tools refusing to vote. My compliments to the 'dead dog' in the White House."

Tennessee's reward came twenty-four hours later, when a resolution was introduced in Congress to admit the state to representation. Thaddeus Stevens thought the haste unseemly, but nevertheless did not oppose the action, and the resolution passed both the Senate and the House. The Tennessee representatives were seated at once, and so was Senator Fowler. But Sumner's searching eye detected a flaw in the record of Andrew Johnson's son-in-law, and Patterson's credentials were referred to an investigating committee. During the war, after being hunted into the hills because of Union sentiments, and in order to protect his family, Patterson had taken the oath of allegiance to the Confederacy, with a spoken reservation. The committee reported, after due study, that Patterson had plainly acted under coercion; and Senator Clark (who had engineered Stockton's expulsion and was a thorough radical) even termed Patterson "not only a Union man, but such a Union man as would put some of us to shame." The judge thereupon was sworn in.

Doubts had been expressed that Johnson would sign the Tennessee resolution, dearly as he wished the admission of his state, because of the offensive preamble, which stipulated that the resolution should not be construed as setting a precedent for other excluded states. Johnson did not hesitate. In an accompanying message he pointed out that the preamble contained statements of opinion having no legal force, and the essential fact—Tennessee's just claim to representation—had been recognized. He then signed the resolution, and Tennessee, which according to Johnson had never been out of the Union and according to Congress had not been in, resumed its status as a full-fledged and equally privileged partner in the nation.

Shortly after this—and after voting four thousand dollars in extra pay for each of its hardworking members, but nothing for the war veterans—Congress adjourned, to reassemble after the autumn election.

3.

During these tense days, Johnson was beset with family anxieties as well as political antagonism. The frequent inebriation of his son Robert had become a Washington scandal. Senator Pomeroy of Kansas had spread a story that he had called at the White House and had seen the President, Robert, and Judge Patterson all drunk together. When challenged, Pomeroy protested that he had been misquoted, that he had said he had seen only Robert intoxicated. Nevertheless, the gossip was repeated as far West as St. Louis.

In desperation, Johnson appealed to Secretary Welles to find a berth for Robert aboard a navy ship bound on a distant cruise. Seward fell in with the scheme and gave Robert semi-official standing. But after weeks of preparation, when the captain of the ship called at the White House to pick up his passenger, Robert had decamped—out on a spree, Martha admitted. The family's grief was profound, for Robert possessed ability and charm when sober. Eventually he was shipped out on a cruise to Liberia, but no cure for his alcoholism was effected.

The President's brother, William Johnson, also was more or less of a problem. Never thrifty, Bill appealed to Johnson for material help. Johnson sent him a thousand dollars, told him to be careful of it, and when that was gone he would send more. But Bill wanted a government position, although Johnson had a rule against nepotism like the one against accepting presents. Bill's pleas, however, finally took effect; one day when the President was telling Ben Truman about his brother's importunities, he concluded:

"He wants some kind of a position down in Texas; maybe a United States marshal. Well, that's not much. I suppose I should give it to him."

Adjournment of Congress had brought no cessation of the political ferment going on all over the country. Secretary Welles had noted how strangely the old parties had become intermixed, and now a process of political realignment was in progress.

Out of the war had risen the Union party, to which the War Democrats had adhered in 1864, when their concern for preserving the Union had coincided with the aims of the Republicans. But since the termination of the conflict these War Democrats had been hankering for their old party affiliation, and the Union party had disintegrated into one that was narrowly Republican, radically dominated. Conservative Republicans deplored the extremism of the radicals, but they were no match for the latter's force and positive action; willy-nilly, the moderates were swept along by superior zeal and energy on the part of the radicals.

Conservative Democrats, on the other hand, after they had abjured their temporary alliance with the Republicans, were finding their own party basically changed. In most sectors, the copperhead element, which had refused to join the Union alliance in the war, retained control of the party machinery. This control they were not at all ready to surrender.

The parties thus were moving in opposite directions—the Republicans towards complete radicalism, the Democrats towards a copperhead triumph—and both were moving away from the Union position of the President. He thought in 1866 as he had thought in 1864; *Union* was still the principle on which his political faith was based, without regard to party labels. Pondering the problem in the early summer of 1866, it seemed to him that the solution lay in the formation of a third party, to which all devotees of constitutionalism and opponents of extremism in any guise could rally, North and South.

To get such a movement under way, Johnson offered to contribute twenty thousand dollars of his own money, and a group of his close advisers soon had plans drawn up for a convention in Philadephia in August. The objective would be to whip up organized support for the election of senators and representatives favorable to Johnson and his policy in the October-November elections.

It was a bold plan, boldly conceived; but carried away by their enthusiasm, the planners failed to perceive that their scheme was impractical. The time remaining before the elections was too short to set up a new political organization, raise funds, appoint leaders, obtain speakers, and carry out the innumerable details involved in such a project. The Democrats and Republicans, on the other hand, were already in the field, with complete organizations and experienced leaders, amply financed.

Johnson failed to grasp the hopelessness of the undertaking, mainly because of his lack of background as a party man. In Tennessee his following had been personal; he had worked with the party organization when it suited his purposes, or campaigned outside it when he felt that to be the better way. In allowing himself to be persuaded that a third party with any vitality could be improvised in a few weeks, he committed a fundamental error. And so did others of the well-meaning but inept promoters of the movement.

The call did, however, serve to bring about a purge of the disaffected members of the cabinet. These had held aloof from the convention scheme, until Senator Doolittle, one of its principal sponsors, wrote to each member soliciting a public expression of support. Forced to take a stand, and unable to approve the call, Speed and Dennison resigned. The President immediately named Henry Stanbery as Attorney General, and Alexander W. Randall as Postmaster General.

Secretary Seward, with Thurlow Weed, had already given his endorsement and was working actively for the convention's success. McCulloch and Welles approved the idea, although the latter foresaw obstacles. Interior Secretary Harlan hung on, despite his disapproval, until Johnson told Orville Browning that he thought the man's conduct was "indecent." Still, he did not wish to dismiss him, for Harlan was influential in the Methodist church, a powerful factor, whose ill will it was not advisable to incur. But Harlan at last resigned, merely asking to hold his post until September. To this Johnson agreed, and appointed Browning as successor.

In making these appointments, the President selected Republicans who had never been Democrats, thereby keeping faith with the Union party that had elected him.

The problem of Stanton remained, and here a drama was enacted behind the scenes—an internal drama involving Stanton's conscience and his deepest convictions—of which the President knew nothing.

Doolittle's letter confronted the War Secretary with a dilemma. His first reaction was one of indignation, and sitting down he dashed off a reply into which he poured all his resentment and hatred of the President, the President's Southern policy, and those who supported it. It was one of the frankest letters Stanton ever wrote.

This convention, he said, seemed gotten up for the purpose of organizing a party consisting of those in the South who had carried on the rebellion, and those in the North who had sympathized and cooperated with them. "I do not approve of the call of that convention. So far as the terms of the call and the purpose and objects of the convention are designed to oppose the constitutional authority of Congress, I heartily condemn them."

After such a letter, but one course would be open—to resign as Secretary of War and go into honorable and open opposition.

But Stanton did not send the letter. Instead, he filed it away, and continued to sit in the President's councils and claim the President's confidence. He made no reply to Doolittle.

This silence did not sit well with the suspicious Welles, and a short while afterwards he had a chance to smoke out Stanton in a cabinet meeting. The latter reported, in a bantering tone, that he had been approached by the convention's promoters for bunting with which to decorate the hall, and that he had told them he had none, but was referring them to the Navy Department.

"My bunting has always been promptly shown," rejoined Welles. "It would be well were you now to let us have a sight of yours."

Stanton flushed, and repeated that he had no bunting available.

"Oh, show your flag!" exclaimed Welles.

"You mean the convention?" snapped Stanton angrily. "I am against it."

Then why had he not said so in reply to Doolittle's letter, Welles asked.

"Because I do not choose to have a *Doolittle* or any other *little* fellow draw an answer from me," was Stanton's sneering reply, and the subject was dropped.

That evening Welles asked Johnson whether he had had any

previous intimation of Stanton's opposition. None whatever, said Johnson.

Welles pointed out that the administration could hardly "get along this way" much longer.

"No, it will be pretty difficult," the President agreed, but said no more.

Stanton did not resign, and Johnson did not demand his resignation.

On Stanton's part, his role was clear in his own mind. It was to be that of an informer for the radicals in Congress. They wanted to keep him in the cabinet to spy on the President's intentions, and stay he would.

"It is best to have someone in that office in whom Congress can trust in case of trouble with the President," one congressman put it, while relaying word that Stanton had assured him, during a confidential conference, that "he fully sympathized with the radicals in Congress, and was remaining in office for their benefit."

A chance to serve the cause of the radicals actively soon occurred. On July 30, on the eve of the Philadelphia "harmony" convention, disruptive and disgruntled elements in the South showed their worst side, and the gutters of New Orleans ran blood.

4.

The long and tragic story of race rioting in the United States had begun, and a century later the chapter would not be ended. In 1866 it was Memphis and New Orleans; one hundred years later it would be New York, Detroit, Los Angeles, Newark, Birmingham, and Memphis again—a widening pattern.

The first serious trouble had occurred in April at Memphis, in Governor Brownlow's radical-ruled Tennessee. There had been hard feeling between the city police and a Negro artillery regiment garrisoned in the city. On April 30 the gunners tried the dangerous sport of jostling policemen off the sidewalks. The Memphis police force was mainly Irish, and Irish tempers being short, fights broke out, with sporadic rioting. The next day—May Day—the police, reinforced by a mob of whites, attacked the

Negro population and for two days killed, burned, and looted. Forty-six Negroes were slain, and twelve Negro schoolhouses and four Negro churches were destroyed.

Northerners denounced the outbreak as evidence of the savagery of the South; but because the "incident" had occurred in the territory of an ally, the radicals forbore to make capital out of it, not wishing to embarrass the picturesque "Parson." But Northern reaction generally was bitter. Wrote diarist Strong:

"Southern arrogance and brutality have revived, lifted up their ugly heads, and seem nearly as rank as ever. The First Southern War may not be the last."

The Memphis upheaval was an expression of crude race prejudice, not essentially political in its origin. The New Orleans disorder at the end of July was politically grounded and inspired, and it directly involved the interests of the radicals, on the one hand, and the supporters of the President's policy, called conservatives, on the other. Most of the conservatives were ex-Confederates.

Louisiana had been reconstructed under Lincoln's "ten percent" plan. A state convention had framed a new constitution, which was ratified by popular vote, and a state government had been installed. While this was not recognized by Congress as entitling the state to representation, it had been functioning for some time in all branches.

The governor was a shifty vacillator who answered to the tripping name of J. Madison Wells.

Elected as a radical, in 1866 he found his position disintegrating under a take-over of local offices by pardoned ex-Confederates. (Up to June, 1866, more than twelve thousand pardons had been issued by President Johnson to former rebels, restoring their voting and officeholding rights in the states.)

Wells and his ring of radical officeholders thought of a scheme to retain power: this was to rewrite the state constitution and enfranchise the Negroes, and with their help outvote the conservatives.

The state's 1864 convention had adjourned subject to recall by its president, in the event that the constitution it had framed should be rejected. But that constitution had been approved, and thereupon the convention presumably expired, its mission fulfilled. Now the radical group proposed to reconvoke the convention and amend the constitution.

The 1864 president of the convention, Edmund H. Durrell, declined to issue the call. He was a judge, and his legal opinion was that the convention was defunct. Some of the delegates were determined to meet anyway, but found they could not muster a quorum. Thereupon they agitated for an election to choose new delegates, and Governor Wells authorized one.

Becoming restless, the agitators decided not to wait for this election, and on June 26 issued a call for the convention to reassemble in New Orleans on July 30.

Judge Edmond Abell, who had been a member of the convention in 1864, was so outraged by this flouting of legality that he instructed the grand jury to indict the men issuing the call; the meeting, he said, was called for the purpose of committing an unlawful action, and therefore was in itself illegal. The grand jury acceded to the judge's views.

Meanwhile, the mayor of New Orleans, John T. Monroe, the Attorney General of the state, A. J. Herron, and the lieutenant governor, Albert Voorhies, all conservatives and enemies of the artful J. Madison Wells, separately and together determined to prevent the meeting, holding it to be unlawful and inflammatory.

On Thursday, July 25, Mayor Monroe wrote to General Absalom Baird, commanding United States troops in the area during the temporary absence of General Sheridan in Texas, pointing out that the meeting was illegal and "calculated to disturb the public peace," and saying that he proposed to arrest the participants unless the military forbade it.

Baird wished to steer clear of a sticky situation, and he told the mayor that he neither approved nor disapproved the meeting; that if it was lawful, it had a right to assemble, and if it was unlawful, the courts would settle that question and it would become merely "a harmless pleasantry." But Baird did arrest Judge Abell for his instructions to the grand jury, an action that encouraged the radicals.

The excitement in the sweltering city was mounting when, on Friday, July 27, A. P. Dostie, a Northern dentist who had settled in New Orleans, delivered a violent harangue before a crowd of Negroes, saying that those who were opposing the convention wanted to deny the freedmen their right to vote.

"We will give them this right," Dostie shouted, "and on Monday I want you to come in your power. I want no cowards to come, I want only brave men . . . We are four hundred thousand to three hundred thousand, and can not only whip but exterminate the other party . . . There will be no such puerile affair as at Memphis, but if we are interfered with, the streets of New Orleans will run with blood! The rebels want you to do the work and they will do the voting; and will you throw over them 'the mantle of charity and oblivion'?"

The contemptuously quoted phrase was Andrew Johnson's. The excited crowd, misunderstanding the question, yelled back, "We will! We will!"

"No, by God!" the speaker corrected them. "We won't! We are bound to have universal suffrage, though you have that traitor, Andrew Johnson, against you!"

The next day Mayor Monroe appealed again to General Baird, saying it was his intention, in which Lieutenant Governor Voorhies concurred, to have the sheriff arrest the members of the convention if they should meet on Monday. Baird replied that in that case he probably would be obliged to arrest the sheriff. But the general was worried, and he telegraphed to Secretary of War Stanton asking for instructions from the President himself.

At the same time, Monroe, Voorhies, and Attorney General Herron each wired separately to the President, stressing the illegality of the meeting and stating their purpose to prevent it. What attitude would the military be instructed to take, they asked.

The President replied promptly that "the military will be expected to sustain, and not to interfere with the proceedings of the court"; in other words, the army should respect arrests made by proper civil authorities. More explicitly, Johnson wired to Herron directing him to ask General Sheridan "for sufficient force to sustain the civil authority in suppressing all illegal or unlawful assemblies." And to Governor Wells the President fired an angry telegram demanding by what authority he had called the defunct convention back into session. J. Madison Wells had made himself invisible for the time being; but from his hideaway he assured the President that he had convoked no convention, he had merely set a date for an election.

The situation was fairly frantic, and so, it may be surmised, was General Absalom Baird, when he received no response to his appeal for instructions. His telegram seemed to have melted away. Actually it was reposing in Secretary Stanton's desk, where it would remain, unseen by the President, to whom it was in effect addressed. Yet the general's wording had been unmistakable:

"A convention has been called, with the sanction of Governor Wells, to meet here on Monday. The lieutenant governor and city authorities think it unlawful, and propose to break it up by arresting the delegates. I have given no orders on the subject, but have warned the parties that I should not countenance or permit such actions without instructions to that effect from the President. Please instruct me by telegraph."

The appeal had reached Washington on Saturday, July 28, which was the day Congress wound up its session and adjourned. The members had not dispersed; the city was filled with them; and on that day, and over that weekend, Judge Durrell—the president of the 1864 convention, who had declined to reconvoke it, but was not hostile to the Louisiana radicals' objectives—was in Washington conferring with radical leaders. Radical spokesmen were at all times in communication with Secretary of War Stanton.

On Monday morning, July 30, New Orleanians were greeted by a municipal proclamation urging everyone to stay away from the Mechanics Institute, where the convention had been called to meet.

General Baird had been shown President Johnson's wire of reply to Mayor Monroe; but that telegram being unofficial (not having come through War Department channels), the general felt privileged to disregard it, and he again cautioned the civil authorities not to interfere with the assembly.

However, the ugly mood of the city was plain, and as delegates began to drift in, Lieutenant Governor Voorhies asked Baird to deploy troops to prevent violence, without necessarily interfering with the convention.

The general himself was increasingly worried by Washington's unaccountable silence, and deciding to act on his own responsibility, he began calling in outlying detachments for riot duty. But in some way or other Baird had "formed the impression" that the convention was to meet at six o'clock in the evening, whereas the call had gone out for noon. The troops moved towards Jackson Barracks without haste and long before they reached the scene, New Orleans had had its bloodbath.

It started about one o'clock. A handful of delegates had been waiting in the hall for an hour, when a band of Negroes, estimated to number anywhere from sixty to one hundred and thirty, came marching along Burgundy Street. At their head was a drummer and a fifer, and a man carrying the American flag. Some of the marchers were armed. The procession crossed Canal Street to the Institute, around which stood a scowling mob. Sullen spectators jammed the sidewalks, and at one point a boy was shoved or knocked off the curb by a marcher. The police rushed to arrest the offender, some of the Negroes fired their guns, and police reserves, heavily armed and under orders to "take no prisoners," swarmed in, followed by the mob.

The Negroes ran for safety into the Institute, and in a few minutes a white flag was hung out of an upper window. The police started to enter the building when someone inside opened fire. The police then charged, with the mob at their heels. A frightful butchery took place. The number of killed was never learned for certain, although it may have reached two hundred, all of them Negroes or radical whites. A few policemen reported slight wounds. Dr. Dostie paid for his rabble-rousing: the mob hacked him to pieces. Race warfare raged throughout the city, and by the time General Baird and his troops appeared, the slaughter was complete.

The nation was appalled. There had been riots before, some even more bloody, such as the draft riots in New York City in 1863, when probably fifteen hundred were slain, Negroes were lynched in the streets, and for three days mobs ruled the city amid scenes reminiscent of the French Revolution. But in that instance the national conscience, the necessity of preserving wartime morale, and the determination of the Irish (who were conspicuously involved) to hush the episode, had all combined to push that horror out of men's minds.

The New Orleans riot was a political manifestation, and almost as if upon signal, the radical press and leaders raised a shout that the guilt lay at a single doorstep—that of the White House. The criminal who was responsible for the tragedy, they cried, was Andrew Johnson.

Thaddeus Stevens said that now all could see the consequences that flowed from the policy of "universal amnesty and universal Andy Johnsonism."

The *New York Tribune*, fugelman for extreme radicalism, denounced the episode in unbridled language as "cold-blooded murder." Why did not the President send troops to prevent it?

The *Independent*, a strongly radical religious weekly, exclaimed that "this man [Johnson] aided and abetted the New Orleans mob." The paper's sincere but harebrained editor, Theodore Tilton, added, "He doubly inspired the murderers."

The *Nation* thought the President was "utterly without palliation . . . [There is] scarcely an act of usurpation . . . he has not committed, and such usurpations will no longer be tolerated."

Senator Sumner assured a correspondent that he might safely judge the character of the President by "the terrible massacre in New Orleans," and confided that Stanton had told him "Johnson was its author."

Forney's *Philadelphia Press* joined the outcry by printing an account said to have been received from an eyewitness, "worth more than all the rebel lies that are repeated by their copperhead friends." After this experience, the Senate Secretary exclaimed, "the rebels, copperheads, and His Accidency, the President 'that Booth made,' ask us to restore these men to place and power!"

The news shocked the President, and he instantly ordered General Sheridan to restore peace and report the circumstances. The general quite accurately said the slaughter was "not a riot, it was a massacre." At first he blamed both parties for inciting the bloodshed; then in amended reports he shifted the blame to the conservatives, largely exonerating the radicals. Navy Secretary Welles thought he saw the influence of radical mentors upon the impulsive Sheridan, who was an officer of the highest gallantry, but young and unpracticed in civil administration. The general was being coached, the navy chief deduced. But most of the generals were playing politics to some extent in the backwash of the war, and Sheridan would not have been unique if his opinions were "influenced" against conservatism.

The riot came before the cabinet at its next meeting, and Stanton, greatly excited, produced an exchange of telegrams with General Sheridan—but not the telegram from General Baird. Stanton referred bitterly to Mayor Monroe and Lieutenant Governor Voorhies as "pardoned rebels," and held them personally guilty of the "terrible bloodshed." To Welles it seemed that Stanton betrayed "marked sympathy with the rioters, and the President and others observed it." Welles himself was convinced that radicals in Washington had fomented the riot as "the commencement of a series of bloody affrays through the states lately in rebellion . . . There is a determination to involve the country in civil war, if necessary, to secure Negro suffrage and radical ascendancy."

The *New York Tribune* took the tack of alleging that the President was withholding dispatches concerning the riot—dispatches which, if produced, would "fix the stain of blood on the hands of their chief so indelibly that all the waters of the Mississippi can never wash it out." The connivance of the President, the *Tribune* claimed, had provided the "warrant which the rebels had sought for butchering the detested radicals."

Johnson's answer to this accusation was to order Stanton to present the entire file of communications in form for publication; and in mid-August the President received the complete documentation. In it he read for the first time of General Baird's appeal of July 28.

When Stanton was challenged to explain why he had so oddly "overlooked" this key telegram, he said airily that he had seen nothing urgent in it.

"There was no intimation in the telegram that force or violence was threatened by those opposed to the convention, or that it was apprehended by General Baird," he stated glibly. "Upon consideration, it appeared to me that his warning to the city authorities [not to interfere] was all that the case then required."

Of course Stanton was horrified by the agonizing results. Bloodshed and death always threw him into a febrile and morbid excitement, often succeeded or accompanied by maudlin senti-

mentalism. To Sumner, Stanton unfolded an intricate train of reasoning by which he arrived at the conclusion that the President
had instigated the disaster. Sumner broadcast these darkling accusations at home and abroad.

Johnson brushed aside Stanton's excuse in silent indignation.
Had he received the suppressed telegram, he told Colonel Moore,
the riot would never have occurred. Of course the incident
brought renewed demands for Stanton's removal, but the President was too deeply involved with the political situation to arouse
the War Secretary's radical supporters further. Nevertheless, the
increasing cabinet muddle worried him, and he burst out impulsively one day to Moore that he could solve the whole difficulty in
two hours. All that he would have to do would be to appoint
General Grant as Secretary of War, Admiral Farragut as Secretary of the Navy, Charles Francis Adams (then minister to England) as Secretary of State, and Horace Greeley as Postmaster
General. The political turmoil that would be stirred up by such a
drastic housecleaning he left Moore to imagine. And he shrank
from wounding certain members of the cabinet of whom he had
become fond—Seward, for instance, and the always dependable
Gideon Welles. Moore saw that the subject was painful and he
did not prolong the conversation.

As everyone, Stanton included, realized, the important business
of August was the preparations being made for the Congressional
elections. The President turned his attention towards that crucial
test, leaving New Orleans to bury its dead, though it could not
bury its shame.

5.

In outward semblance, the setting was one of unalloyed harmony when the hopefully projected National Union convention
assembled in Philadelphia on August 14, 1866. Actually, however,
the facade was cardboard-thin, and from the start an air of un-
reality permeated the proceedings, the stage management being
imperfectly concealed, and wishful thinking substituting for solid
convictions. The meetings were held in a half-finished wooden
arena three miles from downtown. The ramshackle building,

called the "Wigwam," led the *New York Herald* to jeer that it would be spurned as a gift by any self-respecting Indian. Every state in the Union had sent delegates, and Postmaster General Randall, who opened the sessions, achieved a climax of theatricality when he announced the entrance of the delegates from South Carolina and Massachusetts, linked arm in arm, and looking very self-conscious. Heading the file were Governor Orr of South Carolina and General Daniel N. Couch of Massachusetts.

The spectacle was ironically symbolic. Orr was of great bulk and stature, while Couch was puny. Couch by no means represented the predominant sentiment in his state, and Governor Orr was the very same "unwashed rebel" whose election had aroused Ben Wade in the Senate.

Amid thunderous applause and waving of handkerchiefs, the two-by-two procession marched down the center aisle to their seats, setting the tone of the convention and suffusing the eyes of the delegates and spectators with tears.

The eyes of the President were dimmed by tears of thankfulness when he heard of this display of mutual reconciliation. The news came in the midst of his performance of a social duty, which for once he went about with complete enjoyment. The occasion was a White House reception for Queen Emma of the Sandwich Isles. The full cabinet had been urged to attend, but only Welles, McCulloch, and Stanbery showed up. Seward being out of town, the Attorney General deputized for him as the Queen's escort. Stanton had angled to get that place of prominence but had been overruled, and he stayed away in pique.

Making one of her two appearances at public functions during her years in the White House, Eliza Johnson did honor to the royal visitor by receiving at her husband's side, assisted by Martha Patterson. The First Lady, simply but richly gowned, was unable to stand throughout, and after welcoming the Queen she received the other guests seated, explaining the necessity with smiling friendliness. Secretary Welles was quite fascinated by the buxom Emma, whom he judged to be thirtyish, "well developed," with fine bust and figure, a roguishly roving, "round, full eye," and complexion "a shade darker perhaps than a brunette." Reporters found the Queen full of animation and mirthfulness, while the President seemed in a happier mood than he had been for a long time. Graciously attentive to all, he presided with animation and courtesy.

It was owing to Martha Patterson's thrift and industry that the reception rooms were ready for such an occasion. Throughout the summer she had been supervising carpenters, painters, and others engaged in restoring the shabby parlors. She negotiated contracts and purchased materials, stretching to the limit the meager allowance provided by Congress for the work. Her ingenuity had been called into play to find replacements for the original decorative schemes that could not be duplicated, such as the expensive wallpaper of the East Room. The walls there had been refinished in panels and gilt carvings. Carpets and hangings had been renewed, the salvageable furniture repaired and new pieces added, all in good taste.

During the second and third days of the Philadelphia convention, the reports reaching the President continued to give him satisfaction. An address had been read by Henry J. Raymond, leading New York Republican, and a declaration of principles had been adopted, vigorously endorsing Johnson's aims and policy. True, there had been a few untoward happenings, such as the action of Clement L. Vallandingham of Ohio, the super-copperhead of the war. He had been elected a delegate from his district, but had been prevailed upon to remain away in the interest of harmony. However, he succeeded, despite the opposition of the chairman, in having his letter of renunciation read from the floor, and it had been tremendously applauded.

Raymond's address and the declaration of principles had been toned down drastically in committee before being heard by the convention. Southerners on the resolutions committee objected to the use of the words "rebellion" and "insurrection." Was it necessary to speak of the "evils" of slavery? Positively no allusion should be made to the pending constitutional amendment. And with what justice was the "patriotism" of the "American soldier" singled out for praise, without indicating that Confederate soldiers were included, too? On and on the winnowing process went, until address and declaration were reduced to windy generalities, having neither meat nor marrow of conviction.

When the declaration was presented to the delegates, maver-icks tried to debate it, although the rule of "no floor discussion" had been adopted at the start; every possibility of an acrimonious exchange, which would belie the appearance of unity and frater-nity, must be guarded against.

As a result, the convention's sessions unfolded like a well-rehearsed play, its actions deceiving nobody except those who wished to be deceived—the players and their well-wishers. Also, disguise the fact though they might, the delegates were largely Democrats—and Democrats with copperhead records or leanings in that direction. The Republicans attending were repelled, and War Democrats were hardly less ill at ease in finding themselves companioned by an element in their party that they despised. But how could the Peace Democrats be shut out? If former Confed-erates were admitted—and they were present in large numbers—by what rule could the convention refuse to accept Northerners who had merely tried to help the Confederates' cause?

Thus, despite the pretentious pronouncements, the National Union movement was a sham, an image of pseudo-fraternity, a growth without roots; and the opposition exposed its falsity with ridicule. The "bread-and-butter" convention, it had been dubbed, made up of officeholders. Then it became the "arm-in-arm" con-vention, and Thomas Nast in *Harper's Weekly* cruelly cartooned the silenced delegates marching in, arms linked and lips pad-locked, shedding copious crocodile tears. Radical editors turned to Scripture and printed the Biblical story of Noah gathering the beasts into the ark, two by two—"of clean beasts, and of beasts that are not clean, and of fowls, and of every thing that creepeth upon the earth."

Such pungencies did not disturb President Johnson or those who had blinded themselves to the political realities. Had not General John A. Dix, the temporary chairman, pronounced the convention "the most able, harmonious, and enthusiastic body of men of such magnitude I have ever known in my long acquaint-ance with public affairs"? And who could dispute the patriotism and judgment of General Dix, the man who, on the eve of the war, when Secretary of the Treasury in Buchanan's Cabinet, had in-structed a subordinate in New Orleans that if any man tried to haul down the American flag, "shoot him on the spot!"

Orville Browning and Senator Doolittle hastened back from Philadelphia convinced that the convention would have a powerful effect. Directly after them came a delegation headed by Reverdy Johnson, to convey the resolutions voted by the convention to the President.

The President was deeply affected by this demonstration. Standing between General Grant and Secretary Welles (Stanton absented himself), he replied in a speech fraught with emotion, thanking the committee and tracing his efforts to bring about national harmony. He alluded to the source of the opposition of his attempt—"hanging upon the verge of the government, as it were, a body called, or which assumes to be called, the Congress of the United States, while in fact it is a Congress of only a part of the states. We have seen this Congress pretend to be for the Union, while its every step and act tend to perpetuate the disunion and make the disruption of the states inevitable."

Little did he or his auditors dream that these words, prophetically uttered, would be cited one day as a "high crime and misdemeanor" by the very Congress thus described.

The radicals did not confine their counterattacks to ridicule, but hastily assembled a rival convention of "loyalists," North and South. This also met in Philadelphia three weeks later, under the sponsorship of such spokesmen as Carl Schurz, Senator Chandler, Horace Greeley, "Dead Duck" Forney, and "Parson" Brownlow.

After the New Orleans riot, Brownlow had apologized, profusely and publicly, for having helped to nominate Andrew Johnson for the Vice-Presidency. Now the full battery of his invective was trained on the President, and the "loyal" convention was treated to a display of the "Parson's" verbal pyrotechnics.

"Better would it have been," cried the old word-hurler, "for the cause of Republican victory, if the Tennessee delegation, including the speaker, had been in a rebel prison, South, rather than in the Baltimore convention, helping to place Johnson in a position where he, when *his friends* should murder the patriot Lincoln, should become President of these United States! Johnson is a traitor!" He gave numerous reasons for drawing this conclusion, ending with, "last but not least, because he has never been true to anyone but Andrew Johnson."

This "loyal" convention split into opposing factions on the

question of Negro suffrage. The Northern delegates shunned the issue, knowing it was unpopular with their constituents, while the Southern radicals saw in the Negro vote their best hope for survival in office. Brownlow, of course, had his say on the subject, calling for enfranchisement, although no portion of his state was more fiercely opposed to Negro equality than his own East Tennessee.

"I would rather be elected by loyal Negroes than by disloyal white men," he said. "I would rather associate with loyal Negroes than with disloyal white men. I would rather be buried in a Negro graveyard than in a rebel graveyard. And after death, I would sooner go to a Negro heaven than to a rebel's hell."

The convention was addressed also by James Speed of Kentucky, until recently Attorney General, now openly contemptuous of the President whom, while a member of the Cabinet, he had served with surly incompetence.

"Whenever you have a Congress," Speed laid down the rule, "that does not resolutely and firmly refuse, as the present Congress has done, to act merely as the recording secretary of the tyrant of the White House, American liberty is gone forever."

The convention endorsed and circulated throughout the nation resolutions charging that the President had abandoned the "loyal" men of the South. "He has corrupted the local courts . . . He has pardoned some of the worst rebel criminals . . . His policy has wrought some of the most deplorable consequences."

Two other national conventions were held that autumn of 1866 to whip up election fever. These were composed of ex-servicemen. One, held at Cleveland, was sponsored by the Johnson administration; the second, held later at Pittsburgh, was staged by the radicals.

The Cleveland rally drew a galaxy of generals, including Custer, Steedman, McClernand of Illinois, and, as presiding officer, General John E. Wool, co-hero with Generals Scott and Taylor of the Mexican War and the oldest major general in the army. Wool castigated those in and out of Congress who fanned the flames of racial hatred, calling them "revengeful partisans with a raging thirst for blood and plunder, who would leave their country a howling wilderness for want of more victims to gratify their insatiable cruelty."

At the Pittsburgh rally the outpouring of army brass shone with the luster of Generals Ben Butler and John E. Hartranft, who had presided at the hanging of Mrs. Surratt. For a while after Johnson became President, Butler had kept up a flow of advice to the White House, in notes cordial and cautionary, containing repeated bids for appointment to some place of prominence. These more than hints going unregarded, Butler had thrown in his lot with the radicals, and was now campaigning for election to Congress on the one-plank platform of a pledge, if elected, to see that Andrew Johnson was impeached.

Ohio's Governor Cox, who also had deserted the Johnson banner, presided at this convention, and he laid down the issue squarely. Congress, he said, *was* "the representative government of the people. We all know and all traitors know that the will of the people has been expressed in the complexion and character of the existing Congress." And amid ringing cheers he foretold that the next Congress would be of the same character, *only more so*.

Four national conventions in a non-Presidential election year were sensational, but greater shocks were in store. The President had decided to cast aside precedent, and take to the campaign trail himself in a face-to-face-with-the-people electioneering tour. The method had never failed him in Tennessee, and that a President of the United States had never tried it counted for little in his view. The times were revolutionary and the crisis was imminent and urgent. He felt cheerfully confident that the people would harken to him.

On the morning of August 28, therefore, he boarded a special train at Washington that would carry him into ten states during a nineteen-day "swing around the circle."

So began a chapter, which eventually—more in sorrow than in sarcasm—G. T. Strong would title:

"Andrew Johnson's Adventures in Blunderland."

PART SIX

FORAYS IN BLUNDERLAND

THE stated reason for setting out on this first Presidential barn-storming tour was to assist at the dedication of a monument to Stephen A. Douglas in Chicago. The President had been invited to speak at the unveiling on September 6. A group of prominent Wall Street men followed with an invitation to pause in New York City on the way west and accept the tribute of a civic banquet. As other invitations came in, a schedule was worked out that promised to test Johnson's powers of physical endurance. But he had undertaken more grueling campaigns in Tennessee.

The novelty of the expedition evoked almost equal curiosity and censure. Loss of dignity was the most frequent objection; some of Johnson's advisers shivered at the thought of his excitability before a crowd—especially before a crowd. These friends recalled the shock to the nation caused by his Washington's Birthday outburst, and how his words then had been twisted by the radical press and radical orators.

Senator Doolittle, as ardent an admirer as the President had, beseeched him to avoid extempore speaking.

"You are followed by the reporters of a hundred presses who do nothing but misrepresent you," the senator wrote. "I would say nothing which has not been most carefully prepared, beyond a simple acknowledgement for their cordial reception. *Our enemies, your enemies*, have never been able to get any advantage from *anything you ever wrote*. But what you have said extemporaneously, in answer to some question or interruption, has given them a handle to use against you."

Orville Browning and McCulloch added their earnest recommendations that Johnson abstain from off-the-cuff oratory, but the President brushed aside their fears. He knew his powers, as he felt they did not, and the reaction to his February speech had not greatly bothered him; the radicals had maligned and distorted his written messages, too. As for loss of dignity, what could be more undignified than slinking away from a slanderer without uttering a word in reply? In Tennessee a man was expected to stand up and fight, dignity be damned, and there was not a heckler living who could force Andrew Johnson to give an inch.

Seward was confident that Johnson would make out well. Welles feared the radicals might try to blow up the train, and suggested taking Stanton along as a precautionary measure. Stanton approved the trip heartily and promised to accompany the President, but at the last minute he reported his wife was ill and he could not leave Washington.

Nonetheless, the entourage the President assembled was prestigious. It was headed by the two idols of the nation, General Ulysses S. Grant and Admiral David G. Farragut. There were seven other generals, all glamorous figures (Generals Rawlins, McCullum, Stoneman, Steedman, Rousseau, Crook, and Custer), Admiral Radford, Surgeon General Barnes, and Surgeon Morris. Martha Patterson went along as her father's companion, accompanied by her husband, the senator. The cabinet was represented by the Secretary of State and the Secretary of the Navy, and along the way the Postmaster General joined the party. A special guest was Señor Mattias Romero, Mexico's minister to the United States, while Mrs. Farragut, Mrs. Welles, and Mrs. Steedman lent feminine support. There were two presidential secretaries (Colonel Moore and Robert Morrow) and a brigade of newspaper correspondents, headed by the veteran L. A. Gobright of the Associated Press.*

At first the radicals affected to ignore the whole silly junket. *The New York Times* and *New York Herald* carried full advance reports, and the *Times* sent two newswriters along, while the *Herald* sent four. The *Tribune* (which for some time had been calling the President "Judas Johnson") gave no space to the trip in advance, and on the day the party left Washington its front

---

* For a comparable group in our time, imagine President Harry Truman setting out on his whistle-stop tour of 1948 escorted by Generals Marshall, MacArthur, Eisenhower, Arnold, Patton, Bradley, and McAuliffe; Admirals Nimitz and Halsey; several cabinet members, a foreign diplomat, and a bevy of ladies.

page featured Sheridan's denunciation of the New Orleans "massacre" and "Parson" Brownlow's fulminations.

The Presidential party left Washington in bright sunshine at seven in the morning, August 28. The President was in the best of spirits, looking trim in a well-fitting black broadcloth coat. The party traveled in three cars, with one for baggage. The run to Baltimore was made in good time. There a crowd of perhaps one hundred thousand greeted the excursionists; even the critical *Tribune* admitted that the throng was "simply enormous." Johnson tried to speak, but his words were drowned by waves of cheering.

The city authorities of Philadelphia had vetoed a civic reception and the mayor had ostentatiously departed on a vacation; but a monster welcome had been organized privately. General Meade at the head of a military delegation escorted the commander-in-chief to the Continental Hotel, where Johnson was to speak and remain overnight. The factual Associated Press reported the streets bright with flags and streamers, but the *Tribune* insisted they were "bare and destitute of ornament," the sole display at the hotel being "six small and particularly dirty flags . . . stuck out of chambermaids' windows."

Johnson's speech in Philadelphia was a plea for national unity. "Forget that we have been divided into parties," he urged. "Let the interests of the great mass of people be promoted, and let parties sink into insignificance." And don't worry about politicians, "for when the people get right, the politicians are very accommodating."

The next day, crossing New Jersey, the Presidential special was greeted by friendly crowds at every halt. At Jersey City a committee of prominent New York citizens was waiting with a chartered ferryboat to carry the President to Manhattan, and as Johnson stepped ashore at the Battery, Mayor John T. Hoffman clasped his hand. The party piled into carriages and paraded up Broadway to City Hall, where there were addresses and Johnson was rendered almost speechless by the warmth of his welcome.

Then the procession moved up Broadway to Twenty-third Street, thence west to Fifth Avenue, and south on the Avenue to Delmonico's restaurant at Fourteenth Street. All along the way the sidewalks were black with people—the largest turnout ever seen in the city, according to the *New York World*, "several miles of flags, handkerchiefs, and human heads." (According to the *Tribune*, however, the buildings along Broadway were "bare of decoration.")

The President rode in a barouche "drawn by six black horses, magnificently caparisoned," and was escorted by detachments of cavalry and the Metropolitan Police. In a carriage behind the President rode Grant and Farragut, in uniform, and cheers rolled in salvoes as the cavalcade passed.

At the door of Delmonico's the President was greeted by more dignitaries, and was ushered by Lorenzo Delmonico, proprietor of the famous establishment, to reception rooms on the second floor. A reviewing stand had been erected on the Fifth Avenue side of the building, and from this position Johnson reviewed nine thousand New York State troops. Twenty regiments were in line, and the President was observed to be particularly pleased by a band of Highland pipers, and by a regiment of French volunteers led by their saucy *vivandière*.

As the review terminated, and the President started to leave the stand, there was a rush and the frail platform swayed. Johnson looked back, and Welles, at his elbow, exclaimed, "What do you think of that, sir?"

"It's wonderful!" said Johnson; and wonderful was the reception accorded to him at the banquet that night.

People were eager to get a good look at this relative newcomer to the city, and the newspapers elaborately described his appearance. The *World* said he was "in stature square-built, broad-chested, not over-tall, compact, manly. His body seems merely a pedestal for mounting his massive head. A broad brain; hair originally a deep black, but now evenly sprinkled with . . . white; complexion dark; keen black eyes. A face of grave aspect, which strikes the beholder at once . . . a face upon which public responsibilities have deeply graven their lines."

But the President's voice startled the brilliant assemblage of diners most; it was unexpected. Even the *Tribune* conceded that it was "low and sympathetic . . . singularly penetrating . . . He spoke with a reserve of power which made listening to him easy."

His strength, the *Tribune* thought, lay in "the modulation of his clear, mellow voice, the tones of which rose and fell as his passion, interest, or indifference predominated."

The speech covered familiar ground. The Southern states had attempted to break up the government by secession; they had failed, and the Union had been preserved; but now Congress was saying that the Union had been dissolved, and the South was out of it, not entitled to representation, though the lately rebellious states had renewed their allegiance, and reaffirmed their loyalty to the Constitution, "the sacred charter of liberty." The issue before the American people was whether they would submit to this dissolution.

To the accompaniment of applause, Johnson stated the case for the Southerners:

"They are our brethren. They are part of ourselves. They are bone of our bone, and flesh of our flesh . . . We have come together again; and now, after having understood what the feud was, the great apple of discord removed, having lived under the Constitution of the United States in the past, they ask to live under it in the future . . . This government cannot get along without the South . . . large as it is, it is not large enough to divide . . .

"I am one of those who believe that a man may sin and do wrong, and after that may do right. If all of us who have sinned were put to death . . . there would not be many of us left . . .

"The Son of God, when he descended and found men condemned under the law, instead of executing the law, put himself in their stead and died for them. If I have erred in pardoning, I trust in God I have erred on the right side."

Applause continued to interrupt as he went on:

"I fought those in the South who commenced the rebellion, and now I oppose those in the North who are trying to break up the Union. I am for the Union. I am against all those who were opposed to the Union. I am for the Union, the whole Union, and nothing but the Union. I find the Union of these states in peril. If I can now be instrumental in keeping the possession of it in your hands, in the hands of the people; in restoring prosperity and advancement in all that makes a nation great, I will be willing to exclaim, as did Simeon of old of him who had been born in a manger, that I have seen the glory of thy salvation, let thy servant depart in peace . . . I would rather live in history, in the affection of my countrymen, as having consummated this great end, than to be President of the United States forty times!'"

There was not a dissenting voice as the throng rose and cheered this dedication to a faith.

In the street outside, a great crowd had waited, entertained by bands playing patriotic airs, for a glimpse of the President. Coming out on the balcony, Johnson lit into Congress and raked the "subsidized and mercenary press" which charged he aspired to become dictator. "What have I to gain now? From the office of alderman up to that of President of the United States, I have filled all positions." The crowd hurrahed for Andy, many of New York's Irish remembering his courageous stand during the days of the Know-Nothings.

The next day the presidential party boarded the yacht *River Queen* and steamed up the Hudson, pausing at West Point to review the cadets. Throngs—cheers—addresses of welcome—pledges of support—marked every halt, and Johnson glowed.

At Albany, the party encountered another friendly crowd; but although Governor Reuben E. Fenton, a radical, presented Johnson to the Senate, he deliberately snubbed Seward.

By now it was clear to the press contingent that the President was making the same speech over and over, with slight variations. This was the method used in rural Tennessee, where newspapers were few and narrowly circulated. Under such conditions, one set speech would sound fresh to each audience. Now the situation was different; correspondents of the great dailies and the Associated Press were reporting the President's words to millions of readers, day after day, and some of the stereotyped phrases were beginning to sound ludicrous.

Nevertheless, the President was succeeding too well to please the opposition and, dropping the pose of ignoring the excursion, the radicals set to work to counteract its effect. As the party moved across New York State the reports became more biased. In the radical papers what the President said was mimicked and his mannerisms were burlesqued. There was no denying that the crowds were large and well disposed, but the opposition insisted that the people had turned out from mere curiosity. Not counting wayside stops, Johnson spoke at Schenectady, Little Falls, Utica, Syracuse, Seneca Falls, Genoa, Canandaigua, Rochester, Lockport, Niagara Falls, and Buffalo. His voice grew hoarse, and Welles was afraid he would break down; but at Niagara Falls Johnson got his second wind and his voice recovered. At the end of five days, the trip admittedly had been "a continuous ovation," though (the opposition press added) "the President continues to make himself ridiculous and to disgust sensible people by his egotistic and self-glorifying harangues."

The basis for this charge of egotism, which would be pounded on relentlessly, lay in the President's frequent references to "my policy"; in the looseness inherent in extemporaneous speaking, where slips in grammar are inevitable; in his use of the personal pronoun "I"; in his "egotistical" cataloging of the offices through which he had risen to the Presidency as evidence that he had reached the summit of ambition and could aspire to nothing more; and in the recurrence of certain tricks of speech that became noticeable through constant repetition.

The President's usual method of starting, for example, was to disclaim any intention of making a speech—and thereupon launch into one. He harped on the same themes, over and over: assailing Congress for its obstructionism, defending "my policy" as one of peace and restoration, denouncing "traitors" North or South, and concluding with statements that he was leaving the Constitution in the hands of the voters before him, confident that they would preserve and protect it against its enemies.

"Having occupied most positions, from alderman up to the chief magistracy of the United States . . . and at last having been charged with being a traitor . . . I say, what have I to gain?" he asked the crowd at Silver Creek, New York, and repeated this over and over.

"If I were disposed to make a speech, and time would permit me to do it," he prefaced his remarks at Buffalo.

"I say to you, if the worst comes to the worst, if it is blood they want, let them take mine if it be necessary to save the country," he volunteered at Utica, and repeated the offer again and again.

"I tell you, my countrymen, I have been fighting the South . . . and now, as I go around the circle, having fought traitors at the South, I am prepared to fight traitors at the North," he would state and restate.

"In parting with you, I leave the Constitution and the Union in your hands, where I am satisfied they are safe," he told a throng at Fonda, New York, and he would say the same thing at other stops, sometimes adding that he was also confiding to their care "the flag of your country, not with twenty-five stars but with thirty-six upon it."

It was apparent that the President enjoyed this renewal of contact with the people, and those traveling with him were pleased. The reports reaching the office of the *Herald* in New York were so enthusiastic that an editor wrote to the President, "We are all rejoicing in the extraordinary good effect of your journey to Chicago."

One member of the party who especially approved the journey was General Rawlins, Grant's confidential aide during the war. Rawlins was devoted to Grant, and as the party neared Buffalo, he became uneasy. Grant was tipping the bottle again, and Mrs. Farragut had complained that he was becoming "stupidly communicative." Quietly Rawlins succeeded in putting Grant aboard a lake steamer for Detroit, and the scandal was kept from the public.

On leaving Buffalo, the President headed into northern Ohio, where he had been warned he might encounter trouble. The region around Cleveland was the old Western Reserve, settled by New Englanders, and for a generation it had been a center of militant abolitionism. It was Ben Wade's country, and the radicals were entrenched solidly there. Surprised and alarmed by the popular response to Johnson's bold appeals, his opponents mapped their counteroffensive. It was baited with hecklers, and the President walked into the trap.

The crowd waiting at the depot was large and not unfriendly when the President and his party reached Cleveland shortly after dark on Monday, September 3. Johnson was weary. As he had worked his way through the towns along the south shore of Lake Erie, the heckling had started, in a minor way. At Westfield, New

York, not far from the Ohio border, there had been some ribald discourtesy when he made his usual introductory remark about not intending to make a speech. "Don't!" a heckler had shouted.

"Keep quiet until I have concluded," Johnson had rejoined. "Just such fellows as you have kicked up all the rows of the last five years."

When told by Seward, acting as master of ceremonies, that General Grant was not with them, the Cleveland station crowd grew noisy, but there was no serious demonstration.

A larger throng had collected at the Kennard Hotel, where the President was to stay. Though Welles thought that Johnson should not attempt to address this crowd, the President yielded to persistent calls, came out on a balcony, and began with his usual disclaimer. By now this gambit had been exposed in innumerable newspapers, and its repetition brought guffaws. Warmed by this challenge, the President launched into a defense of his actions, well knowing that he had enemies in the crowd.

Suddenly a man shouted, "What about Moses?" This was an allusion to Johnson's celebrated "Moses speech" in Nashville in 1864, when he had promised to lead the Negroes to their reward of freedom.

"Let your own Negroes vote before you talk about Negroes voting in Louisiana," Johnson advised. "Cast the beam out of your own eye before you see the mote in your neighbor's."

Boos and catcalls greeted this, for Johnson had touched a sensitive spot: Ohio did not allow its Negroes to vote.

"What about New Orleans?" came a shout. The President offered to demonstrate that the riot was radical-inspired, but groans and laughter drowned his words. "Why don't you hang Jeff Davis?" came another taunt. "Hang Thad Stevens and Wendell Phillips!"

Now thoroughly aroused, Johnson flung back that Lincoln, had he lived, would have encountered the same opposition from disunionists and merchants of hate that he was meeting. A roar of protest cut him off, but there was some applause, too.

"I love my country," the President resumed when he could be heard. "I defy any man to put his finger on anything to the contrary. Then what is my offending?"

"You ain't a radical!"

"Veto!"

"Traitor!"

"I wish I could see that man," called Johnson angrily, looking towards the source of the last epithet. "Show yourself. Come out here where I can see you. If ever you shoot a man, you will do it in the dark."

The pattern of the disturbance showed that it was organized but Johnson was not intimidated.

"With all the pains this Congress has taken to poison the minds of their constituents against me, what has this Congress done?" he demanded. "Have they done anything to restore the Union of these states? No; on the contrary, they have done everything to prevent it; and because I stand now where I did when the rebellion commenced, I have been denounced as a traitor! . . . I tell you, my countrymen, though the powers of hell, death, and Stevens combine, there is no power that can control me save you . . . and the God that spoke me into existence!"

By now the disorder had become general, and there were shouts of "It's a lie!" Unable to make himself heard, the President turned on his heel and reentered the hotel.

And the next day the radical press sang jubilee. The President was an illiterate, crude, coarse, vulgar Southerner who traded insults with a mob, they chanted. Some said outright that he was drunk. The Muscatine, Iowa *Journal* termed the whole trip "a big drunk . . . When we reflect upon the solemn object of the journey, we just blush crimson at this monstrous impropriety, this cold-blooded impiety . . . A President of the United States reeling to Chicago!"

The *Cincinnati Commercial* echoed the chorus: "The President confessed himself mad . . . His friends excuse the matter today by declaring he was too drunk to be responsible for his actions."

The *Lorain County News* refused even to extend this excuse for conduct "which sinks the President of the United States below a decent contempt."

In the President's party the feeling was mixed. Welles deplored the poor taste, but Seward dismissed the unpleasantness, saying that Andy Johnson was the best stump speaker in the country and was helping his cause. Welles retorted that the President of the United States should not be a stump speaker at all.

From Cleveland onward misfortunes dogged the excursionists. At Niles, Ohio, the platform broke down, leaving Johnson standing precariously on the edge and throwing Seward, Grant, and Farragut to the ground. Luckily they were not badly hurt.

At Elyria, Ohio, a house on a hillside overlooking the railroad station flaunted a large black flag, while at Ashtabula, Wade's home town, the crowd laughed and chattered, cheered the military heroes but showed plainly that they had no intention of letting the President speak. Johnson waited several minutes for the tumult to subside, then gave up the attempt.

At Toledo the crowd was friendly, and again at Detroit, though at Ypsilanti and Ann Arbor, Michigan, Grant was cheered again and again in the midst of the President's remarks.

At Battle Creek the crowd hooted Johnson and hurrahed for Congress. At Michigan City, when he repeated his blast at the "rump Congress," the President was answered with "three rousing cheers" for that Congress. As he entered their states, governors and mayors fled. At few stopping places was there any official reception.

In Chicago, on September 6, Johnson spoke briefly at the Douglas monument dedication, but the governor and lieutenant governor of Illinois stayed away from the ceremonies, and there was no municipal welcome. Pickets carrying anti-Johnson placards circled around the scene, and the contemptuous *Chicago Tribune* reported hisses and general apathy (though in another column it spoke of an immense throng and "loud cheers"). The *Tribune* played up the drunkenness reports. At the start of the parade, it said, "A. Johnson, the 'humble individual,' after one or two ineffectual attempts to land in the gutter, was handed, or rather lifted, into the buggy awaiting his august presence."

Leaving Chicago, the party journeyed to Springfield, where, on a dismal, rainy day, they visited Lincoln's tomb. No state or city official appeared; the streets were empty.

The next day, at Alton, Illinois, the sun shone, and with brightened spirits the excursionists boarded thirty-six steamboats, representing the thirty-six states, for the trip to St. Louis. The steamer carrying the President was named *Andy Johnson*, and the *Muscatine Journal* took another swipe at the President by noting that the *Andy Johnson* carried "a very good bar," so "the President and Seward have not suffered . . . for want of a brandy-and-water."

As the fleet neared St. Louis on Saturday afternoon, they were met by barges loaded with enthusiastic greeters. The streets around the Southern Hotel, where the President was to remain over Sunday, were black with people. The President addressed these briefly, and spoke again in the evening at a banquet in his honor. During this banquet the street crowd outside clamored for another speech, and tired though he was, Johnson finally acceded.

This crowd was noisy from the start, and the give-and-take grew animated. Johnson kept his temper, however, until a voice came out of the darkness chanting, "Judas! Judas!" That angered the President.

"There was a Judas," he shouted, "and he was one of the twelve apostles . . . The twelve apostles had a Christ . . . If I have played the Judas, who has been my Christ that I have played the Judas with? Was it Thad Stevens? Was it Wendell Phillips? Was it Charles Sumner?"

Amid groans and whistles he kept on:

"These are the men that compare themselves with the Savior! And anybody who differs with them is denounced as a Judas!"

"Why don't they impeach him?" cried a heckler, and the din became deafening. Johnson by now had lost contact with his audience, and struggle as he might, they refused to hear him.

"Yes, yes, they are ready to impeach!" he shouted. ("Let them try it!" came a voice.) "And if they were satisfied that they had the next Congress by as decided a majority as this . . . upon some pretext or other . . . they would vacate the executive department of the government!" ("Too bad they don't!")

"But as we are talking about this Congress, let me call the soldiers' attention to this immaculate Congress. Let me call your attention . . . Oh, yes, this Congress that could make war upon the executive . . . because he stands for the Constitution and vindicates the rights of the people . . . exercising the veto power in their behalf . . . because he dared to do this . . . they clamor and talk about impeachment . . . So far as offenses are concerned . . . upon this question of offenses . . . let me ask you what offenses I have committed."

"Plenty, here, tonight!"

Lear-like the President stumbled on, braving the uproar. (Long ago he had foreshadowed this very scene, when he told a group of war veterans at the White House that "the whole pack" of his enemies was being loosed against him—"Tray, Blanch, and Sweetheart, snapping at my heels.") Standing in the torchlight, whipped by insults, facing a mob he could not subdue, Andrew Johnson seemed to lose touch with reality. He babbled. The familiar rallying cries—"Union"—"Constitution"—were the same with which he had stirred a nation in 1861—where was their magic now?

The next day the press carried a complete commentary on the unedifying episode.

"A very remarkable circus," Thad Stevens was quoted as saying, "that sometimes cuts outside the circle and enters into street brawls with common blackguards."

Said the *Missouri Democrat:*

"St. Louis has to thank Andrew Johnson for one of the longest, the meanest, and the most demagogical harangues he has uttered since he became President. A speech as foolish in its statements as it was vulgar in tone, ungrammatical in expression, and muddy and incoherent in style. A reader might suppose the speaker was drunk, but he was not. We must accept this insolent, tricky, illogical, and altogether vulgar harangue as the best the President of the United States can do."

"THE NATIONAL DISGRACE," read the *Cincinnati Gazette*'s headline, under which wound one of the interminable "banks" of the news captions of that period:

"Mr. Johnson Surpasses in Blasphemy and Ribaldry all his Previous Efforts—Compares Himself to the Savior of Mankind . . . Defends New Orleans Murderers—Pours Out a Torrent of Vile and Intemperate Abuse Against the Congress of the United States—Unparalleled Effusion of Profanity, Vulgarity, and Slang—Sense, Decency, and Grammar All Discarded."

This was mild compared with the *Independent*, which "gave thanks to God that the basest citizen of the republic, even though its chief magistrate, is unable to destroy, but only to disgrace it."

This "trickster" Johnson, the *Independent* informed its readers, combined "the face of a demagogue, the heart of a traitor," and "deep-set, lascivious" eyes, and was "touched with insanity, corrupted with lust, stimulated with drink."

To the *Nation*, the Presidential jaunt had become "a melancholy tour." And an Ohio friend gloated to radical Congressman James A. Garfield, "Isn't Andy doing finely?" An Ohio college professor added, "Who ever heard of such a Presidential ass?"

Grant took leave of the party at St. Louis, promising to catch up with them at Cincinnati. He gave as his reason a desire to visit his father, but privately told Rawlins that he did not care to travel with a man who was "deliberately digging his own grave." Already Grant had begun intimating that he had not consulted his own wish in coming along, but had obeyed an order.

From St. Louis, Johnson headed eastward, and the fiasco was repeated at most of the stops.

At Indianapolis the crowd outside the hotel kept chanting for "Grant!" At length Johnson appeared, and he started with, "I should like to say to this crowd tonight," and was cut off by yells of "Shut up!" "We don't want to hear from you!"

That evening he tried again, but the mob still clamored for Grant and jeered the President. Johnson finally returned inside the hotel, and a riot broke out, in which one man was killed and several were wounded, and the casualties were laid at the President's door.

Louisville, for a change, received the President handsomely. But in Ohio, at Columbus and Cincinnati, the crowds were rowdy. Grant rejoined the tour at Cincinnati, and was disgusted by a leather-lunged St. Louis congressman, John Hogan, whom Johnson had unwisely invited to join the party. Hogan had done his best to oppose the war. He delighted in bawling out an introduction of the President at each halt, and Grant growled that he could stand a rebel, but a copperhead, no!

In Steubenville, Stanton's town, the President was not permitted to speak. At New Market, Ohio, hecklers raised a cheer for Thad Stevens, and General Custer gave them a dressing down; he had been born two and a half miles from there, he said, and he was ashamed of them.

Pittsburgh produced another disaster. Stepping out on the balcony of his hotel, as was the custom, Johnson faced a dense mass of people stretching for two blocks. The disturbances began at once, while a radical parade, with drums and a band, marched on the edge of the throng, flaunting placards quoting Johnson's war-time pledge to "make treason odious and punish traitors." He tried to speak, but the mob would only cheer Grant and Farragut. Finally, with "I bid you good night," Johnson retreated into the hotel. There, that evening, at a banquet arranged privately (the mayor having left the city in order, he sent word, to "preserve my self-respect"), Johnson was heard respectfully and was generously applauded.

The tour's mishaps reached a climax at Johnstown, Pennsylvania, when a platform put up beside the tracks collapsed and dropped five hundred spectators twenty feet. Eight were killed outright, more died later, and a hundred at least were badly hurt. The opposition charged that the President callously continued on eastward without a word of sympathy for the victims, although the truth was that he started a relief fund with a five-hundred-dollar donation, and left one of his military aides to render all the assistance possible.

Near Louisville, Secretary Seward had been taken gravely ill with cholera. He had been started back to Washington in a private car, ahead of the President's train, but grew worse, and at Harrisburg the car had been switched to a siding, in expectation of his death. The car was there when the President arrived, and word was received that Seward might not last through the night. Accompanied by Welles, Johnson hurried to the sick man. They found him very weak. His voice was faint and he could speak only in a whisper, but taking Johnson's hand, he murmured solemnly:

"My mind is clear, and I wish to say that your course is right, and that I have felt it my duty to sustain you in it; and if my life is spared I shall continue to do so. Pursue it for the sake of the country. It is correct."

Postmaster General Randall had hurried on ahead to organize a welcome home at Washington, and with this, on Saturday, September 15, the "swing around the circle" came to an end. General Grant had caught a separate train from Baltimore and cut across lots alone to his home. Johnson's train was late, but the crowd waited until it pulled in at seven o'clock that evening.

Attorney General Stanbery and Secretary Stanton were on hand, the latter extending smiling congratulations as he shook the President's hand. A procession was formed along Indiana Avenue and marched to Pennsylvania Avenue, turning there towards the White House. At City Hall Mayor Wallach spoke a civic greeting. Then the bands, the standard-bearers, the fire brigade, and the Johnson clubs fell into line again. The sidewalks were crowded with spectators, and all the way down Pennsylvania Avenue the President stood up in his carriage, waving his hat in response to cheers.

2.

The extent of the debacle which the President had suffered was not appreciated at once. It could hardly have been more complete.

His errors had been many. Throughout his nineteen-day journey through ten states, during which he had spoken more than a hundred times, including twenty major addresses, he had appealed to the voters to send men to Congress who would back his policies. But he had failed to name any candidates. He also had failed to stress the issues on which the radicals were vulnerable. In asserting that Congress had done nothing to bring about national unity, he ignored the Fourteenth Amendment, which was the Congressional plan for reconstruction. The President had neglected to pin down candidates on the question of Negro suffrage, a touchy subject in most of the states he visited. He had not compelled his opponents to state plainly whether ratification of the pending amendment was to be the only condition required of the South. Certainly the matter would not end there if Stevens and Sumner had their way; but while many congressmen avoided a direct commitment, the impression was allowed to grow that nothing more would be asked. And there were economic issues that might have been utilized to drive a wedge between the agrarian West and the high-tariff, manufacturing East.

Also, throughout the trip Johnson had failed to grasp that what the people of the North wanted most was tranquillity, an end of argument. Attitudes had changed since the war. Appeals to the "Union" seemed redundant now, when the Union was no longer in danger. To the average voter the "Constitution" was an abstraction. What was real—the fear of the hour—was that Johnson's policy, if carried to its logical conclusion, would turn the government over to the late rebels, and annul the sacrifices made to win the war.

Johnson failed to appreciate these political facts, or, if he appreciated them, failed to heed them. Instead, he had presented himself to the country in anachronistic terms, in a very present crisis seeming like a holdover from a bygone age, mouthing old slogans; to the tough, cynical, disillusioned, preoccupied postwar generation his values meant little; even his plain speaking and old-fashioned sense of personal dignity were grotesque and drew the inevitable ridicule with which the popular crowd attacks any too-glaring oddity.

In almost every respect Johnson made his moves too late. The six weeks intervening between the Philadelphia convention and the elections was too short a time in which to set a political revolution in motion. The President had allowed Congress to arm itself against him. The patronage teemed with appointees ready to aid the radicals; and when, on returning to Washington, the President began to clean out these disloyalists, the grass-roots outcry frightened those Republicans who still hesitated into the radical ranks for self-preservation. On top of all the Democrats helped to undercut the President's position by nominating candidates who had been wartime pacifists—men for whom no Unionist could conscientiously vote.

Before the end of the tour, Johnson had lost almost the last of his major newspaper support. After St. Louis, the *New York Herald* had recalled its reporters, announcing that the "humble individual" was "played out." The *Herald* always tried to be on the winning side, and the September election results in Maine had convinced it that Congress would carry the day nationally. As the political weathercock of the nation, Maine had been watched intently, and the radicals swept the state, increasing their majorities. This was the handwriting on the wall. The newspapers prospered as they caught the trend. News "butchers" on trains around New York City by the end of Johnson's tour were selling three copies of the *New York Tribune* to one of the *Herald*, although the *Herald*'s circulation had been the largest in the United States. The trend was the same in the Midwest.*

The last metropolitan daily to desert the President was *The New York Times;* but when it lost a third of its circulation and revenue of one hundred thousand dollars within a few weeks, the *Times*, too, "saw the light," recanted, and reluctantly switched over.

Johnson did not take these desertions by the press too seriously. A speaker and not a writer, he tended to be impatient with the press and reporters. They had never been much help to him in Tennessee. What he craved, what he needed, was to be heard, not read; in print, his speeches lost much of their vitality and very much of their effect.

"Would to God my voice could be heard in every hovel throughout the land!" he had exclaimed in Baltimore. And in Columbus, Ohio: "I wish I had a clarion voice to extend to the remotest cabin!" Yet out of the perhaps one million people who saw the President on his speaking tour, only a small fraction heard him at all, and fewer yet heard him coherently and sympathetically; but the travesties of his words, and the vagaries of his conduct, real or fictitious, the newspapers transmitted to five million readers every day.

Meanwhile, the opposition staged a vigorous rebuttal campaign. All issues except two were ignored—the character and personal failings of the President, and the danger of rebel seizure of the government if Johnson's policy prevailed. Neither issue was presented rationally: the appeal was to hysteria and hate, and the technique became known as "waving the bloody shirt." It had been started when a Republican speaker waved a bloodstained shirt, said to have been taken from a slain Union soldier, and demanded whether his listeners were willing to restore to power the men who had shed that blood—who had slaughtered their sons, brothers, husbands, fathers. How far one could go in this

---

* In 1864 the post office in a town near Chicago had been handling sixty-three subscriptions weekly to the radical *Chicago Tribune*, against fifty-two to the *Chicago Times*, a wartime copperhead and postwar pro-Johnson paper. After the President's tour, the same post office handled one hundred and thirty-six *Tribune* subscriptions weekly, against three for the *Times*.

appeal was shown by Governor Morton of Indiana. G. W. Julian, the governor's rival in Indiana Republicanism, once remarked that it had been aptly said of Morton ("and not by his enemies") that no man in public life "ever brought such magnificent resources to the support of both sides of a question." Now as violently opposed to the President as formerly he had been for him, Morton contended that nobody but Democrats wanted Andrew Johnson; and he made clear whom he meant by Democrats:

"Every unregenerate rebel lately in arms against his government calls himself a Democrat. Every bounty jumper, every deserter, every sneak who ran away from the draft calls himself a Democrat. Every 'Son of Liberty' who conspired to murder, burn, rob arsenals and release rebel prisoners calls himself a Democrat . . . Payne and Booth proclaimed themselves Democrats. Every man who labored for the rebellion in the field, who murdered Union prisoners by cruelty and starvation, who conspired to bring about civil war in the loyal states . . . calls himself a Democrat . . . Every wolf in sheep's clothing who professes to teach the Gospel but proclaims the righteousness of man-selling and slavery; everyone who shoots down Negroes in the streets, burns up Negro schoolhouses and meetinghouses, and murders women and children by the light of their own flaming dwellings, calls himself a Democrat. Every New York rioter in 1863 who burned up little children in colored asylums, who robbed, ravished, and murdered indiscriminately . . . called himself a Democrat. In short, the Democratic party can be described as a common sewer and loathsome receptacle, into which is emptied every element of treason North and South, every element of inhumanity and barbarism which has dishonored the age!

"And this party . . . proclaims to an astonished world that the only effect of vanquishing armed rebels in the field is to return them to seats in Congress, and to restore them to political power. Having failed to destroy the Constitution by force, they seek to do it by construction, with . . . the remarkable discovery that the rebels who fought to destroy the Constitution were its true friends, and that the men who shed their blood and gave their substance to preserve it are its only enemies!"

Such blows told. In vain the President might restate his aims, as when he told a delegation of soldiers at the White House:

"Ours is a government of limited powers, with a written Constitution, with boundaries both national and state, and these limitations and boundaries must be observed and strictly respected if free government is to exist; and, coming out of a rebellion, we ought to demonstrate to mankind that a free government cannot live on hatred and distrust."

The public was moved, but not in the direction desired by the President. "My policy" became a byword, a taunt yelled by guttersnipes in the streets.

                                3.

In this process Johnson had the bad luck to become the target of three masters of propaganda, each addressing a different level of public intelligence, and together spanning the social and intellectual spectrum.

The first was the dialect humorist, David R. Locke, who wrote in the character of "Petroleum V. Nasby," an illiterate copperhead ("a Dimocrat uv thirty years standin, who niver skratched his ticket and allus took his likker strate"). The second was the brilliant satirical cartoonist, Thomas Nast, whose savage caricatures in *Harper's* and elsewhere depicted "King Andy" in various unsavory guises, such as a togaed Roman emperor, complacently allowing Seward to crown him while in the arena below mercenaries are slaughtering captives. Third was the Boston intellectual, James Russell Lowell, who, in the *North American Review*, subjected Johnson, Seward, and their associates to masterly denigration for the enlightenment of so-called liberals and the highly educated.

Locke's reporting of Johnson's tour (written originally for the *Toledo Blade* but republished nationwide) was later collected into pamphlets, which were sold on newsstands and appealed to the tastes of the common, very common citizen. One, entitled "Andy's Trip to the West," started with crude cartoons showing the President, Seward, and Grant packing for the junket. Johnson was stowing away jugs, bottles, and a pistol; Seward was cramming his valise with speeches, ink, pens, and foolscap; and Grant was stuffing cigars by the fistful into a carpetbag—"a few of the necessities of life."

The prefatory account of the President's life may be judged by the briefest excerpt:

"The subjeck uv this sketch wuz at an early age apprenticed to the tailorin bizness, wich wuz a most fortunate and appropriate selektion, becuz fust, the aspirant is only required to be the ninth part uv a man . . ."

Following, but not in dialect, were the "Orations of Johnson, When Going to the Douglas Wake (Condensed)." The lampooning was deadlier because it parodied one of Johnson's most effective speaking devices—constant repetition, to drive home a point. This alleged summary of the speeches made by the President on his tour read:

1—He who now addresses you is a Humble Individual.

2—I have filled all the offices which the nation has to bestow, from Alderman up to the President of the United States. I leave the Constitution in your hands.

3—I am very much abused by a subsidized, corrupt, and mendacious press.

4—Pardon my alluding to myself, but I beg leave to inform you that I commenced as an Alderman of one of the small towns of this Nation; I went from that to Mayor, from that to the Legislature, from that to Senator of the State Legislature, from that to the Senate of the United States, from that to the Presidential chair.

5—I am no traitor; Mr. Seward is no traitor; nobody that supports My Policy is a traitor.

6—I have no wish to be egotistic, but I must say that I have occupied all the places from Alderman up to the position I now occupy—President of the United States.

7—The members of Congress who oppose My Policy are all traitors; everybody who opposes My Policy is a traitor. I leave the Constitution in your hands.

8—It is not my habit to make mention of myself, but it is perhaps my duty to say that I have been an Alderman, a Mayor, a State Senator, a Representative, a Senator of the United States, and now I am President. What more do I want?

9—The Union Party may go to the devil.

10—My ambition is satisfied. First I was an Alderman, then a Mayor, then a member of the State Senate, then a member of the House of

Representatives, then a member of the United States Senate, and at the moment I am President of the United States.

11–Seward is my friend and I am Seward's friend; Seward likes me and I like Seward; Seward is a good fellow and I am a good fellow; we like each other. We leave the Constitution in this town.

12–I have served my country in all capacities. I began life as an Alderman, was a Mayor during my infancy, was State Senator in my childhood, became a Representative in my early youth, attained my majority in the Senate of the United States, and now, in the prime of my manhood, I am President.

13–Who wants niggers to vote? If the Northern States want niggers to vote, why don't they let them vote at home? Niggers sh'an't vote; I desire them to have the same chances as white men.

14–Perhaps you are not aware, fellow citizens, that I have been an Alderman, a Mayor, a State Senator, a Representative, a United States Senator, and finally President of the United States.

15–The Congressmen who voted for the Freedmen's Bureau Bill and the Civil Rights Bill are all fools. I should like to fight the whole one hundred and eighty-two of them. I won't leave the Constitution with nary one of them.

16–It is a matter of history that after being an Alderman, a Mayor, a United States Senator, I became President. Lincoln was assassinated and Seward butchered, and so I became President.

17–I have great confidence in the American people, all except Members of Congress, Unionists, and Niggers; they are all traitors, and I mean to fight them with the help of General Grant.

18–Nobody ever held so many offices as I have. I have filled all the various positions in life, such as Alderman, Mayor, State Senator, Member of Congress, United States Senator, and at length I was made President.

19–I repeat that Seward is a good fellow; he stands by me and I stand by him; I am not afraid of a subsidized and mercenary press; all loyal people may go to the devil; the Baltimore platform is my platform; Douglas was a friend of mine; I am going to erect a monument over him; I am not upon an electioneering tour; I have not punished any Southern traitors, but I mean to make it up by punishing lots of Northern traitors; every man who does not go for me is a traitor; I can't be a traitor, because I have been an Alderman, then a Mayor, then a State Senator, then a Representative, then a Member of the United States Senate, and then President.

20–I leave the Constitution in your hands, where it is safer than in mine, for having been an Alderman, etc.

This pamphlet was chuckled over at every crossroads in the North, including the address of the putative author, Petroleum V. Nasby—"Saint's Rest (wich is in the Stait uv New Jersey)."

Another audience was reached by Nast's cartoons—the literate, lower middle class. Lowell addressed the educated, reflective element of society, among whom breadth of view, sobriety of judgment, and tolerance might normally be expected.

That an ignoramus, blinded by partisan prejudice, should swallow the story about Johnson's drunkenness on that grueling Western tour (something which, strangely, the highly respectable women members of the party never noticed, and certainly would not have condoned)—this might not have occasioned surprise; but that James Russell Lowell, writing for an audience proud of its intelligence, should call the trip an "indecent orgy," did provide cause for some astonishment.

Lowell's attack was expert and hard-hitting. Seward was taken to task for having served as "bear-leader" to his "partner in vulgarity," the President. The avowed object of "this indecent orgy," Lowell protested, was "almost as discreditable as the purpose it veiled so thinly." The memory of Stephen A. Douglas, he said, was not associated with "a single measure of national importance, unless upon the wrong side." Though a clever politician, the Illinois senator had been "wholly without the instinct for the higher atmosphere of thought or ethics."

Himself secure upon that lofty plane, Lowell stooped as readily as Petroleum V. Nasby to pun upon the name of Senator Doolittle, Johnson's friend, detecting "something ominously suggestive" in that cognomen. Andrew Johnson he described as "how vain and weak a man . . . sore with such rancor as none but a 'plebeian,' as he used to call himself, can feel against his social superiors . . . the Presidential Punch . . . [full of] jack-pudding tricks and catch-rabble devices."

The pontifications proliferated: "A small politician cannot be made out of a great statesman, for there is an oppugnancy of nature between the two things, and we may fairly suspect the former winnings of a man who has been once caught with loaded dice in his pocket."

From consideration of "the real clown being allowed to exhibit himself at short intervals upon the highest platform in this or any other country," and the pitiable "dry-rot" of Seward's mind, Lowell passed to a firmly reasoned brief for the radical cause. This was convincing if one accepted the basic premise, namely, that the Southern representatives, if admitted to Congress under Johnson's program, would prove to be meanly destructive, vindictive, treacherous, and a permanent stumbling block to the peace and harmony of the nation. Since this assumption was debatable, the argument became purely hypothetical; nevertheless, its effect upon those who perused it was undeniably profound.

Johnson's chief fault, it thus transpired obliquely, was his offensiveness to educated Northerners, as well as to Southern patricians—his inborn "vulgarity." He too painfully embodied the "people," and Lowell was a victim of the dichotomy that commonly plagues intellectuals who are long on political theory and short on human practice; while they extol democracy as the best form of government, from the standpoint of both justice and wisdom, they shrink from mingling with the "demos," the "vulgus," which is the "people." Johnson's closeness to the identifiable "vulgus" repelled the fastidious Bostonians. Throughout the President's tour, for example, the rarefied *Boston Transcript* had headlined its daily report: "I, I, I, My, My, My, Me, Me, Me."

Benjamin Truman had caught the note when he wrote to the President from Massachusetts (where he saw no glimmer of hope for Johnson in the coming election) that "the long-haired men and cadaverous females of New England think you are horrid. I had a conversation with an antique female last night in the course of which she declared that she hoped you would be impeached." When asked what the President had done to deserve that, she had replied: "Well, he hasn't done anything yet, but I hope to God he will!"

Sumner was disseminating letters alluding to "His Vulgarity," and gloating prospectively over the chastisement that was in store for "this poor dead snake."

Governor Brownlow organized what later would be known as "truth squads" to follow up Johnson's "bushwhacking pilgrimage" and "wipe out his moccasin tracks." In the *Knoxville Whig* he published that Johnson had run up whisky bills, some as high as four hundred dollars, in town after town and then decamped without paying them.

The Republican convention of Tennessee resolved that "we cover our faces with shame when we contemplate the disgrace brought upon our beloved state by the defection and degeneracy of her adopted son, who, by the bullet of an assassin, has ascended to the chief magistracy of the nation; and we shall cordially endorse any action of Congress which shall legitimately deprive him of continued power to disturb the peace of he country."

Back at his stand-up desk, Johnson went about his duties, enforcing the Civil Rights Act and meeting other obligations punctually. His staff and the cabinet were astonished by this self-containment. He never lost his dignity, and tourists were gratified to catch glimpses of the embattled President strolling in the White House gardens of an afternoon, frock-coated, top-hatted, swinging a gold-headed cane, seemingly every inch a Southern gentleman of the old school. His associates were indignant at the abuse being shoveled out by the opposition and by the recurrent rumors of intended violence. Johnson himself confided to Orville Browning that he had "no doubt there was a conspiracy on foot among the radicals to incite another rebellion, and especially to arm and exasperate the Negroes in the South."

Two days after Browning was told this by the President, he was called on by an Indiana general who said he had "the most satisfactory evidence" of a plot to "overthrow the government and set up a military dictatorship," in the event of a radical triumph at the polls.

In October several states voted, with Pennsylvania at the top of the list. Fragmentary returns indicated a victory for the President there, but the final tally gave the state overwhelmingly to the Republicans. Ohio, Indiana, and Iowa took the same course, and in November New York and the balance of the states completed the radicals' triumph. It was the first landslide victory in the nation's history. The Republicans increased their majority in the Senate well beyond the two-thirds needed to override any action by the President, and strengthened their already massive grip on the House. The radical press exulted that the President had been checkmated—the snake defanged—and there was mounting talk of getting rid of the encumbrance in the White House altogether.

4.

The day before President Johnson returned to Washington, Secretary of War Stanton wrote a letter to James Ashley, a Republican congressman from Ohio, in which he revealed perhaps as much of his secret thoughts as he did to anyone at this time. Ashley, a monomaniac on the subject of Andrew Johnson's "usurpation," had so often called for Johnson's impeachment that his colleagues nicknamed him "Impeachment Ashley." Stanton's choice of such a confidant was illuminating.

"There is indeed 'danger ahead,' " the secretary wrote, "the most serious being that Johnson and Grant, as you put it, 'suck at the same quill.' The President has for more than a year put forth persistent efforts to capture Grant for purposes that are unmistakeable. Their habits are congenial . . . Grant goes daily, almost hourly, to the White House, in full view of the populace, and at this moment is gyrating through the country on a deplorable joust with Johnson . . . So long as these delinquencies were confined to Washington City, I felt no apprehension . . . but when the great mass of virtuous common people are called out to behold the head of our nation and the head of our armies reeling through the country . . . demoralization must follow."

Increasingly, he sighed, he longed "to be free . . . free as a bird." When Lee surrendered, he recounted, he had begged Lincoln to release him, but had been drafted to remain at his post. When Johnson succeeded, he had proffered his resignation again, only to be told, "No, you must keep the machine running."

"There you have my situation—when I thought it was safe to resign, I could not. Now that I can resign, I dare not. However, as soon as the way shall be clear, which may be soon after the meeting of Congress, I shall retire . . . My physical condition is deplorable. Prostrated by spasms of asthma and tortured by unbearable pains in the head, it is a problem how much longer I can bear up. Come early, I beg of you, for Congress has a heavy task before it . . . *Truly your friend*, Edwin M. Stanton."

Upon his return from the West, pressure was redoubled on the President to get rid of the Secretary of War; indeed, a clean sweep of his cabinet was recommended by numerous advisers. But though Johnson agreed that something should be done, he refrained from acting. At first Welles and others believed he was reluctant to roil the waters further before the election; but the election passed, and still Stanton sat at the council table. The President watched him, and grew exceedingly reticent; it seemed to old Mr. Ewing that procrastination was likely to be Johnson's undoing. Doolittle also was extremely depressed; the President's Washington's Birthday speech, the senator reckoned gloomily, had cost them one hundred thousand votes.

The members of Congress did assemble in Washington early. Although this was a "lame-duck" session, the knowledge of the increased strength they would wield in the Fortieth Congress rendered the Republicans cocksure and belligerent. Representative George S. Boutwell of Massachusetts, an intense, steely-eyed bundle of energy and fount of florid rhetoric, came talking impeachment, and so did Ben Butler, who had won his election to the House, although he would not be seated until the spring.

Boutwell's first call was at the War Department, where Stanton filled him with horrendous stories about Johnson's issuing orders to the army unknown to either the Secretary or Grant. From Stanton's dictation Boutwell wrote down the words of a law that would practically strip the commander-in-chief of authority over the army; this later would be incorporated in an army appropriation bill.

Thaddeus Stevens came back to the capital for the last time. The emaciated old man was so feeble he could scarcely stand, but his spirit and his mental powers were untouched. With sardonic irony he announced:

"I was a conservative in the last session of this Congress, but I mean to be a radical henceforth."

Representative Julian was gratified to find that sentiment in favor of treating the Southern states as conquered territories had gained ground, for the election results were viewed widely as a mandate for dealing sternly with the presumptuous and uncowed rebels.

Congress assembled on December 3, and the President's State of the Union message was heard in sour silence. The draft of the message had been read to the cabinet two weeks before, and had been approved by every member except Stanton; he regretted that it failed to include endorsement of the Fourteenth Amendment, but when nobody supported his position, he dropped his objections. He would not approve, he said, but he would make no objection to the message.

The document was noticeably calm, courteous in phrasing, and logical in its deductions. The President reviewed the national unrest, and stressed that the restoration of "peace, harmony, and fraternal feeling" was the need of the hour. And once more he struck at the continued exclusion of Southerners from Congress.

"A dreary, lifeless document," said the *Nation*. But Sam Milligan termed it "the offspring of a mind conscious of its own rectitude," and congratulated Johnson, whose combativeness he knew, upon having ignored the abuse with which he was being buffeted and resisting the temptation to indulge in "intemperance of language."

Before the session was an hour old, Senator Sumner introduced a bill to impose Negro suffrage on the District of Columbia. The measure was sped through both houses and on December 14 was sent to the President. A veto was predicted. On January 4 Johnson read his veto message to the cabinet, and all approved it except Stanton. He produced a written opinion to the effect that he had examined the bill carefully, found nothing contrary to the Constitution in it, and he recommended that it be signed. Since the question was one of expediency, not of legality, his opinion was mere word-spinning. Grant was present by invitation that day, and he expressed himself emphatically against the bill, not because it disfranchised ex-rebels (he rather liked that, Welles gathered), but because he thought it a "very contemptible business" for members of Congress whose own states denied the ballot to Negroes to force it on the district. Only a short while previously the voters of the district had rejected the proposition by seven thousand to thirty-six.

The veto went to the Capitol on January 7, and was overridden by both houses in jig time, amid sturdy applause.

A contest then developed between two representatives—Benjamin Loan of Missouri, and James M. Ashley of Ohio—to be the first to secure the honor of opening a frontal assault upon the "usurper" of the White House. Loan got the floor, and in disconnected remarks referred to the assassination of Lincoln and to "subsequent developments" which had shown it to be "the result of deliberate plans adopted in the interest of the rebellion . . . An assassin's bullet, wielded by rebel hands and paid for by rebel gold, made Andrew Johnson President," he said. "The price that he was to pay for his promotion was treachery."

This was stealing Representative Ashley's spite and fury, and by adroit parliamentary play he shuffled Loan aside to make his own speech on the same tragic event, invoking "the man who came into the Presidency through the door of assassination," and "the dark suspicion that crept over the minds of men as to his complicity in the assassination plot." With a show of repugnance, Ashley then introduced a resolution which began:

"I do impeach Andrew Johnson, Vice-President and acting President of the United States, of high crimes and misdemeanors."

The offenses listed included usurpation of power, violation of law, corrupt use of the appointive, the pardoning, and the veto powers, corrupt disposal of public property, and corrupt interference with elections. Therefore:

"Be it resolved, That the Committee on the Judiciary be authorized to investigate the official conduct of Andrew Johnson, Vice-President of the United States . . . and to report to this House whether . . . the said Andrew Johnson . . . has been guilty of acts which are designated or calculated to overthrow, subvert, or corrupt the government of the United States."

Stevens blocked debate, and the resolution was passed by one hundred and seven to thirty-nine. To the forty-five Republicans not voting, Stevens promised retribution; one holdout who protested that his conscience would not allow him to vote for such an outrageous proposal drew the snarled ejaculation:

"Damn your conscience! Vote with your party, or I will post you for a coward!"

Such "posting," the culprit knew, meant political excommunication.

During this time Secretary Browning discussed the subject of impeachment with his cabinet colleagues, Seward, McCulloch, and Randall. They scoffed at his fears. Though the threat had come into the open, it generated little concern at the White House.

The day after Ashley's resolution was adopted, the President conferred with the cabinet on the proposed Military Reconstruction Bill, which Stevens had introduced, and which dealt with the defeated South as a conquered territory.

The bill regrouped the ten states not represented in Congress into five military districts, each of which was to be governed by an army general, selected not by the President but by the commander of the army, General Grant. The district commanders were to be invested with powers comparable to those of an absolute monarch. The existing state governments were to be merely provisional until new ones were created; and the commanders could dismiss the governors, suspend elections, and void court orders at their discretion. This legislation was so revolutionary that the President felt it imperative to sound out the cabinet on it while the bill was still under discussion in the House. A show of unity among his advisers, he felt, would carry weight with the country, and might even influence waverers in Congress.

When he put the question to the cabinet, Johnson was unusually "pale and calm," Welles noticed, but his expression was one of "firm and fixed resolution."

Seward was in his place, having almost miraculously recovered from his latest brush with death. The old man seemed a little more deliberate, a little more detached, a little more disabused of illusions, but otherwise hardly changed in appearance, and his mind was as agile as ever. The scars on his right cheek (the sight of which caused Stevens to growl, "What a bungler was Payne!") stood out vividly, and he was sensitive about them; he never allowed himself to be photographed from that side any more.

Confronted by the President's question, the Secretary of State said thoughtfully that the discussion seemed to be premature, inasmuch as Congress had not yet passed the bill; still, never, under any circumstances, would he be brought to admit that a sovereign state could be destroyed or reduced to a territory.

McCulloch echoed Seward's feeling, and Browning was so eager to register his disapproval he broke in ahead of turn, and was brought up short by Stanton. The War Secretary prefaced his remarks by volunteering that he had "communicated his views to no man," although this had not been asked or suggested. Within the cabinet, he went on nervously, he had "cordially approved of every step which had been taken to reorganize the governments of the states which had rebelled," and he saw "no cause to change or depart" from that course. He had not seen the bill under discussion, and did not care to, for he thought it would all "end in noise and smoke." He had discussed the subject with only one member of Congress, he added—Senator Sumner—and that had been a year before; beyond that he had conversed with neither Sumner nor anyone else on the matter. He did not concur in Sumner's views, and he did not think a state could be "remanded to a territorial condition."

Stanton seemed under some compulsion to go on record, and his extensive and overdetailed statement was made in a very positive tone. It was, in fact, so forcefully put that for once Welles and Stanton agreed.

Attorney General Stanbery denied the power of Congress to "dismantle states," and as for expediency, "it is never expedient to do that which we have no power to do."

All having expressed their opposition (Postmaster General Randall was not present), the President then brought up the subject of Ashley's impeachment resolution. Nobody except Browning was inclined to take this seriously. Ashley was known to be as fanatical as he was unscrupulous, and it was thought that his main objective was to attract notoriety.

The debate on the Military Reconstruction Bill rolled along in the House, and in closing the discussion, Stevens rose to impressive heights. This bill would impose the policy he long had advocated, and to urge it he brought irony, wit, eloquence, and invective to bear. None present, spectator or congressman, ever forgot the gaunt, withered, ancient figure, like some Old Testament prophet, uttering with preternatural solemnity:

"If, sir, I might presume upon my age, without claiming any of the wisdom of Nestor, I would suggest to the young people around me that the deeds of this burning crisis, of this solemn day, of this thrilling moment, will cast their shadows far into the future, and will make their impress upon the annals of our history; and that we shall appear upon the bright pages of that history just in so far as we cordially, without guile, without bickering, without small criticisms, lend our aid to promote the great cause of humanity and universal liberty."

At the end he seemed rejuvenated, his eyes flashed, and he exclaimed "with good old Laertes—Heaven rules as yet, and there are gods above!"

The roll was called, and the bill was adopted by one hundred and nine to fifty-five.

The Senate found imperfections in the measure which it proceeded to set right. Selection of the district commanders was restored to the President, as commander-in-chief, and steps were outlined by which the rebel states could regain admission. These included ratification of the Fourteenth Amendment and adoption of new constitutions drafted by conventions elected by all citizens, regardless of color. These constitutions might disfranchise ex-Confederates, but they must give the vote to the Negroes. The constitutions must be ratified by the same electorate that chose the conventions, whereupon Congress would examine them, and if found satisfactory, senators and representatives who could take the "ironclad" loyalty oath would be admitted.

When the Senate agreed to these amendments, Sumner rushed from the chamber, uttering curses.

The House also took umbrage at what it considered a watering down of the original bill; but since the end of the session was near, in order to prevent a pocket veto, Stevens consented to the changes, and the measure went to the President.

A last-minute surprise had been provided by Senator Reverdy Johnson. After speaking against the bill, he had turned around and voted for it, to the disgust of the President's partisans.

Three days previously, another bill of far-reaching implications had been handed to the President for his signature. This was the so-called Tenure of Office Bill, which provided that no officeholder who had been appointed by the President, with the advice and consent of the Senate, could be removed by the President except with the Senate's consent. The bill did allow the President to *suspend* an appointive officer, should Congress not be in session, and report the reasons for the suspension to the Senate within twenty days after its reconvening. Should the Senate approve, the suspension would become dismissal; should the Senate disapprove, the suspended official would thereby be reinstated. Violations would carry a penalty of fine and imprisonment.

This measure was designed to restrict the President's patronage powers, and the debates on it in Congress had become a seminar in semantics. As first drawn and passed by the House, the members of the President's cabinet had been exempted from its provisions. In the Senate, however, an amendment was offered to strike out this exemption. Senator Sumner made a four-day speech in support of this amendment, maintaining that the bill was an answer to the need of the moment to protect the country against its chief executive; a need, he said, which had never arisen before, because there had been "no President of the United States who had become an enemy to his country." Andrew Johnson, he said, was "the successor of Jefferson Davis . . . a terror to the good and a support to the wicked." His "beastly intoxication" was of little moment, compared to his subsequent "treason."

Other senators objected strenuously to the cabinet proposal. How, they asked, could one possibly deprive the President of the right to choose his own constitutional advisers, and to get rid of any who became hostile, faithless, or personally obnoxious?

"If we adopt this amendment," said John Sherman, "we compel the President to retain in office . . . any man who has not the courtesy to retire . . . I cannot imagine a case where a cabinet officer would hold on to his place in defiance of and against the wishes of his chief; and if such a case should occur, I certainly . . . would not protect him."

Finally, a compromise was worked out which provided that cabinet members should "hold their office respectively for and during the term of the President by whom they may have been appointed, and for one month thereafter, subject to removal by and with the consent of the Senate."

Senator Doolittle demonstrated that under this restriction, Stanton, Seward, and Welles were not protected from dismissal because they had been appointed by President Lincoln and had never been appointed by President Johnson, but merely held over; hence, the President might remove them at any time without hindrance.

No senator disputed this contention, and Senator Sherman brushed it aside as immaterial. "We do not legislate in order to keep in the Secretary of War, the Secretary of the Navy, or the Secretary of State," he replied impatiently. "And if I supposed that either of these gentlemen was so wanting in manhood, in honor, as to hold his place after the politest intimation by the President of the United States that his services were no longer needed, I certainly, as a senator, would consent to his removal at any time, and so would we all."

On this basis the bill was passed and sent to the White House for approval.

Even while the measure was being voted upon, Stanton was making trouble in the cabinet. Congress had called on the President to supply whatever information he might have regarding failure to enforce the Civil Rights Act. Johnson passed the request to the heads of the departments, who promptly sent in reports—all except Stanton, that is. He waited four weeks, and then without forewarning, at a meeting of the cabinet, produced a sheaf of papers which he said constituted his report, supplemented and amplified by separate reports from General Grant and General Howard, the head of the Freedmen's Bureau.

Everyone present was astonished by this action. Welles castigated Stanton's report as "an omnium gatherum of newspaper gossip, rumors of Negro murders, neighborhood strifes and troubles, amounting to four hundred and forty in number—vague, indefinite party scandal, which General Howard and his agents had picked up in newspapers and all other ways," without supporting proof of any kind.

Browning denounced the report as a mass of unauthenticated allegations, and pointed out that what Congress had called for was "information that had come to the knowledge of the President," and presumably had been investigated by him.

The motive behind Stanton's action seemed clear: it was to embarrass the President by compelling him either to pass along the report, unexamined, undigested, unverified, yet presumably stating true facts, or to withhold it and be accused of suppressing information. Browning thought Stanton "impudent," "mean" and "malicious," especially since Stanton said there was little doubt that members of Congress already had seen the report—"quite likely had copies." The only source from which copies could come was the War Department.

After a heated discussion, the cabinet advised that the report be transmitted, with a statement by the President that it had been brought to his attention for the first time that day, and that the information it contained would be investigated promptly.

Johnson was visibly angered by Stanton's sly move, and some time later he alluded to it to Welles.

"I wonder if he supposes that he is not understood," the President questioned, and Welles saw latent fire in his eyes, while his manner betrayed intense, though suppressed, feeling. Welles reflected that few men possessed stronger emotions than Johnson, and fewer still had "the power of restraining themselves when evidently excited."

This self-control was telling painfully on the President's health, and he confided to Colonel Moore that he feared a serious return of his old malady, the gravel.

On February 22, a week after the episode of Stanton's surprise report, Johnson laid both the Military Reconstruction Bill and the Tenure of Office Bill before the cabinet and asked their recommendations. On the Military Reconstruction Bill, everyone except Stanton advised a veto. The Tenure of Office Bill was laid aside for later consideration, and the President brought up the impeachment question. A bill had been introduced in the House providing for the arrest and suspension of the President, in the event of impeachment, before his trial by the Senate. Should such an attempt be made to depose him without trial, in violation of the express provisions of the Constitution, the President asked, what course should he pursue? The opinion was unanimous that such an attempt would be revolutionary and he should resist it.

At their next meeting, the cabinet took up the Tenure of Office Bill. Here again unanimity was attained, everyone advising Johnson to veto the measure. Stanton was the most emphatic of all in his objections. "No man with a proper sense of honor would remain in the cabinet when invited to resign," he agreed, but the whole bill was obnoxious. His earnestness was so pronounced, Johnson asked him to write the veto. But Stanton begged off because of rheumatism in his arm, which made writing painful. Johnson then applied to Seward, who consented to take on the task if Stanton would furnish the authorities. And so the message was written.

The veto of the Military Reconstruction Bill, a more elaborate document, meanwhile was being put into shape with the help of Jeremiah S. Black, a superb advocate and formidable legal authority. Draft after draft was made, Johnson and Attorney General Stanbery assisting, until the twenty-thousand-word message was completed.

On Saturday, March 2, the last day of the session, both vetoes were sent to the Capitol. Without ado, both were overridden, amid congratulations of the majority upon having at last scotched the viper in the White House.

The spite of Congress against Andrew Johnson, "acting President of the United States," found other legislative expression that day.

A supplementary thirty-five thousand dollars was voted to complete repairs and refurnishing of the Executive Mansion (a task being carried out under the thrifty supervision of Martha Patterson), with the stipulation that "no further payments shall be made on any accounts [for this purpose] until such accounts shall have been submitted to a joint committee of Congress and approved by such committee." The President's bookkeeping was not to be trusted.

Also, more money was voted to push work on a new district jail.

5.

"What do you suppose the vulgarian of the White House thinks of his fight with treason 'at this end of the line' by this time?" gloated Charles Sumner to a friend while the President was sustaining these fresh reverses. "How very contemptible he must appear just now, even in his own villainous eyes! Our only purpose in retaining him even a day longer is simply to compel him to fill the measure of his shame by draining to the very dregs the cup of bitter, blasting humiliation that shall be held remorselessly to his lips . . . until he complete the degradation of his *own accursed section* by executing the high behests of that body he presumed to denounce and affected to despise!"

Lawmakers whose minds traveled in such grooves were scarcely the ones to weigh dispassionately the President's most recent veto messages. Yet those arraignments of the course of Congress were worth weighing. Early in January General Sherman had indicated as much to his brother the senator, warning:

"If the President is impeached and the South reduced to territories, the country will, of course, relapse into a state of war, or quasi-war, and what good it will do passes my comprehension."

The veto of the Tenure of Office Bill was based on the precedent followed by the government since 1789, and it referred to President Lincoln's wholesale removals, which had never been challenged. The bill was held to be without constitutional warrant, and the message appealed for cessation of attempts to rewrite the Constitution by statute, or by any means except the processes it laid down.

The Military Reconstruction Bill veto, a more extended protest, breathed intense concern. The bill, the President said, placed "all the people of the ten states therein named under the absolute domination of military rulers." The bill's preamble averred that legal governments did not exist in those states, whereas in fact they all had governments organized as regularly as the government of any state of the Union. The allegation that life and property were inadequately safeguarded in the South the President denied, on the basis of all the information procurable. By prescribing the steps that the people of the ten states must take to regain their place in the Union, after they had already complied with the demands made upon them, the bill did not, as it erroneously contended, contribute towards peace and promote harmony; it had, rather, been enacted not "for any purpose of order, or for the prevention of crime, but solely . . . [for] the purpose of coercing the people in the adoption of principles and measures to which it is known that they are opposed, and upon which they have an undeniable right to exercise their own judgment."

The powers of the military district commanders were exposed as more than kinglike. The commander's "mere will is to take the place of all law . . . He may make a criminal code of his own . . . He is bound by no rules of evidence; there is indeed no provision by which he is authorized or required to take any evidence at all. Everything is a crime which he chooses to call so, and all persons are condemned whom he pronounces to be guilty." Even worse, the commander could delegate his power, amounting to "absolute despotism," to as many subordinates as he wished, creating a multitude of petty despots, and reducing the population of the ten states "to the most abject and degrading slavery." For five hundred years, no British monarch had ruled with such power, the message expostulated, nor during all that time would English-speaking people anywhere "have borne such servitude."

This was a time of peace; there was no war, no rebellion, no insurrection in any state; the federal courts were open and functioning; and the President cited the Supreme Court's categorical decision that martial law could constitutionally obtain only under conditions of invasion or warfare, and where recourse to the civil courts was impeded or impossible.

Reverting to a fundamental objection, the President maintained that the people of the South were entitled to a hearing on measures that would decide "the destiny of themselves and their children." Moreover, here was involved a principle vitally important "not only during the life of the present generation, but for ages to come." The bill had been passed while ten states were denied representation, and this very fact justified its rejection as legislation that, "looking solely to the attainment of political ends, fails to consider the rights it transgresses, the law which it violates, or the institutions which it imperils."

That most members of Congress actually heard this solemn exhortation when it was read in the droning voices of reading clerks in the House and Senate—or that they heard it with any feeling except exacerbation and resentment—was doubtful. In the Senate, certainly, the more self-important senators (and no self-importance equals that of a United States senator who is aware of his importance) unanimously sputtered at being thus "lectured like dullards" and told to mind their constitutional p's and q's; why, there was not a member of that august body who was not better educated than the tailor Andy Johnson!

The depth of the President's feeling against the bill he showed in conversation with his secretary, Colonel Moore. Rather than sign a measure which in time of peace deprived American citizens of the right of habeas corpus, said Johnson fervently, "I would sever my right arm from my body." And after the bill had been enacted over his veto, he returned to the subject, exclaiming: "Too bad, too bad, this law which practically breaks up the government to satisfy bitter partisan feelings. If by leaving my right arm upon this battlefield, and having it severed from my body with a cleaver, I could settle this question, it would soon be disposed of."

Obviously Johnson was tired, but his opponents gave him no respite. In order to be available for instant action, should the executive require further disciplining, the Fortieth Congress was organized immediately on the expiration of its predecessor, on March 4. And the motive behind Senator Reverdy Johnson's surprising switch to the radical side on the Military Reconstruction Bill came to light on that day. At one o'clock on March 4, a letter from the senator was handed to the President; it requested the appointment of the Marylander's son-in-law as United States attorney at Baltimore—an appointment which would have to be confirmed by the radical Senate.

"As cool a piece of assurance as I have ever witnessed!" ejaculated the President on reading the request. Nevertheless he made the appointment, and the radical Senate confirmed it—causing the crusty Welles to mutter about "political prostitutes."

Ben Butler was sworn in as a member of the new House—the same Butler whom the detective, Allan Pinkerton, had once characterized in a report to the War Department on wartime financial scandals, as "the biggest villain God Almighty ever put guts in." The impeachment investigation by the House Judiciary Committee claimed Butler's earnest attention, the incoming Congress having authorized a continuation of that so far fruitless search for evidence of presidential high crimes and misdemeanors. Soon committee sleuths were scouring the country to uncover possible wrongdoing in Johnson's past, public or private. A detective was sent to Tennessee to dig up testimony that Johnson was known there as a drunkard. In Greeneville, Lewis Self, who had long been foreman of the Andy Johnson tailor shop, was sounded out by this consensus-taker on Andy's drinking habits. The "Squire" eyed the questioner up and down, spat, and drawled:

"Well, I'll tell you this: Andy Johnson never got so drunk he disremembered his friends."

A star witness before the committee was Lafayette C. Baker, recent general and former head of Stanton's secret police, whom President Johnson had kicked out of the White House after catching him in the act of setting spies there. Baker swore that he had seen a letter that Johnson wrote, while military governor of Tennessee, to Jefferson Davis; unfortunately, the letter could not be found, and the "reliable persons" whom Baker named as able to confirm its existence turned out to exist only in Baker's imagination.

An attempt was made to implicate Johnson in shady railroad financing in Tennessee, but Stanton assumed responsibility for the operations in question. Rumor persisted that Johnson had a fortune tucked away in railroad bonds, and the committee summoned the cashier of the First National Bank of Washington, where the President maintained his personal account, and ordered him to produce the records. The cashier demurred, contending that such information was confidential. Going to Johnson for advice, he was met with cheerful permission to show the committee anything they wanted to inspect, to hold back nothing. The investigation revealed that Johnson's modest fortune was invested, not in railroad bonds, but in securities of the United States.

This fishing did wound Johnson, however, though only his secretary Moore was allowed to see it. One day, speaking of the indignity, the President came as near to bitterness as Moore ever heard him, saying:

"I have had a son killed, a son-in-law die during the last battle at Nashville, another son has thrown himself away, another son-in-law is in no better condition, and I think I have had sorrow enough without having my bank account examined by a committee of Congress."

He was not to be spared. Long since, he had been moved to

protest to General Thomas, commanding in Tennessee, against the despoiling of his home in Greeneville. The fences had been broken, the glass knocked out of the windows, the walls were scribbled with obscenities against "Andy the traitor," and at one time the building had housed a Negro brothel. This final degradation had brought a preemptory order to Thomas to rectify matters; but the house was still technically held as "abandoned property" by the War Department, in the jurisdiction of the Freedmen's Bureau.

At times he grew weary of the struggle, and then the quiet, unassuming support of Eliza, Martha, and Mary sustained him. Isolated in the White House, Eliza Johnson yet knew how the winds of passion were beating upon her husband, and she never allowed him to consider departing from the course that he judged to be right, and best for the nation. So long as he followed his conscience, Eliza comforted him, they should not worry about the outcome.

In the midst of all the criminations, Martha filled her position as White House hostess with unruffled tact and propriety. She took charge of her mother's mail, which often was large; she saw every petitioner, listened to every complaint, and presided socially with dignity and complete competence. The state dining room had been redecorated and was now the scene of entertainments worthy of the President's House. At banquets, every detail was in good taste, the food, wines, service, and table appointments of the finest. The President was a genial host, seated in a high-backed chair behind which proudly stood the attentive Sam, his body servant; his conversation was easy and varied, both surprising and pleasing some of the distinguished guests.

The President met every demand of etiquette his position imposed. When George Peabody, the nation's first grand-scale philanthropist, announced his gift of three and a half million dollars to reestablish schools in the devastated South, the President called at Peabody's hotel immediately to extend the nation's thanks.

Such activities the radicals were willing to allow him, since they had shorn him of power, had tamed, corralled, and hobbled him, as they thought. They could pass laws as they wished; so let him go his ignominious, ceremonial way, bowing on cue, uttering vapid amenities, enacting the pantomime of a phantom President. The Military Reconstruction and Tenure bills were not the only vetoes that Congress had hooted down. A second Freedmen's Bureau bill had been passed, containing most of the objectionable features of the first; it had been vetoed; and it had been repassed without either House or Senate paying the veto message the courtesy of a reading.

Congress also had taken away the President's effective control of the military establishment, although constitutionally he remained commander-in-chief. A rider attached to the Army Appropriation Bill provided that all orders must be routed through the commanding general, who was Grant; and further, that the commanding general's headquarters must be in Washington. Johnson had wished to veto this provision, but had been unable to without vetoing the entire bill and running the risk of leaving the men in the ranks unpaid for lack of funds. Under protest, he had acquiesced in this humiliating condition—which was the precise measure Stanton had dictated to Boutwell, months before.

One objective of Congress in passing this act was to retain Grant in Washington, where he could be wooed, and, the radicals hoped, won to their side. Grant's behavior had been enigmatic for some time. Celebrated for his taciturnity, he maintained a cryptic silence, and his actions were watched from day to day to descry the bent of his sympathies. The Republicans were dangling a glittering bait—the presidential nomination in 1868—and Grant was not unresponsive. Unfortunately, he was not inured to political intrigue, and his ineptitude hampered both his well-wishers and his own far from subtle moves. In the judgment of the man who possibly knew him most thoroughly, General Rawlins, Grant was apt at only one human activity—fighting.

Browning was startled to receive a visit from Rawlins one day and to hear him analyze Grant unsparingly as a man headed for a fall. This Rawlins would like to prevent, if possible. He was convinced that Grant at heart was conservative, but he was no match for clever politicians, let alone statesmen. "He knows how to do nothing but fight," said Rawlins. The radicals wanted to use him for their own ends, and he was "a little unsettled about it"; the temptation was "beginning to make an impression." Grant was a man "of strong passions and intense prejudices," Rawlins went on, and if pushed into politics would probably make a spectacle of himself.

Browning himself thought Grant was veering towards radicalism, and the fact certainly was that the general had been a failure at every occupation he had tried in civilian life. Now plunged into the heady atmosphere of Washington, and tempted by the lure of the presidency, at the same time aware that the outcome of the raging constitutional struggle might well depend upon himself and the army, Grant was in a vulnerable position. He was unschooled in government, and because of his phenomenal success in the war, without having had any prophetic preparation, acquiring skill as he went along, he had become imbued with the belief that he could succeed at anything. That he was developing an itch to take a hand in the game of politics, and at a table where the stakes were highest, was evident; but so far he had played somewhat like the yokel who fancies he can outguess the thimblerigger at the county fair, or the sandlot pitcher who undertakes to strike out the hitters of the big league. Washington was no place for fledgling politicians; there assembled the big-timers who played rough, as the little general was in a fair way of learning.

In May the long-sustained agitation for closing the books on the case of Jefferson Davis brought results, when the former President of the Confederacy was remanded to the civil authorities to stand trial for treason at Richmond. For weeks his case had been under study by the President and cabinet. The December decision of the Supreme Court in *Ex parte Milligan* had forced the action. The court had ruled that military tribunals could not try civilians in time of peace in regions where civil courts were operating. Davis had been held by the military authorities for two years, under indictment for treason; but now Attorney General Stanbery was adamant that he could not be tried by a military commission, but must be turned over to the civil courts. Since no one could imagine a Virginia jury bringing in a conviction, such a course would be tantamount to unconditional release of the man whom Johnson had denounced again and again as the arch traitor of all.

Every time the subject was broached, Stanton had become excited. He vehemently opposed letting Davis out of the clutches of the military. He insisted that the army could hold the Confederate ex-President as long as it wished and could do with him whatever it cared to. On the topic of Jefferson Davis, in fact, the War Secretary seemed unbalanced.

Johnson never doubted that Davis ought to hang. But the law was binding; and after searching consultations, the transfer was made, although reluctantly. As expected, Davis was at once freed on bail (Horace Greeley signing the bond) and was never brought to trial.

This incident was seized upon by the impeachment investigators, but again they were stymied when it transpired that the only two persons who still desperately wanted to hang Jeff Davis were Edwin Stanton and Andy Johnson.

About this time word was brought to the President, through the wife of a Judiciary Committee clerk, that if valid evidence to impeach the President could not be found, some would be manufactured. Sinister moves were being disclosed. "Impeachment Ashley" was visiting the prison where a perjurer named Conover was confined. Conover had been a government witness in the 1865 trial of the Lincoln assassins, and later had been convicted of perjury and subornation of perjury in that case. In great indignation, Conover wrote to the President saying that Ashley had promised remission of his sentence if he would swear that Johnson was implicated in the assassination and "find" proofs to back up the accusation. Conover revealed this activity only after he came to suspect that Ashley intended to renege on his promise. Ben Butler became involved in the clandestine attempt, but nothing of value to the impeachers was uncovered.

While this tragic farce was being enacted, a former congressman from Indiana dropped in on Secretary Welles to renew their acquaintance. He had just come from the White House, he said, where he had been reminded of something that had occurred in the summer of 1861. He was then in Cincinnati, on the way to Washington for the extra session of Congress called by President Lincoln at the start of the war. He had finished his breakfast, and was sitting on the piazza of the hotel, when a troop of cavalry clattered up. Both riders and horses looked jaded. The column opened up, and a civilian in a dusty coat trotted forward and dismounted.

That man, Welles's caller said, was Andrew Johnson, and he looked exhausted. A senator from Tennessee, he was on his way to Washington at the call of the President, and the military authorities had provided the escort to guard him through the state of Kentucky. He had just come from Tennessee, where the rebel authorities had posted him as a fugitive and a traitor.

Now there was talk of impeaching that man.

"I little thought," the speaker said, "that I should ever hear Andrew Johnson denounced as a rebel, or a sympathizer with rebels—that partisan malice would ever accuse him of want of fidelity to the Union. But God only knows what we are coming to in these radical times! Such a patriot as Johnson, who has suffered so much and done so much, deserves better treatment from his countrymen."

Tears of shame trickled down the man's cheeks.

6.

At the White House, there were moments when the President's patience wore thin. When during a cabinet meeting Secretary McCulloch urged a course of action on the ground that it would tend to head off impeachment, Johnson flared up. "Impeach and be damned!" he exclaimed; he was tired of being threatened, and he intended to "go forward in the conscientious discharge of my duty, without reference to Congress, and meet the consequences."

Johnson was coming to rate McCulloch and Browning as excessively timid under Congressional rumblings. Although both were devoted to the President and his policy, they were not combative. Browning, as a lawyer, was too habituated to looking at both sides of a question, while McCulloch, a banker, had never been involved in a no-holds-barred political gouging match. And everything these days took on a political tinge. Moore was amused one Sunday afternoon when the doorkeeper came in to ask the President whether he would require the carriage; Cooper, the coachman, wanted to know. To himself the President muttered, "I wonder how he wishes to spend his afternoon." Then

lifting his head, "Tell him I will not want him." And again solilo-
quizing, "I might interfere with some of this gentleman's 'rights.' "

The President often relaxed with Moore; he was lonely in his
isolation. The conversation covered many subjects.

"I missed my vocation," said the President once. "If I had been
educated in early life, I would have been a schoolmaster. I have
always had the sense of the importance of instructing people in
the right ideas. Ministers and schoolmasters—consider their responsibilities. You educate one little girl in proper ideas, and
some day she may transmit to her child the good you have sown.
Yes, I ought to have been a schoolmaster and a chemist. It would
have satisfied my desire to analyze things, to examine them in
separate periods and then unite them again to view them as a
whole." After a moment of reflection, he added, "Heroics and
mysteries always seem to thrive with the artful."

Moore was impressed by the President's responsiveness to literary beauty. During a discussion of poetry, Johnson recited with
much feeling Gray's "Elegy in a Country Churchyard":

> "Let not Ambition mock their useful toil,
>   Their homely joys, and destiny obscure;
> Nor Grandeur hear with a disdainful smile
>   The short and simple annals of the poor."

The line, "the dark, unfathom'd caves of ocean bear," he repeated over and over, savoring its "grandeur and solemnity," un-
approachable, he thought, in all literature. At other times he
reeled off passages from Wendell Phillips's literary orations,
which he greatly admired—the tribute to Washington, the words
on Napoleon, and "The Irish Orator." In his opinion, Phillips
could be faulted on the monotony of his style; he "would mount
his Pegasus and soar above the clouds from the beginning to the
end of his speeches, with no variation in thought"; and this kept
him from being appreciated as highly as he merited, in Johnson's
view.

The President's range of information surprised his staff. Coming into the outer office late one evening, he found a youthful
secretary immersed in a book. Inquiring the subject and being
told it was China, Johnson sat down, put his feet up on the desk,

and discoursed for half an hour on the history of China, its people, and the philosophy of Confucius.

This same secretary, who was something of a wag, ran afoul of the President's imperviousness to jokes. Johnson opened the door of his private office and asked what was the Christian name of a man to whom he was dictating a letter. The wag answered:

"Mr. President, he had no Christian name; he is Jewish."

Johnson stared, said nothing; but a moment later, through the closed door, was heard inquiring what was the "first name" of the man in question.

In the secretaries' room there stood a tall, awkward desk which was not used and was in the way. One of the secretaries ordered it to be removed, but the President happening to enter just as the desk was being carried out, sharply countermanded the order.

"That desk was used by General Jackson," he instructed. "I revere Andrew Jackson, and as long as I occupy the White House that desk will remain in its place."

Remain it did, and the rebuffed secretary was gratified every time Johnson barked his shins on it.*

After the strain of the major vetoes, the President's vigor seemed to return, and he displayed a cheerfulness unusual for him. A fight always invigorated him. A woman writer for the ultra-radical *Independent* was amazed by both his vitality and his serenity when she glimpsed him strolling the White House lawn one afternoon. "His step was strong and comfortable and slow," she reported, and he did not look tired at all. "A smile brightened the clogged lines of his face," which actually was "not unkind." In every way he typified to her "a gentleman of leisure, gloved, caned, his iron-gray hair rolled smoothly under," taking his promenade with placid composure. The picture hardly resembled the ogre she had been told she would find.

By midsummer the impeachment bugaboo seemed headed for limbo. There was a momentary flurry of excitement when Ben Butler brought to light the hitherto concealed diary that had

---

* Johnson was not witty and had little understanding of wit in others, although he was capable of humor. A man who dressed flashily and seemed to prance, rather than stride or walk, he described jocularly as "like a stud horse in springtime, with a red surcingle and a broad forehead band studded with brass tacks."

been found on John Wilkes Booth's body. Several pages had been cut or torn out, and Butler demanded to know "who spoliated that book?" Drawing sinister conclusions, he proceeded to infer that the motive for the mutilation had been to remove evidence of Andrew Johnson's connection with Lincoln's murder.

The book had not been produced at the conspirators' trial in 1865, Butler charged, because it would have shown conclusively that Mrs. Surratt knew nothing whatever about the plot to kill Lincoln, but only about a previous plot to kidnap him. The responsibility for this concealment he hurled at Representative John A. Bingham, one of Mrs. Surratt's prosecutors, after the latter had taunted Butler with having voted fifty-seven times to nominate Jefferson Davis for President of the United States in 1860.

Butler retorted that he had never made any secret of those votes, and that he could live with the memory of them more comfortably than Bingham could with the knowledge that he had shed the blood of a woman "convicted without sufficient evidence." This he followed with a series of insinuating questions: "Who was it that could profit by assassination who could not profit by capture and abduction [of Lincoln]?" Who was it whom the conspirators "expected . . . would succeed Lincoln, if the knife made a vacancy?"

But this sensation faded when even Bingham repelled "with scorn and contempt" the inference that the President was an assassin.

Johnson had immediately ordered Secretary Stanton to provide an accurate copy of the mysterious diary, about which he had known nothing until then, together with "a succinct statement of all the facts connected with its capture, and its possession by the War Department." After looking over the documents, and showing them to the cabinet, Johnson inquired whether there could be any objection to their publication. Stanton violently opposed publication; the others saw no reason to forbid it.

The would-be impeachers had suffered a setback already in the election of Ben Wade to be president *pro tempore* of the Senate. By law, should Johnson be impeached and removed from office, the president of the Senate would succeed, there being no Vice-

President. But while Wade as a fighter for reforms was admirable, he was suspected of so many heretical notions that the thought of him in the White House frightened businessmen and political conservatives. The *Washington Chronicle* believed that most Republicans, "sooner than Wade should be President, will welcome the deluge." Wade had protested that he was no parliamentarian, but the radicals wanted to have a man in the chair who would know how to rule in their favor when the necessity arose.

Among Wade's vagaries was his belief that women should be allowed to vote. He also meditated a crusade to bring about a more even distribution of wealth. To a reporter he said openly that "a system which degrades the poor man and elevates the rich, which makes the rich richer and the poor poorer, which drags the very soul out of a poor man for a pitiful existence, is wrong." In an impromptu speech in Kansas, he would say that "Congress, which has done so much for the slave, cannot quietly regard the terrible distinction which exists between the man that labors and him that doesn't. And if you dullheads can't see this," he flung at the crowd of men, "the women will, and will act accordingly."

These things were remembered and chalked up against the sentiment for impeaching Johnson and making Wade President, to the discomfiture of Ashley, Boutwell, and a few others as fanatically inclined.

The Fortieth Congress had found it necessary to enact a second Reconstruction Bill, to correct blunders in the first. When this, too, received the Presidential veto, it was repassed without delay. Butler fought to hold Congress in continuous session after that, averring that "Andrew Johnson is a bad man, and this House and this Senate should sit here and take care of his acts"; but though Sumner in the Senate also pronounced Johnson "a bad man . . . search history and I am sure that you will find no other ruler who, during the same short space of time, has done so much mischief to his country," a recess was taken until July.

In the cabinet circle, tension had increased. Since the Tenure of Office Act, Stanton had tended more and more to show hostility to the President's views. After his emphatic disapproval of the Tenure of Office Bill, Johnson had hinted repeatedly that Stanton's resignation would be acceptable, but the Secretary was impervious to hints. The President disliked to ask for the resignation for several reasons: he did not like publicly to advertise the division among his advisers, and he still could not credit that Stanton could be utterly untrustworthy. About the competency of the War Secretary the President had never been in doubt.

When selection of the generals to command the five military districts under the Military Reconstruction Act was first debated, McCulloch and others had cautioned Johnson to choose dependable men, and they had been appalled when the President allowed Stanton to name the choices. To Johnson this seemed reasonable, since the commanders would be operating directly under the Secretary of War; but at least two of Stanton's choices were definitely unreliable from the President's point of view. These were General Daniel Sickles, to command in the Carolinas, and General Philip Sheridan, in Louisiana and Texas. Both men immediately gave trouble.

Hardly had he been installed when Sheridan removed from office Mayor Monroe of New Orleans, the Attorney General of Louisiana, and Judge Abell—three men who had tried to prevent the bloody rioting of a year before. Next Sheridan ousted the Board of Levee Commissioners, and when Johnson asked by what authority he had done so, replied arrogantly that he possessed the right, given by Congress, to make removals without consulting the President. A little after this he removed the governor, J. Madison Wells.

Meanwhile, at Charleston, General Sickles had stirred up a hornet's nest by setting aside court orders.

Attorney General Stanbery submitted his opinion that this action was illegal, and the cry went up from the radicals that the President was obstructing the operation of the Reconstruction laws.

This charge cut to the quick, for Johnson had hewed to the line of executing the laws passed, with or without his consent, to the best of his judgment and ability. That he was being accused of dereliction of duty stung, and he requested the Attorney General to submit a comprehensive interpretation of the Reconstruction Acts for the guidance of the military commanders.

In a series of protracted cabinet discussions, this interpretative opinion was gone over, point by point, and point by point Stanton controverted Stanbery's conclusions. Stanton was especially vehement in maintaining that the military commanders were omnipotent in their districts, that the President had no power to interfere with their actions. Although he could appoint and remove them, their actions were outside his control.

A renewed tussle with Congress to settle this issue was foreseen, and finally the cabinet voted (Stanton dissenting) to have the Attorney General's interpretation of the law sent out as his legal opinion, and not as an order from the commander-in-chief.

Among the things which Stanbery's opinion affected was the registration of voters that the commanders were obliged to carry out for the purpose of electing constitutional conventions. Sheridan conducted the registration in his district within a time limit that many believed was too short, and a multitude of protests came to the President. He ordered the general to extend the time, and Sheridan complained to Grant that the President's order practically opened "a broad macadamized road for perjury and fraud to travel on." This impertinence angered Johnson, and a rumor that Sheridan would be displaced gained currency. Against this possibility a howl went up from the camp of the radicals, where Sheridan was valued as the loyal liege of Congress; his popularity as a war hero was immense. The *Independent* cried out indignantly that "the people would throw a thousand Andrew Johnsons into the sea rather than permit one Phil Sheridan to walk the plank."

Congress returned in fighting mood, and swiftly passed a third reconstruction bill, which wiped out Stanbery's interpretation. This law not only empowered the district commanders to remove state officials, and set aside state laws, but enjoined upon them the duty of throwing out "all disloyal persons," and specifically made the commanders accountable for their actions not to the President, but to the General of the Army, Grant. The law said plainly that the commanders were not to be bound "by any opinion of any civil officer of the United States," starting with the highest.

The schism between the President and Congress thus became

absolute, and although lawyers argued the merits of the opposing positions there was no consensus of agreement. Although no lawyer, Johnson was able to see the issue clearly, thanks in part to his habit of narrowing his view so as to concentrate on one essential fact or set of facts. The prize for which he and Congress were contending, he grasped, was the independence and integrity of the presidency. He personally was incidental, of importance only because he happened to be the current embodiment of the presidency. But he—Andrew Johnson, the onetime bound boy of Raleigh—was the obstacle that Congress must get around before the legislative branch could absorb the total power of the government.

With this realization in mind, Johnson vetoed the latest reconstruction bill in a stern message. How absurd, he wrote, to require the President, under solemn oath, to execute the laws, and take away from him the power to perform that duty. By this bill the military commander in each district was "made to take the place of the President . . . and any attempt on the part of the President to assert his own constitutional powers may, under the pretense of law, be met by official insubordination." This he would never consent to. "I can never give my assent to be made responsible for the faithful execution of the laws, and at the same time surrender that trust, and the powers that accompany it, to any other officer, high or low, or to any number of executive officers."

Repassage of the measure over the veto was the contemptuous answer of Congress, and Johnson's declaration that he would not contribute to making the President a glorified stamp-licker for a rampaging legislature was taken as evidence of obduracy, "pigheadedness," and all-consuming ambition. General Robert Schenck, a representative from Ohio, called Johnson an "irresolute mule," and other epithets as colorful were showered upon "the man at the other end of the Avenue."

In a glow of satisfaction, Congress then recessed again until November.

In the meantime, counteractive measures taken by the President's friends had failed to create sentiment in his favor. By diligent cultivation of influential radicals like Sumner and Stevens, Secretary of State Seward had managed to secure ratification of the treaty to purchase Alaska from Russia for seven million dollars in gold. Expansion of the national territory seemed the sort of accomplishment that would arouse public enthusiasm, but instead, "Seward's folly" became a byword. Strong was disgusted by the acquisition of a "summer resort" which produced nothing but "a few furs diminishing in quantity as the otters and seals and so forth are yearly persecuted toward extermination." Ridicule swept the nation.

Strong noted at about the same time that "A. Johnson the Pigheaded" had passed through New York, but had "kept himself tolerably sober this time." The occasion was Johnson's visit to Boston, where he had been invited to take part in the dedication of the new Masonic Temple. Johnson had always been keenly interested in Masonry, and told his secretary once that he regretted that he had not been able to give more time to it, for he believed in its ideals of universal brotherhood. Before leaving Washington for Boston, the President had been invested with the degrees from fourth to thirty-second in a ceremony in his White House bedroom. He was deeply affected by the tribute, noting that several presidents before him had been Master Masons—Washington, Jefferson, Madison, Monroe, Jackson, Polk, and Buchanan.*

In New York and Boston on this trip the President was received with every mark of respect. He made no political speeches, no governors fled at his approach, and he returned in a happy mood.

Just previous to this outing he had journeyed to Raleigh, North Carolina, at the invitation of the governor and other state dignitaries, to preside at the unveiling of a monument over his father's grave. In 1865, when Sherman's army occupied Raleigh, the surgeon of an Ohio regiment had visited the cemetery where Jacob Johnson was buried, and found the grave marked with only a little stone on which were chiseled the initials "J. X. J." He suggested to the mayor of Raleigh that, in honor of the son Jacob Johnson had given to the nation, the appearance of the plot might be improved, and he had himself made the first contribution to a fund for that purpose.

The President had not seen his birthplace for many years, and

* He perhaps did not realize that a fellow Master Mason was Benjamin F. Butler.

his return was marked by elaborate celebration. He was accompanied by Seward and Randall, and was particularly touched by the demonstrations of affection on the part of the common people —the people of whom he was a part. His rise from insignificance to the highest dignities of the land, under the beneficent auspices of the Constitution, was the theme of earnest meditation during the journey. The contrast between "then" and "now" was brought home again after the return to Washington, by a pencil-scrawled letter from a hatter in Raleigh, named Neal Brown. It was addressed to "Mr. Andrew Johnson, P. of the U.S.," and read:

"It affords me Great pleasure to write to one who in our Boyish days spent so many happy moments in our Boyish plays many an hour have we spent at Cat and Base Ball and Bandy whitch was my choyest game . . . While on your visit to Raleigh I had a Great Desire to have seen you that we might have had a social chat. But there was such a desire of all to see you that I could not Rush up."

The writer recounted the "great troubles" he had suffered when Sherman's men stripped him of everything, even the tools of his trade, and "I was left without one muthful of any thing to eat all around where I lived fared as I did and my old woman is very much afflicted I am nearly blind . . ." He asked for nothing, merely wanted to wish Andy "a long life and a happy one and When you come to change worlds I pray that you may be recevd up to Glory where the wiced cease to trouble and the weary are at rest fare well."

From this evocation of an almost forgotten simplicity to the crosscurrents stirred up by the Reconstruction Acts was a sharp transition. Reports continued to reach the White House that General Sheridan was carrying things with a high hand in his district; an "ungovernable temper" and bad advice were blamed. The deposed governor, J. Madison Wells, did not hesitate to say that Sheridan had succumbed to an "inordinate ambition to make himself a great man"—which J. Madison Wells was not. Grant, whose special favorite was Phil Sheridan, seemed to Johnson to be covertly egging on his subordinate. When the latter applied to Grant for a positive instruction about obeying directions coming from the President, Grant had replied that such orders "had probably better be complied with," but Sheridan could use his judgment, because Congress might override anything emanating from the wrong end of Pennsylvania Avenue.

All this was muddying a situation already murky, and behind it, as the authority responsible, was the War Department, which meant Stanton and Grant. If it had not been for the War Department's backing "this damned extreme gang during the last session of the Thirty-ninth Congress, all this trouble would long since have been brought to a close," Johnson told Colonel Moore in a burst of candor. "If Stanton had proved all right at the beginning of Congress, senators and representatives from the excluded states would have been admitted before that Congress adjourned."

Of this the President was at last convinced. Yet taking punitive action was not only risky (it was bound to stir up a great commotion, and the country was plagued by commotion already), it was distasteful to Johnson. He could not forget that Stanton and he had stood shoulder to shoulder during the war; such services deserved consideration, no matter what their aftermath. He also knew that Lincoln had been sorely tried by the intractable War Secretary time and again. From the final step of requesting Stanton's resignation, therefore, the President held back as long as possible.

At this juncture the ghost of Mary Surratt intervened. That uneasy spirit had hovered accusingly over the White House for two years; now the spectral wraith moved in another direction.

John Surratt, the hanged woman's son, had been captured in Egypt and returned to this country, where he was on trial for his life as a conspirator in Lincoln's murder. During argument, a defense attorney made reference to a recommendation for mercy which had been presented on Mrs. Surratt's behalf. The startled prosecutor immediately queried the War Department, and Joseph Holt, the judge advocate general, personally delivered to the prosecutor a copy of the complete file in the case, accompanying it with his account of what had taken place.

In the file, in proper sequence, was indeed the recommendation for clemency signed by five judges of the military court. Holt vouched for the fact that the file, as he produced it, was the same that had been placed before the President on the day he signed the death warrants.

The prosecutor, relying on Holt's statement, announced in court:

"President Johnson, when the record was presented to him, laid it before his cabinet, and every single member voted to confirm the sentence, and the President with his own hand wrote his confirmation of it, and with his own hand signed the warrant . . . He signed the warrant with the paper [the clemency recommendation] right before his eyes—and there it is!"

This sensational disclosure blazed in headlines across the nation the next day, and President Johnson read it with disbelief, and then with wrath. It was impossible not to perceive behind this travesty of the truth, and the incredible concealment of the recommendation, an act of malicious treachery, committed by Holt and connived in by Holt's superior, the chief instigator of the 1865 military trial—Edwin Stanton.

The day on which the news was broadcast was Sunday.

On Monday morning, August 5, the President addressed a curt note to the Secretary of War:

"Sir:—Public considerations of a high character constrain me to say that your resignation as Secretary of War will be accepted.

"Very respectfully yours,
"Andrew Johnson,
"President of the United States."

Johnson directed Colonel Moore to deliver the note personally at once. Moore had once served as confidential secretary to Stanton, and he was embarrassed by his errand. Finding the secretary closeted with a visitor, Moore intruded long enough to hand the letter to Stanton, and withdrew before the latter read it.

At the same time Johnson demanded from the War Department the complete record on Mrs. Surratt. It was brought. He leafed through it minutely, and saw, in its proper place, the recommendation for clemency. At the top of the page were the telltale marks, the tears which indicated that it had once been ripped out, then restored. The yarn about the record having been submitted to the cabinet was false, as the President and every member of the cabinet knew.

"Very emphatically" Johnson told Moore that he had never seen the mercy petition, and had never heard of it until then. He recalled vividly how Holt had brought the file to him privately, when he was recovering from a severe illness; he recalled that the death warrant was already written out, in Holt's handwriting (there it lay in the file), ready for signature. He recalled positively that Holt had made no mention of any recommendation for commuting the sentence or otherwise extending mercy; and he clearly remembered that the judge advocate general had gathered up all the papers directly after Johnson's signature was affixed to the warrants, and had carried them away.

The conclusion was ineluctable: Holt had tricked him into sending to her death a woman about whose sentence even her judges had qualms; the mercy petition had been deliberately concealed, held back; and anyone who knew the subservient Holt would know that he was incapable of perpetrating so bold a fraud without the knowledge and sanction of his superior, the Secretary of War. Stanton was audacious; Holt was merely vindictive.

Monday passed with no reply from Stanton. The President was moody and nervous. He sought the opinion of others as to whether Stanton would bow out, and Welles thought he would. But the Navy Secretary feared the action had come too late. Johnson expressed regret that he had not heeded Welles's advice long before. He was now satisfied, he said, that Stanton had been "the prolific source of difficulties. You have alluded to this, but I was unwilling to consider it—to think that the man whom I trusted was plotting and intriguing against me."

Colonel Moore, from his knowledge of Stanton, doubted that he would resign; but the President was unable to see how any man with a spark of self-respect could refuse to quit under the circumstances. On Tuesday morning Stanton's answer came. It was dated the day before; the Secretary had taken time to consider his action carefully. The note was brief. It read:

"Sir—Your note of this day has been received, stating that public considerations of a high character constrain you to say that my resignation as Secretary of War will be accepted.

"In reply, I have the honor to say that public considerations of a high character, which alone have induced me to continue at the head of this department, constrain me not to resign the office of Secretary of War before the next meeting of Congress.

"Edwin M. Stanton,
"Secretary of War."

This was not brevity, this was insolence. Stanton proposed to take refuge behind the Tenure of Office Act and hold his ground until his friends in Congress should return to Washington to defend him.

Johnson seemed not to be surprised at the tenor of the note; if anything, he was relieved. His next step had already been decided upon. As he told Moore:

"I will leave Mr. Stanton hanging on the sharp hooks of uncertainty for a few days, and then suspend him."

Under the Tenure Act, since Stanton was invoking its protection, the President had the right to *suspend* him during the absence of Congress. He went about the business methodically.

First he had to make sure where Grant stood in the matter. Johnson had in mind appointing Grant secretary ad interim, to hold down the position until a final disposition was reached. But Grant's behavior lately had been equivocal, and Johnson deemed it wise to put the situation squarely, and find out whether Grant would play an assigned part in the drama. On the last day of July, the President had had a long talk with the general, chiefly concerning the impropriety of Sheridan's actions in Louisiana, and about the prospects of replacing Stanton. The next day the President had received from Grant a letter filled with strikingly radical views; the general wrote that it certainly was the intention of Congress to place a cabinet minister "beyond the power of executive removal, and it is pretty well understood that . . . the Tenure of Office bill was intended specially to protect the Sec. of War . . . The meaning of the law may be explained away by an astute lawyer, but common sense, and the mass of loyal people, will give to it the effect intended by its framers."

Sheridan, Grant further said, was "universally, and deservedly, beloved by the people who sustained this Government through its trials; and feared by them who would still be enemies of the Government." Therefore the "loyal people of this country" would not submit quietly to seeing "the very man of all others, who they have expressed confidence in, removed."

This letter the President had not replied to.

Now, calling Grant to the White House, Johnson explained his intentions regarding Stanton and asked whether Grant would accept appointment as secretary ad interim.

Confronted with the direct question, Grant answered ("with the hectic smile peculiar to him," Johnson later described the scene) that he would obey an order. This was not exactly an answer to the President's question, but Johnson accepted it. He then asked Grant plainly whether there was "anything between us," any cause of friction, that is, pointing out that there had been rumors of disagreement, and he believed he had a right to know; he wanted a straight answer.

Grant responded that there certainly was nothing personal between them, though there might be differences of opinion regarding the Fourteenth Amendment and the interpretation of the Reconstruction laws.

Acting on this reassurance, Johnson directed Moore to faircopy a notice already drafted, to be served on Stanton forthwith. This read:

"By virtue of the power and authority vested in me as President, by the Constitution and laws of the United States, you are hereby suspended from office as Secretary of War, and will cease to exercise all functions pertaining to the same. You will at once transfer to General Ulysses S. Grant, who has this day been authorized and empowered to act as Secretary of War ad interim, all records, books, papers, and other public property now in your custody and charge."

Another note was prepared officially informing Grant of his appointment as temporary Secretary. Both letters were dated Sunday, August 11, and were delivered personally by Moore on Monday morning.

Already Stanton had the word. On Sunday evening, after his talk with the President, Grant had appeared unexpectedly at Stanton's home, and taking the secretary into a room alone, had informed him of the pending action. The two men emerged from the room flushed and constrained in manner; and immediately after Grant had left, Stanton broke into wails to his wife that she had been right, he should have retired two years before; that now he was being tossed on the scrap heap, a broken man, without health, without money, discredited and dishonored.

By morning he had regained control of his nerves, and he received Colonel Moore politely when the latter called at ten o'clock. Handing Stanton the President's letter of suspension, Moore this time remained while the secretary read it slowly. Then the latter said, "I will give an answer."

The colonel then went to Grant's office nearby and delivered the President's note naming him temporarily to the secretaryship. Grant read the letter, folded it up, and responded laconically, "Very well."

Thereupon Moore left, and Grant composed a letter to Stanton, informing him officially of his appointment (which he designated an "assignment," in other words, an order), and appending somewhat effusively:

"I cannot let the opportunity pass without expressing to you my appreciation of the zeal, patriotism, firmness, and ability with which you have ever discharged the duties of Secretary of War."

Stanton's reply to Johnson, delivered the next morning by the hand of an aide, was defiant. He denied the right of the President to suspend him "without the advice and consent of the Senate and without legal cause"; but "inasmuch as the General Commanding the Armies of the United States has been appointed *ad interim*, I have no alternative but to submit, under protest, to superior force."

This seemed to intimate that the combined might of the armies of the United States had been required to expel the lone secretary from his office.

The President read the communication with a sense of relief. The prospect of a fight always affected him like a tonic, and to Moore he exclaimed:

"The turning point has at last come. The Rubicon has been passed."

Then, with deep feeling:

"Colonel Moore, you have no idea what Mr. Stanton has said and done against me!"

Headlines across the country sizzled with the dramatic announcement, and torrents of imprecation, congratulation, and muddled debate rolled off the presses.

Stanton, with a display of joyousness, left Washington for a long-postponed holiday in New England (where he would be a guest at the seaside cottage of that same Representative Hooper who had played the parsimonious host to President Johnson in 1865). Outwardly professing satisfaction at sloughing official burdens, inwardly he fretted. Grant sent never a word. What could the silence mean? wondered Stanton. Was Grant trustworthy? Doubt brought on racking pains, and between aches and chagrin the ex-Secretary sank into hypochondria.

"Parson" Brownlow thought the prospect—impeachment surely—just dandy. "Soon," said he, "Wade will be President *ad interim*, and Johnson will be President *ad outerim!*"

PART SEVEN

DEFENDER OF THE CONSTITUTION

BY suspending Stanton the President believed that he had stopped "the fountainhead of the trouble," as he put it; next he turned his attention to General Sheridan in Louisiana. Sheridan had written a defiant letter, taking issue with Johnson's "interference," and the President resolved to send the graceless "Phil" to fight Indians on the Western plains. When he brought the question before the cabinet, however, the reaction was a near panic: Sheridan was a national hero, and the outcry that would be raised against any rebuke from the White House, even to the general's vanity, which was immense, was bound to be tremendous. (Johnson later said that McCulloch and Browning had blenched at the suggestion, and Browning's face "actually grew thin.")

Nevertheless, Johnson drew up orders transferring Sheridan to St. Louis, replacing him with General George Thomas, and assigning General Hancock to Thomas' command. This shifting about was sure to be regarded as a reprimand of Sheridan, and the President intended that it should be so regarded. The cabinet's opinion was that Sheridan should have been relieved immediately after his insolent letter, and that now it was too late—that the crisis had blown over, and it should not be revived. But at the time of Sheridan's insubordinate action Johnson had been taken up with Stanton; now he was free to act, and he handed the order of transfer to General Grant. In a covering note he indicated he would welcome Grant's comments.

Back came a reply urging that the order be rescinded, "in the name of a patriotic people who have sacrificed hundreds of thousands of loyal lives and thousands of millions of treasure." Then Grant launched into a political lecture.

"It is unmistakeably the wish of the country that Gen. Sheridan should not be removed from his present command," he stated.

"This is a republic, where the will of the people is the law of the land. I beg that their voice may be heard . . . General Sheridan's . . . removal will only be regarded as an effort to defeat the laws of Congress. It will be interpreted by the unreconciled element in the South—those who did all they could to break up this government by arms and now wish to be the only element consulted as to the method of restoring order—as a triumph . . . There are military reasons, pecuniary reasons, and, above all, patriotic reasons why this order should not be insisted on."

Such a primer of politics offered by a military man who had proved maladroit in civilian affairs invited a retort from controversialist Andrew Johnson. In a letter matching Grant's, the President reduced the general to his place and function. First, as to "the will of the people" requiring that General Sheridan remain at New Orleans, Johnson was "not cognizant that the question had ever been submitted to the people themselves for determination." The sarcasm continued. "It certainly would be unjust to the army to assume that, in the opinion of the nation, he alone is capable of commanding the states of Louisiana and Texas, and that were he for any cause removed, no other general in the military service of the United States would be competent to fill his place."

Next Sheridan's removal could not be regarded "as an effort to defeat the laws of Congress," when the whole purpose was to facilitate their execution. This Sheridan had bungled. His transfer could not be interpreted by "the unreconciled element of the South" as a "triumph," for they must know that the "mere change of military commander cannot alter the law . . . They are perfectly familiar with the antecedents of the President, and know that he has not obstructed the faithful execution of any act of Congress . . .

"You remark," the President went on, "that 'this is a republic, where the will of the people is the law of the land.' and 'beg that their voice may be heard.' This is, indeed, a republic, based, however, upon a written Constitution. That Constitution is the expressed will of the people . . . While one of its provisions makes the President commander-in-chief of the army and navy, another requires that 'he shall take care that the laws are faithfully executed.' Believing that a change in command . . . is absolutely necessary for a faithful execution of the laws, I have issued the order . . . and in thus exercising a power that inheres in the Executive, under the Constitution, as commander-in-chief of the military and naval forces, I am discharging a duty required of me by the will of the nation, as formally declared in the supreme law of the land . . . Any other course would lead to the destruction of the republic; for, the Constitution once abolished, there would be no Congress for the exercise of the legislative powers; no executive to see that the laws are faithfully executed; no judiciary to afford to the citizen protection for life, limb, and property."

Having instructed the commander of the armies of the United States in the basics of politics, the President concluded that he perceived no " 'military,' 'pecuniary,' or 'patriotic reasons' why the order should not be carried into effect."

Grant, as stubborn as Johnson, then procured a medical opinion that General Thomas' health would suffer from the Louisiana climate; and in the face of this, and of Thomas' expressed reluctance to leave his current command, the President altered the order so as to send General Hancock to Sheridan's district, and shift the latter to Missouri. And at the same time, Johnson relieved General Sickles in the Carolinas and replaced him with General E. R. S. Canby, an officer who was not noticeably political-minded.

In cabinet the next day, Grant proceeded to deliver what lawyer Browning scornfully called "crude opinions upon all subjects, especially legal questions, as if they were oracles and not to be contradicted." Browning thought the usually laconic general had been "stuffed for the occasion." Grant remonstrated again against the transfer of both Sheridan and Sickles, saying that the law placed the enforcement of the Reconstruction Acts in his hands; yet he was receiving orders from the President that ran counter to his own. Therefore, while he wished to enter into conflict with nobody, he must make clear that he had a duty to perform, namely, the enforcement of the Reconstruction Acts, and he intended to see that they were properly executed.

Welles thought that Grant's speech showed it had been "studied and premeditated." The President heard the general out, then coolly replied that it was the duty of the President, not of Grant,

to see that the laws were executed, and also, "when I assign officers to their duty, my orders must be obeyed." The orders in
respect to Sheridan and Sickles had been prepared deliberately,
he added, and they must be carried out "with as little delay as
possible."

At this rebuke Grant seemed crestfallen, and he backtracked on
his objection to Sickles' removal, even agreeing that Sickles had
exceeded his authority. In a pouting tone, Grant then announced
that he was no politician, and he should prefer not to sit in on
cabinet discussions of political questions, especially those outside
his department. Johnson replied that he could do as he liked, and
Grant withdrew, apparently in a chastened mood.

But he did not desist in his attempts to overrule the commander-in-chief. The next day Johnson received a long letter in
which Grant rehashed his stated protest, but closed by saying
that against his own judgment he was deferring to the President's
opinion and would carry out the order.

The arrogance of this letter astonished Johnson, and it was
rendered more offensive when the *Washington Chronicle*, Forney's bitterly hostile paper, published the contents in a way most
slighting to the President. The publication produced widespread
excitement, reflected in the comments of Francis Lieber, scholar
and radical pamphleteer, to another of the President's haters, that
Grant's letter was "revolutionary . . . but we are in the midst of a
revolution . . .

"The person who is President fears impeachment," Lieber ran
on, "and has taken again to intoxication. The day before yesterday [the day of the cabinet meeting], so I am positively informed, wholly intoxicated. You know he has never given up deep
and constant drinking . . . Many calm and well-meaning men
believe that he who is the boldest pettifogger and meanest man of
power combined, that history has any record of, thinks of resisting impeachment by force."

Lieber might be excused for talking wildly, because his job as
keeper of the war archives had just been abolished by Grant as an
economy measure. Others were remarking on how Grant was
"ripping out Stanton's toadies and parasites" in the War Department, and the feeling among the service employees there cer-

tainly had become easier since Stanton's departure. Lieber insured wide circulation of his libels against "*that* man—a faithless, ruinous, and rebellious executive"—by cautioning his correspondent to hold the remarks in strict confidence, although they might be shown to "discrete friends."

Johnson's impulse was to publish Grant's letter intact; instead, he summoned the general to a heart-to-heart talk, during which he set Grant straight on the workings of the government. Congress, he made clear, had *not* superseded the President in respect to enforcement of the Reconstruction laws; Congress had *not* restricted the commander-in-chief in appointing or removing the military district commanders. While Grant had been protesting to the cabinet that he wished to stay out of political discussions, his letter—which was nothing more or less than an extended policy essay—had been lying in his office awaiting signature. If every order the President gave were to provoke a similar disquisition, it would be impossible for them to work together, Johnson pointed out. Moreover, Grant must be aware that there were persons who would like to create misunderstandings between them, especially in reference to the Reconstruction laws. In passing, Johnson remarked that he was not a candidate for the Presidency in 1868, and Grant hastened to say that he was not either.

At the end of the conversation, Grant, apparently contrite, asked permission to withdraw his letter, and took it away with him.

Two days later the order changing commands was promulgated, and, as had been predicted, Sheridan's removal provoked radical howls.

Colonel Moore, Johnson's secretary, had little confidence in Grant's permanent reformation; he told the President that by the time the general got back to his office he probably had become "as obstinate as ever." Indications that Moore might be right cropped up quickly thereafter. On the basis of many complaints, Johnson directed Grant's attention to secret drilling carried on quite illegally by armed bands of Negroes. Grant's reply was either flippant or insulting, for he merely called the President's attention to reports of secret drilling by armed bands of white men.

The President's mail was filled with warnings and offers of help from veterans who professed their eagerness to raise troops for his defense, should Congress move against him. On the other side, throughout the Midwest, an organization of Union veterans, called the Grand Army of the Republic, was active in preparations to defend Congress against the President at the November reconvening.

The tension was greatest at the time of the October elections, in which the Republicans were severely rebuffed. The party had mobilized all its forces, temporal and spiritual, and when Granville Moody, the itinerant evangelist who had prayed so rousingly with Johnson at the siege of Nashville, invoked divine blessing upon "our noble Congress" at the Ohio state Republican convention, one delegate told his wife that only a sense of propriety had kept the convention from applauding.

Moody's prayers seemed to have become less effectual than they had been in sterner times, for the voters swept Democrats and Johnsonites into every state office in Ohio except the governorship, and the Republican winner of that post, Rutherford B. Hayes, barely squeaked in. In Pennsylvania, also, the Democrats scored marked gains, and the October trend was confirmed by Republican upsets elsewhere in November.

Tennessee was an exception. There Governor Brownlow, bidding for a second term, boldly induced his legislature to enfranchise the state's Negroes, and with their votes, and by wholesale proscription of ex-Confederates, pardoned or not, the "Parson" won reelection. Shortly thereafter he engineered his election as United States senator to succeed Patterson, though the latter's term would not expire for two years yet.

The Democratic victories in the North stimulated the reckless talk of another civil war, but at the same time the impeachment agitation died down. The House Judiciary Committee had been unable to discover any grounds on which to base an impeachment action; and even a separate "smelling committee," headed by Ben Butler, set up to delve into every aspect of Lincoln's murder (in hope of implicating Johnson), turned up nothing of use. The efforts of this group, in fact, proved so flat a failure that no report was filed, and Butler, in his egotistical memoirs years afterwards, would go out of his way to put on record that he had tracked down not a scintilla of evidence that the President had any connection with the assassination plot.

Finally the Judiciary Committee called Representative Ashley, who had started the inquiry, and demanded proofs to back up his repeated assertion that Johnson had committed impeachable offenses. Ashley confessed that while he possessed evidence, it was "not the kind that would satisfy most men; it would not amount to legal evidence."

"I have a theory," he said. "I have always believed that President Harrison and President Taylor and President Buchanan were poisoned, and poisoned for the express purpose of putting the Vice-President in the presidential office. The attempt on Mr. Buchanan failed; the other two succeeded. Then Mr. Lincoln was assassinated, and from my viewpoint I could come to the conclusion which impartial men, holding different views, could not come to."

At this crackbrained admission, the majority of the committee threw up their hands and let it be known that they would recommend that the investigation be dropped.

Throughout all this, Johnson had remained so imperturbable and attentive to the daily routine that Welles was moved to admiration of his self-containment. For three years the Navy Secretary had associated with the President intimately, almost daily, and his judgment of the man was that he possessed great ability, was conversant with public affairs "beyond most men," had wide experience, "great firmness, sincere patriotism, a sacred regard for the Constitution," and was "humane and benevolent.

"Extreme men and extreme measures he dislikes," Welles set down in his delineation. "The radicals accuse him of being irritable and obstinate, but the truth is he has been patient and forbearing, almost to an infirmity, under assaults, intrigues, and abuse."

One of the President's handicaps, Welles thought, was his inability to take people into his confidence. "Many of his most important steps have been taken without the knowledge of any of his Cabinet, and I think without the knowledge of any person whatever. He has wonderful self-reliance and immovable firmness

in maintaining what he believes to be right; is disinclined to be
familiar with men in prominent positions, or to be intimate with
those who fill the public eye."

Because of this isolation, Welles noted with approval the in-
stalling of Colonel Edmund Cooper as a special friend of the
President. Cooper had served Johnson in confidential capacities
at Nashville and later in Washington. He had then been elected to
Congress from Tennessee, but had been defeated for reelection,
and his return to the White House circle was in the role of family
counselor.

Cooper was less sanguine than Johnson about the political outlook. He especially feared that in the event of a disagreement
between Johnson and Grant, General Sherman, whose prestige
was second only to that of the commanding general, would side
with Grant. That would be fatal for the President, because the
army's choice of sides would determine the outcome in such a
crisis.

As the time approached for Congress to reassemble, the Judiciary Committee set to work on its report to the House. Word was
passed that the report would state that no grounds had been
found on which to base impeachment.

It was a surprise, therefore, when, on the evening of November
21, the day Congress reconvened, Cooper appeared in great excitement at the White House and informed the President that
the committee would recommend impeachment. One member
had changed sides, and the majority now stood five to four for the
recommendation. The chairman and one other Republican would
oppose it, together with the two Democratic members; but five,
under the leadership of George S. Boutwell, lean, crafty, and
fanatical in his hatred of the President, were preparing their
report.

Johnson doubted the accuracy of Cooper's information, but the
latter said his informant had offered to bet one thousand dollars
to ten dollars that it would stand up. Whereupon Johnson became
grave.

"If it is so, so let it be," he finally said.

Cooper's information was correct. On November 27, Boutwell
reported to the House of Representatives. On seventeen separate

counts, he held the President guilty of usurpations and violations of law meriting impeachment and removal from the office that he had besmirched and disgraced. The two dissenting Republicans, in a separate report, tore to shreds every one of Boutwell's contentions, found no ground for impeachment, but recommended that the President be censured for general bad conduct. In a third report the two Democratic members charged that Johnson had been "hunted down by partisan malice as no other man was ever hunted and hounded before," and disowned the heresy hunt *in toto*.

When the House was informed that it would require ten hours just to read Boutwell's voluminous report, they waived the reading and proceeded to debate.

On December 7, a vote was taken, and by one hundred and eight to fifty-seven the report was rejected. Of the votes cast against it, two-thirds were by Republicans, many of them radicals, but unable to find any promise of success in the mishmash Boutwell had cooked up. The plain words of the Constitution in every instance sustained the President.

"Impeachment is dead," said Thad Stevens. "I'll never talk impeachment again."

At the White House the President received the news "with some little show of exaltation," and told Moore that the time for defense had passed; now he could "stand on the offensive in view of the Constitution and the elections."

About this time Stanton returned to Washington to await the Senate's action on his suspension.

The enigmatic Grant went to and from the White House, saying nothing.

2.

The fact was, the hero of Appomattox was playing a tricky game, and not adroitly. He had taken the lure dangled by the Republicans—expectation of the party's presidential nomination in 1868—and was doing his best to keep in good standing with the party's leaders, while not disengaging himself from the security of the establishment, as represented by the White House and the administration. In October, the Democratic victories gave him pause, and for a while he appeared to be veering towards the President. In an exceptionally frank conversation at that time, he had told Johnson that should Stanton endeavor to regain possession of the office of Secretary of War on the strength of action by Congress, the attempt would have to go to the courts for adjudication; and even if the Senate should *order* Stanton's reinstatement, he would still be *out*, and would have to appeal to the courts.

This was Johnson's hope. He told Grant that he did not believe Stanton was covered by the Tenure of Office Act, but he would welcome a test of the law's constitutionality. He added candidly that he was determined to keep Stanton out, no matter what, and in spite of the Senate. Grant said he had not studied the Tenure Act closely, but he still thought Stanton would have to turn to the courts for a definition of his rights. Should he change his opinion, he would let the President know in sufficient time to make his arrangements. Meanwhile, it was understood between them that in the event of the Senate acting to reinstate Stanton, Grant would either retain the office and force a court test, or would resign as Secretary ad interim and turn the office back to Johnson in time for the latter to install a successor who would submit to legal proceedings.

Despite this assurance of compatibility of views, Grant's behavior during the last weeks of 1867 grew increasingly dubious. He undercut the President in orders to the new military district commanders, forbidding them to reinstate officials who had been ousted by Generals Sheridan and Sickles, thus in effect signifying his approval of the actions that had led to those generals' removal. The silence Grant habitually maintained encouraged speculation as to his intentions. The radicals plied him with flattery, after the scare of October '67 relying more and more on his popularity to save them in the autumn elections of '68.

In November the cabinet was given a reading of Johnson's State of the Union message, and endorsed it without exception. Then, with great earnestness, the President submitted a series of carefully phrased questions bearing on the course he should adopt in the event that an attempt should be made to arrest him and suspend him from his official functions, after impeachment articles had been voted but before his trial by the Senate. A bill to accomplish this was pending in Congress, and impeachment talk at the Capitol had by no means died out, in spite of the House vote.

It was the cabinet's unanimous opinion that such an attempt would be in the highest degree revolutionary, whether made by Congress or by private parties, and that it ought to be resisted. Grant joined in this opinion, saying that the President certainly should not submit, and that "a mere law by Congress would not justify such a step; an amendment to the Constitution would be necessary."

This unanimity pleased Johnson, and after the meeting he told Moore that the day had "produced great results."

On December 3 the President's message went to the Capitol. It was a forceful statement of conditions and principles, and merited the closest attention, but Congress was not even listening.

"Candor compels me to declare that at this time there is no Union as our fathers understood the term, and as they meant it to be understood by us," the President stated. On the momentous question of reconstruction, he had had "the misfortune to differ with Congress," and had expressed his convictions without reserve. "Those convictions," he repeated, "are not only unchanged, but strengthened by subsequent events and further reflection."

The injustices of the Reconstruction Acts he again capitulated: the denial of the protection of habeas corpus and trial by jury, the failure to provide security of property or person against the "passion, prejudice, or rapacity" of military rulers. Such wrongs, "being expressly forbidden, cannot be constitutionally inflicted upon any portion of our people, no matter how they have come within our jurisdiction, and no matter whether they live in states, territories, or districts."

Striking at the assumption of omnipotency by Congress, he served notice that should the legislative branch of the government "pass an act, through all the forms of law, to abolish a coordinate department of the government, in such a case the President must take the high responsibilities of his office and save the life of the nation at all hazards."

This was not mere theoretical supposition: a bill to do away with the Supreme Court was on file in the House of Representatives, and "all the forms of law" already had been employed to strip the executive branch of its constitutional powers and convert it into a minor agency, without vigor of its own. The meaning of the message was clear enough: under sufficient provocation the President would feel obligated to resist these unwarranted encroachments in order to prevent a total overthrow of the tripartite system of governmental checks and balances established by the Constitution.

Wrathful rhetoric greeted this able exposition. The President was grandiloquently described as "the nightmare that crouches upon the heaving breast of the nation," while Senator Sumner denounced the entire message as "incendiary . . . calculated to provoke civil war." Without deigning to controvert, Congress turned to more profitable business, and no great flurry was produced when, on December 12, Johnson sent to the Senate a statement of his reasons for suspending Stanton.

This, too, was a comprehensive document, compiled under the scrutiny of the Attorney General; Browning called it "clear, powerful, and I think unanswerable."

Stanbery's care had been that the public should be reminded of the obstructions that Stanton had placed in the way of the President's discharge of his duties; and among other things the whole story of the New Orleans "massacre" was recited, including Stanton's suppression of General Baird's appeal for instructions, which might have prevented the bloodshed. To clinch the case, Johnson recalled that the first business before the cabinet after he became President had been "a plan or scheme of reconstruction . . . prepared for Mr. Lincoln by Mr. Stanton . . . It was approved, and at the earliest practical moment was applied . . . to the state of North Carolina, and afterwards became the basis of action in turn for the other states.

"There is perhaps no act of my administration for which I have been more denounced than this," Johnson summed up. "It was not originated by me, but I shrink from no responsibility on that account, for the plan approved itself to my own judgment, and I did not hesitate to carry it into action."

For good or ill, the Johnson policy towards the South was Stanton's brainchild, yet Stanton had obstructed its fulfillment by collusion with that policy's bitterest opponents.

Without debate, the Senate referred the statement to its Military Affairs Committee, and recessed over the holidays.

The season was not festive for Stanton, hanging in suspense. He was cut off from reliable sources of information, his network of spies being no longer available to him, and Grant remaining inscrutable. A soldier on duty at the White House did keep the ex-secretary posted on the visitors who passed in and out, and how long each stayed, and from these scanty clues Stanton tried to piece together the plots against himself that he was sure were being woven inside those forbidden walls. He was hard up for money, his salary having been stopped (the New England trip had been made on borrowed funds), and his wife had grown despondent and complaining. Never personally popular, he was largely ignored by radicals who remained in the city over Christmas.

In anticipation of the crisis, Johnson had called General Sherman to Washington in hope that he might be able to hold Grant in line. Sherman's devotion to Grant was absolute; for Stanton he naturally had antipathy. Sherman found Grant thoroughly imbued with radical ideas, so much so that he told Sherman he had accepted the War Department portfolio temporarily not to help the President, but to "protect the army against Johnson."

Meanwhile, the President made ready for swift action. On January 7 he had Colonel Moore draw up a letter dismissing Stanton (instead of merely suspending him), together with a notification to be sent to the Senate. The President kept these papers at hand for instant signing. Reports from the Capitol indicated that the Senate committee would recommend nonconcurrence in Stanton's suspension. On Friday, January 10, the committee did report to this effect. Democratic senators challenged the report in speeches lasting all that day, and all day Saturday, while the Republicans sat in stony silence.

On Saturday Grant came to the White House in considerable agitation. He had just told Sherman that should the Senate reinstate Stanton under the Tenure Act, he would not remain as secretary ad interim. Sherman urged him to tell the President this without delay, and Grant had come to do so. Having at last examined the Tenure Act, he said, he had found that it carried penalties for violation—a ten thousand dollar fine and five years in prison. He had no wish to incur such a risk, he explained, and therefore would not participate in a court test of the law.

Johnson listened patiently, then went over the legal ground again. He had not suspended Stanton under the Tenure Act, he explained, but by his constitutional authority. He had appointed Grant under the same authority. The legal basis for the action went back to 1795, and the Tenure Act was not at issue. However, since the Senate was invoking that law—improperly and unconstitutionally, as he believed and as he felt the courts would decide —he then and there offered to pay any fine that might be levied against Grant for violating it, and would gladly serve any term of imprisonment. The talk lasted some time, and Grant finally gave way and indicated he would abide by their previous agreement, namely, either to stick as secretary ad interim until the courts could rule on the law, or to resign and turn the office back to the President in time for the latter to install a successor. The men parted with an understanding that Grant would return and give Johnson a final decision on Monday.

The next day, Sunday, was taken up with frantic efforts by Sherman, abetted by his father-in-law, old Thomas Ewing, to provide a way out of the dilemma. Their proposal was for Johnson to nominate former Governor Cox of Ohio as Secretary of War to succeed Stanton the minute the Senate should meet on Monday. Cox, a Republican, had been in and out of the radical camp, and Ewing was certain that the Senate would confirm him. This would eliminate Stanton and relieve the senators of the necessity of placing themselves on record in regard to him. The success of the plan would depend on careful timing, Sherman explained to the President; but Johnson was indifferent; he was banking on Grant.

Sunday passed and nothing was accomplished. Thereupon Ewing advised Sherman to stand clear of the blowup that could not fail to come.

On Monday the Democratic senators resumed talk, but by

afternoon they had run out of words, and the vote was taken. By thirty-six to six (thirteen not voting), the committee's report was adopted, stating that Stanton had been suspended without the concurrence of the Senate and ordering his reinstatement.

A messenger sped the decision to Stanton's home, and within minutes telegrams of congratulations began to arrive, and then jubilant congressmen.

Forney, as Secretary of the Senate, also sent Grant immediate notification. On reading this, the general wrote a letter to the President stating that Grant's authority as secretary ad interim had expired as of the moment of the Senate's action. This letter he signed and laid aside; it would be delivered to the White House Tuesday morning. Grant had not called at the Executive Mansion during Monday nor did he have any communication with Johnson. That evening the general and Mrs. Grant attended the regular White House reception and chatted with the President; nothing was said on either side about Grant's resignation.

Tuesday morning, January 24, Grant and Stanton arrived separately at the War Department. Stanton went to a room on the second floor, while Grant entered the secretary's office. There he gathered up his personal papers, then bolted one door on the inside, and went out the other door and locked it on the outside, taking the key with him. Retiring to army headquarters nearby, he gave the key to the assistant adjutant general, E. D. Townsend. This was about ten o'clock in the morning.

At noon Grant dispatched an aide, General Comstock, to the White House with his letter of resignation.

Meanwhile, informed of Grant's departure, Stanton had called for the key of the office, which General Townsend handed over with a mock "present arms." Stanton unlocked the door and took possession of the room from which he had been excluded since August 12. A throng of senators and representatives swarmed after him, among them the House delegation from Tennessee.

The restored secretary's first action was to draw three thousand dollars of salary due him. Then, assuming an air of industriousness but really doing nothing, he waited for some sign from Grant. None came, for Grant was passing one of the most uncomfortable hours of his life.

When General Comstock handed Grant's letter of resignation to President Johnson, with its statement that the general's functions as ad interim secretary had ceased the day before, the aide watched while the President read it. Colonel Moore saw Johnson's face flush. The President did not (as the radical press would aver later) "storm and swear and kick the furniture" but Moore had never seen him so furious. In an angry voice Johnson ordered General Comstock to tell Grant that he would be expected to attend the cabinet session that afternoon.

After Comstock had left, Johnson broke into denunciation of Grant's "duplicity," repeating to Moore the understanding that had been arrived at, that Grant would either retain the office pending a court test, or would turn it back to the President in time to make a new appointment. Instead, he had turned it back to Stanton, and the latter was already in possession. Only the Saturday before, Johnson exclaimed, Grant had repeated his understanding of the agreement, and had promised to give a final decision on Monday.

When the cabinet assembled, they were startled by the news, and were astonished when Grant walked in. The general explained stiffly that he was there by request, and when the President addressed him as "Mr. Secretary," he replied that he no longer bore that title. Then Johnson, in Moore's language, "brought the matter home" to him. Moore recorded the scene.

The President asked Grant to state distinctly whether his surrendering the office to Stanton without the knowledge of the President was in accordance with the agreement between them. Browning noticed that though the President was excited and indignant, he maintained perfect self-control.

According to the account set down that day by Secretary Welles, Grant did not answer the question directly, but admitted that there had been an understanding, although at the time when they had entered into their compact he had not looked into the Tenure Act; and that when he did finally read it, and discovered the penalty clause, he was unwilling to incur a fine and imprisonment.

Determined that Grant should not evade, Johnson asked whether he himself had not assured Grant that he would gladly assume any penalties, and had not Grant repeated that he would give the President his final decision on Monday?

Grant's reply was rambling; he stammered and hesitated, while the cabinet looked on intently. Yes, they had talked over the situation on Saturday, he conceded, and he had not resigned at that time because the Senate had not yet acted, although both he and the President had anticipated that they would reinstate Stanton. He mumbled something about "if the subject was delayed until Monday it would be too late," and he "therefore avoided seeing the President on Monday, as he promised," and on Tuesday moved back to his own quarters as the law required.

"All the members of the Cabinet were astonished" by Grant's "equivocation and bad faith," Welles recorded, as the President sought a straight answer.

"Was it not our understanding—did you not assure me some time ago and again on Saturday, that if you did not hold on to the office yourself, you would place it in my hands that I might select another?" Johnson repeated.

"That," said Grant, "was my intention . . . Mr. [Reverdy] Johnson and General Sherman spent a great deal of time with me on Sunday. Didn't Mr. Johnson come to see you? I sent General Sherman yesterday after talking the matter over. Didn't you see Sherman?"

Yes, he had seen both those gentlemen, the President said, but what did their visits have to do with the case? Neither one had spoken about Grant's resigning. "Why did you give the key to Mr. Stanton and leave the department?"

He had not given the key to Stanton, but to General Townsend, Grant answered sulkily. And he had sent word to the White House.

"Yes," exclaimed Johnson, furious at Grant's squirming, "but that was not our understanding."

Well, said Grant, he had been very busy on Monday; Sherman had "taken up a great deal of time," and he had been occupied with "many little matters," and he had intended to call. Browning found the general growing unintelligible, and at length Grant excused himself and left.

(In order to fasten the scene in mind and "do injustice to

neither man," Browning and Welles set down the extraordinary episode in their diaries immediately upon returning to their offices. Their accounts jibed.)

Grant had retreated to army headquarters, boiling at his humiliation in front of the cabinet. Shortly after reaching his quarters, he received a peremptory order from Stanton to report to the secretary's office. In a surly mood, the general complied, and for an hour the two men were alone together. What was said could only be conjectured, but the apparent result was a series of letters between Grant and the President on the question of who was a liar.

Upon Grant's departure from the cabinet session, all those who had witnessed his shifting and dodging had declared themselves unqualifiedly against both Grant and Stanton, Welles recorded. All except Seward, that is; with his philosophic imperturbability, the Secretary of State had suggested that they all sleep on the incident; that was his rule, he said, before making an important decision.

The next day the *Intelligencer* carried a circumstantial account of the scene, concluding:

"Upon being reminded by the President of his reiterated promise made only on Saturday morning last, General Grant admitted the promise in the presence of members of the Cabinet. We content ourselves at present with a simple statement of the facts . . . from which our readers will draw their own conclusions."

Upon reading this, Grant hurried to the White House, accompanied by Sherman, to protest that his honor had been impugned. He was emphatic and bitter. Johnson had not read the article in question, but after the generals withdrew, he called for the *Intelligencer* and found the account to be substantially correct. Grant refused to allow the imputation of bad faith to stand, and a few days later Johnson received a belligerent communication from the commanding general, requesting that the President put in writing the verbal order that he had given instructing Grant to obey no order issued under the name or authority of the Secretary of War, unless Grant was satisfied that it came from the President. Stanton was giving orders without consulting the President; there was no communication at all between the White House and the War Department a stone's throw away.

Johnson put the order in writing; but back came a long epistle bearing Grant's signature but not in Grant's style, stating that the order would not be obeyed, inasmuch as the Secretary of War had not been informed officially of it. This was a trap set for the President, for if Johnson should communicate with Stanton officially, he would thereby recognize the validity of the secretary's reinstatement. The President sedulously avoided doing this, but Grant created further difficulty by including in his refusal to carry out the order of his commander-in-chief a detailed, point-blank denial of having betrayed the President's confidence. He denied that he had ever promised to call at the White House on Monday, denied that he had misled Johnson in regard to his proposed course of action, and in effect called Johnson a liar.

This insolence on the part of the head of the army found its way into the newspapers, and it demanded an answer. To fortify his position, the President called on the members of the cabinet who had been present at the interview to state their recollection of what had happened and what had been said. First Moore read to the cabinet the *Intelligencer* article, then Johnson asked each man in turn whether that account tallied with his recollection. McCulloch, Randall, Browning, and Welles (Seward was not present) concurred, feeling only that the newspaper account "fell short of what really" had happened. Welles and Browning offered to submit their diaries in confirmation. The remarks of each person were taken down in shorthand by Moore. Here are excerpts:

Said Browning: "He [Grant] admitted all . . . He admitted that when the interview terminated on Saturday, he was to have seen the President Monday on the subject."

Said McCulloch: "He admitted that if he changed his views, the President was to be notified in season to enable the President to put the office in the same position as it was when he was appointed Secretary ad interim."

Said Welles: "The President said, 'I expected to see you Monday. Why did you not call?' Grant replied that he was too much occupied by Genl. Sherman and 'many little matters.'"

Said Randall: "I did not suppose that a man occupying his position would so sneak and prevaricate. He knows now that we all know that he lied and played the sneak. That is the unadorned English of it."

Said the President: "I desired to know what he would do and did not think it possible that he could act in such bad faith."*

The President passed along to the general this confirmation of his own recollection of Grant's words and attitude during the Tuesday questioning as sufficient refutation of the latter's complaint that the *Intelligencer* article teemed with "many and gross misrepresentations." This evoked from Grant an even more officious letter, in which he said that he regretted that the cabinet should "suffer their names to be made the basis of charges in newspaper articles. You know that we parted on Saturday," he lectured the President, "without any promise on my part, either expressed or implied . . . that I would see you at any fixed time on the subject . . . The course you would have it understood I agreed to pursue, was in violation of the law . . . while the course I did pursue . . . was in accordance with the law, and not in disobedience of any orders of my superior.

"And now, Mr. President, where my honor as a soldier and integrity as a man have been so violently assailed, pardon me for saying that I can but regard the whole matter, from the beginning to the end, as an attempt to involve me in the resistance of law, for which you hesitated to assume the responsibility in orders, and thus to destroy my character before the country."

Grant's "character before the country" at that moment was his stock in trade, for he had fully determined to seek the presidency; his ambition, therefore, as well as his integrity, was involved.

This extraordinary communication, upon being read to the cabinet, was met with mingled "indignation or ridicule," according to Moore, and at the conclusion all joined in a hearty laugh. Browning thought the letter "the weakest and most disreputable" Grant could have written; Stanbery found its whole "tone and taste" offensive; McCulloch was amazed that Grant should repeat, as the general did, first his denial of having promised to call at the White House on the critical Monday, and then his labored excuses for not having called. Said Johnson, "If he did not promise, there was no necessity for an excuse," and on Stanbery's ad-

---

* These quotations are from Moore's transcript, endorsed at the foot of the page: "Handwriting of Col. W. G. Moore, Private Sec. of President Johnson, written at the time of the meeting." Paper filed in the Andrew Johnson Papers, Library of Congress, Washington, D.C.

vice the President drafted a circumstantial rebuttal, exposing Grant's inconsistencies and closing with a stinging reprimand.

There were "five Cabinet members present at the conversation" in dispute, Johnson reminded Grant once more; and to obviate any possible misconception, he enclosed copies of written statements submitted by the five. Four bore out Johnson's version absolutely. Seward alone qualified his verification slightly, saying that he believed he had heard Grant's words correctly, but he might have been mistaken. (Seward occasionally succumbed to diplomatic deafness.)

The President went further than this simple refutation. Grant's treachery had angered him clear through, and Moore had been given a glimpse of the intensity of his feeling when the President first read Grant's insolent defiance.

"I have tried to be decent," the President had exclaimed, "but I know my nature, and I'll be damned if some things haven't gone about as far as they can go! Grant has been spoiled. I am tired of having his views thrust upon me; this is the fourth time! I really wanted to be his friend, for I knew some of the difficulties he labored under, and he had my sympathy. But I'll be damned! . . ."

And in the scorching response, Johnson this time accused Grant of deliberately breaking faith, and of having acted in bad faith from the start.

"You admit that from the very beginning of what you term 'the whole history' of your connection with Mr. Stanton's suspension, you intended to circumvent the President," Johnson wrote. "It was not in obedience to the orders of your superior, as has heretofore been assumed, that you assumed the duties of the office . . . You accepted the office not in the interest of the President, but of Mr. Stanton . . . In the ethics of some persons such a course is allowable . . . Your connection with this transaction, as written by yourself . . . shows that you not only concealed your design from the President, but induced him to suppose that you would carry out his purpose to keep Mr. Stanton out of office . . . If the President had reposed confidence *before* he knew your views, and that confidence had been violated, it might have been said he made a mistake; but a violation of confidence reposed *after* [our] conversation was no mistake of his, nor of yours . . . The point is, that . . . you had secretly determined to do the very thing which at last you did—surrender the office to Mr. Stanton. You may have changed your views as to the law, but you certainly did not change your views as to the course you had marked out for yourself from the beginning."

These sentences outraged Grant, but a concluding paragraph touched his professional conscience as a soldier:

"Without further comment upon the insubordinate attitude which you have assumed, I am at a loss to know how you can relieve yourself from obedience to the orders of the President, who is made by the Constitution the commander-in-chief of the army and navy, and is therefore the official superior, as well of the General of the Army, as of the Secretary of War."

To a West Pointer, "insubordinate" is an ugly word, and the next day brought Grant's sulky denial of any such intention; but he would obey any *legal* order coming from the Secretary of War, he insisted stubbornly, unless it was expressly countermanded by the President.

That day Johnson, responsive to a resolution of the House of Representatives, submitted the entire correspondence to Congress. Thad Stevens looked it over, gave his opinion that both men probably were lying, and suggested they go out in the back-yard and settle it with dung forks.

"What the devil do I care about the question of veracity?" the old man said. "That has nothing to do with the law. Grant isn't on trial; it's Johnson." And but for the "pack of wincing politicians" in the House, impeachment would have been voted long ago "without further palaver."

Throughout the country Grant's popularity remained unshaken, though his reputation suffered stains of the sort that would mottle the record indelibly before his public career was ended. But Johnson's position had become utterly untenable. Though still nominally President, he had been so stripped of constitutional powers that the general of the army flouted his authority with impunity, and the Senate by its fiat could force an avowed enemy into his cabinet. His methods were maligned, his motives befouled by slander to the point where he was being accused of atrocious crimes.

There were two courses open to him. He could stand ineptly,

bewailing his helplessness and wringing his hands like the pitiful
Buchanan during the last months of that tragically futile administration, or he could resist, and risk condemnation and expulsion in
an effort to preserve the government bequeathed to the whole
nation—a government by representatives of all the people,
within the limits of plainly defined rules safeguarding reciprocal rights, and not a government by any clique, party, minority,
vested interest, or "central directory" of headstrong and selfish
men.

Being the man he was, Johnson could only choose to resist; his
whole life had been a combat, his character was that of a fighter;
and character, as has been said, is fate. The virtue and manliness
of the office of the presidency had been entrusted to him, and he
would not connive in its emasculation. He would not consent to
be revolutionized by party despotism. His closest friends wanted
him to make an accommodation, bow to the inevitable, submit
without further struggle to rule by Congress. In this way, he was
told, agitation would be allayed, the country would be pacified,
and he could finish out his term in peace if not with respect.
Submission offered the easy way; to him it was the way of betrayal. The test must come, and he must invite it. As he once had
staked everything on the struggle to preserve the Union, now he
must risk all again on an attempt to preserve constitutional government. He told Colonel Moore:

"If the people do not entertain sufficient respect for their Chief
Magistrate to uphold me in this, then I ought to resign."

He had decided upon his next step. On Friday, February 21, all
business at the Capitol was abruptly halted and both houses were
thrown into uproar when notification arrived from the White
House that the President had that day *dismissed* Edwin M. Stanton as Secretary of War, and had appointed Major General
Lorenzo Thomas secretary ad interim. Thad Stevens was galva-
nized into action by the news. Grounds for impeachment of that
"bad man" had been found—provided by Andrew Johnson himself.

3.

Johnson had encountered difficulty in finding a man who would collaborate in a court test of the constitutionality of the Tenure of Office Act. Although the President had *suspended* Stanton in August on the basis of his constitutional right, and without reference to the Tenure Act, the Senate had thrown the protection of that law around him, and therefore could be expected to shield him from *dismissal* by the same law. The President required an ad interim substitute who would become a party to a prosecution, if necessary, and run the risk of a heavy fine and imprisonment.

For nearly a month Johnson hunted in vain. He sounded the chief clerk of the War Department, but that functionary begged to be excused. He tried to induce General Sherman to accept nomination as Stanton's successor, but Sherman refused to take precedence of Grant, and said bluntly that rather than obey a command to do so he would resign from the army. Sherman did more: he telegraphed his brother, the senator, to oppose confirmation should his name be sent to the Senate in spite of his expressed objections.

Johnson finally lighted upon General Lorenzo Thomas, a desk warrior of sixty-two, who, although adjutant general of the army, had long been shunted aside by Stanton. Vain, foppish, foolish, and frequently tipsy, the general, Johnson admitted, would bring no strength to the cabinet; but he was willing and even eager to take the assignment. Therefore Johnson had Moore prepare the documents removing Stanton, appointing Thomas secretary ad interim, and notifying the Senate of these actions. On Friday, February 21, he summoned Thomas and handed him his appointment and the notification of Stanton's removal, to be delivered at once. The President cautioned the old beau to take along a witness, and with a crony the general set out, preening himself on his mission.

Stanton accepted the President's note calmly, sat down on the worn sofa in his office and read it slowly. Then he asked mildly whether he must vacate at once, or would be allowed time to remove his personal property?

"Act your pleasure," said Thomas gallantly, and then, to complete the record, he showed Stanton his own appointment as secretary ad interim. Grant entering the room just then, Thomas displayed his authority to the commanding general also. Stanton asked if he might have a copy, and the ad interim appointee departed to have one made. Grant and Stanton were left alone.

When Thomas returned with the copy, duly certified by himself, Stanton seemed to have changed his mind.

"I wanted some little time for reflection," the secretary said vaguely. "I don't know whether I shall obey your orders or resist them."

It was then nearly one o'clock, and Thomas sallied back to the White House to report progress. Johnson listened attentively, then said:

"Very well. Go and take charge of the office and perform the duties."

Thomas departed, promising himself to take possession the next morning; that would allow Stanton a decent interval to clear out. The old soldier, whose shoulder straps were a familiar sight in the capital's barrooms, informed every friend he met of his promotion and his intention to enter actively upon his new duties the next day, whether Stanton liked it or not. Answering hypothetical questions as to what he would do should Stanton resist, why, he said, he would simply break down the door and take possession by force.

Meanwhile, two messages reached the Capitol almost simultaneously at about half past two. One was the President's notification to the Senate of Stanton's dismissal and the appointment of General Thomas; the other was a cry for help from Stanton. Thomas, the secretary wrote hastily, was bragging that he would take over on Saturday morning, and "if the Senate does not declare its opinion of the law, how am I to hold possession?" To Senator Conness, California radical, Stanton sent separate word that he was still at the War Department and meant to stay there "until expelled by force."

Both ends of the Capitol were plunged into disorder. The Senate went into executive session behind closed doors, while messages of encouragement were sped to Stanton. Sumner was shocked into brevity for perhaps the only time in his life; his message read, "Stick!"

Hours passed in angry debate. A reporter prowling the corridors averred that every time the door of the Senate chamber opened, out darted a Senator "fit to set the republic ablaze with indignation."

At about five o'clock, by strict party vote, a resolution was adopted declaring that "under the Constitution and the laws" the President had "no power to remove the Secretary of War and to designate any other officer" to perform his duties.

This, in effect, pronounced the President guilty of violating a law that both he and eminent legal minds believed was itself a violation of the Constitution of the United States.

Having done its duty, the Senate adjourned, and attention shifted to the House of Representatives.

Under the Constitution, the impeachment process starts in the House, which, upon the evidence, can impeach or indict the President for "high crimes and misdemeanors." The impeachment, expressed in "articles," is then referred to the Senate, which, resolving itself into a high court of justice, tries the case. If found guilty, the President is removed from office and disqualified from holding public office again. After his removal, he may still be prosecuted on criminal charges if the evidence warrants, and perhaps sentenced to fine and imprisonment.

In the House, Thad Stevens seemed literally recalled to life by the development. Months before he had suffered a physical collapse, and since then his corpselike figure had groped through the Capitol, haggard and trembling, the image of a dying man. But Thad was determined to hang on until he got rid of the "great criminal," and he grasped this heaven-sent opportunity. Speaker Colfax had interrupted debate to announce that the President had defied Congress, and burly John Covode of Pennsylvania at once rose to a privileged question and offered a resolution, short and to the point:

"Resolved, That Andrew Johnson, President of the United States, be impeached of high crimes and misdemeanors."

Amid the excited speeches that followed, Stevens, leaning heavily on the arm of Representative Bingham, shuffled from desk to desk, croaking, "If you don't kill the beast now, it will kill you!" The House referred Covode's resolution to the Reconstruction Committee and adjourned until the next day.

That evening Secretary Welles's son attended a dance, and was startled when between waltzes a messenger in uniform ordered all officers attached to General Emory's command to report to headquarters at once. General William H. Emory commanded the troops in Washington. What could this nocturnal mobilization mean?

At a masquerade ball that evening, General Thomas was spotted by his shoulder straps, and soon was spouting his plans for the morning to eager listeners. He got home about midnight— at about which hour Colonel Moore, the President's secretary, was roused from sleep by the editor of the *Intelligencer*, who said that Thomas was making a fool of himself and that the President wanted Moore to get hold of the old dodderer and calm him down, as Moore could handle him better than anybody else. Moore promised to attend to the matter the first thing in the morning.

Johnson was seriously irritated, and early Saturday morning, when Welles brought word to him of what Welles's son had overheard, he sent for General Emory to find out who had issued the midnight order and why. The wildest rumors were flooding the city: the army was about to arrest Johnson; the President was massing troops to arrest Congress; a force in Confederate gray was marching on the capital from Maryland.

General Emory appeared at the President's summons and answered Johnson's questions in a manner half respectful, half insolent. The purpose of the order was simply to make certain that Washington was well guarded against possible disorder, from whatever source, he said, and the order had come from the general of the army, as the law required.

"Am I to understand that the President of the United States cannot give an order but through General Grant?" demanded the President.

That was the opinion of leading lawyers, Emory answered cockily, and after naming a couple of these authorities he retired.

Early that morning Johnson had appeared nervous, but he soon regained his calm. Word was brought that Stanton had spent the night locked in his office, and then that General Thomas had been arrested on Stanton's complaint, alleging violation of the Tenure of Office Act.

The arrest had been made at eight o'clock. Judge Cartter and his night clerk had been routed out during the early hours to issue the warrant, and two United States marshals awakened the groggy adjutant general and marched him off to court. They did permit him to stop at the White House and tell the President of his predicament.

The crestfallen warrior in custody was a welcome sight to Johnson; the visit restored his spirits completely. For months he had been hoping to get the situation before the courts; now Stanton himself was taking it there.

"Go see the Attorney General," Johnson told Thomas, "and then make your court appearance." To the arresting marshals the President injudiciously added:

"That is just the place I want him—in the courts."

Stanbery also told Thomas to go ahead to court. Unfortunately, the Attorney General failed to advise Thomas to follow the procedure that Colonel Moore was prepared to urge, namely, to refuse bail, go to jail, and thus enable the administration at once to start habeas corpus action and bring the Tenure of Office Law before the Supreme Court without delay. Instead, Thomas appeared before Judge Cartter and made bail, and Moore, pursuant to his midnight promise, caught up with the befuddled general just as the bail bond was being signed.

Released on bail, Thomas headed for the War Department and walked into Stanton's room in righteous dudgeon. The secretary (or ex-secretary) had passed a fitful night. After engineering the arrest of his would-be successor, Stanton had catnapped on the sofa, protected by a cordon of soldiers thrown around the building and a sentry outside the door. Senator Thayer had stayed with him as a further bodyguard. Every sound had thrown Stanton into a sweat. Excessively timid by nature, he imagined that Welles was sending marines to evict him, and mistook the tramp of his own guards for their tread.

Stanton and half a dozen senators and congressmen with him

had observed Thomas' approach through the window. When the general entered, he found them standing in a row facing the door, Stanton in the middle. Stanton inquired Thomas' business. The latter said he had come to take over. Stanton denied his authority to do so and ordered him to his own office. A congressman took down the interesting colloquy:

Thomas: "I will stand here. I want no unpleasantness in the presence of these gentlemen."

Stanton: "You can stand there if you please, but you cannot act as Secretary of War. I am Secretary of War. I order you out of this office and to your own."

Thomas: "I refuse to go and I will stand here."

And so back and forth until Thomas got tired and wandered across the hall to another room. Stanton and several of his witnesses followed, and handed Thomas a written order commanding him to abstain from exercising authority illegally. To which Thomas replied that he would act as secretary and would not go to his own office. The scene degenerated into low comedy, and Thomas himself ended it by complaining about his early arrest. The next time, he begged Stanton, please do not arrest him before breakfast.

At this tension eased, and Stanton called for a bottle. One was produced, nearly empty. Stanton measured out two exactly equal drinks in tumblers, gave one to Thomas, took the other himself, and they drank together. The secretary seemed frisky, sent for a full bottle, and poured a second round. Breathing a sigh of refreshment, Thomas said, "This, at least, is neutral ground!"

While this was taking place at the War Department, excitement prevailed at the other end of Pennsylvania Avenue. It was George Washington's birthday, February 22. A raw, wet snowstorm pelted the streets, but hundreds of spectators had trudged through the slush to jam even the corridors of the Capitol. The crush was so great that reporters pushing through the packed mass of people were an hour reaching their seats in the House gallery.

The Senate had met at noon, heard its chaplain drone through a prayer commencing, "Thou settest one up and puttest another down," and then adjourned. Most of the senators trooped over to the House wing, to watch the show there. Ben Wade, president *pro tempore*, was accommodated with a seat on the rostrum beside Speaker Colfax. For Wade this was a critical moment. He had just been denied reelection to the Senate by the Ohio legislature. Should Johnson be removed, he would become President. But should impeachment fail, Wade's days in Washington would be numbered.

When the session came to order the Reconstruction Committee was still deliberating. It was reported to be for impeachment, and Stevens was exerting all his influence and finesse to bring in that recommendation. The dawdling representatives did rouse themselves sufficiently to rebuke a Democrat who moved that in accordance with annual custom Washington's "Farewell Address" be read. Out of order, ruled "Smiler" Colfax, and a wag in the gallery yelled, "How about Johnson's farewell address?" The gavel banged, but chuckles of merriment greeted the quip. The Democrat said he would move the reading of the Constitution of the United States, but that would probably be out of order, too.

At twenty minutes past two, Stevens led the Reconstruction Committee into the chamber. He did not take a seat on the floor, but was given a chair at the left of the Speaker. From that elevated position he submitted the committee's report—a simple resolution to impeach the President. He saw no reason for debate, he added, but if "the other side" wished to say something, there would be no objection on his part, provided he might have the last word. At first no limit was set on the speeches, but later they were held to half an hour. A week might have been consumed, so eager were the members to vent their spleen on "the man at the other end of the Avenue." Throughout the harangues, Stevens remained in his commanding position, slouched in his chair, sometimes standing, now and then withdrawing to a cloakroom to lie down. It was his show, and it was at his beck that Colfax recognized members on the floor.

Andrew Johnson had been denounced many times, but never so unsparingly, never so vituperatively, never at such length as on that Washington's Birthday. Speakers invented opprobrious epithets when the supply of old ones gave out.

"Who is this Andrew Johnson?" cried Representative Farnsworth, leading the radical attack. A Democrat called out, "A President you elected!"

"I deny it!" retorted Farnsworth. "He is your President, not mine. I admit I voted for him. We were cheated by the loud professions and lying promises of this ungrateful, despicable, besotted, traitorous man . . . this accidental President, made so by an assassin's pistol, this man who, in an evil hour, was thrust upon this country. Too long has he been an incubus and a disgrace to this great and glorious country! Let him be removed!"

"The turpitude of Andrew Johnson!" shouted "Pig Iron" Kelley of Pennsylvania. "The arraignment is too circumspect for me. I hold . . . that we are about to bring to trial the great criminal of our age and country, a man who for two years has been plotting with deliberate and bloody purpose the overthrow of the institutions of our country . . . Sir, before God and the people I affirm my belief that it was his intention to overthrow the government . . . before leaving Tennessee! . . . Possessed by the thought of the Presidency . . . there stood between him and [that] position . . . but one life, that of Abraham Lincoln, and that life, a few days after Mr. Johnson was inaugurated as the President's constitutional successor, violence removed! . . . Lincoln was murdered, and other distinguished patriots may be! It is known that men ascend to power over bloody steps, and that they may do it in this country and yet be tolerated!"

The Democrats got in their say, though the galleries and the Republicans on the floor punctuated their indignation with ironical laughter.

Brooks of New York, minority leader, warned that the country was in the midst of a revolution. "A legislative power not representing the people seeks to depose the Executive Power . . . We are traversing over and over again the days of Cromwell and Charles I and Charles II." He cautioned the majority to observe every form of law in their impeachment. "If, as threatened, you suspend him; if you throw him out of office by any other process than impeachment, I tell you in behalf of thousands and tens of thousands and millions of the people of this country, we will never, never, so help me God, never, never submit!"

Derisive laughter swept the Republican side.

"Go on, go on, if you choose!" Brooks shouted. "Suppose you succeed; suppose you settle that hereafter a party having a sufficient majority in the House and Senate can depose the President of the United States"—with or without cause—"for the hat he wears, or the color of his coat. You establish a precedent which all future parties in all time to come will look to. Andrew Johnson has no power now as President of the United States. He is without authority or influence or patronage . . . By your violent acts . . . you may succeed . . . in immortalizing him on the pages of history as the most glorious defender of liberty that ever lived under any constitutional government . . . You may strip him of his office, but you will canonize him among those heroic defenders of constitutional law and liberty!"

Representative Spalding of Ohio sneered at Brooks's "gasconade," and Stevens had the penalty clause of the Tenure Act read aloud ominously. Bingham asserted that "the President of the United States has deliberately, defiantly, and criminally violated the Constitution, his oath of office, and the laws of the country."

General John A. Logan of Illinois, one of the most accomplished wavers of the bloody shirt, cried that Johnson "has dragged, as a demagogue, the robes of his high official position in the purlieus and filth of treason! . . . He has done every act which can be enumerated in the English language which is an obstruction to the prosperity of this nation and the preservation of the harmony of its people . . . He has done every act a man can conceive, not only to degrade himself, but to destroy the rights of the American people!" Mimicking the defiance of Brooks, "Blood, blood, Mr. Speaker, will flow!" Logan groaned; and "laughter" and "renewed laughter" spangled the reporter's notes.

"Andy won't stand fire a minute!" jibed a member. Another, from Illinois, read a telegram just received from Governor Oglesby of that state:

"Andrew Johnson's last act is the act of a traitor. His treason must be checked. The duty of Congress is plain . . . Millions of loyal hearts are panting to stand by the Stars and Stripes. Have no fear. All will be well."

"Ignorant, cunning, and unscrupulous," Representative Ingersoll termed Johnson's character. A colleague called for tearing

"the mask from the man who was made President by an assassin."
Representative Washburne of Illinois, Grant's mentor and spokesman, spaciously described Johnson as "the opprobrium of both
hemispheres, as mendacious as malignant," the personification of
"perfidy and treachery and turpitude unheard of in the history of
the rulers of a free people." Congressman Julian of Indiana all but
thanked Johnson for the "stupid rebel malignity" which had at
last given Congress "the courage to hurl him from the White
House . . . His capacity for evil stands out in frightful dispropor-
tion to his other gifts. He is a genius in depravity!"

So many members desired to add to the torrent of invective
that the debate was continued till Monday. But to make sure that
the seventeenth President of the United States should be impeached on the anniversary of the first, the House clock was set
back, so that the date in the journal would read February 22.

On Monday Colonel Moore found a tremendous crowd at the
Capitol, and extra guards of police everywhere. How ridiculous,
he thought; how different from the quiet prevailing at the White
House. No troops, no policemen there.

In the House, the tirades rolled on. Representative Blair recalled the "swing around the circle," when "the mouth of the
President was vomiting forth against the representatives of the
people of the United States." More telegrams from Republican
organizations at home were read. It was an orgy of hate. Representative Shanks grew tired of the clamor and called for "the
official death of Andrew Johnson without further discussion. I am
not surprised that one who began his Presidential career in
drunkenness should end it in crime."

By agreement, the vote was to be taken at five o'clock. At four-
thirty Stevens arose to make the closing speech. The House grew
hushed, for the skeletal figure suggested a wraith speaking from
the brink of the tomb. A few members tiptoed forward to catch
the feebly uttered words.

Stevens wasted none. Impeachment was a purely political
process, he said, and though the resolution was based on a violation of the Tenure Act, impeachment had been justified by a
multitude of misdeeds. Without quibbling or legal niceties, he
declared that impeachment was "intended as a remedy for mal-
feasance in office, and to prevent the continuance thereof. Beyond

that, it is not intended as a personal punishment for past offenses or for future example." Yet let none forget that there were penalties which might be visited upon an offender. Once more he stated, even as his breath failed and he was compelled to hand the speech to a clerk to finish:

"The sovereign power of the nation rests in Congress, who have been placed around the President . . . as watchmen to enforce his obedience to the law and the Constitution . . . Never was a great malefactor so gently treated as Andrew Johnson. If Andrew Johnson escapes with bare removal from office, if he be not fined and incarcerated in the penitentiary afterwards under criminal proceedings, he may thank the weakness or the clemency of Congress, and not his own innocence."

The reader became silent, and an eerie hush hung all over the crowded chamber. The soughing wind outside, whistling through the porticoes of the Capitol, and the scratching of the reporters' pens were plainly audible.

The roll was called, and on straight party lines, one hundred and twenty-six to forty-seven, the resolution was carried and the President was impeached. Not one Democrat voted "aye," not one Republican voted "nay." Horace Maynard, Andrew Johnson's companion in exile during the war, was absent, but he recorded his vote as "aye."

At the White House, the President had continued the day's routine of business calmly. He seemed a trifle more talkative than usual, and asked Moore to remain for dinner. The two were alone together when word of the vote was brought, shortly after six o'clock. The secretary thought that Johnson took the news "very coolly." He simply remarked that he thought many of those who had voted for the resolution felt "more uneasy over the position in which they had put themselves," than he did over the position in which they put him.

4.

The House had appointed a committee of two—Stevens and Bingham—to inform the Senate of their action, and shortly after one o'clock on Tuesday, February 25, the pair presented themselves at the door of the Senate chamber. Stevens, pale and grim, was leaning on a cane and Bingham's arm, but he straightened up, dramatically flung his hat on the floor behind him, handed his cane to a doorkeeper, and advanced firmly to the bar. There, drawing a paper from his pocket, he read in solemn tones, while Ben Wade sat listening with glittering eyes and owllike frown:

"Mr. President, in obedience to the order of the House of Representatives, we appear before you and in the name of the House of Representatives and of all the people of the United States we do impeach Andrew Johnson, President of the United States, of high crimes and misdemeanors in office; and we further inform the Senate that the House of Representatives will in due time exhibit particular articles of impeachment against him and make good the same; and in their name we demand that the Senate take order for the appearance of the said Andrew Johnson to answer said impeachment."

The president *pro tempore* replied:

"The Senate will take order in the premises."

The House had voted to impeach without having formulated any specific charges. The task of drawing up articles of impeachment was assigned to a committee of seven, and this committee at once ran into snags. One of the members, the glory-hunting Boutwell, wanted to deny Johnson even the title of President, maintaining that he was merely acting as such; but Bingham impatiently pointed out that if Johnson was not legally President, then nobody was, and there was nobody to impeach.

Then the question became one of what high crimes and misdemeanors could be proved against Andrew Johnson. This raised ticklish legal points; but goaded relentlessly by Stevens, the committee did succeed in patching together nine separate articles, or counts of indictment, all of which, in one form or another, dealt with violations of the Tenure Act committed by the dismissal of Stanton and the appointment of Lorenzo Thomas "when no vacancy existed." Ben Butler was insistent that another article be included, one that he had drawn up himself, quoting Johnson's speeches, especially those made in the 1866 "swing around the circle," in which the President—"unmindful of the high duties of his office, and the dignity and proprieties thereof . . . did make and deliver, with a loud voice, certain intemperate, inflammatory, and scandalous harangues" designed to bring into "disgrace, ridicule, hatred, contempt, and reproach the Congress of the United States . . . [to] destroy the regard and respect of all the good people of the United States for the Congress . . . and to excite the odium and resentment of all the good people of the United States against Congress and the laws by it duly and constitutionally enacted."

The article trailed on, but Butler got it adopted.

Stevens regarded the total result with unfeigned disgust. He added an eleventh article which swept together all the charges in a catchall wording that he hoped would give every senator plagued by a conscience some loophole to slip through and pronounce the President guilty of something or other.

The articles—the grounds for impeachment, that is—were reported to the House five days after the President's impeachment had been voted.

That day Johnson's temper got the better of him.

"Impeach me for violating the Constitution!" he muttered to Moore. "Damn them! Haven't I been struggling ever since I have been in this chair to uphold the Constitution they trample under foot!"

His special friend, Edmund Cooper, brought on another storm by suggesting that patronage might be used to predispose some senators to acquit.

"How would I feel after acquittal if I had bought it?" he flung back. "How would I feel if my conscience told me that I owed my acquittal to bribery? I will do nothing of the kind. I will not seek to use any unfair means for my vindication."

The President did resent keenly the injustice of the impeachment and the constant maligning of his motives. His cabinet watched him and were surprised when he never seemed despondent. Sometimes he did betray irritation and anxiety, but not despair. He bore the setback without much distress when General Thomas appeared for trial on Stanton's complaint and Judge Cartter dismissed the case; Stanton had realized his blunder, and declined to prosecute. So Thomas was set free, and the hope of an immediate appeal to the Supreme Court went glimmering. The impeachment would have to be fought out to the end.

The night of this reversal for the President, numerous radical congressmen attended a reception at the home of Chief Justice Chase, and they were startled when Johnson and his daughters were announced. The President circulated among the guests, at ease and smiling; but the visit stirred up rumors that Chase was about to desert the radicals and assist the President in the trial. From then on the Chief Justice was under suspicion.

Johnson was never more alert than when in the midst of a fight. His secretary, Moore, understood this. On the Sunday before the impeachment process started, Moore had accompanied the President to church, and on their return to the White House Johnson had requested Moore to read aloud passages from Addison's *Cato*, after which he "descanted quite clearly" on the character of Cato, a man who would "not compromise with wrong, but being right, died before he would yield." Moore inferred that the President drew a parallel between Cato and himself, forced to pursue a similar course "in his attempt to discharge his duties." While the House was vilifying him, the President had assured Moore that "self-respect" demanded that he force the issue raised by Stanton's disloyalty; that if he could not be President in fact, he would not be President in name only.

"What advantage would it be for me to do wrong?" he had argued. "I have nothing to gain by this step. But I am right and I intend to stand by it. I don't want to see this government lapse into a despotism. I have always battled for the right of the people and their liberties, and I am now endeavoring to defend them from arbitrary power."

He was not without support among the people. The White House mailbag bulged with messages of confidence and encouragement. Offers of armed protection against Congress poured in. A letter from Ohio read: "The hostility you are meeting from many of our representatives leaves us, the people, no other way but to approach you personally, and assure you of our sympathy and approbation." A group of Indiana citizens offered to pay the cost of his legal defense. "Old Bunker Hill sends greetings." "Be firm." "Stand for the Constitution and the people." "If you require brave hearts and stout arms to aid you, give the word." "If you want troops, let us know; this county will furnish a regiment in ten days." Such phrases studded the messages from high and low, together with frequent quoting of Sumner's famous advice, "Stick!"

Even the radical press expressed doubt of the wisdom of Congress' action. Anything to get rid of Andy Johnson, they agreed, but the articles of impeachment inspired no enthusiasm. A humorous correspondent for the *Brooklyn Daily Eagle* reported that the President was to be thrown out of office for violating the law against cruelty to animals, "in trying to kick a dirty dog out of the War Office," and "for being Andy Johnson." New York's prize-fighter congressman, John Morrissey, was said to be cogitating a resolution that "Andy Johnson fight Ben Wade for the presidency at catchweights in the rotunda of the Capitol."

Few people were happy over the prospect as the time for opening the trial of the President approached. A newspaper carried a story that Grant's wife had "cried her eyes out" over the trouble the general had involved himself in; but on the other side, General Sherman's wife was furious at Congress.

Johnson did draw one bit of satisfaction from Ben Butler's excerpting of the presidential speeches in his Article X.

"I am much obliged to him for bringing them again to public notice," the President said. "There is really even more truth in them than I supposed."

That day the President was in good spirits, and the next day— the day on which the impeachment articles were laid before the Senate—he took time to drive to the home of William Slade, the White House steward, who was dying of dropsy. The President had high regard for Slade, a colored man. Sitting down on the bed, he took the sick man's hand and did his best to comfort him. Slade could barely speak, but said gratefully that the President's daughters had been taking care of him, and Mrs. Johnson had sent messages and comforts. Two days later Johnson repeated the visit; and when Slade died shortly afterwards, the President, in the midst of his trial, attended the humble funeral.

The cabinet had favored the Attorney General's conducting of the President's defense. Stanbery was eager to do so, but he insisted on resigning in order to devote his entire time to the case and also to forestall criticism that the President was being defended at the public expense. (Nobody seemed to notice that the

President was being prosecuted at the public expense.) Selection of associate counsel presented a touchy problem; but after some casting about, Benjamin R. Curtis of Boston, a former Supreme Court justice; Jeremiah Black; William S. Groesbeck of Cincinnati, and William M. Evarts of New York were retained. To these Johnson added as his personal choice T. A. R. Nelson of East Tennessee.

At one point a group of prominent New Yorkers proposed to assume responsibility for the fees of this expensive array of counsel, but Colonel Moore told them they would have to do it secretly, because if the President got wind of their plan he would stop it. No help was needed, however; all the attorneys served without fee.

Seven managers had been named by the House of Representatives to prosecute the case before the Senate. These included five who had helped to draw up the articles of impeachment—Boutwell, Bingham, Butler, Logan, and Stevens as chairman. Old Thad was kept alive only by his unquenchable will. During the formulation of the articles, he would sit for hours, crouched over the table, occasionally sipping from a glass of wine or brandy; only his eyes seemed alive. By the time the trial commenced he had grown so weak he was carried in a chair to the Capitol from his home by two stalwart House attendants.

On March 4 the House reported (or "exhibited," as the legal phrase ran) its charges. On March 7 a summons to appear was served on the President by the Senate's sergeant-at-arms, George T. Brown. Johnson accepted the summons in his office, with only Moore present; the President said merely that he would "attend to the matter," but Moore saw that he was deeply moved by the event. The Senate ordered him to appear at one o'clock on March 13.

Meanwhile, a complication had arisen through what Johnson considered a highly improper attempt to maneuver him into buying the good graces of some of his principal accusers. As a result, Black was eliminated from the defense counsel. The affair concerned an islet off Santo Domingo, the island of Alta Vela. It contained valuable guano deposits, which an American company had exploited until expelled by Santo Domingo authorities. The group wished to have a United States warship repossess them of their property, and Black's law firm had been retained to push this claim. Meanwhile, a New York group, in which Thurlow Weed, Seward's "alter ego," was interested, had made a deal with the Santo Domingans and were mining the guano. Seward had consistently disapproved the application by Black's clients for armed intervention. Suddenly the President was handed a legal opinion endorsing their claim—the opinion signed by, among others, Butler, Bingham, and Thaddeus Stevens, all managers of the impeachment trial. And the opinion was dated *after* the impeachment process had started.

The President construed this as scarcely veiled blackmail, confronted Black with the document, and although the latter denied having any knowledge of the matter (a partner had solicited the signatures), he withdrew as counsel in the impeachment. Rumors flew that he had pulled out because he thought the President's case was hopeless.

The remaining counsel were having difficulty with their client because he insisted that his defense be conducted in his way, not theirs. He wanted to defend himself before the nation, he said, and would "care nothing for conviction by the Senate if I stood acquitted by the people." Also, if he directed his own defense, "then, if I should be convicted, I alone can be blamed if it follows as a result of plain speaking."

One rule his counsel did enforce, and that was that he should not appear in person at any time because of his hot temper and his propensity to answer back. The counsel were unanimous in requiring this, and Johnson gave in reluctantly.

On March 13, with all the pomp they could muster, the Senate, sitting as a court of justice, opened the trial. The galleries were crowded; this was expected to be the show of the century. Admission was by ticket, and the clamor for seats had been so tremendous that Senator Anthony, who was in charge, had been compelled to call the police to clear the crowds away from his home. The members of the House were on hand, seated behind the senators, and all the managers were present, although Stevens was so weak he could not stand without aid.

Already the Senate had organized itself as a court, and had had

several brushes with the Chief Justice, who was to preside. Chase
was a man of awesome dignity, and intensely ambitious politically. The Presidency was always in his mind, as a goal to be
attained and a distinction to which he felt he was entitled. In
1860 and 1864 he had tried to sidetrack Lincoln in the race for
the nomination, and his eye was fixed on the nominating conventions, which were to meet soon. However, another side of his
character was at odds with his ambition: he was profoundly religious, and scrupulous in matters of moral judgment. Should he, as
the radicals hoped, allow partisan prejudice to control the impeachment trial, he would be false as a judge, but he might expect to receive a political reward. Ambition told him that. But
already he had reached his decision. He had written to a friend:

"Whatever I may have formerly thought, or even desired, in
connection with the Presidency, I wish now to have my name
completely disconnected from it . . . I cannot be a party judge; I
must express an honest opinion of the Constitution and the law. I
must do my duty without fear and without favor."

Such honesty, he realized, would bring down the wrath of the
Republican leaders, but he went ahead. At the very start he had
insisted that he be permitted to rule on points of law; otherwise,
he intimated, he would withdraw from the trial. Since the Constitution prescribes that the Chief Justice shall preside at impeachment trials, this would have raised an obstacle to impeachment,
and the Senate had grudgingly given way. But it ruled that
should any senator object to a decision made by the chair, the
point would be put to a vote. Under this provision, Chase's rul-
ings would be set aside many times, to the detriment of the defense.

An extended brush developed over the propriety of allowing
Ben Wade to cast a vote on the President's guilt or innocence.
"How can he cast a vote that will raise his salary from eight
thousand to twenty-five thousand dollars a year?" wondered old
Sam Ward, gentleman lobbyist who was an inured to the antics of
politicians as a man could get. But Charles Sumner, who had felt
it incumbent upon him to redeem the honor of the Senate when
Stockton voted in his own case, defended Wade's right to exercise
all the prerogatives of a senator; and John Sherman claimed the

right of Ohio to have two votes in the Senate, irrespective of the matter in hand. Innuendoes were passed regarding the impropriety (if Wade's participation was censurable) of Senator Patterson, the President's son-in-law, voting in the interest of a kinsman. The decision was never in doubt: Wade was sworn, taking the same oath as the other senators and the Chief Justice himself— "in all things pertaining to the trial of the impeachment of Andrew Johnson, President of the United States, now pending, [to] do impartial justice according to the Constitution and the laws, so help me God."

On March 13 the President made appearance by counsel, Stanbery, Curtis, and Nelson attending. They requested forty days to prepare their answer to the charges, and were granted ten. That meant daily and often nightly sessions with the President, the cabinet, and witnesses to prepare the case. The cabinet had rallied firmly behind the President, and Seward, notorious for his diplomatic slitherings, proved the most practically helpful of all. Observing that "too many cooks usually spoil the broth," he announced that he would volunteer no advice unless asked, and he placed his resignation in the President's hands, to take effect the moment Johnson thought it might be of help. Seward made no secret of where he stood; when approached by the radicals with a promise that, if he would desert the President, he would be kept on as Secretary of State by Wade, he snapped:

"I'll see them damned first. The impeachment of the President is the impeachment of his cabinet."

Johnson also was the target of continual attempts to induce him to "buy off" conviction by accepting a radical cabinet.

"I shall have to insult some of these men yet," the President told Moore after one such brazen suggestion.

The ten-day preparatory period produced one positive result: the President's counsel formed a high opinion not only of his character but of his mental powers. Curtis, who had never met Johnson before, soon after reaching Washington was writing to his brother in admiration of the President's calmness, honesty, and sincerity. To his uncle, George Ticknor, the historian, Curtis was specific in his praises, writing:

"The President firmly believes he has been and is right; he

knows he is honest and true in his devotion to the Constitution. If he is expelled from office, he will march out with a firm step and a strong heart . . . My respect for the moral qualities of the man is greatly enhanced . . . He is a man of few ideas, but they are right and true, and he could suffer death sooner than yield up or violate one of them. He is honest, right-minded, and narrow-minded; he has no tact, and even lacks discretion and forecast. But he is firm as a rock; and if he should be convicted, he will go out with a firm reliance that the time will come when a 'black line' will be drawn around that senatorial record, by the command of the people of the United States."

None of his counsel had suggested that Johnson resign, and Curtis felt that even if they all advised it, "the President would not listen to such advice."

Removed from the turmoil at the Capitol, but within sight of the White House, Stanton kept vigil in his barricaded office. At first his wife had refused to supply him with either food or bed-clothing, angrily telling him to come home and stop making himself ridiculous; with an indulgent chuckle, Stanton had sent for a pot and some meat and tried his hand at cooking a stew in the fireplace. But he fell asleep, and the stew boiled over and burned. Then his wife relented and sent his meals in. He took short walks on the path outside the door, not daring to venture far and always on the *qui vive* to scuttle back inside at the first sight of an enemy.

General Sherman, having business at the War Department one day, started to leave by a side door and found it locked. He tried another, and it was locked, too. A sentry advised that he would have to use the front door, because all the others were locked ("the general can guess why"), and Sherman went away laughing heartily. Why, he exclaimed, Stanton was more heavily guarded than he himself ever thought of being when riding through hostile Indian country.

On March 23 the President's counsel entered his answer to the charges, repelling them all. That evening Johnson gave his annual reception for members of Congress, and the White House staff expected the attendance would be light. On the contrary, congressmen showed up by the scores, including many who had been foremost in stigmatizing their host. Crook, the President's body-guard, who acted as usher on such occasions, came upon a knot of these in the East Room, where they had gathered after being welcomed by the President and Mrs. Patterson in the Blue Room, and thought they sounded like giggling children.

"What are you here for?" asked one.

"What are you doing here yourself?"

"Wanted to see how Andy takes it."

Crook reflected that they were getting small satisfaction, for the President's manner was impeccable; one might have supposed the affair a surprise party in his honor, to congratulate him upon a victory.

The next day the impeachment managers filed their "replication" to the defendant's answer, and announced their readiness to submit testimony. Whereupon Ben Butler made the opening statement for the prosecution.

Butler would always consider this the high point of his career, but a fellow lawyer who heard him thought Ben showed up poorly. Butler's appearance was not in his favor. With his pot-belly, bald head, and drooping eyelids, he reminded cartoonists irresistibly of a buzzard. Being nearsighted, he held his speech close to his nose and read it nervously. The argument was clever, but it contained nothing new; it said again everything that had been said before, and said it offensively. "By murder most foul," he concluded, Andrew Johnson had become President; but Congress, thank God, could and would remove him. "The future political welfare and liberties of all men hang trembling on the decision of the hour."

Impressed by the historic significance of the proceedings, some of the managers attempted to observe strict legal decorum. Not so Butler; he proposed to conduct this trial "like any horse case." The handicap was that he had little case to try, and throughout the ensuing weeks he would attempt to make up for lack of argument by bluster. (Long afterwards he would confide to Evarts that as a lawyer he would rather have been on the opposite side.)

Among the points on which the prosecution hammered was their contention that the President had never thought of testing the Tenure Act in the courts until he rowed with Stanton and needed a blind to cover up his illegal action. The prosecution also claimed that Johnson had planned to use force in evicting Stanton; and a third charge was that he had issued orders personally to General Emory, in disregard of the law requiring all orders to go through the commanding general, Grant.

As witnesses were paraded before the senators, the trial at times took on the zaniness of a farce. Reporters were summoned to testify to Johnson's drunken and licentious habits; they swore that though they had known the President for years, they had never noticed that he was much of a drinker. His speeches on the "swing," these reporters thought, differed in no way from the kind of speeches he had been making for years, without serious objection.

"Ad Interim" Thomas, as Washington had dubbed the opera-bouffe general, added to the gaiety by gravely and minutely describing how he had split drinks with Stanton and had protested the inhumanity of before-breakfast arrests. He also had told a chap from Delaware, who cornered him at a ball and beseeched him not to fail their native state, that he would stand firm.

"The eyes of Delaware are upon you," the rustic interloper had exhorted. "Stand firm!"

"Yes, I'll stand firm," the general had answered obligingly. By way of illustrating how he stood firm, he drew himself erect on his tiptoes in a demonstration; then went on to confess that he had told somebody that if Stanton didn't get out soon, he would "probably kick the fellow out by and by."

The general was so eager to tell the whole truth that he embarrassed the prosecution. Try as they might, they could not elicit one word that showed that Johnson had contemplated using force at any time. But "the eyes of Delaware are upon you" became a catchphrase and helped the impeachers none.

Witnesses were gagged, time and again, by the Senate's overruling Chase when their answers promised to help the President. The defense tried repeatedly to introduce testimony by the cabinet showing that Johnson had expressed a wish to have the Tenure Act tested in the courts long before Stanton's suspension. Welles was put on the stand, but the Senate would not allow him to testify regarding this. Finally General Sherman, after two days of sparring, did get the fact into the record.

Butler played to the gallery continually. On April 16 the defense requested a delay in view of the serious illness of Stanbery, whereupon Butler launched into a tirade that recalled to some Lincoln's description of Ben—"as full of poison gas as a dead dog."

"We cannot wait now for the sickness of the learned Attorney General," Butler protested. "And why should we?" Counting up the days and hours of postponements already granted—always to the defense, he insisted—he said that "the whole legislation of the country is stopping; the House of Representatives has to be, day by day, here at your bar. The taxes of the country cannot be revised because this trial is in the way. The appropriations for carrying on the government cannot be passed because this trial is in the way . . . Gentlemen of the Senate, this is the closing up of a war wherein three hundred thousand men laid down their lives to save the country . . . More than that, I have in my hand testimony of what is going on this day and this hour in the South. While we are waiting for the Attorney General to get well, our fellow citizens are being murdered day by day. There is not a man here who does not know that the moment justice is done on this great criminal, these murders will cease!"

Curtis rose to object, but Butler hurried on.

"I cannot be interrupted . . . Mr. Chief Justice, in Alabama your register of bankruptcy . . . is driven today from his duties and his home by the Ku Klux Klan, upon fear of his life . . . and shall we here delay this trial any longer, under our responsibility to our countrymen, to our consciences, and to our God, because of a question of courtesy? While we are being courteous, the true men of the South are being murdered, and on our heads and on our skirts is this blood if we remain any longer idle."

He then accused Johnson of being implicated in a ring of gold speculators, and when one of his associate managers, Logan, tried to correct his figures, waved him back with, "No; I mean what I say. I never make mistakes in such matters . . . For the safety of the finances of the people, for the progress of the legislation of the people, for the safety of the true and loyal men, black and white, in the South, who have periled their lives for four years; yea, five years; yea, six years; yea, seven years, in your behalf; for the good of the country, for all that is dear to any man and patriot, let this trial proceed!"

Nothing could halt the flow of indignation.

"I open no mail of mine that I do not take up an account from the South of some murder—or worse—of some friend of the country. I want these things to stop! Many a man whom I have known standing by my side for the Union I can hear of now only as laid in the cold grave by the assassin's hand . . . I say nothing of the threats of assassination made every hour and upon every occasion, even when objection to testimony is made by the managers. I say nothing of the threats made against the lives of the great officers of the Senate and against the managers . . . We have not the slightest fear of these cowardly menaces; but all these threats, these unseemly libels on our form of government, will go away, when this man goes out of the White House!"

Instead of answering in kind, Evarts—lean, learned, precise, whose wit upon occasion could cut like a razor—replied with steely calm:

"Mr. Chief Justice and senators . . . I have never heard such a harangue before in a court of justice; but I cannot say that I may not hear it again in this court. All these delays . . . seem to press upon the honorable managers except at the precise point of time when some of their mouths are open occupying your attention with long harangues . . . And now twenty minutes by the watch are taken up with this harangue of the honorable manager about the Ku Klux Klan."

There was a hush as the rebuke sank in. Then Senator Cameron of Pennsylvania, a stalwart radical, rose to object that the word "harangue" was out of order.

Not the word, but the harangue itself, was out of order, Senator Doolittle countered. Whereupon a peacemaker moved that the Senate do adjourn, and it did.

Evart's mildness did not sit well with the President. His stump-speaker blood was fired by Butler's rant, and he deplored that he had not been at hand to give the "Beast" a dressing down he would never forget.

"The idea of not one of the counsel replying to him as he should have been answered!" Johnson grumbled. "I was charged with murder and robbing the Treasury, and the only reply was the word 'harangue'!"

The next Sunday the President returned from church fretting

about the "mismanagement" of his case. He told Moore that he
had even received word that the other side thought it was being
botched.

"Look at Mr. Evarts' reply to Butler the other day," the President repeated. "When he let loose his tirade of abuse, when he
opened his billingsgate on me, all Mr. Evarts had to say was that
it was a 'harangue!' And I believe he thought he did a most smart
and dreadful thing when he so termed Butler's references to me.
Then was the chance to have administered a rebuke that would
not only have told upon the Senate, but upon the whole country!
What has such rubbish to do with the merits of the case? And
when it was lugged in, why wasn't it answered fittingly? The
managers allude to me as a 'criminal.' Why hasn't that been replied to by my counsel?"

In disgust at the pusillanimous ways of lawyers, the President
sulked, and became argumentative and captious. When his counsel asked for certain documentary data, Johnson burst into
Moore's office wondering aloud why some people always wanted
others to do their work for them. The secretary thought the President seemed worried. But nothing would induce Johnson to utter
a guess as to the outcome of the trial. It was all speculation, he
insisted; the same as in an election; you could never be sure how
the vote would go.

Analyzing the opposition, he put the people who were against
him in three categories. First, those who wanted him removed
because he was an obstacle to their selfish designs; these people
were abusive. Second, those who more or less agreed with him
on policy, but resented that they were not able to control him.
Third, those who carried a grudge because of the part he had
played during the war; these were the copperheads.

Johnson frequently reverted to Grant's behavior. The general
was lobbying for conviction and predicting that the President
would be found guilty; he told Senator Henderson that Johnson
deserved impeachment if for nothing else than because he was
"an infernal liar." On his part, Johnson told Moore that General
Lee would go down in history as a greater man than Grant.

At the time of passing this judgment, Johnson did not know
that Grant had in his pay a White House janitor who ransacked

the waste baskets for incriminating papers. At least one highly compromising letter was found, torn into bits, which Stanton painstakingly pieced together. Unfortunately, the letter compromised not Johnson but a senator who was one of the loudest in demanding conviction.

Grant's influence was operating in another way. The Republican national convention was to be held at Chicago in May, and Grant's nomination for President seemed certain. Eager to get aboard the bandwagon, state conventions and other party units were lining up in favor of Grant and against Johnson, his "detractor," and this back-home pressure was being applied to doubtful senators.

Not all of the President's judges cowered under the party whip, even though the *Independent* screamed that "if Mr. Johnson is acquitted, Reconstruction and the Republican party are destroyed together!" Fessenden received warning that "any Republican senator who votes against impeachment need never expect to get home alive." Neal Dow, Maine's apostle of prohibition, advised Fessenden to "hang Johnson up by the heels like a dead crow in a cornfield, to frighten all his tribe." But the senator replied that he had taken an oath to do impartial justice, and "I would rather be confined to planting cabbages for the remainder of my days" than break it. What he thought of Andrew Johnson politically was beside the point; actually he thought very little of him, and believed that if the President were being tried for "general cussedness" he would be convicted overnight. But the law and the evidence must decide the case, and Fessenden served notice on his constituents that "I, and not they, am sitting in judgment upon the President."

Chase was receiving the same sort of vilification. He was followed in the street, his mail was filled with abuse, spies watched his house, and he was threatened with political annihilation. He was cut socially, a heavy blow to him; but he continued to preside honestly and to rule according to the law. His personal opinion of the case he divulged in a letter to a friend, writing:

"How can the President fulfill his oath to preserve, protect, and defend the Constitution, if he has no right to defend it against an act of Congress sincerely believed by him to have been passed in violation of it? To me, therefore, it seems perfectly clear that the President had a perfect right, and indeed was under the highest obligation, to remove Mr. Stanton, if he made the removal not in wanton disregard of constitutional law, but with a sincere belief that the Tenure of Office Act was unconstitutional, and for the purpose of bringing the question before the Supreme Court."

Wade, who daily sat beside Chase on the rostrum, treated the stately Chief Justice with coarse familiarity. "Chase is all right," he once remarked, "but his theology is loose: he thinks there is a fourth member of the Trinity." Chase used the Vice-President's room to assume his judicial gown before entering the Senate. One day the robe was missing, and Chase and several pages hunted it in vain. Wade, who was watching silently, spied something black under something else, and fishing it out with his cane, held it out on the tip of the stick, with, "Here, Chase, here's your damned robe." The mortally offended Chief Justice presided that day in a manner more stately than ever.

Passion, not sense, ruled the hour. To young Henry Adams, home after eight years of diplomacy in Europe, it seemed that periodically the entire Senate would "catch hysterics of nervous bucking." Congressman Julian, hot for impeachment and one of the authors of the articles, would remember years afterward the "relentless" feeling against Johnson, which he had shared to the full. "Party madness was in the air," it seemed to him as he looked back in amazement. "No extravagance of speech or explosion of wrath was deemed out of order . . . The exercise of calm judgment was simply out of the question . . . The spirit of intolerance among the Republicans against those who differed with them set all moderation and common sense at defiance."

In such a fever of crimination and unreason, the time when the Senate would render its verdict drew close. Hopes on both sides rose and fell. Washington swarmed with strangers. Some of them were office seekers, eager for the jobs to be passed out by the Wade administration; with an election in sight, the patronage promised to be lush. Others were gamblers, laying odds for and against impeachment; money to back either side was plentiful. Then there were the dispensers of advice, the seers and mediums with messages from the quick and the dead, surefire counselors on how to win. These, including spiritualists and table-rappers, kept at Johnson even in the midst of the trial. His legal counsel professed to see victory in sight. G. T. Strong encountered Evarts in New York and found him "cocksure of his illustrious client's acquittal." Strong hoped Evarts was wrong. As a lawyer he thought the managers had made their case, and he was for Johnson's "conviction and degradation."

Sumner foresaw universal woe if impeachment should fail. An abolitionist of long standing told Julian, on the eve of the voting, that he was so despondent he felt "as if he were sitting up with a sick friend who was expected to die." Two evenings before the vote, the managers were so jubilant that Wade met with Grant and selected his cabinet, Ben Butler, as was expected, being tapped for Secretary of State.

At the White House, Colonel Moore was fidgety and gloomy. To him it seemed that the Senate was devil-bent on crushing Johnson, right or wrong, and even men of previous integrity— Senator Sherman, for instance—were caving in under the party demands. The cabinet itself was divided as to the outcome, Browning sure the President would be convicted, the others uncertain. Only Seward remained optimistic; between pinches of snuff he offered to bet Browning two hampers of champagne that the President would be acquitted, but the wager was declined.

"Ad Interim" Thomas, who had been making a nuisance of himself in cabinet meetings, grew restive, and said he couldn't wait much longer, he ought to "go across and demand possession of the War Department." Johnson commanded him to do absolutely nothing, and Browning, who was acting as Attorney General, added the caution to *say* nothing either.

Johnson remained inscrutable. He seldom discussed the trial any more, but often talked about his early youth. One day he brought out a battered copy of *The American Speaker*, and asked Moore to read the passages from Chatham's speeches from it. He had learned to read from a copy of that book, the President said; it had been given to him by William Hill. "How ardently I wished I could read like Bill Hill!" Another time he showed Moore a large-print Bible he had brought from Tennessee, and with feeling read aloud a verse (I Samuel, 12:3):

"Behold, here I am: witness against me before the Lord, and before his anointed: whose ox have I taken? or whose ass have I taken? or whom have I defrauded? whom have I oppressed? or of whose hand have I received any bribe to blind mine eyes therewith? I will restore it you."

Moore saw the application the President was making mentally to his own case.

Occasionally the President would philosophize on the subject of public gratitude, commenting that he had encountered ingratitude so often he had ceased to expect anything else.

"I don't know anything more depressing than for a man to labor for the people and not be understood," he expatiated. "It is enough to sour his very soul. He may have nothing else at heart than the interest of the mass; he may struggle for their elevation; he may have nothing selfish in view; he may not look to his own or his relations' aggrandisement; and yet he may be deserted by the very persons in whose behalf he has given all that he has."

Yet there was no self-pity in the observation. Johnson divulged no real clue as to his estimate of the chances of acquittal, though he did tactfully suggest that Moore look around for some appointment he fancied; he could have any place the Senate would confirm him in.

The President still relaxed by driving into the country, with or without the grandchildren, and on these outings it seemed to Crook that he was more reserved and meditative than usual. Apparently his thoughts were melancholy, but no matter how withdrawn he appeared, Crook knew that Johnson was constantly aware of all that went on around him. Crook had realized this on a day in the previous summer, when, on their way back from a drive to what is now Rock Creek Park they were caught in a sudden shower. The carriage overtook a young woman, cheaply dressed, struggling through the downpour, carrying a baby. Johnson stopped the carriage and invited the forlorn wayfarer in. She lived on a dingy street not far from the White House, and the President directed that they drive there. During the ride, while the woman huddled on the seat, trying not to soil the cushions with her dripping garments, Johnson said hardly a word, but Crook noticed that his eyes rested on her and the child very kindly. At the door of her frame cottage, Crook helped her out;

she was still unaware that she had been riding in the President's carriage. Then, at the White House, Crook overheard Johnson quietly instructing the steward to make sure that the drenched coachman got a hot toddy. The President was not oblivious of his surroundings.

Tuesday, May 12, was the day appointed for the Senate to vote. The day before, Welles feared the worst. And so, on their side, did the impeachers. The vote was bound to be close, and the radicals felt they needed more time to put pressure on the waverers. When the court convened, therefore, Senator Chandler immediately moved for a postponement until Saturday, because of the sudden illness of Senator Howard, Chandler's Michigan colleague. Howard was delirious, Chandler said; he could not possibly attend until the end of the week.* Howard was an ultra radical and would vote for conviction. The majority of the Senate approved the delay, to the disappointment of Browning, who believed the President could have been acquitted had the vote been taken that day.

On Friday, the fifteenth, government business came to a virtual standstill as employees in the departments gathered in knots to discuss the outcome of the voting the next day. On the streets, whenever two acquaintances met they stopped and exchanged guesses. Lists of senators known, or suspected, to be "for" and "against" were drawn up, scrutinized, altered, amended, and redrawn, never coming out the same. No two lists agreed. The gamblers were happy, and rumors of "big money" invading the town gave a fillip to the betting. The consensus of the cabinet gave the victory to the President, but by a slender margin, and little outright confidence was expressed.

Saturday, May 16, dawned, a lovely spring morning. In bright sunshine crowds trooped to the Capitol—among them a Tennessee boy who had called at the White House with his father the day before, and had received a ticket to "go see the show on the Hill." The President had smiled as he handed out the coveted pasteboard. The moment of decision had been reached.

---

* Secretary of the Navy Welles did not doubt that Senator Howard was delirious; probably, he wrote in his diary, delirium tremens.

5.

Three interlocking dramas had been unfolding during the hectic weeks of April and May, 1868. There was the daily forensic spectacle on Capitol Hill. There was the behind-the-scenes activity of undercover workers for both sides. And there was a private drama being played out at the White House in the family of the man who stood in the vortex of the storm.

Johnson's family was his steadfast support in the crisis. Following his invariable custom, the President paid his regular morning call on his wife, in her sitting room, and discussed the program for the day. Eliza Johnson counseled cheerfully, never doubted the outcome, but told Andrew over and over that as long as he obeyed his conscience, he had nothing to fear.

Martha ran the domestic establishment without a ripple of interruption. Every levee, every state dinner, every social courtesy was carried out imperturbably. Martha greeted callers as usual, managed her mother's bulky mail, and never faltered in tact or poise. She watched jealously over her father's welfare, and when consultations with counsel stretched into the early hours, sometimes till dawn, she was on hand with chafing dish, coffee, and sustaining snacks, no matter what the time. The White House staff could detect no alteration in the smooth routine of the household, though among themselves there was constant speculation.

The President was able to get his side of the case before the public in his own words, despite the Senate's gagging of his trial witnesses, by means of newspaper interviews. These sometimes were indiscreet, and caused his attorneys anguish because he gave away secrets of strategy; nevertheless, they served a useful purpose.

Before the trial began, in an interview with the *New York World* reporter, Johnson had made clear the grounds on which he based his right to dismiss Stanton both constitutionally and under the Tenure of Office Act. He scoffed at fears being expressed that he aimed to subvert the government.

"What nonsense!" he said. "It's very likely that *I* am anxious to start a revolution! No, I'll leave that responsibility with those who have already undertaken it."

A month later, the same correspondent had a second talk with Johnson, and reported that the President showed in no way that he was feeling the strain.

"No," the President replied to a question as to whether his health was affected. "I may have lost a little weight, if anything. The rack used to be called in Venice, you know, a great appetizer."

When the reporter probed for Johnson's estimate of his chances in the trial, he got a return question as to the reporter's guess.

"My opportunities for communication with the parties [concerned] are not, just now, quite so favorable as yours," the President pointed out drolly.

The newsman replied that he thought if the matter were put to a vote quickly, impeachment probably would carry; but the longer the decision was put off, the brighter the prospect for the President, because public opinion was bound to turn in his favor.

Johnson laughed.

"You take a rather gloomy view," he said, and launched into a statement of his position. The reporter noted that as he became engrossed, "he leaned forward in his chair, and enforced what he said with vigorous gestures."

"Congress assumes that the President is merely an executive, compelled by his oath to execute any law passed . . . over his veto," the President explained. "There is a limit to such an assumption as that . . . Suppose Congress should pass a law abolishing the veto power . . . suppose it should pass a dozen laws of this character . . . would the President be constitutionally bound to execute them as laws? Would it not be his duty, as in the present instance, to seek immediate judgment in the Supreme Court?"

To another interviewer Johnson defended the speeches he had made during the "swing around the circle." When great questions are before the people, he said, "it is more important that they be understood than that anybody's dignity should be preserved . . . Do they propose to impeach me on a question of taste and dignity? Is it dignified of Mr. Wade to go around the country, calling me a damned traitor, and must I be impeached if I say a word in reply?"

By such expositions, the President elicited public sympathy to a widening extent, while the shoddiness of the impeachers' motives and case was being exposed before the Senate. On the basis of the legal arguments alone, several senators felt that they could not vote for conviction. On every point the managers were outmatched, outmaneuvered, and outdebated by the far abler defense counsel, and the emptiness of the allegations was laid bare tellingly.

In lieu of valid proofs, the party leaders redoubled the pressure on doubtful senators. The belief was spread that should Johnson be acquitted, he would wage a fiercer war on Congress and the result would probably be civil conflict. To dispel this fear the defense enlisted the help of Reverdy Johnson, who contrived to bring the President and Senator Grimes together by apparent accident, and in the course of a general conversation made allusion to the disturbing rumors. Johnson denied energetically having any such ideas; there was no warranty in anything he had ever said or done for believing he would not conform strictly to the Constitution and the laws, he pointed out. This reassuring word Grimes carried back to the Senate, where it had good effect.

The Senate met again on May 16 to render their verdict. Uncertainty still prevailed regarding the outcome. The managers believed they could count on thirty-five votes—one short of the two-thirds needed for conviction. The senator on whom they had concentrated their efforts of persuasion or intimidation was Edmund G. Ross, of Kansas. Young for a senator (he was forty-one), Ross had succeeded to the seat of Jim Lane when the latter blew his brains out in despondency over financial woes. Ross had no fortune and no influential connections outside of the party leadership in Kansas, and Kansas was perhaps the most radical state of all. Ross stood at the commencement of his political career. Though he had been under extreme pressure from his Kansas colleague, Senator Pomeroy, he had steadily refused to commit himself. The evening before, however, Pomeroy had elicited a half admission that if Ross were to convict on any of the articles, it would probably be on the eleventh—Stevens' catchall. Still, he had declined to commit himself positively even to that extent.

This faint admission altered the impeachers' strategy.

When Chase opened the court on May 16, the radicals moved and carried that Article XI should be voted on first. This scrapped a previously agreed rule that the articles should be voted on in numerical order.

Solemnly the Chief Justice cautioned the galleries to maintain absolute silence during the calling of the roll. The warning was superfluous; a profound hush had settled over the chamber packed with fifteen hundred senators, representatives, reporters, and spectators.

Suddenly this was broken when Senator Fessenden excitedly moved for a half-hour delay because Senator Grimes was not in his seat. Grimes was known to be for acquittal; he had said so openly and often, and in a way so offensive to the impeaching party that three days before, the *New York Tribune* had wound up a volley of abuse directed against the Iowan with the words: "We have had Benedict Arnold, Aaron Burr, Jefferson Davis, and now we have James W. Grimes." The atrocious slander had brought on a stroke of apoplexy; but though he was partially paralyzed, Grimes had vowed to be in his place on Saturday when the vote was taken, if it cost him his life.

(Senator Howard actually was brought to the Capitol on a stretcher, but managed to stagger to his seat.)

Fessenden was still making his appeal when Reverdy Johnson cried, "He is outside the door! He is here!"

Supported by four friends, Grimes shuffled to his desk, and the roll call commenced. The senators' names were called in alphabetical order. Each was required to rise and remain standing while the Chief Justice propounded the question:

"How say you? Is the respondent, Andrew Johnson, President of the United States, guilty or not guilty of a high misdemeanor, as charged in this article?"

The only answer that could be given was either "guilty" or "not guilty." Nothing more could be said, and no senator could decline to render judgment; those who cared to file written opinions could do so, and these would be included in the journal.

The first name was called:

"Senator Anthony of Rhode Island."

At the White House, McCulloch, Welles, and General Thomas

sat waiting with the President. Willard's Hotel, a stone's throw away, was connected with the Capitol by telegraph, and Moore had posted an orderly to hurry across with the dispatches as they arrived. The President seemed cool, showed little excitement, and merely observed that he hoped the contest would be settled; it had dragged on too long. Word of the change in the order of voting caused surprise. Then the balloting was reported as it progressed.

Congressman Julian, seated in the Senate chamber behind a double row of senators, marked the "indescribable anxiety" on the faces of the representatives around him when Senator Anthony rose to respond to the Chief Justice's question. His answer came, "Guilty." That had been expected. The roll continued, and men "grew pale and sick under the burden of suspense," while "such a stillness prevailed that the breathing in the galleries could be heard," Julian recorded. This was especially noticeable each time a doubtful senator voted, "the people holding their breath as the words 'guilty' or 'not guilty' were pronounced, and then giving it simultaneous vent."

Fessenden paused before answering, and in the silence the tinkle of a woman's earring was plainly heard. His vote was "Not guilty."

Hearts throbbed when Senator Fowler's turn came, and in his excitement the Tennessean stammered something like "Guilty." The Chief Justice asked him to repeat, and this time Fowler audibly acquitted the President.

Grimes's name was called. Chase suggested that he remain seated, but Grimes pulled himself to his feet, heard the question through, and voted, "Not guilty."

At Henderson's name, tension built up again, for the Missourian had been subjected to the most intense pressure to convict. He looked haggard, and when he voted "Not guilty," scowls crossed the faces of radical senators.

Up to this point the tally showed twenty-four votes to convict. The impeachers were sure of ten more, and were fairly sure of Willey of West Virginia. Trumbull of Illinois and Van Winkle of West Virginia were among the Republicans pledged to acquit, and the Democrats of course were solidly for acquittal. If Willey voted to convict, as expected, the impeachers would have thirty-five votes—one short of two-thirds. The result, therefore, hinged upon a single vote—that of the mild-looking senator from Kansas, Edmund Ross.

During the voting Ross had sat abstractedly tearing up slips of paper, which littered the floor around his seat. His future was at stake, for he had been threatened by Pomeroy with political ruin if he upheld Johnson. Worse, word had been brought of a plot to seize him, convey him to Baltimore and either hold him there until after the vote had been taken, or if necessary assassinate him. Ross was not a heroic man; he had no wish for martyrdom.

The Chief Justice called his name. Ross arose, scraps of torn paper fluttering from his lap to the floor—prophetically symbolic of his shattered future if he made the wrong response.

After putting the question, Chase himself leaned forward to catch the reply, anxiety written on his features.

In a slight voice, conversationally, Ross replied, "Not guilty."

A groan went up from the radicals seated around him. Ben Butler glowered. Wade buried his chin in his collar and looked grim.

Thereafter the roll call produced no surprises, and the final tally stood—thirty-five for conviction, nineteen for acquittal. Impeachment on Article XI had been beaten by one vote.

Under the previously adopted rules, voting was to proceed on the other articles in numerical order, starting with Article I. But Ross's defection had thrown the radicals into confusion, and they determined to play for time. A motion therefore was presented that the Senate adjourn for ten days. The motion was carried, over the protests of both Democrats and a few Republicans, and the court adjourned.

When the result of the vote on the eleventh article was brought to the little group sitting in the President's office, their thought was (in Moore's words) that they were "out of the woods." The next dispatch, telling of the postponement until May 26, destroyed that optimism. Ten more days of suspense were looked forward to gloomily.

Johnson took the delay philosophically. When friends began dropping in to offer congratulations, he displayed no elation.

What did please him was the swift arrival of a single line in Seward's handwriting, sent over from the State Department, expressing gratification at the result. Seward, Johnson told Moore, had been absolutely true all through the impeachment crisis, he had never wavered once.

The managers had gained ten days in which to pick up one additional vote, somewhere, somehow, by means legitimate or illegitimate. The House empowered the prosecution to throw out a dragnet in hope of snaring some fact or knowledge that might be used to influence at least one of the seven Republican senators who had voted "not guilty" to recant. Bank accounts were pried into, telegrams impounded, the mails violated, a swarm of spies was turned loose, witnesses were bullied and harassed, and the most private relationships were ruthlessly revealed.

Senator Ross was hounded. Agents offered him any amount of money to change his vote. "If it's money the damned scoundrel wants, tell him there's a bushel!" roared Ben Butler. A letter was found indicating that a senator *had* offered to sell his vote to the defense for thirty thousand dollars—but unfortunately the senator proved to be not Ross, but Ross's colleague, Senator Pomeroy.

The imprecations of the church were called to assist, and Methodist Bishop Matthew Simpson, a radical in politics, secured the adoption of a resolution at his church's General Conference calling for a day of prayer to "save our senators from error."

Senator Henderson of Missouri was subjected to the most intense pressure, Grant himself indicating to Henderson the danger of his stand for acquittal, and hinting at a cabinet position should Henderson reconsider. The hint meant something at this juncture, because on May 21, while the Senate stood in adjournment, the Republican convention in Chicago had nominated Grant for the presidency, and, passing over Ben Wade, chose "Smiler" Colfax as running mate. (The day before the convention opened, a speaker at a Republican rally had declared that Senator Trumbull would be wise not to show himself on the streets of Chicago, or he would be strung up at the nearest lamppost.)

In the case of Senator Ross, the influence of a woman, Vinnie Ream, was sought. Ross boarded with Vinnie's mother, and Vinnie, pert and twenty-one, was a sculptress who was working on a statue of Lincoln to be placed in the rotunda of the Capitol. She had been assigned a tiny room in the crypt of the Capitol for use as a studio, and she believed that President Johnson was both great and good. Seeking to escape his hounders, Ross occasionally took refuge in her studio, and the impeachers suggested to her that she persuade the senator to vote as desired. When she refused, General Dan Sickles was called in to charm her. Sickles fancied himself as a lady-killer; but Vinnie was proof against his one-legged gallantry and not only succeeded in resisting his blandishments, but prevented him from speaking with Ross until the day of the resumed voting, on May 26.

As before, the President received the results by telegraph from the Capitol and by courier from Willard's. This time, it being a regular cabinet day, the entire cabinet was on hand. Seward was cheerful as usual, but the others looked uneasy. Johnson was calm and self-possessed.

The first message announced that the Senate had again changed the order of voting, and would take up the second article ahead of the first. In a closed-door session of the Senate, Senator Sherman had stated that he simply could not stultify himself by voting "guilty" on the first article. This charged Johnson with violating the Tenure Law by dismissing Stanton. After all he had said in the Senate at the time of the bill's passage about the law's not applying to Lincoln holdovers in the cabinet, Sherman could not and would not maintain the opposite now. On the second and third articles, however, he might see his way clear to convict, for these charged that the President had illegally appointed General Thomas Secretary of War ad interim, when there existed no vacancy in the office, and that the President had issued orders to Thomas unlawfully.

In consequence, as soon as the Senate met on May 26, a motion was put and carried to vote on the second article, and then the others in numerical order, skipping the first article altogether.

Again the suspenseful drama unfolded. When Senator Ross rose to respond to Chase's fateful question, he looked down, as he would later testify, "literally into my open grave." But he voted "not guilty." No senator changed his vote, and the tally stood again at thirty-five for conviction, nineteen for acquittal. On that article the President was cleared, and the news brought a sigh of relief to the cabinet assembled in the White House.

Then the roll was called on the third article, which was only a rehash of the second. Nothing changed: the result again was thirty-five to nineteen.

The radicals were enraged. They had used up their best chances, and to prolong the voting would only invite more conspicuous disaster. Senator Williams of Oregon, the floor manager, threw in the sponge by moving that the court adjourn *without day*, ending the trial altogether. There was some quibbling over whether the Chief Justice should be permitted to record a verdict of outright acquittal—or of acquittal on three articles only—but Chase prevailed, and judgment of full acquittal was entered, and the court was dissolved.

Carried out of the Senate in his armchair, Thaddeus Stevens brandished his pipestem arms and croaked, "The country is going to the devil!"

As dispatches reporting each of these moves were received by Johnson, Secretary Browning noted his deportment intently. The President was "calm, dignified, placid, and self-possessed, with no outward sign of agitation," Browning recorded. "When the final result was announced, and we all knew that the atrocity had ended . . . he received the congratulations of his Cabinet with the same serenity and self-possession which have characterized him throughout the terrible ordeal."

Crook, the bodyguard, who had been posted at the Senate by the President, ran all the way back to the White House with the news, and after bursting in on the President, dashed upstairs to inform Mrs. Johnson.

She was in her rocking chair, sewing, and as she looked up, Crook cried, "He's acquitted! The President is acquitted!"

Tears of joy came to the eyes of the frail little woman, and rising, she took the messenger's hand between both hers and said with a voice that did not quaver:

"Crook, I knew he would be acquitted; I knew it. Thank you for coming to tell me."

At twenty-five minutes past three o'clock, a letter arrived at the White House from the War Department. It contained the resignation of Edwin Stanton as Secretary of War. But he made plain, in bowing out, that he was yielding not to the President, but to the authority of the Senate, which had not seen fit to uphold him.

The general who brought the letter thought Johnson read it with anger, but the President made no comment.

By that time the mansion was overflowing with people hastening to extend congratulations. An "avalanche of cards" poured in, and the reception rooms took on the air of "a royal palace after a coronation." Reporters noted many faces that had not been seen at that end of the Avenue for a long while. The President bore himself with dignity and restraint, offered no recriminations, and praised the seven Republican senators who had stood out for acquittal.

"Never," commented one onlooker, "did a man behave himself more without arrogance, or an appearance of unseemly joy."

In Congress, the utmost fury of the radicals was loosed upon those who had thwarted their will, and Vinnie Ream was summarily evicted from her basement cubbyhole.

6.

Governor Brownlow did public penance for Johnson's acquittal.

"Tennessee, including Johnson, Patterson, and Fowler, has acted so treacherously," he announced contritely, "that I am ashamed to ask the loyal North any longer to confide in any of us."

The anger of the frustrated impeachers did not subside swiftly. At the close of the trial, the President sent Stanbery's renomination as Attorney General to the Senate, but in a fit of peevishness the Senate rejected it. Johnson then submitted Evarts' name, and because he was a radical, albeit not a pronounced one, Evarts was confirmed.

Two days after the verdict, the stricken Grimes expressed a hope to Browning that the administration would conduct itself thenceforward "wisely and prudently." The President had no contrary intention, and Evarts schemed a way out of the Stanton-Thomas muddle. At the time General Thomas had been appointed secretary ad interim, the President had sent to the Senate the nomination of Thomas Ewing to be Stanton's permanent replacement. Ewing was highly regarded, but he was nearly eighty years old, and the Senate had taken no action on the nomination. Evarts suggested that Johnson send in the name of General John M. Schofield as Stanton's successor. Schofield was a popular middle-of-the-roader with a fine service record, who had many senatorial friends. Before consenting to accept the appointment, he insisted on consulting Grant, and the latter strongly urged him to decline, warning that Johnson could not be trusted. In spite of this Schofield did accept; and after some petty quibbling about the wording of the resolution, the Senate confirmed him. Johnson had not thought highly of Schofield at first, but they got along very well together.

Meanwhile, the President's confidence in McCulloch had lessened. The Treasury Department had become staffed and stuffed with radical partisans, and the secretary appeared overzealous in defending these. McCulloch also seemed unable to comprehend the corruption that had proliferated in his department. Johnson believed he was too timid to take corrective action, but McCulloch maintained that the Tenure of Office Act tied his hands.

The disagreement came to a head in the case of the Commissioner of Internal Revenue, E. A. Rollins, whose involvement with the infamous Whisky Ring was notorious. This conspiracy already had defrauded the government of millions of dollars in taxes, but McCulloch refused to move against Rollins. Johnson finally lost patience, demanded and received Rollins' resignation, insolently worded, and then procured Rollins' indictment and trial. But the prosecution was hamstrung by apathy at the Treasury (where McCulloch allotted a mere one thousand dollars to defray the expense of an extraordinarily complex case) and by the not irrelevant consideration that the Whisky Ring controlled the judge and the jury. Rollins was acquitted.

The general breakdown in public morality caused Johnson intense concern. Corruption was everywhere; one carpetbag politician gaily proclaimed that "corruption is the fashion" and publicly preened himself on being as venal as his competitors. The shady transactions of the Credit Mobilier already were besliming the

Capitol, although the full story of its swindles would not be disclosed for some time yet. Johnson repeatedly sought action to curb the cynical looting of the public treasury, but Congress preferred to devote time and energy to promoting more or less open schemes of peculation.

Seward, also, after his steadfastness during the impeachment trial, was causing the President misgivings. The Secretary of State seemed to have reverted to his incorrigible habits of compromising; he invited Grant to dinner, and was seen in the general's company in New York. Grant had not spoken to a single member of the cabinet who had condemned him in the altercation over his loss of memory at the time of Stanton's reinstatement; but Seward, it was recalled, had hedged his account with a possible doubt, and Grant did unbend to him somewhat.

Brushing aside the demands that still beset him to make over his cabinet, the President, in spite of rising difficulties, decided to make no change.

For Thaddeus Stevens, the collapse of the impeachment was the collapse of hope. His anger against the "man at the other end of the Avenue" burned on, and he worked over a speech which was read for him in the House on July 7, as his valedictory. In it he presented five new articles of impeachment, stating that he did not expect them to be acted upon, but he wished his arraignment to stand in the record. Never again, he predicted, would a usurping executive be removed by peaceful means. "If he retains the money and the patronage of the government, he will be found, as has been found, stronger than the law, and impenetrable to the spear of justice." No, in the future "let the block be brought out and the axe sharpened . . . and if tyranny become intolerable, the only recourse will be found in the dagger of Brutus."

Against this grisly prospect he opposed his vision of the unattainable ideal that had haunted and warped his existence. Addressing Speaker Colfax, he concluded:

"My sands are nearly run, and I can only see with the eyes of faith. I am fast descending the downhill of life, at the foot of which is an open grave. But you, sir, are promised length of days and a brilliant career. If you and your compeers can fling away ambition and realize that every human being, however lowly

born and degraded by fortune, is your equal, that every inaliena-
ble right which belongs to you belongs also to him, truth and
righteousness will spread over the land, and you will look down
from the top of the Rocky Mountains upon an empire of one
hundred millions of happy people."

The ideal was the same that Andrew Johnson held throughout
his life.

When Congress adjourned, Stevens was too weak to return to
Lancaster, and on August 11 he died. By his instructions he was
buried in a Negro cemetery as a protest against discrimination
and a final vindication of the brotherhood of all men.

On July 4 the President issued an amnesty proclamation which
pardoned everyone who had participated in the rebellion except
those few who were under indictment. Foremost among these
was Jefferson Davis, awaiting trial in Virginia. Johnson had
wished to include even Davis, but his cabinet demurred; they
feared that such action would arouse the radicals to make another
attempt at impeachment.

"I suppose there will be a howl," Johnson admitted. "But I
don't care for that. The question is, is such a step right? If it is, I
am going to take it. I will not mince matters."

As a matter of expediency, however, he yielded to the entreat-
ies of the alarmed cabinet and made the few exceptions.

The seven Republican senators who had defied the party whip
and voted to acquit the President were suffering every form of
vengeance which the enraged radicals could take. Enlightened
public opinion, however, approved their courage. Said the *Nation:*

"We believe, for our part, that the thanks of the country are
due to Messrs. Trumbull, Fessenden, Grimes, Henderson, Fowler,
Van Winkle, and Ross, not for voting for Johnson's acquittal, but
for vindicating . . . the sacred rights of individual conscience . . .
We shall hear no more of impeachment, and we are glad of it."

Other responsible journals—the *Chicago Tribune, Harper's
Weekly, Boston Advertiser, Providence Journal, Cincinnati Com-
mercial, Hartford Courant*, all staunchly Republican—echoed the
Nation's commendation.

By irresponsible elements, however, unbridled abuse was

heaped upon the dissenting seven. Grimes was hissed on the street in Iowa; Ross was hanged in effigy, beaten, impoverished, and shunned socially in Kansas; Fessenden was tongue-lashed in Maine. Without exception, their political careers were ended; those who did not die before their terms expired were denied reelection and never held public office again.

For Johnson the acquittal was tinged with bitterness. After all, a majority of the Senate had voted him guilty of official crimes, and nothing could wipe that from the record. Crook thought the President was a little more somber on the days when they drove into the country, during that summer of 1868. Johnson had taken a fancy to visiting the Soldiers Home, north of the city, and meditating in a summer arbor that overlooked the cemetery there; cemeteries seemed to have a fascination for him.

"Look," he said once to his bodyguard, indicating with his cane the rows on rows of white headstones. "It's a city—a city of the dead."

When the Democratic party met in national convention in New York in July, there was a flicker of expectation that they might nominate Johnson for the presidency, to oppose Grant. He saw no reason why not. The Democrats had adopted his policy and praised his course of action, he pointed out. "They say I have stood by the Constitution and made a noble struggle."

Why, then, asked Moore, did he not join the Democrats outright?

"Why don't they join me?" he retorted.

The possibility was momentarily tempting, though at first he had reacted to the idea with revulsion.

"Before God," he told Moore, "I would rather this moment pack up and leave this house and go to my old business of tailoring again, than remain here subject to the insults and annoyances of the place!"

But nomination would be a vindication, and his interest was evident when the convention opened. On the first ballot he received the second highest number of votes; but then Horatio Seymour of New York was nominated, with young Frank Blair his running mate. Behind Seymour was arrayed the old copperhead element of the party, with whom the President could have nothing in common; the Democrats still were not ready to join him. The day after the decision, Moore found Johnson in good spirits, and all through that summer and fall he seemed to relax.

The White House levees and receptions grew popular, and there was a stream of distinguished visitors, especially from Europe, where Johnson's conduct had evoked the warmest praise. Charles Dickens, in Washington for a reading of his works (in quest of American dollars), met the President and was impressed by his presence and personality. Nobody could meet Andrew Johnson without realizing that he was an extraordinary man, Dickens wrote home. Young Henry Adams was brought to the White House by Evarts, and his impression of Johnson would have startled that man. To Adams, Johnson fitted perfectly with his ideal of "an old-fashioned Southern senator and statesman."

"He sat in his chair at his desk with a look of self-esteem that has its value," Adams would recall. "In that world none doubted. All were great men; some, no doubt, were greater than others; but all were statesmen and all were supported, lifted, inspired by the moral certainty of rightness. To them the universe was serious, even solemn, but it was their universe, a Southern conception of right . . . The Southerner could not doubt; and this self-assurance not only gave Andrew Johnson the look of a true President, but actually made him one."

The Republican sweep that autumn caused no tremors at the White House. Seward and Evarts, it was true, had showed signs of being a little too friendly with "that Grant crowd," but Johnson did not allow their obvious impatience to be on with the new regime to estrange him. He could take a measured view of loyalties now. In a long letter to Ben Truman, his wartime newspaper friend, he set down his judgment of some of the men who had impinged sharply upon his career. Thaddeus Stevens he had already summed up as "honest" and "open," though unbalanced on the Negro question. He thought Sumner was plain mad, but had "no sordid motives." Lincoln he ranked as "the greatest American that has ever lived." This was not detracting from Washington, he explained, but after all Washington was really an Englishman. "I doubt whether there will ever be another Washington or another Lincoln."

The President considered Ben Butler "the most daring and unscrupulous demagogue the country has ever produced." But Butler's services to the Union during the war could "never be overestimated," and Johnson could "never thoroughly despise him on that account."

Were he to live his administration over, he told Truman, he might accept the advice given to him to add Morton of Indiana, Andrew of Massachusetts, and Horace Greeley to his cabinet. "Morton would have been a tower of strength, and so would Andrew." But Greeley was "a sublime child . . . all heart and no head . . . like a whale ashore."

The President also ranked the military leaders of the war by his own standards. George Thomas he deemed "the greatest general the war produced, and the only one who annihilated an army. He will continue to grow great as long as he lives, and long after he dies. Yet Thomas would not have done as well as Grant under the circumstances. Grant has treated me badly; but he was the right man in the right place during the war, and no matter what his faults were or are, the whole world can never write him down— remember that.

"I have always liked Sherman. He is our greatest military genius. He is erratic and stubborn, but he doesn't know how to lie.

"The time will come when Sheridan will be looked upon by many distinguished military men as greater than Grant. But Sheridan would not have had his great opportunity had it not been for Grant."

Grant—Grant—the name haunted Johnson. Yet with all his detestation of the general's "duplicity," he could judge him fairly.

"Grant was untrue," he told Truman. "He meant well the first two years, and much that I did that was denounced was through his advice. He was the strongest of all in support of my policy for a long while . . . But Grant saw the radical handwriting on the wall, and heeded it. I did not see it, or, if seeing it, did not heed it. Grant did the proper thing to save Grant, but it nearly ruined me. I might have done the same thing under the circumstances. At any rate, most men would.

"I shall go to my grave with the belief that Davis, Cobb,

Toombs, and a few others of the arch-conspirators and traitors should have been tried, convicted, and hanged for treason. I would show coming generations that, while the rebellion was too popular a revolt to punish the many who participated in it, treason should be made odious and arch-traitors should be punished."

Now Grant was President-elect, and Johnson was on the way out. At least he would leave in orderly fashion, and with a flourish.

The orderliness took the form of carefully packing all his documents and personal possessions. Nothing except what was undeniably his own property was boxed for shipment to Tennessee.

"I found nothing here, and I am going to leave nothing here when I go," he told Crook.

The flourish introduced a novelty to Washington society—a children's ball. It was held at the White House on December 29, the President's sixtieth birthday. Every bit of ceremony was trotted out to give grown-up brilliance to the occasion. Nearly three hundred engraved invitations were sent to sons and daughters of the nation's dignitaries and to those of the White House servants, requesting the pleasure of the recipient's company in the name of "The Children of the President." Grown-ups were not included. The carriages began to arrive at six o'clock, and the guests alighted on a red carpet rolled out to the carriage block. The rooms were decorated with masses of flowers, and the chandeliers were aglow.

The only adults on hand were the parents and grandparents of the hosts. Eliza Johnson came downstairs for this event and received the guests smilingly seated in an armchair. The President welcomed them with outstretched arms, the little ones with a hug and a kiss, and those conscious of their greater maturity with a hearty handclasp. The Grant children, although invited, did not attend; the newspapers had announced that the general and his family were spending the holidays out of the city, in order to avoid the embarrassment of Grant's obligatory appearance at the President's New Year reception.

Never did Johnson appear happier than at that "Juvenile Soirée." The dancing was in the East Room, and fiddles played as merrily as they had played sixty years before, in a tavern yard at

Raleigh; but now the fiddlers were musicians of the United States Marine Band. Marini's dancing class showed off their fanciest steps, and the engraved programs listed an "Esmeralda," "Varsovienne," "Basket Quadrille," "Quadrille Sociable," a "Waltz" and a "Polka-Galop." At the intermission the state dining room was thrown open for the refreshments—cakes, ices, confectionery, and everything delicious that the steward, Martha Patterson, and Eliza Mitchell, the White House head cook, all together could contrive. The affair was voted a marvel of social elegance, and children's balls, heretofore unknown, became a bright feature of capital entertaining.

Other social events of note marked Johnson's final months in the Executive Mansion. On the day when the Chinese embassy was to be entertained at a formal dinner, a woman caller on Martha Patterson was invited to see the preparations in the great dining room. The table was set for forty; everything was in order, fruits, flowers, Sèvres china, fragile glassware, massive plate, fine linen. A photographer was taking a picture as a souvenir for the children. The visitor was impressed by the tastefulness of the display, ornate yet distinguished, in every detail bearing the stamp of Martha's discrimination.

Martha cheerfully confessed that she looked forward with relief to her imminent release from such responsibilities.

"Mother is not able to enjoy these entertainments," she explained. "Belle [her daughter] is too young, and I am indifferent to them, so it is well that they are almost over."

While they were talking, the curtains parted and the President looked in to ask whether Martha had shown her friend the portraits of the Presidents. Johnson himself acted as guide, identifying each subject and telling anecdotes of that administration. The rain was falling softly outside, and the house, with an occasional rumble from the children's rooms above, and the President's mellow voice, seemed to the caller to be snug and habitable—a place that was lived in. To the Johnsons it was not.

The Chinese magnificoes dined with the President that evening, resplendent in their mandarin robes, and fascinated the other guests by eating ice cream with chopsticks.

On Christmas day Johnson extended unconditional pardon to

everyone who had taken part in the rebellion, Jefferson Davis included. Let Congress howl: it was time to wind up that episode. The pardon did not remove the civil disabilities imposed on thousands of the South's leading citizens by Congress under the Fourteenth Amendment, which had been ratified, Georgia consenting. But property and citizenship rights were restored by this act of oblivion.*

In numerous ways, a softer side of Johnson's character found expression during those final months in the White House. He complained of no one, and now and then showed a quaint sense of humor. One day when Moore entered his bedroom, the President picked up a basket from the floor containing flour, and asked the secretary whether he had ever seen whiter. It was ground, he said, in a mill near Greeneville which he had bought. Pointing to where the flour appeared to have been nibbled, Johnson explained that while he was getting ready for bed, the night before, a mouse had scampered across the hearth; so he had put the basket of flour on the floor for it and its friends to enjoy.

"Now," he said, "I am filling it again for them."

A couple of days later Moore asked whether he was still feeding the mice, and the President replied that yes, the little fellows had given him their confidence, and he had given them their basket and poured a little water on the hearthstone, in case they were thirsty.

Other instances of an Indian-summer serenity in the President's mood occurred in his orders to the Secretary of War to release to their relatives the remains of Mrs. Surratt, Booth, Azterodt, and Payne, for reburial in consecrated ground.

The White House New Year reception of 1869 drew the largest crowd ever seen, though even Johnson was nonplussed when walrus-like Ben Butler coolly entered the Blue Room. But the laws of hospitality were not repealed, and the President extended his hand to his traducer as pleasantly as to any stranger.

At that time, in Tennessee, another foe of Andrew Johnson, and one of longer standing than Butler, was bidding farewell to one career to embark upon another. "Parson" Brownlow was resigning

---

* The last of these disabilities were not removed until the McKinley administration.

the governorship in order to take his seat in the United States Senate. He was a physical wreck, shaking with palsy, crippled by paralysis, capable of speaking only in a whisper, kept alive apparently by vindictiveness alone. For months his death had been expected daily, and it was everywhere said that he would never survive the trip to Washington.

The "Parson" did not share this conviction. His flesh was feeble, but his mind was jocund and his spirit was robust. In a farewell editorial (he had sold the *Knoxville Whig*) he raised his battlecry once more:

"Had I my life to live over, I should pursue the same course I have pursued, ONLY MORE SO!"

They carried him aboard the train. At each stopping place his car was besieged by crowds come to gape at the terrible "Parson" —"Old Proc," they called him, because of his avalanche of proclamations. Brownlow had become as legendary in Tennessee and Virginia as Andy Johnson himself.* Waving spectrally to the awed crowds, he looked forward with relish to entering into Washington as Johnson slunk out of it in disgrace.

On the eve of Grant's inauguration, the general upset the arrangements committee by stating that he would not ride in the same carriage with the outgoing President, and would not even speak to him. The cabinet cast about for a suitable procedure, in view of this; two carriages and even two processions were proposed, but ruled out as grotesque. Up to March 4, Johnson had announced no decision as to his own course.

Eliza Johnson had gone to the home of John Coyle, owner of the *Intelligencer*, where she and the President planned to stay a few days. Mary Stover, Robert, and the children had returned to Tennessee to make things ready for the President's return. Martha had been detained by last-minute housekeeping responsibilities,

---

* Brownlow's governorship had degenerated into a carnival of corruption and misrule. Honest himself, he was surrounded by men who could not claim that virtue, and under such indubitable Unionists Tennessee suffered as cruelly as any state of the Reconstruction subjected to carpetbag rule. General Nathan Bedford Forrest considered Brownlow's tenure "more trying to the brave men and women of Tennessee than four years of terrible war," while a North Carolina critic said of the "Parson" that "in times to come children will shrink from his polluted touch, and lonely women will shun him as they would a rattlesnake."

for she was determined that the Grants should find the house in perfect order. On the morning of March 4 she, too, departed.

Usually the outgoing President spends the last hours of his term at the Capitol, signing bills. When McCulloch, Welles, and Browning arrived to escort Johnson to the Capitol, they found him at his desk, signing bills as they were brought to him. A little before noon Evarts bustled in, in haste to be on the way. Without taking off his overcoat, he reminded Johnson that the hour was late; hadn't they better be starting?

The President replied quietly that he thought he would wind up his business there.

Then Seward sauntered in, puffing his everlasting cigar, and fidgeted when Johnson repeated his decision.

At a little after twelve o'clock the President pushed back his chair and stood up.

(At about that moment, in the Senate, "Parson" Brownlow, having been carried into the chamber, was taking the oath seated at his desk, his palsied upraised arm supported by a page, while spectators and fellow senators stared in fascination.)

The President shook hands with each member of the cabinet and spoke a cordial good-bye. Then he walked down the stairs to the front portico, where the White House staff was waiting.

Johnson waved to them, called out "God bless you," and stepped into his carriage.

Slowly, without haste, he was driven away, alone.

EPILOGUE

The End and a Beginning

No, the story was not all told. Life has its revenges.

When Andrew Johnson left Washington in the spring of 1869 he left no unfinished business there. He had called for all his bills and paid them. He had drawn the last of his salary and settled his account with the Treasury. His administration was ended, and the record was stowed in boxes and crates already on their way to Tennessee.

That record had been amassing up to the last day. There had been Johnson's State of the Union message to Congress in December. He had prepared that message without consultation, and it restated his views in one comprehensive final exposition. Again he reviewed the headlong course of Congress and traced the baleful effects being wrought in the South. Again he recorded that he had never knowingly swerved from his duty to defend the Constitution. Again he proposed reforms which he had advocated for years—the direct election of the President, Vice-President, and United States senators; a single six-year term for the President; popular election of federal judges. More startling was his suggestion for reducing the load of national debt by paying off government bonds in a manner that would be less adverse to the wage earner and less favorable to the banks and capitalists. This attempt to "tamper with the credit of the nation" was denounced as "repudiation"—something more dangerous and reprehensible than all Andrew Johnson's heresies heretofore.

In the House of Representatives, the message was received with contemptuous silence, and Schenck of Ohio (who as Republican national chairman had just engineered Grant's election victory) moved to prevent its printing. In the Senate, the clerk had barely read the opening paragraph when the senators refused to listen to any more, termed the document an insult, and adjourned in a rage. The next day they allowed the reading to be completed, for the sake of the record.

On the last day of his term, the President released to the press his own farewell address to the nation, defending his course and warning of griefs to come.

The ex-President was honored with a civic reception in Baltimore immediately after his retirement from office. Tens of thousands cheered him in a parade, and he spoke at a banquet. It seemed that the people liked him, if politicians did not, and he returned to Washington with a right hand swollen and raw from handclasps.

On April 18 the family started for home. Everywhere along the route they were met with effusive welcomes. Lynchburg, where in 1861 Johnson had been hanged in effigy, tendered him municipal honors; at Bristol a delegation of Tennesseans boarded the train; and at Greeneville the town turned out, led by Blackston McDannel. On Main Street, where in '61 a sign had been stretched reading, "Andrew Johnson, Traitor," a new sign was strung, "Welcome, Andrew Johnson, Patriot."

The old home was ready for them. Mary Stover had been busy restoring the house, repapering the walls to hide the scrawls, and placing the heavy, substantial, but tasteful furniture that had been bought in Washington and shipped on ahead.

Scarcely was the family settled again, when Johnson was stricken by a bilious fever, and the word went out that he had died. He recuperated rapidly, however, and was able to attend the marriage of his daughter Mary to William R. Brown of Greeneville. The couple moved into a house across the street from her parents' home, and they provided daily companionship for Eliza. Mary still owned the Stover farm in Carter County, and would spend the summers there.

Almost at the same time as Mary's marriage, Robert Johnson, who had come home with his father and mother, died suddenly. He was only thirty-three, and had been a prey to melancholia for some time. Eliza, by now ethereally frail, turned her affections towards her grandchildren.

The political situation in Tennessee drew Johnson's attention. Brownlow had left things in turmoil, and a campaign was on for his successor as governor. The radicals nominated their candidate, and the moderates backed the current Speaker of the legislature. Invited to help, Johnson stumped the state in opposition to the radical, and found that he had lost none of his appeal for Tennesseans. The campaign was in the unruly tradition of the state, and Johnson was sometimes howled down by hostile crowds; but gradually his hard-hitting presentation of facts and figures won him a hearing, and the result was a victory for his man.

Word spread that at the convening of the legislature Johnson would be elected to the United States Senate.

Edmund Cooper had been elected to the legislature, and he assumed charge of Johnson's campaign. In Washington, Brownlow stirred up the administration and Grant announced that he would consider Johnson's election "a personal insult." Money was poured into the state; but after eight ballots were taken, Johnson led the field and lacked but two votes of winning.

In desperation, the radicals hit upon a new strategy. Edmund Cooper's brother, Henry, was a member of the legislature. The radicals proposed to withdraw all their candidates, and unite behind Henry Cooper. In this way they believed they could win the votes of both Cooper brothers and shut out Johnson. The strategy worked; the double appeal of family loyalty and party regularity won over Edmund Cooper, and he agreed to go along with the scheme.

That evening a former railroad president had called on Johnson at the Maxwell House, and told the President that he positively would be elected the next day; he had rounded up the two votes necessary. Johnson asked how.

"I promised to pay a thousand dollars apiece for them," was the unblushing reply.

Johnson's eyes flashed.

"You will do no such thing!" he demanded. "Go tell those rascals the deal is off! If I am elected by those purchased votes, as sure as God lets me live, I will go before the legislature and expose the fraud and refuse to accept the election!"

The next day the vote was taken, and the defection of Edmund Cooper swung the election of his brother.

This act of treachery, like Grant's deceit, Johnson could not forgive. When Cooper tried to excuse his falling away, the ex-President looked him in the eye and said coldly:

"Caesar had his Brutus, Jesus Christ had his Judas, Charles I had his Cromwell, George Washington had his Benedict Arnold, and I have my Ed Cooper!"

Johnson returned to Greeneville and devoted himself to business affairs.

One day a former clerk of the House impeachment committee happened into Greeneville on business, and decided to look up the ex-President, against whom he still had intense prejudice. Trudging a quarter of a mile "in the thick dust of the highway, between thickets of burdock and Mayweed," this visitor reached the Johnson home—"a very small and very plain brick structure." The front door stood open, and there was no answer to his knock; so the stranger walked through to the back and there saw Johnson, in his shirt sleeves, hoeing in the garden.

Johnson greeted the caller politely, pulled on his coat, and led the way into the front parlor. This was furnished "in the conventional village style, with black haircloth-covered sofa and chairs, a marble center table holding a family Bible and a few books, and framed photographs on the walls."

The talk ran on politics for half an hour; then Johnson took his caller up the street to the weather-beaten tailor shop. As he unlocked the door, he explained that he had never allowed the building to be torn down because "he had a fondness for it." Inside were stacked boxes of papers, containing, Johnson remarked grimly, "letters which would ruin the reputations of many of the leading Republicans in Congress." Some day he might print them, he said.

The visitor left "a good deal impressed by the simplicity of the ex-President's life at home. He was not ashamed to hoe in his kitchen garden, or to harness his horse to an old buggy when he wanted to drive. I do not think he had a servant about the place, unless it was a woman to wait on his invalid wife." But the man left hating Johnson as thoroughly as ever.

After the stir of Washington and national events, Johnson found Greeneville at times hard to bear. The town was "as lifeless as a graveyard," he told a friend at the start of 1870; and in June of '71 he wrote to Martha that "there is nothing of interest transpiring in Greeneville. All is dull and flat, I long to see a return of Spring when I will be set free from this place forever I hope."

Occasionally letters from Sam Milligan posted him on events in Washington. Johnson had placed Milligan in the capital as a judge of the Court of Claims. As Grant's administration lurched deeper into the mire, Sam wrote despairingly that "things are going at a hard gallop to the Devil . . . The people are honest, and want to do right, but experience has taught me that they are easily misled."

The summer of 1872 brought a return to the political arena. In an election for congressman-at-large, the Republicans nominated Horace Maynard, and the Democrats put forward a hero of the Confederate cause, Major General Benjamin F. Cheatham. A class of politicians had sprung up that was derisively known as "Confederate brigadiers." Their sole political capital was their war records, and Cheatham typified this class. When his nomination was made known, Johnson entered the race as an independent.

That three-cornered campaign would be talked about in Tennessee for half a century. Nothing so physically grueling, so rowdy, so tempestuous had been seen since the heyday of the Know-Nothings. Johnson seemed endowed with the energy of youth as he waded streams, drank in country taverns, braved mobs, and defied death threats. The three candidates spoke from the same platform in many places, and once Maynard threw up to Johnson the execution of Mary Surratt. Johnson answered:

"In 1865 the city of Washington was an armed camp; Lincoln was our commander-in-chief; he was foully murdered, and a court duly organized sat upon the case and convicted his murderers, a woman included; I was unwilling to pardon her; and that is all there is to it."

At one of these encounters the same unfriendly Northerner who had found the ex-President in his garden saw Johnson in action. Maynard spoke first, he wrote, "in a dry, argumentative way, intellectual but dull. Cheatham followed in the regulation Southern style of oratory, fiery and bombastic. Then Johnson closed in a shrewd . . . practical talk adapted to the comprehension of the men who had come from the mountains to attend the meeting. His points all told, and the audience which had been cold grew uproariously enthusiastic . . . The roughly clad mountain folk felt that he was from their class, and was one of them."

Maynard won the election, as Johnson had expected, but he was satisfied that he had accomplished his objective—"to reduce the brigadiers to the ranks." Sam Milligan wrote that Andy had "taught the whole South to feel that treason is not honorable, or a ground for political promotion in the government against which it was committed."

To the common people of Tennessee Andy Johnson was again a political idol. They "gloried in his spunk." But now, paradoxically, his greatest popularity was in Middle and Western Tennessee, for in East Tennessee the feeling against ex-Confederates was too deep-rooted for Johnson's generosity to find favor. There was talk that he would run for the Senate again, and he was willing. However, the next vacancy would not fall for a couple of years, until Brownlow's term should expire.

In the summer after the Congressional race, East Tennessee was visited by an epidemic of Asiatic cholera, and in Greene county more than a hundred persons died. Those who could fled the contagion of the towns; but Johnson remained at home, nursing the sick and assisting the destitute. Then he was stricken and for a while his life was despaired of. During this illness, facing death, he set down in a crabbed pencil scrawl his inmost thoughts:

"All seems gloom and despair. I have no fear. Approaching death to me is the mere shadow of God's protecting wing. Here I know can no evil come; here I will rest in quiet and peace beyond the reach of calumny's poisoned shaft; the influential, evil, and jealous enemies; where treason and traitors in States, where backsliders and hypocrites in the church, can have no place, where the great fact will be realized that God is Truth, and gratitude the highest attribute of man."

He survived, but won his health back slowly, and he would never completely recover.

In the spring of '74, a telegram from Washington told him that death had taken Sam Milligan. The loss of his best adviser keyed him to make one more effort to obtain the vindication that would

vindicate Sam Milligan's confidence in him, too: he announced
his candidacy to succeed Brownlow in the Senate. To arouse popular support he stumped the state once more. Every tactic of
intimidation that the radicals could devise was used against him,
and his life again was often in danger. When he announced his
intention to speak in Columbia, where Edmund Cooper lived, he
was warned that a repetition of his "Judas" brand on Cooper in
that town would result in his death.

On reaching Columbia, Johnson found that an ally of Cooper
had taken over the courthouse, and was speaking inside. Johnson
called for packing boxes and had a makeshift platform set up
directly under the window of the room where the orator was
holding forth to a group of Cooper's partisans. Johnson had his
partisans outside.

Mounting the stage, he announced that he had been told he
would be shot if he repeated certain remarks there; then he deliberately repeated his scornful accusation, only this time including
Henry Cooper with his brother. He paused, and in the silence
eyes and cocked pistols were trained on the window, from which
a fusillade was expected. Nothing happened, and Johnson went
on with his speech.

Wherever he went in that campaign, he swept the crowds as he
had not for years. Now he spoke without resentment of anyone
except the Coopers and Grant. In Memphis he addressed a throng
that packed the theater and represented every class; step by step
he accounted for his stewardship as a tribune of the people, told
his ups and downs, and replied to taunts that he was supposed to
be ambitious. Of course he was ambitious, he said:

"I would not be worthy to be called a man unless I was ambitious. I am ambitious, ambitious of acquiring a name in the minds
of the people that I have been a faithful representative; that I
have stood upon the watchtowers of my country, and defended
and vindicated and guarded their rights when they were not in a
condition to do it for themselves . . . I have lived and toiled for
the people because I wanted their approbation and esteem; and
when the time shall come that my connection is to be severed
with this people and all things that are mortal . . . the most
pleasant thought that can pass through my mind will be to feel

that I occupied a place in the respect and hearts of my country-men.

"I know that when a man gets a little old, he is regarded as a cinder, something that won't generate any more heat, and he is thrown out on the ash pile . . . But, thank God, there is a little of the fire of youth running through my veins and in my heart yet; and as time sets all things even, I look to the future to judge me."

The crowd answered with a shout, and they became deeply moved when he went on, without rancor:

"I feel that my state was wronged, I feel that I was wronged in 1868, and I am free to say that the deepest wound inflicted upon me, yes, I may say, was by a member of my own household."

All in all, that stumping campaign was probably the most successful and the most gratifying of his life.

It was the legislature, however, that would elect a senator, and when the session convened in January of 1875 there was a shoal of candidates in opposition to Andy. Included were three Confederate major generals. Against such a field, no one but Johnson believed he could possibly win. But he had the people behind him, and his supporters poured into town to put pressure on their representatives. The balloting went on for several days, and at one time General W. C. Bate, one of the "brigadiers," came within a single vote of success. Johnson's friends despaired, but he told them confidently that Bate would be beaten. "No man who comes within one vote of winning ever picks up that extra vote," he said, speaking from experience.

General Forrest, the greatest war hero of Tennessee, was in Nashville to lend his support to Bate. Johnson called on Forrest and explained why such relatively insignificant military men had been trotted out to oppose him: it was because the party leaders knew they could be controlled.

"These damn fellows are just using you and your influence against me," Johnson said with a bluntness which Forrest could appreciate. "If they want a sure-enough general for senator, why don't they bring out you?"

Forrest saw the point, went back to Memphis, and Johnson's prospects improved.

Finally, on January 26, 1875, and on the fifty-fifth ballot, Johnson distanced the field and was elected to the United States Senate.

Pandemonium broke loose in Nashville, and letters and telegrams flooded in from the whole country. Suddenly, far beyond Tennessee, Andy Johnson was a hero.

"Wild with excitement," came the first flash from Clarksville, Tennessee. "The town is in a blaze, bonfires, rockets," Bolivar reported. Memphis fired one hundred guns from the bluff in Johnson's honor, and so did the citizens of Buffalo, New York. From Chicago: "In this city men meeting each other stop and congratulate the *country* upon the event. We look upon your election as a national blessing." The sergeant-at-arms of the Ohio House of Representatives telegraphed: "News of your election received during noon recess. Your friends here gave three times three cheers." From Mrs. William Tecumseh Sherman (on official stationery of "Headquarters of the Army of the United States, St. Louis, Mo."): "We rejoice to see you returned to the Senate. Ellen Ewing Sherman." From Philadelphia: "When I looked in the *Ledger* this morning, I found you were elected, and I said, Glory to God." In Michigan, Zachariah Chandler had been defeated for reelection to the Senate, and from Bay City came the shout: "The defeat of Chandler and the election of Andy Johnson is glory enough for once!" General Custer, fighting Indians on the Plains, was delighted. Political pundits in the East were dumbfounded. "No common man," Thurlow Weed wrote in the *New York Tribune*, "could have dug himself out of a pit so deep and dark as that into which he had fallen." Ordinary folk just bubbled with joy. "In the name of Liberty, 'amen and amen'!" came a Washington greeting. "May you live to be an impeacher yet!" was another. "Good-bye Grant!" And, from Boston, the essence of brevity: "Greeting. Thank God! Now give them hell down there!"

Most affecting to the winner was a note scribbled on rough paper which arrived from Lawrence, Kansas:

"I am rejoiced to learn . . . this evening of your election to the Senate. Your vindication from the slanders born of the hatred & malice of the impeachers in 1868 is now well nigh complete . . . I trust that the reign of hate has gone by & that a better day is coming."

There was a postscript:

"Excuse the unconventional form of this note. I write it in haste at my journeyman printer's desk as I am able to snatch a moment from my evening's labor."

It was signed, "E. G. Ross"—the onetime senator from Kansas, who was paying the bitter price of poverty for having obeyed his conscience and voted Andrew Johnson "not guilty."

Another letter Johnson cherished. This was addressed not to him, but to Eliza Johnson:

"While telegrams are pouring in upon your honored husband from every quarter, permit a stranger to you, but a friend of his, to tender to you his earnest congratulations for this 'crowning victory' in his career. In the first speech I ever heard him make, he attributed to your influence his success in life."

Johnson understood that not the legislature, but the support of the people of Tennessee really had elected him. To a youthful legislator he passed along the kernel of all his political wisdom:

"If you would continue in public life, be sure of one thing . . . that you always strive to keep in touch with the *common people*. With them for you, corporations and combinations may organize against you . . . but they will war in vain . . . Keep the common people on your side and you will win."

Strangest of all, it seemed to some who had all but lost faith in Johnson's ability to reach the top again, the press of the nation, conservative and radical, in dazed acknowledgment welcomed his return to the Senate. Newspapers that had scourged him now blossomed with tributes to his courage and indomitability. The *New York Herald* termed his election a "national victory." The *St. Louis Republican* called it "the most magnificent personal triumph which the history of American politics can show." The *Nation* observed, in belated apology, that Johnson's "personal integrity . . . and his respect for the law and the Constitution make his administration a remarkable contrast to that which succeeded it." Said *The New York Times:* "He went out of the White House as poor as he entered it, and that is something to say in these times. We shall not be sorry to see him again in public life."

By 1875, most of the evils against which Johnson as President had warned had come to pass. The Grant administration, in its second term and with the President grasping at a third, had established a record of venality, corruption, and moral rottenness which, happily, has never been equaled in this country, exceeding even the sorry showing of the Harding regime.

Grant had called Congress into special session to act on a treaty with the ruler of the Sandwich Islands (Hawaii). The session met on March 5, and the Senate organized the next day. The galleries were filled to watch the entrance of the new senator from Tennessee. Already Brownlow was on his way home, more dead than alive in appearance, but still full of venom.

Shortly after noon, Johnson walked into the chamber, and spectators craned as he advanced slowly down the aisle to his old desk, which was heaped with flowers. Senator Edmunds of Vermont was speaking, and noticing the commotion, he turned and saw the man whom he had voted guilty of high crimes in office. His voice trailed away, and jerking up his arm he knocked over a stack of books, and abruptly sat down. Roscoe Conkling, New York's Republican machine boss—he of the "Apollo curls" and "turkey-gobbler strut," who in the House of Representatives had deeply damned Andrew Johnson—pretended to read a letter, but watched out of the corner of his eye. Senator Freylinghausen of New Jersey, who had voted for impeachment, ducked under his desk, groping for something there. Boutwell, one of Johnson's prosecutors, now a senator, stared straight ahead. Logan of Illinois, another impeachment manager, affected to pay no attention. Anthony of Rhode Island, Sherman of Ohio, Cameron of Pennsylvania, Morrill of Maine, who all had voted "guilty," appeared not to see. Morton of Indiana, who first had supported Johnson then turned against him, hesitated; noticing this, Johnson put out his hand, which Morton grasped gratefully.

"There are not many men who could have done that," Morton said later. "He wore the same kindly smile as in times before."

Reporters thought the ex-President bore himself with composure. He seemed little changed, his hair whiter but not thinned, his step firm, his face marked by neither harsh lines nor deep wrinkles. His expression seemed mingled earnestness and sadness; but that had been his habitual expression since 1865.

The clerk called the names of newly elected senators, and Hannibal Hamlin, Lincoln's first Vice-President, came down the aisle. When "Andrew Johnson" was called, Henry Cooper, Tennessee's

other senator, advanced, as etiquette required, bowed stiffly, and
with Senator McCreery of Kentucky escorted Johnson to a place
beside Hamlin.

The Vice-President, Henry Wilson, was in the chair. In 1868
Senator Wilson had voted not only for Andrew Johnson's conviction of the charges preferred, but for "his disqualification from
hereafter holding any office under the Constitution he has violated and the government he has dishonored." Wilson arose and
stepped down to administer the oath, an uncustomary mark of
great respect. The oath was taken. Then Johnson turned to Hamlin and without embarrassment shook hands warmly. Then he
shook hands with Wilson, and applause burst from the galleries.
Hamlin and Wilson were tall men, Johnson was short, and the
contrast was striking; but as one onlooker said, "to everyone
present there was no taller man in the Senate that day than Andrew Johnson."

As he was returning to his seat, a page handed him a bouquet,
and his eyes suffused with tears. To avoid further demonstrations,
he retreated to a cloakroom, where friends followed. He did not
seem elated; rather, he spoke wistfully of the faces he missed.
Grimes, Fessenden, and Seward were dead; Sumner was dead;
Chase, dead. Henderson, Fowler, Trumbull, Reverdy Johnson—
all were missing. Of the thirty-five senators who had voted him
guilty, only thirteen remained. Stanton had died long ago, and
was not mourned. For Johnson the homecoming was weighted
with grief, and he spoke gently of some of those who in times past
had vilified him.

The next day he made clear to a reporter that he had returned
to Washington with no thought of revenge.

"I have no wrongs to redress but my country's," he said. "My
election settled all personal injuries inflicted. I come now to deal
only with the present issues."

These issues were momentous. In a conflict between two
equally corrupt political factions in Louisiana, Grant had intervened and arbitrarily installed one claimant to the governorship.
Violence had resulted, and in the "Battle of Canal Street," infuriated victims of long-continued carpetbag rule marched on the
state Capitol and turned out Grant's governor. The President

thereupon sent troops and warships to New Orleans, expelled the legislature, and put General Sheridan in charge. Johnson, when President, had removed Sheridan from that command because of incompetency, and his restoration was viewed as a direct slap at the ex-President. Sheridan proceeded to show his ineptness by appealing to Congress to rule the "outs" mere "banditti," and allow him to deal with them in his own way.

This final arrogance produced a revulsion throughout the nation. People had grown sick of the stench of radicalism; yet, as the *New York Tribune* indignantly declared, not one of the self-styled moderate Republicans in Congress had spoken out against "a crime against a state, the Constitution, and against liberty, committed by the President . . . Not a mother's son of them dares open his mouth except to tell some inquisitive reporter that he is 'waiting to hear both sides'!"

Senator Johnson did dare to open his mouth. He had come to Washington to make a speech against Grant's colossal misgoverning; not a personal attack, but a denunciation of grasping ambition and condonation of unparalleled corruption in office. He prepared the speech with care, enlisting the help of his old body-guard, William Crook, to comb scrapbooks for materials.

On March 22 he made the speech, again before packed galleries. It was one of Johnson's best, and one of his most timely. In bold language he assailed Grant's arrogance, his greed for a third term, his assumption of arbitrary power, his violations of the Constitution, his shielding of malefactors even in his official household, and his perpetuation of tumult and bloodshed in the South. Every charge was backed by irrefutable evidence. But Congress was in no mood to listen; Grant still rode high.

The brief session closed and Johnson lingered a while in Washington; then returning to Greeneville, he remained there until the dog days of July drove him to seek relief at the Stover farm in Carter County. Eliza was already staying there, with her daughter and grandchildren.

On the train ride, Johnson fell in with friends from years back, and entertained them with anecdotes of his political ups and downs.

"More than a hundred times," he told them, "I have said to

myself, what course may I pursue so that the calm historian will say one hundred years from now, 'He pursued the right course'?"

At Carter's Station he alighted from the train, and was driven six miles to the farm. There he found all well, and joined in a cheerful lunch. Afterwards he went to his room and sat chatting with his granddaughter, Lillie Stover, who was soon to be married.

As she was leaving the room, she heard a thud behind her, and turning, saw her grandfather on the floor. It was apoplexy; his left side was paralyzed and he could not rise. Lifted into bed, he refused to let the family send for a doctor, saying that either he would get well or he would not, and that was the long and the short of it.

For the rest of that day and the next morning he lay quietly, talking sometimes about his youth, about the tailor shop days. He made no mention of anything that remained to be done; his work was finished; it was to the distant past that his mind reverted, recalling incidents of half a century before.

That afternoon a second stroke left him unconscious, and although doctors were summoned, in an hour or two Johnson was dead.

Three cities—Memphis, Nashville, and Knoxville—competed for the privilege of providing his sepulture. But he had chosen the spot himself, on a hill overlooking Greeneville and the mountains and valleys beyond. There he was laid a few days later. The whole town turned out again, and the mountain folk—the same mountaineers and their families who had trekked in from the distant clearings in response to his earliest spellbinding speeches —came by the thousands to pay their respects.

The wish he had expressed years before ("let the Stars and Stripes be my winding sheet, and pillow my head on the Constitution of the United States") was carried out: his body was wrapped in a bright new flag, with all its stars intact, and under his head was placed one of his own dog-eared, penciled, underlined copies of the Constitution. The plain silver coffin plate was engraved:

ANDREW JOHNSON
Seventeenth President of the United States.

The services were Masonic, conducted by Mother Lodge 119, of which he and Andrew Jackson had been members. Blackston McDannel was chief pallbearer. Special trains brought dignitaries and mourners from other states; but mainly the throng was made up of those "mudsills of society"—the hardworking artisans, mechanics, tradesmen, laborers, and farmers—whose interests and thoughts had been his own.

For several years his grave remained unmarked. Then the family—not by any public subscription but at their own expense —erected an impressive monument—a shaft of marble, draped with the Stars and Stripes, and on its crest an American eagle. Cut into the base was a hand, resting on the Constitution, and an inscription:

HIS FAITH IN THE PEOPLE NEVER WAVERED.

On the day this monument was unveiled, the little rebel of Nashville in 1863—the girl who had vowed that she would dance on Andy Johnson's grave—strewed flowers instead.

NOTES ON SOURCES

THE accompanying Bibliography is offered as indicative of the scope of the sources drawn upon in the preparation of this work. It is not necessarily complete.

The primary source of information about our seventeenth President, of course, is the Andrew Johnson Papers in the Library of Congress. Andrew Johnson directed that every scrap of paper relating to him and his activities be preserved intact, and in that extraordinary jumble the momentous and the trivial jostle each other in a wholly lifelike fashion. Drafts of state documents appear side by side with the White House grocery accounts and Johnson's personal whisky bills (very modest).

Included in the collection, and of invaluable service to the biographer, are the transcripts of the shorthand diaries of Colonel William G. Moore, the President's executive secretary during most of his term. No man was in closer daily contact with Andrew Johnson than Colonel Moore, and the latter's candid jottings provide searching insights into Johnson's character, emotions, meditations, and beliefs that are obtainable nowhere else.

A word about the intent of this book may be helpful. This is the life story of a man who became President of the United States during a tumultuous period of our national history. It is not a history of an administration or a history of the Reconstruction.

The concern here—the sole concern—has been to present Andrew Johnson the man; to make plain what formed, prompted, and sustained him at different stages in his life; to portray his defeats and achievements, his successes and shortcomings, as he lived them and expressed himself through them. The accent is on the effect of his actions on himself and those around him, rather than on their effect on the nation. Reconstruction is a subject for the historian. The life of Andrew Johnson meshes with that larger subject, but does not include it.

No judgments are offered as to the ultimate wisdom or unwisdom of Andrew Johnson's policies. Judgments aplenty abound, but they are judgments of actions, not judgments of a man. To remark that the conclusions reached by historians after a century of debate on the merits or demerits of Andrew Johnson's course differ from one extreme to the opposite is to state the well known. Nor is any final agreement possible, for in each interpretation of the ineluctable "what really happened" there must be the inevitable "ifs," based on the shifting foundations of second-guesses.

Special gratitude is expressed to the staffs of the Manuscript Room, Library of Congress, the Henry E. Huntington Library at San Marino, California, and the New York Public Library for their cheerful and efficient cooperation.

Mrs. Margaret Johnson Patterson Bartlett of Greeneville, Tennessee, great-granddaughter of President Andrew Johnson, has been generosity itself in contributing to the authenticity of the narrative.

And to numerous correspondents who lent their suggestions and encouragement during the long and complex task the word is "thanks."

SELECTED BIBLIOGRAPHY

Manuscript Sources

Andrew Johnson Papers, Library of Congress, Washington, D.C.
S. L. M. Barlow Papers, Huntington Library, San Marino, California
Montgomery Blair mss., Huntington Library, San Marino, California
Gideon Welles mss., Huntington Library, San Marino, California
Francis Lieber mss., Huntington Library, San Marino, California
Transcripts of "Short" and "Long" shorthand diaries of Colonel
   William G. Moore, Library of Congress

Periodicals

American Historical Review
American Heritage
Atlantic Monthly
Century Magazine
Current History
*East Tennessee Historical Society
   Publications*
Galaxy
Harper's Weekly
Independent
Indiana Magazine of History
Leslie's Illustrated Weekly
Masonic Review
Mississippi Valley Historical Review
Nation
North American Review
Overland Monthly
South Atlantic Quarterly
Taylor-Trotwood Magazine
Tennessee Historical Magazine
Tennessee Historical Quarterly

Newspapers

Albany (New York) Argus
Boston Advertiser
Boston Transcript
Chicago Times
Chicago Tribune
Cincinnati Commercial
Cincinnati Gazette
Knoxville Whig
Lorain County (Ohio) News
Missouri Democrat
Muscatine (Iowa) Journal
Nashville Banner
Nashville Press
Nashville Union and American
National Daily Intelligencer
New York Herald
New York Times, The
New York Tribune
New York World
Philadelphia Press
Philadelphia Times
Washington Chronicle
Washington Star

PUBLISHED SOURCES

ABERNATHY, THOMAS PERKINS, *From Frontier to Plantation in Tennessee.* University of North Carolina Press, Chapel Hill, 1932.

ADAMS, HENRY, *The Education of Henry Adams.* Massachusetts Historical Society, Boston, 1918.

ALBJERG, MARGARET HALL, "The New York Press and Andrew Johnson," *South Atlantic Review,* October, 1927.

ALEXANDER, THOMAS B., *Political Reconstruction in Tennessee.* Vanderbilt University Press, Nashville, 1950.

AMES, MARY CLEMMER, *Ten Years in Washington.* Hartford Publishing Co., Hartford, 1883.

ANDREWS, RENA MAZYCK, "Johnson's Plan of Reconstruction in Relation to That of Lincoln," *Tennessee Historical Magazine,* April, 1931.

Assassination of President Lincoln and the Trial of the Conspirators: Courtroom Testimony Compiled and Arranged by Benn Pitman. Moore, Wilstach & Baldwin, Cincinnati and New York, 1865.

AVARY, MYRTA LOCKETT, *Dixie After the War.* Doubleday, Page, New York, 1906.

BACON, G. W., *Life of Andrew Johnson.* Bacon & Co., London, n.d.

BADEAU, ADAM, *Grant in Peace.* S. S. Scranton, Hartford, 1887.

BAKER, LAFAYETTE C., *History of the United States Secret Service.* L. C. Baker, Philadelphia, 1867.

BANCROFT, FREDERIC, *The Life of William H. Seward.* Harper, New York, 1900.

BARROWS, CHESTER L., *William M. Evarts.* University of North Carolina Press, Chapel Hill, 1941.

BATES, DAVID HOMER, *Lincoln in the Telegraph Office.* Century Co., New York, 1907.

BEALE, HOWARD K., *The Critical Year: A Study of Andrew Johnson and Reconstruction.* Harcourt, Brace, New York, 1930.

——— "On Rewriting Reconstruction History," *American Historical Review,* July, 1940.

BELDEN, THOMAS GRAHAM and BELDEN, MARVA ROBINS, *So Fell the Angels.* Little, Brown, Boston, 1956.

BELMONT, AUGUST, *Letters, Speeches, and Addresses.* Privately printed, New York, 1890.

BELMONT, PERRY, *An American Democrat*. Columbia University Press, New York, 1940.

BIGELOW, JOHN, *Retrospections of an Active Life*. Baker & Taylor, New York, 1909–1913.

BINCKLEY, J. W., "The Leader of the House," *Galaxy*, July 15, 1866.

BLAINE, JAMES G., *Twenty Years of Congress: From Lincoln to Garfield*. Henry Bill, Norwich, Conn., 1884.

BLAY, JOHN S., *After the Civil War*. Crowell, New York, 1960.

BOUTWELL, GEORGE S., *Reminiscences of Sixty Years in Public Affairs*. McClure, Phillips, New York, 1902.

BOWERS, CLAUDE G., *The Tragic Era: The Revolution After Lincoln*. Houghton Mifflin, Boston, 1929.

BOYKIN, EDWARD, *Congress and the Civil War*. McBride, New York, 1955.

BRADFORD, GAMALIEL, *Union Portraits*. Houghton Mifflin, Boston, 1916.

BRIGANCE, WILLIAM NORWOOD, "Jeremiah Black and Andrew Johnson," *Mississippi Valley Historical Review*, September, 1932.

BROWN, GILBERT PATTEN, "The Unique Personality of Andrew Johnson," *Masonic Review*, December, 1931.

BROWNING, ORVILLE H., *The Diary of Orville Hickman Browning*. Edited by James G. Randall and Theodore C. Pease. Illinois State Historical Library, Springfield, 1933.

BROWNLOW, WALTER P., "Defense and Vindication of Andrew Johnson," *The Taylor-Trotwood Magazine*, September, 1908.

BROWNLOW, WILLIAM GANNAWAY, *Sketches of the Rise, Progress, and Decline of Secession, With a Narrative of Personal Adventures Among the Rebels*. Childs, Philadelphia, 1862.

BUCK, PAUL H., *The Road to Reunion, 1865–1900*. Little, Brown, Boston, 1937.

BURGESS, JOHN W., *Reconstruction and the Constitution*. Scribner's, New York, 1902.

BUTLER, BENJAMIN F., *Butler's Book*. Thayer, Boston, 1892.

BUTTERFIELD, ROGER, *The American Past*. Simon & Schuster, New York, 1947.

CAIN, MARVIN R., *Lincoln's Attorney General, Edward Bates of Missouri*. University of Missouri Press, Columbia, Mo., 1965.

CALLENDER, E. B., *Thaddeus Stevens, Commoner*. Williams, Boston, 1882.

CARLSON, OLIVER, *The Man Who Made News—James Gordon Bennett*. Duell, Sloan & Pearce, New York, 1942.

CASKEY, W. M., "The First Administration of Governor Andrew Johnson," *East Tennessee Historical Society Publications*, No. 1, 1929.

――― "The Second Administration of Governor Andrew Johnson," *East Tennessee Historical Society Publications*, No. 2, 1930.

CATTON, BRUCE, *The Coming Fury*. Doubleday, Garden City, 1961.

――― *Never Call Retreat*. Doubleday, Garden City, 1965.

――― *A Stillness at Appomattox*. Doubleday, Garden City, 1954.

——— *Terrible Swift Sword*. Doubleday, Garden City, 1963.

——— *This Hallowed Ground*. Doubleday, Garden City, 1956.

——— *U. S. Grant and the American Military Tradition*. Grosset & Dunlap,

New York, 1954.

CHESNUT, MARY BOYKIN, *A Diary From Dixie*. Houghton Mifflin, Boston, 1949.

CLARK, ROBERT D., *The Life of Matthew Simpson*. Macmillan, New York, 1956.

CLARKE, GRACE JULIAN, *The Life of George W. Julian*. Indiana Historical Commission, Indianapolis, 1923.

CLARKE, JAMES FREEMAN, *Memorial and Biographical Sketches*. Houghton, Osgood, Boston, 1878.

CLAY, MRS. CLEMENT C., *A Belle of the Fifties*. Narrated by Ada Sterling. Doubleday Page, New York, 1905.

CLEMENCEAU, GEORGES, *American Reconstruction 1865–1870, and the Impeachment of President Johnson*. Edited by Fernand Baldensperger. Translated by Margaret MacVeagh. Dial, New York, 1928.

CLEWS, HENRY, *Fifty Years in Wall Street*. Irving, New York, 1908.

COIT, MARGARET L., *John C. Calhoun: American Portrait*. Houghton Mifflin, Boston, 1950.

COLEMAN, EVAN J., "Gwin and Seward—A Secret Chapter of Ante-Bellum History," *Overland Monthly*, 1891.

Compilation of the Messages and Papers of the Presidents, 1789–1897. Edited by James D. Richardson. Bureau of National Literature and Art, Washington, 1896–1899.

CONNALLY, ERNEST ALLEN, "The Andrew Johnson Homestead at Greeneville, Tennessee," *East Tennessee Historical Society Publications*, No. 29, 1957.

COULTER, E. MERTON, *The South During Reconstruction*. University of Louisiana Press, Baton Rouge, 1947.

——— *William G. Brownlow, Fighting Parson of the Southern Highlands*. University of North Carolina Press, Chapel Hill, 1937.

COWAN, FRANK, *Andrew Johnson, President of the United States: Reminiscences of His Private Life and Character*. Greensburg, Pa., 1894.

COX, S. S., *Union—Disunion—Reunion: Three Decades of Federal Legislation, 1855–1885*. Reid, Providence, R.I., 1885.

COX, W. V. and NORTHRUP, M. H., *The Life of Samuel S. Cox*. Northrup, Syracuse, N.Y., 1899.

CRAVEN, JOHN J., *Prison Life of Jefferson Davis*. Carleton, New York, 1866.

CROOK, WILLIAM H., *Memories of the White House*. Little, Brown, Boston, 1911.

——— *Through Five Administrations*. Harper, New York, 1910.

CURRENT, RICHARD N., *The Lincoln Nobody Knows*. McGraw-Hill, New York, 1958.

—— *Reconstruction—1865–1877.* Prentice-Hall, Englewood Cliffs, N.J., 1965.

CURTIS, GEORGE TICKNOR, *The Life of James Buchanan.* Harper, New York, 1883.

DALY, MARIA LYDIG, *Diary of a Union Lady.* Edited by Earl Hammond. Funk & Wagnalls, New York, 1962.

DAVIS, ELMER, *History of the New York Times 1851–1921.* New York Times, New York, 1921.

DAVIS, JEFFERSON, *The Rise and Fall of the Confederate Government.* Appleton, New York, 1881.

DENNETT, JOHN RICHARD, *The South As It Is.* Edited by Henry M. Christman. Viking, New York, 1965.

DENNETT, TYLER, *John Hay: From Poetry to Politics.* Dodd Mead, New York, 1934.

DEPEW, CHAUNCEY M., *My Memories of Eighty Years.* Scribner's, New York, 1922.

DERBY, J. C., *Fifty Years Among Authors, Artists, and Publishers.* Carleton, New York, 1884.

DEWITT, DAVID MILLER, *The Assassination of Abraham Lincoln and Its Expiation.* Macmillan, New York, 1909.

—— *The Impeachment and Trial of Andrew Johnson.* Macmillan, New York, 1903.

—— *The Judicial Murder of Mary E. Surratt.* Murphy, Baltimore, 1895.

—— "Vice President Andrew Johnson," *East Tennessee Historical Society Publications,* November 1904 and January, March, May, July, 1905.

DONALD, DAVID, *Charles Sumner and the Coming of the Civil War.* Farrar, Straus & Cudahy, New York, 1929.

DOOLITTLE, JAMES R., "Andrew Johnson," *Harper's Weekly,* September 15, 1866.

DORRIS, JONATHAN T., *Pardon and Amnesty under Lincoln and Johnson: The Restoration of the Confederates to Their Rights and Privileges.* University of North Carolina Press, Chapel Hill, 1953.

DUKE, BASIL W., *A History of Morgan's Cavalry.* Edited by Fletcher Holland. Indiana University Press, Bloomington, 1960.

DUNNING, WILLIAM A., *Essays on the Civil War and Reconstruction and Related Topics.* Macmillan, New York, 1898.

—— "More Light in Andrew Johnson," *American Historical Review,* April, 1906.

—— *Reconstruction, Political and Economic, 1865–1877.* Harper, New York, 1907.

EISENSCHIML, OTTO, *Why the Civil War?* Bobbs-Merrill, Indianapolis, 1958.

—— *Why Was Lincoln Murdered?* Little, Brown, Boston, 1937.

ELLIOTT, MAUD HOWE, *Uncle Sam Ward and His Circle.* Macmillan, New York, 1938.

ESKEW, GARNETT LAIDLAW, *Willard's of Washington*. Coward-McCann, New York, 1954.

FERTIG, JAMES WALTER, *The Secession and Reconstruction of Tennessee*. University of Chicago Press, Chicago, 1898.

FORNEY, J. W., *Anecdotes of Public Men*. Harper, New York, 1873.

FURNAS, J. C., *Goodbye to Uncle Tom*. William Sloan Associates, New York, 1956.

—— *The Road to Harper's Ferry*. William Sloan Associates, New York, 1959.

GERARD, JAMES W., *My First Eighty-Three Years in America*. Doubleday, Garden City, 1951.

GOBRIGHT, L. A., *Recollections of Men and Things at Washington During a Quarter of a Century*. Claxton, Remsen & Haffelfinger, Philadelphia, 1869.

GORHAM, GEORGE C., *The Life and Public Services of Edwin M. Stanton*. Houghton Mifflin, Boston, 1899.

GOUVERNEUR, MARIAN (Mrs. M. C.), *As I Remember*. Appleton, New York, 1911.

GRAF, LEROY P. and HASKINS, RALPH W., "Blackstone McDannel to Andrew Johnson: An East Tennesseean in the Mexican War," *East Tennessee Historical Society Publications*, No. 32, 1960.

GRANT, U. S., *Personal Memoirs of Ulysses S. Grant*. Webster, New York, 1886.

GUROWSKI, ADAM, *Diary*, 3 vols. Vol. 1, Lee & Shepard, Boston, 1862; Vol. 2, Carleton, New York, 1864; Vol. 3, Morrison, Washington, 1866.

HALL, CLIFTON R., *Andrew Johnson, Military Governor of Tennessee*. Princeton University Press, Princeton, N.J., 1916.

HAMER, MARGUERITE BARTLETT, "The Presidential Campaign of 1860 in Tennessee," *East Tennessee Historical Society Publications*, No. 3, 1931.

HAMILTON, GAIL (Mary A. Dodge), *Gail Hamilton's Life in Letters*. Edited by H. Augusta Dodge. Lee & Shepard, Boston, 1901.

HAMILTON, J. C. DEROULHAC, *Life of Andrew Johnson* (Pamphlet). Greeneville, Tenn., 1928.

HANCOCK, CORNELIA, *South After Gettysburg: Letters of Cornelia Hancock 1863–1868*. Edited by Henrietta Stratton Jaquette. Crowell, New York, 1937.

HASKINS, RALPH W., "Andrew Johnson and the Preservation of the Union," *East Tennessee Historical Society Publications*, No. 33, 1961.

HAYES, WILLARD, "Andrew Johnson's Reputation," *East Tennessee Historical Society Publications*, Nos. 31 and 32, 1959 and 1960.

HENDERSON, JOHN B., "Emancipation and Impeachment," *Century Magazine*, December, 1913.

HENDRICK, BURTON J., *Bulwark of the Republic: A Biography of the Constitution*. Little, Brown, Boston, 1937.

—— *Statesmen of the Lost Cause*. Literary Guild, New York, 1939.

HENRY, ROBERT SELPH, *"First With the Most" Forrest*. Bobbs-Merrill, Indianapolis, 1944.

—— *The Story of the Confederacy*. Bobbs-Merrill, Indianapolis, 1931.

—— *The Story of Reconstruction*. Bobbs-Merrill, Indianapolis, 1938.

HESSELTINE, W. B., *Civil War Prisons*. Ohio State University Press, Columbus, 1930.

—— *Lincoln and the War Governors*. Knopf, New York, 1955.

—— "Methodism and Reconstruction in East Tennessee," *East Tennessee Historical Society Publications*, No. 3, 1931.

HEWITT, EDWARD R., *Those Were the Days*. Duell, Sloan & Pearce, New York, 1943.

—— *Ulysses S. Grant, Politician*. Dodd Mead, New York, 1935.

HIBBEN, PAXTON, *Henry Ward Beecher: An American Portrait*. Doran, New York, 1927.

HIGDON, HAL, *The Union vs. Dr. Mudd*. Follett Publishing Co., Chicago, 1964.

HOLDEN, W. W., *Memoirs*. Seaman Printery, Durham, N.C., 1911.

HOLLOWAY, LAURA CARTER, *The Ladies of the White House*. United States Publishing Co., New York, 1872.

HOWELLS, WILLIAM DEAN, *Years of My Youth*. Harper, New York, 1916.

HUNT, GAILLARD, "The President's Defense," *Century Magazine*, December, 1913.

Impeachment Trial of Andrew Johnson. 3 vols. Government Printing Office, 1868.

JOHNSON, ANDREW, *Speeches of Andrew Johnson, President of the United States*. Edited by Frank Moore. Little, Brown, Boston, 1865.

JONES, JAMES S., *Andrew Johnson*. East Tennessee Publishing Co., Greeneville, Tenn., 1901.

JONES, KATHARINE M., *The Plantation South*. Bobbs-Merrill, Indianapolis, 1957.

JULIAN, GEORGE W., "George W. Julian's Journal—The Assassination of Lincoln," *Indiana Magazine of History*, December, 1915.

—— *Political Recollections, 1840–1872*. McClurg, Chicago, 1884.

—— *Speeches on Political Questions*. Hurd & Houghton, Boston, 1872.

KECKLEY, ELIZABETH, *Behind the Scenes*. Carleton, New York, 1868.

KENDRICK, BENJAMIN B., *The Journal of the Joint Committee of Fifteen on Reconstruction*. Columbia University Press, New York, 1914.

KENNEDY, JOHN F., *Profiles in Courage*. Harper, New York, 1956.

KEYES, ERASMUS DARWIN, *Fifty Years' Observation of Men and Events*. Scribner's, New York, 1884.

KIMMEL, STANLEY, *Mr. Lincoln's Washington*. Coward-McCann, New York, 1957.

—— *Mr. Davis's Richmond*. Coward-McCann, New York, 1958.

—— *The Mad Booths of Baltimore*. Bobbs-Merrill, Indianapolis, 1940.

KORNGOLD, RALPH, *Thaddeus Stevens: A Being Darkly Wise and Rudely Great*. Harcourt, Brace, New York, 1955.

KOUWENHOVEN, JOHN A., *Adventures of America: A Pictorial Record from Harper's Weekly, 1857–1900*. Harper, New York, 1938.

KUNHARDT, DOROTHY MESERVE and KUNHARDT, PHILIP B., Jr., *Twenty Days*. Harper & Row, New York, 1965.

LAMON, WARD HILL, *Recollections of Abraham Lincoln, 1847–1865*. McClurg, Chicago, 1895.

LASKI, HAROLD J., *The American Presidency: An Interpretation*. Harper, New York, 1940.

LECONTE, EMMA, *When the World Ended, Diary*. Edited by Earl Schenck Miers. Oxford University Press, 1957.

LEECH, MARGARET, *Reveille in Washington, 1860–1865*. Harper, New York, 1941.

Letters of J. R. Doolittle and L. I. Farwell on Events of Assassination Night (ms). Wisconsin State Historical Society, 1866.

LEWIS, LLOYD, *Sherman, Fighting Prophet*. Harcourt, Brace, New York, 1932.

LINDSEY, DAVID, *"Sunset" Cox: Irrepressible Democrat*. Wayne State University Press, Detroit, Mich., 1959.

LOGAN, JOHN A., *The Volunteer Soldier of America*. Peale, Chicago and New York, 1887.

LOMASK, MILTON, "When Congress Tried to Rule," *American Heritage*, December, 1959.

——— *Andrew Johnson: President on Trial*. Farrar, Straus & Cudahy, New York, 1960.

LOWELL, JAMES RUSSELL, "The Seward-Johnson Reaction," *North American Review*, October, 1866.

MACARTNEY, CLARENCE EDWARD, *Grant and His Generals*. McBride, New York, 1953.

McCALL, S. W., "Washington During Reconstruction," *Atlantic Monthly*, June, 1901.

McCLURE, ALEXANDER KELLY, *Abraham Lincoln and Men of War-Times: Some Personal Recollections*. Times Publishing Co., Philadelphia, 1892.

McCULLOCH, HUGH, *Men and Measures of Half a Century*. Scribner's, New York, 1888.

McKITRICK, ERIC L., *Andrew Johnson and Reconstruction*. University of Chicago Press, Chicago, 1960.

McPHERSON, EDWARD, *Political History of the United States During Reconstruction*. Philip & Solomons, Washington, 1880.

MARTIN, EDWARD WINSLOW, *Behind the Scenes in Washington*. Continental Publishing Co., Philadelphia, 1873.

MILTON, GEORGE FORT, *The Age of Hate: Andrew Johnson and the Radicals*. Coward-McCann, New York, 1930.

——— "Andrew Johnson—Man of Courage," *East Tennessee Historical Society Publications*, No. 3, 1931.

——— *The Eve of Conflict*. Houghton Mifflin, Boston, 1934.

Mirror of War: The Washington Star Reports the Civil War. Compiled and edited by John W. Stepp and I. William Hill. Prentice-Hall, Engle-wood Cliffs, N.J., 1961.

MOORE, JOSEPH WEST, *The American Congress: A History of National Legislation and Political Events, 1774–1895*. Harper, New York, 1895.

MOORE, POWELL, "James K. Polk and the 'Immortal Thirteen'," *East Tennessee Historical Society Publications*, No. 11, 1939.

MORGAN, JAMES, *Our Presidents*. Macmillan, New York, 1959.

NASBY, PETROLEUM V. (David R. Locke), *The Struggles of Petroleum V. Nasby*. Introduction by Charles Sumner. Lee & Shepard, Boston, 1868.

—— *Swingin' Round the Cirkle: Andy's Trip to the West* (Pamphlet), 1866.

NEVINS, ALLAN, *Frémont, the Pathmarker of the West*. Longmans, Green, New York, 1955.

—— *Hamilton Fish: The Inner History of the Grand Administration*. Dodd Mead, New York, 1937.

—— *Ordeal of the Union*. Scribner's, New York, 1947.

—— *The War for the Union*. Scribner's, New York, 1959–1960.

"New Facts About Mrs. Surratt: Correspondence of Judge Holt and Hon. James Speed," *North American Review*, July, 1888.

NICHOLS, ROY F., *The Disruption of American Democracy*. Macmillan, New York, 1948.

——*The Stakes of Power, 1845–1877*. Hill & Wang, New York, 1964.

NICOLAY, HELEN, *Our Capital on the Potomac*. Century Co., New York, 1924.

NICOLAY, J. G., and HAY, JOHN, *Abraham Lincoln, A History*. Century Co., New York, 1890.

OBERHOLTZER, ELLIS P., *A History of the United States Since the Civil War*. Macmillan, New York, 1917–1937.

OLMSTED, FREDERICK LAW, *The Slave States Before the Civil War*. Edited by Harvey Wish. Putnam's, New York, 1959.

OTIS, HARRISON GRAY, "The Causes of the Impeachment," *Century Magazine*, December, 1913.

PARTON, JAMES and others, *Men of Progress*. New York & Hartford Publishing Co., 1870–1871.

PATTON, JAMES WELCH, "The Senatorial Career of William G. Brownlow," *Tennessee Historical Magazine*, 1931.

——*Unionism and Reconstruction in Tennessee*. University of North Carolina Press, Chapel Hill, 1934.

PHIFER, GREGG, "Andrew Johnson Argues a Case," *Tennessee Historical Quarterly*, June and September, 1952.

—— "Andrew Johnson Loses a Battle," *Tennessee Historical Quarterly*, December, 1952.

—— "Andrew Johnson Takes a Trip," *Tennessee Historical Quarterly*, March, 1952.

—— "Andrew Johnson versus the Press in 1866," *East Tennessee Historical Society Publications*, No. 25, 1953.

PHILLIPS, ULRICH BONNELL, *Life and Labor in the Old South*. Little, Brown, Boston, 1929.

PIATT, DONN, *Memories of the Men Who Saved the Union*. Belford Clarke, Chicago and New York, 1887.

PIERCE, EDWARD L., *Memoir and Letters of Charles Sumner*. Roberts Bros., Boston, 1893–1894.

POLK, JAMES K., *Polk: The Diary of a President 1845–1849*. Edited by Allan Nevins. Longmans Green, New York, 1929.

POORE, BEN: PERLEY, *Reminiscences*. Hubbard, Philadelphia, 1886.

POST, MARIE CAROLINE, *The Life and Memoirs of Comte Régis de Trobriand*. Dutton, New York, 1910.

PRATT, FLETCHER, *Stanton, Lincoln's Secretary of War*. Norton, New York, 1953.

PRYOR, MRS. ROGER A., *My Day: Reminiscences of a Long Life*. Macmillan, New York, 1909.

—— *Reminiscences of Peace and War*. Macmillan, New York, 1904.

RAMAGE, BURR R., "Andrew Johnson's Administration," *South Atlantic Quarterly*, April, 1902.

RANDALL, RUTH PAINTER, *Mary Lincoln*. Little, Brown, Boston, 1953.

Reconstruction: A Documentary History of the South After the War, 1865–1877. Edited by James P. Shenton. Putnam's, New York, 1963.

Reconstruction in the South, 1865–1877: First Hand Accounts by Northerners and Southerners. Edited by Harvey Wish. Farrar, Straus & Giroux, New York, 1965.

REID, WHITELAW, *After the War: A Southern Tour, May 1, 1865, to May 1, 1866*. Sampson Low, Son, & Marston, London, 1866.

Reports of Committees of House of Representatives, 40th Congress, Report #44 (May 25, 1868) "On Raising of Money to be Used in Impeachment." Washington, 1868.

REYNOLDS, WILLIAM D., *Miss Martha Brownlow: or, the Heroine of Tennessee*. Barclay, Philadelphia. n.d.

RHODES, JAMES FORD, *History of the United States 1850–1877*. Macmillan, New York, 1906.

RIDDLE, A. G., *The Life of Benjamin F. Wade*. Williams, Cleveland, 1886.

ROSS, EDMUND G., *History of the Impeachment of Andrew Johnson*. New Mexican Printing Co., Sante Fe, N.M., 1896.

ROSS, ISHBEL, *Proud Kate*. Harper, New York, 1953.

ROTHSCHILD, SALOMON DE, *A Casual View of America: Letters, 1859–1861*. Translated and edited by Sigmund Diamond. Stanford University Press, Stanford, California, 1961.

RUSSELL, WILLIAM HOWARD, *The Civil War in America*. Boston, 1861.

—— *My Diary, North and South*. Harper, New York, 1863.

—— *Pictures of Southern Life, Social, Political, and Military*. New York, 1861.

—— "Recollections of the American Civil War," *North American Review*, 1898.

SADLER, CHRISTINE, *Children in the White House*. Putnam, New York, 1967.

SANDBURG, CARL, *Abraham Lincoln*. Scribner's, New York, 1940.

SAVAGE, JOHN, *Life of Andrew Johnson*. Derby & Miller, New York, 1866.

SCHUCKERS, J. W., *The Life and Public Services of Salmon Portland Chase*. Appleton, New York, 1874.

SCHURZ, CARL, *Reminiscences*. McClure, New York, 1907–1908.

SEITZ, DON C., *The James Gordon Bennetts*. Bobbs-Merrill, Indianapolis, 1928.

SEWARD, FREDERICK W., *Andrew Johnson*. Lippincott, Philadelphia, 1890.

—— *Reminiscences of a War-Time Statesman and Diplomat*. Putnam's New York, 1916.

SHERMAN, JOHN, *Recollections of Forty Years in the House, Senate, and Cabinet*. Werner, Chicago and New York, 1895.

SHERMAN, W. T., *Memoirs*. Webster, New York, 1891.

SMALLEY, E. V., "Recollections of Andrew Johnson," *Independent*, September 6, 1900.

SMITH, J. FRAZER, *White Pillars*. Welburn, New York, 1941.

SMITH, WILLIAM ERNEST, *The Francis Preston Blair Family in Politics*. Macmillan, New York, 1933.

STAMPP, KENNETH M., *The Era of Reconstruction*. Knopf, New York, 1965.

STEINER, BERNARD C., *The Life of Henry Winter Davis*. Murphy, Baltimore, 1916.

STERN, MADELEINE B., *Purple Passage: The Life of Mrs. Frank Leslie*. University of Oklahoma Press, Norman, 1953.

STERN, PHILIP VAN DOREN, *An End to Valor: The Last Days of the Civil War*. Houghton Mifflin, Boston, 1958.

STODDARD, HENRY LUTHER, *Horace Greeley: Printer, Editor, Crusader*. Putnam's, New York, 1946.

STRODE, HUDSON, *Jefferson Davis: American Patriot, 1808–1860*. Harcourt, Brace, New York, 1955.

STRONG, GEORGE TEMPLETON, *The Diary of George Templeton Strong*. Edited by Allan Nevins and Milton Halsey Thomas. Macmillan, New York, 1952.

STRYKER, LLOYD PAUL, *Andrew Johnson: A Study in Courage*. Macmillan, New York, 1929.

SWANBERG, W. A., *First Blood: The Story of Fort Sumter*. Scribner's, New York, 1957.

—— *Sickles the Incredible*. Scribner's, New York, 1956.

TAYLOR, RICHARD, *Destruction and Reconstruction*. Longmans, Green, New York, 1955.

TEMPLE, OLIVER P., *East Tennessee and the Civil War*. Clarke, Cincinnati, 1899.

—— *Notable Men of Tennessee*. Cosmopolitan Press, New York, 1912.

TENBROEK, JACOBUS, *The Antislavery Origins of the Fourteenth Amendment*. University of California Press, Berkeley, 1951.

THOMAS, BENJAMIN P. and HYMAN, HAROLD M. *Stanton: The Life and Times of Lincoln's Secretary of War*. Knopf, New York, 1962.

THOMPSON, CAROL L. "Andrew Johnson and the Lost Cause," *Current History*, June, 1948.

TOURGÉE, ALBION W., *A Fool's Errand*. Harvard University Press, Cambridge, Mass., 1961.

TREFOUSSE, HANS LOUIS, *Ben Butler*. Twayne, New York, 1957.

TRIETSCH, JAMES H., *The Printer and the Prince*. Exposition Press, New York, 1955.

TROWBRIDGE, JOHN T., *The South: A Tour of Its Battle-Fields and Ruined Cities*. Stebbins, Hartford, 1866.

TUCKERMAN, CHARLES K., *Personal Recollections of Notable People*. Bentley, London, 1895.

TRUMAN, BENJAMIN C., "Anecdotes of President Johnson," *Century Magazine*, January, 1913.

United States 44th Congress, First Session, 1875–1876. Memorial Addresses on the Life and Character of Andrew Johnson (a Senator from Tennessee), Delivered in the Senate and the House of Representatives, January 12, 1876. Government Printing Office, Washington.

United States Statutes at Large, 39th and 40th Congresses. Government Printing Office, Washington.

VAN DUSEN, GLYNDON G., *Thurlow Weed: Wizard of the Lobby*. Little, Brown, Boston, 1947.

——— *William Henry Seward*. Oxford University Press, New York, 1967.

VESEY, JOHN HENRY, *Mr. Vesey of England*. Edited by Brian Waters. Putnam's, New York, 1956.

VILLARD, HENRY, *Memoirs of Henry Villard*. Houghton Mifflin, Boston, 1904.

Volcano Under the City, The. By a Special Volunteer. Ford, Howard & Hurlbert, New York, 1887.

WARMOTH, HENRY C., *War, Politics, and Reconstruction*. Macmillan, New York, 1930.

WATTERSON, HENRY, *"Marse Henry," an Autobiography*. Doran, New York, 1919.

WEED, THURLOW, *Autobiography and Memoir*. Houghton Mifflin, Boston, 1883.

WEISBERGER, BERNARD A., *Reporters for the Union*. Little, Brown, Boston, 1953.

WELLES, GIDEON, *The Diary of Gideon Welles*. Edited by Howard K. Beale. Norton, New York, 1960.

West Point Atlas of American Wars, The. Edited by Colonel Vincent J. Esposito. Frederick A. Praeger, New York, 1959.

WHITMAN, WALT, *Walt Whitman's Civil War*. Compiled and edited by Walter Lowenfels. Knopf, New York, 1961.

WHYTE, JAMES H., *The Uncivil War*. Twayne, New York, 1958.

WILKINS, WILLIAM GLYDE, *Charles Dickens in America*. Scribner's, New York, 1911.

WILLIAMS, HARRY T., *Lincoln and His Generals*. Knopf, New York, 1952.

—— *Lincoln and the Radicals*. University of Wisconsin Press, Madison, 1941.

—— *P. G. T. Beauregard, Napoleon in Gray*. Louisiana State University Press, Baton Rouge, 1954.

WILSON, LOUIS D., *Andrew Johnson as He Really Was* (Pamphlet). Richmond, Va., 1911.

WINSTON, ROBERT, *Andrew Johnson, Plebeian and Patriot*. Holt, New York, 1928.

INDEX